SIDNEY BECHET

THE WIZARD OF JAZZ

SIDNEY BECHET
THE WIZARD OF JAZZ

by

JOHN CHILTON, 1932 -

NEW YORK
OXFORD UNIVERSITY PRESS
1987

In memory of the Horton family
who were so kind to a wartime evacuee
and for Eddie Lambert
who loved Bechet's music

© John Chilton 1987

First published in 1987 by
The Macmillan Press Ltd
London
Great Britain

Published in 1987 in the United States by
Oxford University Press Inc
200 Madison Avenue
New York
NY 10016

ISBN 0-19-520623-1

Typeset by Rowland Phototypesetting Ltd
Bury St Edmunds, Suffolk
in 10/11½pt Caledonia

Printed in Hong Kong

Bechet to me was the very epitome of jazz . . . everything he played in his whole life was completely original. I honestly think he was the most unique man ever to be in this music.

Duke Ellington

Also by John Chilton:

Who's Who of Jazz: Storyville to Swing Street
Billie's Blues: a Survey of Billie Holiday's Career, 1933–1959
Stomp Off, Let's Go! The Story of Bob Crosby's Bob Cats & Big Band
Teach Yourself Jazz
McKinney's Music: a Bio-discography of McKinney's Cotton Pickers
*A Jazz Nursery: the Story of the Jenkins' Orphanage Bands of Charleston, South
 Carolina*
Louis: the Louis Armstrong Story (with Max Jones)

Contents

Acknowledgements		xi
Introduction		xv
1	Creole Ancestry	1
2	The New Orleans Truant	9
3	Jazz Prodigy	18
4	Restless	27
5	Transatlantic Triumphs	35
6	Deportation Blues	45
7	The Wizard on Wax	55
8	Duel of the Giants	64
9	Mayhem in Paris	75
10	Gigging and Sewing	85
11	Big-band Days	98
12	Summertime	110
13	The Jazz Revival	124
14	One-man Band	135
15	Farewell to Louisiana	149
16	Bunk and Boston	162
17	King Jazz	174
18	Absent Enemy	189
19	Chicago Showdown	201
20	European Acclaim	212
21	Beating the Ban	224
22	Monsieur Bechet	241
23	Stardom in France	254
24	The Birth of a Ballet	269
25	The Final Bows	282
Coda		294
References		295
Bibliography		308
Selected Discography		311
Index		315

Acknowledgements

This book could not have been completed without the help of the following people. Their kindness and generous assistance was inspirational; I shall always be grateful to them.

Jeff Atterton, Emelda Bechet-Garrett, Lawrence Gushee, Richard Hadlock, Mike Hazeldine, Franz Hoffmann, Mary Karoley, Robert Lewis, Claude Luter, Evelyn McCoy (Arkansas Arts Center), Johnson McRee Jr, Brian Peerless, William Russell, Howard Rye, Françoise Venet, Terkild Vinding, Bob and Joanne 'Pug' Wilber.

I would also like to express my gratitude to the following: Bernard Addison, Richard Allen, Ernie Anderson, George Avakian, Christian Azzi, Jean-Claude Baker, Chris Barber, Eddie Barefield, Danny Barker, Everett Barksdale, Alan Barrell, Collin Bates, Josephine Beaton, Ken Bell, Tommy Benford, Clyde Bernhardt, Cuff Billett, John Blowers, Marcel Bornstein, Arthur Briggs, Michael Brooks, Eric Brown, Lawrence Brown, Beryl Bryden, Teddy Buckner, Garvin Bushell, James Butts, John Ciardi, Buck Clayton, Bill Clark, Derek Coller, James Lincoln Collier, Mal Collins (Sidney Bechet Appreciation Society), W. Mercer Cook, Peter Cripps, D. Criscuolo, Charlie Crump, Michael Cuscuna, Patti D'Arta, Stanley Dance, Kenny Davern, Russell Davies, Demas Dean, Charles Delaunay, Guy Demole, John Dengler, Dave Dexter, Ray Diehl, Derek Drescher, Frank Driggs, Ake Edfeldt, Jack Egan, Roy Eldridge, Nesuhi Ertegun, Wally Fawkes, John Featherstone, John Field, Kansas Fields, Dr Desmond Flower, Clarence Ford, Charles Gabriel, Bob Glass, James Goggin, Lorraine Gordon, Jeffrey Green, Laurie Green, David Griffiths, Eddie Grossbart, Marty Grosz, Adelaide Hall, Hammersmith Central Library, John Hammond, Harry Hayes, J. C. Heard, Art Hodes, Dick Hughes, Joan Hulbert, George Hurley, Jazz Archive (Tulane University, New Orleans), Norman Jenkinson, Dr Helen Johnson, Mrs Lemuel Johnson, Jonah Jones, Max and Betty Jones, Wayne Jones, Max Kaminsky, George W. Kay, G. E. Lambert, the Honourable Gerald Lascelles, John Lawrence, Jack Lesberg, Henry Levine, Harry Lim, Lincoln Library (Springfield, Illinois), Alfred W. Lion, Rainer Lotz, Humphrey Lyttelton, Alan Macmillan, Oscar Madera, Don Marquis, Adele Girard Marsala, Barry Martyn, Jim McGraw, Pierre Merlin, Tony Middleton, Bob Mielke, Max Miller, Johnny Mince, Kurt Mohr, Fred Moore, Dan Morgenstern, David Mylne, Joe Muranyi, Newspaper Guild of New York, Louis Nussbaum, Ray Oehler, Dave R. Ogden, Gerard W. Organ, Bob Osgood, Mary

Osgood, F. Wynne Paris, Grace Wynne Paris, Johnny Parker, Sidney Parker, David Perry, Nat Pierce, Arthur Pilkington, Mike Pointon, Lewis Porter, James T. Powell, Dorothy Prescott (New Hampshire Library of Traditional Jazz), Sammy Price, George Probert, Ruth Reinhardt, Barbara Reid, Roy Rhodes, Charles 'Red' Richards, Trevor Richards, Shirley Rickards, Al Rose, Bob Salt-marsh, Lou Savarese, Phil Schaap, Walter Schaap, Peter Schilperoort, Arvell Shaw, Alyn Shipton, Mrs James Shirley, Johnny Simmen, Hal Smith, John Smith, Keith Smith, Kenneth Smith, Stephen W. Smith, Don Sollash, Monty Sunshine, Ronald Sweetman, Mike Sutcliffe, The British Broadcasting Corpora-tion, Clarence Todd, Eric Townley, Christopher Tyle, Alfred Van Straten, Steve Voce, Al Vollmer, Arthur Wang, Matt Walsh, Benny Waters, James Weaver, Harold 'Buddy' Weed, George Wein, Dick Wellstood, John Whitehorn, Brian Willan, Bert Willcox, Johnny Williams, Spencer P. Williams, Laurie Wright, Dan Wyllie, Sol Yaged, Bernard Zacharias.

The following magazines and periodicals were consulted:

Great Britain	Band Wagon, Crescendo, Dancing Times, Dancing World, Eureka, Footnote, Holborn Guardian, Hot News, Jazz Express, Jazz Forum, Jazz Journal, Jazz Magazine, Jazz Monthly, Jazz Music, Jazz News, Jazz Scene, Jazz Tempo, Jazzology, Melody Maker, Musical News and Dance Band, Pickup, Popular Music & Dancing Weekly, Rhythm, The Stage, Storyville, Swing Music, Tune Times, West London Observer, The Wire
France	Bulletin du Hot club de France, Jazz hot, Jazz magazine, Jazz, La revue du jazz, Les cahiers du jazz
Holland	Doctor Jazz
Eire	Hot Notes
Australia	Jazz, Australian Jazz Quarterly, Jazz Notes, Quarterly Rag
Canada	Coda
Germany	Berolina (das Magazin der Kempinski-Betriebe)
USA	American Jazz Review, Amsterdam News, Baltimore Afro-American, Basin Street, Boston Herald, Cadence, Chicago Defender, Clef, Down Beat, Esquire, HRS Rag, IARJC Journal, Illinois State Journal, Indianapolis Freeman, International Musician, Jazz, Jazzfinder, Jazz Information, Jazz Music, Jazz Quarterly, Jazz Record, Jazz Register, Jazz Report, Jazz Review, Jazz Session, Jazz Today, Jersey Jazz, Journal of Jazz Studies, Metronome, Mississippi Rag, Music & Rhythm, Needle, New York Age, New York Clipper, New York Times, New

York World, New Yorker, Orchestra World,
Pittsburgh Courier, Playback, Record Changer,
Record Research, Second Line, Sounds and Fury,
Swing, Tempo

Introduction

Sidney Bechet's autobiography *Treat it Gentle* is without doubt the most poetic of all jazz books. It is a work that I have read and reread with enormous pleasure, but some years ago, when I began assembling a chronological survey of Bechet's career for the original edition of *Who's Who of Jazz*, I realized that long periods of his life were not touched upon in his memoirs. Dr Desmond Flower, the editor of *Treat it Gentle*, made valiant efforts to get Sidney to fill those gaps and to explain various anomalies, but by that time (in the late 1950s) Sidney's health was failing and the task remained uncompleted at the time of his death in May 1959.

I have always been fascinated by Sidney Bechet's music; he was featured on the first jazz recording that I consciously heard, and his was the first photograph that I ever stuck in a scrap book. Over the years I have talked and corresponded with many people who knew Sidney; any references to his work or articles about him were carefully retained. Eventually I decided to research his life as thoroughly as I could. My findings do not always tally with Sidney's own account of events.

ONE

Creole Ancestry

The first of Sidney Bechet's ancestors to enter New Orleans was Françoise Cocote, a negro woman born around 1760 in the state of Illinois. She remained unmarried, but had three children: two daughters, Eulalie, born c1800, Marie Jeanne, born c1805, and a son, Jean Becher, born c1802. Francois lived on St Pierre Street in New Orleans on a plot of land that formed part of the inheritance she left to her children in a will made in May 1817, shortly before she died. In a document dated 10 May 1817 (signed by Marc La Fitte, Notary Public, New Orleans) she also bequeathed 50 piasters each to Jean Becher and to Marie Jeanne "for them to be made free by their respective godmothers".

Somewhere in the course of time Jean Becher's name became changed slightly, first to Beschet, then to Bechet. In the Louisiana Census of 1850 he is described as a mulatto, and his wife Marie Gabrielle (born c1815) as black. Jean was a carpenter by trade, a successful one, described in the 1860 Census as owning property with 2500 dollars and with personal funds of 800 dollars. In the 1861 City Directory his name was printed as J. B. Beshé. Jean and Marie had a large family. Six of their children thrived, among them Omar, who was born about 1855 (his age is given as 24 in the 1880 Census). Because many early documents were transcribed phonetically, Omar's name was also entered at various times as Omer and Homer.

Omar adopted the trade of shoemaker and continued to live at home with his mother after she was widowed. Later he introduced his bride, Josephine Michel, into the Catholic household that dwelt in the 7th Ward of New Orleans at 414 Girod Street (this being the old Girod Street, now known as Villere). Josephine bore Omar ten children in all, but three died in early infancy. The surviving sons were Homer (b1884), Leonard Victor (b1886), Albert Eugene (b1887), Joseph (b1890) and Sidney Joseph (b1897). The two daughters were Bertha (later Mrs Taylor) and Albertine (who died during adolescence).

Sidney Bechet's age has been the cause of a vast amount of speculation. On the 1910 Census form his age is clearly given as 12 and he is described as a schoolboy. His baptism took place in a ceremony conducted by the Reverend Joseph Subileau at St Augustine's Church in New Orleans on 26 September 1897, and his date of birth was then given as 14 May 1897.[1] The saga of misunderstandings concerning Sidney's age is dealt with later. These became so recurrent that Sidney himself gave up trying to set the record straight and taciturnly agreed with almost any date that was put forward. He himself was in no doubt, and 14

May 1897 was the date of birth that he put down on the first application he ever made for a passport, back in 1919.

The history of New Orleans, that most cosmopolitan of cities, is well detailed in many books. Its occupancy by French and Spanish administrators and its subsequent development as part of the United States of America meant that many widely differing ingredients went into its make-up. Immigrant groups of German, English, Italian, Scottish and Irish people also settled there. An influx of black slaves, either direct from Africa or from the Caribbean islands, and the entry of ex-slaves made it into a racially mixed city.

The proudest, and perhaps the most insular, of all the various racial groups was that of the Creoles. During the mid-19th century the term 'Creole' was used to describe colonial families who had come from France to settle in Louisiana, but this definition gradually lost its original meaning and the word became applied to anyone whose lineage showed both negro and French (or Spanish) ancestry. The offspring from these mixed unions were sometimes spoken of as "Creoles of colour" (*gens de couleur*), but eventually the word Creole became common parlance for any light-skinned Negro.

During the 19th century the Creoles played an important part in the growth of New Orleans, providing the city with a good percentage of its craftsmen and tradesmen. In the last decade of that century the racial intolerance that had been increasing in the southern states since the end of the Civil War (1865) took the form of positive action. In Louisiana, as in many other places in the South, new legislation made it difficult for the Creoles (being part black) to thrive as they had done in the past. New Orleans had always been more tolerant of racial differences than most other southern cities, but any of its inhabitants who had a discernible negro heritage were soon made aware of new repressions.

The Bechet family, living in down-town New Orleans, had developed a bourgeois life style during their decades of relative prosperity. In the 1890s some of the family conversation was still carried on in French, or at least the local patois. Their direct dealings with black people who lived in the up-town section of the city were few and far between, and, even though no formal segregation existed between Creoles and Negroes, most of the Bechet family's neighbours were of French extraction. The changing laws and restrictions introduced in the 1890s meant that the Bechets, and countless other Creole families, found themselves reclassified in a way that they themselves considered to be a form of relegation. This metamorphosis brought drastic changes, one of them being the music-making of the various non-white sections of the population. A Creole teaching a black pupil would have been a rare occurrence in the Reconstruction years following the Civil War, and the reverse even more unusual. But by 1900 this cross tuition – particularly in music – was taking place in several parts of New Orleans, and, as a result, the old down-town and up-town sections gradually lost their definite boundaries when it came to the making of music.

Music played a big part in the life of the Bechet household. Omar liked nothing more than to play a flute for relaxation (he also played the trumpet a little). Besides his shoemaking activities, he was also active in local politics and helped organize the Citizens' League, but he always found time to play music and encouraged his sons to do likewise. All of Sidney Bechet's brothers showed an aptitude for music-making, but the playing of their various instruments was regarded solely as a hobby – something to be enjoyed when the serious work of the day was over. Homer was a janitor who played string bass, Leonard a dentist and trombonist, Albert Eugene a butcher's assistant who played violin, Joseph a plasterer by trade and a guitarist by inclination. Sidney, much younger than his brothers, listened enviously to their musical efforts, and looked on in awe when Benny Raphael, the trombonist with the Imperial Band, came to the house to give Leonard his lessons.

Leonard recounted to the Belgian author Robert Goffin what he described as "Sidney's remotest memoir of syncopated music".[2] During the spring of 1903, as Leonard was walking with Sidney on Liberty in the vicinity of Hope's Hall, they heard music: "Children were dancing on the pavement, there on the side of the road was an accordeon player, a mandolinist, a bassist and a clarinettist, and other musicians, described by the infant Sidney as 'some men behind'. The kid stood there for an hour listening to this music."[3]

Sidney's desire to play music like his brothers made itself clear when he was little more than a toddler. One of his earliest memories was of finding a douche that belonged to his mother and attempting to blow the nozzle of it like a clarinet.[4] This innocent experiment provided his parents with shocked amusement, but it also made them well aware of their youngest child's ambitions. They bought him a small fife, and soon all of the neighbours were introduced to the sound of Sidney's diligent practice. One of these was Elizabeth Landreaux (later the famous singer Lizzie Miles). She recalled: "Sidney was my neighbour and school mate, as kids we'd play together in the evenings when work was done. He owned a little nickel-tin flute, that's what he'd play. I'd sing and another neighbour, Wilhelmina Barth, would play the piano. He was younger than me, and Wilhelmina older."[5]

The urge for Sidney to be a performer manifested itself in various ways, and when he was about seven or eight he sang *I wish I was in heaven, sitting down* at a children's talent contest held at the Economy Hall on Ursulines Street. The earnestness of his presentation rather than the sweetness of his voice won him a prize, and this same earnestness marked his approach to playing the fife. Young Bechet made amazing progress. He was too young to play paid engagements, but he soon linked up with the Rena brothers, a couple of aspiring young musicians who were doing their best to make music on home-made instruments.

Years later Joe and Henry Rena graduated on to proper musical instruments. Joe became a clarinettist and drummer, and Henry (who was nicknamed 'Kid') became a widely respected trumpeter. During their childhood the Rena brothers had to make do with what they could afford; Kid played a paper-covered comb, and Joe made himself a drum from a cheese-box covered with the skin from a round of beef. Joe recalled that the youngsters, with Sidney, rehearsed in a coffin-making shop owned by the father of one of their friends.[6]

Sidney's musical prowess rapidly outstripped the technical limitations of his 'toy' instrument and he became eager to move on to something more challenging. One day, when the home was empty, Sidney went up to Leonard's room and borrowed his brother's C clarinet. Leonard's main instrument was the trombone, but he also had aspirations to double on clarinet. As most of his time was devoted to studying dentistry, finding opportunities to practise the trombone often proved difficult; the clarinet had been packed away for more leisurely times. Sidney began practising on his brother's clarinet whenever he felt that the coast was clear. One day he was overheard by his mother, who realized immediately that the sound, and the flowing runs, were not being played on a fife. She castigated Sidney for being devious, but was proudly impressed by what she heard.

Mrs Bechet discussed Sidney's ambitions with her husband and the two of them decided to broach the subject of the clarinet with Leonard. They did so, being careful not to emphasize Sidney's amazing progress on the instrument. Leonard soon realized that he was expected to pass on the clarinet to his youngest brother, but made the proviso that it was to be given as a formal Christmas present. The bestowing of this gift probably took place around Christmas 1905. Sidney was inclined to stress his status as a prodigy by sometimes putting the date at 1903, but this doesn't tie in with a chronology suggested by the comments of Joe Rena, who clearly remembered Sidney receiving the C clarinet.[7] Bechet himself said that the first tune he ever learnt to play on clarinet was *I don't know where I'm going but I'm on my way* (written and published by Joseph Bren in 1905).

If Sidney's practice on the fife had been conscientious and determined, his routine for improving his clarinet playing was even more arduous and enthusiastic. He practised morning, noon and night, making even his music-loving neighbours a little restless; they found no faults with the child's growing skills, but it seemed that he never stopped trying to improve. All of this diligence built a formidable technique, and Sidney's brothers soon realized that the youngster had more musical talent than all of them put together. Other adult musicians conceded that a brilliant young musician had emerged in down-town New Orleans.

During Sidney's early childhood, around the turn of the century, the music that became known as jazz began to take definite shape. It was to be some years before the new style was given its name; the early music improvised by black pioneers such as Charles 'Buddy' Bolden (1877–1931) was classified as ragtime, even by the performers themselves. Yet this new way of playing had elements that were not part of ragtime: it was full of 'blue' notes, the sound of which fell somewhere between adjoining notes on a piano. A blue note was inflected in a way that, for instance, made it too low to be a true D but not low enough in pitch to be called a D flat; it was an in-between sound that had no place in formal European notation. These blue notes instantly made the music sound different. The effect became startling when the self-taught musicians from up-town New Orleans, blowing blue inflections, deliberately created a rough, burring effect in their throats.

Even more remarkable were the innovative rhythmic patterns that formed the basis of the 'new' music: jazz used time values that were entirely different from those of the waltzes, mazurkas and schottisches that had long been the standard music of the New Orleans dance halls. Elements from the African-style dancing that had been a feature of the slave gatherings in Congo Square, New Orleans, during the early part of the 19th century drifted through the following generations as an atavistic memory and linked up with exotic rhythms brought into the city from South America and the Caribbean islands. These rhythms were transplanted into European metres of two- and four-beats in a bar with dramatic results.

The new rhythms and the new timbres married easily and were funnelled into the burning desire for musical self-expression that swept through New Orleans in the last part of the 19th century. These revolutionary ideas were performed, in the main, on European-type instruments and superimposed on European harmonies. The end-result was the creation of a music that was subsequently to bring pleasure to the lives of people everywhere. Jazz, as the music became known, flowered throughout the world from seeds that originally ripened in New Orleans.

Sidney Bechet had a remarkable memory, so his claim to have heard Buddy Bolden (who played his last engagement in New Orleans in 1906) is probably true. He recalled hearing the great pioneer play a street parade, leading a band that took part in a musical 'battle' with the Imperial Band. Bechet said, "I was six or seven. I had just started to learn the clarinet."[8]

The rough-and-ready ways of Bolden did not charm the average Creole family in New Orleans. Even Leonard Bechet, a part-time musician, said he disapproved of "low-down type of music", adding, "Us Creole musicians always did hold up a nice prestige."[9] Guitarist Johnny St Cyr confirmed that the old insularity died hard, and that during his early years he didn't know any up-town musicians.[10] Happily, attitudes gradually changed, but even today it is not unknown for a venerable member of an old Creole family to dwell on racial differences.

Sidney recalled that during his childhood his mother got annoyed when he stayed out to listen to "rough music", but at that stage of Sidney's life he could guarantee that his mother would not remain angry with him for long. His brothers looked on unamused as Mrs Bechet fussed around her youngest son with "my dear, this, and my dear, that". As a special treat she took Sidney to the circus, but, unlike most of the children there, he was far more interested in the accompanying band than he was in the acts. He always retained fond memories of visiting the Opera House with his mother, and from childhood loved the sound of the tenor voice. Some of the first gramophone recordings that he ever heard were of Enrico Caruso;[11] the dramatic vibrato and the panache of the great singer made their mark on the youngster's imagination.

Not long after Sidney had begun to learn the clarinet, his brother Leonard took him to a reunion of Des France Amis held at their hall (situated at the junction of Robertson and St Antoine). There he heard clarinettist George Baquet improvising, and was "overwhelmed". A few weeks later the two brothers went to a ball at St Catherine's Hall featuring John Robichaux's Orchestra and the Superior Band. On this occasion Sidney heard the influential sounds of 'Big Eye' Louis Nelson's clarinet playing, and Leonard recalled that they made the child "delirious with joy".[12]

Mrs Josephine Bechet seems to have been a remarkable woman. She organized her own lawn parties at the family home on Marais Street (whence they had moved from St Antoine Street soon after Sidney's birth). On several occasions she hired bands and charged revellers to enter the house's big yard (the price of admission included unlimited helpings of Creole food). For one of these gatherings, held ostensibly to celebrate Leonard's 21st birthday in April 1907, Mrs Bechet booked a notable band led by cornetist Manuel Perez (Emile Emanuel Perez), but Perez sent a deputy in the shape of Freddie Keppard, a young up-and-coming Creole cornet player.

The band's clarinettist, George Baquet, was late for the engagement and the group started without him. Baquet's tardiness presented young Sidney with a golden opportunity: he got out his clarinet and joined in with the band, but from the safety of an inner room, since he did not want to risk the chance of an instant rebuff from any of the adult musicians. Keppard heard the sound of the clarinet drifting out and, according to legend, thought it was Baquet warming up his instrument. He went to investigate and found that the sounds were being made by a child. Keppard's discovery coincided with Baquet's arrival at the function.

The other musicians teased Sidney about his attempts to do Baquet out of a job, but all of them were deeply impressed by what they had heard; Keppard (only 18 years old himself) smacked the boy on the shoulder as though he were a grown-up, and in doing so elevated himself to the position of a hero in Sidney's eyes. George Baquet, who was a well-respected musician, showed his kindly disposition by offering to coach Sidney on the clarinet. He invited him to call at his house whenever he needed technical guidance.

Sidney always retained considerable respect for Baquet, and years later (in 1940), at a reunion in New Jersey, warmly acknowledged the help that Baquet had given him. The lessons never fell into a regular pattern, however. Sidney called on Baquet occasionally and handed over a pouch or two of Bull Durham tobacco as payment for the tuition. One day George invited the youngster along to hear him play at the Economy Hall; the visitor was vastly impressed, not only by the music-making but also by the life style of the patrons. A renowned New Orleans clarinettist, Emile Barnes, who was a few years older than Sidney, said he thought that Bechet played like "early Baquet", but also praised his individuality. Barnes said that Baquet "took great pains to attempt to teach Sidney the right fingering, but he had developed his own technique to such an extent that he was never able to change."[13]

Sidney willingly listened to advice from Baquet concerning embouchure, reeds, mouthpieces, and legato and staccato playing, but any talk about reading music (which Baquet did expertly) and studying harmonies seemed to be quite pointless. Sidney could follow intricate chord changes quite easily without knowing their names, and to sit poring over a piece of music that he could re-create after one hearing seemed a total waste of time.

George Baquet wasn't Sidney's only music teacher. In addition he received some advice from Paul Chaligny (who also instructed Leonard Bechet), and some technical guidance from clarinettist Alphonse Picou, who claimed that he gave Sidney lessons soon after the youngster graduated from fife to clarinet.[14] The most important influence on Sidney seems to have been the clarinet playing of 'Big Eye' Louis Nelson (who was born in 1880, and whose original name was Delile or Delisle).

Nelson was largely self-taught, though he did receive some guidance from Lorenzo Tio, who first persuaded him to buy a clarinet. Nelson leaned away from the academic approach to playing the clarinet, and instead helped create the rougher up-town style that soon gained popularity with dance-hall listeners. Bechet said, "I myself learned to play by patterning my work after 'Big Eye' Louis Nelson. In fact, Nelson gave me my first formal instruction on the clarinet. After I had learned the rudiments from him I had to learn the rest for myself. That's what every young person has to do."[15] Older, more staid, musicians called Nelson's style of playing "ratty", but for young Sidney it had qualities that he admired: "Some musicians played the tune prettily, but I like the playing that makes me want to dance."[16]

Soon after Sidney's introduction to Baquet and Keppard, the youngster began entering talent contests regularly (often singing, dancing and playing). He recalled: "I began taking my clarinet when I wanted to make a bigger hit."[17] On one such occasion, when his clarinet developed a fault on stage, things almost went drastically wrong; fortunately Lorenzo Tio, one of the city's most famous clarinettists, was in the accompanying orchestra and he loaned his instrument to the young contestant. The startling music that emerged was responsible for Sidney's gaining the first prize of 25 dollars. Lorenzo Tio suggested that Sidney should take some tuition from his elder brother, Luis 'Papa' Tio; Lorenzo's son, Lorenzo, Jr (b1893), was already one of the brightest musical prospects in New Orleans.

Sidney dutifully turned up at the Tio household for a brief series of lessons; but Luis 'Papa' Tio's approach to the reed family was too legitimate for the young pupil, while Sidney's was much too rough and husky for the 'professor' (who used to run into his house when he heard a jazz band playing in his street).[18] Years later, Sidney, his eyes twinkling, used to recall Papa Tio's roar of disapproval: "No! No! No! We do not bark like a dog or meow like a cat!"[19] But doubtless some of the sage advice that Papa Tio gave stayed with Sidney. Luis Tio, Jr (a son of Lorenzo Tio, Sr), said that Sidney got "many pointers both from Luis 'Papa' Tio and Lorenzo Tio, Jr".[20]

Johnny St Cyr spoke of this period of Sidney's life: "I met Sidney Bechet through his brother Joe, who was a plasterer [like St Cyr himself]. He told me about his younger brother and the clarinet and that he just couldn't keep time. I told him to bring Sidney over to my house and see if I could help him. Sidney was then about 13. He was fine, especially on blues, but he had a tendency to gain or lose a beat occasionally. He came around to remedy that. He caught on rapidly."[21]

Johnny St Cyr invited the youngster to accompany him to the Artisan Hall one Sunday afternoon when Manuel Perez and 'Big Eye' Louis Nelson were playing there. Sidney sat in for a few numbers and made a favourable impression. Big Eye told St Cyr that he thought Sidney was "terrific", and agreed to give him "some pointers". Nelson was noted for his willingness to help others: drummer

Baby Dodds said, "He'd show a youngster all he knew, but he had a glum disposition."[22]

Bechet's first lesson gave Big Eye little to smile about. He tried to get Sidney interested in working on some solfeggio exercises from a standard tutor, but first sight of the manual was enough for Sidney – he left it at Nelson's house and never bothered to pick it up again. Big Eye and Sidney laughed over the incident years later (at a meeting in 1944), but Nelson could not have been too amused at the time. Nevertheless, he always praised Sidney's extraordinary skills, and said, "He wouldn't learn notes, but he was my best scholar."[23]

TWO

The New Orleans Truant

Sidney's brothers were proud of his musical achievements, even though they were slightly irritated by his lack of interest in their advice; one of them became angry enough to kick the youngster's roller-skates from under him. Fortunately, Leonard was close at hand instantly to repair the damage to Sidney's teeth.[1] Leonard always took a special interest in Sidney's well-being, particularly his general education. The youngster hated going to school. Years later, in 1938, Sidney told historian Bill Russell of a ruse he used to avoid attending school. Before leaving home laden with school books, Sidney would put his clarinet on a window sill. As soon as he was outside he would hide the books under the stilts of the house, then reach inside the open window, grab the clarinet, and run off to spend the day blowing as and where he could.[2] Leonard warned his brother that he was heading for trouble in playing truant so often. Sidney pointed out that he wasn't being idle during school hours, he was using the time to practise the clarinet. A compromise was reached whereby a cousin came to the Bechet household to give Sidney lessons on general subjects.

When Sidney felt like taking a rest from practising the clarinet he often went fishing, and he liked nothing more than being allowed to cook what he had caught. Even at an early age he was always curious to know how a certain dish was cooked, what its ingredients were, and how long it took to prepare. He subsequently became an excellent cook; friends from later in his life suggest that he could have been a master chef. As a teenager, whenever he ate at another household, he always complimented good cooking – a habit that didn't fail to charm mothers of his friends. Sidney also showed an interest in tailoring and gained a detailed knowledge of needlework and the merits of good cloth. But there was no question of cooking or tailoring replacing music as the foremost interest in young Sidney's life.

Both of Sidney's parents began hinting, softly at first, that it would soon be time for Sidney to start thinking about becoming apprenticed to a trade: bricklaying and hairdressing were mentioned, but both suggestions were flatly rejected by Sidney. "My mind was on other things," he explained.[3]

Omar and Josephine Bechet, like most other Creole parents, felt that music was a pleasurable hobby; it was not considered a worthy profession. Mr and Mrs Bechet pointed out that even the most eminent home-town musicians, such as Manuel Perez (a cigar-maker) and Alphonse Picou (a tin-smith), had respectable trades. The parents emphasized to Sidney that all of his brothers had the opportunity to play music, but they also had the security and dignity of a steady day job. The rift between Sidney and his immediate family concerning his working future began to widen and deepen.

The Bechet brothers felt that this might be the opportune time for Sidney to join them in their musical activities. Leonard, as ever, was particularly anxious to restore a happy family atmosphere. The senior brothers had recently organized their own group, which they called the Silver Bell Band. It consisted of Leonard on trombone, Joe on guitar, Homer on string bass, Albert on violin, and a young fellow Catholic, Sidney Desvigne (b1893), who was studying cornet with Manuel Perez.

Desvigne recalled the rehearsals that the Silver Bell Band held at the Bechet home on Marais Street: "We used to get in the back yard and just blow so loud that the policeman used to have to come around and tell Bechet's mother that 'those kids have to stop playing that loud, they're disturbing the peace'. I remember the first job we played. We played for Leonard Bechet's mother, they gave a little house party. We started playing about 8 o'clock at night and wind-up at 3 o'clock in the morning. It was sort of a subscription affair, they paid fifty cents to come in to eat and drink and dance. Well, she made out pretty good. I guess she made over a hundred dollars, she gave us five dollars, extra one for me. So then we began taking engagements."[4]

Leonard Bechet obviously did not regard this home gig as the official début of the band. He cited the Silver Bell's first date as a Carnival Day parade, which used the three-piece front-line and brother Joe on guitar. Sidney Bechet was by this time a regular member of the group and its star performer, but from the onset he didn't enjoy the experience. Leonard was as quick-tempered as Sidney, so there were a number of violent discords before and after the band's performances. The young newcomer made it plain that he thought the group had chosen a foolish name for itself.

Sidney still showed no inclination to attend school regularly, despite various admonitions. The school inspector called to investigate the reasons for Sidney's repeated absences, and this led Leonard Bechet to take action that he had long threatened. He made Sidney accompany him to the Junior Court on Carondelet Street, where Captain Pierce, the magistrate, issued a warning to the young errant.[5]

Disregarding the threat, Sidney carried on with arduous practice schedules. He also found a new port of call where he could get musical advice and also sit up half the night listening to anecdotes about musicians. The tutor and teller was a fine multi-instrumentalist, Dave Perkins, who was light-skinned enough to 'pass' into white bands without any problems. Sidney was prepared to listen to anyone imparting good musical advice, whatever the colour of their skin.

Sidney, increasingly eager to perform in public, used to walk from the Bechet family's new home on St Bernard Avenue to John Rexach's bar on Saratoga and Gravier to play a few numbers on his clarinet for the customers. His payment was ten cents' worth of beer. The bar was a hangout for bass player Bob Lyons and trombonist Frankie Dusen, both of whom managed bands, so, although Sidney's immediate reward was tiny, he did his long-term prospects no harm at all.

Gradually Sidney began to be offered paid gigs with various young local musicians. He played for lawn parties with trumpeter Willie Hightower and at house parties with Clarence Todd, a young pianist and singer who lived on St Phillips. He also appeared as a 'novelty guest' with John Robichaux' band at St Catherine's Hall.

As a diversion, Sidney began playing the cornet (he had tried out Sidney Desvigne's instrument and found it easy to play). But blowing the cornet never took up very much of Sidney's time. The clarinet had to come first; his enthusiasm for it was undiminished and he played whenever and wherever he could. Albert Nicholas, a few years younger than Sidney, was inspired by this dedication: "We all came up at the same time. Sidney would sit on the sidewalk playing. I heard him when he was in knee pants and 14 years old. Sidney was playing in with men, so that gave me a lot of inspiration."[6]

Sidney's youthful ways became more harum-scarum. He either arrived home at dawn or not at all. Most of his time was spent amongst his heroes, the talented clarinet players of New Orleans. Several of these men met up after they had finished work to talk of problems they were having with a new reed or a new woman, and both subjects had come to fascinate Sidney. Clarinettist Emile Barnes remembered these dawn gatherings: "Alphonse Picou, George Baquet, Lorenzo Tio [Jr], Sidney Bechet, 'Big Eye' Louis and Sidney 'Vigne used to meet up-town musicians in the Alley, a bar-room at St Bernards and Claiborne. They would play and party. If anyone had any money, the others could be sure of continuing their pleasure – sometimes until 7 a.m."[7]

All of these adults respected young Sidney's talents and each of them did his best to help him understand the ways of the world. Sometimes the cornetist Freddie Keppard called in at these reed players' gatherings. One of Sidney's happiest memories of these early years was of deputizing temporarily for George Baquet in the band that Keppard led at the 101 Ranch. But some staid veterans were not impressed by Bechet's approach to playing. Paul Barnes (brother of Emile) spoke of this attitude: "At the age of 14 Sidney Bechet was very good, but not rated by old musicians, as he couldn't read music."[8]

Emile Barnes struck up a friendship with Sidney, who began calling regularly at the Barnes household so that the two of them could play clarinet duets. (By this time Sidney had swopped from a C clarinet to a B flat Albert system 13-key Buffet.) The two would practise together "every day and half the night", stopping only to eat. Often Bechet was enjoying himself so much that he "forgot" to go home, and by now his attitudes were causing despair within his family. He cared nothing for his appearance, and Emile Barnes remembers "patches in his pants".[9]

Inevitably Sidney left the Silver Bell Band. His departure wasn't the result of one dramatic incident; instead he eased himself out by not turning up on time for the band's gigs and generally appearing uninterested. Leonard said, "Sidney just played so well we could not hold him in the Silver Bell Band."[10] During the last stages of his stay with the family band, Sidney had been invited to join a group that had been formed by one of the most talented young cornetists in the Crescent City, Buddy Petit. Petit (born Joseph Crawford, in White Castle, Louisiana) was the step-son of a valve trombonist, Joseph Petit. At this stage of his life, Buddy, like Bechet, didn't read music. He was a Creole, born about the same year as Sidney, and just as precocious. The two young talents, both short of stature (Bechet plump and Petit lean) struck up an easy friendship and a successful musical partnership within the Young Olympians (named after the city's illustrious Olympia Band).

The permanent nucleus of the Young Olympians consisted of Petit, Bechet, Simon Marrero on string bass, and John Marrero on guitar. Yank Johnson and Ernest Kelly played trombone with the band at various times, and the original drummer was 'Little' Mack Lacey, whose place was taken first by Arnold DePass and then by Eddie 'Rabbit' Robertson.

Junior though it was, the Young Olympians band could hardly go wrong with such an array of talent. The only time that things went seriously awry was when Sidney, or Buddy, or both of them, had too much to drink. As teenagers, their outlook on life was similar; so too was their taste for alcohol.

Both youngsters also played other gigs with various leaders – some of them for Ernest 'Ninesse' Trepagnier, one of the best bass drummers in New Orleans. Trepagnier was frequently asked to provide bands to play at the Sunday all-day picnics that were held out at Lake Pontchartrain, and he often booked Bechet and Petit. Trepagnier asked the musicians to assemble for a 9 a.m. call at the old down-town railway station in New Orleans; this was so they could all proceed together on the 15-minute ride along the single track.

Trepagnier told writer George Hoefer of the problems he had in getting Bechet and Petit to the station on time.[11] On Sunday morning he would pick Bechet up from his home before moving on to Buddy Petit's house, which was usually locked up. If there was no reply to his heavy knocking, Trepagnier usually had to break into the house to rouse Petit. Then the three musicians would run to the station with Petit dressing on the way.

Many of the Young Olympians' own engagements were at various picnic camps at Milneberg or at Lake Pontchartrain. These gatherings provided a regular source of income for most New Orleans musicians. The music played at them consisted of popular songs of the day, old folk tunes, military airs, and, occasionally, the blues. No bookings, even in this wide-open city of New Orleans, offered as much scope and musical freedom for the participating musicians; the important part they played in the development of jazz has been largely overlooked.

Paul Barbarin (who occasionally played drums in the Young Olympians) worked at many of these outdoor engagements during his formative years. His highly evocative memories of them were published posthumously: "Each camp had its own boardwalk, like a driveway or walkway, leading from the main walk. A band would be hired for a group at one camp. In the next camp another band would be working. Some played for pay. Some were just a bunch of neighbours having a good time, playing, singing, dancing."[12] Barbarin went on to explain that the most popular days for these jaunts were Sundays and Mondays (most people then worked all day Saturday and were allowed to take Monday off):

> On Mondays at Lucian's Pavilion there was always an attraction. You would find a picnic plus the Imperial, the Superior or the Olympia Band. Imagine the bright

summer sunshine, the blue lake, the camps white, green, yellow, every color of paint. The white summer dresses, many colored parasols. The gold lettering on the brewery trucks, the harness shining . . . About five or six bands playing five or six different tunes, and not over 100 yards apart. Laughing men rolling a half keg of beer along the boardwalk to a camp. Hot dogs, oysters, crawfish, green crabs and fat lake trout. Everybody eating, singing and making music. This was a friendly place and a friendly time. Maybe two camps away there would be a white band. Don't think we didn't have many great white jazzmen in those days. We had 'em. And they played great. But there was honest, musical rivalry.

The shadow of segregation fell across these gatherings. By the early years of this century every non-white Louisianian accepted that prejudice could affect almost every sphere of life. There was a little fraternization between white and black musicians, but no 'sitting in' whatsoever – a state of affairs that was to last for decades. By 1915 white bands were creating fascinating jazz styles of their own – not all of them hybrids. Back in 1919, when arguments were beginning about the origins of jazz, a letter from pianist Bob Aquilera was published in the *Dramatic Mirror*. It read: "Some of the claimants should think back years ago when all-day picnics, or one-dollar-fifty a couple picnics as they were called, used nothing but Negro orchestras, who played what we now call jazz."[13]

A follow-up letter, from 'C. S. K.', was published by the same journal a month later: "Long before Stale Bread* and his band became popular, all-day picnics were given at Milneberg and Pecan Grove, near the city. It was here that Negro jazzing could be heard every Sunday."[14] Tony Sbarbaro, the white drummer of the Original Dixieland Jazz Band (from New Orleans) said, "A colored band could play for a white picnic, and did, but no white band ever played a colored picnic."[15]

Paul Barbarin confirmed that the Young Olympians were occasionally booked by white people. On one occasion Paul, Sidney Bechet, Buddy Petit and others played for a group from the Irish Channel section of New Orleans. Things became very high-spirited and someone took all the coats that belonged to the band and tied them together in a huge ball.[16]

Barbarin was one of a large Creole family (his sister Rose became the mother of the celebrated guitarist Danny Barker). The Barbarins were similar in many ways to the Bechets. Paul's grandmother spoke nothing but French. Sidney felt quite at home with all of the family and often dropped into their house on Urquhart Street when he was at a loose end.

Things were still unsettled at Bechet's own home. His parents, with great reluctance, had come to accept that their youngest son was going to follow his own intentions, come hell or high water. Omar had sometimes dealt out physical punishments to his sons, but in Sidney's case he thought that approach would be useless. All of Sidney's brothers had grown weary of trying to guide him onto what they saw as the right path. Parents and brothers devised an ultimatum to Sidney concerning his nocturnal habits; they decreed that anyone wishing to

---

* Emile 'Stalebread' Lacoume (1885–1946). The blind leader of the Razzy Dazzy Spasm Band, a group of white youngsters who performed on the streets of New Orleans around the turn of the century using home-made musical instruments.

book Sidney for a gig had to call for him and return him to the Bechet house. Leonard later summarized the family viewpoint: "We didn't want to jeopardize our family by mixing with the rough element. We worried a lot about Sidney when he'd be out playing."[17]

But guardianship was not always possible. Sometimes the Young Olympians moved out of New Orleans to play weekend gigs at nearby towns. Bechet said (in 1939) that his first tour with the Young Olympians occurred when he was 14: "All this was before records and radio so we didn't know what jazz was being played anywhere else. We just played our own style."[18]

One of these trips took them out to Mandeville, where they played at a rural dance-hall (probably the Sons and Daughters Hall). There Bechet first met the young Jimmie Noone, who was learning the guitar but also dabbling on a clarinet that his brother had discarded. Freddie Keppard, who was courting Noone's sister, popped up out of the audience and introduced Sidney to Jimmie.

Later that same year Noone's family moved into New Orleans and Jimmie lost no time in locating Sidney and asking him for guidance on the clarinet (even though he was three years older than Bechet). Noone said later that Bechet gave him "priceless instruction" and also showed him "the ropes around Storyville"[19] – the notorious red-light district.

Sidney's successes with the Young Olympians led him to work within the famed Olympia Band, with which he stayed for "three or four months"[20], replacing his former tutor 'Big Eye' Louis Nelson. By then Nelson had fallen in with general fashion and changed from playing a C clarinet to a B flat model; it was said that the move slowed him down, because he couldn't execute as fast on the slightly larger B flat model. Most New Orleans clarinettists played B flat Albert system instruments (and those that did a lot of orchestral work also carried an A clarinet). Lorenzo Tio, Jr, and George Baquet also played the small E flat clarinets for parade work, since the shriller qualities of the smaller instrument had cutting powers that were at their most effective when played in the open air in an ensemble heavy with brass instruments.

As part of the disciplinary regime at Sidney's home it was decided to put his clarinet under lock and key, so as to ensure that he didn't attempt to break the rule about an employer having to collect him at the house. Sidney got around this strategy by going to a gig and borrowing any clarinet he could lay hands on. On several occasions he simply asked the bandleader to get him a clarinet out of the local pawn-shop; he played the gig and then returned the instrument to the bandleader. Peter Bocage recalled the technical agility that Bechet showed in these circumstances: "He'd take an E flat clarinet and play in the orchestra. He didn't know what key we was playing in, but you couldn't lose him. That's the truth. Never saw anything like it."[21]

Johnny St Cyr also remembered a pawn-shop emergency which led to Sidney procuring an instrument from Jake Fink's hock-parlor. On this occasion Bechet and Buddy Petit were booked to play 'an advertisement' aboard a horse-drawn wagon. Because of problems at home Sidney was without his clarinet. Bob Lyons, then working at a pawn-shop on Rampart and Perdido, loaned Sidney an ancient model. Paul Barbarin observed the transaction and heard the resultant music: "I don't know how long that clarinet had been in that pawn shop. It looked like a banana, the colour of a banana . . . some of the notes didn't blow. Wow! What come out of that clarinet! And the notes that didn't work, he didn't mind that at all. That man was great."[22]

Bechet and Petit began going their separate ways. They continued to play occasional gigs together for some years, but by now each was being booked individually. Sidney's next regular unit was the Eagle Band, whose star cornetist was Willie 'Bunk' Johnson, a legendary figure of New Orleans jazz. Most members of the Eagle Band had formerly been sidemen with Buddy Bolden, so Johnson was occupying a prestigious place. Bunk was not a Creole, but he was a Catholic; he had been born to negro parents in New Orleans during the 1880s.

Bunk was impressed by Sidney's clarinet playing and persuaded Frankie Dusen (the manager of the Eagle Band), to bring him into the group. Dusen agreed, despite the youngster's age, so at sometime around 1911 (according to Sidney), but possibly two years later, he joined Bunk, Dusen, Brock Mumford (guitar), Henry Zeno (drums) and Dandy Lewis (string bass). (For marching dates Dandy played the bass drum, a role that bass player Ed Garland also took during his days with the Eagle Band.) It was a prestigious move for Bechet – he was replacing Lorenzo Tio, Jr – but all went well. Frank 'Big Boy' Goudie heard Bechet play alongside Bunk in a carnival, which led him to say: "Sidney Bechet was the best clarinetist I heard. He was considered a phenomenon."[23]

Bunk Johnson dutifully collected Sidney for the various evening gigs that they played together. According to Bunk the first of these took place at Pitman's, where the two front-line musicians worked with a drummer called Two Bits and a pianist unflatteringly known as Bogus.[24] The Eagle Band played several residencies at venues within Storyville, which was always referred to by the musicians simply as 'the District'. Two of the band's regular haunts were Buddy Bartley's place and 'Fewclothes' (the slang name for George Foycault's club at 135 North Basin Street). Sidney, who became a fastidious dresser in later life, looked so scruffy at this time that Buddy Bartley went out and bought some new clothes for him.

The aspect of the Eagle Band's music that marked it apart from its rivals was its ability to play the blues effectively. Sidney commented on this: "The Eagle Band was much more of a barrelhouse band – a real gutbucket band – a low-down band which really played the blues, and those slow tempos. To tell the truth the Eagle Band was the only band that could play the blues. That was really a band."[25]

The music of the Eagle Band had a rougher edge than that of its rivals. Its followers also tended to be rougher, and more prone to wild behaviour than the average New Orleans dance-hall patron. There were lively scenes at the 'Funky Butt' (Kinney's Hall) and at Liberty Hall, where Frankie Dusen used to promote dances, at which the Eagle Band played, three times a week. Trumpeter Lee Collins heard it play for a very rough crowd at the Masonic Hall (a regular Saturday-night booking for the band). By that time the rhythm section consisted of Tubby Hall on drums, Pops Foster on string bass and Cliff Stones on guitar. Collins recalled that the band's repertoire was extremely varied; it featured various ragtime favourites, including *Maple Lead Rag*, *Rose Leaf Rag* and *Frog Legs*.

Bechet was not tied exclusively to the Eagle Band, and often worked as a freelance with others: he played at George Foycault's with a band led by pianist Richard M. Jones (which at various times had Freddie Keppard and Joe Oliver on cornets); he worked with Manuel Perez in the Imperial Band, and he performed occasionally with the Superior Band. On one occasion Bechet worked alongside Lee Collins at another 'tough place' – the Red Onion. Buddy Petit was supposed to have played on the date but got so drunk he sent Collins in his place; the deputy recalled that the venue was packed with "out-of-town women". [26]

Sidney had begun to take a notably active interest in the opposite sex. 'Big Eye' Louis Nelson recalled: "We could never keep our hands on that Sidney. Regular little devil, always running off down the alley after them little women." [27] Sidney was regularly observed hugging and nuzzling the heavily rouged, daringly dressed females who frequented the rough joints where he worked, and he always made sure there was large glass of gin at his elbow.

Inklings of these activities naturally reached the Bechet home, and the *entente cordiale* that had been arrived at by acquiescence began to disintegrate. Bechet resumed his nocturnal wanderings and sometimes slept the night away (or what was left of it) on a meat stand at the back of the old Circle market. [28] Bunk Johnson was a noted tippler, so the two key members of the Eagle Band often got drunk together and sought female companions in tandem.

Next morning he might have a fearful hangover, but, despite that, Bechet usually managed to play any day-time gigs that he had accepted. Some of these were out on the picnic sites and involved his taking the 15-cent ride on the old Smokey Mary steam train that puffed its way along the 4½ miles of track. The trip was just long enough for the exhausted Bechet to fall asleep. Guitarist (and bass player) Eddie Dawson remembered the consternation that these slumbers caused: "The band would wait for Bechet to arrive on the Smokey Mary, but he'd ride back and forth to and from town because he was sleeping. Somebody would finally go to the train and take him to the job." [29]

Bechet also continued to play dates with Freddie Keppard. For one of these he asked Jimmie Noone to loan him a clarinet. Noone dutifully turned up with the instrument, but Bechet failed to arrive. Noone filled in for him, working alongside Keppard, Zue Robertson (trombone), Richard M. Jones (piano) and Jean Vigne (drums). It was Noone's first paid engagement, but he played so well he was offered the job permanently, and remained in the band until Keppard moved to California in the spring of 1914. [30]

The usual rate for a New Orleans gig in the early 1910s was around one dollar, 50 cents, so Sidney was probably earning at least 15 dollars a week – a little more than the average wage for a working adult. Sidney gave some of his money to his mother, or at least he did when his sprees left him in credit. Incoming funds were welcome at home because Sidney's father had temporarily given up shoemaking to open an ill-fated restaurant (eventually he got a job working for the New Orleans Mint). But no amount of money compensated the family for the fact that Sidney was working regularly in 'the District': such employment was thought of by them as a stigma. The situation was described by Buerkle and Barker in their book *Bourbon Street Black*: "For many Creoles of Color, playing in Storyville meant a loss of status within their own community."[31]

Sidney could not understand why his family worried about him. From an early age he felt independent and quite able to look after himself. He seems to have changed from being an innocent boy to a mature young man in an amazingly swift time, somehow avoiding the uncertainties of adolescence. Traits that stayed with him through life had taken shape by the time he reached puberty. Peter Bocage, who worked with Sidney both as a lad and as a middle-aged man, said, "He was always fiery. He's just a naturally fiery guy, it's his make-up. He don't sit still one minute. There's always something he's got to be doing. And when he plays he's the same way. He's fired up all the time."[32]

Bass player Albert Glenny described Sidney, not without affection, as a "bad boy". Following a particularly stormy incident at home Sidney went off to live with an aunt on Derbigny Street. Glenny saw him regularly and took him to gigs, but by then Sidney's wanderlust was obvious. Glenny recalled: "Tonight he might live here, and tomorrow night, there."[33]

Bechet's parents became more and more disenchanted, but years later Leonard Bechet adopted a philosophical attitude when he told Alan Lomax: "A person has to go through all that rough stuff like Sidney went through to play music like him. You have to play with all varieties of people. You have to play real *hard* when you play for Negroes. You got to *go* some if you want to avoid their criticism. You got to come up to their mark. If you do, you get that drive. Bolden had it. Bunk Johnson had it. Manuel Perez, the best ragtime Creole trumpet, he didn't have it."[34]

The young Sidney Bechet could be soft spoken and charming; he retained these appealing qualities throughout his life and they made him a permanent favourite with the opposite sex. He usually remained quiet in the company of strangers but once he knew someone he was always the first to give a friendly nod. When he was with his own clique he often adopted a jovial, almost jaunty, style of conversation – one that was laden with nicknames – but all of his friends were well aware of Sidney's short-fused temper. As he approached manhood, both friend and foe discovered that an ultra-suspicious attitude could quickly surface and turn Sidney into a fiend.

For the first half of his life Bechet could be, and sometimes was, an aggressive drinker. A few glasses of gin made him the liveliest of companions, eager to dance and joke. A few more made him maudlin, and any thereafter usually brought an antagonistic glint to his eyes that meant trouble was only a hair's breadth away. But truculence and tipsy brooding were only a part of Sidney's character, and in general he was liked by most of his fellow musicians. Even those who were irritated by his restlessness and alarmed by his belligerence always found time to praise his marvellous musicianship.

THREE

Jazz Prodigy

Bunk Johnson seems to have been the one who suggested to Sidney that it would be advantageous to redevelop his earlier interest in the cornet so that he could make himself extra money by playing in marching bands. Bechet took Johnson's advice and occasionally played cornet in street parades. One of his employers was the brass-band leader Henry Allen, Sr, whose son Henry, Jr, had vivid memories of hearing Bechet's startling cornet playing, and was impressed by his exceptional range. Henry, Jr, then only about nine years old, thought for some while that the Sidney Bechet who played cornet was a different person from the Sidney Bechet who played clarinet. He couldn't believe that any young man could be outstanding on both instruments, but when he saw Bechet playing the clarinet he realized his mistake.[1]

It seems that Bechet's cornet playing was not only flexible, it was also remarkably forceful. During one parade (on which Bechet was working as a clarinettist) a heavy rainstorm caused the band to disperse. Bechet and 'Wooden' Joe Nicholas (one of the most powerful of all New Orleans brass players) took shelter in a disused house. During their enforced wait Sidney borrowed Joe's cornet and, according to Nicholas, blew as loudly as he himself could have done.[2]

Any differences that existed between Creoles and Blacks were forgotten when a pick-up marching band assembled. Albert Nicholas recalled: "Brass bands were mixed bands. Creole and uptown in a brass band – they were solid. They were one, Joe Oliver and Manuel Perez, see?"[3]

About 1913 Bechet's long-standing dispute with his parents reached a head: the mature youngster moved up-town and began working in a band led by trombonist Jack Carey. Jack's brother Mutt played cornet in the band, which had a shifting personnel. Amongst the various musicians who went through its ranks were Ernest Rodger (drums), Charles Moore (guitar), and an ex-Bolden sideman, Jimmy Johnson, on string bass. Jack Carey did not make an ideal bandleader. He was, according to drummer Baby Dodds, "a wild and quick tempered fellow, loud and boisterous."[4] Bass player Jimmy Johnson was replaced by George Foster, who became one of the most illustrious bassists in jazz history. Foster recalled Bechet's stay with the Carey band: "Sidney played the 'District' with Jack Carey. Sidney was an ear musician and a wonderful jazzman. One night we ended up in jail together. He was fooling around with a chick at a dance out at the lake. She pulled a knife and stabbed him. I grabbed a stick and started after her. When the cops came we told them we were playing.

They took us to jail and then let us go. When he got back to the dance she thanked us for not getting her in trouble. Sidney was always wanting to fight but they never came off."[5]

Working with Jack Carey was only part of Bechet's hyperactive musical life. He was kept so busy playing various gigs that sometimes he 'tripled', or played three engagements each day – none of them lasting for less than three hours. He had achieved his ambition of earning a living solely from playing music. In the 1914 edition of Soards City Directory he was listed as a musician, living on Cohn Street. His reputation was growing steadily, and he was recognized as the best improvising clarinettist in all of New Orleans.

Sidney was always fiercely competitive, ever willing to engage in a musical duel with a clarinet-playing rival. Bechet and his friend Emile Barnes used to operate together in seeking out any challengers; Barnes called these musical contests "cutting hay".[6] Barnes and Bechet went to dances with their clarinets hidden in their back pockets. Barnes usually sat in with the band first and proceeded to cut his opponent with a display of superior skills, but if the home clarinettist proved difficult he would then have to face the overwhelming power of Bechet's playing.[7]

Emile Barnes said that clarinettist Johnny Dodds used to run away when he saw Bechet and Barnes approaching a bandstand on which he was working. Dodds lived to fight another day, and became one of Bechet's own favourite jazz players. He was an up-town Negro, one who showed no compromise in his passionate approach to improvising; Sidney admired this reflection of his own attitude.

Louis James, a clarinettist several years older than Sidney, worked out a plan to keep young Bechet at bay. Whenever Sidney entered Villa's Cabaret (where James worked with Manuel Manetta on piano and Joe Howard on cornet), in order to discourage the visitor from performing, the resident clarinettist would play the fastest, most intricate music that he knew.[8]

During the late spring of 1914 several famous New Orleans musicians left for California, where they formed the Original Creole Orchestra (under the leadership of bass player Bill Johnson). The group soon embarked on a series of tours that took them from coast to coast. Three of the departing musicians, Freddie Keppard, George Baquet and Eddie Vincent (trombone), were members of the New Olympia Band. They were replaced by Joe Oliver, Sidney Bechet and Alvin 'Zue' Robertson (cited by Bechet as the most underrated of all New Orleans musicians). The newcomers joined Armand J. Piron on violin, Henry Zeno on drums, Willie Marrero on string bass and Louis Keppard (Freddie's brother), on guitar. An eye-witness account of the Olympia Band in action comes from the New Orleans historian, musician and medical man Dr Edmond Souchon:

In 1914 I vividly remember the Tulane Gymnasium scrip dances, held almost every Saturday night (8pm–midnight). One dollar per couple, stags one dollar. One band that always packed the house was the Olympia, otherwise known as the 'monocles' band. The latter name was derived from the protruding eye of the cornetist. When he reached for a high note, his bulging eye gave the effect of wearing a monocle. The man who held the crowd spellbound with his horn was none other than Joe 'King'

Oliver. The quiet leader of this band was Armand J. Piron, with the following famous men: Sidney Bechet, clarinet, Louis Keppard, guitar (later replaced by Johnny St Cyr), Henry Zeno, drums, and Clarence Williams, piano, later replaced by Steve Lewis.[9]

Souchon's recollections show that from time to time the line-up of the Olympia Band varied. In fact, there was a great deal of flexibility in New Orleans concerning personnels and specific instrumentations. The format of a six-piece band (depending on circumstances) might consist of various permutations of instruments: cornet, clarinet and four rhythm; cornet, clarinet, trombone and three rhythm; cornet, two clarinets plus trombone and two rhythm; and so on. There was no question of the rigid use of a front line consisting of cornet, clarinet and trombone, and in a six-piece band a violinist was often given the task of playing the melody. A wealth of tone colours was available because most musicians doubled on other instruments.

Very few New Orleans bands automatically used the same number of musicians for every engagement that they played; they took only the number of men they were being paid to bring. Johnny St Cyr pointed out that even those bands who were playing residencies were often asked by the management to pare off one, two, or even three members of a band on 'quiet' nights of the week. Sidney Bechet rarely found himself made redundant, however. He played many casual dates with various groups in New Orleans during the years 1914 to 1917. One such booking, which was on a semi-regular basis, marked the professional début of drummer Minor Hall (brother of drummer Tubby Hall). Minor, Sidney and pianist Arthur Campbell played in Guidrey and Allen's Upstairs Club on Perdido Street.[10]

Joe Oliver and Bechet played a residency together at the "25" Cabaret (a club managed by Johnny Lala) in the District. They worked there with Arthur Campbell on piano, Buddy Christian on banjo, Lewis Matthews on string bass, and Jean Vigne on drums. Vigne was a respected drummer, but late hours did not suit him. During the day he worked in his own coal yard, and towards the end of a night's playing he often fell asleep across his drum kit.[11] Johnny Lala's "25" was one of the few cabarets in the District which did not operate a "whites only" customer policy. Another club that served people of any race was Pete Lala's club.[12] (The Lalas were not related; Pete's real name was Ciaccio.)

Violinist Peter Bocage replaced banjoist Buddy Christian at the "25". In an interview in 1959 for the Tulane Jazz Archive, he recalled his days at the club: "Bechet was there. Just full of talent, and never had two weeks good schooling in his life. But man could he play that clarinet. We was playing on Basin Street, the 'Big 25' on Franklin Street there. And one night he came there, he was nothing but a kid, and he didn't have no reed. He took a piece of cigar box and shaped a reed and played all night with that thing." Dr Souchon heard Oliver's band at the "25" and described it as "hard-hitting, rough and ready, full of fire and drive."[13]

Pete Lala's cabaret was at the corner of Iberville and Marais. Bechet also worked there with Joe Oliver, together with Ferdinand Valteau (violin), Henry Zeno (drums) and Manuel Manetta (piano). Others who occasionally played with Oliver and Bechet at the club included Joe Pierre (drums), Herb Lindsay (violin) and Frank Ahaynove, a pianist from Mobile, Alabama. Sometimes 'Big Eye Louis Nelson deputized for Bechet and this cabaret, which was soon to be turned into a dance-hall.[14] It was there that Bechet developed a quaint party trick which greatly amused the customers: he gradually took his clarinet to pieces, but continued to play a tune on the remnants, dramatically completing the act by playing on the mouthpiece only.

Violence often surfaced in the District cabarets. One evening in 1915, while Bechet and Oliver were standing in John Lala's on North Franklin enjoying a drink, one of the customers was shot dead. Both musicians appeared in court to give eye-witness testimony.[15] Two years earlier in an infamous shoot-out, two club owners, Billy Phillips and Harry Parker, had been shot dead in the Tuxedo Saloon.

Sidney regarded mayhem as one of the hazards of a musician's working life. In some ways it seems as though he was stimulated by violent behaviour; for much of his life he was fascinated by gangsters and hoodlums and often went out of his way to drink and chat with them.

Not all of Bechet's working hours were spent in sleazy clubs. He continued to play for picnics, lawn parties and various parades. He also occasionally played at funerals, where his talents greatly impressed Louis Keppard, who considered that Sidney was vastly superior to Lorenzo Tio, Jr, at this type of work.[16] But Tio, who was skilled at reading music, had opportunities to play engagements in theatre orchestras, a line of work that Sidney shunned. Sidney's inability, or rather unwillingness, to learn to read music also meant that he didn't play in bands organized by the Streckfus family for their steamship excursions. The Streckfus family was prepared to take on 'slow' readers, but refused to consider employing musicians whose fame rested solely on their ability to improvise. Bechet's riverboat work was limited to playing occasionally in a three- or four-piece band aboard smaller boats on 'moonlight excursions'.[17]

Most New Orleans musicians benefited from work that was available aboard the advertising wagons that often rolled through the streets of the city. The music played on these horse-drawn vehicles was used to call attention to various promotions; most often it was a forthcoming dance, but the 'ballyhoo' (as the musicians called it) was also used to announce the opening of a new theatrical show, a boxing match, or even the merits of a proprietary medicine.

On one occasion Sidney acquired a wagon job advertising the Ivory Theatre on Marais Street, and he was given money enough to provide a trio. The line-up he chose was 'Little' Mack Lacey on drums and a young cornet player called Louis Armstrong; he paid the two sidemen 50 cents each and kept a dollar for himself.[18]

Louis Armstrong gave his recollections of 1917 in his autobiography *Swing That Music*: "One of the hottest clarinettists then was a young genius named Sydney Bachet."[19] Louis's phonetic spelling of 'Bechet' highlights the different pronunciations of Sidney's surname: his New Orleans contemporaries said 'Bash-ay', later jazz fans opted for 'Besh-ay', but in France it was always 'Besh-ett'.

In his later autobiography *Satchmo*, Louis said that he was still working in the coal yard when he first heard Sidney play an up-town date at Gravier and

Franklin. He also retained vivid memories of Bechet's cornet playing, particularly the time when Henry Allen, Sr, was a man short and borrowed a cornet from Jake Fink's pawnshop for Sidney to play on a parade. Louis said of the incident: "Bechet joined the band, and he made the whole parade, blowing like crazy. I marvelled at the way Bechet played the cornet, and I followed him all that day."[20]

Sidney had known Louis by sight for several years before they ever worked together. He remembered the youngster hanging around various bands, listening avidly to the cornet players – particularly Bunk Johnson and Joe Oliver. Bunk Johnson took Sidney to hear Louis singing in a kerbside quartet. Sidney was impressed with what he heard and later asked Louis if he would visit the Bechet home to sing for the family. Louis seemed reluctant to do this, explaining to Sidney that his shoes were so badly worn that he couldn't walk any distance in them. Bechet gave Louis 50 cents to get the shoes repaired, but for some reason or other Louis never appeared at the Bechet household.

A few years later, on the advertising wagon, there were no footwear problems. Louis climbed aboard with Sidney and the drummer and proceeded to blow hell out of the cornet, even playing the fast-flowing 'clarinet' chorus on *High Society*, a technical feat unheard of in those days. The highly competitive Bechet must have screwed up his eyes a little at this musical onslaught, but according to his own recollections he felt nothing but unalloyed admiration. Louis said that he was thrilled to have worked with Sidney, but thereafter, for the rest of their lives, the two geniuses of early jazz treated each other with the utmost caution.

Bechet played for various leaders aboard advertising wagons during the mid-1910s. Sometimes he worked with Clarence Williams, a young pianist who was already earning money from his composing activities. But few wagons used a piano, not only because of the difficulties of getting one up onto the vehicle, but also because the instrument would soon be shaken out of tune during a journey over the rough streets of New Orleans. On one piano-less ride Clarence Williams decided that he would play a C-melody sax in the band alongside Sidney's clarinet. Another pianist, Joe Robichaux, was standing at one of the places at which the wagon stopped, and saw Bechet fooling around with the saxophone during a lull in the promotional work. Bechet told Williams that he was sure it would be easy to learn the saxophone, so Clarence allowed Sidney to take the instrument home for the night. Next day Bechet turned up at the Rosebud Hall able to play a tune on the C-melody sax.[21]

Peter Bocage recounted a similar anecdote, perhaps, since Clarence Williams also figured in the story, based on the same incident. Bocage quoted Bechet as saying, "Man, I can play this thing." He then took the instrument away and mastered it easily. Bocage added, "He was just that type of boy, never says 'quit'."[22]

In an interview on Radio KRE, California, in 1953, Bechet recalled his first experience of playing the saxophone: "I was engaged for this job because the clarinet player didn't show up. So they asked me, would I come over to play at the Roof Gardens? I said, 'Yes'. But I didn't have a clarinet, so this Armand J. Piron, he had a C-melody sax. He said, 'Do you think you could play a saxophone?'. I said, 'Yes, get it'. I meant it, but I didn't know whether I could play it or not. It was a little trouble, but it came out alright." As Piron later partnered Clarence Williams in a publishing company, this may well have been the very same saxophone on which Bechet had previously practised.

Although they were comparatively rare, saxophones had been seen in New Orleans long before Bechet's first attempts to play one; they were no more or less popular in New Orleans than anywhere else, however, and, contrary to some viewpoints, their usage created no musical crises. The soprano saxophone was then one of the rarest of the saxophone family, but both Willie Humphrey, Sr, and Alphonse Picou owned soprano saxophones during the 1910s. What is certain is that Sidney Bechet had made efforts to play the saxophone long before he ever acquired his first soprano instrument.

Clarence Williams played a part in the next big move in Sidney's life – one which took him outside Louisiana for the first time. Bechet joined a travelling show as part of a quartet that accompanied Williams's comedy and vocal routines. Williams also played piano in the show, but most of the keyboard work was done by Louis Wade, whose brother Clark was one of the most celebrated pimps in all New Orleans. A former colleague of Bechet's, Henry Zeno, was on drums. All of the musicians took acting parts in various sketches; this greatly pleased Sidney, who had always enjoyed himself immensely in the talent contests of his childhood. He was also given a feature spot of his own in which he performed his clarinet dismantling trick.

The troupe polished its routines during a two-week booking at the Lincoln Theatre in New Orleans. The *Chicago Defender* of 7 October 1916 reported: "Williams and Wade Stock Company consists of Lela Dudson [probably Dusen], vocals, and Mr. Williams' Creole Four Orchestra: Mr. Henry Zeno (traps), Sidney Basha [sic] (clarinet), Lee Braxton (trombone), and Mr. Clarence Williams (piano)." The *Defender* also noted: "Mr Basha [sic] is screaming 'em' every night with his sensational playing. All send regards to the Creole Band. Basha says look out Louis Nelson I am coming."[23] ('Big Eye' Louis Nelson had left New Orleans in June 1916 to join the Original Creole Orchestra, replacing George Baquet.)

The tour prospered for a while, but eventually floundered in Texas for want of bookings. Sidney joined up with a touring carnival which took him to Beaumont, Texas, where he worked with a unit he described as "the Jones Band".[24] The personnel of that group is unknown, but it may be connected with the mellophone player and saxophonist David Jones (who was one of Louis Armstrong's tutors). Jones made his home in Port Arthur (which is close to Beaumont) for several years.[25]

Sidney's guitar-playing brother, Joe, had been added to the Williams and Wade line-up before the tour left New Orleans. After the show became stranded Joe and a girl-friend moved on with Lee Braxton to Braxton's home town, Galveston. Sidney eventually joined them there, but Joseph and he soon decided it was time to return to New Orleans. They counted their money and discovered that there were only funds enough to pay for one railroad ticket; Sidney won the toss and his brother was forced to 'ride the rods' on the train journey back to his home city.

Back in New Orleans Sidney soon began working again with Joe Oliver, this time at Toodlum's Bar in the District (on the former site of Buddy Bartley's Club). They also played for lawn parties that Toodlum organized. The timing of their work also allowed both men to play regularly at the Claiborne Theatre (owned by Pete Lala, and situated on Claiborne and St Louis). Even this hectic schedule wasn't enough for Sidney. He used his spare time playing countless gigs in all sorts of groups, including dates with Buddy Petit at the Poodle Dog on Liberty and Bienville.

On one parade date he resumed his activities as a cornetist. He was nothing if not bold, for his two colleagues in the cornet trio were Buddy Petit and Louis Armstrong. Sidney was assigned the high note that ended one particular piece; he hit it good and true, and this time it was Louis Armstrong's turn to blink in astonishment.

With Buddy Bolden long retired (through ill health), and Freddie Keppard and Bunk Johnson out of the city, Joe Oliver's services were much in demand, and he began working regularly with trombonist Kid Ory. There was a plan to feature both Johnny Dodds and Sidney Bechet within the group, but the idea was abandoned, and Dodds became the sole reed player. However, when Dodds left town temporarily to go on tour, Sidney was the obvious man to replace him. Ory, already developing a reputation for being a firm disciplinarian, had problems with Bechet. Clarinettist John Casimir recalled: "Sidney led Ory something of a dance. Bechet would get drunk and not come on the job. If you want Bechet to play tonight you've got to bring him here, then you had to get him half-drunk to keep him."[26] In later years Bechet and Ory never strived to be reunited.

During this period Sidney might well have gone to California. Clarinettist James Williams died whilst working on the West Coast with the Black and Tan Orchestra, and an urgent request for a suitable replacement reached New Orleans. Sidney was one of the candidates, but he declined and the job was taken by Willie F. Humphrey, Sr. The Blacks and Tans worked regularly on film sets, playing background music to help the 'silent' actors and actresses play their roles in a congenial atmosphere. Thirty years later Bechet mused on his decision not to move west: "I never went into the movies. I could have gone, back in 1917. That's when I was really playing clarinet – but I didn't want to tip my hat to nobody."[27]

In 1917 Bechet's main source of employment was Pete Lala's Theatre (which was then functioning as a movie house). On 5 June 1917, whilst working for Lala, Bechet was called to register for possible service in the US forces. On registration form 228, Bechet stated that he had to support both his father and his mother. He described himself as single and gave his race as "colored"; he wrote that he was "short and stout with black hair". All the physical descriptions could be seen to be true, but there are three oddities on the card. Firstly, Sidney gave his occupation as "Labor". Secondly, he gave his date of birth as 14 May 1896. It seems that he added a year to his age (making himself 21) so as to add strength to his claim that he was supporting both parents. He also gave the family address, 1240 St Bernard Avenue, as his home.

There is nothing to suggest that Sidney was any less patriotic than the next man, but soon after he had registered for possible recruitment he developed what he called "itchy feet".[28] An opportunity for him to begin travelling again presented itself during the early part of July 1917. A Mrs Bruce, who ran a stock company with her husband Arthur, journeyed to New Orleans to recruit musicians for her travelling company. The *Indianapolis Freeman* of 14 July 1917 noted that Mrs Bruce had gone to "New Orleans on Wednesday to engage a jazz band". A month later (on 18 August 1917) the same journal reported that the mission had been successful: "Mrs Bruce has secured a Jazz Band from New Orleans, including Louis Wade, Sidney Bechet, Frank Keeling and Johnnie Sawyer. They are all red hot, and the tremendous crowds howl and rave to hear them play the *Livery Stable Blues.*"

Sawyer was a drummer, Keeling a cornetist, and Louis Wade the same pianist who had toured previously with Bechet. As before, the musicians played roles in the stock company's sketches. Sidney was pleased to get another chance to develop his acting technique; he was apparently ever willing to take advice from various old vaudevillians. Bechet recalled that the Bruce and Bruce Company "toured through Alabama, Georgia, Ohio and Indiana".[29] The *Indianapolis Freeman* noted that the group was in Macon, Georgia, in September 1917, and announced subsequently that its booking at the Monogram Theater, Chicago, in November 1917 was so successful that it had been held over for a second week.

A critic, Sylvester Russell, reviewed the troupe during the Chicago booking and commented: "The clarinet player should have sense enough to play soft for soloists, so people can hear the words also the voices."[30]

Sidney's routine at the Monogram Theater allowed him enough time to seek out various pals from New Orleans who had made the move to Chicago – where they could earn more money than they ever did in Louisiana. A vast influx of black workers entered Chicago during the 1910s, most of them rural folk from the South seeking employment in the factories and plants of the city. Those who found work soon had money to spend on entertainment; they thronged into the black theatres and dance-halls and created a boom time for black artistes and musicians.

White Chicagoans had earlier welcomed the sound of New Orleans music presented to them by Tom Brown's band (in May 1915), and more lastingly by the five-piece Original Dixieland Jazz Band (led by cornetist Nick LaRocca), whose widespread successes began in Chicago in 1916. Brown's six-piece band did not use a piano; the line-up of cornet, clarinet, trombone, guitar, string bass and drums was a common instrumentation for New Orleans sextets. LaRocca's group created a different sound by using a three-piece front line (cornet, trombone and clarinet) supported by a rhythm section consisting only of piano and drums. The ODJB's instrumentation was not one that had been featured regularly by any other New Orleans band, black or white, though Freddie Keppard had briefly used it when forced to cut down a group for economic reasons.

LaRocca spent a good deal of his later life claiming to have invented jazz. The preposterous nature of this boast tended to make most jazz lovers regard the ODJB's music as something that was equally false, but the band's music had merit, even though none of its members was a first-rate improviser. LaRocca's group provided the world with a bold pastiche of sounds that had long been heard in New Orleans, and it did so with a vigour and enthusiasm that appealed to the dancing public. It was originally billed as the Original Dixieland Jass Band, but in Chicago 'Jass' became 'Jazz', and this name rapidly adhered itself to any attempts to play the 'new' music. Even black New Orleans musicians began using the term, phasing out the word 'ragtime'. Bechet himself had contempt for the sounds of the ODJB, and said so: "Some of the white musicianers had taken our style as best they could. They played things that were really our numbers . . . it's awful hard for a man who isn't black to play a melody that's come deep out of black people. It's a question of feeling."[31]

Nevertheless, the Original Dixieland Jazz Band achieved a degree of popular success that had eluded Freddie Keppard and the Original Creole Orchestra during the theatre and club bookings they had played in Chicago. Several other black New Orleans musicians had also tried their luck in Chicago before the début of the ODJB, but their successes were limited and most of them soon made their way back to their home city. The success of the ODJB in Chicago encouraged promoters, white and black, to import more and more jazz musicians from New Orleans.

Sidney's old friends from New Orleans urged him to stay in Chicago to take advantage of this lucrative situation, but he decided to move on with the Bruce and Bruce company. In his own account of his travels Bechet simplifies the situation by saying he left the show whilst it was at Chicago's Monogram (mis-transcribed as the Mardi Gras), but this was not so. Newspaper reports mention Bechet with the group in Cincinnati (December 1917), in Indianapolis (February 1918) and in Cleveland (March 1918). A report in the *Indianapolis Freeman* of 2 March 1918 mentioned that the Bruce and Bruce company had been laid off in Cleveland but was preparing to move to Detroit on Monday 4 March 1918. This seems to mark the point at which Sidney decided to quit the show. He was soon back in Chicago, where he joined a band that was led by two Louisianians, clarinettist Lawrence Duhé and trumpeter 'Sugar' Johnny Smith.

In Chicago Bechet's talents soon won him many new admirers. There was fierce competition for his musical services, and amongst the many offers that reached him was one that took him away from America for several years.

FOUR

Restless

The migration of New Orleans musicians to Chicago is usually conveniently linked to the closing of Storyville, the bordello area which had been named after the zealous and prominent New Orleans administrator Alderman Sidney Story. In November 1917 the US Department of the Navy, determined to ensure that its sailors kept away from the brothel area, put Storyville out of bounds. The move was an attempt to stop the occurrence of vicious brawls within the area, and to minimize the incidence of venereal disease amongst the servicemen. As a result of the restrictions, some of the 'sporting houses' went out of business and many of the itinerant prostitutes, who had previously found seasonal trade good in New Orleans, moved on.

The history of jazz was not drastically affected by the closure of Storyville. Only a few brothels employed the services of a regular band, for even the plushest whorehouses were content to have music provided by a resident pianist. Most of the work for improvising musicians was in dance-halls and cabarets, and these had suffered diminishing returns before Storyville closed. Business had been hit by various trade recessions that occurred as an aftermath of the outbreak of World War I in Europe (in 1914). Drummer Paul Barbarin said: "The music business was at a standstill long before the District closed."[1] In later years Bechet could get quite testy if he heard the Storyville 'theory' expounded. He said, "The way some people talk, you'd think we all sat and waited for Storyville to close."[2]

Poor rates of pay was the main reason for New Orleans musicians seeking work outside Louisiana. When various veterans recalled what they earnt in the Crescent City during the period 1910–16, the quoted rates usually ranged from $1.50 to $2.50 per engagement. George Foster said, "We made a dollar and a half a night or nine dollars a week. We were the best paid band in the District."[3] Multi-instrumentalist Manuel Manetta said, "We got $2.50 for an 8 p.m. to 4 a.m. cabaret gig, about the same for a dance, plus an extra dollar for playing an advertising job from 1 p.m. until 6 p.m."[4] Alphonse Picou recalled getting $1.25 for his 8 p.m. to 4 a.m. engagements, but said this low amount was supplemented by tips. Sonny Henry said a funeral usually paid $2.50 per musician. Even a highly successful leader like Kid Ory only paid his sidemen $17.50 a week, and a star player like Joe Oliver only got $25 a week at Pete Lala's.[5] The white bands fared no better. Drummer Tony Sbarbaro, later with the Original Dixieland Jazz Band, recalled his early days in New Orleans: "We got 15 dollars for five parades, or 12 dollars for seven nights' work."[6]

Admittedly, in the early 1910s a good steak could be bought at a New Orleans market for ten cents and a loaf of bread for only five cents, but, when Paul Barbarin worked as a lift-boy in New Orleans (in 1915), he got $17.50 a week. The musician's life might have seemed glamorous, but mundane occupations were as well paid.

So there were good economic reasons for Sidney Bechet not to return to New Orleans. Chicago was particularly inviting because it seems that the musicians' union there did not require Lousianians to undergo any stringent probationary restrictions. New Orleans violinist Charles Elgar was one of the earliest black musical emigrés to settle in Chicago. He soon became an important figure in Local 208, the so-called Colored branch of the American Federation of Musicians (white musicians belonged to Chicago's segregated Local 10; the two branches did not amalgamate until the 1960s). The President of Local 208, Alexander Armand, was also from New Orleans, and, although there is no suggestion of connivance in favour of home-town arrivals, it does seem that black New Orleans musicians who moved to Chicago found authorized work almost immediately.

Sidney Bechet's pursuit of employment was not impeded by his having to undergo any test of his ability to read music (an examination that usually formed a vital condition of entry to the musicians' union). As soon as he returned to Chicago he joined up with Duhé and Smith's band, then performing at the De Luxe Cafe, 3503 State Street. The practice of using two clarinettists in a New Orleans band was not uncommon and Sidney's prowess would certainly have been an asset to the group. Duhé admitted that Bechet was a better player than he was: "Sidney could always outplay me – but he didn't."[7]

Lawrence Duhé (1887–1960) was from La Place, Louisiana. He had arrived in Chicago during April 1917 with a band consisting of Herbert Lindsay (violin), Ed Garland (string bass), Louis Keppard (guitar), Roy Palmer (trombone), Tubby Hall (drums) and a cousin of the Marrero family, 'Sugar' Johnny Smith (cornet). Duhé and his colleagues had not arrived on spec, but had been contracted to appear at the De Luxe (which was managed by Isidore Shorr) by promoters Mitchell Lacalzi and Lee Krauss.[8] Soon after they arrived Duhé added a pianist, Lil Hardin (who later married Louis Armstrong), from Memphis, Tennessee.

By the time Sidney Bechet joined the band in 1918 there had been several changes of personnel: drummer Tubby Hall, drafted into the US Army, had been replaced by his younger brother, Minor Hall; Wellman Braud had taken the place of Ed Garland on string bass; and Gilbert 'Bab' Frank had been added on piccolo to re-create the parts the violinists Herbert Lindsay and Jimmy Palao had played during their stays with the group.[9]

According to Duhé, Bechet was "the featured hot man". Duhé himself concentrated on reinforcing the melody, allowing Bechet to embellish; both men played B Flat Albert system clarinets. "Sidney couldn't read, but he only had to hear a piece once to be able to play it," said Duhé. "He used his lips to get effects like chicken cackles," (Bechet had been taught this trick by 'Big Eye' Louis Nelson.)[10] By the time Bechet had settled in the band at the De Luxe it was being billed as the "Lawrence Dewey [sic] Orchestra".[11] Lil Hardin said that the job with Duhé paid her 55 dollars a week.[12]

Cornetist 'Sugar' Johnny Smith was in poor health (he died a short time afterwards from the scourge of that era – tuberculosis), and his condition made it impossible for him to work the full schedule with Duhé's band. This was causing Duhé some worry, as he was shortly to begin a new residency at the Dreamland Cafe (run by Bill Bottoms) at 35th and State Street. A new arrival, in the bulky shape of Joe Oliver, temporarily solved the problem.

Oliver had moved to Chicago from New Orleans, ostensibly to join the band that bass player Bill Johnson was organizing for the Royal Gardens, a dance-hall and bar-room at 459 East 31st Street (by Cottage Grove Avenue). Oliver was not Bill Johnson's first choice; the bass player had originally wired an offer to Buddy Petit, who failed to answer. Johnson then tried Oliver, who accepted, as did clarinettist Jimmie Noone.

Duhé, learning of Oliver's impending arrival, made plans to entice the cornetist into his band. In order to do this he asked Sidney Bechet to accompany him to the railway station to meet the morning train (knowing of Sidney's unpunctuality Duhé made him stay the night at his apartment).[13] Oliver listened to Duhé's offer, then decided to have the best of both worlds by doubling between the Royal Gardens and the Dreamland Cafe.

This arrangement did not entirely suit Duhé. His Dreamland booking was from 9.30 p.m. until 1 a.m., but Oliver was expected (by the Royal Garden bosses Virgil Williams and James Griffin) to be on stage at his other gig by 1 a.m., in order to play his three-hour stint there. Under this pressure Oliver was inclined to start packing his cornet and mutes away well before 1 a.m., so that he had ample time to negotiate the distance between the two jobs.

Whilst Bill Johnson had been waiting for replies from New Orleans, he had utilized the services of his long-time colleague cornetist Freddie Keppard. Both Johnson and Keppard were in Chicago because the Original Creole Orchestra's trombonist, Eddie Vincent, had been forced to quit that group unexpectedly to undergo an appendicectomy. It so happened that all three of these musicians found the Chicago atmosphere congenial, and they never went back on the road again as a unit.

Duhé decided to ask Keppard to join his band. The proud Keppard did not want it to appear that he was anybody's second choice, so he demanded – and received – 50 dollars a week, which was more than Oliver had been paid.[14] Keppard only used this sort of work as a stop-gap, since he had ambitions to be a successful bandleader. By the end of 1918 he was leading at the De Luxe Gardens and was billed as King Keppard, obviously as a challenge to Joe Oliver (who was now always referred to as King Oliver).

Bechet was not unamused by the rivalry between the two ace cornetists. Although he was closer to Keppard socially, he also kept in with Oliver and frequently played pool with him. Tommy Ladnier, a young trumpeter (also from Louisiana), often saw the two men enjoying a game together, but was too shy to make himself known.[15]

Oliver persuaded Bechet that he too should double jobs between the Dreamland and the Royal Gardens, so for a brief while Bechet did the late-night dash with Oliver to work alongside the now-recovered trombonist Eddie Vincent.

Paul Barbarin was on drums and Bill Johnson on string bass. Following a new fashion that had been inspired by Lil Hardin's successes with Duhé's band, the Royal Gardens group introduced a pianist, Lottie Taylor (from Kentucky), who took the place of a violinist simply remembered as Geraldine.[16] According to Paul Barbarin, Oliver used Keppard on second trumpet at the same venue (in much the same way as he later employed Louis Armstrong).[17]

At some point during this period Oliver and Bechet had a bitter quarrel, and thereafter, for the rest of his life, Bechet found it hard to speak with any warmth about Oliver. But Freddie Keppard always remained something of a hero in Bechet's eyes and he rarely talked for long about the old days without bringing Keppard's name into the story.

The musician and writer Richard Hadlock recalled sharing a journey with Bechet in the early 1950s, during which Sidney spoke warmly about his old friend: "We were riding from Philadelphia to New York City, Bechet talked a lot about one of his heros – Freddie Keppard. He loved Keppard's big-tone lead horn and complete command. I had the feeling he was saying *that's* what it would take for a cornet to lead him through a performance. Sidney had an interesting rationale about lead playing. He said the melody belonged to the violin in the old days. Lacking a violin the clarinet would take over (and of course the soprano could be considered an extension of that)."[18]

One of Keppard and Bechet's off-duty haunts in Chicago was the Asia Cafe on 35th and State Street. There were no colour restrictions at that venue, but many Chicago bars and after-hours clubs practised segregation. Clarinettist Johnny Dodds, who made his home in Chicago after moving there to join King Oliver, said (in a rare interview): "It's hard for a colored person down South – so much discrimination. That's why most of us never went back except for a short trip sometimes. But a lot of us found it hard up North too. I mean the number of jobs you can get is limited because of discrimination, and then there are places you can't live in, eat in or go to, because you're colored."[19]

Sugar Johnny's health rallied and he returned briefly to play cornet in Duhé's band, but he was terminally ill. After his demise Keppard resumed playing with the group. As Bechet said, "Sugar Johnny's death threw me and Freddie Keppard together again."[20] The two men were kindred spirits. According to Bechet, Keppard "wasn't all serious, he was hell of a go-round man, they just don't come any better."[21] In Chicago the two musicians got so drunk in their dawn visits after work to "8 or 9 saloons"[22] that neither could remember where they had left their instruments.

To many people, Keppard appeared haughty. Trumpeter Charlie Gaines described him as "a stuck-up sort of fellow",[23] and he had what Johnny St Cyr called "that independent Creole temperament".[24] Keppard actively encouraged clannishness amongst New Orleans Creoles. Singer Lizzie Miles, who met up with him in Chicago, recalled that he always spoke to her in patois so that eavesdroppers couldn't follow the conversation.[25]

It seems that the remarkable aspects of Keppard's musical talents were never captured on record. He made a number of recordings (some under his own name), but none of them indicates any degree of genius. On record his playing has a rugged, forthright quality, but his staccato phrases are rhythmically closer to ragtime than to the 'jazzy', 'swinging' phrasing that is apparent even on early recordings by Sidney Bechet and Louis Armstrong. All the same, Keppard must have been a highly effective player in person, one whose gifts simply did not transfer to recording wax. Johnny St Cyr said, late in life: "It has been my good fortune to play with three of the geniuses of jazz, Freddie Keppard, Sidney Bechet and Louis Armstrong."[26]

Keppard is most often remembered now for declining an offer to record for the Victor Talking Machine Company, the acceptance of which would have made the Original Creole Orchestra the first jazz band to have recorded. The reason usually cited for the refusal (which probably occurred during the band's visit to New York in December 1915) is that Keppard didn't want anyone to steal his ideas by copying what he played on a recording. Most descriptions of Keppard suggest he was a shrewder character than that, but he was a highly suspicious person and (like Sidney Bechet) inclined to lose his temper easily.

According to George Baquet (the clarinettist in the band) Keppard began to get annoyed with the Victor company when they expressed doubts as to whether Bill Johnson's string bass playing could be recorded on the primitive, fragile recording equipment of that era. The recording company wanted the band to go into the studios to make a test to ascertain this point, but the 'audition' was to take place without payment. This greatly incensed the trumpeter; "Keppard couldn't understand playing a date and not being paid for it", said Baquet. Keppard delivered an ultimatum to the recording company: "We've been kicked around so much we don't want to record. We'll do it if you give us money, right away."[27] Victor declined the terms, and the course of jazz history was altered. It was a few years before Keppard finally made his recording début, long after the Original Dixieland Jazz Band's successes, and it was 1921 before a black jazz band, Kid Ory's Sunshine Orchestra, made its first recordings; that session took place in California. The history of jazz is full of 'if only', but it seems a tremendous pity that none of the intense jazz activity on the South Side of Chicago before 1920 was ever recorded. The New Orleans bands were working in an environment that was very different from that of their home city; they no longer worked for parades, funerals or picnics, and most of their playing was done in night-clubs or dance-halls.

Sidney Bechet continued to work with Lawrence Duhé's band at Dreamland, but when the Royal Gardens closed temporarily his after-hours 'doubling' spot became the Pekin Cafe, an upstairs club on State Street, near 27th. Bechet often worked there with the New Orleans pianist and singer Tony Jackson. Jackson was not only a fine pianist; he also sang beautifully, and composed highly melodic tunes (including the evergeen *Pretty Baby*). Bechet always retained the utmost admiration for Jackson's musicianship: "He was a wonderful piano player and entertainer. I worked at the Pekin with him; just him and I, piano and clarinet. Lots of times Tony didn't need me. He could entertain three or four hundred people just with his piano."[28]

During his trip to Galveston, Texas, in 1916, Sidney heard a recording by the Six Brown Brothers, a touring vaudeville act that featured six saxophones of varying registers, from bass up to soprano. For Bechet the appeal of their version of *Bull Frog Blues* was the sound of the soprano saxophone; he resolved to buy one for himself if the opportunity arose. Sometime during the winter of 1918, after he made his home in Chicago, Bechet saw a curved soprano saxophone in a pawnshop window. The asking price was 20 dollars, which was then less than half what Sidney was making a week, so he decided to buy it: "I took it on the job, and I was doing pretty good, but it didn't *give*. It had no volume, so I sold it to Darnell Howard."[29]

Darnell Howard confirmed that the transaction took place, but indicated that the purchase was completed in a more roundabout way: "Sidney sold me the pawn ticket for the soprano for five dollars, and that's how I got hold of it."[30] Howard, a native of Chicago, was one of the few non-Louisianians to be accepted in the various New Orleans cliques that were formed in the city. He told writer Johnny Simmen: "These men were great artistes and gentlemen who always treated me like a brother. Sidney especially, he invited my mother and me to his home and showed me anything on the clarinet and saxophone that I wanted to know. And there was never a question of paying him." Howard was an exception. During the late 1910s there was considerable resentment and jealousy between the Chicago musicians and the New Orleans newcomers.

Ill feeling could also brew easily within the ranks of those who were from Louisiana. When Sidney Bechet was accidentally given Lawrence Duhé's wage packet at Dreamland, he saw, to his anger, that Duhé was earning a lot more than he was. This discovery led to heated words between the two men, and Bechet left the band forthwith. By this time Freddie Keppard was leading a band at the Deluxe Cafe on the other side of State Street. Sidney joined Keppard (who was replaced shortly afterwards as leader by Manuel Perez at the Deluxe), but continued to 'double' by playing an after-hours stint at the Pekin.

Bechet had developed a formidable reputation amongst the jazz musicians in Chicago, but, according to violinist Robert 'Juice' Wilson, he was forced to admit defeat on one occasion. This was when his old friend Lorenzo Tio, Jr, came into Illinois. Wilson recalled: "Tio came up from New Orleans and cut Bechet to strips."[31] Happily this contest did nothing to diminish the mutual respect that the two clarinet players had for each other's talents.

Noble Sissle first heard Sidney play on the South Side of Chicago in 1919. Sissle was then an assistant to Lt James Reese Europe, a black musician who had returned to the USA in February 1919 after leading his Hellfighters Band in France during World War I. Jim Europe and Noble Sissle, then released from the army, were looking for outstanding musicians and had been advised to hear Sidney Bechet. They made contact with him and asked if he would mind giving an audition. What happened next astonished both Europe and Sissle. As the latter recalled: "Bechet agreed and pulled half of his clarinet from his right coat pocket, half from the left and his mouthpiece from the inside coat pocket. 'He's not going to try and play that, is he?', Europe asked, for the instrument's keys were held together with tape, and rubber bands were used to replace broken springs."[32] Noble Sissle never forgot the spectacular performance that Bechet gave on the dilapidated instrument.

Wellman Braud also spoke of Bechet's meeting with Jim Europe: "Bechet was invited by James Reese Europe to join his band. Bechet told him he didn't read, but Europe asked him to come to a rehearsal. Bechet sat in and played a cadenza in the *Poet and Peasant* overture, cutting the twelve clarinettists that Europe already had in the band."[33]

Early in 1919 Will Marion Cook, one of the outstanding black musicians of his generation, appeared in Chicago with the New York Syncopated Orchestra – a vast unit consisting of a huge choir and a big orchestra. Cook, formerly a violinist, was a shrewd talent spotter who was always on the look-out for gifted musicians to feature within his touring ensemble. After his group had given a concert at the Orchestra Hall in Chicago, Cook, his star trumpeter Arthur Briggs, and a saxophonist, Mrs Mazie Mullins, went to the Deluxe, where they heard Sidney playing in a band that also featured cornetist Manuel Perez (who had been lured from New Orleans by offers of big money) and trombonist George Filhe (also from New Orleans, and like Perez a cigar-maker by trade).

Will Marion Cook was astounded by Bechet's creative musicianship and immediately offered him a place in his orchestra. Cook was then negotiating to take his company on a tour of Europe and realized that Bechet's playing would be a startling attraction. Bechet told Cook that he didn't read music, but this didn't deter the leader, who offered Sidney 60 dollars a week (not much more than he was making in Chicago). Sidney had begun to feel restless in Chicago, and accepted the chance to travel. Bechet suggested to Cook that he might be able to find a place within his troupe for the remarkable talents of pianist Tony Jackson. Cook didn't dismiss the idea and visited the Pekin to hear Bechet and Jackson play together, but Jackson was not offered the job. Bechet always believed that Cook had been deterred by apparent signs that Jackson had venereal disease.

Will Marion Cook's plans for his overseas engagements ran into contractual difficulties (his main partners in the enterprise were the orchestra's manager, George W. Lattimore, and a sponsor, composer Joe Jordan), and, after the group had finished its tour by playing in New York City, he asked all the musicians and singers to remain on call so that he could assemble them quickly when the right time arrived.

Bechet now had the task of getting a passport. He had made preliminary enquiries in Chicago, where Manuel Perez had offered to be his guarantor.[34] But in New York rumours were rife that Will Marion Cook's proposed tour had been cancelled. Sidney felt that he had burnt his boats by leaving Chicago, so he decided to accept an offer to play with the band led by drummer Louis Mitchell at the Casino de Paris, in the French capital. Accordingly, on 28 April 1919 Louis A. Mitchell backed Bechet's passport application by sending a formal letter and sight of the contract that he held for the Paris engagement to the US Secretary of State's office in New York. Bechet duly signed his passport application on 13 May 1919 (giving his date of birth as 14 May 1897). His guarantor was the singer and bandolin player Henry Saparo, who signed an affidavit stating that he had known Sidney Bechet "for the past 20 years, as I lived in the same house as his Mother and Father for the last 23 years and have known the said Sidney Bechet ever since he was born."

To cover various contingencies Bechet wrote that he desired a passport for use in visiting France, which he crossed out, and Br Isles (British Isles), which he did not alter. He said that he intended to leave the United States of America on board the SS *Espagne*, due to depart New York harbour on 15 May 1919.

News of Sidney's extraordinary musical talents had preceded his arrival in New York, and he soon had a job working in Lieutenant Tim Brymn's orchestra (known as the Black Devils), which was playing a residency at the Shelburn Hotel at Brighton Beach, Coney Island. Brymn, who had recently returned from leading an army band in France, later achieved success as a songwriter. Wearing an elaborate uniform, Bechet was given feature numbers in Brymn's programme, but, just to amuse himself, learnt by ear the entire repertoire of the orchestra. The item in the show that most fascinated him was an instrumental version of *Song of Songs*, played on soprano saxophone by Nelson Kincaid. The performance rekindled Bechet's interest in the instrument.

Drummer Jasper Taylor, a veteran of the Chicago music scene (reminiscing in the issue of *Down Beat* magazine dated 1 July 1940), said that Freddie Keppard also went to New York to work with Tim Brymn, but neither Bechet, nor anyone else, mentioned that visit. Another larger mystery concerns Bechet's matrimonial state at this time. On an official document, completed in London in 1922, Bechet claimed that he had a wife, Norma, living in Chicago. This could have been a common-law partnership, but in view of Bechet's sexual proclivity it seems odd that he would have cited any unofficial liaison. No more details have been discovered.

Eventually, Will Marion Cook sent word to all of his company telling them to be ready to sail for Europe in early June 1919. Bechet was still in New York because Louis Mitchell's European booking had fallen through. This cancellation prompted him to have second thoughts about crossing the Atlantic with Cook. Bechet had no particular desire to return to his home on South Dearborn Street, Chicago, but he had settled into a comfortable groove in New York, and was being paid 80 dollars a week by Tim Brymn. However, Will Marion Cook made it plain to Bechet that he would not stand for any procrastination. He arrived at Sidney's place of work and pointed out that Bechet had agreed to make the trip and, accordingly, his passage had been booked. There would be litigation if Bechet refused to go, and Cook made it clear that he would seek reimbursement of monies already advanced. Bechet relented and went back to his apartment at 150 West 131st Street to pack his bags for the long trip.

The Southern Syncopated Orchestra (as Cook's group was now known) crossed the Atlantic in two parties; half of the troupe (which included Henry Saparo) sailed on the SS *Northland* and the remainder aboard the SS *Carmania*. Bechet and Cook travelled on the SS *Carmania* for what proved to be an uncomfortable nine-day crossing. The boat docked at Liverpool, England, on 14 June 1919, at the very time that the city was experiencing some of its worst-ever race riots. Fortunately Bechet's stay there was very brief, and within 24 hours he was taking his first look at London.

FIVE

Transatlantic Triumphs

London in 1919 was a city that was ready to enjoy itself. The sufferings and hardships that its inhabitants had undergone during World War I had created a mood that craved gaiety. The feeling affected all strata of society; after four years of carnage and tension the time had come for everyone to relax. Problems of unemployment and material shortages were looming, but even those who realized this were determined to enjoy themselves. For Britain, the jazz age was about to begin.

As in Chicago, the members of the Original Dixieland Jazz Band acted as missionaries for the new music; the group had arrived in London in April 1919. In some quarters its music met with stiff opposition, and derision, but it was rapturously received by the young dancers, who were fascinated and stimulated by the choppy syncopations that were the group's trademark.

The words 'jazz' and 'jazzy' were on many British lips during this time. They were used to describe anything that was new and daring: there was much talk of jazzy clothes and jazzy behaviour. Will Marion Cook was determined not to use the word 'jazz' for any of the music performed by the Southern Syncopated Orchestra (though several of its members could produce jazz that was superior to anything the ODJB played). Cook felt that the SSO's music would receive more careful listening, and more lasting acclaim, if it was not described as jazz. But he made no attempt to limit the jazz content of Bechet's main feature, *Characteristic Blues*; he respected the young man's creativity and accorded the clarinet solo a prominent part in the SSO's programme by making it the penultimate number in the show.

Cook was a fine composer who had previously toured Europe with his show *In Dahomey*. Educated at Oberlin College, he had aspirations to be a concert violinist, and to this end he studied with Joseph Joachim in Berlin and with Antonín Dvořák in America. But during Cook's early years of manhood there were no prospects of a negro musician becoming a concert artiste in the USA, or even a member of one of the leading American symphony orchestras. Cook diverted his artistry and wrote songs for various theatrical productions; he also organized his own troupe of musicians and singers, the Memphis Students, which was a forerunner of the Syncopated Orchestra. During his travels in the USA Cook always took a keen interest in regional differences of music created by black Americans, and was one of the first to comment in print on the unique rhythmic qualities of New Orleans music.

For Sidney Bechet, Europe was full of novelty. His status had suddenly been elevated: for years he had worked in dubious clubs and seedy cabarets, and now he was a concert artiste. He always maintained that his tour with Will Marion Cook was a highlight in his life, and 30 years later often used his descriptions of it to inspire his pupils to practise so that they might find themselves featured in eminent surroundings.

With the SSO, Bechet had to contend with several innovations, not the least being that for the first time in his life he was in a musical unit that had a minority of musicians from Louisiana. Will Marion Cook had recruited his talent from all over the USA, and from Cuba and Haiti. Bechet's only home-town companion was Henry Saparo, who was 12 years older than Sidney; a musician nearer Bechet's age, trumpeter Arthur Briggs, became the young clarinet player's close friend.

Briggs and Bechet, and several others from the SSO, found living accommodation at a hotel run by Mr Horatio Botacchi at 1 Grenville Street, London, WC1 (in the Bloomsbury district, close to Russell Square). Bloomsbury adjoins Soho, and for the next few months most of Bechet's life, at work or at play, was spent within this square mile. Had Bechet and his companions tried some other hotels in London, they would certainly have encountered racism. Even during the early 1930s black entertainers such as the Mills Brothers, Louis Armstrong and the Peters Sisters found difficulty in booking rooms. The black clarinettist Rudolph Dunbar wrote of his experiences in London during that era: "In most lodging houses where there are 'rooms to let' signs, if a black man should apply the reply will be 'I am sorry but that room I had vacant has just been let'."[1]

The Southern Syncopated Orchestra performed at the Philharmonic Hall, 95 Great Portland Street (a short walk from Oxford Street). After a series of rehearsals it opened there on Friday 4 July 1919. Throughout its booking at the hall the band played twice daily, at 2.45 p.m. and 8.30 p.m. (the show lasted for approximately two hours). The unit was presented there by impresario Andre Charlot as the Southern Syncopated Orchestra (under the management of George W. Lattimore); Will Marion Cook was billed as the group's Musical Director and John C. Payne as the Chorus Master. The ensemble was organized in two units, the Singers and the Orchestra (some of the musicians were members of both sections). The personnel of the SSO at the Philharmonic Hall was detailed in a printed programme:

Violins	Paul Wyer, Angelina Rivera
Cello	Joseph Porter
Double basses	Santos Rivera, Pedro Vargos
Clarinets	Anthony Rivera, Sydney [sic] Bechet, John G. Russell
Saxophones	Ferdinand Coxcito, Frank A. Dennie
Tympani	Benton E. Peyton
First bandolins	Lawrence Morris, Joseph Caulk
Second bandolins	Henry Saparo, Carroll Morgan
Pianos	Pierre de Caillaux, Ambrose Smith, Mattie Gilmore
Cornets	James Briggs, Robert Jones, Edward Patrick
French horn	Milford Warren
Trombones	John Forrester, Jacob Patrick, George Rogers
Drums	Buddie Gilmore, Robert Young

The singers were listed:

Sopranos	Mrs H. King Reavis, Miss Lottie Gee, Miss Angelina Rivera
1st tenors	Earl C. McKinney, Joseph Caulk, Wm. D. Burns, Frank A. Dennie, George Baker
2nd tenors	Henry Saparo, Joseph Hall, Carroll Morgan
Baritones	Joseph Porter, E. C. Rosemond, J. C. Payne, B. E. Peyton, Lawrence Morris
Basses	Robert Williams, Robert Young, Wm. T. Tatten.

This line-up was similar to the personnel that had played at the group's London début, but some of the musicians listed in the programme, notably the star percussionist, Buddie Gilmore, had joined the SSO after the Philharmonic opening. The instrumentation remained broadly the same throughout the booking, and so too did the basic programme:

Part I

1.	Sally Trombone	Filmore
2.	Hungarian Dance no.5	Brahms
3.	Go Down Moses	Traditional
	Jessamine	Williams
	O, Mary	Traditional
4.	Spring	Tyers
5.	Mighty Like a Rose	Nerin
6.	Pan Americano	Herbert
7.	I got a Robe	Traditional
8.	Ramshackle Rag	Snyder
9.	Swing Along	Cook
10.	Plantation Melody	Lannin
11.	Swanee River	Foster
12.	Couldn't Hear Nobody Pray	Traditional
13.	Swanee Ripples	Blanfuss
14.	Joshua Fit the Battle	Traditional

Part II

1.	Deep River	Burleigh
2.	Drum Solo	Buddie Gilmore
3.	Exhortation	Cook
4.	Russian Rag	Cobb
5.	Rose of No Man's Land	Burleigh
	It's me, O Lord	Traditional
	Peaches down in Georgia	Meyer
6.	Humoresque	Dvořák
7.	Mammy o' Mine	Pinkard
8.	Peach Jam Making Time	Kendis
9.	Characteristic Blues (Clarionet Solo)	Sydney [sic] Bechet
10.	Rain Song	Cook

Very few of the items in the SSO's repertoire had anything to do with jazz. Arthur Briggs said that Bechet was the only real jazz improviser in the band's line-up (modestly not including himself): "We had various players who could embellish melodies and play variations in the symphonic style, and we also had musicians who could re-interpret a melody with ragtime phrasing, but Bechet could, and did, play pure jazz and blues. He was sensational, and I think he could improvise jazz on any sort of theme, whether it was classical or not."[2]

Sidney Bechet came down to the front of the orchestra for his feature. For the rest of the time he sat amongst his colleagues in the reed section, all of whom were able to play from a written orchestration. Bechet's method of joining in didn't involve his improvising a counterpoint; instead, he usually played a harmony part that moved in parallel motion to the melody. His marvellous musical ear enabled him to 'fake' his part with ease, and he did so with such skill that he rarely bumped into the written parts played by the other musicians.

During a later series of London concerts, Sidney's desire to play a more prominent part in the proceedings got the better of him. As the band's flautist, Bertin Salnave, told writer Bertrand Demeusy: "Will Marion Cook's wife, Abbie Mitchell, who sang with the orchestra, began performing Puccini's *Madame Butterfly*. Without saying anything to anyone Sidney Bechet left his place and came to the front of the stage and played an obbligato on his clarinet. When the number ended he started to return to his place to the acclaim of the audience. He knew he would have to face the director's anger, but Abbie Mitchell rushed towards him, threw her arms around him and embraced him, crying, 'Ah, Sidney, only you could have done it like that!' Somewhat mollified, Will Marion Cook asked, 'But still Sidney, why didn't you ask me?' 'If I had warned you,' replied Sidney, 'you would never have allowed it.'"[3]

Will Marion Cook liked every detail of a new arrangement to be perfected before any embellishments were added. Elliott Carpenter, who worked with Cook, said: "We'd play around with it, and then old man Cook would say 'Take it'." However, most of the classical numbers in the programme were played exactly as per the orchestration. An English musician, Natalie Spencer, who deputized in the SSO, described one of its rehearsals: "One day we had a preliminary run through a new and rather formidable 'Blues', and the band, feeling pleased with itself that day, played it through with great gusto and as we thought, rather creditably. Mr Cook stood quietly by and let us go right on to the bitter end, and then all he said was, 'Alright, now we'll do it my way'. Mr Cook does not use a baton for conducting – only his hand – a glance and a raising of the eyebrows gives a cue, while facial expressions are a great factor, a vigorous nod signifies 'All out – as loud as you like'."[4]

But, although the music was highly unlike what he had performed in New Orleans or Chicago, Sidney was stimulated and intrigued by what the SSO played, and often sat listening intently to the solo singers, whose repertoires were based mostly on plantation songs and spirituals. Bechet always retained a love of traditional negro songs, and said late in life, "Those spirituals are really the pure blues that bring sadness and gladness to you."[5]

In Britain, published reviews gave preference to the vocal numbers. One of the first critiques (in *The Referee* of 6 July 1919) typified this reaction. After commenting on the curious instrumentation of the orchestra the critic wrote: "Some of the playing of the band was often more noisy than musical but in some pieces delightful delicacy and refinement were attained, and always a keen sense of rhythm and emotional significance. The musical value of this body lies in its singers and their rendering of genuine coloured music, particularly old Negroe plantation ditties. We have had so much imitation coloured music that it is refreshing to hear the real thing."

A little later, in *The People* of 27 July 1919, a reviewer noted: "The SSO has caught on well at Philharmonic Hall. Old folk songs of the South are a special feature of the programme and most of the vocal and instrumental items are vociferously encored at each performance." The *Daily Herald* of 4 August 1919 reviewed the SSO whilst they were playing at a special Sunday concert at the People's Palace in the East End of London. Under a headline "REAL RAGTIME BY REAL DARKIES" (which indicated the naïveté that existed, even amongst well-wishers) an unnamed critic, bursting with enthusiasm, wrote: "I don't know which took the most exercise, the audience or the performers. As the music grew raggier and raggier they swayed and we swayed . . . they snapped their fingers and clapped their hands and we clapped more, and were all quite excited." The excitement produced a few mis-spellings, but one name is clearly recognizable: "Mr Sidney Becket [sic] did some strange things with the clarionet, aptly called *Characteristic Blues*."

The *Cambridge Review* of 6 September 1919 said: "Mr Sidney Bechet positively revels in the ululations of his skilful clarionet." Mr Edward J. Dent in *The Athenaeum* of 26 September 1919 was also struck by Bechet's performance: having likened the ensemble to a "nightmare entertainment", he conceded that "like a nightmare it has in the midst of its fantastic oddities unexpected moments of contact with real experience." Dent then cited as a "queer link with reality" the clarinet solo on *Characteristic Blues*.

Some London critics were not quite sure what to make of Bechet's playing. C. Dutorsdoit in the *Musical Standard* of 2 August 1919 was one: "Those who believe there is no humour in music should listen to Mr Sidney Bechet's clarinet solo *Characteristic Blues*. There has never been anything like that latter item since John Sousa's Band convulsed an audience with *Has anyone here seen Kelly?*."

The most important review of the SSO in London, however, was not written by a British writer, but by the Swiss conductor Ernest Ansermet (1883–1969), who was in London with the Ballets Russe. Ansermet, who was the resident conductor of L'Orchestre de la Suisse Romande, visited the Philharmonic Hall on several occasions and subsequently put down his thoughts on what he heard there in an article that was published in the *Revue Romande* of 19 October 1919. Ansermet's article (in translation) has been reprinted in dozens of jazz magazines and several anthologies. It thoroughly deserves that singular honour, because its initial publication marked the first occasion on which a jazz performance was seriously and skilfully reviewed in print.

Ansermet's review is not only important from a pioneering aspect; it remains one of the most incisive examples of jazz analysis ever conceived. After writing about the birth of syncopation and its usages in ragtime Ansermet describes the timbre deliberately produced by black instrumentalists: "The Negro takes a trombone and he has a knack of vibrating each note by a continual quavering of the slide, and a sense of glissando, and a taste for muted notes which makes it a new instrument; he takes a clarinet or saxophone and he has a way of hitting notes by which he discovers a whole series of effects, produced by the lips alone. . . ." After commenting on blue notes and various harmonies ("which many European musicians should envy") Ansermet saves pride of place in his article for Sidney Bechet's remarkable talent:

> There is in the Southern Syncopated Orchestra an extraordinary clarinet virtuoso who is, so it seems, the first of his race to have composed perfectly formed blues on the clarinet. I've heard two of them which he had elaborated at great length, then played to his companions so that they could make up an accompaniment. Extremely difficult, they are equally admirable for their richness of invention, force of accent, and daring in novelty and the unexpected. Already, they gave the idea of a style and their form was gripping, abrupt, harsh, with a brusque and pitiless ending like that of Bach's second Brandenburg Concerto. I wish to set down the name of this artist of genius; as for myself, I shall never forget it, it is Sidney Bechet. . . . What a moving thing it is to meet this very black, fat boy with white teeth and that narrow forehead, who is very glad one likes what he does, but who can say nothing of his art, save that he follows his 'own way', and then one thinks that this 'own way' is perhaps the highway the whole world will swing along to-morrow.

It seems bizarre that Sidney Bechet had to travel to Europe to receive the sort of expert acclaim that was worthy of his vast talents, but Ansermet's perception at that time was unique, and it was to be some years before any other piece of writing about jazz (on either side of the Atlantic) measured up to it. However, many people who heard Bechet with the SSO recognized that here was a musician of extraordinary capabilities. One of these was the Prince of Wales, heir to the throne of England; the future King Edward VIII (later the Duke of Windsor) was a devotee of 'hot' dance music and jazz during the years immediately following World War I.

At the Prince of Wales's suggestion the SSO played at Buckingham Palace on 10 August 1919. This has been described as a "command performance", but it was actually a royal garden party held in the grounds of the palace during the afternoon. Bechet, on clarinet, was also featured in a small unit consisting of Lawrence Morris on bandolin, Arthur Briggs on cornet, William Forrester on trombone and Robert Young on drums. The singing troupe performed for the 1100 guests as well. The palace lake had been drained during World War I and its dry, flat bed made a fine natural amphitheatre. Apparently the royal listeners were pleased with what they heard, but it is probably just as well that the Prince of Wales did not let enthusiasm get the better of him. At one supper dance in 1928 he had a band play *A Room with a View* nine times.[6]

Not all of Bechet's activities were accompanied by gloved applause and the glitter of coronets. During his off-duty hours he maintained a hedonistic schedule that was scarcely less lively than his after-hours routine in Chicago and New Orleans. Sidney's friend Arthur Briggs recalled their days together in London: "Bechet was a good friend and a fine fellow, but he just couldn't trust himself. He was so impetuous." Bechet had by then developed his life-long habit of giving people nicknames, and to him Arthur Briggs was always 'the Kid'. Briggs continued: "Despite being older than I was, he asked me to keep an eye on him, because he might get drunk or get in with the wrong crowd. But he was so easily tempted that when the time came nothing on earth would stop him from doing what he wanted to do. Arriving on time meant nothing to him, but he didn't like to be hurried. Yet we always remained good friends. He wasn't unpopular with the rest of the orchestra, but I would say that he kept his distance from them. He liked to make his own way."[7]

Despite the favourable reviews, the SSO never really conquered London, and some of its performances were poorly attended. English trombonist Lew Stone remembered going to a concert at the Philharmonic Hall where the audience was "twenty people or less".[8] The musicians of the SSO sensed, with consternation, that their administrators were having financial problems, and they also knew that contractual wrangles were developing between Will Marion Cook and the group's manager, George Lattimore. Business at the Philharmonic Hall began to improve steadily, but the rift between Lattimore and Cook widened to the point where Cook left. His place as conductor of the SSO was taken by a former member of the Memphis Students, Egbert E. Thompson, who had been born in Sierra Leone, grew up in Jamaica, and was educated in the USA (where he eventually became a US Army bandmaster).

In October 1919 the SSO, having played more than 200 performances at the Philharmonic Hall, reduced their schedule there slightly by giving afternoon shows only, on Monday, Wednesday, Thursday and Saturday. But the musicians were kept just as busy because they began playing a series of matinées at the Prince of Wales Theatre. They also played occasionally for private functions, notably the Armistice Ball held at the Royal Albert Hall in November 1919.

The eminent South African Nationalist Solomon Plaatje (1876–1932) was at the Armistice Ball (which ran from midnight until 4.30 a.m.), and wrote an account of it for *The Clarion* (Cape Town): "When the black band struck up their first bar they seemed to lift that huge swarm of dancers and sent them swinging and swaying in rhythmic glides around the hall. Vociferous applause from the spectators and revellers greeted the end of their pieces. They would repeat a piece two or three times, then strike up a better one while the throng still clamoured for more of it."[9]

The SSO's long run at the Philharmonic Hall ended on 6 December 1919. Originally it was hoped that the band could move straight on to the Continent to begin a series of engagements there, but the tour failed to materialize. On 8th December the group began playing for a week as part of a variety bill at the Huge Coliseum Theatre in London (working alongside Mme Haru Onuki, Billy Wells and the Eclair Twins, and the Three Neslos). The SSO was paid £580 for the week's work (which was about the amount it averaged at the Philharmonic Hall)[10]; not much of this money reached the musicians, however, and they began demanding their back-pay. The issue of unpaid wages had already caused ill feelings, and some of the entourage had left during the last part of the Philharmonic Hall booking.

As early as September 1919 a small group from the ranks of the SSO had begun playing for dancing at the Portman Rooms, London W1. Manfred Coxcito, the group's Haitian saxophonist, had been part of this enterprise from its inception; he was later joined by Henry Saparo and a new arrival from America, violinist

George Mitchell Smith. The engagement at the Portman Rooms ended abruptly on 20 December 1919; the musicians turned up to work and were sent home by the management.

The nucleus of this group, together with Sidney Bechet, drummer Benton Peyton, and pianist Pierre de Caillaux, became a new unit known as the Jazz Kings, and in December 1919 began a residency at the Embassy Club, 6–8 Old Bond Street. The background to this booking began when George Lattimore (the SSO's manager) was approached by impresario Albert De Courville (who had brought the Original Dixieland Jazz Band to London) to provide him with a band to play at the Embassy. The band, formed from SSO members, received a total of £92 per week from Lattimore, but after three weeks of employment the musicians discovered that Lattimore was charging £140 a week for their services. The Jazz Kings refused to work with Lattimore as a go-between and negotiated a new contract with De Courville for £120 per week. By this time drummer Benton E. Peyton had assumed leadership of the group.

George Lattimore considered that the ex-SSO musicians were still under contract to him and promptly took legal action against Peyton, Coxcito, Saparo, Smith and the booker Albert De Courville. Bechet was not involved in the litigation – during the band's first weeks at the Embassy he had been fired. In the court proceedings Lattimore said that Bechet's dismissal did not meet with his approval: "Peyton informed me he had substituted John George Russell for Sidney Bechete [sic]. This was without my knowledge or authority." No reason was given for Bechet's dismissal, but he was, at this stage of his life, wildly unpunctual.

Although Bechet's stay with the band on this occasion was short, it was not without its importance. He claimed, and there is no reason to doubt him, that he made his first recordings whilst working with Benny Peyton at the Embassy Club. Bechet's comments on the subject were first printed in the *Melody Maker* of 3 June 1939, where in answer to a question from writer Leonard Feather he said: "The first records I ever made? Well that must have been with Benny Peyton's Jazz Kings in London." Almost ten years later, when *Melody Maker* writers Max Jones and Sinclair Traill were in Paris for the 1949 Jazz Festival, they asked Bechet for more details and then summarized his comments: "Bechet says that during the time they played at the Ambassador's [sic] Club, in the tail end of that year, they cut eight sides for Columbia. He cannot remember the titles, but he is certain of the company and that he took a soprano *or* clarinet chorus on each of them. The personnel of the band was: Bechet, Fred Coxcito (alto sax), George Smith (violin), Pierre de Caillaux (piano), Henry Saparo (banjo) and Benny Peyton (drums). He doesn't think that all the sides were issued, in fact, he is certain that they weren't. But he is sure that at least one side was released, although it is possible it may have been put out under a pseudonym."[11]

British discographers and record collectors did their best to track down any of these recordings, but to no avail. Bechet was grilled again and again over the years about this session, and he told one inquisitor that he thought two of the tunes were *High Society* and *Tiger Rag*. It is conceivable that these two tunes formed part of the lost session, but it is just as likely that Bechet cited two jazz standards just to get people off his back. Everything else he said about the session has the ring of truth, even to the season – "at the tail end of the year" – but unfortunately the recordings have never been discovered.

Bechet's first stint with the Jazz Kings at the Embassy Club coincided with the SSO's first trip to Scotland, which took it to Glasgow, Edinburgh and Dunfermline in late 1919 and early 1920. Thus his name does not figure in any of the press reviews of that tour. The skills of drummer Buddie Gilmore (who had joined the SSO in September 1919) were lauded wherever the band went. One Scot, writing in *The Bailie*, commented: "And if the syncopated fellows would just lend their drum and drummer to the Glasgow Police Pipe Band you couldna match the like of yon for music anywhere."[12]

George Lattimore lost his court action against various members of the Jazz Kings, and the group was able to fulfil the contract it had with De Courville. Early in 1920 Lattimore faced further problems in his dealings with the members of the SSO. The tour reached Liverpool in February 1920, but after playing a few concerts there the group's musicians, most of whom were still owed their back-pay, went on strike, and the rest of the performances had to be cancelled.

During April 1920, in the London High Court of Justice, George William Lattimore (described as the proprietor of the SSO) battled with Will Marion Cook (who had returned to England from the USA) and impresarios Andre Charlot and Ernest C. Rolls over the use of the orchestra's name. The outcome was that Cook did not use the Southern Syncopated Orchestra billing for a rival group that he formed (which contained some of the original SSO members). Cook's ensemble played a number of engagements in London, Bristol, Liverpool and Sheffield during the period April to September 1920. This group was billed as "Marion Cook's Band" or "Will Marion Cook's Syncopated Orchestra".

Lattimore also sued Albert De Courville over a contract that was to have taken the SSO to France to play an engagement (from 14 January to 17 February 1920) at the Folies Marigny in Paris. Despite the fact that De Courville had verbally agreed that the orchestra would receive an overall salary of £3400, the booking never materialized. In May 1920 the action was heard in London before Mr Justice Bray, who awarded Lattimore £1733 and costs.

Bechet played no direct part in any of these court cases, though several of his colleagues and ex-colleagues were called as witnesses. Somehow Sidney seems to have remained on friendly terms with all the parties involved in these various disputes: his admiration for Will Marion Cook never waned, he stayed on equable terms with Lattimore, and he was soon working again with the Jazz Kings.

Following the strike several of the SSO musicians were placated by Lattimore, and as a result they joined a reformed SSO for a residency at the Albert Hall, Nottingham, from 19 April until 1 May 1920. Perhaps feeling that he needed a respite from the intrigues that were enveloping his former colleagues, Bechet left England briefly during June 1920 to play an engagement in Belgium with Louis Mitchell's band (the group with which he had originally planned to travel to Europe in May 1919). Bechet's presence in Belgium at this time has been questioned, but when Sidney applied for a passport renewal in October 1921 he listed the two countries in which he had worked during the period 1919–21 as England and Belgium. Bechet soon returned to England and rejoined the Jazz Kings, whose residency at the Embassy Club ended when a fire damaged the building during the night of 10 August 1920.[13]

SIX

Deportation Blues

Sometime during 1920 Bechet was out strolling in the West End of London with his pal from the SSO, Arthur Briggs. As the two men walked along, Bechet looked into the window of J. F. Lafleur's music shop at 147 Wardour Street and caught sight of the musical instrument that was to change his life. There, glinting against a dull backcloth, was a brand-new straight soprano saxophone. Bechet went into the shop with Briggs and enquired about its price. On being told that it was 30 guineas, he asked if he could try out the instrument. There in the shop he demonstrated on the saxophone a hit song of the moment, the tune *Whispering*. Briggs fidgeted while Bechet played through hundreds of arpeggios and runs, but in his own good time Sidney called the assistant and said that he would buy the instrument, providing a double-octave key could be added to it. The salesman agreed to this and Bechet called back later to pick up the specially altered instrument.[1]

Soprano saxophones – both straight and curved models – were then still something of a novelty. Because of tuning problems inherent in their manufacture they were, for a long time, almost the least popular of the saxophone family (the real outcast being the smaller E flat sopranino). Early B flat sopranos were built in low pitch (where a' was tuned to 435 Hz) and high pitch ($a' = 454$ Hz). Jazz and dance-band musicians favoured the low-pitched version, but all of them (including Bechet) found that when the instrument's mouthpiece was pushed in (so as to get in tune with a piano tuned to $a' = 440$), the whole upper register became extremely sharp. Strong lips and a broad vibrato were needed to cloak this in-built deficiency, and Bechet had both. The vibrato (or wavering pulsation) that Bechet produced on the soprano saxophone was markedly similar to the one he imparted to his clarinet playing. It was not applied accidentally, or haphazardly, but was part of his way of expressing music. He said, "Like vocal soloists I believe that the vibrato plays an important part in any solo that has to build up to a real effect."[2]

Bechet loved listening to operatic tenors, and one of his particular heroes, Enrico Caruso, often used a vibrato no less broad than Sidney's. The soprano saxophone was the perfect instrument for such an embellishment, since its pitch problems were conveniently disguised by the use of a wide, controlled vibrato. For Bechet's admirers the vibrato was the perfect accessory to his passionate and imaginative improvisations, a pulsating effect that symbolized the intensity of the man's music, no more distracting than the regional accent of a great orator. No listener could doubt Bechet's musical abilities, but for some people his wide vibrato was anathema, an aural hardship that prevented them from enjoying any of his work.

Within days of buying the new instrument Bechet was producing sensational music on it. His skills on the clarinet had made him an outstanding performer in every band he had worked, but the increased power offered by the soprano saxophone meant that he could now dominate by power as well as by artistry. Some of Bechet's colleagues in London regarded the purchase as a mixed blessing, but Sidney was determined to achieve prominence on the instrument and began featuring himself on the tune *Song of Songs*, which he had first heard Nelson Kincaid play in New York. He was aware that there was opposition to his new instrument, and said later: "Boy, when I first started that soprano, I'm telling you that guys used to tell me, 'Please play the clarinet'. I used to say, 'Please leave me alone.'" Sidney subsequently gave his reason for preferring the soprano saxophone to the clarinet: "I could express myself, and I had a better audience."[3]

Sometimes Bechet argued with his colleagues in London, but there were no violent altercations. He was keen to learn as much as he could about every aspect of music and was never afraid to ask questions. He often sat at the piano keyboard working out various harmonies; he could also pick up a guitar and play the right chords for quite complicated songs. However, he ignored those who advised him to learn to read music. This attitude disappointed, and annoyed, some of the older musicians, who felt that if Bechet could read music there would be no limits to his performing skills. Sidney simply shrugged off any such talk; he felt that if he were to learn to read music his powers of improvisation would leave him.

The conception that 20th-century London remained totally staid until the so-called Swinging '60s is laughed at by people old enough to have revelled in that city during the early 1920s. There was, if one knew where to look, opportunity for wild abandonment embracing drugs, alcohol and sex. There was no 'Prohibition' in Britain concerning drinking, but there were stringent regulations governing the hours in which alcohol could be sold. This meant that there were vast profits to be made by anyone who devised a successful 'club' system that enabled them to sell drinks after the public houses had closed (usually at 10.30 p.m.).

Bechet knew both the pub and club side of London life. He and some of his ex-SSO colleagues used to frequent a public house called The Bell, at 15 Little Titchfield Street (only a few hundred yards from the group's old stamping ground at the Philharmonic Hall). Black people were not welcome in every London pub during the 1920s, but there were no problems at The Bell because one of Bechet's acquaintances, a black saxophone player named Daniel Kildare, was married to the landlady, Mary Rose Kildare. Originally from Jamaica, Kildare had been a member of the Clef Club Orchestra in New York, but had moved to London in 1915, subsequently becoming leader of the band at Ciro's Club. His brother Walter, a pianist, was also known to members of the SSO.

Arthur Briggs remembers Dan Kildare as "a quiet, pleasant man", but in June 1920, after a heated row with his estranged wife, Daniel Kildare shot her and her sister dead. He badly wounded a barmaid before committing suicide, blowing his brains out. A month later another acquaintance of Bechet's, a Jamaican musician named Edgar Manning (who was a notorious drugs dealer) was involved in a shooting affray in Shaftesbury Avenue, where he wounded 'American Frank' Miller and Charles Tunick. Manning lived at 22 Regents Park Road, NW1; Bechet came to know him through visiting other black musicians who lived in the same area. As ever, hoodlums and gangsters had something of a fascination for Sidney.

Regents Park Road, an eminently respectable thoroughfare, housed many reputable professional people, and it was this factor that appealed to John C. Payne, the choirmaster of the SSO; he took a long lease on a property at no. 17. The address became the centre of a cultured coterie of black artists, writers, musicians and singers during the 1920s and 1930s. Bechet was never out of his depth intellectually on the occasions he attended soirées there; he was not well read, but his inquisitive intelligence charmed people into discussing a wide range of subjects with him. Bechet's personality was diverse enough, however, for him to feel just as much at ease with the villains who lived in the same road.

During the early 1920s a number of aristocratic young women were developing a keen interest in the performances of the London-based black musicians – mostly their horizontal efforts, said one black artiste wryly. Some of the bright young things who hung around the late-night clubs where the musicians worked were also eager to try another imported vogue – cocaine. Bechet took no part in this trade; he obtained his 'lift' from the spirit hipflask that he always carried. He did his best to save the randy young debutantes from sex-starvation, but remained positively against the use of hard drugs.

Of the considerable number of black musicians working in London, most were from America, some were West Indians (many of whom had served in British army bands), and others were African. A reason for the initial demand for black bands in London was put forward in the *Chicago Defender* of 22 May 1915: "Race musicians are being called from America to take the place of Germans in London hotels and cafes." Theatrical managers also wanted to book black musical acts to add flair to the music-hall bills, and by 1915 the first signs of the coming craze for ballroom dancing, which also increased the demand for exotic bands, were becoming apparent.

All these various trends meant that black musical aggregations (like Louis Mitchell's group and the Versatile Three) found employment in London long before the Original Dixieland Jazz Band arrived. But it was the ODJB's enormous successes at the vast Hammersmith Palais (where the group played from October 1919 to June 1920) that tipped the scales in favour of American bands and led many agents and ballroom managers to wire to the USA for the services of small jazz bands similar in line-up to the Dixielanders.

The demand for these imported bands exceeded the supply, and this gave many young British musicians the opportunity to secure bookings in London by pretending to be from the USA. Harry Roy and his brother Sid were two of many. Harry explained: "We decided to cash in on the American tendency then apparent in dance music. London dancers wanted American musicians. We bought ourselves American collars, invested in 'Harold Lloyd' spectacles and some chewing gum, and then adopted nasal American accents."[4]

The Palais at Hammersmith in West London became, and remained, the most important single venue in the growth of interest in British ballroom dancing. It had originally been a roller-skating rink, but after reconstruction it opened as a dance-hall on 28 October 1919. Its huge Canadian maple-wood floor covered 27,000 square feet, and in 1919 it boasted 80 dance instructors (50 women and 30 men). The ballroom was open for two sessions a day, from 3 p.m. until 6 p.m. (admission 2/6d) and from 8 p.m. until midnight (admission 5/-). There was room for 2500 patrons to dance in comfort, but sometimes attendances topped 5000.[5] During its early years the Palais employed two bands, each placed on a different bandstand, so that as one group finished its set the other could begin playing immediately.

The company that organized events at the Hammersmith Palais was headed by two men from across the Atlantic: a Canadian, William F. Mitchell, and an American, Howard E. Booker. These two men, whose agency in nearby Kensington High Street had the telegraphic address 'Bazzjand', had been quick to realize that postwar London was hungry for diversion. In addition to the Palais, they also owned Rector's, the night-club that flourished at 31 Tottenham Court Road. (A Rector's in New York, named after dancer Eddie Rector, had been successful in pre-Prohibition days.)

The Original Dixieland Jazz Band played for Mitchell and Booker both at the Hammersmith Palais and at Rector's. When its contract ended on 26 June 1920 the company had difficulty in finding a follow-up attraction with the same appeal. Various permutations of home-grown and imported musical talents were tried as replacements, but it wasn't until the Jazz Kings took up residency there on 3 October 1920 that the problem was solved. Mitchell and Booker's publicity manager, Byron Davies, was also the editor of *Dancing World*, which enabled the Jazz Kings' leader, Benny Peyton, to publicize the group's intentions:

> We do our best to render jazz music in a manner, sufficiently good, we hope, to make the public like it, and to free it from monotony. But further than that, the Jazz Kings can entertain with tricks, stunts, solos and so on. First of all I would like to mention Mr. Sidney Bechet, our clarionettist, and it is no exaggeration to say that he is in a class by himself. Bechet is regarded by many who are competent to judge, as the most original and possibly the greatest of known clarinet players (at least for dance music) in the world, in saying that, I would like to emphasis that this is a statement of fact and I am not speaking merely for advertising purposes. He is, in many respects, the pride of our Band, and the envy of his rivals.[6]

The Jazz Kings quickly proved to be a huge success at the Palais, and one of its main attractions was the power and beat engendered by Bechet's playing. The group's line-up was Peyton (drums), Bechet (soprano saxophone and clarinet), Manfred Coxcito (alto saxophone), Pierre de Caillaux (piano), George Smith (violin) and Joseph Caulk (bandolin and vocals).

Arthur Briggs saw less of Bechet during this period; Sidney had moved to the Paddington district of London so that it would be easier for him to make the twice-daily journeys to Hammersmith. At the Palais, Bechet rapidly established himself as a favourite with many British musicians, particularly those who worked opposite him in other bands. Trombonist Bernard Tipping retained vivid memories of hearing Sidney during this period:

> Berchet [sic] was a real "jazz" artist if ever there was one. He would conceive the most weird and clever ideas quite spontaneously while he was playing, and out they used to come all on the spur of the moment, as it were. Some of his ideas used to strike one as being a little far-fetched, but as crazy as his tricks might at first appear, when one analysed them one found that they always fitted properly and were always musically correct. One great thing that tickled my fancy more than anything else was his glissando playing. I had never heard glissando played so well on a clarinet before, but here was a man who could glide and slide about on the clarinet as easily as if it were a slide trombone. I have seen scores of musicians listening in amazement to Berchet [sic] playing his clarinet.[7]

Although Mitchell and Booker advertised the Hammersmith Palais regularly in various London newspapers, their policy was not to mention the names of the bands who played at the venue. The style they adopted for their advertising copy was positively genteel: "Visitors to the Palais de Dance, Hammersmith constantly eulogize the 'perfect' music rendered by the two jazz bands always in attendance. Each is a perfect syncopated orchestra, comprised of specialist musicians. The effect is both novel and pleasing, and provides the best of good dancing."[8] Sidney's arrival seems to have had a strong impact. In January 1921 the Palais advertisement began: "The piper loud and louder blew. The dancers quick and quicker flew."

Soon after the Jazz Kings began their residency, Howard Booker left the Palais company (he later ran the Cosmos Club in London). This meant that William Mitchell became the principal director. Mitchell liked the spirit of the Jazz Kings and decided to use them at his night-club, Rector's. So for many months the band did a 'doubling' schedule, performing at the Hammersmith Palais before making their way to Tottenham Court Road (about five miles away), where they played at Rector's until the early hours of the morning. Bechet did not want to make a long journey after finishing at Rector's, so he moved into lodgings near the night-club, at 27 Southampton Street (now Conway Street) in Fitzroy Square.

Rector's* was thought of as an 'in' place amongst the smart set of the early 1920s. Saxophonist Harry Hayes was taken there as a teenager, and he described the clientele as consisting of "mugs and birds" – rich male customers who were fleeced by wily hostesses. The London County Council tried to keep a strict eye on the premises, and in order to do so employed the services of the Arrow Detective Agency, whose sleuth, a former police official, failed to gain entry. A report to the LCC Theatre and Music Hall Committee said: "He is told that the place is frequented by wealthy kept women and wealthy men who are associated with them, and that it is extremely difficult to get admission without satisfactory introduction."

---

* Rector's operated in Tottenham Court Road until 1928, when the venue became known as the Carlton Dance Hall; a later version of Rector's functioned at 207 Regent Street in the late 1930s.

Even with stringent conditions of admission the management still had trouble with its clientele. Alfred Van Straten (later to become a bandleader) delivered to Rector's, for William Mitchell, a suit which had been tailored by his father. The teenager stood by as Mitchell threw a cheque back at a customer. The club owner pointed to the walls of his office, which were plastered with 'bounced' cheques, and said to the reveller, "I don't want to see yours up on that wall. Please pay me in cash."[9]

Professional dancer Josephine Bradley gave a description of Rector's in her autobiography *Dancing through Life*. Comparing it to Murray's Club and the Grafton Galleries, she wrote: "This was of a highly different character, not so health giving as it was underground, but there was a certain amount of space. The dances at Rector's were the foxtrot, the waltz and the one step."[10]

At both the Palais and at Rector's the Jazz Kings shared the work-load with another band; a whole succession of small groups played opposite them at both venues. The musicians found that the brief sets left them with a lot of time to kill, and most of the intervals at Hammersmith were spent in the small band-room, where high-stake card games often took place. Lew Davis recalled that, even though the usual weekly wage for doubling between Hammersmith and Rector's (for British musicians) was £27 10s (£15 for the Palais and £12 10s for the club), it was not unusual to see a five-pound bet made on a single call of cards.

Sidney Bechet almost became enmeshed in gambling during this stage of his life. Something in the impulsive side of his nature loved the thrill of wagering, but Sidney was not a good loser. One of his card-playing opponents had to take pity on him after a late-night game. Violinist George Hurley recalled: "My brother Sam Hurley was one of the original members of Rector's club. He wasn't a musician, he was in business, but he liked night-life and dancing. He got to know Bechet at Rector's, and played cards with him, usually poker, after the musicians had finished work. One night Bechet lost disastrously and ran out of money. The only thing he had to gamble with in the end was his clarinet, which he was carrying with him. He put the instrument in as a stake and lost that too. Sam, who knew a musician's life well, said, 'Well how are you going to earn your living?' and gave him his clarinet back."[11]

Bechet took on pupils during his stay in London. One of these, Charles Henry Maxwell Knight, was an extremely colourful character who is said to have been the inspiration for the novelist Ian Fleming's creation of James Bond's boss, M. Maxwell Knight, it transpired, was indeed an important figure in British espionage (he was also an eminent naturalist), but Knight's burning ambition was to be a jazz musician, and during Bechet's stay in London he became one of the latter's pupils. In 1965, on BBC radio, he told presenter Roy Plomley why he had chosen *Softly awakes my heart* from *Samson and Delilah* as one of his "Desert Island Discs": "It was a great favourite of Sidney Bechet, who taught me to play the clarinet. He liked to play it, and one day he and I combined in a sort of jam session. He played *Softly awakes my heart* on the soprano saxophone, and I did my best on the clarinet."[12] Maxwell Knight never blossomed as a musician but he always remained a passionate fan of Bechet's work, and in the same broadcast said: "Bechet was the jazz genius of all time, and probably will remain so."

Knight's biographer, Anthony Masters, wrote in *The Man who was M*: "Most of his domestic animals (including snakes, bush babies and parrots) were brought up on a musical diet of Sidney Bechet."

Harvey Astley, writing in the December 1949 issue of the British *Jazz Journal*, provided an eye-witness account of Bechet in action during the early 1920s: "Bechet's playing with the Jazz Kings was a sensation. Always arriving late, with a bulge in his hip pocket, he set the band alight as soon as the first few notes had fallen like rain from his magic clarinet. The King of Jazz had arrived. That was the signal for a number of dancers to gather round the band for the remainder of the evening and listen to real New Orleans music in the raw. The bright spot of the evening was when Bechet sat down in the middle of the dance floor, legs crossed, tailor-fashion, and proceeded to give us solos on his soprano sax, usually starting off with the Prologue from *Pagliacci*."

The Jazz Kings took a break from their London routine in order to play at the re-opening of the Birmingham Palais de Dance, in Monument Road, on 1 September 1921. As this was one of William Mitchell's enterprises there were no problems about the band taking leave from the Hammersmith Palais or Rector's. The band remained in Birmingham for almost two weeks, playing opposite an American college unit called the Southern-Rag-a-Jazz Band. The Jazz Kings' visit was mentioned in "Some recollections of a Birmingham Palais Dancer", which the *Melody Maker* published in February 1931; the writer particularly remembered the band's version of the 1920 pop song *Bright Eyes*.

It is apparent from the various recollections of those who heard the Jazz Kings that most of the group's repertoire consisted of songs of the moment. Their most featured member was the bandolin player Joseph Caulk, who crooned numbers like Irving Berlin's *All by Myself* and *Beautiful faces need beautiful clothes*. The band rarely played dixieland numbers or tunes that were later to be regarded as 'jazz classics'. Apparently Coxcito and Bechet took it in turns to play the melody, each of them moving alternately onto a harmony part (usually a third away from the tune). On certain numbers both reed players dropped out whilst the violinist emphasized the melody, but sometimes they played quiet background figures behind his lead. The final chorus was usually left open to allow Bechet space in which to improvise.

During these formative years Bechet rarely played alongside a trumpeter, and accordingly he developed the feeling that taking the lead was his prerogative. This sense of autonomy often resurfaced in later years, much to the ire of some of the trumpeters who worked with him. In September 1962 the British *Jazz News* published a letter from Fred N. Hunt, who wrote: "I was a pupil of Sidney Bechet who was playing with the Jazz Kings at the Hammersmith Palais de Danse. In my opinion he was playing at his best then. Having no competition with a trumpet, the soprano sax was of course the lead instrument and in fact should never be used in any other way." Writer Iain Lang heard both the Original Dixieland Jazz Band's clarinettist Larry Shields and Bechet in London in 1920, and, although he found Shields "most impressive", he greatly preferred Bechet's playing: "He had a range Shields lacked, and I think he was definitely ahead in jazz development."[13] Bechet was apparently the ideal sort of player for William

Mitchell, owner of the Palais, who once said: "I don't want musicians in my band, I want jazz bandsmen."[14]

The Southern Syncopated Orchestra (under George Lattimore's management) had continued to work in Britain during 1921. After playing a round of seaside concerts in Southern England the orchestra moved north to take up a residency in Scotland, at the Lyric Theatre, Glasgow. It finished its three-week booking there on 8th October and left Scotland that night to sail to Ireland aboard the *SS Rowan*. A fatal collision occurred at sea and several musicians were killed, including drummer Pete Robinson, who had worked in London clubs with Bechet.

Tragedy moved closer to Bechet. On 27 January 1922 pianist Mope Desmond (whose real name was Caleb Jonas Quaye), who had also worked with Bechet in London, was killed in a freak railway accident whilst on his way to play a gig (with Arthur Briggs) in Wolverhampton. By a bizarre coincidence Desmond had just taken out an insurance policy in favour of his English-born wife, Doris. Mope's son, who was four months old at the time of his father's death, thrived and grew up to be the noted singer and pianist Cab Kaye.

Reminiscing years later, Bechet thought that he was back in America at the time of the *SS Rowan* disaster, but in October 1921 he was still firmly in Europe. There was a reason for his confusion. He had played some dates with Lattimore's version of the SSO during its period at the Kingsway Hall, London, during July 1921 (possibly during a quiet period for the Jazz Kings), but Bechet made it clear to Lattimore that he had no intention of touring with the unit.

During the SSO's residency at the Kingsway Hall one of its saxophone players was taken ill; no other negro musicians in London were available to fill the vacancy. Violinist Leon Van Straten, who sometimes led a band at Rector's, had a dark-complexioned, curly-headed brother, Joe, who played the saxophone. George Lattimore saw and realized that he could easily 'pass' in the SSO, even though he was Caucasian, so Joe became a temporary member of the orchestra. When the group found that it was a saxophone player short for its impending tour of Scotland, again the call went out for Joe.

Joe's brother Alfred Van Straten picks up the story: "Very early one Sunday morning a big, dark man came to where we were living in High Holborn. He banged heavily on the front door. My father went down to answer, still in his dressing gown. He was alarmed because the man was bellowing out, 'I want Joseph. I want Joseph'. My father told him that Joe wasn't at home, and the man went away. Joe actually was in, he was still in bed, but something made my father tell the man that Joe was out. Joe found out later they wanted him to go on a tour of Ireland with the SSO, but, as it happened, the boat sank on the way over, so Joe always felt grateful that my father hadn't said that he was in."[15]

During the early 1920s William Mitchell nursed an ambition to open dance-halls and night-clubs in France, just as he had done in England. As a result he opened a branch of Rector's in Paris during the latter part of 1920, but the Jazz Kings did not play there. However, in the autumn of 1921 the band did cross the Channel to play a brief residency at the Apollo on the rue de Clichy in Paris (Bechet also recalled that it played at "a large hotel" on this trip).[16] The musicians' stay in France was brief, and they returned to London to begin another residency at Hammersmith Palais in January 1922. By this time they had made one of their rare changes in personnel, Bert Romaine having replaced Pierre de Caillaux on piano. After playing another booking at the Birmingham Palais de Danse in February 1922, the Jazz Kings returned to London and began another residency at Rector's.

William Mitchell occasionally introduced new groups on to his circuit; when he did, he usually allowed a resident band to rest. At some point in 1922 this policy led to the Jazz Kings being 'rested', which allowed Sidney Bechet to work again at the Embassy Club, this time in a line-up consisting of George Clapham (piano), Bertin Salnave (saxophone), Andy Clarke (drums), Arthur Briggs (trumpet), and Jacob Patrick (trombone).

Bertin Salnave was greatly impressed by Bechet's powers of musical organization at the Embassy. After a song called *When the sun goes down* had been requested, Bechet began instructing the musicians on how it should be played. Salnave described the scene: "Picking up his saxophone he spoke to the trombonist, Jacob Patrick, 'You have to play your part like this', then turning to me he said, 'You Salnave, you do it like this. You, piano man, you've got the piano part? Good! Now we can play it. Let's go men.' He gave the signal to start and that's how the arrangement was put together."[17]

After Bechet returned to work at Rector's he kept in touch with pianist George Clapham. The two musicians used to go off to paint the town after they had finished their respective jobs. George Ruthland Clapham, born on St Kitts in the West Indies in 1889, had arrived in Britain during World War I. He was, according to Bechet, "a classical man", but he played in various small bands (and in the SSO) during the period around 1920, and also took a band to Norway in 1921. He later led his own band at various London clubs, including Romano's, and briefly worked as an accompanist for Paul Robeson. Clapham's main interest was in composing and he had a number of works published in Britain before moving back to St Kitts in 1937. Like Bechet he had a taste for high-spirited night-life.

In the early hours of Saturday 2 September 1922, both men went to an all-night rendezvous, the Breakfast Room, in Percy Street. They observed two women at another table and got into conversation with them. The women, Ruby Gordon and Pauline Lampe, later described themselves as dancers, but Bechet claimed that Ruby Gordon was a prostitute with whom he had previously had relations. At the Breakfast Room Bechet told the two women that he had some whisky, so they accompanied Sidney and George Clapham to the latter's apartment in the boarding house at 1 Grenville Street (where Bechet had stayed when he first came to London).

Events in the upstairs room at the boarding house led to Bechet and Clapham being tried later that day at Clerkenwell Police Court in front of magistrate H. T. Waddy. Both were charged with unlawfully assaulting Ruby Gordon, who alleged that Bechet "pushed me in a room and knocked me on the bed". She further alleged that Bechet had struck her and that Clapham had helped to hold her down; she said that she screamed after attempts were made to rip off her clothes. Gordon's friend Pauline Lampe said that the two of them visited the flat for "2 or 3 hours. I went downstairs to try to get help but didn't." Eventually the police were called.

In court Clapham, who like Bechet pleaded not guilty, said that the altercation arose between Ruby Gordon and Bechet "because he wouldn't have copulation with her. I got out of the room but they made such a row they disturbed occupants."[18] Bechet in his evidence said: "We were all lying down when I saw one girl sniffing something. I didn't want to do as Ruby Gordon wanted and I went to get away, but she punched me and I had to hit her to release myself. The landlord came and tried to get Ruby Gordon out but she wouldn't go, she wanted to stay. It was suggested to send for the police to get her out, but when the policeman came he took me."[19]

Police Constable Eagleton confirmed that a complaint had been telephoned to the Hunter Street police station at 8.40 a.m. He went to the Grenville Street boarding house and found the two defendants and the two women on a landing: "Ruby Gordon accused Bechet and said Clapham had tried to force whisky down her throat. There were marks on her face so I made an arrest."[20]

Bechet was found guilty as charged and was sentenced to 14 days imprisonment with hard labour; it was also recommended by the magistrates that he be deported back to the USA. Clapham received the same sentence, but no deportation order was made against him because he held a British passport. Notice of appeal was lodged and both men were granted bail, but in Bechet's case, as he was the subject of a deportation order, there was a delay in obtaining his release. Eventually he left Brixton Prison in London on 26 September 1922. The two men's appeals were heard at Newington Court on 10 October 1922, but they were unsuccessful and the verdicts remained unaltered.

Benny Peyton organized a petition against the deportation order and lodged it with the relevant authorities. Amongst the various people who signed the petition were Joseph Caulk and Manfred Coxcito (both of the Jazz Kings), Julius Nussbaum* (a Polish-born musician who had settled in London and who later worked at the Embassy Club with the bandleader Ambrose), the violinist James Horton Boucher from Sierra Leone (a former member of the SSO), and Gerard Mainz (who was employed by Mitchell and Booker, the owners of Rector's). The petition was to no avail and the deportation order was confirmed. It was noted on the petition that Sidney Bechet had on two previous occasions been fined £2 by a Court of Summary Jurisdiction, but no detail was given of these offences.

Bechet was taken from Brixton Prison to the port of Southampton, where he was placed aboard the SS *Finland* (the ship on which the ODJB had returned to the USA in 1920). He had only one shilling on him when he was arrested, so "in accordance with instructions" he was given ten shillings before he left the prison for subsistence during his voyage; he sailed for New York on 3 November 1922.

---

* Nussbaum, according to his son Louis, was dark-complexioned enough to work in various negro bands that came to Britain, including the Blackbirds Orchestra.

SEVEN

The Wizard on Wax

During Sidney Bechet's long absence from the USA his parents had died, but the returned traveller chose not to make a pilgrimage of condolence to New Orleans. Bechet's family ties had grown progressively weaker during the latter stages of his rebellious adolescence, and they were further damaged when he moved north. Being in Europe had prevented him from appearing at either of his parents' funerals, but the fact that he chose not to pay a visit of homage was taken badly by his relatives in New Orleans. As a salve to his conscience Sidney later inferred that he returned home soon after his father's death, but both his brother Leonard and his niece Emelda were adamant that he did not do so. In fact Sidney was still in England when his father died.

Sidney was never a zealous correspondent and his family in New Orleans often lost track of his whereabouts, both in Europe and in the States. News of his progress usually came to them in a roundabout way – sometimes from Lizzie Miles, who included anything favourable that she had heard about Sidney in the letters that she wrote home. Bechet's family was understandably irked by his lack of consideration, but it didn't diminish the pride they felt in his musical achievements – a feeling shared by many young black musicians in New Orleans. For these youngsters, Sidney had become a travelling hero whose musical skills had taken him half-way around the world. Danny Barker remembers the awe with which Bechet's name was mentioned: "When I was a child he was already a legend in New Orleans."[1]

Jazz musicians in New York were also aware of Bechet's achievements in Europe, and soon after his return from overseas (on 13 November 1922) he began working regularly. Rumours reached New York concerning Sidney's problems with the English police, but few people broached the subject. Sidney was both guarded and vague about his tribulations and hinted, perhaps with justification, that his arrest had racial overtones. Some people gained the impression that Bechet had been deported for a firearms offence and he did nothing to dissuade them of that belief. Their supposition was not wildly fanciful: in New York during the early 1920s many musicians, including peace-loving men such as Garvin Bushell and Louis Metcalf, carried guns. Metcalf gave his reasons: "It was heck of a deal to try and get paid on a lot of jobs and most of the places were gangster dominated. A lot of musicians had to carry sidearms, not for aggression, but for protection."[2] Bushell said, "You were supposed to have a licence to carry a gun, but nobody ever had one."[3] Back in New York, Sidney soon adopted the habit of carrying a pistol, which for him proved to be long standing. Even when he was a silver-haired old man he often toted a revolver, and when this was impractical, or likely to be detected visually, he carried a switch-blade knife.

Sidney's first gigs in New York were with a society orchestra led by Ford Dabney, which also featured the talents of cornetist Joe Smith (soon to join Fletcher Henderson), and alto saxophonist Hershel Brassfield, whose playing impressed Bechet. Work of a more permanent nature transpired after Bechet met up with the pianist and composer Donald Heywood. Heywood, who was casting for a show called *How Come*, could see the possibilities of employing a sensational instrumentalist who was also willing to act. Accordingly he gave Bechet the role of How Come, a Chinese laundryman who happened to be a brilliant jazz improviser; Sidney also played the role of a police chief in another sketch. The show, for which rehearsals began in New York on 18 December 1922, opened at the Attucks Theatre in Norfolk, Virginia, on 15 January 1923 and played there for a week.

The principal role in *How Come* was played by singer Georgette Harvey (whose name was mistakenly transcribed as Gloria Harven in *Treat it Gentle*); Sidney shared an on-stage version of a theme from *I Pagliacci* with the contralto. Early in 1923 the show was further strengthened by the inclusion of another magnificent singer, the Empress of the Blues herself, Bessie Smith. The circumstances are vague. Bechet said he first met Bessie at the home of singer Virginia Liston in Washington, and that she joined the *How Come* show there (the production did play for a week at the Howard Theatre, from 22 to 28 January 1923). On another occasion he said Bessie joined the show in Philadelphia (where the troupe played at the Dunbar Theatre for over a month, beginning on 29 January 1923). Sidney said that he and Bessie shared an on-stage duet on *St Louis Blues*, and he also hinted that they practised another sort of liaison off-stage. This must have been a highly surreptitious affair, because Bessie was closely attended by the burly Jack Gee (whom she married on 7 June 1923). The performers' affair would have had no time to develop because after a week with the show Bessie rowed with the principal comedian, Eddie Hunter, and was sacked.[4]

The show's booking at the Howard Theatre provided one young Washingtonian, Duke Ellington, with his first hearing of Bechet. It left an indelible impression on him, which he recalled almost 50 years later: "My first encounter with the New Orleans idiom came when I heard Sidney Bechet in my home town. I have never forgotten the power and imagination with which he played."[5]

There was a marked degree of impermanence in the cast listings for *How Come* that were published in contemporary advertisements. Even Georgette Harvey had left the show by the time it played at the Apollo (the old Apollo on West 42nd Street), New York, where it appeared for 32 performances in April 1923. There the production was billed as "a girly musical darkomedy"; Will Vodery directed the 20-piece orchestra, Eddie Hunter wrote the book and Ben Harris the score. The show's main performers were listed in an advertisement in the *New York Age* on 28 April 1923 as Eddie Hunter, George W. Cooper, Chappelle and Stinette and Sidney Becket [sic]. The cast also included Alberta Hunter (billed as Bertha Hunter).

In the *New York Age* of 21 April 1923, Sidney received specific mention:

"Sidney Bechet, as How Come, a Chinaman, gave a clarinet jazz solo as a novelty speciality and was well received." However, critic Heywood Broun summed up the general reaction to the show in the *New York World* of 18 April 1923: "We found much of *How Come* rapid and strident rather than exhilarating." The show's organizers took heed and prepared to revamp the production by calling for new rehearsals. When Bechet heard about these plans he decided to quit the show to chance his arm in New York. He did not have to spend much time looking for work and was soon being featured as "The Wizard of the Clarinet" in a series of theatre engagements with his former employer Will Marion Cook.

Clarence Williams, an old friend from New Orleans, was also quick to contact Sidney when he learnt that he had left the show. Like Sidney, Williams had moved from New Orleans to Chicago in the late 1910s. He ran a publishing company there, on South State Street, but was soon enticed by prospects in New York, which was rapidly developing into the most important centre of entertainment in the USA. Williams, always a good businessman, quickly established links with various recording companies in New York. Most of these organizations had been slow to perceive the potential of black talent, but the situation altered dramatically after the singer Mamie Smith recorded her hugely successful version of *Crazy Blues* in August 1920.

Williams had no plans to book Bechet for public engagements. Although they did play at a few together before the year had ended, his main intention was to feature Sidney's fine talents on record, and his connections with the Okeh recording company made this easy. So on 30 June 1923, as a member of Clarence Williams's Blue Five, Sidney Bechet recorded two titles – *Wild Cat Blues* and *Kansas City Man Blues*. The long wait was over, both for Sidney and for all the people who only knew of his talents through hearsay or by the printed word. All the disappointments and frustrations that Bechet must have felt when he realized that less gifted artists were gaining fame and fortune simply by being on record were soon to evaporate. On his début with Williams, Sidney released his pent-up emotions with a controlled passion, playing his soprano saxophone with such style and bravura that no one could have guessed that here was a musician new to the recording game.

Wild Cat Blues, a brisk tune composed by Clarence Williams and Thomas 'Fats' Waller, becomes a *tour de force* for Bechet. He is featured throughout the recording, from the first note of the introduction through to the final phrase of the coda. The dominant sound of his soprano saxophone establishes the three main themes, and he plays these various strains in a way that highlights the effectiveness of his ingenious rhythmic phrasing. His skill is brought into sharper focus when Sidney plays a series of dramatic two-bar breaks; the rest of the band (Clarence Williams on piano, Buddy Christian on banjo, John Maysfield on trombone and Thomas Morris on cornet) is heard only in the subsidiary role of accompaniment. Morris, a lauded player in his day, gains some prominence in the final sections of the performance, but the power and invention of Bechet's flowing counterpoint continues to hold the listeners' attention. The concluding phrase of the piece is a stunningly conceived two-bar break by Bechet which ends on a boldly blown seventh note.

Wild Cat Blues was not actually a blues; it was given that appendage to its title (as were many other non-blues of the period) as a sales fillip, to link it with the success of previously recorded hits such as *Crazy Blues* and *Livery Stable Blues*. However, *Kansas City Man Blues* is a genuine blues, constructed on the time-honoured 12-bar pattern (which in its most basic form consists of four bars on a tonic chord, two bars on a subdominant chord, two further bars of the tonic followed by two bars of the dominant 7th, resolving on to the final two bars of the tonic). Bechet was a master of the blues. Sometimes when improvising on a blues Bechet took a sophisticated, near-rhapsodic approach, but most often he sobbed out the most primitive sounds to emphasize the mood of the music. Throughout his career, Bechet always sounded at his supreme best when playing the blues; his recorded début in this form is truly monumental.

On *Kansas City Man Blues*, Clarence Williams again makes sure that Bechet's talents are given especial prominence. Sidney takes the lead throughout the first three choruses and remains firmly in the centre of stage when the cornetist and trombonist step forward (somewhat tentatively) in the final two choruses. Here Bechet's performance on soprano saxophone is absolutely magisterial. The breaks that he plays are imbued with that special quality of having all the time in the world, which is the mark of truly great jazz performances, but further qualities are obvious: they are delivered with a telling sonority and superb technical skill. Such individual prowess had not been apparent on any previous jazz recordings; even the masterful début sides by King Oliver's Creole Jazz Band, though models of jazz ensemble playing, have only fleeting glimpses of the solo skills of its talented members.

Wild Cat Blues and *Kansas City Man Blues* took Bechet's music to thousands of enthralled listeners. In New Orleans the recordings had a formative, inspirational effect on many young musicians. For Barney Bigard the disc was an introduction to Bechet's playing: "I heard Sidney Bechet's records while I was in New Orleans, and I used to copy him note for note.[6] Everybody had that record. That was all you could hear. Every time you passed someone's house that had the door or windows open they would be playing that on their victrola."[7] In many distant parts young musicians listened to Bechet's playing on the recording and gained the conception of jazz improvising from it. In Boston, Johnny Hodges and Harry Carney (long before they became stars in the Duke Ellington Orchestra) wound their record players countless times to replay the record. Further west, Lionel Hampton was doing the same thing, and 40 years later he could still remember every detail of *Wild Cat Blues*: "Bechet was one of my idols as a kid."[8]

Bechet's skills as a blues player made him a sympathetic accompanist for the growing number of women singers who were recording the blues, or blues-orientated songs. A few weeks after his recording début Bechet began a long series of sessions for Okeh (with Clarence Williams), where his principal task was to accompany various singers, including Sara Martin, Mamie Smith, Rosetta Crawford, Margaret Johnson and Clarence Williams's wife, Eva Taylor.

By then the great Bessie Smith had already begun her illustrious recording career; in February 1923 she made her first sides for the Columbia label – Okeh's rival. Late in life Bechet claimed that he had played an important part in getting

Bessie her first opportunity to record. He maintained that he took her to the Okeh company soon after the two of them had worked together in *How Come*. As a result (he said) Bessie and Sidney, together with a small group, cut a test recording of *I wish I could shimmy like my sister Kate* (which has never come to light). But Bessie's husband Jack Gee insisted that Charlie Carson, a record-store owner of 518 South Street in Philadelphia, made the first connections that led to Bessie's recording début.[9] Writer John Hammond, who knew Bessie and Sidney, said categorically that Bechet's account of these events was fallible.

None of the singers that Bechet recorded with during this busy period (1923–4) was in the same class as Bessie Smith, but several of them had commendable individuality. Sara Martin sings *Blind Man Blues* with genuine feeling aided by Bechet's apt and sensuous fill-ins. The soprano saxophonist's imaginative mood is not helped by having to follow the trombonist's lugubrious solo, but he sounds inspired and inventive. Bechet's work on *Atlanta Blues* is more distantly placed as far as the balance is concerned, but he still sounds mighty effective and his vigour adds most of the merit contained in the muddled ensemble.

On the trio sides with Mamie Smith (a notably flexible vocalist) Bechet shines more because he has fewer colleagues to clog up the proceedings. Clarence Williams on piano and Buddy Christian on banjo play simple, unobtrusive harmonies that allow Bechet plenty of space in which to demonstrate his skills. His solo on *Lady Luck Blues* opens with a series of long notes, creating a mood that is profound but not ponderous, full of expression without being melodramatic, and the way in which he soars up to his high notes is enthralling. Thirty years later Bechet cited this as being one of his favourite recorded performances. The original reverse side of *Lady Luck Blues* was Mamie Smith's version of *Kansas City Man Blues*. This contains some vibrant instrumental interludes by Bechet, which he plays by shifting in and out of double-time phrases with all the ease of a top-class distance runner changing pace.

Very little seemed to ruffle Bechet's concentration – not even indifferent musical company. Within him burnt a fire that always ignited his phrases, regardless of cross-winds blown by lesser talents. The combination of Eva Taylor's light, graceful vocal lines and Clarence Williams's enthusiastic 'singing' does not make a particularly stimulating musical blend, but, undaunted, Bechet plays triumphantly on their version of *Oh Daddy Blues*. Here Bechet performs on clarinet (instead of soprano saxophone) and does so in exemplary fashion, utilizing his powerful 'woody' tone and his ample technique. During the ensemble his improvisations move onto some attractively deft harmonies, showing the sensitivity of his musical ear, and the deliberate pitch variations he creates in his blues-tinged break underline the depth of his expression. His emotions were just as potently displayed on clarinet as they were on soprano saxophone.

Both *Oh Daddy* and the wordy but trite *I've got the Yes We Have No Bananas Blues* (which is basically a feature for Eva Taylor) are played by an unchanged Blue Five. This same personnel also recorded an instrumental version of *Achin' Hearted Blues* two weeks later, in August 1923. Bechet is again on clarinet and is featured on the breaks that serve as an introduction. The band sounds more cohesive than on its previous recordings; cornetist Thomas Morris was rarely as bold and assertive as he is here. The trombonist also radiates more confidence, playing a part that sounds as if it was inspired by the style of King Oliver's trombonist Honore Dutrey, but the outstanding feature of the recording is Bechet's work on clarinet, which effortlessly combines a scorching timbre and ingenious timing. His solo begins with a thrilling entry note, and there is no lessening of tension throughout the next two choruses; these are full of complicated phrases, all of which are perfectly resolved. Bechet rarely used his technique to show off.

Although this series of recordings is an important link with what Bechet was doing in 1923, their creation was only a brief part of his professional activity. For most of the summer of that year he worked as a freelance around New York, performing in clubs and cabarets, undertaking stage work at various midnight matinées, and occasionally playing in theatre orchestras. When work was done he was as restless as ever, roaming Manhattan and doing his best to acquaint himself with every aspect of New York's night-life. Reed player Garvin Bushell first met Sidney during one of his reconnaissance excursions:

> In 1923 I joined Sam Wooding at the Nest Club on 133rd Street in Harlem. We had a very good band and the place was packed every night. At the time Bechet was looking for a place to establish himself in New York, so he made his rounds every night to all the Harlem clubs. One night he came to the "Nest" and played. After which he came to the band stand and said to me "Hello namesake, I hear you've been using my name". I merely laughed and told him in no uncertain terms that the name Bushell in New York was big and important enough, we didn't have to change it. That didn't hit him too well, but he calmed down and said "I was only joking". He then asked me to play on the soprano sax, well I was in good form that particular night, I played well, at least the audience thought so. Sidney and I became very good friends after that.[10]

During this period Bechet began composing regularly. Sometimes the act of composition was merely a patient repolishing of themes he had devised earlier, but more often his tunes came to him in a sudden burst of inspiration. Then he began a frantic search to find someone who could write down in musical notation what he hummed at or played to them.

Bechet's regular recording sessions with Clarence Williams meant that the two men rebuilt social contact, and Sidney often called at Williams's home in New York. Williams was always on the look out for publishable material and he actively encouraged Bechet to bring him his songs. Williams also acted as a go-between in finding lyricists to add words to Sidney's melodies. The first tune that Bechet seems to have copyrighted is *Ghost of the Blues* (registered on 5 September 1923), an atmospheric piece written in a standard 32-bar format, but containing bold unexpected notes; the lyricist for this song was Bechet's former employer Lt Tim Brymn. Within a month of copyrighting that song Bechet had registered a further seven compositions, some with his own lyrics, others with words by collaborators such as Alfred Knight, Charles Matson and Clarence Williams. Later, in 1925, his chief collaborator was Rousseau Simmons.

After a summer respite Bechet began a new series of recordings with Williams (beginning in October 1923). In a trio (Williams on piano and Buddy Christian on banjo), Bechet provided superb backings for two expressive performances by Eva Taylor, *Irresistible Blues* and *Jazzin' Babies Blues*. Sidney is in triumphant form during his solos. Once again the clarity afforded by the smaller line-up reveals that Bechet's tone and articulation (as well as his musical ideas and harmonic sense) were all fully developed, so much so that, if it were possible to transplant these solos alongside his later work, the effect would not sound incongruous. Bechet's rephrasing of the melody of *Jazzin' Babies Blues* has all the rhythmic poise of a supremely talented, fully mature artiste.

At this stage of the development of jazz no other saxophonist in New York had successfully grasped the music's unique phrasing, and none of them could match the speed and power of Sidney's improvisations; even a young virtuoso like Coleman Hawkins still sounded stiff and unswinging. Bechet, by example, demonstrated a new way of articulating notes on the saxophone (both staccato and legato), and his amazing breath control inspired others to begin constructing long, smooth-running phrases. Great music falls thick and fast from Bechet during late 1923; lesser moments only occur when he has to play trite unison figures with other players, or when he is poorly balanced. Bechet was an extremely powerful player, and wary sound engineers of this period often felt that he was too loud for their recording equipment. Bechet couldn't fail to observe their apprehension: "When it got to my chorus the needle would jump. I couldn't play the way I wanted to. The engineers would almost go crazy when they saw me coming into the studios. They'd say, 'Here comes trouble itself.'"[11]

Shreveport Blues (by Clarence Williams's Blue Five) seems to have been one of the titles affected by the engineer's caution: Sidney's playing is very much in the background, but even so he can be heard cutting loose effectively. A few days later, on *House Rent Blues*, his stop-time chorus comes through loud, clear and magnificent. One of the couplings from this batch of recordings in late 1923 was *E Flat Blues* and *If I let you get away with it*, on which Bechet (and the Blue Five) accompany the deep, powerful voice of Margaret Johnson. Bechet is splendidly audible in the backings to the vocal part and quite dominating in the instrumental interludes, his break on *If I let you get away with it* being absolutely spectacular.

Something about this recording caught the attention of the Parlophone Company in England (who had access to Okeh material), and in June 1924 it was issued in England with a publicity handout promising that "the rhythm will get you". The merits of the two sides certainly did 'get' the local jazz fans: the recording sold well for many years and became the foundation stone of many Bechet collections in Britain.

Bechet is alleged to be amongst the personnel that accompanies singer Virginia Liston on Clarence Williams's session of 7 January 1924, but the musician who plays the *alto* saxophone on *I don't love nobody* and *Tain't a doggone thing* is not Bechet. Bizarrely enough, Bechet claimed to have recorded with Virginia Liston later that week, on guitar! The record label supports his contention, but guitarist Bernard Addison, an ex-school friend of Virginia Liston and someone who saw Bechet "practically every day" during this period, thinks it highly unlikely that Sidney played on the date.

Clarence Williams adroitly chose not to promulgate musicians' names on his record labels. He occasionally relented, but usually felt that he just might be held to ransom if, after gaining fame through appearing on one of Williams recordings, a particular musician began demanding extra fees. Bechet later complained bitterly about this wanton omission. The Okeh record company, however, was proud to advertise that they were using Sidney's skills, and in their press advertisements for Christmas 1923 published his photo captioned "King Bechet".

At the beginning of 1924 Bechet became involved in a project that was the brainchild of Will Marion Cook's wife, Abbie Mitchell. Sidney's contribution to *Negro Nuances* produced a glowing tribute from Cook, who wrote in the *Chicago Defender* of 22 March 1924: "The play was written by Miss Abbie Mitchell, with most of the music by me. Additional music is by Sidney Bechet and Jimmie Johnson. The music for the last 22 minutes is by these two. Sidney Bechet is the most beautiful song writer in the world today. At least three of his numbers will be world wide successes. You possibly know that he is the writer of *The Ghost of the Blues*. I want you to make more of Bechet than you do of me. I am going, Bechet is coming."

Unfortunately *Negro Nuances* never progressed much further than the embryo stage. The long-running production that Bechet became involved with in 1924 was headed by Jimmie Cooper, and it comprised 70 artistes and musicians, 35 of whom were white and 35 black; the troupe became known as the Black and White Revue. One of the dancers in the show was Bessie Dessieur, also known as Bessie De Sota (her name was mistakenly transcribed in *Treat it Gentle* as Bessie Descheux), with whom Bechet struck up a friendship. On tour he also made the acquaintance of a Miss Hodges from Massachusetts, who told Bechet that her young brother was a fan of his, and that he had started to learn the saxophone. Bechet said, "Bring him along", so, there in a backstage dressing room in Boston, Sidney Bechet and Johnny Hodges had their first meeting. Sidney asked Johnny to play something and he obliged with a chorus of *My Honey's Loving Arms*.[12]

The younger man often reminisced about this experience. The exact circumstances of the initial meeting were subject to variation in the various retellings, but Hodges's eternal admiration for Bechet's talent was obvious. Towards the end of his life Hodges said: "Sidney Bechet is tops in my book – he was my favourite! He schooled me a whole lot and I'll say that if it hadn't been for him I'd probably just be playing for a hobby."[13]

In 1924 there was a gap in Bechet's recording activities, and for a period of ten months he made no recordings at all with Clarence Williams. His only session during this hiatus produced a curio: it is a recording of one of his compositions sung by a white vaudeville artiste, Maureen Englin, who reminisced about the session in 1962. Whilst visiting a New York publisher she heard "beautiful soft saxophone music". She asked who was playing and was told it was Sidney Bechet. After the two had been introduced Maureen Englin said: "That was a beautiful tune you were playing. Is it new? I'm looking for some new songs for my act." Bechet told her that it was his own composition *Foolin' me*. Englin took a copy of the song away so that she could use it for a recording date she was contracted to do on the following day. She asked Bechet if he would join pianist Art Sorenson in accompanying her for the recording and he readily agreed. Next day Bechet turned up at the studio on East 52nd Street and played some unobtrusive, mellow phrases behind the singer; the results were first issued on the Pathé label.[14]

The publishing house referred to by Maureen Englin belonged to Fred Fisher who issued several of Sidney's songs in 1924, including *Foolin' me, Do that thing* (which was recorded by Fletcher Henderson), and *Pleasure Mad*, a big early hit for Sidney which was recorded in the mid-1920s by Charlie Creath, Ethel Waters, Bennie Krueger, Whitey Kaufman and others.

EIGHT

Duel of the Giants

Throughout the first year of his recording career Bechet was the star performer of every band session in which he took part, and even when his role was that of accompanist he usually emerged as the premier performer. The situation changed during 1924. Bechet's talents were not eclipsed, but the skills of a young rival jazzman, new to New York, soon caused musicians and other listeners to argue about which of the two was the greater player. The newcomer to New York was no stranger to Sidney Bechet – his name was Louis Armstrong.

Louis, like Bechet, played every sort of gig in New Orleans before moving on to Chicago. He left for Illinois in 1922 to join his mentor Joe 'King' Oliver, and served a notable apprenticeship playing second cornet in the Creole Jazz Band, making his recording début with the group in April 1923. In September 1924 he was persuaded to move to New York to become a featured soloist in one of the leading black bands of the era – Fletcher Henderson's orchestra. News of Louis's arrival caused a stir amongst local musicians, vividly remembered by one of them, Louis Hooper: "I was at the Lafayette Theatre the night Henderson introduced Louis Armstrong to New York at a midnight show. Sidney Bechet was in the pit band that night as a guest, they introduced Louis and he played *What-cha-call 'em Blues*."[1]

Fletcher Henderson had no exclusive claims on Armstrong's recording activities, and this allowed Clarence Williams to conceive the idea of pairing the two supreme improvisers of their era in a series of sessions during 1924 and 1925. Whenever Armstrong and Bechet met, each man knew instinctively that he was facing his closest rival in the jazz hierarchy. In those days they always greeted each other effusively, but they made no effort to meet socially. They might share an animated conversation about the merits of New Orleans food, but such talk never took place around a meal table. No one recalled ever seeing them out on the town together.

Socially they were from widely differing backgrounds and, although a darker shade of skin did not prejudice Bechet, Louis would have good cause to remember that Bechet knew of his humble origins and shoe-less days. Both men were of similar build – short and stocky – but in temperament they were vastly different. Bechet had a fiery temper; Louis was generally complacent. Bechet could be a honey-voiced, soft-spoken charmer; Louis tended to talk in gruff, short sentences. At this time Bechet was apparently very much the man about town, dressing in a debonair fashion; he was restless by nature and eager to chance anything for a good time. In contrast, Louis was basically a shy man, with nothing, as yet, of Bechet's panache. If Armstrong was with people he knew, he could lapse into easy, free-flowing banter; otherwise he stood by, quietly amused by the antics of others. There was nothing of the kill-joy in him, but during his early years in New York he rarely visited lively clubs after he had finished work; yet, when he did so, he showed that, like Sidney Bechet, he was a superb dancer. Also like Bechet, he could instantly improvise over any chord progression that was played to him, even if it was one that he hadn't encountered before. But whereas Bechet was not interested in learning to read music, Louis had an avid desire to develop this skill (he eventually became an accomplished reader). Each man shared an amazing capacity for improvising sublime solos, a fact underlined by their work on the remarkable recordings with Clarence Williams, which began on 17 October 1924.

On *Texas Moaner Blues*, Armstrong's lead sounds stately against the heavy vamping of the piano and banjo on the beat; he carries the melody as if he were leading a noble procession. Bechet, sounding equally assured, seems content temporarily to play the role of prince regent. Trombonist Charlie Irvis is unobtrusive but effective in the ensemble and blows a forthright, economical solo; in the classic New Orleans manner, Armstrong and Bechet continue to play, creating soft, telling lines behind the trombonist's improvisations. The two paragons share a sombre break, then Louis steps forward to create a sublime solo, marking his phrases with heartfelt blue notes; in the background the clarinet and trombone weave a brocade of sounds. Bechet, now on soprano saxophone, begins his solo with a dramatic downward phrase; descending with a heavier tread than Armstrong would have used for a similar phrase, he moves on and embosses an element of drama onto every motif. Just as Louis had done in his solo, Sidney manages to encapsulate a microcosm of his talents in a startling mid-chorus break. The final ensemble achieves a rocking momentum created mainly by the combined rhythmic energy of Armstrong and Bechet. Sidney's clarinet coda achieves a suitably climactic finish.

The group's task on *Early in the Morning* is to back the attractive vaudeville-blues singing of Virginia Liston. Armstrong uses the verse to demonstrate the power and surety of his upper register. One tiny corner of a canvas can reveal a painter's genius, and here a mere six-bar segment shared by Armstrong and Bechet confirms their extraordinary talents; their playing during this brief interlude reveals that they were far in advance of any of their contemporaries. Bechet's ascending two-bar clarinet break amply illustrates his masterful sense of form.

Virginia Liston is also featured on *You've got the right key*. Armstrong's huge tone is superbly captured and Bechet shows that he and Johnny Dodds shared many similar ideas about projecting the sound of a clarinet. Another brief instrumental interlude produces startling music: Sidney's soprano saxophone drives the band along, but this time it is Louis's turn to create a breath-taking two-bar break.

Bechet's next great moments in the studio occurred on a date with Sippie Wallace when he worked in a trio consisting of himself on soprano saxophone and clarinet, Clarence Williams on piano and Buddy Christian on banjo. Sidney turns in a stirling performance, playing all through both tunes recorded. He begins *I'm so glad I'm a brownskin* sounding triumphant in the top register of his saxophone, and goes on to construct a commanding solo that shows how skilful he was becoming in the use of tonal variations. Bechet plays clarinet throughout *Off and On Blues*, again tipping his cap to Johnny Dodds and also, it seems, to 'Big Eye' Louis Nelson, who taught him the near-comical 'chicken cackling' effects he deliberately inserts in his 12-bar solo.

Later during that same month, December 1924, Bechet took part in a session with Clarence Williams that included the only jazz performance on sarrusophone ever recorded. On *Mandy make up your mind* Bechet's innate musical skill somehow conquers the problems posed by this unwieldy hybrid instrument. None of the sarrusophone family (in its various registers) ever caught the public's imagination or the interest of many composers or performers. Where Bechet found his bass model is conjectural – it was rumoured that he borrowed it from a pawn shop; Sidney himself usually laughed off serious enquiries about this matter. It is just conceivable that the unusual instrument which Darnell Howard recalled a relative of Bechet's playing in the 1910s[2] was actually a sarrusophone. It is also rumoured that Sidney experimented on the sarrusophone during the time he lived in London. He certainly played the bass clarinet during his stay in Britain.[3]

Whatever the background, Bechet's efforts on the sarrusophone are remarkable. He was always serious when it came to music-making, and made no attempt to create hokum effects on the double-reeded rarity. Louis, for his part, also reveals a sense of musical dignity by playing a delightful obbligato to Bechet's low-note excursions; Charlie Irvis on trombone carries on as though nothing untoward were happening. Despite the comically visual presence of the sarrusophone, there are no banal moments, and when Bechet picks up his soprano saxophone the momentum is increased, giving the eminently pleasant voice of Eva Taylor an inspired accompaniment.

Armstrong's lead on the opening of *I'm a Little Blackbird* (another vocal feature for Eva Taylor) is peerless, but fortunately Bechet was on hand to create a series of exhilarating follow-up phrases; the two men take turns in playing lead and harmony parts. Eva Taylor's stop-time vocal part engenders a charming surprise effect. The band backs her assiduously before being swept into a fervent ensemble by the stirring sound of Irvis's trombone glissandos. Again Armstrong's phrasing of the tune is exemplary, but Bechet has the last word, constructing a neat little three-note ending figure.

Louis Armstrong's wife, Lil Hardin Armstrong, takes over the piano-playing duties of the group for titles it made as the Red Onion Jazz Babies (a billing inspired by a notorious New Orleans club). Alberta Hunter (using the name Josephine Beatty for contractual reasons) sings *Nobody knows the way I feel 'dis mornin'* and *Early Every Mornin'* with gusto and feeling. The band's task on the first title is limited to the repetition of an insistent answering phrase, but on the reverse there is a pearl of an eight-bar ensemble. Lil was never a highly accomplished pianist, but her heavy touch adds a welcome degree of keyboard activity that seems to be missing when Clarence Williams is with the group.

The Red Onions concluded the session with an exciting version of *Cakewalkin'*
Babies. A vocal duo, consisting of Alberta Hunter and Bechet's old friend from
New Orleans Clarence Todd, provides an interlude that sounds determinedly
vaudevillian, before the band gets down to business by producing some highly
charged ensembles. Armstrong's unflagging talent gives the melody an impact,
and Bechet's counterpoint is created with an air of flamboyant invention;
trombonist Irvis sounds much niftier than usual. Allowed the luxury of a second
ensemble chorus, the band achieves a penetrating intensity, with both Bechet
and Armstrong adding to the aura of excitement by blowing an array of fiery tonal
effects – the sort that would never be heard in a conservatoire. Even more
extraordinary were the intensely involved rhythmic patterns that Louis and
Sidney were introducing.

Throughout 1924 Bechet had managed to dovetail his time recording and
playing live engagements. After he had finished his stint with the Black and
White Revue he returned to New York and found a place in a show by Noble
Sissle and Eubie Blake called *In Bamville*, which opened at the Lyceum Theatre
in Rochester, New York, on 10 March 1924. A stage photograph from the
production shows Bechet (dressed as a policeman) playing the alto saxophone and
trumpeter Joe Smith (wearing a kilt). Smith remained with the show for several
months but Bechet decided he didn't want to go on tour, so he stayed in New
York and went to work in clubs whose schedules allowed him time to take part in
various recordings and freelance dates.

By 1924 Bechet's devoted admirer Johnny Hodges had gained enough proficiency on saxophone to make the journey from Boston to New York in order to
pick up weekend gigs; these trips allowed him good opportunities to see and hear
his hero in action. Hodges found that during this period Bechet was moving from
one cabaret to another, playing a feature number in each and staying long enough
to pick up the resultant tips, but moving on whilst the applause was at its loudest.
Hodges commented, "He would play just long enough to pick up about 40 or
50 dollars, then he'd go along to the next club. Man, he was just terrific."[4] The
scope in New York City for such a wandering performer was enormous. In 1924
there were 238 licensed dance-halls in New York City,[5] besides hundreds of
unregistered late-night clubs. Bechet's main area of activity was around 134th
Street, where Smalls', Leroy's, Fritz's, Connie's and the Owl Club all thrived
within the space of one block.

Duke Ellington's Washingtonians were establishing a reputation at the Hollywood Club (soon to be renamed The Kentucky) at 203 West 49th Street. In the
spring of 1924, when Ellington's band interrupted its residency to do some
touring, the club's management brought in a group led by another famous pianist
and composer, James P. Johnson. Saxophonist Benny Carter was in that band,
and so too was Sidney Bechet. In an interview in 1936 Carter recalled the deep
impression that Bechet's playing made on him: "One of the very few men who
ever played really marvellous soprano was Sidney Bechet, who was amongst
the most original artistes I have ever heard on any saxophone and created the
style which inspired Johnny Hodges. Bechet was playing alto and soprano with
Jimmy Johnson's Band, of which I was also a member when we followed Duke

Ellington into the old Kentucky Club."[6] Bechet's stay with James P. Johnson was a brief one. Apparently the leader wanted the music he presented to be based on written arrangements, while Sidney felt certain that the club's clientele was more eager to hear improvisations. The two men parted company.

Bechet decided to accept an offer to play a residency at the Rhythm Club, a basement venue on 7th Avenue and 132nd Street in New York. This spot (managed by Bert Hall) became a popular rendezvous for musicians eager to swop stories and news of impending gigs. It was also one of the first places in New York City (along with the Garden of Joy at 7th Avenue and 140th Street – at which Bechet had also worked) where improvising musicians could take part in informal jam sessions. Bechet soon assumed leadership of the Rhythm Club's resident band, which played a four-hour session, usually from 3.30 a.m. until 7.30 a.m. Trumpeter Louis Metcalf and drummer Tommy Benford worked with Bechet at this venue, together with a variety of pianists, including Willie 'the Lion' Smith and Bechet's friend from New Orleans Buddy Christian.

The resident group at the Rhythm Club was constantly being joined by various sitters-in, and at times there were as many as a dozen musicians on the tiny bandstand. But no matter how big the line-up was, the strong sounds of Sidney's soprano saxophone could be heard soaring above the ensemble. Bechet rarely played clarinet during this period. He later said that the instrument had gone out of fashion by the time he returned to New York from Europe.[7] Bechet brought his Lafleur soprano saxophone back across the Atlantic from London, but this didn't stop several British musicians from claiming later that they owned Sidney's instrument. The only explanation is that Sidney was doing some wheeling and dealing in soprano saxophones during the latter part of his stay in Britain. He subsequently played a Conn soprano, but after a number of years he made a permanent change to a Buescher.

The added power of a soprano saxophone certainly came in useful during the various musical combats that occupied Bechet during the period 1923–5. He had always thrived on competition, and he found plenty in New York, where willing contenders were arriving from all over the land. One night Sidney became particularly vexed by the over-brimming confidence of Coleman Hawkins, a young tenor saxophonist who was already a star in Fletcher Henderson's orchestra. The subsequent encounter between Bechet and Hawkins provided Duke Ellington with an unforgettable experience: "In the old days they had cutting contests where you defended your honor with an instrument. I remember a great night at the Comedy Club. We arrived late one Sunday morning but Sidney Bechet and Coleman Hawkins had hooked up, and they went at it all night long."[8]

Wellman Braud, Ellington's long-time bass player, also recalled this meeting in a conversation with guitarist Danny Barker: "Hawkins, they said, remarked that New Orleans musicians can't play, 'they ain't no hell'. The slander was relayed to Bechet who sent word that the great Hawk come by the Band Box [sic] and bring his ax – his golden horn, the tenor saxophone – so that the New York Harlem critics could judge if New Orleans musicians could play. So the date was set, and the two reed giants met at the over-packed Band Box. Bechet blowing like a hurricane embarrassed the Hawk, he played and continued to play as Hawkins packed his horn and as he walked out angrily Bechet followed him outside and woke up the neighborhood, it was six o'clock in the morning."[9] The encounter produced a lot of mutual respect, and ever after the two men always exchanged friendly greetings, though neither showed any great desire to share a bandstand with his former adversary.

One Leonard Bernstein, who owned the Hollywood Club, hadn't failed to notice the dramatic appeal that Bechet had on his audiences, so when Duke Ellington returned to the club he suggested that Bechet be added to the Washingtonians. Duke was delighted by the idea – he was one of Sidney's staunchest admirers. In the mid-1920s, however, Ellington was still a junior bandleader, and he soon found that Bechet was something of a handful – both in New York City and during a brief tour of New England. Sidney's musicianship created no problems, but his disregard of punctuality and of discipline proved to be a headache. In later years Duke would probably have smiled benignly at the inconveniences that Bechet's non-musical failings caused, but as a 26-year-old leader he found the unreliability extremely troublesome. He was also bemused when Bechet insisted on bringing his huge German shepherd dog, Goola, to work with him.

The suspiciousness that had been part of Bechet's adolescent character developed more sinister roots when he was in his twenties, and he often felt that people were plotting against him; he invariably suspected various musicians he worked with. In Ellington's group Bechet saw two enemies, trumpeter Bubber Miley and trombonist Charlie Irvis. Miley had been serving a brief jail sentence when Bechet first joined Ellington. On his return to the band he and Irvis (according to Bechet) began making personal asides, and – sin of sins – commented unfavourably on New Orleans musicianship. Bubber Miley, like Bechet, was a self-possessed character, game for musical combat with anyone. Harry Carney said of him: "He was a man who liked to battle,"[10] and Tricky Sam Nanton added, "He was loaded with personal magnetism and dominated any situation."[11]

Duke Ellington knew that every session that Bechet and Miley shared was going to be a lively one, and he was shrewd enough to realize that their competitiveness added excitement to his band's music. He said, "Bechet and Bubber used to have what we called cutting contests. One would go out and play ten choruses then the other would do the same. And while one was on the other would be back getting a little taste to get himself together and finding a few new ideas. It was really something."[12]

Unfortunately none of the music that Bechet made with Ellington was ever issued on record. Sidney told an interviewer that he had recorded two titles (*Twelfth Street Rag* and *Tiger Rag*) with Duke Ellington for the Brunswick label in 1924, but these have never been traced. Sidney may have been trying to add some spice to the interview by mischievously hoodwinking the questioner. When asked about these recordings, Duke Ellington was positive that Sidney was mistaken. In 1944 (in answer to queries raised by a British collector, Norman

Evans) Ellington wrote: "There was no recording session in 1924 (or any other year) with Sidney Bechet."[13]

However, Bechet's influence had a permanent effect on Ellington's approach to composition and to the way he featured instrumentalists: Bechet-like themes crop up in various of his works – as in the fast-moving passage in *Daybreak Express* – and many of his rhapsodic passages would seem to have been inspired by Bechet's phrases. Duke later found that it took two skilled musicians to fulfil the role in his arrangements that Bechet had undertaken during his brief stay in the band. The two players were Johnny Hodges on alto saxophone and Barney Bigard on clarinet. Both were nurtured by Ellington and became jazz giants; his inspiration for featuring them as he did came from ideas that germinated as he listened to Bechet displaying his talents within the Washingtonians.

The Ellington–Bechet union ended after Sidney went missing for three days. A good excuse was needed to evaporate the bandleader's vexation. "Where the hell have you been?" he asked Bechet, who coolly replied, "I jumped in a cab and we got lost, and I just now finally found out where I was."[14] Duke was exasperated by Bechet's nonchalance and, as a result, gave him his marching orders. Bechet showed no signs of smarting over the dismissal; nor did the incident diminish his admiration for Ellington, either as a person or as a musician.

Bechet casually resumed his work in late-night clubs, and again secured the job as leader of the Rhythm Club's resident group. His first recording assignment in 1925 was an unadventurous affair. It consisted of providing accompaniment (as part of Clarence Williams's Blue Five) for singer Margaret Johnson, whose firm but slightly adenoidal voice may be heard on one of Bechet's compositions, *Who'll chop your suey when I'm gone*. The opulent melody and *double entendre* of the lyrics are earnestly sung by the vocalist, with Bechet seemingly directing the background effects. Subsequently Sidney gives a fairly straightforward rendering of the melody and is answered by stock phrases from the brass duo. The coupling, *Done made a fool out of me*, is instrumentally even less eventful.

Half-way through that session there was a change of trumpeter; Bubber Miley left the studio and was replaced by someone who sounds like Joe Smith. Later that same day yet another trumpeter took over, but his identity was unmistakable – it was Louis Armstrong. Armstrong, Bechet, Charlie Irvis, Clarence Williams and Buddy Christian pooled their skills to create another version of *Cakewalkin' Babies*. All except Williams had been on the eminently successful recording of the same tune two weeks earlier, but that had been for the Gennett label; Clarence Williams wanted a version for issue on Okeh.

Eva Taylor takes the vocal part. She performs the song well, with admirable clarity and charm, but the performance of the band achieves a quality that places this track amongst the finest jazz recordings of all time. The group tackles the opening chorus with rare inspiration: Armstrong and Bechet create an infectious sense of swing as they improvise a series of superbly balanced rhythmic phrases. After the vocal the band regroups and performs with an intensity that borders on the ferocious, but even during the passages of white heat both Bechet and Armstrong keep a firm grip on their technique, and, despite the excitement, retain the ability to create daring phrases the split second they are conceived.

If this performance were viewed as a contest between Armstrong and Bechet, the result would be considered a dead heat, but, although the two supermen remain fiercely competitive throughout, nothing they attempt lessens the overall appeal of the performance. A startlingly original phrase from one produces an astonishing counter from the other, and the rest of the group is carried along by the creative energy that is circulating. The final number of the day was a sentimental ballad by Eva Taylor. *Pickin' on your baby* begins in a sweet, uneventful way, with Bechet wailing out some sympathetic high notes whilst the two brass players quietly guard the low register. After the vocal Armstrong seemingly appears from nowhere to begin playing the melody way up in the stratosphere, almost losing his balance in alighting on such a high ledge. He quickly recovers to give a passionate high-register performance of the melody that is similar in concept to his 1929 version of *When you're smiling*; for good measure he also plays a totally perfect break. On this occasion Sidney decided to take a back seat.

In March 1925 the same group, augmented by two reed players, Buster Bailey and Don Redman, performed an innocent waltz, *Cast Away*, which is sung by Eva Taylor. The main feature of this is the trembling sound achieved by the reed trio. Things revert to swinging normality on *Papa De-da-da*, where Louis Armstrong firmly establishes the melody against a background of arranged reed passages. This time only Clarence Williams accompanies the vocal part, but Armstrong is again prominent in the final chorus, blowing joyously. Unfortunately Bechet's efforts are submerged within the over-organized reed trio.

In the spring of 1925 Bechet left New York to tour with a theatrical troupe. The *Baltimore Afro-American* of 9 May 1925 reported: "Bechet, the clarinet wizard, has been added to the musical unit in Seven-Eleven." One of Sidney's colleagues in this show was his friend from New Orleans (and Chicago) bass player Wellman Braud. After playing in Newark, New Jersey, the troupe (which the *Chicago Defender* described as the first of the "racial burlesque companies") played at the Empire, Baltimore, and the Gayety, Washington, DC, before beginning a three-week stay in Boston. The band's line-up in 1925 was Thornton Brown and Louis Prevost (trumpets), Sidney Bechet, John Howell, Alex Poole, Jerome Don Pasquall and William Paris (reeds), Stanley Bennett (piano), Wellman Braud (bass) and a drummer.

The show finished its Boston run in June 1925, moved first to Providence, Rhode Island, then on to New York, where (in early July) it began a summer residency at the Columbia Theatre. Bechet quit the show there. On his arrival in New York he had been greeted by a bonanza in the shape of a big payment of royalties earnt by his various compositions. He decided to use this lump sum to set up his own night-club. Johnny Hodges recalled the developments: "Bechet had a club that he was going to open at 145th Street called Club Basha and he came by one night and approached me and said he wanted me in his band right away. That was my big chance, so I quit Fritz's Club and went to work for him. And it was then he used to show me different things on the soprano. You see each club used to go to the Lafayette Theatre every Friday for the midnight show and advertise, you didn't get paid for this, it was just an advertisement for your club. So Bechet and I did this duet. I think it was *Everybody loves my baby* or *I found a new baby*, I'm not sure which, but this was one of the things he taught me."[15]

For much of his life Bechet saw himself as an enterprising businessman, who only needed capital to make a success of his various dreams and schemes; he always listened intently when anyone outlined a smart money-making idea. He pondered on such stories and sometimes half-imagined that he had been involved in some of the wily deals he heard about. Such was the case when veteran musicians told him about the money made in Europe during the soap shortages of World War I. Sidney convinced himself that he too had pulled off a sensational coup by bringing vast crates of soap to Britain. His good friend Arthur Briggs described Bechet's 'soap story' as "baloney". Indeed, if Sidney had arrived in England with a huge quantity of soap in 1919 he would have found no shortage, since production was higher than it had been for many years.[16]

But there was nothing imaginary about the Club Basha – so named because all of Sidney's New York acquaintances pronounced his surname 'Bash-a'. It operated on the former site of Hermit's End (2493 Seventh Avenue), a basement club which had employed various bands during 1924, including one led by Cecil and Lloyd Scott. Bechet's partner in the enterprise was someone he chose to refer to only as 'George'. The partner apparently had good contacts for the supply of bootleg liquor – vital for any night-club's success in the era of Prohibition.

The organization and setting up of the club took much of Bechet's time that summer. He did apparently play on one recording session in July 1925, however, as part of an inauspicious pick-up group called the Get Happy Band, which makes a miserable job of playing a jerkily phrased version of *Junk Bucket Blues*. The only true musical merit from the session comes when Bechet takes a series of fine breaks during the concluding chorus of the band's other offering, *In Harlem's Araby*. Bechet later said that he couldn't remember taking part in this session, but that may have been wishful thinking.

Bechet persuaded drummer Tommy Benford to join the band he was forming for the Club Basha, and on piano he engaged one of the legendary New Orleans players, Sammy Davis (a great favourite of Jelly Roll Morton). The trombonist was Jacob Patrick, and the banjoist and guitarist, Smithy Frasier. Sidney enlisted Johnny Hodges to share saxophone duties with him. By this time Hodges was living in New York, sharing an apartment with Cecil Scott on 135th Street.

The *Baltimore Afro-American* of 22 August 1925 reported: "Club Basha, New York. Sidney Basha [sic], house manager and orchestra leader with his New Orleans Creole Jazz Boys performed alto saxophone solo on *Dear Old Southland*." This item seems to confirm the point that Benny Carter made about Bechet temporarily playing the alto instrument during the mid-1920s.

After a slow start the Club Basha quickly achieved success. It seemed likely that Bechet's invested royalties would soon be quadrupled, but the figure of dancer Bessie Dessieur cast a shadow over the relationship between Sidney and his partner George. Bessie, who had worked in the *Plantation Days* show and in the Black and White Revue as part of a dance trio, had ambitions to become a solo artiste (she did subsequently become a successful 'Egyptian novelty dancer'). Seeking glamour for his new club, Bechet hired Bessie (with whom he had been on friendly terms for a couple of years), but his partner George soon struck up a close relationship with the dancer and sided with the frequent complaints she made about her work schedule.

This liaison irritated Bechet: one night, when Jerry Preston (a friend who owned the Log Cabin Club) asked Bessie to dance for him and she refused, his volcanic temper erupted. Bechet insisted that the dancer was to be fired, but George disagreed; the two men almost came to blows, and each threatened to call on the services of various 'heavies' that they knew. Bechet went as far as to enlist the aid of one Bub Ewley, but then realized that violence would be met by violence. Accordingly he decided to abandon his share of the club. Bechet was legally bound to pay half of the bills that the club incurred, and as a result he engaged George Lattimore's brother, who was an attorney, to make a settlement offer, which was accepted by partner George. The club continued to thrive after Sidney had relinquished his interest, and as late as 24 March 1926 an advertisement in *Variety* listed Bernie Roberson's Maryland Ramblers as "the musical attraction for the Club Basha's nightly revue".

Following the ill will engendered by the Club Basha enterprise, Sidney must have thought that New York City was an unhealthy place to be in. Via a recommendation by Will Marion Cook, he was offered a chance to put thousands of miles between himself and his potential adversaries. The offer came from the bandleader and pianist Claude Hopkins, whose band had been given the job of accompanying a show that was due to leave New York for Europe in September 1925. The production was called *The Black Revue* (*La Revue nègre*), and it was the brainchild of Mrs Caroline Dudley Reagan, a wealthy white Chicagoan then in her middle-thirties. Mrs Reagan auditioned Hopkins's band during a residency that it played in New Jersey. She was suitably impressed and signed the musicians there and then. Hopkins recalled the details: "After we finished up on Labor Day in Asbury Park I took the band to New York for two weeks' rehearsal with the show. It was comprised of eight chorus girls, a comedian, three novelty acts, a dance team, and my band. But we didn't have a lead attraction, finally Spencer Williams (the composer) suggested Mrs Reagan try the end girl in the *Shuffle Along* chorus . . . the girl was Josephine Baker."[17]

The Black Revue proved to be the springboard that launched Josephine Baker's international career. Her gorgeous figure and comic antics had made her the attraction of *Shuffle Along*, but she never graduated out of the chorus line in that production. With *The Black Revue* she was given the chance to blossom.

Aboard the Cunard liner *Berengaria* (which sailed from New York harbour in late September 1925) Josephine and Sidney Bechet soon struck up a warm friendship, which was welded by the sympathy that Sidney displayed when Josephine got herself into a musical tangle whilst singing at one of the concerts the troupe gave for the ship's passengers. Recalling the circumstances in her autobiography, Josephine Baker wrote: "Sidney was the only musician who hadn't made fun of me after my disastrous rendition of *Brown Eyes*. Ten or so years my senior he was cafe-au-lait like me. Sidney had traveled widely. My spirits lifted when he talked about Paris. I shouldn't be afraid he said. Parisians didn't notice people's skins."[18]

Josephine Baker was a highly sensual woman with an abundance of lovers and countless admirers. Claude Hopkins himself had an affair with her in Europe, but, although Josephine and Sidney remained friends for some while after their sea voyage, it seems that the apex of their affair took place aboard the *RMS Berengaria*. A friend of Josephine's said, "She was looking for the perfect penis."[19] So who can blame bold Sidney for helping the lady in her quest?

Concerning Bechet's musical exploits, it is often said that he played in the session led by Clarence Williams that produced *Coal Cart Blues* and *Santa Claus Blues*. Under pressure from discographers Bechet didn't deny being on the date, but in truth he had already landed in France by the time that session was recorded, on 8 October 1925. The playing on the two tracks, so similar to that of Bechet, is by one of Sidney's disciples, Buster Bailey. Bechet must have been suitably impressed by the sound of Bailey's work, because years later he bought the soprano saxophone that Buster had used in the session.

NINE

Mayhem in Paris

The *RMS Berengaria* docked at Cherbourg after its five-day transatlantic crossing, and the cast of *The Black Revue* caught a train to Paris. At the Gare St Lazare they were met by a reception committee of old friends and representatives of the Théâtre des Champs-Elysées, where they were soon to make their European début – on 2 October 1925.

Will Marion Cook had given Mrs Caroline Dudley Reagan advice and assistance during the initial formation of the production. Cook's daughter Marion and her husband Louis Douglas were featured in the show; on arrival in Paris they were met at the railway station by Cook's son, Mercer, who was studying French at the Sorbonne. Mercer Cook knew several of the cast and had been at school in Washington, DC, with trombonist Daniel Doy, who was in Hopkins's band. Mercer soon got to know everyone in the show: "A few days later during a rehearsal at the Theatre I convinced Mrs Dudley that the show needed a quartette. As a result I sang tenor in what was undoubtedly the world's worst warblers, but I welcomed the 15 dollars it paid every week. More importantly, it gave me an opportunity to hear Bechet play each and every night."[1]

For most of the show's duration Bechet sat in the orchestra pit with his fellow musicians, but he appeared on stage to back some of the speciality dancing and for his big feature number. As in his previous sojourns in travelling shows he had a role to play; this time it was that of a jazz-playing fruit seller. One report said: "Sidney Bechet strolled out, pushing a brightly painted vegetable cart, took up his clarinet and blew a wild improvisation."[2]

Years later the show's organizer, Mrs Dudley, realized that Sidney could have been featured more prominently. Her biographer Jean Claude Baker wrote: "Caroline's regret until the day of her death was that she never built Sidney Bechet as one of the stars of *La Revue nègre*."[3] Mrs Dudley, whose husband was a commercial attaché at the American Embassy in Paris, successfully got the show talked about amongst the smart set in the city, and soon the revue was being commented on throughout the theatrical world. The critics were generally favourable to the show – mainly because of its vitality – but they saved special praise for the amazing personality of Josephine Baker, who was soon to become the toast of every European capital.

Although the show didn't really click with the general public, its season at the Théâtre des Champs-Elysées lasted for several weeks. The music in the production caught the attention of Oscar and Ralph Mouvet, two brothers who ran the famous Moulin Rouge night-club, and they engaged Hopkins's band and

Josephine Baker to appear for them after the evening's work at the theatre was over. Bechet also remembered playing a benefit show with Josephine Baker, in which he was featured playing a "special number with a symphony orchestra".[4]

The Black Revue moved to a different section of Paris and played for some weeks at l'Etoile, a much smaller theatre than the Champs-Elysées. Bechet, and others in the band, found that there were plenty of opportunities to play late-night gigs in Montmartre after they had finished working in the show.

As in London, Bechet continued to revel in both the high and low stratas of society. A reporter from the newspaper *Comoedia* observed him at a tea party held at Mrs Caroline Dudley's elegant house overlooking the Seine: "Sidney Bechet in evening clothes lounges at the piano, humming and tapping his foot. Bechet is improvising as usual. The saxophonist and flautist [sic] of the Charleston Jazz Band can't read a note of music. If asked when he learned to play the piano he grinningly replies 'at birth'. At his side in an elegant pastel suit sits Louis Douglas."[5]

From Paris *The Black Revue* moved into Belgium to play in Brussels as part of the Cirque Royal, where the cast was working with tight-rope walkers, clowns and aerialists. They stayed there for a few weeks providing the finale for each of the three shows a night. After their final performance in Brussels they hastily packed their bags and the props so that they could catch the late-night train that was to take them to Germany. Claude Hopkins picks up the story:

> To save time and trouble when we crossed international borders, Mrs. Reagan Dudley kept all the passports for safe keeping. This meant that all you had to do was step forward when your name was called so the border guard could check the picture on the passport. In this case everything went along fine until Sidney Bechet's name was called. Sidney was nowhere to be found. So the officers insisted on taking all of us off the train while they made telephone calls to Brussels. This took two or three hours. Finally they traced Sidney. He had gotten on the wrong train and had wound up back in Paris, where he was promptly arrested for not having a passport. Once again Mrs. Reagan's connections came to the rescue. She phoned the right people in Paris and finally we were back on the train and headed towards Berlin, and Sidney was put on the next train for Berlin out of Paris.[6]

Claude Hopkins was giving Sidney the benefit of the doubt. The story about his accidentally finding himself in Paris sounds suspiciously like the 'wandering Bechet' of old, going wherever inclination took him. One of his colleagues in the band, trumpeter Henry Goodwin, recalled that Sidney often unaccountably missed various performances of *The Black Revue*. Goodwin also described Bechet's feature number: "He would come out on stage wheeling a fruit cart, with imitation fruit piled high on it, and dressed in a long duster [dust coat]. He'd come shuffling along slow, and then he'd leave the cart and start to play the blues, and he could really play the blues. I learned a lot from Bechet about the blues and I could play those things too. Sometimes Bechet wouldn't be there for his act and I used to take his place."[7] After work was over Bechet and Goodwin often played card games that lasted all night: "I remember a poker game Bechet and I were in in Berlin. We were playing deuces wild, and then Bechet turned up with five deuces that broke up the game."

In Berlin *The Black Revue* played at a theatre on the splendid Kurfürsten-damm. The cast gave one performance on stage each evening, after which the seating was altered so that the auditorium was converted into a dance floor; the band then reassembled and played for dancing in this mock night-club setting until 1 a.m. Josephine Baker also sang at these late-night events.

Josephine's reputation had grown swiftly and by early 1926 she was being bombarded with offers from various theatrical impresarios and agents. The famous Folies Bergère in Paris won the contract for her services, and her departure meant that *The Black Revue* lost its most potent attraction. The show floundered and eventually died. As Claude Hopkins said, "Her loss wrecked our revue."[8]

Hopkins's musicians scattered. Doy and Goodwin went off to work elsewhere in Germany, as did saxophone player Joe Hayman and Claude Hopkins himself, but Bechet's next port of call was far away – in Russia. In early 1926, just as *The Black Revue* was coming to an end, trombonist Frank Withers (a former member of the SSO) organized a black jazz band to take into the USSR to fulfil bookings for the Russian Rosfil agency. Bechet knew all of the musicians in Withers's band, which comprised saxophonist Manfred Coxcito, drummer Benny Peyton, pianist Dan Parrish and cornetist Cricket Smith.[9] Withers met up with Bechet in Berlin, heard that he had no immediate plans and offered him a place in the Russian-bound band, which Bechet readily accepted.

The band made its way to Moscow by train, where it played its first engagements of the tour on 22 February 1926. Sidney made an immediate impact on the Russian listeners, and (according to Garvin Bushell, who also visited Moscow in 1926 as a member of Sam Wooding's band) on the Russian ladies. The group did not play for dancing; it performed at the Dmitrovka Cinema for a seated audience, most of whom were having their first encounter with jazz. Bechet also said that the band played at the Moscow Grand Opera House.[10] The group added one member to its personnel in Moscow. This was singer Coretty Arley-Teets (also known as Coretti Arley-Tiz), a black-American woman who had lived in Russia for more than ten years at the time of the band's visit. Bechet was delighted by the ecstatic receptions accorded him. As the tour progressed large posters appeared showing Sidney in action, announcing that "the Talking Saxophone" would be appearing at such and such a venue.

Years later Bechet's friend Mary Karoley asked him where he would choose to settle down permanently to play his music. She recalled the conversation: "He replied instantly 'Russia' and said they treated him as royal (of all things). I should say categorically that no one could be less interested in politics than Sidney."[11] The aspects of Russia in the mid-1920s that did not please Sidney were the food and the accommodation, which he described as "poor"[12], but the travelling conditions pleased him least of all. Fortunately Withers's band played a two-month residency in Moscow, so the latter hardship didn't spoil Bechet's early days in the country.

A large band led by black pianist Sam Wooding arrived in Moscow on 1 March 1926 and the musicians soon linked up socially with their compatriots from Frank Withers's group. In Moscow, Garvin Bushell renewed his friendship with

Bechet. He recalled that Sidney became deeply interested in the classical music that they heard together in Russia – not only contemporary works but also the music of Tchaikovsky: "Monday was a holiday in Russia in those days. Every Monday we would go to a symphony concert, after that we would go to the night-clubs. Monday night was the time for all musicians and actors and dancers to meet at various clubs. We had a wonderful time in Moscow. The women loved Sidney."[13]

Bechet first made the acquaintance of the Louisiana trumpet player Tommy Ladnier in Moscow. Ladnier, who had been too shy to speak to Sidney in Chicago, was one of the stars of Sam Wooding's band. Bechet, who was developing what turned out to be a life-long interest in cameras, heard on the musicians' grape-vine that Ladnier had a Pathé cine-camera for sale. Bechet already had a projector, but no camera, so he bought Ladnier's. The transaction was the start of a warm friendship. But the two musicians didn't play a note of music together in Russia; soon after their initial meeting Bechet left Moscow with Withers's band to play a series of concert dates in Kiev, Odessa and Kharkov. Wooding's group moved out of Moscow to play a tour that eventually took it to Leningrad, where it played its final date in Russia on 23 May 1926.

In the last stages of Withers's tour Bechet seriously misjudged the Russian night air. Although it was spring-time, there was still snow on the ground, and the temperature dropped rapidly after dark. Bechet, out on a spree, decided not to wear an overcoat or a hat. He wound up with an attack of bronchitis that forced him to stay behind in Russia to recuperate whilst the rest of Frank Withers's band left for its next booking in France. In an interview broadcast by the BBC on its radio programme "The Silver Bell", Bechet recalled his frosty stroll: "One day the vodka told me that I could go out and walk without my coat. Was it madness? I walked for two or three hours in the snow and two days later I landed up in bed."

Bechet somehow got his visa extended, then decided to make his own way to Berlin. Back in Germany he seems to have worked briefly in a show organized by one Joe Baher (according to Garvin Bushell, who is vague about the precise name). But Bushell had good reason to remember in clear detail a visit that Sidney made soon after he had returned from Russia: "At 5 a.m. in Berlin there came a knock on my door at the hotel. I asked who it was, the reply was 'Sidney, open up!' With all of that talking, my Great Dane, Caesar, began to roar, then another dog began barking out in the hall. Sidney had brought his Dobermann to challenge my Great Dane to a fight. Since my Dane had recently killed two dogs in Danzig I thought it best not to let Sidney and his dog in; he left making all sorts of threats to me and my dog if ever we met again, so I made it my business to stay out of his way while he was in Berlin."[14]

Garvin Bushell's deliberate avoidance of Bechet soon proved unnecessary. Sidney left Berlin with a new version of *The Black Revue* touring party, organized by Will Marion Cook's son-in-law Louis Douglas and featuring some of the original cast. Once again Sidney found that his talents were displayed in solo numbers; these took place against various backdrops depicting a Mississippi cotton plantation, a Harlem cabaret, or a New York street scene. His big feature number in the production was *Old Fashioned Love*.

Bechet became the music director of *The Black Revue*, which was later billed as *Black People* and *Black Flowers*. The show's orchestra consisted of 14 musicians, "mostly Frenchmen, Germans and Cubans", said Sidney;[15] they played theatre bookings in Greece, Turkey, Sweden, Spain, Egypt, Hungary, Czechoslovakia and Italy, but there were gaps in the itinerary and in the summer of 1926 Bechet briefly 'guested' with Benny Peyton's band at the Hotel Apollo in Rome. Wherever he went, Bechet did his utmost to hear local musicians, and years later often surprised listeners by playing various folk themes that he had heard during his travels in the 1920s.

In many of the places that Sidney visited on those tours, the sight of a Negro was a rarity, and he became used to being stared at in the street. Sometimes the curiosity became physical: "We were playing some place in Germany. Big crowd, and after the concert some white woman came up to me, wet her finger and wiped it across my cheek, she had to make sure."[16]

The Louis Douglas tour eventually ended in Munich. By then Bechet had temporarily had his fill of touring, and he decided to organize his own small band to play a residency in a beer garden in Frankfurt am Main. He also played at the Beethoven Hall in Frankfurt as part of an American exhibition within a trade fair. But quite the most important event for Sidney during this period of his life was meeting his future wife, Elisabeth.

Sometime during the spring of 1928 Bechet decided to return to Paris. He soon linked up with various musicians that he knew and played briefly at Bricktop's club (replacing reedman Frank 'Big Boy' Goudie), but his main endeavour at this time was working on an extended composition, *The Negro Rhapsody* (subtitled *The Voice of the Slaves*). By then Bechet had had many songs published, and several had achieved success, but the deep interest in classical music that he had developed in Russia made him determined to write something more substantial.

During the second half of the 1920s many professional jazz musicians, black and white, flirted with the classics. It was also an age in which orchestration became more important than improvisation in many big 'jazz' groups. The public, ever eager for change, welcomed this smoothing process; so too did most of the critics, who unreservedly praised the quasi-sophistication of 'symphonic jazz'. A reviewer in the December 1926 issue of the *Melody Maker* was typical. Commenting on the Parlophone issue of *Mandy make up your mind* (by Clarence Williams), he wrote: "Well played of the kind, but a little too blue for me. They are a reversion to what was getting stale two years ago."

Singer and composer Noble Sissle was one of the bandleaders who benefitted from the change of attitudes. Sissle had enjoyed considerable success as part of a stage act, first with Eubie Blake and later with the English composer and pianist Henry Revel. In the spring of 1928 Sissle and Revel were called over from London by French agent Henri Lartigue to sing and play for a week at the famous Les Ambassadeurs club in Paris. Their task at the club, on the Avenue des Champs-Elysées, was to fill intermission spots in support of the main band, Fred Waring's Pennsylvanians. It transpired that Waring's band did not want to fulfil a contractual clause that gave it a second eight weeks at the club, so after playing

Les Ambassadeurs for two months it left in order to take part in the Broadway show *Hello Yourself*. Sissle recalled the dilemma that the club's manager, Edmund Sayag, faced: "They were stalled for a band because Ted Lewis was to come in for the third eight weeks. For the eight weeks of July and August they couldn't send to America to get a band. The fellow who wrote the show I happened to know. He was a Yale man and he became one of our greatest song writers – Cole Porter. Instead of singing, it turned out that I was to put in a band."[17]

Noble Sissle cabled to the States for musicians, which resulted in the arrival of saxophonists Otto Hardwicke and William Blue and trumpeters John Ricks and Dave Richards. In order to recruit a full complement of musicians Sissle had hastily to visit various night-clubs in Paris to sign up players, American and European. The stars of this mixed band were Sidney Bechet and trumpeter Johnny Dunn, both of whom were recruited in Paris, as was the group's pianist, Charlie Lewis. Lewis recalled the circumstances: "Sissle had been forced to form his band in a hurry, and we had no repertoire, to make matters worse Fred Waring's band had taken the music that was used to accompany the show, so we had a difficult start. The orchestra was so bad that Clifton Webb, the American dancer (who later became a film actor) left the stage in the middle of a feature. By the third day things got a little better. Our 'pièce de résistance' was *St Louis Blues*, Sidney Bechet played the soprano sax with a little apron and a bonnet on his head, having a musical conversation with trumpeter Johnny Dunn. This number was a great success until the day that Ted Lewis forbade us to use it because it was one of his specialities."[18]

Despite the show's talented cast, which included George Gershwin's sister Frances, the production wasn't hailed as a triumph for the composer, Cole Porter. Of the 20 tunes he wrote for the show, only one, *Looking at you*, achieved any degree of lasting success. Nevertheless the show marked the emergence of Noble Sissle as a successful bandleader. In late July 1928 a band led by the pianist and composer Fred Elizalde was added to the Les Ambassadeurs production.

Noble Sissle was content only to use Bechet's talents on special feature numbers; jazz solos were few and far between in the show's commercial orchestrations. But, rather than have Sidney just sitting there whilst the rest of the band played from the written arrangement, a strategy was devised that kept him fully occupied. Many of Fred Elizalde's scores featured the bass saxophone (having been written to display the talents of the American player Adrian Rollini). Noble Sissle liked the sound and bought a bass saxophone for Bechet to play. Creating two-in-a-bar bass saxophone parts was simple work for someone with Bechet's superb musical ear, and he soon became adept on the huge instrument. For one bizarre period Sissle hired the largest saxophone of all, the E flat contrabass model, for Sidney to chug away on, but mercifully Bechet left the unwieldy leviathan in Paris (though some while later the very same instrument turned up in Boston).[19]

For his initial spell of bandleading Noble Sissle adopted a style of leadership – blending traits of a sternish uncle, a jovial headmaster and a conscientious sergeant major – that was to remain constant throughout his career. Sissle's concepts of discipline were built on his experiences as a soldier during World War I, first as a drum major then as a commissioned officer. Show business camaraderie eventually mellowed him but he always kept a close watch on business matters and on the behaviour of his musicians, whose life styles he felt should be just as clean as the white gloves he always wore to conduct. Outsiders hearing him speak curtly to his 'men', as he called them, imagined him to be uncaring and ruthless, but all those who worked with him for any length of time regarded him with affection.

With Noble Sissle, Bechet soon realized that he would have to curb his tendency casually to miss performances. He was happy to fall in line because the money was good and the venue had the sort of sparkle that he found stimulating. His relationship with his colleagues in Sissle's band was variable; most of the other musicians were wary of him, because it was whispered in the band-room that he had fought with someone in every group that he had ever worked in. But, as ever, to those whom Bechet liked and trusted he was affable, kind and helpful. Pianist Charlie Lewis assisted Bechet by transcribing his ever-developing musical tone poem. Lewis said, "He loved to compose, even though he couldn't write music. During this period he concentrated on *Rhapsodie nègre*, which I helped to edit." Lewis also commented on Sidney's general attitude: "Bechet was not sociable, he often argued with other musicians because he thought they were stealing one of his choruses."[20]

In September 1928, when Sissle's booking at Les Ambassadeurs came to an end, he travelled back to Britain to resume working in a duo with Harry Revel; the orchestra disbanded in Paris. By then Bechet had connections in various clubs in Montmartre – even during the time he was with Sissle he doubled in a club on the rue Caumartin. He had also worked in the Latin Quarter with reed player Fred Adler. After the stint with Sissle, Bechet decided to join Opal Cooper at a club on the rue Blanche.

The habitués of French night-clubs (unlike their British counterparts) regularly gave gratuities to a band, whether or not they had made requests. These tips meant that jobs at successful venues were lucrative. However, probably because of his romantic attachment to Elisabeth Ziegler, Bechet soon decided to make his way back to Frankfurt, and from there (on 10 October 1928) he first copyrighted *The Negro Rhapsody*. The piece was later published, and Bechet was genuinely proud to show copies of the sheet music to fellow musicians. The work itself did not cause a sensation, and Bechet's amanuensis, Charlie Lewis, later revealed that he never wholeheartedly liked what he had been transcribing: "It was a composition without a definite form and the only thing Negro about it was the title."[21]

Before the end of October 1928, Bechet was back in Paris, this time bringing Elisabeth with him. He resumed playing at the exclusive Chez Florence at 61 rue Blanche, and that was where his boyhood friend from New Orleans Albert Nicholas found him. Nicholas, who had been on a wide-ranging tour that had taken him as far as China, was returning to the USA (via France) after playing a residency in Egypt. Years later Nicholas said, "The musicians that I saw in Paris were just hanging around and playing corn, gambling amongst each other. I found out where Sidney was playing and I said I'll go that night. So around ten o'clock I went there and sat at a table. I sat alone and I was looking at Sidney playing on the stand and he looked up . . . then he said, 'You know I think I know that boy. He looks like somebody I knew in New Orleans'."[22]

The two expatriates had a happy reunion. On the next night Nicholas returned to the club to sit in on tenor saxophone (he had recently changed from playing an Albert system clarinet to a Boehm model and didn't feel he was quite ready to display his progress in public). Nicholas must have played well because he was offered a permanent place in the band; he declined because he already had a ticket for the sea voyage home.

The sitting about, the gossiping, the gambling and the drinking were very much a part of the life of American musicians in Paris during the late 1920s. Bechet enjoyed the bistro scene as much as anyone, and, despite being a grumpy gambler, he rarely avoided the chance of a card game. He also frequented the billiard halls, and loved the ambience of a boxing gymnasium that was situated on the corner of Faubourg and rue Bergère.

One of Bechet's particular friends at this time was a flamboyant black American named Eugene Bullard. Originally from Columbus, Georgia, Bullard settled in France and during the early days of World War I joined the French Foreign Legion. He was later transferred to the 170th Infantry Regiment, and after being wounded he became a pilot in the Lafayette Flying Corps. His brave, reckless exploits against German war planes made him a hero, and he was nicknamed "the Black Swallow of Death".[23] When the USA entered the war in 1917 Bullard was transferred to the American forces, but whereas the white American fliers who had also served in French units were immediately commissioned as pilots, Gene Bullard was henceforth grounded. The French Government recognized Bullard's bravery and awarded him medals. He decided to stay in France and remained for many years, sometimes working as a club manager, occasionally as a drummer, and also as a professional boxer. The famous night-club owner Bricktop Smith wrote of Bullard in her autobiography: "I once saw him beat up three sailors with absolutely no help."[24] This was Sidney's kind of man. One night Bricktop and Bullard had a violent disagreement. Bricktop admitted she was bent on revenge: "I went home, got my pistol and went back to the pool hall. Luckily Gene was gone by then. I don't know what I would have done if I'd found him."[25] Life in Paris for Sidney and his circle was no less armed than it had been in New York during Prohibition. Recalling that era in the French capital, Bechet said: "You could be surer if you had a gun on you. There was tough times back there."[26]

From Paris, in 1928, Bechet typed a letter to his brother Leonard in New Orleans. The contents make it apparent that the two brothers had not corresponded for years. From an address at 25 rue Hermel, Paris 18, Sydney headed his letter, Bechet's Mississippi Jazzers c/o American Express:

My dear brother,
  I was very glad when I received the answer of my letter from you, things are starting to be very good for me and I will be able to do what I have in mind. So you

have boy and girl*, I am very proud to know that and I know you and your wife are happy.

Leonard, I am going to get married and I know if you would see my intended wife you would know that she is a good girl and from a very good family and they like me very much. I had a hard time but I succeeded, the first time the mother and brother had heard that I was a black man they thought it was a crime, but the girl loves me so much they had to let me come to the house so I went there and became lighter and lighter, now I'm just as a white man to them. I wish you would get my Birth Certificate and sent it to me. I must have it and don't forget to send me the picture of your children. Give your wife my best regards, I will let you have the clipping in my next letter this is all I have found. My best wishes to my family and friends. Hoping to hear from you soon. From your brother Sidney.[27]

But before Bechet's matrimonial plans were finalized he became involved in mayhem. Often, when he had finished work, he called in at Bricktop's club, partly for a night-cap but also to find out about local events and to discuss job prospects. Many other black expatriate musicians followed the same routine and called in at Bricktop's during the early hours of the morning. Bricktop, who as Ada Smith had enjoyed success in the States as a singer and dancer, was well used to the ways of jazz musicians (in 1929 she married the New Orleans clarinettist Peter Du Congé), and she raised no objections to the dawn congregations in her club.

In the early morning of 20 December 1928 a group of black musicians gathered as usual in Bricktop's, but on this occasion a violent argument developed between banjoist Gilbert 'Little Mike' McKendrick and Sidney Bechet. The exact cause of the dispute is still in doubt. Pianist Charlie Lewis was one of the musicians at the fateful gathering. He said, "Bechet and Mike started arguing about the harmonies on a number we had just played. Mike pretended that Bechet was unfamiliar with the correct harmonies, one word led to another and the argument got very bad. Mike got his gun out. Sidney disappeared then came back armed as well."[28] Many serious incidents are sparked off by a triviality, but if the playing of a wrong chord automatically led to a shoot-out the world would be full of wounded jazz musicians. It seems there were other reasons for the flare-up, which came to a climax not at Bricktop's but at a café in Montmartre.

Another pianist, Glover Compton, was also involved in the dispute. Bechet had known Compton in Chicago but had never considered him a friend. In July 1926 Compton had accepted an invitation to become the resident pianist at Bricktop's, so he and Bechet saw one another regularly in France. Bechet treated Compton with suspicion: "He really liked to talk big . . . It was like he was looking for a reputation as a bad man . . . He was always acting like he wanted to stir up trouble."[29] Bechet remained convinced that Glover Compton acted as the *agent provocateur* in the dispute with Mike McKendrick.

Glover Compton's side of the story was that Bechet took offence when McKendrick made a remark about Bechet's habitual unwillingness to pay for a round of drinks. Later, according to Compton, Bechet accosted McKendrick outside a bistro: "Sidney evidently went out and got a revolver. Mike had one in

---

* Leonard's first two children, Emelda (*b* 30 Jan 1925) and Leonard, Jr (*b* 16 Aug 1927)

his pocket, but didn't nobody know it. Sidney must have passed the Costa Bar and looked in there for Mike. Mike stepped out on the sidewalk and I stepped out, right behind Mike. And when I stepped out that's when the shooting started."[30] It was, said Charlie Lewis, "like the scene of a fight straight out of a cowboy movie. It provided a talking point for years for the Montmartre musicians."[31]

Bechet, beside himself with fury, saw McKendrick coming out of the bar and opened fire. The net result was that Glover Compton was shot in the leg, a 22-year-old Australian dancer, Dolores Giblins, was wounded in the lung, and a French passer-by, Madame Radurea, was hit in the neck by a ricocheting bullet. McKendrick, unhurt, returned the fire. Years later Bechet claimed that only the stiffness of his shirt-collar had saved him; a bullet lodged in his clothes without doing any harm.

Both Bechet and McKendrick were swiftly arrested and charged with offences connected with the shooting. McKendrick obtained a lawyer through the efforts of writer Nancy Cunard, her cousin Victor Cunard and writer Louis Aragon. Bechet acquired his legal aid through the auspices of his friend Eugene Bullard. Bullard spoke up for Sidney at the trial, and so too did Aragon, who apparently gave character references for both Bechet and McKendrick. Despite these efforts, the two musicians were found guilty and sentenced to imprisonment. Bechet was given 15 months, but remission meant that he was out of prison in under a year. He and McKendrick actually became friends (of a sort) after the case, but Bechet never forgave Glover Compton. As soon as Bechet was released from prison he learnt that Compton was planning to sue him for compensation. This news so incensed Sidney that he sent word to Compton advising him to watch out for his other leg; Compton abandoned his plans for litigation.

The violence might not have taken place had Mike McKendrick not been quite such a ladies' man in the late 1920s. Nancy Cunard supplied a pertinent description of him: "As attractive as a panther and rather like one – young, with a beautiful light brown skin, rippling blue-black hair. He has innate courtesy, beautiful clothes."[32] Bechet himself was ultra-keen to be noticed by women and he would no doubt have regarded McKendrick as a rival, if not a threat, in certain romantic situations. Everett Barksdale, a guitarist who knew both men well, feels that a dispute over a woman was probably the root cause of the violence. McKendrick continued to live in France until he returned to the USA in 1939, but Bechet was apparently ordered to leave the country after he had completed his prison sentence.

TEN

Gigging and Sewing

One of the first tasks that Bechet had to do before he could move out of France (in compliance with the court order) was to get his passport renewed. On 5 December 1929, at the US Consulate General's office in Paris, he collected new credentials, valid for two years. He could easily have chosen to leave immediately for the United States, but he did not. Apparently a divorce from his wife, Norma, was being processed in America and Bechet probably felt that it was injudicious to be anywhere near the scene of that action. Long-term plans to marry Elisabeth seemed to have disintegrated (but not for ever, as it transpired).

Just before Bechet began his jail sentence he had accepted an offer to rejoin Benny Peyton's band (then playing in Nice), but that offer melted during his term in prison. After his release Bechet pondered on which country to go to next. The two European capitals that he knew best were London and Paris, but he was barred from being employed in either. In December 1929 he resolved to try his luck by making a return visit to Berlin.

Bechet had found Berlin to be a lively spot during his earlier stays, but in the interim the decadence that indelibly marked the pages of that city's history was in full flow. Restrictions concerning the employment of foreigners were on the increase, but Sidney found a niche for himself by joining a band that worked at the Haus Vaterland, a huge entertainment complex built on the principles of a department store – each floor serving a different whim of the public. Sidney estimated that at least six different bands played residencies in various restaurants and night-clubs within the vast building. His main place of work was in the Wild West Bar, where the band played for dancing and for a cabaret that was heavily laden with beautiful chorus-girls.

The whole enterprise was organized and managed by the Kempinski company, whose intention was to present every style of popular music within the same building. A mandolin band played in the Bodega section; on the Lowenbrau floor, German national melodies were the order of the day; in the Palmensaal, 'Jazzmeister' Bill Bartholomew and his orchestra performed. The Wild West Bar billed "The McAllan Blackband, Saxophon-Virtuso Sidney Bechet".[1] Bechet also worked in the same hall with a group called the Tom Bill Nigger Band, and with the New Yorkers. The McAllan [sic] band was led by drummer William 'Willi' Mac Allan (1909–69), whose father was a musician from British Somalia (Willi's mother was German).

Perhaps because this period of his life followed soon after his prison trauma (a subject that Bechet understandly never dwelt on), Sidney was not revealing about his days in Berlin. But several young men who later developed a life-long love of jazz, including Ernest Bornemann, Horst Lange and Desmond Flower, heard Bechet play at the Haus Vaterland. Other than brief mentions in the Haus Vaterland magazine *Berolina*, little appeared in print about Bechet in Germany during the early 1930s.

Unfortunately no one seems to have had the foresight to record Bechet during his days in Germany, though one film maker did briefly feature his playing. This was in 1930 in the production by UFA (Universal Films Company) entitled *Einbrecher* (*Burglar*), which starred Lilian Harvey and Willy Fritsch. In the film, which was released in France as *Flagrant délit*, Bechet's main appearance shows him in a top hat, playing his soprano saxophone in a seven-piece band; the set was said to be based on the décor of the Haus Vaterland's Wild West Bar. The band's main feature is a fast and furious opus (based on the chords of *Tiger Rag*), which accompanies some wildly exuberant dancing. Bechet's playing is clearly a feature, but it is interesting to see that an alto saxophone stands in front of him (as does a clarinet and a spare soprano saxophone). Although some of the other musicians indulge in frantic movements for the camera, Bechet stands relatively still.

This was not Sidney's only connection with the German film industry. In January 1959 I was travelling on a slow overnight train from Liverpool to London, having played a one-night stand in the northern city. My companion was a trombonist, John Mumford. We found vacant seats, put our instruments on the luggage rack and attempted to get to sleep. We were soon joined by a noisy, drunken stranger, who managed to recognize the trombone case. He began imitating slide-actions by throwing his right arm out as far as it could go, accompanying his energetic movement by blowing loud 'raspberries'. This appalling noise gave way to a series of mumbled reminiscences. On and on he droned, but eventually, as he sobered up, the sentences became coherent.

Esoteric names of various American jazzmen who had visited Europe in the 1920s emerged. I sat up to listen more closely, so too did John Mumford. A clear story formed. The man, who was English, had been an alto saxophonist and clarinettist on the Continent in the late 1920s and early 1930s. He had played at various clubs in Berlin, including one called the Barberini; he had also played on German film sets. Although the 'talkie' age had begun, a particular studio in Berlin had reverted to making silent films, and all the attending musicians were required to do was to provide 'atmosphere' music.

One morning the musician turned up, took his place on the studio bandstand, and found himself seated next to Sidney Bechet, whom he knew only by sight. He was adamant that Bechet had only an alto saxophone with him; as the stranger (who refused to give us his name) also had only an alto instrument, the two men made a joke about the situation, then began playing, by ear, a series of various standard tunes. As the studio lights got hotter and hotter, so the English musician became increasingly enamoured by one of the flimsily dressed film extras. Eventually he told Bechet that he wanted to go outside to cool down.

When he returned Bechet couldn't stop chuckling, and said, "Why man, if I felt like that about a girl I'd go up to her and tell her so." The musician pleaded shyness, whereupon Bechet said, "Don't worry. When we've finished I'll go over and tell her how you feel." At the end of the day's filming Bechet went over and began talking to the young beauty. The eager musician looked on as Bechet and the girl smiled at each other. Then they walked out of the door together, and that was the last that the stranger saw of either of them.

Eventually Bechet became restless with the regimented afternoon-and-evening routine at the Haus Vaterland, but somehow, despite a lack of musical stimulation, he kept up his standards of performance. Desmond Flower, who heard Bechet at the Haus Vaterland, remembers him playing superbly. For most of his stay in Germany, Bechet worked with bands that comprised musicians of various nationalities. Some of these were technically gifted, but only a few could play jazz convincingly; whatever their colour, they could best be described as dance-band musicians. Years later Bechet told saxophonist Bud Freeman that he played with many black musicians in Europe who actually hated jazz and had no feeling for it.[2]

As the year 1930 approached its end, Bechet's immediate plans were shaped by an offer to return to the USA to rejoin Noble Sissle. Sissle was just completing a tour of Europe and sailed back from England to New York on 16 December 1930. Bechet sailed from Holland and arrived back in America on the same day as Sissle – 22 December 1930.

Noble Sissle's career as a bandleader had made considerable strides since Bechet had worked for him in France during the summer of 1928. Despite the initial problems at Les Ambassadeurs, Sissle had returned there to play subsequent summer seasons. The band had also played a hugely successful booking in London at Ciro's Club. Sissle, who was a wily strategist, realized that the impact of Sidney's playing would also help the band to gain a following in the United States. He used Bechet's vivid talent sparingly, allowing him to burst out of otherwise tepid arrangements. When Bechet wasn't being featured on soprano saxophone or clarinet, he reverted to his role of playing an innocuous and economical part on the bass saxophone.

Several of Bechet's old friends were in Sissle's band, including trumpeters Arthur Briggs and Tommy Ladnier. His reunion with them came at the band's first New York date – a booking at the Rockland Palace on 24 December 1930. In the audience that night was agent Harrison Smith: 'I had arranged with the manager, Andrew Clarke, to have a girl, Naomi Price, audition with the orchestra. I was at the entrance to the hall and who do you suppose walked in? None other than Professor Ferd (Jelly Roll) Morton with his consort Fussy Mable (Queen of the Dips). Though I greeted them most cordially they resented my presence. Jelly's prime purpose in coming to the hall was to raid Sissle of Bechet and Ladnier."[3]

Jelly Roll Morton didn't succeed in wooing Bechet and Ladnier away from Sissle's band, which moved off to play a series of dates around Chicago before returning to New York to begin a residency at Pierre's Club on 27 January 1931. Three days before the group began that booking, it took part in a New York recording session for the Brunswick label. The two sides that were issued soon afterwards, *Got the bench, got the park* and *Loveless Love* (both with vocals by Noble Sissle) give a good indication of the band's style.

Got the bench, got the park, a 'pop' song of the period, is given a commercial treatment in an undemanding arrangement. The power of Edward Cole's bass playing rocks the rhythm section but the intonation of the saxophone secton is decidedly shaky. Sissle's light tenor voice is inoffensive and his diction is, as usual, exemplary; his vocal here is backed by a distant clarinet obbligato and rippling arpeggios from the pianist. Bechet can be heard pumping away on the bass saxophone during the final chorus, while above him the brass section is particularly impressive. The one jazz solo (by the tenor saxophonist) is competent but uninspiring.

Loveless Love is more loosely arranged. Once again the power of the string bass playing is evident from the first notes of the introduction. The saxophone section plays a bland chorus of the melody, which is repeated in a mundane fashion by the muted brass section. Sissle's vocal is notably brief and gives way to an incisive muted chorus from Tommy Ladnier. The turgid arrangement rumbles on, but after a spiky clarinet solo (not by Bechet) the excitement starts to build and is consolidated by a change of key. The best moment, a brief gem of a solo by Bechet on soprano saxophone, comes near the end: eight bars full of majesty and passion are embossed with searing blue notes. Musically it would have made more sense to allow Bechet's solo to 'ride out' the chorus; instead he reverts to the bass saxophone and plays a minor role in an unspectacular ending.

The third title from the session, *In a café on the road to Calais,* was finally released in 1983. Sissle's vocal phrasing never sounds quite comfortable, and the arrangement itself is poor; there is, however, another expressive solo (lasting for 16 bars) by the redoubtable Ladnier on trumpet. Bechet again excels himself in his eight bars of improvisation, but as before he finishes the piece astride the mighty bass saxophone.

During his years as a stage performer and producer Noble Sissle gained many valuable contacts with theatrical managers, and these links provided a whole series of theatre bookings for the band. Billed as "Noble Sissle and his Paris Ambassadeurs Orchestra", the group played the theatre circuits in the States until the spring of 1931, when it was time to leave for Paris to play a return booking at Les Ambassadeurs.

On 21 April 1931, just before the band departed for Europe, it again visited the Brunswick studios to record another three numbers. *Basement Blues,* the first of these, has some excellent instrumental interludes and a set of woefully naive lyrics for Noble Sissle to contend with. Arthur Briggs plays two emotive 12-bar blues choruses, sounding unflurried and assured, then Bechet enters, on soprano saxophone, and soars up to even greater heights of feeling, creating a chorus that radiates intensity. Subsequently Tommy Ladnier, not sounding the least bit overawed, blows a beautifully constructed 12-bar solo. The final ensembles are powerfully integrated, and sound not unlike the Luis Russell band's work from the same period. There are brief solos on the brisk version of *What ja do to me,* but the emphasis is on arrangement and vocal. The final side of the session, *Roll on, Mississippi, roll on,* is a happy two-beat affair, with Noble

Sissle sounding suspiciously like Ted Lewis. Ladnier's trumpet solo never strays far from the melody but remains piping hot, and Sidney's brief eight-bar outing is a triumphant miniature. The bass saxophone is not heard in this session; either the idea of its use had been shelved temporarily or the big instrument had been crated up for the forthcoming sea voyage.

Although Bechet had been deported from France, he had not, it seems, been formally banned from re-entering the country; accordingly, on 22 April 1931 he obtained a one-month visa from the French Consul General in New York.

Sissle's entourage arrived at Le Havre on 1 May 1931. The musicians proceeded to make their way to Paris, where they began their engagement at Les Ambassadeurs on 7th May. At this time the French authorities were making determined efforts to reduce the number of foreign workers, including overseas musicians, in their country. Bechet got wind of a rumour that suggested that Sissle's band would only be permitted to fulfil the second half of its booking if 50 percent of its personnel was replaced by French musicians. This proved to be the truth, but it was a stipulation that Sissle would not accept, and as a result his band was replaced by Lud Gluskin's orchestra.[4] By then Bechet was far away, having moved on to Berlin, where he resumed his place as a featured soloist at the Haus Vaterland.

Bechet stayed at the Haus Vaterland for some weeks, during which time Sissle and his group ran into insoluble problems concerning the possible extension of their work permits; they remained in France for only six weeks before returning to the USA. Soon after they sailed Bechet made his next move, which was to rejoin Louis Douglas's touring company, now with a show called *Black Flowers*. Bechet worked with this production in various German cities and in Spain, Portugal and Holland.

Sissle's band, having arrived back in the USA ahead of schedule, did not have any immediate contracts to fulfil, but as soon as Sissle received confirmation of a residency at the prestigious Park Central Hotel in New York he cabled Bechet in Europe and asked him to rejoin the group as soon as possible. The message reached Sidney in Amsterdam. He immediately made plans to sail back to the USA and arrived in New York on 21 September 1931. Eighteen years were to pass before Bechet returned to Europe.

Noble Sissle's band was playing at the Pearl Theatre in Philadelphia when Bechet arrived back in New York, but he soon linked up with the group as it prepared to start its booking at the Park Central Grill. The band was well received there and, on the promise that it would soon return, the management at Park Central waived its exclusive contract to allow the musicians to work at New York's Lafayette Theatre in *The Rocking Chair Revue*. Marion Hardy's Alabamians (another black group) 'subbed' for Sissle's band at the Park Central and continued to do so while Sissle took his troupe to Cleveland, Ohio, to appear in a production with Eddie Cantor and George Jessel.

For the first months of 1932 Sissle's band alternated between residencies at the Park Central and brief theatre tours, mostly on the East Coast. The distinguished jazz writer John Hammond met up with Bechet during one of the stints at the Park Central and still remembers how downcast Sidney felt about being trapped in the big-band routines. Hammond, in common with almost every other jazz critic, was not impressed by the musical qualities of Sissle's band; he also felt that the red uniform jackets the group wore did nothing for presentation. (The red outfit was an innovation; previously the band had worn green velvet suits with orange coloured bows.)[5] During this period Bechet ceased playing the bass saxophone; instead he 'doubled' on the slightly smaller E flat baritone instrument.

Bechet eventually decided that he needed better rewards for the musical restrictions that he endured, and he asked Sissle for a lot more money, half-knowing that the leader would refuse the raise. Sissle wouldn't comply, so Bechet left the band. He was not immediately swamped with offers of work, as he undoubtedly would have been had he made such a move ten years earlier. By 1932 most leaders of big bands insisted that the musicians they employed were good readers, or at the very least readers. New York, still suffering from the Depression, was no longer full of thriving clubs which could afford to pay five or six resident musicians; the few that had continued with a live-music policy usually made do with a solo pianist.

New styles of playing had come into fashion during Bechet's various sojourns in Europe, as he found out when he sat in at various jam sessions. Musicians at these New York gatherings agreed that Sidney's improvisations were as dynamic as ever, but many young jazzmen were seeking something new. Trumpeter Roy Eldridge, who greatly admired Bechet's 'battling' qualities, played at many of the informal musical contests that took place in New York at this time. He said, "It wasn't that Bechet wasn't playing good. He was. But saxophone players like Coleman Hawkins and Benny Carter were attracting the attention of all the young cats, and these youngsters just weren't interested in anything that had happened earlier."[6]

Sam Wooding, whose orchestra had recently returned from Europe, employed Bechet briefly during this period for some theatre dates. Years later, when I talked with Wooding about Bechet, I formed the impression that his interlude with Sidney was not amongst his happiest experiences. Despite the traumas of his prison sentence, Sidney could still be truculent. Trombonist Clyde Bernhardt met Bechet at the Lafayette Theatre during the brief stint with Wooding: "Sidney Bechet started talking to me and my brother Paul and teasing both of us because we was wearing those derby hats. Bechet told us that we was too young to be wearing derby hats, because they was for old men. All of us had to laugh at the way Sidney Bechet was teasing me and my brother. Bechet was from New Orleans and he had the same ways like King Oliver, and most of the New Orleans people have. They like to laugh at your appearance, if you don't look to please them. They are very critical. It pays to always be well dressed when you are in their company."[7]

Bechet regularly called in to see pianist Willie 'the Lion' Smith at Pod's and Jerry's Club, situated at 168 West 132nd Street. Smith said later that, although 'sitting in' was discouraged there, an exception was made in Sidney's case (later on Bechet worked regularly with Smith at this venue). A steady job materialized at the Nest Club (on 133rd Street) where the band was led by Sidney's old friend the clarinettist (and saxophonist) Lorenzo Tio, Jr, who had made his home in New York. The Nest Club was famous for its flexible hours and its informal musical policy; dawn jam sessions were practically inevitable. Although Tio was just 40 years old, his health was poor, but this did not stop him and Bechet toying with the idea of opening their own 'bootleg' club. Mercifully they didn't, because Prohibition was soon to end.

Health problems eventually forced Tio to leave the Nest Club and Bechet assumed leadership of the band for a while, during which time he employed Danny Barker, a fine young guitarist recently up from New Orleans. Barker told writer Jean Roland Hippenmeyer about this: "When Bechet was full of whisky he'd start fighting. One night we had an argument. I was working with him at the Nest Club for about two months and he got in the habit of getting drunk every night. The boss got very angry."[8] Not surprisingly Bechet and the Nest Club manager parted company and Sidney began looking for other work. When Duke Ellington heard that Bechet was available he seriously considered bringing him into the band again. He chose not to, but invited Bechet to come along with the band to Philadelphia so that he could help Johnny Hodges re-create a spectacular chorus that Sidney usually played on *The Sheik of Araby*. Juan Tizol transcribed what Sidney played, and this 'theme' became Hodges's solo on the recording of the piece that Ellington's band recorded in May 1932.[9]

At about this time Bechet again met Tommy Ladnier. During their stay in Noble Sissle's band the two Louisiana musicians had become close friends. They decided to pool their talents and become co-leaders of their own band. Their first effort was to organize an eight-piece group to fill in at the Saratoga Club in New York, but when their plans were finalized they chose a sextet format: Bechet on reeds, Ladnier on trumpet, plus a trombonist, pianist, bass player and drummer. They decided to call the band the New Orleans Feetwarmers.

The musicians played their initial gigs in Jersey City and in White Plains, New York. When they had worked up a repertoire they applied for, and obtained, a residency at the Savoy Ballroom (140th–141st Street at Lenox Avenue), then New York's most spectacular ballroom, with a capacity for 4000 dancers. On Wednesday 14 September 1932, at what was billed as "the Savoy's Grand Fall Opening", the sextet made its major début, supporting the Mills Brothers and Fletcher Henderson's orchestra. For this booking the band was billed as "Ladnier and Bechet's New Orleans Feetwarmers. Dixie's Hottest Band – The Newest Note in Blazing Jazz".

By this time the group had a stable personnel. During some of the initial out-of-town gigs Lil Hardin had played piano and Sumner 'King' Edwards was on bass[10], but thereafter the regular pianist was Hank Duncan and the permanent bass player Wilson Myers. The drummer was Morris Morand (brother of Herb and one of Bechet's neighbours in New Orleans). Bechet and Ladnier also tried to get another New Orleans musician, trombonist Albert Wynn, into the band. Wynn, just back from working in Europe, did several rehearsals with the Feetwarmers, but as he lacked a local 802 New York Musicians' Union card he couldn't join the band, so Theodore 'Teddy' Nixon from Philadelphia secured the job.

Something of a compromise had been effected concerning the "Ladnier and Bechet" part of the band's billing. Apparently Moe Gale (Maurice Galewski), the booker for the Savoy, wanted Bechet advertised as the leader of the group, but Charlie Buchanan, the ballroom's black manager, wanted Ladnier to have sole billing. Gale, an experienced agent, felt that Bechet's dominant stance and powers of musical projection made him the only choice as leader, but Buchanan, and his wife Bessie, had good reasons for preferring Ladnier. Buchanan had gained first-hand experience of Ladnier's musicianship and his personality during the trumpeter's stay in Fletcher Henderson's orchestra some years earlier; Buchanan had been impressed. Buchanan's wife (formerly Bessie Allison) had worked in shows with girls who had known Bechet (including Josephine Baker). Bessie had nothing against Bechet personally, but she was well aware of his reputation for ignoring responsibility and of his unpunctuality. The Buchanans needed some convincing, but eventually they agreed to Ladnier and Bechet sharing the billing.

Besides being an admirable trumpeter, Tommy Ladnier was also the possessor of a rare brand of charm. Cornetist Muggsy Spanier, who had known Ladnier in Chicago, spoke of meeting up with the latter in Europe: "We spent a lot of time together, that is when Tommy wasn't hobnobbing with the upper crust. I've never seen a more popular guy with the higher ups, the dukes and counts and things."[11] Clarinettist Mezz Mezzrow described Ladnier as "philosophical and sincere".[12] The trumpeter had a relaxed way of making droll, cryptic remarks and, unlike Bechet, his temper had a low boiling point. However, in the manner of many musicians from Louisiana, he had a good deal of pride and was quick to guard what he considered were his rights. Garvin Bushell recalled: "When Tommy Ladnier joined us in 1925 he clearly had the feeling that nobody could play trumpet like the guys in New Orleans."[13] Another member of Sam Wooding's band, trombonist Herb Flemming, remembered Ladnier hotly disputing a point with Willie Lewis, after the reedman had butted in during one of the trumpeter's solos: "Tommy, usually the mildest of men, got to his feet and slowly walked across the stage and thrusting his trumpet in Willie's face said 'Here you want to play my solo, go take my horn and get on with it'."[14]

Perhaps it was this hard centre that caused Bechet always to treat Ladnier with respect. The two men established a highly effective partnership, and on the day following their début at the Savoy Ballroom they had the chance to prove it in the recording studio. There were no disputes about the group's name at the RCA Victor Sound Laboratory so, on 15 September 1932, the New Orleans Feetwarmers created its mark in jazz history.

The first tune of the day, *Sweetie Dear* (written by Joe Jordan in 1906), was one of Freddie Keppard's old favourites.[15] The Feetwarmers take it at a bright, lilting tempo, with Ladnier punching out an emphatic lead, one that is entirely devoid of schmaltz. Against this acrid, effective trumpet playing, Bechet, on clarinet, weaves a lively counterpoint, his tone sounding tough and vibrant; drummer Morand's press rolls add to the zest of the opening ensembles. Bechet's clarinet breaks serve as a bridge to lead the band into a new key, which Ladnier greets with an emphatically blown high note. Some expert musical duelling then gives way to a piano solo, and, amidst shouts of encouragement, Hank Duncan plays a two-handed chorus which is sturdy rather than cerebral. Bechet begins his clarinet chorus with a bold, wide trill, maintaining a feeling of exhilaration throughout the solo. Ladnier, cleverly emphasizing the beat, plays a delightful solo, then the front line drops its volume whilst Myers on string bass comes to the fore. Myers, a skilled multi-instrumentalist, was a relative newcomer to the bass; nevertheless he acquits himself well. The front line plays a series of riffs that build effectively without threatening to become frantic, and the resultant tension is a marvel. Only in this final section are we aware that trombonist Nixon has turned up for the date. The last bars of the piece owe something to the ending that Luis Russell's band played on *Jersey Lightning*, but all else is stimulatingly original.

I want you tonight, a ballad written by Bechet and vocalist Billy Maxey, is introduced by four bars of chime-like piano playing from Hank Duncan. Bechet on clarinet (sounding like Johnny Dodds) plays the melody with a passionate intensity, swooping onto notes that he wants to emphasize, all the while adding a throbbing, sensual vibrato. Ladnier, whose role in the early stages was to provide softly muted long notes alongside trombonist Nixon, emerges to play a supremely relaxed middle eight. Bechet remains on clarinet to play a rich sounding obbligato to Maxey's vocal (which seems inspired by the phrasing, if not the timbre, of Louis Armstrong's singing), then quickly changes to soprano saxophone to be ready for a triumphant eight-bar solo. Ladnier's playing swells up as the band enters the final eight bars and he and Bechet almost collide, but team spirit saves the day and a smooth ending materializes.

Bechet and Ladnier again demonstrate their musical compatibility on the first two choruses of *I found a new baby*. Ladnier plays the lead for the opening 32 bars, with Bechet (on soprano saxophone) adopting a bustling role that takes him over and under the trumpeter's line; Bechet then assumes the dominant role and Ladnier begins skilfully weaving an accompaniment. Trombonist Nixon is again almost inaudible but his sound does peep through during the verse. Bechet's solo is full of power and spirit, but Morand (perhaps over excited) sounds relentless on drums. Hank Duncan rattles through his solo, which is given a sudden lift when Myers's bass playing swings into a four-in-the-bar pattern. Teddy Nixon has his moment and responds by playing a shouting half chorus, which unfortunately is badly under-recorded. Ladnier sparks the final chorus with some rubato upper-register phrases and Bechet counters with swift-flowing riff patterns.

There are no unexpected harmonic twists in Bechet and Maxey's composition *Lay your Racket*. Sidney allocates the melody to himself. Hank Duncan plays another energetic solo, and by this time drummer Morand has mercifully picked up his brushes. Maxey's vocal reveals his vaudevillian background but this doesn't deter Bechet, who re-enters with an inspired burst of flaming ideas. The band's riffs continue to stoke the fire until the firm brakes of an intricate ending call a halt to the piece.

Scott Joplin might not have liked the adventurous treatment that the band imparts to his *Maple Leaf Rag*, but any jazz fan who likes passion, ideas, technique and swing in his music could not fail to respond to the performance.

Bechet, on soprano saxophone, takes the lead through most of the first half of the piece; he plays each theme with a commanding assurance, helped here and there by the brass players' staccato riffing. Pianist Duncan sounds more dextrous than usual and again Morand uses his brushes, but this time the off-beat effect he creates is slightly worrying. Bechet resumes his blistering attack, pouring out a ceaseless flow of penetrating ideas. The band's equilibrium falters slightly after the final modulation but Bechet's pulsating high notes ensure that there is no anticlimax.

There is no opening melody to *Shag*, which makes it one of the first, or perhaps the first, non-thematic jazz recording. The band launches straight into a series of group improvisations on the harmonic sequence of *I got rhythm*. A spirit of daring and invention prevails and Bechet plays ideas the like of which had never previously been recorded. Nixon's muted solo is adept but conventional, as is Maxey's scat singing, but the creative abandon resumes when Bechet takes over. Sidney's long notes sound as though they were almost torn out of the soprano saxophone and the effect created is one of boundless energy. The rest of the band responds, trying to match what seems like the work of a superman.

Thus ended a superbly exciting session. If there is one regrettable point about the date it is that Ladnier wasn't accorded more prominence. A few years later he told the French writer Hugues Panassié that he felt badly served by the recording balance. Ladnier was satisfied with the sound of the first tune of the day, but thereafter he felt that Eli Oberstein, who supervised the date, deliberately gave Bechet emphasis.[16] Oberstein, who had worked with Columbia and Okeh before moving to RCA Victor in 1928, may have realized that Bechet was in sensational form and didn't want to miss any nuance of his performance.

But, despite the excellence of its music, the New Orleans Feetwarmers was a short-lived group. There were various reasons for its demise, but probably the most important one concerned its musical style. The rough bite of the Depression had been felt in most American homes, and its effects were still hitting the music world when the group emerged. In 1932 most of the money that was spent on entertainment bought escapism. Undiluted jazz, which had been the perfect beverage for the carefree dancers of the early 1920s, was too rough a brew for the worried people of the early 1930s. Crooners singing romantic songs, lush saxophone sections warbling saccharine harmonies, helped to provide a relief from harsh realities – for both Whites and Blacks. Attendance figures for various nights at a Harlem ballroom in 1932 underline this trend:

Isham Jones	3500
Rudy Vallee	2800
Guy Lombardo	2200
Ben Bernie	2000
Vincent Lopez	1700
Duke Ellington	700
Cab Calloway	500
Louis Armstrong	350[17]

Bechet's and Ladnier's impassioned improvisations were too vivid for the taste of their audiences. Mezz Mezzrow said that the reason why the Feetwarmers lasted only briefly at the Savoy Ballroom was "because the East had gone modern by then"[18]; the average New Yorker's conception of hot jazz was that it was a thing of the past. Some jazz-orientated groups kept intact through the bleak years of the early 1930s, but those that did had been well established before the financial crash of 1929, and thus had capital or assets on which to feed during lean times. Neither Bechet nor Ladnier had the sort of money that bandleaders need to ride comfortably through bad periods. A band, like any other sort of business, needs capital to get established and to thrive. For transport to and from its initial engagement at White Plains, New York, the Feetwarmers had to use the only vehicle that the leaders could afford to buy – a 1919 Ford.[19]

The Feetwarmers' stay at the Savoy lasted only for a matter of months, and during the last part of this time the group was employed only intermittently at the ballroom. The British writer and composer Patrick 'Spike' Hughes, who was in New York from January until May 1933, wrote about a visit to the Savoy: "I remember being completely taken in at the Savoy in Harlem, where there was a soprano player of moderate ability who used to make his instrument sound exactly like a trumpet in the higher register. The illusion was enhanced by his playing a number of pseudo-Armstrong codas."[20] Clearly Hughes was not a devotee of Bechet's style of playing.

During the Feetwarmers' final dates there was a change of drummer. Morris Morand had a reputation for aggression and he lived up to it after Bechet had criticized him. Morand's half-sister was Bechet's old friend Lizzie Miles, who said of Morris, "When he drank enough he imagined he was Joe Louis."[21] Morand ignored the rules of boxing in his fight with Bechet, and actually threatened to kill him. He was speedily replaced by Kaiser Marshall.

At the end of the group's stay at the Savoy, Bechet became involved in another dispute, but this was nothing like the violent scene created by Morand. Sidney's arguments were with Tommy Ladnier's wife, who was critical of the part that Bechet had played in the joint leadership of the group. Sidney later recalled: "Tommy's wife wasn't satisfied. She wanted Tommy to be the sole boss. That's where we lost the job at the Savoy. That was the end of the Feetwarmers."[22]

Bechet, on the loose again, secured a regular job with Willie 'the Lion' Smith at Pod's and Jerry's Club, working with drummer Arthur 'Traps' McIntosh. Billie Holiday often sang at this club during the early 1930s, but only banjoist Elmer Snowden even mentioned seeing Bechet and Billie there together.[23] Bechet, always suspicious where money matters were concerned, was impressed by Smith's habit of making a three-way even split of the money, and the two became life-long friends.

By this time Lorenzo Tio, Jr, who lived in Mount Vernon, New York, had become seriously ill. Acrimony developed between his wife (who was looking after Lorenzo's affairs) and Bechet. In his autobiography Bechet said that Mrs Tio claimed that he owed her husband "money or something".[24] Apparently the "something" was an important item. According to Tio's daughter Rose, her father's soprano saxophone was at the bottom of the dispute; it had been borrowed and never returned.[25] Tio died in New York on 24 December 1933, and was buried in New Orleans.

Bechet's disputes with Mrs Tommy Ladnier ended when the Feetwarmers left the Savoy. Ladnier himself had observed the various arguments between his wife and Bechet without saying much, and his silence had so embittered his spouse that she eventually left him and moved away from New York. This development seems to have reunited Bechet and Ladnier. Ladnier had been doing some touring in Chick Webb's band, but neither he nor Bechet had any lucrative prospects in sight – not, that is, until Sidney conceived another of his business schemes. Years later he recounted how he had outlined the plan to Ladnier: "So I told [sic] Tommy, 'What you say we open up a tailor's shop? All we have to do is get an apartment and do a lot of pressing early in the morning, and after 12 all we have to do is put on one of those old pot of beans and stuff and get that good old King Kong whisky and we'll have everybody coming round.'"[26]

At first Ladnier didn't seem to go for the idea, but he was soon swept away by Sidney's enthusiasm. The site for the great enterprise was in Harlem, on St Nicholas's Avenue at 128th Street; the venture was called the Southern Tailor Shop. According to Willie 'the Lion' Smith, who went there – not for sartorial improvements, but simply to take part in the jam sessions that were held in the back room – the place was "a dark, damp, beat-up cellar".[27] Bechet had no plans to make suits there, and the main business was to be repairs and cleaning. Smith observed the early problems: "Sidney had the women chasing him all the time, and he never got much chance to press the suits brought in by the customers."[28] Trombonist Clyde Bernhardt was one of these customers:

> I would take my clothes to his cleaning and pressing place. I often asked Sidney Bechet when was he going to start to play again? He would laugh and say when he got tired of pressing clothes like he was tired of playing music, then he would play again! Sometimes I would visit Bechet and eat his good food. He would have a different wife every time I visited him. He told me that when his different wives started to get nasty and act-up he would whip their ass and put them out. He said that he was rough on his women.
>
> He liked to cook different kinds of Gumbo, 'Creole Beef', 'Chicken' and 'Spare Ribs cooked Creole style'. Sidney Bechet didn't like to hear me say that John Marrero or Simon Marrero, or any other New Orleans people could cook good Creole food. He wanted to be rated the best Creole food cook![29]

In an early interview Bechet spoke of this period: "All the cats used to drop in to have a jam session in the back room, and I used to cook for them. We had some good food and good music too; that was when I really felt I was playing the way I wanted to."[30] The information that Bechet had gleaned by asking about recipes and the preparation of food had come to be very useful; so too had his inquisitive attitude towards tailoring. Even before the opening of the shop he successfully repaired and altered various colleagues' band uniforms, and sometimes their best suits. Tommy Ladnier, although he was a partner in the shop, showed no aptitude for sewing, cooking or ironing. In the cause of jazz the two men had gone through thick and thin together with very few arguments, but there, in the steamy cellar, tempers became as frayed as some of the customers' pants.

Bechet reviewed the situation 20 years later: "I was the one who was working like the devil because Tommy couldn't press. So I was the one. I even had to go out and make deliveries. He wouldn't do that. He wanted to be the shoe-shine boy, that's all he wanted to do was shine shoes and stay there. I'm telling you we went through something in the place."[31]

It is almost funny to think of these two men struggling to run their ill-fated enterprise, but not so when one considers the plight that made Bechet contemplate carrying out the original idea. Here were two great black artists, one of them possessing talents that placed him amongst the finest natural musicians that America had produced, and they were forced by circumstances to become menials. Like true artists they had done their best to present the world with work that was untainted by commercialism, but they found no takers. They had played their music with supreme skill and it had lacked neither emotion nor expression, but their reward, for the time being, was to be ignored.

Noble Sissle, playing bookings at New York's Lafayette Theatre (in May 1934), heard about the plight of his former sidemen and asked Bechet to return to the fold (apparently Bechet was, by this time, considering becoming an undertaker).[32] Bechet agreed to return if Sissle would also reinstate Tommy Ladnier. Sissle raised no objection, but Ladnier (much to Bechet's disappointment) wasn't interested in the offer. Bechet said, "I begged Tommy, but he didn't want to come back. So I went back to Noble Sissle's band and I left Tommy in charge of the pressing shop, but when I came back to New York there was no pressing shop."[33] Bechet accepted this last development philosophically. He would have been pleased to see Ladnier under any circumstances, but it was to be a few years before their paths crossed again.

ELEVEN

Big-band Days

Bechet found several new faces in Noble Sissle's personnel when he rejoined the band in Chicago in 1934.

The full line-up was: Wendell Culley, Demas Dean, Clarence Brereton (trumpets); Chester Burrill (trombone); Harvey Boone (alto saxophone), Ramon Usera (tenor saxophone), James Toliver (alto saxophone); Oscar Madera (violin); Harry Brooks (piano); Howard Hill (guitar); Edward Coles (string bass); Jack Carter (drums). There were also three singers: Noble Sissle, Billy Banks and Lavada Carter (wife of the drummer Jack Carter and sister of the vocalist and trumpeter Valada Snow). Sissle no longer wore white gloves to conduct but all else was similar, including the musical policy and the style of the arrangements.

After what seems to have been a whirlwind romance Bechet married Mari-louise Crawford in Chicago on 3 July 1934. The bride, a beautiful woman (some inches taller than Sidney) from Cleveland, Ohio, was only 19.[1]

Noble Sissle and his orchestra worked at Chicago's French Casino (at Clark and Lawrence) and appeared in an imported version of the French revue *Folies Bergère*, which had been brought to Chicago as part of lingering celebrations connected with the 1933 World's Fair. The 100-strong company consisted mostly of French artistes and mannequins; besides Sissle's group there was another American orchestra that was led by Carl Hoff.

Sidney was on his best behaviour throughout the Chicago run and had only been with the show for a week or so when he achieved a permanent place in Noble Sissle's good book. Demas Dean recalled the incident: "Carl Hoff's Orchestra played the show up to the Grand Finale, then both bands played together. The show lasted over an hour, so Sissle's Band were off the stand until the Finale. On this particular night when Carl Hoff turned to bring Sissle's Band in and gave the down beat there was no one on the stand but Bechet. Sissle wasn't on the stand because Hoff was conducting. We tried to make it back but were too late. Sissle chewed all of us out except Bechet. He gave Sidney a watch and made him our time-keeper. We never missed another finale."[2]

Noble Sissle did not approve of his musicians sitting in with local bands, but on one occasion Bechet ignored the embargo and joined four other clarinettists from New Orleans in a memorable Chicago jam session. Trumpeter Natty Dominique told historian Bill Russell the details of the incident, which took place when Dominique was working in a band led by Johnny Dodds. Barney Bigard, in town with Duke Ellington, and Omer Simeon, working locally with Earl Hines, visited the club where Dodds's group was working. Jimmie Noone was amongst the listeners and so too was Sidney Bechet. It was Sidney who suggested that they all get their clarinets in order to join in with Dodds's band. A spectacular cutting contest developed, and, according to an admiring Dominique, it was Bechet who blew the other reedmen off the stand. On another occasion Natty said, "Bechet makes stuff on his clarinet that Barney Bigard and all them break their fingers to make. He doesn't know what he's doing but he's been doing it, and don't forget he plays a straight chorus too, beautiful tone."[3]

The *Folies Bergère* (which had been imported by the Music Corporation of America) achieved considerable success in Chicago, playing there for almost six months. That booking was followed by residencies in New York, first at the Casino Theatre (beginning on 25 December 1934) and then at the Supper Club of the Ziegfeld Theatre. Billed as "the French Folies Bergère", the show, which was compèred by film actor Emil Boreo, retained Carl Hoff's orchestra and Sissle's group for the New York run. A reviewer, commenting on the New York production, wrote: "Noble Sissle provides the torrid dance music, with a rumba thrown in for good measure every once in a while."[4]

Before Sissle's entourage had left Chicago it recorded four titles for Decca, in August 1934. All three of the band's singers, Sissle, Billy Banks and Lavada Carter were featured, and a fine instrumental, *Polka Dot Rag*, was also recorded.

Sissle's vocal on *Under the Creole Moon* is, as usual, clearly enunciated, pleasantly sung, and 'stagey'. The entire arrangement (played as a rumba) is devoted to ensemble playing. *The old ark is moverin'* consists of a light-hearted 'sermon' delivered by Billy Banks, with congregational answers from the band. Banks ends his vocal by urging the band to "swing it", which it does quite effectively during the final 12 bars of the arrangement. As on the previous title, there are no solos.

The band's remake of *Loveless Love* has some good jazz interludes. Lavada Carter sings with a coy, relaxed charm, but the main interest is created by Brereton's elegant muted trumpet solo and Bechet's soprano saxophone improvisations, which are full of stirring phrases but marred slightly by some unexpected misfingerings. The tenor and alto saxophone solos both contain worthwhile ideas and the band achieves a good deal of flair and swing in the last two choruses.

The instrumental number, *Polka Dot Rag*, provides the most memorable music of the session. The piece was composed by Sidney Bechet and James Toliver, but Noble Sissle, in the manner of most bandleaders of that era, became a co-composer on the day that the song was recorded. The complex first theme is entrusted to the saxophone section, whose fingers are not quite nimble enough to do justice to the fast-running melody. Sidney's clarinet leads the band into an equally attractive second theme, but this too is replete with mistakes by the saxophonists. The tenor saxophonist falters in his solo but manages to keep going, handing over to Madera on violin, who plays confidently without achieving any remarkable jazz heights. The saxophonists pick up clarinets and play as a trio, sounding more chirpy and more accurate than they had done earlier, then Sidney (on soprano saxophone) blazes into action, pouring out a blend of brief, staccato phrases and long, supple arpeggios. Midway through his solo he inserts a series of 'test' triplet phrases that often figure in the work of most great New Orleans reed players. By this time inspiration has lifted the band and the players zoom into a final chorus built on a series of call-and-answer phrases. Ultimately it is the brass section's turn to stumble, but none of the various mistakes (by brass and reeds) diminishes a performance that is full of vitality. The tune achieved some success aside from Sissle's recording, being featured by the bands led by Andy Sanella and Maurice Spitalny.[5]

James Sumner Toliver, Bechet's collaborator on *Polka Dot Rag*, became his close friend and his chief musical transcriber for many years. Toliver (whose nickname was Buster) was from New England and had grown up with Johnny Hodges and Harry Carney. He played all the reed instruments and was also an excellent pianist.

Sidney, in his usual way, had entered the band warily, but soon warmed to Buster Toliver. He did not, however, feel over friendly towards the other members of the saxophone section. As in the past, Bechet became convinced that two men were plotting his downfall: this time it was Raymond Usera and Harvey Boone, both of whom, according to Bechet, "het up in this jealousy business".[6] Bechet was incensed by "all those off-runs", but became angrier when Usera went to Sissle and told him that he refused to arrange anything for Bechet. Fortunately Toliver was a skilled orchestrator and he took over the task of writing arrangements for Bechet's feature numbers. This smoothed things over, and by the time the band had finished its Chicago run everything was equitable.

This was one of the happiest periods of Bechet's life. He realized that the music he was part of was not of the highest standard, but he was acknowledged as the band's leading instrumentalist. Domestically everything was settled and happy. Noble Sissle, always anxious to have stability and decorum within his group, actively encouraged his musicians to bring their wives with them on tour, so Bechet and Marilouise travelled happily together on the wide-ranging journeys that the band undertook in 1935 and 1936.

Bechet's contentedness showed in his relationships with fellow musicians. Sissle's band was, to use Demas Dean's expression, "a family affair". Apart from his initial ill feelings towards Usera and Boone, Bechet did nothing to disturb that atmosphere (he actually collaborated with Usera in composing *Under the dreamy creole moon*). The violinist Oscar Madera (who also doubled on tenor saxophone with the band) said of Sidney:

He was a very friendly human, with a joke and a smile always. He got on fine, not only with Mr Sissle, but with all the members of the band. He was a nice man, one of those natural God-made musicians, a real artist with such marvellous musical ideas, and mastery of his instruments. As far as I could appreciate he had what we would call a photographic mind. We used to rehearse arrangements for the orchestra and believe me he would memorize the complete melody and bass parts of each arrangement. Such a marvellous mind, because as far as I knew he couldn't read a note of music. He himself once said that music was born inside of him and that he could never understand how to read music, no matter how hard he tried. He really was a terrific 'get-off' man with the soprano saxophone and the 'C' clarinet. Of course he was terrific too on the bass saxophone which he played in unison with the string-bass, and every note was exactly right. Sidney was also a very good 'get-off' piano player.[7]

On one occasion, when the band was playing in Philadelphia, Bechet and his wife visited a club where Bessie Smith was singing. Bessie, who had been drinking, came over to their table and began to get over friendly with Sidney. The atmosphere began to turn nasty but fortunately the club owner intervened.

Out on tour Bechet loved looking at, and occasionally buying, second-hand jewellery and perfume bottles (which he collected). He was happy to spend hours browsing through trinkets and baubles, and nothing would induce him to leave a second-hand camera behind. Occasionally he demonstrated his culinary gifts, cooking for the entire troupe. Demas Dean recalled: "On some theatre dates we would chip in and he'd buy all the things he'd need to fix up a good old Creole dinner."[8] Several members of the band were keen fishermen, and each of them was given a piscatory nickname. Clarence Brereton, being a tiny man, was called 'Minnow', but Bechet's plump frame led him to being called 'Flounder'.

The Sissle band's dates varied from theatre engagements to private bookings, which included performances at country clubs and university balls. The most regular bookings were at big theatres such as the Lincoln in Philadelphia and the Howard in Washington, and at night-clubs like Billy Rose's French Casino in New York, where the group played in 1935. One of the band's radio programmes (transmitted on NBC and WBR) was reviewed in the March 1935 issue of *Metronome* by George T. Simon, who noted: "Bechet with his bass sax, English Horn, etc, gives the section plenty of variety and of course aids the rhythm section no end." Simon also wrote: "The three trumpets and fourth sax all double on fiddle, while the fiddler can come back by playing fifth sax." The line-up for the broadcast was the same that had made the recordings in 1934.

Simon had mistaken the sound of Bechet's soprano saxophone for that of an English horn, an understandable error in that, by 1935, the instrument had become something of a rarity in the jazz world. Alto saxophonists like Johnny Hodges, Don Redman and Charlie Holmes occasionally played the soprano saxophone, but Emmett Mathews (a disciple of Bechet) was one of the few players to specialize on the instrument during this period. By then Bechet was playing much more on soprano saxophone than he was on clarinet, though his colleague Madera made the point that for a while Bechet temporarily reverted to his first love, the C clarinet.

All the members of Sissle's band were used to the hazards of touring, which at times included overt racism. Sometimes the band bus went miles out of its way to avoid any hint of trouble. This strategy was part of Sissle's "ambassadors of good will theory", which meant that he expected his musicians to look straight ahead, no matter what insults might be hurled at them. One newcomer to the troupe found this attitude hard to accept: her name was Lena Horne. She had formerly been at the Cotton Club, but auditioned for Noble Sissle and successfully replaced Lavada Carter. Despite not seeing eye to eye with Sissle on all matters, Lena retained an enormous respect for his professionalism and his skills in interpreting an audience's mood. She later wrote: "In Noble's defense I must say that no one else thought in any other terms in those days. Noble and people like him did the best they could."[9]

Sissle himself (who had been educated at white schools) said in one interview:

"All this prejudice is more or less generated by managers and men who make up their minds that this is the pattern they are going to set. I've played all over the South. For six or seven years I travelled from one end of the South to the other, I never had any trouble."[10] Nevertheless, as Lena Horne pointed out, Sissle's musicians and his singers usually had to enter by the back door at most of the plush hotels in which they worked. In many towns they found that getting a hotel, or a hot meal, or a taxi, was fraught with difficulties.

It was the versatility of Sissle's orchestra that made it such a popular 'live' attraction; had the musicians been forced to rely on money from their record sales they would quickly have starved. A period of 18 months elapsed (after the session of August 1934) before Decca invited the band back to record further titles.

The session on 11 March 1936 produced five titles. *That's what love did to me* is a slow, romantic ballad which marks Lena Horne's recording début. The best music on this title is the high-register muted playing of the opening melody by trumpeter Wendell Culley. Lena, who said of her early vocals that she was only able to "carry a simple tune simply", was being too modest, but here the song isn't strong enough to support the quasi-dramatic treatment. Billy Banks's infectious high-pitched singing is well featured on *You can't live in Harlem.* Bechet has a characteristically exciting solo on soprano saxophone that lasts for half a chorus, and trombonist Burrill gives a good account of himself in his brief spot. It is obvious that the band is more cohesive and in tune than on its 1934 recordings. The new drummer, Wilbert Kirk, plays a more exuberant role than his predecessor, which sometimes helps and sometimes hinders the group.

I wonder who made rhythm is a commercial pot-boiler sung enthusiastically and stylishly by Billy Banks, but *Tain't a fit night out*, despite Sissle's jokey vocal, has a superb solo from Bechet. The piece is in a minor key and brings forth from Sidney the sensual expressiveness that became obvious when he improvised over minor chords. Brereton on trumpet also plays a penetrating 16-bar solo, which is more effective by far than the alto saxophonist's brief excursion.

The bright version of *I take to you* also has a good rough-edged half chorus from Brereton which is marred by a lapse of concentration in the last few bars. On this title Lena Horne sings a careful, theatrical vocal, as does Sissle on *Rhythm of the Broadway Moon.* Burrill on trombone blows lustily, but Bechet's solo shows improvisation of a totally superior class. Sidney, on soprano saxophone, is in overwhelming form, leaping out of the ensemble as though he had springs on his heels.

Noble Sissle was always keen, and proud, to be the first black bandleader to play in venues that had previously engaged only white groups. In the summer of 1936 the band was due to achieve one of these 'firsts' at the Moonlight Gardens ballroom in Cincinnati. As sometimes happened, Noble Sissle chose to travel by car – on this occasion riding with vocalist Billy Banks and guitarist Jimmy Miller. Near Delaware, Ohio, a tyre on the vehicle blew out, causing an accident in which Noble Sissle was serious injured. He was taken to hospital where a fractured skull was diagnosed.[11] Sissle, who had observed the infallible appeal that Lena Horne had for her audiences, sent word to the group, which had arrived in Cincinnati, that Lena was to front the band at the Moonlight Gardens. His only condition was that Lena had to be billed as Helena (a name he much preferred). The musicians did all they could to help Lena with her task, and she remained ever grateful.

Helena Horne did such a marvellous job fronting the band and acting as MC, that the management at the Moonlight Gardens agreed without hesitation that the band could fulfil the three-week contract that they had signed with Sissle. The only unhappy time that the group suffered during this booking was on 19 June 1936. Someone brought a radio to the dressing room and there the band heard that the German boxer Max Schmelling had defeated their idol, Joe Louis. Most of the musicians, including Bechet, were in tears as they got onto the bandstand to play.

Noble Sissle made a swift recovery from his injuries. As a gesture of his appreciation to the hospital that had nursed him he asked the band to visit Delaware to play a special concert for the doctors and staff. They did so, and on 30 June 1936 were photographed (with their wives) and the medical team of the Jane M. Case Hospital. Sissle was able to resume full duties by the time the band played at the Ritz-Carlton Ballroom in Boston during August 1936.

Despite Lena Horne's growing eminence she was not happy with touring conditions. After playing various dates in and around New York (including a week at the Apollo Theatre in October 1936) she elected to stay in New York with her husband, Louis Jones. Sissle decided not to replace her immediately. Saxophonist Jerome Don Pasquall gave the background:

> When I joined Noble Sissle he had four entertainers with his band, Lena Horne, Edna Mae Harris, the versatile Billy Banks, and a comedian named Buddy Doyle. The guitar player, Jimmy Miller, and other members of the band all collaborated to put on an hour's show at each dance that was of Broadway calibre. Lena Horne was just leaving the band as I arrived so that left Sissle with just two vocalists. Sidney Bechet was the instrumental star of the band. His improvisations were always electrifying. Even though he would set a chorus and play it the same way every night it was always a moving experience for the dancers – and the musicians – to listen to him. He was so great . . . Sissle had a lot of confidence in Bechet, which Bechet was careful not to abuse.[12]

Although Sissle was conservative by nature he was not cut off from events that were taking place in the music world. By 1937 he was well aware that there was a growing interest in jazz music and its history. Music magazines in America and in Europe were beginning to mention the important part that Sidney Bechet had played as a pioneer in developing jazz. Paul Eduard Miller (in the January 1937 issue of *Down Beat*) mentioned Sidney's "twenty continuous years of peerless performances". In a subsequent issue he wrote: "Discophiles and critics of Le Jazz Hot have acclaimed Bechet to have had more influence on modern saxophone playing than any other personality in the history of rhythm music."

Sissle was also fully aware that most big swing bands were successfully featuring a band within a band: a contingent of jazz musicians from various sections would form a specialized small group to play an interlude within the main programme. Sissle decided to utilize Bechet's growing appeal by featuring him with a small group drawn from the orchestra's personnel. This unit was billed as Noble Sissle's Swingsters.

At the orchestra's next recording session, on 16 April 1937, the small group recorded two numbers that Sissle had originally featured in the show *Shuffle Along* in the early 1920s. *Bandanna Days* is a charming anachronism, having all the qualities of an overture from the pre-microphone era, but during its early stages Bechet's new status in the organization becomes obvious. He is allocated an entire chorus to play his solo, blowing with a clarity of tone that suggests he had either changed the model of his saxophone or was using a new mouthpiece. In the closing stages Sidney again takes the limelight, this time on clarinet.

The next tune recorded, *I'm just wild about Harry*, was the famous work that Sissle had composed with Eubie Blake. The first chorus is played rather straight by muted trumpets, then the saxophones, phrasing in a manner inspired by Benny Carter's style of writing arrangements, prepare the way for Sidney's high-note entry on clarinet. Bechet creates a *tour de force* which is a tantalizing mixture of melodic paraphrases and bold excursions that superimpose new harmonies on the existing sequence. The ensemble re-enters and Bechet, as in years past, reverts to the bass saxophone for the final chorus.

Two versions of each of these numbers were released. They show that once Sidney had formulated the outlines of a chorus he often used it as a blueprint for further renditions. But, like a master craftsman, he often honed away at a phrase until he was totally satisfied with it.

Dear Old Southland, recorded by the full orchestra, is a feature for Sidney, and one that he had played in public for many years. It begins with a series of dramatic, unaccompanied phrases on soprano saxophone, after which Bechet glides into a ravishing version of the melody. Brereton's solo demonstrates his skill with the plunger mute, and then Sidney resumes his dominant place at the centre of the arrangement.

Bechet was familiar with all aspects of *Dear Old Southland*, but he could perform just as brilliantly on a song that he had heard only once before. Drummer Wilbert Kirk described how Sidney's amazing musical reflexes came into action at a band rehearsal: "His ear was terrific. We could be playing a song he'd never heard before. We'd pass out the music because all the musicians were good readers. We'd start playing. We'd change key. Now, this was a song he'd never heard before, but he'd jump right up and play a chorus on it just like it was nothing. I mean fast, not slow. We didn't know it ourselves, we had to read it. I said, 'How does he do it?' Amazing!"[13]

The recording session in April 1937 was for the Variety label, which had been formed shortly before by the agent Irving Mills (who was also Duke Ellington's manager). Helen Oakley, then working for Irving Mills's publicity department, was a staunch champion of authentic jazz, and pointed out to Mills that recordings by Bechet in a small group would have more impact than Noble Sissle's often ponderous arrangements. Helen had two valuable allies: both Duke Ellington and Johnny Hodges had never lost their overwhelming admiration for Bechet's talents and they were emphatic in supporting Helen's recommendation. The net result was that Noble Sissle's Swingsters returned to the Variety studio after the full band session to record two amazing tracks, *Okey Doke* and *Characteristic Blues*.

In this session, for the first time in his recording career, Bechet was left to his own devices. Even on early tracks like *Wild Cat Blues* his performance had been to some extent governed by surroundings, and on the sides that he accompanied blues singers (splendid though his performances were) he was restricted by the obvious prominence of the vocalists. On *Okey Doke* and *Characteristic Blues* he was free to present himself exactly as he wished, and the results are minor masterpieces of jazz.

The intensity of Bechet's opening breaks on *Okey Doke* sets the performance going with dramatic impetus – the phrases he plays are grandiloquent examples of his skill at 'bending' notes. He deliberately shades the pitch of his clarinet, creating eerie 'blue' notes that have no part in the chromatic scale. Some of these notes, after they have served their purpose of creating a mood, are resolved into transcribable sounds, but others are left suspended, creating a raw tension. Every phrase in Bechet's performance (on clarinet and on soprano saxophone) is packed with vitality and swing.

Characteristic Blues begins with a long, three-and-a-half-bar clarinet trill, suggesting some primitive call signs. This shrill effect gives way to a series of warm, smooth phrases as Bechet descends into his woody-sounding low register. Vocalist Billy Banks shouts exhortations as Bechet blows a ferocious slow chorus, which suddenly doubles in tempo to become a thrilling work-out. Bechet reverts to the original speed for Banks's two vocal choruses, which are backed by the voices of the other members of the quintet (Bechet may be heard singing enthusiastically). Banks then yodels a chorus which is answered by smouldering clarinet phrases. The roundabout starts up once more and the piece again whirls into double tempo. Sidney inserts a quote from *High Society* at the start of the final chorus, then romps through the concluding bars to end on a dramatic high glissando.

The performance by Bechet was nothing less than sensational, and quite unlike any sort of jazz that was being played at that time. Its roots were certainly in New Orleans, but its foliage had been gathered in the hundred and one towns that Bechet had played in since he had left his native city. Some theorists felt that these recordings demonstrated a perfect blend of African and European music, but even the most adept African griot had never created music that was similar, and nothing in Europe, even counting the bold improvisations of talented Magyar gipsies, could be mistaken for Bechet's art. He was a true original.

In America those record critics who were trying to stem the ever-growing popularity of the big swing bands gave Bechet's recording nothing but praise. Marshall Stearns, in the May 1937 issue of *Tempo*, said: "It's the real thing and strictly terrific." In France Hugues Panassié, editor of *Jazz hot*, wrote of the disc: "It fills a serious gap for all those who have never heard the old, now unobtainable records by Sidney Bechet." In England some reviewers, and a good number of record collectors, were bemused and even alarmed by Bechet's direct thrust at the emotions. But the new recordings meant that everyone who was interested in small-band jazz could readily obtain a sample of Bechet's work, not overwrapped by the sounds of a middling big band, but brilliantly highlighted in the Swingsters.

All of a sudden Bechet was news, and sketches and photographs of him appeared regularly in music magazines. These included one bizarre publicity shot (taken on tour in 1937 by Sissle's new alto saxophonist George Mathews) which showed Bechet serenading a lion in Sioux City. Readers were expected to suspend their disbelief as they read the caption: "Some of the boys became alarmed until Sidney Bechet stepped forward with his magic soprano saxophone and charmed the beast with his own melody *The Pied Piper of Harlem*."[14] The obliging and music-loving king of the jungle was apparently the pet of a prize fighter.

Bechet had long been used to tumultuous applause, but his newly won fame meant that complete strangers came around to Noble Sissle's band room to shake his hand and ask him about jazz events of long ago. The discographers made their initial attacks. Bechet might have been able to capitalize on this publicity had he been more often in New York, but most of his time was still spent on the road with Noble Sissle. Sissle's engagement book was as full as ever.

In the autumn of 1937 the band played a residency at the Chez Paree in Louisville, Kentucky. A prom at the University of Indiana followed, and the group then moved on to play at a private ball in Milwaukee. A string of one-night stands in Indiana and Ohio led on to a four-week engagement at the exclusive Look Out House in Covington, Kentucky. By now Sissle was featuring Bechet on every possible occasion, even taking him along (with the new pianist, Erskine Butterfield) to play at the Mount Zion Church in Cincinnati on the band's day off.

The charms of touring had come to an end for Bechet's young wife, Marilouise, who felt happier staying at home, particularly since her mother had moved into the Bechets' New York apartment. Bechet, on his own, also began to weary of the constant travelling, and he devised his own way of unwinding when the band bus finally reached its destination. Wilbert Kirk explained: "He'd have a couple of drinks and he'd go hide some place. Couldn't find him – the band would be looking for him. He would get in a mood and he wouldn't talk to anybody, but then pretty soon he'd start coming round. This was when we were travelling."[15]

Sometimes the exhausting touring schedule affected the band's music. Writer Dave Dexter heard Noble Sissle's orchestra play at the Fairyland Park Ballroom, Kansas City, during the summer of 1937, and thought the performance was "atrocious". On this occasion Bechet seems to have wearied of people calling to see him backstage; Dexter found him to be "a proud, almost haughty man, who answered questions with brief sentences".[16]

Officials at the Decca recording company, having seen the effusive reviews that greeted the 1937 Variety sides, decided to invite Noble Sissle to recommence recording for their label. They requested that he did not bring the full orchestra, but asked him to select instead a small line-up that was to feature Sidney Bechet. The results, recorded by a septet (billed as Noble Sissle's Swingsters), produced four memorable sides.

Bechet was accorded label credit (as Sidney 'Pops' Bechet) for this recording session in February 1938, and put a lot of care and attention into the preparations. He carefully rehearsed the unit from the main band, which consisted of himself (soprano saxophone and clarinet), Clarence Brereton (trumpet), Gil White (tenor saxophone and clarinet), Harry Brooks (piano), Jimmy Jones (string bass), Jimmy Miller (guitar), and Wilbert Kirk (drums). O'Neill Spencer, the drummer with John Kirby's band, was brought into the session as vocalist.

Viper Mad is a medium-tempo reworking of Bechet's song of 1924, *Pleasure Mad*. The composer takes the melody throughout the opening chorus, projecting it with a nonchalant flamboyance, while his colleagues gently blow a neat riff in support. Bechet modulates into the vocal, which is sung in a relaxed manner by Spencer. Brereton's hot-toned, sparse phrasing (reminiscent of Ladnier's work) provides a fluent link, then Bechet provides a powerhouse in a bold, high note that announces 16 bars of ingenuity. Spencer returns to sing a half-chorus vocal before the band signs off with a stock jam-session type ending.

During *Blackstick* Bechet proves how speedily he could swop from clarinet to soprano saxophone; he concentrates on the former for most of this intriguing arrangement. The main theme (another of Bechet's original compositions) is a simple motif which relies on insistent repetition for effect, and the same melody (taken up a fourth) forms the middle section of the piece. The overall feel is exotic, emphasized by the growling trumpet and the tom-tom patterns of the introduction. Kirk's crisp stick work inspires some surging phrases from Bechet's clarinet, but suddenly Sidney reveals his masterful sense of dynamics by dropping his volume by half. Tenor saxophonist White struggles through a couple of interludes, then Bechet makes a swift change to soprano saxophone and rocks through the final section, which he concludes with a cadenza based on diminished-chord arpeggios.

The majestic first theme of *Southern Sunset* finds Bechet (on soprano saxophone) in full flow, his powerful approach being matched by Brereton's plunger-muted growling. Both Bechet and White play clarinet briefly, then the piano intervenes to allow Bechet to revert to saxophone. On this occasion he produces a near tender sound, not unlike that of the Eastern *sharnai*, but in contrast he adopts an almost brutal tone to reintroduce a variation of the main theme that concludes the piece.

Bechet was a firm believer in the use of backing riffs, and they occur almost continually throughout this session, both as subsidiaries to the themes and as backings for improvised solos. Their effectiveness is typified by the soft background figure that supports Bechet's positive clarinet phrasing on the opening melody of *Sweet Patootie* (a 12-bar blues). O'Neill Spencer sings two smooth, sardonic choruses, then Gil White (on tenor saxophone) does his best to construct an effective solo; he does not succeed, however, and is overshadowed by trumpet improvisations that are rough-hewn but artistic. Another droll vocal chorus precedes Bechet's flawless soprano saxophone solo, which reaches its climax on a vibrant single note that is held for three tremulous bars. In surveying his recorded work, Bechet selected this performance as one of his own favourites.

The reviews of these four titles were even more favourable than those evoked by the quartet recordings of the previous year, and they were more widely issued – in America by Decca, in Europe by Brunswick. The demand for more examples of Bechet's recorded work was enterprisingly met by RCA Victor, which reissued the New Orleans Feetwarmers sides of 1932 on their less expensive Bluebird label.

For Bechet it was a time of reflection. He had worked in Savannah, Georgia, with Noble Sissle's orchestra soon after the death there (in April 1938) of Joe 'King' Oliver, who, within the space of a decade, had slipped from being a nationally famous bandleader to become a poverty-stricken pool-room attendant. Bechet returned to New York and said that Oliver had "died of heartbreak".[17] Sidney may well have contemplated also the progress of King Oliver's most celebrated pupil, Louis Armstrong, whose reputation in 1938, via hundreds of recordings and radio shows (and several appearances in feature films) had already reached international proportions.

Bechet came to the conclusion that time was not on his side. If he was to capitalize on the publicity and acclaim that he was receiving, he must soon move out of Noble Sissle's band. Sissle accepted Bechet's notice with regret but no rancour. He pointed out that there was a strong possibility of the band's playing a residency at Billy Rose's Diamond Horseshoe Club (which was situated in the basement of New York's Paramount Hotel), but Sidney was unswayed and left the band in October 1938.

Whilst Bechet was still with Sissle he had played as a freelance for a session at the Decca studio in May 1938. He was part of a small band that accompanied the singer Trixie Smith and also backed the fine duo of Coot Grant and Wesley Wilson.

Developing alongside the growing interest in small-band jazz there was an emerging awareness of the merits of various blues styles. Decca had given a black entrepreneur, J. Mayo Williams, a free hand to act as recording manager for sessions featuring blues singers (both urban and rural). Williams's right-hand man in this enterprise was the Texas pianist Sammy Price: "I had known of Sidney Bechet for years, but our paths never crossed until we made those records together. J. Mayo Williams was a college man, and one of the unsung heroes of black music. He was from Chicago and had worked for other record companies before he started the project at Decca. We picked the personnel together. Bechet was suggested and everything worked out fine. Bechet and I became close friends later; I was his business manager for a while. He was easy to get along with as far as I was concerned, but he was *dangerous* if he thought you didn't like him."[18]

There is nothing epic about Trixie Smith's vocal line, but she phrases with conviction and swings easily on the fast numbers, implanting a wry message into her interpretation of the blues. Her performances reflect both the vaudeville tradition and the country experience of earlier black singers, and she was one of the artistes whose work contained elements that later surfaced in vocals by the Chicago rhythm-and-blues performers. The backing that the studio group produces is like a smoother (and more complex) version of the music produced for Decca by the Harlem Hamfats group. Bechet is on clarinet throughout, supported by a buoyant rhythm section which features the immaculate brush work of drummer O'Neill Spencer and the energetic and skilful bass playing of Richard Fulbright. Teddy Bunn's brief single-string guitar solos provide a filigree, as do pianist Sammy Price's fleeting individual spots, but each of them plays a sterling part in the excellent rhythm team. The oddest aspect of the session is the heavy reliance on the cup mute of the trumpeter Charlie Shavers.

Shavers and Bechet later developed into cohesive front-line partners, but only the outlines of their musical compatibility show through here. Bechet, without throwing his weight about, regularly assumes the dominant role in the fill-in phrases that they share, but it must be borne in mind that Shavers was only 20 years old at the time of this session. He was already a brilliant and articulate trumpeter, but he was unused to this type of work, frequently showing signs of the musical impishness which later delighted – or exasperated – his listeners. This panache is more apparent on the three sides on which the group accompanies the vocal duets of Coot Grant and Wesley Wilson; Shavers's open work on *Toot it Brother Armstrong* is spectacularly impressive.

The most effective moments for the front-line duo come when they play preconceived riffs and unison phrases – particularly noticeable on *Trixie's Blues*, a track which shows the vocalist at her superb best. The tonal blend that Shavers and Bechet achieve made nonsense of the contention that Sidney's vibrato was incompatible with the playing of more orthodox musicians. Shavers had nothing but admiration for Bechet's musicianship: "He was a bitch. He played hell out of that clarinet and saxophone."[19]

TWELVE

Summertime

Bechet's departure from Noble Sissle's orchestra was a bold move considering that he had no definite plans or firm offers of work. He had enjoyed the security of regular wages for more than four years, and working as a freelance in New York meant that his income dropped drastically. During the first few weeks of his new status his main source of revenue came from appearing as a guest at the Sunday afternoon jam sessions which Joe Marsala organized at the Hickory House (a restaurant owned by the Goldman brothers) at 144 West 52nd Street. In his own quiet way Joe Marsala did as much as anyone on the New York jazz scene to break down racial barriers.

At the Hickory House Bechet renewed his acquaintanceship with a former infantry-band musician from Brooklyn, Herman Rosenberg. Almost every jazz musician in New York knew Rosenberg, who contributed news items to various music magazines. Rosenberg also did his best (usually for nothing) to let musicians know when a job became vacant, or when a club owner was looking for a new group. Through Rosenberg, Bechet met Nick Rongetti, one of New York's most colourful club owners, who ran a restaurant in Greenwich Village. Nick's Tavern, at Seventh Avenue and 10th Street, was one of the main gathering points for white jazz musicians during the late 1930s; they went there more for the music than for the club's speciality, "sizzling steaks".

Nick Rongetti, a New Yorker of Italian extraction and former student of medicine and law, was a frustrated pianist, who installed four pianos in his club (one grand and three upright) so that there would always be an instrument available if he chose to sit in. Despite holding a Local 802 Musicians' Union card, he was not an adept man at the keyboard. One musician said, "Nick plays great – for a cafe operator."

By late 1938 the term "Nicksieland" was being used to describe the sounds heard on Rongetti's bandstand. It was a stylistic blend of dixieland and jam-session music, and its main purveyors were the resident band led by cornetist Bobby Hackett and featuring Pee Wee Russell on clarinet and Eddie Condon on guitar; the resident 'guest star' was another musician from New Orleans, drummer Arthur 'Zutty' Singleton. Nick was well satisfied with Hackett's band, but offered Bechet the chance to appear as guest with an intermission group, the Spirits of Rhythm (featuring Teddy Bunn and Douglas Daniels).

The Spirits of Rhythm soon moved on, but Bechet stayed at Nick's and led his own quartet, which originally consisted of himself, Zutty Singleton, Wellman Braud on string bass (soon replaced by Henry Turner), and Leonard Ware on electric guitar (then very much a novelty instrument). The noted French jazz critic Hugues Panassié, paying his first visit to the USA, called into Nick's regularly during October and November of 1938 and watched Bechet establish himself at the club. Panassié also heard Bechet taking part in a momentous jam session (organized by Joe Marsala) which was transmitted via CBS radio and broadcast in Britain by the BBC.

The broadcast took place in the Viennese Roof Room of the St Regis Hotel, New York, and its compère was an excited young man who became one of the greatest of all radio commentators, Alistair Cooke. A star-studded line-up assembled consisting of Max Kaminsky, Yank Lawson, Marty Marsala and Hot Lips Page on trumpets, Bobby Hackett on cornet, Mezz Mezzrow, Pee Wee Russell and Joe Marsala on clarinets, and Sidney Bechet on soprano saxophone. Tommy Dorsey was on trombone, Bud Freeman on tenor saxophone, and the various rhythm sections were formed from Jess Stacy and Joe Bushkin (piano), Carmen Mastren and Eddie Condon (guitar) Zutty Singleton and Dave Tough (drums), and Artie Shapiro (string bass). Each musician worked for the union scale, 25 dollars a man.[1] The audience consisted of enthusiastic jazz fans and eminent people from the music world, including the composer W. C. Handy and the writer Ernie Anderson. For some reason (probably to gain publicity) Alice Talton, the current 'Miss Georgia', attended the clambake.

Bechet's main contribution to the programme was a brief version of *China Boy*, which he played with a rhythm section composed of Bushkin, Mastren, Shapiro and Singleton. Sidney opens in confident, rhapsodic mood, then re-enters (after Singleton's crisp-sounding drum solo) to play an intricate chorus consisting of his "pre-set variations"; these were phrases which he had practised to perfection, knowing that whenever he performed them in public they always impressed his audiences. In common with many other great jazz musicians, Sidney would 'frame' a particular solo chorus when he thought it was as good as any he was ever likely to conceive; he did this on most of the feature numbers he had played in Noble Sissle's band, and he continued to follow a similar procedure for the rest of his life. But his set solos were always delivered with the alacrity and freshness of spontaneous improvisations, and Bechet's masterful jazz talent allowed him, at whim, instantly to replace a set solo with newly conceived musical ideas. Often his solos contained set phrases *and* daring improvisations.

On the day following the St Regis jam session Bechet made his début as a recording bandleader. Billed as Sidney Bechet and his Orchestra, his six-piece group consisted of three colleagues from Nick's – Ware, Turner and Singleton – and two musicians from Bobby Hackett's band – Ernie Caceres on baritone saxophone and Dave Bowman on piano. The session (for the Vocalion label) took place in the studios at 1780 Broadway. Amongst assorted visitors who dropped into the session were the vocalist Mildred Bailey, Hugues Panassié and the trombonist Dickie Wells, who was recording in an adjacent studio with Count Basie's orchestra. Bechet was determined to create a new small-band sound and used an instrumentation that had not previously been tried in a jazz sextet. His front-line partnership with Ernie Caceres certainly produced innovative tone colours, but overall the music from the session has an uneven quality.

What a Dream, one of Bechet's own compositions, is more interesting harmonically than melodically. Bechet's strategy here is to play the tune on soprano saxophone, leaving Caceres (on baritone) ample space to create a low-register counterpoint. After a chorus of melody the two front-line musicians swop a series of improvised phrases (an early example of the four-bar 'chase' being used). Guitarist Leonard Ware takes an amplified half-chorus, then shares a duo with Caceres before the leader re-enters by swooping on the first notes of a chorus that is rich in flamboyantly presented ideas.

Sidney changes to clarinet and blows a stimulating introduction to *Hold Tight*, a vocal feature for Eddie Robinson and Willie Spottswood (billed as the Two Fishmongers), who make the most of the lively lyrics. In the background Bechet's probing phrases provide fill-ins, which he follows up by playing an absorbing clarinet chorus. Ware tastefully splashes blue notes throughout his half-chorus, and then the singers repeat the simple words. Drummer Zutty Singleton is effective throughout the session, but is at his best on the introduction to *Jungle Drums*. The two reed players pick up the theme and share a lively opening chorus. Ware's guitar solo is poorly recorded but the nuances of Singleton's snare-drum work are nicely captured. Caceres plays a pithy solo, then Bechet growls out some powerful lines, tonguing some of the phrases with awesome force.

Pianist Dave Bowman's only solo is the four-bar rolling boogie introduction to *Chant in the Night*. This minor-keyed theme has an Ellingtonian feel, with Caceres sounding almost like Harry Carney beneath Bechet's poised rendering of the melody. Caceres continues to play a counter-melody under the guitar solo, but this does not blend effectively; Singleton is playing rim-shots at the same time, so a confused sound-picture emerges. Bechet puts things firmly back on course by extemporizing a concluding chorus that reasserts the melody. The two reed players finish on a long harmonized note, but Sidney's intonation wobbles a little at the crucial moment, making the final phrase sound out of tune.

Sidney's tactics for this important session were commendably bold, but they lacked rehearsal: Bechet and Caceres needed more time together to achieve effective ensemble rapport. The arranged passages have a disjointed quality and often fail to build into any sort of climax; another factor is that Bechet's compositions are not memorable enough for what should have been an auspicious date. The participants play satisfactorily but the results are indifferent. The item that Bechet held high hopes for was *Hold Tight*. He judged correctly that the song had commercial potential, and even took a magazine advertisement to plug the fact,[2] but to his disappointment another group's version made its way into the best sellers.

Bechet's search for a new small-group sound did not end with the November 1938 recording session. Soon afterwards he changed the instrumentation of his band at Nick's in a way that was quite revolutionary. He brought in Jimmy Shirley on electric guitar to join Leonard Ware, thus making the group one of the first (if not the first) to use two electric guitars – predating the 'beat groups' by a quarter of a century.

British trumpeter Nat Gonella sat in with this line-up at Nick's during a visit to

Bechet at the time of his arrest in London, September 1922 (by permission of the Public Record Office, London: document HO45/24778)

Sidney's brother Dr Leonard Bechet

Sidney's niece Emelda Bechet-Garrett
(*courtesy Bob and Pug Wilber*)

An early portrait of Bechet

Sidney Bechet with his Creole Orchestra, 1924; the personnel includes Hamp Benson (trombone) and Wellman Braud (double bass) (*courtesy David Mylne*)

Noble Sissle's band in the Moonlight Gardens, Cincinnati, 1936 (left to right): Billy Banks, Chester Burrill, Buster Toliver, Jimmy Miller, Wilbert Kirk, Clarence Brereton, Gilbert White, Jimmy Jones, George Mathews, Jerome Pasquall, Demas Dean, Sidney Bechet, Sissle (*courtesy Demas Dean and Peter Carr*)

DESCRIPTION OF APPLICANT.

Age: *21* years.

Stature: *5* feet, *3* inches, Eng.

Forehead: *Low*

Eyes: *Dark Brown*

Nose: *Broad*

Mouth: *Small*

Chin: *Pointed*

Hair: *D Black*

Complexion: *Light Brown*

Face: *Round*

Distinguishing marks: ....

AFFIDAVIT OF IDENTIFYING WITNESS.

I, *Henry Saparo*, solemnly swear that I am a {native / naturalized} citizen of the United States; that I reside at *150 - W - 131st St. N.Y. City*

(Home address.)

that I have known the above-named *Sidney Bechet*. personally for *20*.

(Name of applicant.)

years and know {him / her} to be a native citizen of the United States; and that the facts stated in {his / her} affidavit are true to the best of my knowledge and belief.

Henry Saparo

(Signature of witness.)

Musician

(Occupation.)

....

(Firm, corporation, or organization, if any.)

150 - W - 131st St N.Y.

(Business or professional address.)

Sworn to before me this .... day

of ...., 19......

[SEAL.]

J Hay

Passport Agent, Department of State.

Applicant desires passport to be sent to the following address:

Louis A. Mitchell

2251 - 7th Ave.

New York City

A signed duplicate of the photograph attached to the original application must be affixed in the space marked below.

The application form for Bechet's passport

Photograph of bearer

Sidney Bechet

The attached photograph
bears the signature and is
a likeness of the person to
whom this passport is issued

This passport is good for travel in all
countries unless otherwise limited.

This passport is valid for two years from
the date of issue unless limited to a shorter
period. It is not subject to extension beyond a period of two years from the date
of issue.

Pages from Bechet's passport

Bechet at Jimmy Ryan's, c1938, with Wellman Braud (double bass), ? Gene Fields (guitar) and Zutty Singleton (drums)

Right: Tallulah
Bankhead
(*courtesy Dick
Hughes*)

To Sidney
love again
Tallulah

Left: Bechet
around the time
he recorded *Blue
Horizon*

Bechet with the Port of Harlem Jazzmen, 1939 (left to right): J. C. Higginbotham (trombone), Bechet, Sid Catlett (drums), Teddy Bunn (guitar), Johnny Williams (double bass), Frankie Newton (trumpet)

Bechet with Clarence Williams and Louis Armstrong, 1940

Bechet at Camp Unity (*courtesy Bob and Pug Wilber*)

Bechet with Bunk Johnson in Boston, 1945; the other members of the band are Ray Parker (piano), Pops Foster (double bass) and George Thompson (drums)

Bechet and his friend Laura opposite Emelda and Elmo Bechet, Club Zanzibar, New York, *c*1946 (*courtesy F. Wynne Paris*)

Bechet with the trombonist Bill Harris at Kimball Hall, Chicago, 26 January 1947

Bechet with Bill and Ruth Reinhardt (*courtesy Dick Hughes*)

Bechet at the time of the New York Newspaper Guild Award, 1949, with (left to right) Joe Marsala (clarinet), Bobby Hackett (cornet) and Brad Gowans (valve trombone) (*courtesy Dick Hughes*)

At Jazz Ltd, Chicago (left to right): Bill Reinhardt (clarinet), Danny Alvin (drums), Bechet, Mel Grant (piano) and Munn Ware (trombone)

New York in late 1938. He reported back to readers of the British magazine *Rhythm*: "At Nick's Tavern the relief band was led by 'Pops' Bechet with two electric guitars, bass and drums, and although the instrumentation may sound screwy the results were very effective."

During one of Hugues Panassié's visits to Nick's, Bechet mentioned the article that Ernest Ansermet had written back in 1919. Ansermet's review had never been published in English, but this omission was soon rectified when Walter Schaap translated it for the French magazine *Jazz hot* (which was administered and edited by Panassié and Charles Delaunay). It was published in the issue of November-December 1938 and was soon reprinted in the British *Melody Maker*, followed by dozens of other publications. The wide circulation of the review increased Bechet's reputation; Panassié was soon to add further to it.

One of the purposes of Panassié's visit to the USA was to record small hand-picked jazz groups. He pondered on the personnel for these dates and kept returning to the idea that the ideal trumpeter would be Tommy Ladnier. The main problem was in finding him, but eventually, during the first week of November 1938, Ladnier, who had been working in Newburgh, New York, was located. Before the month was out he had teamed up with Mezz Mezzrow and Sidney Bechet to create a remarkable series of recordings. Tommy Ladnier and his Orchestra consisted of these three front-line musicians plus Cliff Jackson on piano, Teddy Bunn on guitar, Elmer James on string bass, and Manzie Johnson on drums. The four titles they recorded soon introduced Tommy Ladnier's name to a new generation of listeners, and their wide distribution firmly cemented Bechet's reputation throughout the jazz world.

Ladnier's name was used on the record labels as the leader of the group by force of circumstances. When Panassié, Mezzrow and Ladnier arrived at the recording studio they found Bechet already there with a note from Irving Mills's office granting permission for Bechet to record but stipulating that his name was not to be used on the label. The recordings served to gain Mezz Mezzrow a permanent place in jazz history. Milton 'Mezz' Mezzrow's desire to steep himself in black music began during his upbringing in a white, middle-class area of Chicago. In his dramatic autobiography *Really the Blues*, Mezz recalls the excitement of hearing Freddie Keppard and Bechet playing at the De Luxe Cabaret. Bechet became something of a hero for him, and one of the inspirations for his becoming a clarinettist. Mezz moved to New York in the late 1920s and became a well-known figure in both black and white jazz circles, not principally through his musical prowess but mainly because he could supply copious quantities of top-grade marijuana.

Had Mezzrow been required to depend solely on his skills as a jazz musician, his life would have been a very lean affair; as it was he encountered hardships because of his staunch belief in the superiority of black jazz. He was quite vociferous on this point, and suffered as a result of his candour. However, he successfully badgered recording companies into allowing him to organize sessions featuring black and white musicians playing together, and the results were often superb. Mezzrow had toyed with the idea of using Bechet on one such session in 1936. He later complained that the A & R man (John Hammond) had thwarted the scheme, but Bechet was working exclusively for Noble Sissle at that time and could not have taken part in the date; nevertheless he dropped into the studio as gesture of goodwill.[3]

In 1938 Tommy Ladnier's lip was not as strong as it had been and he was suffering from heart problems, but he still managed to play a vital part in these outstanding recordings, which made an important contribution to the growing interest in what was termed 'hot jazz'. The drummer in the session, Manzie Johnson, said: "I believe these records we made for Hugues Panassié and Madeleine Gautier (Panassié's long-time companion) had more to do with the dixieland revival than any others."[4]

Ladnier's positive articulation of the first notes of *Ja da* give an immediate indication that the session is quite different from other small-band dates of that era. The trumpeter's succinctly timed phrasing acts as a lynchpin that coordinates rhythm section and front line. Bechet, sounding relaxed, begins the piece by playing a quiet counter-melody (on soprano saxophone); gradually he becomes more assertive and is in top gear by the end of the first 16-bar theme. Mezzrow (on tenor saxophone) fills in the remaining spaces.

Cliff Jackson takes a heavy-handed but driving solo. Bunn's guitar work is, in contrast, light and pungent; it is also beautifully supported by Bechet's clarinet whisperings. Ladnier's tightly muted solo is little more than a sparse rephrasing of the melody, but its effect is exhilarating. Mezzrow takes a cumbrous solo on tenor saxophone (one that Panassié loyally maintained sounded better in the studio), but Bechet elevates the excitement with a fiery clarinet chorus. The concluding ensemble romps home, rocked by the vastly under-rated drumming of Manzie Johnson.

Teddy Bunn's elegiac guitar introduction to *Really the Blues* acts as a preview to a moving chorus from Ladnier, whose expressive tone is enhanced by the gently blown long notes of the two reed players. Mezzrow then takes the lead part in an epic clarinet duet with Bechet. This part of the recording proved to be the main talking point for reviewers, and eventually led to Mezzrow and Bechet being featured in a series of recording duos. Ladnier re-emerges to play an incisive muted chorus, spurred on by the impetus of the drummer's snare work. The stage is set for two monumental blues choruses from Bechet (on soprano saxophone); he sweeps his way majestically through them, creating a fitting climax to a magnificent recording.

The musical cohesion among the players is plainly apparent, but on a personal level things were not going too smoothly in the studio. Bunn and Mezzrow had a row, so too did Panassié and the RCA Victor executive Eli Oberstein. Bechet stood aside, his eyes twinkling, and Ladnier looked on with a frown; still remembering the bad balance he had been accorded on the sessions in 1932, he was quite prepared to take sides against Oberstein. Despite the turmoil, a fine spirit marks the group's version of the 19th-century air *When you and I were young Maggie*. Ladnier's terse phrasing is again supremely effective, like the short-distance punching of a champion boxer. There is nothing frantic, or even spectacular, about the trumpeter's work, but his rhythmic drive is engraved on every phrase he plays. Mezzrow on tenor saxophone does his indifferent best to share his love of jazz, but fortunately Bechet is on hand to add the master touch by playing a superb solo. Panassié noticed that Bechet was edging closer and closer to the recording microphone during this stage of the session, but decided not to make an issue of it since time was precious.

For its final number the band performs the plus-perfect version of *Weary Blues* (organized, according to Panassié, in less than five minutes). Manzie Johnson's springy drum breaks launch a lively, extended ensemble which features both Bechet and Mezzrow on clarinets. Bechet takes two 16-bar choruses, unhesitatingly creating long, sinuous phrases and attacking his high notes with true verve. Ladnier again reveals his ingenuity, this time backed by Johnson's percussive striking of the drum-set's cow bells. The front line regroups for a joyous sounding finale which serves to prove that great jazz can be produced by a combination of musicians with unequal techniques.

Bechet and Ladnier had a chance to shine (without being joined by Mezzrow) in a concert entitled "From Spirituals to Swing" that was organized by John Hammond at New York's Carnegie Hall on 23 December 1938. At the concert (dedicated to the memory of Bessie Smith) Bechet and Ladnier played in a sextet with James P. Johnson on piano and three men from Count Basie's band (drummer Jo Jones, bass player Walter Page and trombonist Dan Minor). Two of their numbers, *Weary Blues* and *Sister Kate*, were eventually released on an album more than 20 years later.

Both these items have some wonderful moments. Ladnier performs admirably on *Sister Kate*, constructing a break that emphasizes his wonderful rhythmic balance. Bechet plays soprano saxophone on this tune, which unaccountably, but effectively, moves into a 12-bar blues sequence during its latter stages. *Weary Blues* does not achieve the *élan* and spirit of the studio recording, but it allows Bechet some exciting moments on the clarinet. Hugues Panassié was backstage with Bechet and Ladnier and had a good opportunity to observe the differing reactions of the two men as they prepared to go on stage. Bechet was pacing up and down and appeared agitated, whereas Ladnier seemed nonchalant and at ease. Although Bechet was a life-long victim of stage fright, he usually managed to shake it off the moment he appeared before the public, but not, apparently, on this occasion. Panassié wrote: "Bechet seemed uncomfortable on stage but Tommy Ladnier sounded at his best."[5]

Bechet admitted, "I didn't feel quite right. I wanted the band with me. They put the rhythm section up on the platform."[6] Bechet's apprehension about playing concert dates stayed with him forever. Years later he said, "I like to just go out of this world and play just the way I feel. I have trouble to get into that feeling when I'm playing these jazz concerts."[7]

As Bechet's wife had returned temporarily with her mother to Cleveland, Ladnier moved in briefly with Bechet. One of their near neighbours was drummer Zutty Singleton, who described the shared quarters: "They called their place the House of Meditation and they had a picture of Beethoven on the wall. One day Ladnier said to Bechet, 'You know something Bash? You're the dead image of Beethoven', and that pleased Bechet. Bechet and Ladnier would stand in front of this big old mirror they had and watch themselves whilst they practised. They listened to classical music and they talked a lot about their travels – when Bechet wasn't talking about the Rosicrucians. He was hell of a cat. He could be mean. He could be sweet. He could be in between."[8]

The House of Meditation functioned until Bechet's wife and her mother returned. Ladnier then moved out to dwell for the rest of his brief life in Mezz Mezzrow's apartment at 1 West 126th Street, where he died (of a heart attack) on 4 June 1939. Bechet lost a good friend, and by the time of Ladnier's demise he had also lost another, Zutty Singleton. Fortunately it wasn't death that parted these two men – it was Creole pride.

Singleton had gained a devoted following at Nick's long before Sidney had appeared on that particular scene. Zutty was a star attraction at the club and the only negro musician who worked there regularly before Sidney joined the pay-roll. Sidney's performances within the intermission group soon began to gain more publicity than Zutty's efforts, which irked the drummer, but Zutty's spectacular drum solos drew just as much applause from the club's patrons as anything that Bechet played, and this didn't please Sidney. Pianist Kay C. Thompson, who visited Nick's regularly, witnessed the growing tension between the two Louisianians: "The united front which Zutty and Sidney presented nightly at Nick's had commenced to reveal cracks indicative of the more subterranean strains and stresses. For a variety of reasons their brief musical alliance, at best an uneasy truce, was doomed to be short-lived but during its brief existence it was productive of some of the finest small band jazz I ever heard."[9]

Drummer Johnny Blowers, who worked in Bobby Hackett's band at the club, recalled: "The trio were our relief – half an hour on, half an hour off, 9 p.m. until 4 a.m. I used to sit in with them after my set because I loved the trio and Zutty wanted the rest."[10] By this time guitarist Leonard Ware had been replaced by pianist Hank Duncan. Sidney came to the conclusion that it was time to replace Zutty permanently, and optimistically enlisted his old antagonist Morris Morand. History repeated itself and Morand ended his brief stay by trying to strangle Bechet.

Meanwhile another storm was gathering about Sidney's head. It concerned the song *Hold Tight*, for which Bechet was claiming part-authorship. Sensitive guardians of public morals claimed that the song's message was sexual (albeit in a heavily disguised manner), and it was subsequently banned by various radio stations. Kay Thompson had been using the song on a children's show that was broadcast on WHN, "blissfully unaware of its obscenities. We were required to repeat it for some weeks until at last the censors took cognizance banning the number once and for all."[11]

Kay Thompson gave more details of the saga: "Though few people realise it the original copies of *Hold Tight* had listed Sidney amongst its several composers, but as I recollect, since the composition had been put together out of spare parts that had long been in public domain, a dispute soon arose over its authorship. As a result of conflicting claims, earlier copies were withdrawn and when newer ones were issued, by some alchemy peculiar to the publishing business, Sidney's name was deleted. In spite of this, Sidney continued to play *Hold Tight* at Nick's as though his life depended on it. Indeed without too much urging he would frequently get up and sing it as well."[12]

The background to the dispute over who composed the tune was as complex as the piece itself was simple. In 1938 Leonard Ware, Edward Robinson and William Spottswood had featured the number in their group act. They were heard performing it by pianist Jerry Brandow and dancer Leonard Kent. Ware and his colleagues acceded to a request from Brandow and made a demonstration disc of the song for him. Brandow added more lyrics and then Leonard Kent took the results to the Andrews Sisters, who liked the song. Vic Schoen prepared an arrangement of it for the sisters, and one of them, Patti, adjusted one of the existing lines of the lyrics and added a further line of her own. The girls introduced the song during their Christmas show at the Paramount, New York, in 1938, and soon afterwards made a recording of it. In the meantime Leonard Ware had joined Bechet's group on guitar; he played the song for Sidney, who decided to record it.

When Lou Levy, manager of the Andrews Sisters, discovered that Bechet had recorded the number, he went to the song's publishers to try and ascertain who had actually written the item. A series of claims and counter-claims began circulating, and a compromise was achieved whereby Ware, Robinson, Spottswood, Kent and Brandow were allocated shares of the composers' royalties. Bechet felt aggrieved, claiming that the basis of the song came from his opus of 1924 *I want some seafood mama*, which, according to Bechet, Clarence Williams had refused to publish because the words were too obscene.[13]

The Irving Mills Agency, which had recently been acting as Sidney's management firm, took up the case on his behalf. No sooner was that action taken than up jumped another person claiming to have composed the song – Joseph 'Taps' Miller. *Swing* magazine reported in its issue of June 1939: "So many suits on *Hold Tight*, now 'Taps' Miller, coloured musician, has an injunction restraining payment of royalties to any of the writers until he's proved he wrote the song, in court." A wag in the same magazine wrote: "It might be cheaper to say 'Words and Music by anyone on 52nd Street', or 'Words and Music by sheer luck'." Unfortunately Bechet didn't win his claim for a share in the considerable money that the hit song earned; by May 1939 the Andrew Sisters' Decca recording had sold a quarter of a million copies.[14]

Bechet continued to work at Nick's during the early part of 1939, but gradually his relationship with the club owner deteriorated. Nick could be just as volatile as Sidney, and even more vociferous; he was also a tight man with money and refused to increase Bechet's pay, even though many people were visiting the tavern just to hear Sidney play. Bechet himself was not keen to pay his sidemen more than the union minimum. As a result his group frequently underwent personnel changes as various musicians went off, for a night or for a week, to play a more lucrative job. Incoming players included bass player Edward Robinson and drummer 'Sticks' Magee. Bechet toyed with the idea of adding one of his protégés, vocalist Dell St John, to the group, but Nick vetoed the idea. During this period Bechet's income was supplemented when he took part in a film by Donald Heywood, *Moon over Harlem*.

The February 1939 issue of *Down Beat* announced the end of Bechet's stay at Nick's: "After receiving considerable notice and publicity as a result of praise and mention made of him, Sidney Bechet and his group have been given notice and will exit from Nick's Tavern by the end of this month. Although credited with top ranking ability and virtuosity as a real exponent of le jazz hot, Bechet's prospects are not too good, and it's still a mystery why his services were discontinued when they seemed so successful."

The magazine's point about Bechet's future prospects was all too true: the early months of 1939 looked bleak. Bechet worked as and where he could, and he also took part in a series of jam sessions that Paul Smith and Ernie Anderson organized on Fridays at New York's Park Lane Hotel. At this time Bechet began rehearsing a new version of the Feetwarmers, using Jabbo Smith on trumpet. As a result the following line-up recorded a test session for Baldwin Records in the spring of 1939: Bechet (soprano saxophone), Jabbo Smith (trumpet), Billy Bowen (alto saxophone), Walter Blount (tenor saxophone), Clarence Kaister (piano), Bill Casey (drums), Joe Brown (string bass) and Eva Sharpe (vocals).[15] Unfortunately the results of this interesting-looking session have never come to light. The group played some gigs out at the site of the New York World's Fair, but then Sidney decided he didn't want the responsibility of leading the band and passed over its leadership to Jabbo Smith.

During the spring of 1939 Bechet played a few dates in Philadelphia, appearing as guest for the local Hot Club. He also worked with Willie 'the Lion' Smith on piano and Dinah Taylor on drums (at that time a female percussionist was a rarity) in a trio employed at the Momart Cafe, in Astoria, Long Island. But gigging had its hazards: the pay was often low and sometimes a club owner's cheque bounced. Bechet seriously considered quitting full-time music again, this time to open a "quick order hash house" on Philadelphia's south side.[16] Happily he changed his mind and stayed in New York, where he took part in a momentous recording session for the newly organized Blue Note company.

Blue Note's founder, Alfred Lion, first heard jazz in his native Berlin, where the sounds of Sam Wooding's band (which was touring Germany in 1925) caused him to become a passionate collector of jazz records. In 1938 he settled in New York and was thrilled by the music he heard played at the "From Spirituals to Swing" concert in December. He decided to record two of the participants, the boogie-woogie pianists Albert Ammons and Meade 'Lux' Lewis. Subsequently he pressed up 50 copies of the record – using the less common 12-inch 78 r.p.m. format. They sold quickly, and this success caused Lion to launch what proved to be one of the most important independent jazz record companies. Lion said, "When I started Blue Note there were only two other labels in the jazz record world: Commodore and HRS."[17]

On 8 June 1939 Lion assembled a hand-picked group consisting of trumpeter Frankie Newton (whose band was playing a residency at the newly opened Café Society in New York), Newton's bass player, Johnny Williams, pianist Meade 'Lux' Lewis, guitarist Teddy Bunn, trombonist J. C. Higginbotham, and two Sidneys – Bechet and Catlett (whose drumming was featured on almost every Blue Note session for the next five years).

Bechet had what might be called a 'joshing' relationship with trumpeter Newton. The two men were different in many ways. Newton, towering almost a foot above Bechet, was deeply interested in politics and often propounded left-wing views. Sidney nodded a lot when such discussions took place but never showed any real interest, and often made bystanders laugh by sarcastically commenting on every politician, living or dead. Newton took these ripostes in good part. He was not frightened of Bechet, and got his own back by gently asking Sidney, in mock innocence, for an eye-witness account of some event that happened long before the Civil War. The two men respected each other's musicianship, but somehow they never blended into a memorable front-line coupling.

Bass player Johnny Williams first met both men when they were jamming together at one of the 'Breakfast Dances' that were held at Small's Paradise every Monday morning, beginning at 3 a.m. Subsequently Williams played on several private jobs with Newton and Bechet, including wedding parties. He enjoyed the experience and said of Bechet: "He would kid around with you at times and later he'd get angry. He was 'a moody one' but my association was always nice and it was a pleasure to work with him. At that time some musicians would say he was old fashioned, but not after the Blue Note recordings."[18]

When the participants assembled for the Blue Note session the atmosphere was tinged with sadness: Tommy Ladnier had died four days earlier. Billed as the Port of Harlem Seven, the group settled down to record a tribute entitled *Blues for Tommy*. If only the heart-felt mood created by Bechet's opening phrases could have been maintained, the valediction might have been a worthy one. The main theme, which is devoid of poignancy, is partly to blame. Bechet's wailing soprano saxophone solo is rich in feeling, but Lewis's piano playing sounds uncommitted and Newton (who rarely hit his best form on a blues sequence) meanders, first high and then low. In contrast, Bunn on guitar produces stark patterns that sound eminently appropriate. Higginbotham's burnished trombone shouts are bold and passionate and should have served to fire a memorable last chorus; instead a muddle occurs in which each member of the front line tries to find 'air' by rising to his top note. Higginbotham wins the battle by ending on a powerfully blown high tonic F.

Bunn's evocative introduction on guitar aptly sets the mood for one of Bechet's most celebrated recordings, *Summertime*. Sidney, on saxophone, first produces a subdued rendering of the tune, then (after inserting a snippet from his old favourite *I Pagliacci*) creates four magnificent choruses full of diverse variations. Bunn takes the role of principal accompanist, and in the third chorus stresses the melody in a way that adds even more vividness to Bechet's improvisations; Williams and Catlett play quiet, subsidiary roles and Lewis's piano is inaudible. A series of highly dramatic phrases lead inexorably into a clamactic final chorus which is packed with boldly played 'unexpected' notes that are extensions of the basic chord sequence. Catlett's press rolls add to the heightened mood, which is perfectly resolved by Bechet's final upward glissando.

Alfred Lion had placed no restrictions on the way that Bechet performed *Summertime*. Whereas RCA Victor had fought shy of a five-chorus soprano saxophone solo, Lion encouraged the bold idea. It paid off and provided the Blue Note company with its first success – a small one in national terms, but big in view of the size both of the jazz market and of the record (a 12-inch 78 r.p.m., which generally sold fewer copies than the more usual 10-inch issue).

Summertime was labelled as being by the Sidney Bechet Quintet, so the star of the performance received the publicity that was due to him. Frankie Newton was not in the best of health at the time of this session (he had not long returned from recuperating in Hot Springs, Arkansas), so he was quite willing for Bechet to take over the group for part of the date. This was not a normal session with leader and sidemen, so no ill feelings resulted. Teddy Bunn told writer Peter Tanner how much he enjoyed making the Blue Note recordings: "They were just informal jam sessions, drinks were provided and except for a time limit the musicians scarcely knew that they were being recorded."[19]

The full septet recorded *Pounding Heart Blues*, which bursts into life with a scintillating break from trombonist Higginbotham. Newton's opening chorus again reveals his anomalous approach to the blues. Higginbotham remains characteristically assertive in his chorus, benefitting from the rugged power engendered by Catlett, Williams and Bunn, but the efforts of these three rhythm men do not seem to suit Lewis's piano playing and he again sounds well below his best. Sidney's clarinet solo is both forceful and ingenious and his linking of fake-fingerings and 'lippings' produce eerie, penetrating blue notes. The ensemble fails to muster an appropriate final chorus. Despite the rhythm section's stimulating triplet figure and the vigour of the front line, nothing substantial emerges.

When the 18-hour session had finished – at 9 a.m. – Bechet and Alfred Lion strolled along Third Avenue and went into a small delicatessen for breakfast. They sat down in the minuscule back section of the restaurant, which was stacked high with rolls of toilet paper. Bechet turned to Lion and said, "Well Alfred, we're really in the shit-house now."[20] Fortunately this was not the case; the issue of *Summertime* marked the turning-point in Lion's life and became, in his own words, his "first little hit". One critic, George Frazier, complained about the high price ($1.50) of the record, but in general the coupling *Summertime/Pounding Heart Blues* was greeted with favour. It even gained (what was then a rare distinction) a glowing review by the influential critic Deems Taylor in the *New York Times*.

Soon after the Blue Note session Bechet heard about prospects of regular work: auditions were being held for a band to fill a summer booking. Bechet rounded up a group of young musicians and secured the job, which was for a season at the Spruceland Inn in Stamford, New York. Bechet's quartet (Sonny Williams on piano, Eddie Price on string bass, and Stubby Sebastian on drums) played there from 1 July until 2 September 1939.

Six days after that season ended the same group, sometimes billed as Sidney Bechet's Feetwarmers, sometimes as Sidney Bechet and his Decca Recording Orchestra, began a new residency at the Log Cabin roadhouse on Route 5 (situated six miles west of Fonda, New York). Advertisements for the opening on Friday 8 September announced: "Bechet, the World's Hottest Soprano Sax

Player Will Please Music Lovers and Swing Fans Throughout the Mohawk Valley". Sidney lived up to that promise and soon the club owner added a Sunday afternoon matinée performance to the band's schedule. Charlie Howard, who specialized on guitar but also played trumpet, joined the group during its season at the Log Cabin.

During his first week at the Log Cabin Sidney made the journey down to New York to take part in a recording session for Victor which was led by the legendary pianist, composer and bandleader Ferdinand 'Jelly Roll' Morton. Morton was even lower down on his luck than Bechet, but his outward mood reflected cheerful confidence as he gathered an all-star line-up in his attempt to regain the glories that he had known in the 1920s. Stephen W. Smith, who ran the Hot Record Society (which had its own record shop in New York and its own magazine, the *HRS Rag*), was called in by RCA Victor to help organize this momentous session on 14 September 1939. The session started at 1.30 p.m., but as Sidney had to journey from Fonda it was agreed that he could arrive late; he duly made his entrance and was warmly welcomed by Morton.

Frederic Ramsey, Jr, who wrote the notes for the session, said: "Jelly seemed to know him [Bechet] pretty well and to realize just the proper amount of discipline necessary to get the best work out of him as well as the other members of the band." Steve Smith recalls that Morton went out of his way to be helpful to the late-comer, and quickly spotted the look of apprehension that crossed Bechet's face when he saw that written arrangements were being used: "Bechet, who was known not to read picked up his part and was making a good pretence of reading it. Jelly, who was sitting at the piano and watching him, yelled, 'Sid, you remember how it goes, don't you?', all the while playing Bechet's part on the piano and Sidney who was a quick student and had one of the keenest ears in the whole jazz world listened and said, 'Oh sure, I remember'."[21] Morton summarized this incident by saying of Bechet, "He plays more music than you can put down on paper."[22]

The musicians were placed on platforms of various heights, and initially New Orleans protocol also kept some of them apart. According to Frederic Ramsey, Jr, "Sidney didn't go right over and sit down besides Nicholas [clarinettist Albert Nicholas]. Jelly whispered to us, 'I know the two should be together but they won't like it if *I* tell them'. Sure enough, after the boys had rehearsed a bit one of the engineers came out and suggested that Bechet and Nicholas stand together on a platform directly under the mike. So it was arranged."[23]

The session began with a version of the New Orleans funeral theme *Oh didn't he ramble*, which, as per tradition, was prefaced by Mary Dana's solemn composition *Flee as a Bird*. On the first take (which remained unissued until the microgroove era) there was hesitancy among some of the musicians, particularly trumpeter Sidney De Paris, when playing the middle theme. On this same first take, trombonist Claude Jones, who was given the job of preaching the valediction, says, "If the women don't get you, the liquor must." On the second, generally issued, take, however, he specifies that the potentially fatal brew is "whisky". After Jones's speech there is much wailing from the musicians, acting their role as mourners; then the trumpeter's single rallying note ushers in a break from Zutty Singleton, whose drums provide an invigorating pulse for the subsequent trumpet-led ensemble. Bechet takes the lead for the next 16 bars, then hands over to De Paris, who provides a fiercely growled lead. As the lead shifts to and fro, the sound of Morton's piano playing emerges clearly, but he doesn't play a solo; in fact, his role throughout the date is more one of bandmaster.

The recording of *Oh didn't he ramble* represented the jazz world's growing fascination with the customs and history of New Orleans. The band's next item, *High Society*, also had close links with the Crescent City. Wellman Braud, the bass player in the session, stressed the tune's importance: "It wasn't a dance in New Orleans till they played *High Society*."[24] The set clarinet solo (in the middle section of the tune) has long been regarded as something of a test piece, and its inclusion has become almost obligatory. Steve Smith could see trouble looming over which of the two reedmen (Nicholas or Bechet) was to play the solo, and he side-stepped trouble neatly by having them both do it: "Knowing Bechet's penchant for not allowing anyone to cut him, I craftily had him play a chorus on the sax and then had Albert Nicholas follow with a chorus on the clarinet. At that, I think Albert made the finest rendition of the clarinet chorus ever recorded."[25]

Nicholas also plays delightfully during the opening ensemble, but Claude Jones on trombone seems irresolute and Bechet, except for his flowing 32-bar solo, sounds subdued. Morton himself suffers badly from the recording balance and is only heard in the distance. The lack of prominence for the piano is a disappointment of the session, but fortunately Morton's vocal part comes through sweet and clear on another New Orleans anthem, *I thought I heard Buddy Bolden say*. Guitarist Lawrence Lucie makes his presence felt during the introduction, and then Morton takes over for two choruses with his inimitable and perfectly phrased singing, expounding the doings of the legendary trumpeter. Bechet, on saxophone, leans on the melody during his 16-bar solo, but introduces some spiky variations, particularly the octave jump in bar 12. Claude Jones makes amends for his previous lethargy by playing a brilliant solo, so good it even pleased its diffident creator, who, when asked about his recorded solos, replied, "I don't like any of them much. I did my best work with Don Redman's Band. I guess I like that *Buddy Bolden* side as good as any."[26] Sidney De Paris's tightly muted solo is brief but magical. Morton referred to De Paris's muted effects as "coughing", but chose to back the catarrhal sounds with supportive delicacy. There is no hint of telepathy in the front line's playing of the final chorus, but neither is there a sign of chaos. Bechet releases a flamboyant run in the fifth bar, but for the most part plays restrained backing notes.

The melody instruments blend well on *Winin' Boy*. Their introduction launches the tenor saxophonist Albert 'Happy' Caldwell on his task of playing the lovely melody; his technique creaks a little but overall the effect is not unpleasant, and the rhythm section backs him admirably. Claude Jones performs the melody more eloquently than Caldwell, and his sound is supplemented by Bechet playing a rich obbligato. Morton again proves that he was one of the greatest of all jazz vocalists by singing two deeply felt choruses (ably backed by De Paris on trumpet). De Paris is a model of relaxation during the final ensemble, but even the *élan* of his lead playing cannot hide the fact that the ensemble fails to move gracefully; Bechet again chooses not to push against the wall of congested sound. Two similar takes of this item were issued, and the second has a little more spark and presence. The delightful trombone and soprano saxophone duet on *Winin' Boy* was inspired by music that Stephen Smith had heard a year before the session with Morton took place. Smith explained:

> It was quiet Monday nite at Nick's in the Village with Bechet's Trio (Zutty Singleton, drums, Wellman Braud, bass), playing to an empty house except for my wife Lee and I, and Nick Rongetti sitting at our table relaxing after a hard week-end. In walks Jack Teagarden and his wife, they took a table right next to the Trio and listened for awhile. Then Jack went outside to his car and came back with his trombone. Sitting at his table with his elbow resting on its top he played a duet with Bechet for more than an hour, the Trio not even stopping to take a break. Lee, I and Nick heard some of the most beautiful and inspired music that I am sorry to say the world will never hear. The voices of the trombone and soprano sax stayed with me, so that when I was doing the Jelly Roll Morton sides for Victor I had Jelly put in a spot for Claude Jones, trombone, and Bechet on sax.[27]

Despite minor shortcomings, Morton's session provided a good deal of fine jazz, and Morton himself proved that he was still a very capable music director. A certain amount of tension developed in the studio, partly caused by the problems of paring down a lengthy version of *Buddy Bolden* to the time limits of a 10-inch 78 r.p.m. disc. According to Zutty Singleton, Sidney eased things with a quip. Morton asked Bechet good humouredly about the unexpected octave jump that he had inserted in his solo by saying, "What was that little thing you made?" Bechet replied, "That was that funky air going out underneath the window."[28] But personal animosity between Morton and De Paris began to make itself obvious during the session. Jelly Roll (in a letter to a friend) subsequently described the trumpeter's attitude as being "hateful as could be".[29] It was also rumoured that Zutty Singleton and Bechet were not overjoyed with each other's company on the date. For whatever reason, Sidney chose not to make the journey down from Fonda for the follow-up session a fortnight later.

THIRTEEN

The Jazz Revival

During the latter part of his season in Fonda, Bechet again travelled into Manhattan for a recording session. This time it was to lead the Haitian Orchestra for the Variety label on 22 November 1939. The pianist was Willie 'the Lion' Smith, the string bass player Olin Alderhold, the drummer Leo Warney, and the trumpeter Kenneth Roane (who also wrote the arrangements). It was the most bizarre recording date of Bechet's career, in that all of the tunes were Latin-American themes, several exemplifying the music of Haiti. Almost every item was strictly arranged with little or no scope for improvisation. Bechet had a pronounced interest in music from various regions of the world and had become fascinated by some 'field' recordings made by Haitian reed players. Years earlier Willie 'the Lion' Smith and Duke Ellington had discussed, with admiration, various aspects of Haitian music. It was conceivable that Smith had mentioned these talks to Bechet, for the latter certainly went out of his way to ask Smith to play on the date. According to the pianist, Bechet met him on St Nicholas Avenue (Bechet lived at no. 783, Apt. B), and said, "We should make some West Indian records because everyone is laughing and enjoying the calypso songs."[1]

After some painstaking rehearsals the group committed a total of 14 titles to wax, most of them rumbas and meringues. Except for brief solo interludes for bass, drums and piano, the arrangements feature the two front-line instrumentalists playing a harmonized version of the melody, not always immaculately. In his autobiography *Music on my Mind*, Willie 'the Lion' Smith said: "The album was good musically but no one bought it. We were just about twenty years early." Most jazz reviewers were nonplussed by the recordings. However, musicologist Ernest Bornemann praised the session, saying that it was "the first deliberate reunion of jazz and Afro-Spanish folk music in history".[2] The oddest aspect of the date is that Bechet didn't make use of his skills as an improviser; dozens of other reedmen in New York could probably have done the Haitian date as satisfactorily as he did. It was a bold experiment, but Sidney chose not to include any of the songs in his regular repertoire, and in later years showed no interest in discussing the session.

The season at the Log Cabin in Fonda had not gone as smoothly as Bechet had hoped. The proprietor of the club, Allen Armstrong, wanted to negotiate a new contract with Bechet at a reduced fee. Bechet was angry at the suggestion but became furious when he discovered that the rhythm section was preparing to sign a new contract with Armstrong that excluded Sidney. Bechet promptly fired the players and went into New York to find replacements. He returned with pianist Ellerton 'Sonny' White and his young cousin, Kenny Clarke, who played drums and vibraphone. Wilson Ernest 'Serious' Myers (a former member of Bechet's Feetwarmers) joined on string bass and Charlie Howard (who doubled on amplified guitar and trumpet) remained, being the sole survivor of the earlier group.

When the Log Cabin contract ended in January 1940 Bechet's quintet played a brief residency at a club in Johnstown, New York, which was run by a former musician, Saxie Marshall. Bechet stayed nearby in lodgings on Wills Street, Gloversville. By February 1940 the group was back in New York, where Bechet made his peace with Nick Rongetti and effected a truce with Zutty Singleton. As a result (from Sunday 18 February 1940) Bechet's quintet alternated with Singleton's sextet (which featured Albert Nicholas on clarinet) at Nick's Tavern.

During 1940 Bechet played in several sessions organized by Harry Lim, who booked Nick's as a venue for his Sunday afternoon clambakes. Lim, who had arrived from his homeland of Java a year earlier, soon established himself as an authority on jazz and a good friend of jazz musicians. He has always regretted not having recorded Bechet: "I met Bechet at Nick's. When I started the Sunday session there he always played for me. He and Zutty were always fighting: about tempos, tunes, money, you name it. Yet the old man played the most beautiful blues, both slow and fast. One blues for the whole half-hour set. We all used to cry, including Bud Freeman and Max Kaminsky. Also the old man had a drive and power you never heard in anybody's playing. If you had Red Allen and Bechet in the band you know you had plain sailing."[3] Lim's gatherings were certainly star-studded. For example, the two pianists who shared duties on his session at Nick's on 17 March 1940 were James P. Johnson and Jelly Roll Morton.[4]

In his dealings with Harry Lim, Bechet showed his penchant for allocating people a nickname: he always called him "Mr Jim". Harry remembers one of Sidney's regular requests: "Mr Jim, I need your Shuick and twenty dollars this weekend to see my girl in Connecticut" (the Shuick was Lim's Buick). The Connecticut affair was only one of several that Bechet was carrying on. He was, however, still married to Marilouise, whose reaction to Sidney's romantic escapades was described by an onlooker: "She was taller than he, light-skinned, unemotional to the point of vagueness, attractive, not jealous of his other ladies. I never heard them quarrel. I'm sure she didn't know she was married to a genius."

The revival of interest in the origins of jazz grew swiftly during 1940. Record companies, keenly aware of sales tendencies – even in minority markets – not only stepped up the issue of jazz recordings by contemporary bands but also began dusting off old master-pressings so that they could organize regular reissues from the so-called Golden Era of the 1920s.

Bechet's output of recordings in the 1920s was numerically smaller than that of other reed players such as Buster Bailey and Don Redman, but during the early days of the 'jazz revival' the balance swung Sidney's way; his talents were featured in a number of celebrated and historic sessions, among them epic encounters with the cornetist Muggsy Spanier and with the trumpeter Louis Armstrong.

Spanier (a great admirer of Tommy Ladnier's work) had been one of the stalwarts of the white Chicago jazz scene during the 1920s. In the same way as Bechet had 'buried' himself in Noble Sissle's band, so Spanier spent most of the 1930s working in Ted Lewis's orchestra. He reverted to small-band work in 1939, leading his Ragtimers, which recorded 16 fine titles for Bluebird before disbanding through lack of work. Pairing Spanier with Bechet was another of Stephen Smith's ideas. Smith recalls the background to the dates in 1940:

> Bechet was in the habit of dropping in at the HRS record shop so we saw each other quite often. I was inspired by the French Swing label recordings of the quartet of Django Reinhardt, Rex Stewart, Barney Bigard and Billy Taylor. But my plan was to use men who would give an older, more traditional flavor. Muggsy Spanier had recently arrived in New York. His lip was not in perfect shape but he would try to do his best (his lips were bleeding at the end of the first session). Carmen Mastren, a great guitarist and fine arranger was in town and would sketch out some intros, bridges and endings. Wellman Braud was in and out of the shop and was a sentimental favorite of mine. I picked out some tunes for a variety of tempos. All four men were such consummate, workmanlike musicians that we had no incidents on the date.[5]

Late in his life, bass player Wellman Braud, a vastly experienced musician not given to hyperbole, described the Bechet–Spanier Big Four sides as "the best four-piece recordings ever made".[6] Guitarist Carmen Mastren was only too happy to be reminded of the date:

> I had played alongside Sidney Bechet at various jam sessions, but I had never worked regularly with him, or travelled with him, or with Muggsy Spanier, so I didn't know either of them socially, and I didn't know Wellman Braud at all. The thing that struck me was the attitude of these musicians. I was part of what might be called the swing world, usually playing in big bands. Either the bandleader or the arranger gave you a sort of pep talk. This could sometimes produce inspired performances, or create tenseness, or horseplay or even ill feeling. But the session with Bechet and company was entirely different. Bechet and Braud arrived wearing big old coats and hats; I think Bechet had a beret on. They sat down opposite one another and exchanged pleasantries. It was like an ancient ritual between chieftains. Muggsy joined in whilst he was warming up – same sort of approach. Being used to the razzmatazz that I've mentioned, I wondered what was going to happen: one, two, three, four, and wham! This music explodes all around me.[7]

The group's first session on 28 March 1940 began with a delightfully unified version of *Four or Five Times*, heralded by a pretty introduction that is shared by Bechet and Spanier. The feeling of accord is plainly apparent during the first chorus as Bechet's soprano saxophone plies apt counter-phrases to Spanier's ripe lead; after a fast change to clarinet Bechet creates a series of fascinating paraphrases. Spanier's elegant muted solo is embroidered with his expressive 'shakes' at the end of the phrases. Subsequently Bechet (back on saxophone) joins the cornetist for a series of spontaneous call-and-answer phrases which beckon a chordal solo from guitarist Mastren. After an ultra-relaxed ensemble passage the group wraps things up by repeating the attractive opening figure.

Sweet Lorraine is also full of charm and skills. Spanier phrases the slow opening melody almost without embellishment, relying on tone and feeling for effect. In turn, Bechet also remains faithful to the composer's tune, but occasionally clips a line or expands one; the rich sound of Braud's bowed bass carpets the bright chording of the guitar. The final chorus is a model of give and take, full of a non-cloying, fragile sweetness. On *Lazy River* Bechet's clarinet sounds full and voluptuous, both in his solo and in the mosaic he improvises against Spanier's muted lead. Spanier's solo doesn't reach the Olympian heights of his colleague, but the cornetist shows that the inclusion of well-placed minor-third blue notes can enhance apparently simple phrasing.

Carmen Mastren's comment about a musical explosion seems hard to understand until one hears the group's version of *China Boy*, the apotheosis of the quartet's achievements. Muggsy's forthright phrasing adheres firmly to the melody, allowing Bechet space to weave a daringly rhythmic decoration. Sidney's soprano saxophone solo begins with some effortlessly played legato phrases which give way to brisk on-the-beat lines. The dynamics of his second chorus are majestically controlled, so too are the solo's contours, which peak at exactly the right moments, highlighting the player's innate sense of musical form. A multitude of Bechet's tonal shadings are apparent here, ranging from growls and near honks to light filigree hums. Spanier never sounded truly relaxed when playing solos at a fast tempo, but his tenseness here somehow adds to the growing excitement. He resumes his terse lead whilst Bechet garlands the cornetist's phrases with cascades of ornamental runs. Just at the point where it seems a climax is inevitable the group gathers momentum and moves into a final chorus of unfaltering ebullience. A second take embracing the same format, but with markedly different solos, almost matches the team work and inspiration of the first attempt.

On 6th April the quartet reconvened for a session that was almost as brilliant as the first. *If I could be with you* has Bechet, on saxophone, presenting a series of near-romantic musings, but he cleverly changes the mood by playing a husky mid-chorus break. A guitar solo (which includes some graceful single-string work) is backed by long plaintive notes from Bechet's clarinet, then Bechet and Spanier combine to play a thoughtful final chorus, each musician sounding respectful of his partner's efforts, yet neither playing with untoward restraint.

A brisk sense of urgency fills the opening bars of a pulsating version of *That's a plenty*. Sidney, on clarinet, plays a harmony part that follows the contours of Muggsy's lead, but soon branches out to create some lively polyphony. Every nuance of his compelling clarinet tone is captured during the first bridge passage. Spanier plays the second bridge open, then swiftly inserts a small straight mute for the follow-up phrases before applying the plunger for the succeeding phrases. He goes on to produce a warm, song-like chorus, which contains segments of a melody that sounds amazingly like *I wanna be like you*, a popular song written some years later. Both the first and the longer second take are magnificent.

Spanier is at his most engaging on *Squeeze me*. The mood throughout radiates amiability and Bechet makes no attempt to whip up any undue excitement. Mastren's solo, and his guitar runs in the coda, underline his relaxed consistency. The quartet, by now irrepressible, enlivens a medium-tempo version of *Sweet Sue*, playing it first in two-beat style, then moving emphatically into four in a bar. Spanier's usual drive is apparent, and, even though he doesn't sound enormously inspired, all Bechet's phrases link together so purposefully that even familiar ideas take on a fresh dimension. A series of shared breaks between Bechet and Spanier complete both the piece and a brace of sessions that produced one masterpiece, *China Boy*, and seven other outstanding tracks.

Wellman Braud also took part in the recorded reunion that Sidney Bechet and Louis Armstrong shared in May 1940. The music from that historic session didn't achieve the exuberance, or the charm, of the Spanier–Bechet recordings, but it was full of intriguing moments. There was no guarantee that the rematching of the two giants would produce the sort of epic music that they had effortlessly created 15 years earlier, but both men were still in the prime of their musical lives, and each of them was renowned for his stamina and consistency. Everything looked promising. Braud and Zutty Singleton were certain to provide a solid keel, Addison on guitar was steady and accurate, and trombonist Claude Jones, whilst not a small-band specialist, was technically gifted and the possessor of perfect pitch. The one slight doubt concerned the choice of Luis Russell as pianist. Russell was a highly effective bandleader, but his tendency to lose, or gain, tempo disqualified him from being an automatic swinger. But in their sessions in 1924 Bechet and Armstrong had worked with Clarence Williams on piano, who was no more gifted at the keyboard than Russell, and the results had been a resounding success. (Clarence Williams actually attended the later session in his role as publisher of songs used on the date.)

The Bechet–Armstrong reunion has been analyzed on many occasions. Most critics regard the results as disappointing, but perhaps everyone, including the participants, was expecting too much. Few musical reunions recapture the fertile atmosphere of the original sessions. Years later Bechet blamed Louis Armstrong for altering the routines after the tunes had been rehearsed, but no one else in the session ever mentioned such a drama. It is possible, and even probable, that Bechet was referring to a later get-together that he and Louis shared in 1945. As Bechet had a reputation for following the most intricate routines with the utmost ease, it is surprising that he was flummoxed no matter what had happened; furthermore, the second takes from the date reveal no radical changes of plan. Bechet's comments were made long after the session, and during the interim his feelings towards Louis had cooled.

Charles Edward Smith, who was at the recording session, told Bill Russell that a happy spirit prevailed throughout the date, and that Armstrong, behaving as per the custom of New Orleans musicians, was deferential to any of Bechet's suggestions on the grounds of Sidney's seniority. Participant Bernard Addison described the atmosphere in the studio as "distinctly harmonious, particularly between Louis and Sidney", and, although Zutty Singleton is said to have refused to discuss the session with Barney Bigard, he did tell his friend Robert Lewis that he thought the date produced "some of the greatest recordings ever made in jazz".

One person who felt left out of things was trombonist Claude Jones, who said, "I was the only one who wasn't from New Orleans"[8], though actually Luis Russell was only raised in New Orleans and Bernard Addison was from Maryland. Jones also said, "Everybody except me knew all the tunes they were playing, but Louis

Armstrong said, 'Don't worry about it. You'll do alright'."⁹ He went on: "Louis and Bechet were in peak form that day, but the recording manager just wore me down. He kept coming out of his sound-proof box and shouting, 'Give that horn more tailgate, Jones, more tailgate', and he got me so mad in the end that I messed up my solo in *Down in Honky Tonk Town*."¹⁰

On *Perdido Street Blues* the band revives the format that graced the New Orleans Wanderers' recording of 1926, which gives immediate prominence to the incisive sound of Bechet's clarinet playing. After a series of supercharged phrases from Bechet, Louis Armstrong, blowing with profundity and power, establishes the first main theme. Bechet improvises a heartfelt chorus, the swinging flow of which contrasts sharply with Luis Russell's stiffly executed piano solo. Addison's guitar work sounds forthright, and he gives way to a slightly flustered Claude Jones; in the background Bechet plays quietly on the soprano saxophone, but quickly reverts to clarinet during a one-bar drum fill-in. Clarinet and trombone create a backing riff that cushions the force of Armstrong's three architectural choruses. Bechet plays an apt four-bar tag that is full of decisive blue notes. The session was off to a fine start.

The group's version of *2:19 Blues* suffers from the time restrictions of the 78 r.p.m. era, and there is no opportunity for Armstrong and Bechet to play solos of any length at such a slow tempo. After an ensemble chorus Louis Armstrong sings warmly, the sound of his voice being nicely complemented by Luis Russell's treble-register tremolos and the subtle fill-ins created by Jones and Bechet. Bechet's soprano saxophone solo is powerfully delivered but somehow conveys a feeling of duress. Armstrong restores the equilibrium with his phrasing of the closing theme, but there is no obvious denouement.

Down in Honky Tonk Town was not an ideal vehicle for a Bechet–Armstrong reunion, simply because the tune itself does not allow gaps for the sort of counter-melody that Bechet liked to improvise. Armstrong fulfils his task admirably by sticking to the theme, but he ingeniously cocoons each phrase of the verse and the chorus with an amazing rhythmic impetus. Beneath the trumpet lead, trombonist Jones plays a series of hopeful glissandos; Bechet's thrusts provide a spasmodic counterpoint, but overall there isn't much musical empathy. Bechet's main contribution is his 32-bar solo, in which he creates a mood of urgency but not many momentous phrases. Jones and Addison construct smooth-sounding solos, then the band, after playing stop-time chords that punctuate Singleton's agile drum feature, picks up on the last eight bars of his chorus. Armstrong instantly moves away from the melody and in doing so dominates the exact territory that Bechet usually occupied in culminating situations.

Armstrong did not take his chosen course of action deliberately to spite Bechet; he was simply playing in what had become his natural small-band style. On fast numbers this was busier and more in the upper register than his earlier work with the Hot Fives and Hot Sevens, but it still contained all the unique attributes that had so distinguished his previous performances. By 1940 the trumpeter was well on his way to creating the style that became the vital component in the music of the All Stars.

Singleton, Russell and Jones dropped out of the final number so that Bechet and Armstrong could work in the quartet format that had proved so successful on the Bechet–Spanier date, but unfortunately the Bechet–Armstrong foursome does not achieve the same rapport. Even so, Armstrong's phrasing of the attractive first theme is wonderfully expressive, and Bechet's counter-melody is clever without being distracting. The two musicians combine effortlessly on the equally lovely second theme, then Louis uses his vocal skills to triumph over some indifferent lyrics. The closing cadenzas are allocated to Bechet, who phrases them with grandeur.

If the session was a failure, it was a glorious one, and many bands would have loved to have created jazz of such durable standards. The results were not as homogeneous as might have been expected, but this was because both Bechet and Armstrong had become jazz supremos. In achieving this status each man had moved away from the ensemble role he had filled to perfection in earlier days.

In late 1939, while Bechet's group was working at the Log Cabin in Fonda, it was visited by a record company executive, John Reid, who later became one of Bechet's closest friends. Reid, then 32 years old, worked for RCA Victor; he was also a devoted admirer of Bechet's playing and was determined to get his company interested in recording Sidney's group. He took mobile recording equipment to Fonda, where Bechet and a quartet recorded 'audition' titles that were submitted to Leonard Joy, the recently promoted Manager of Artistes and Repertoire at the company. These performances (later issued by NEC Plus Ultra in France) show the group in a careful mood, but there are some very fine tracks, including a brief, spirited version of *Limehouse Blues* and a fascinating clarinet and guitar duet on *Mood Indigo*.

Leonard Joy, who had led his own orchestra during the early 1930s, saw the group's potential and offered Bechet a recording contract. The first session covered by this agreement took place on 5 February 1940, and featured the line-up that had played the final stages of the booking in Fonda: Bechet, White, Howard, Myers and Clarke. The musicians were used to working together, and their compatibility is obvious on *Indian Summer*. Bechet pours his heart into Victor Herbert's lush melody, and then launches into variations that radiate passion and bravura. Sonny White's piano solo reveals his admiration for Teddy Wilson's work, though he never quite achieves Wilson's *élan* or matches his technique. Bechet steps forward again and plays a stirring final chorus. The number became one of Sidney's 'set-pieces'.

White's sturdy left hand distinguishes the opening piano chorus on *One O'Clock Jump*; he modulates and Sidney enters on clarinet, sounding eager and inspired. Howard, on guitar, takes over and produces some efficiently played standard 'licks', then the full line-up moves into top gear to produce a finale that could be called the *One O'Clock Stomp*. Clarke's imaginative drum work gained him a place amongst the first modern percussionists. He later spoke about this period of his life: "Drummers were hung up with the feeling that they had to keep a steady 4/4 rhythm going all the time. I wanted to punctuate, to make the music more interesting. There was quite a bit of opposition to my ideas. My reason for shifting the rhythmic emphasis to the cymbal from the bass drum was so that I could hear and understand the soloists much better."[11]

The session ended with two blues, the first a medium-paced 'sermon' delivered by bass player Wilson Myers called *Preachin' the Blues*, which has Bechet in authoritative mood on soprano saxophone, particularly during the emphatic concluding riffs. In contrast, *Sidney's Blues* is slow, and features a vocal by Bechet; it also contains some superbly strident clarinet playing. This number, which had been a big favourite with the audiences at Fonda, is sung in a conversational style that borders on recitative. The earthy abandon of the clarinet work is memorable and Bechet's tone is beautifully captured by the recording (bearing out Duke Ellington's view that Bechet on clarinet had "the world's greatest wood tone").[12] The other star of the session is Wilson 'Serious' Myers, who plays superbly throughout, occasionally picking up his bow to create an effect that sounds like the purring of a contented tiger.

The fine music on these four sides encouraged the RCA Victor officials to map out a systematic plan for the 24 titles that Bechet was contracted to record for them. Besides having Bechet record in a quartet with Jelly Roll Morton, the plans included sessions with Lionel Hampton, Erskine Hawkins, Charlie Barnet, Tommy Dorsey, Wingy Manone, Fats Waller and Duke Ellington. The original RCA memo on this subject suggested that the two sides with Ellington should be *Rent Party Blues* and *The Sheik of Araby*, "or preferably two Ellington originals written to feature Bechet".[13]

Unfortunately none of these potentially fascinating sessions ever took place. By the early months of 1940 the jazz 'revival' had moved a stage nearer and more people were asking for recordings of 'authentic' jazz, by which they usually meant a line-up of trumpet, trombone and clarinet playing material from yesteryear. RCA Victor was in business to sell records, so naturally went with the market trend; thus the majority of Bechet's recordings for the company featured a traditional line-up (though Bechet did play soprano saxophone on several occasions). Sidney was originally encouraged to record tunes associated with the 1920s, but later, in an effort to tap the juke-box market, he made various novelty themes. At the very time that Bechet was to be recorded in contexts worthy of his talents as a star soloist, a revival of interest in the music that he had played such a part in creating denied him his big chance.

In general Bechet was delighted to observe the growing interest in the music of his home city. He might have had love-hate relationships with many of his fellow New Orleanians, but he was always quick to defend them and to praise their talents to others. He was also glad to help the compilers of the book *Jazzmen*, an early monumental study of jazz history and its personalities. The work (which was originally published in October 1939) was edited by Charles Edward Smith and Frederic Ramsey, Jr, with chapters by Otis Ferguson, Wilder Hobson and William Russell (who was to become the doyen of jazz historians).

Before Bechet's contract with RCA Victor came into effect he recorded several sides for Blue Note, amongst them an unusual coupling on which he and bass player Wilson Myers accompanied the blues singer and guitarist Josh White. Bechet (on clarinet) sounds almost reticent behind the vocal part on *Careless Love*, but he adopts his usual bold approach during his solo. He sets out on soprano saxophone for *Milk Cow Blues* but, sensing that White's guitar backings could cause tuning problems, swiftly changes to clarinet and plays some restrained but inimitable backing phrases.

Restraint also marks *Lonesome Blues* (a composition by Louis Armstrong), one of four titles Bechet recorded with Teddy Bunn on guitar, George 'Pops' Foster on string bass, and Sid Catlett on drums. It is not one of Sidney's broader performances, but it contains a steady flow of episodic blues ideas. The recording is a little unkind to the group, never conveying a unified sound; Sidney's clarinet tone is piping when he plays in the upper register. Bechet performs on saxophone for *Dear Old Southland*, a tune he recorded several times; this is his least dramatic presentation of the song, and he views it in a mellow light. Bunn's chord sequence sounds a little more basic than it should have been, and unhappily his inversions and Foster's bass notes do not blend well.

The group swings effortlessly through the medium-tempo blues *Bechet's Steady Rider*. Sidney's clarinet work has an attractive swagger and mobility; Bunn's guitar solo is eloquent and his backing here is pert and appropriate. The group sounds even better on *Saturday Night Blues*, an evocative eight-bar sequence that inspires a moving clarinet exposition; Catlett's rocking, off-beat drumming forms the basis of the formidable swing. Like everything on the date this performance was aimed more at the jazz connoisseur than the general public.

Bechet's booking at Nick's Tavern ended in May 1940. During the last weeks of his stay acrimony entered the group that had played together since the residency at Fonda. Sidney was not well paid for leading the band, but the sidemen's wages were downright poor (often less than 30 dollars a week). One by one the grumbling musicians left to work in better-paid jobs or in more congenial surroundings. A whole string of temporary players came in to perform with Bechet during his final weeks at Nick's: guitarist Charlie Howard was replaced by Bernard Addison, whose place was soon taken by Jimmy McLin, and so on, throughout the group.

Bechet decided to form a new band consisting of George Thigpen (who had worked in big bands led by Walter Barnes and Rex Stewart) on trumpet, Bernard Addison on guitar, Marlowe Morris on piano, Ernest Hill on bass, and Toby Grace on drums. As soon as this group was organized Bechet changed his mind about leading it, and decided instead to spend the summer working as a freelance from his home at 783 St Nicholas Avenue.

During this period he encountered an ex-colleague from Clarence Williams's band who had joined a religious sect. Bechet related the anecdote to Wynne Paris during a radio interview: "I happened to be walking down 132nd Street near Seventh Avenue when I saw Thomas Morris, and I was tickled to death to see him. I say, 'Hello Thomas.' He said, 'Not no more. I'm St Peter.' I said, 'You might be St Peter to Father Divine, but you're Thomas Morris to me.'"[14]

One of the most memorable freelance dates that Bechet ever played took place in May 1940, when he was reunited with his old clarinet teacher, George Baquet. In February 1940 Bechet was elected Honorary President of the Philadelphia Hot Club; he had played at the club's inaugural session, "exhausting the musicians accompanying him".[15] For a return visit (on 26 May 1940) Bechet took his own, more resilient, accompanists: Wellman Braud, Zutty Singleton, Willie 'the Lion' Smith and Sidney De Paris. During the band's Sunday afternoon session at the Hot Club (held at the Mayfair Hall, near Camden, New Jersey), they were visited by George Baquet, who made an emotional speech that paid tribute to Bechet's talents.

Baquet had lived in Philadelphia for a long time, and for more than 14 years he led his Swingsters at George Wilson's Cafe. Baquet usually played tenor saxophone with the group, but at a further reunion with Bechet (on 17 June 1940) he proved that he was still a fine clarinettist. The two New Orleans musicians (Bechet on soprano saxophone, Baquet on clarinet) played a touching duet accompanied by Baquet's rhythm section: Harold Holmes (bass) Billy Carter (piano) Shorty Williams (drums) and an unknown guitarist. John Reid, who had become something of a Boswell to Bechet – collecting archival material, both on paper and on record – mercifully had his recording machine with him and captured the five-chorus blues duet. Baquet takes the lead initially and is backed by Bechet, sounding at his most tender. Bechet gently glides into the foreground for the next chorus and Baquet drops into a warm-sounding low register. The two men courteously pass the lead back and forth, creating elegant, bitter-sweet music. Baquet leads throughout the mellow final chorus, which ends with a smooth rallentando.

Two of Bechet's regular cohorts, trumpeter Sidney De Paris and bass player Wellman Braud, were on Bechet's next RCA Victor session (on 4 June 1940). They were joined by Cliff Jackson on piano, Bernard Addison on guitar, Sandy Williams on trombone and Sid Catlett on drums. One of the titles recorded was Duke Ellington's success of 1930, *Old Man Blues*, but the other four items were from earlier times. Both De Paris and Williams had worked mostly in big bands during the 1930s, and were only just becoming reacquainted with the art of small-group work. Skills in improvising a solo are the same whatever the size of the unit, but the main difference in small units concerns the performance of the improvised ensembles. De Paris and Williams later developed their small-band skills to a fine art, but on early sessions with Bechet they are feeling their way. They were not familiar with most of the material that Bechet chose, but this suited Sidney, who did not want to use musicians who simply rattled off a performance that was based on an earlier recorded version.

The session of June 1940 got off to a bad start. Bechet's friend Mary Karoley described it as being the only occasion on which she saw Sidney truly depressed; the reason for his mood was not connected with the music, however:

> I attended many record sessions and was accustomed to see Sidney on his usual high (no drugs, remember), kidding the other musicians, laughing, full of fun and playing gloriously. But it was obvious that the session was going sour. I watched take after take going down the drain. When they came out for a break, Sidney Catlett said to Sidney, angrily, 'What's the matter with you, man?'. I began to search my mind as to what could possibly be wrong. And, at last one possibility dawned on me. When Sidney started to earn some money he became obsessed with owning a car. He didn't know how to drive and his friends tried to dissuade him from this notion. We were terrified that he'd get out on the highway (he thought he could drive) and that in the first few miles Sidney would come to his end in a smash-up. But this man had a mind of his own and no one could change it.

He acquired a late model Packard and he was as proud as punch. All he wanted to talk about was his car. The car sat out front of his apartment. He had to go out of town and when he came back the car was gone. It had been repossessed for non-payment of the monthly stipend. He was so bereft that a group of his fans and friends started to negotiate with the car dealer. The matter was still in the air when it was time for the session. After I got my idea I went to a public telephone and called the dealer. He told me that everything was straightened and Sid could have the car back any time. I dashed into the studio and asked the recording engineer to signal Sidney to come out. He asked me a bit grumpily what was up. I said, "The car is yours again and can be picked up any time."

I can't convey properly the extent of his jubilation. Everyone was amazed at the change – musicians and engineers – as he picked up his horn and led the rest of them by playing with drive, spirit, imagination and sheer beauty.[16]

The aftermath was a formal letter to Sidney from the CIT Corporation confirming that there would be no further repossessions of the car, providing that 33 dollars a month was paid to them.[17]

Bechet certainly exceeds his habitual excellence on *Shake it and break it*. De Paris on trumpet shapes an effective, loosely phrased lead, but the piece sounds over-arranged. Sandy Williams, his tone husky and emotive, plays some stirring solos in the session (particularly on *Old Man Blues*), but often sounds aimless during the improvised ensembles. Bechet is at his very best (both on saxophone and clarinet) during *Nobody knows the way I feel dis mornin'*. Stirred by a hauntingly repetitive simple riff, he takes two choruses on saxophone that display the dramatic way he utilized blue notes. De Paris plays a delicate but heart-felt plunger-muted solo in this title and some fiery breaks on *Wild Man Blues*, which is a loosely arranged feature for Bechet's compelling clarinet playing.

Sidney sings the final item of the day, *Make me a pallet on the floor*, in his usual informal style, but makes up for it by playing soprano saxophone in a flawless manner. This number was recorded simply with Cliff Jackson on piano, Wellman Braud on bass, and someone at the drums. Sid Catlett is in commanding form on earlier titles from the session, but the brush work here does not sound like the work of this master percussionist; perhaps he left for another engagement.

On 16 June 1940, soon after these recordings, John Reid persuaded Bechet to undergo an aural test of the kind that was given to music students. It involved pitch, loudness, time, timbre and tonal memory. Sidney went along with the idea good humouredly and gained "superior" marks in every section. He made only 23 mistakes in the 260 tests, and was judged "perfect" in the tonal memory section.[18]

Bechet's recording contract with RCA Victor did not make him rich, but he was granted a royalty of one cent on each side recorded, and there was an advance payment of 720 dollars. By now John was getting to know Bechet well, and he deemed that it would be in his friend's interest to receive the payment in 12 monthly instalments of 60 dollars each. That way, he reasoned, Bechet would not get involved in any madcap business schemes. Bechet trusted Reid and went along with the idea, but this did not stop him from using all the money he had saved during his residency at Fonda as an 'investment' in a mink farm. Bechet entered into a deal that made him a partner in a fur-producing enterprise; his business luck ran true to form and he lost all his money.

FOURTEEN

One-man Band

By now Bechet's name was known to jazz fans everywhere, but he still had to go out looking for gigs. His only regular employment in the summer of 1940 was a Monday night residency (with Sidney De Paris) at the Enduro Restaurant in Brooklyn. Trumpeter Henry Levine, who organized a regular weekly radio programme, the "Chamber Music Society of Lower Basin Street", came to hear of Bechet's availability: "Jazz players were having a rough time trying to find work and we could get fine players to play for union scale, about 25 dollars a program. I was always an admirer of Sidney's playing, especially on soprano saxophone, and asked our program department to book him. This was very early in the program's existence and Bechet made a big hit with our radio audience. He did several other guest shots with my band and then I lost sight of him."[1] A lasting memento of this brief interlude in Sidney's life was a recording (with Levine's band) of *Muskrat Ramble*, which shows him in adventurous form. Airshots of his performances on radio with the group include a bustling interpretation of *Shake it and break it* and a roaring version of *St Louis Blues*.

In late August 1940 Bechet pondered on an offer he received from Dave Stuart (who ran the Jazz Man Record Shop in Hollywood). Stuart invited Bechet to play at a "From Spirituals to Swing" concert scheduled to be held in Los Angeles in October, but the deal involved coast-to-coast rail journeys, which Sidney's restless nature vetoed. He declined the offer, but half-heartedly toyed with plans to move out to California, possibly influenced by the fact that two old friends, pianist Jelly Roll Morton and trombonist Frank Withers, had recently settled on the West Coast.

Bill Russell and Herman Rosenberg visited Sidney in his Harlem apartment during a Saturday afternoon in September 1940. They were privileged to hear what Bill later described as "probably the greatest performance I ever heard Sidney give". Bechet stood in the middle of a fairly bare room and played an unaccompanied version of the aria *Vesti la giubba* from *I Pagliacci*, which Bill recalled "was done in the same grand manner which Caruso sang it".[2] Sidney's interest in classical music was still intense; at that time he was assembling a set of 78 r.p.m. recordings of Tchaikovsky's Fourth Symphony.[3]

During the time that Bill Russell had been researching information for the book *Jazzmen*, the name of Bechet's old friend Bunk Johnson had figured in various listings of important New Orleans trumpeters. Johnson was eventually located in New Iberia, Louisiana, and equipped with a second-hand trumpet (he no longer had an instrument) and a set of false teeth. The trumpet, and a cornet, were purchased from Fink's second-hand store in New Orleans. The dentures were also from the Crescent City, and made by Sidney's brother Dr Leonard Bechet.

Sidney followed these events with great interest, and managed to get RCA Victor interested in a scheme to record Bunk at Bechet's next session, which was scheduled to be held in Chicago. The ambitious plan failed to materialize for two reasons. Firstly, Bunk didn't, at that stage, hold an AFM union card, and secondly, he didn't feel ready to make his come-back. Bechet perversely blamed Louis Armstrong for the fact that Bunk didn't attend the recording session. According to Sidney, Louis was at fault because he had told a magazine about Bunk sitting in with his big band during their tour of Louisiana; this, Bechet felt, destroyed the surprise element that would have been a big factor in publicizing Bunk's first recordings. This was an imaginary grievance, because Louis, without any mischievous intent, told *Down Beat* about his meeting with Bunk in time for their issue of 15 August 1941 – *after* the Chicago recording session had taken place.

Whilst plans were being finalized for Sidney's trip to Chicago, bad news from that city hit the jazz world. It concerned the death, on 8 August 1940, of clarinettist Johnny Dodds, whose work Bechet greatly admired. Sidney said, "I felt sad to hear about his death. He was one of the boys who really kept up the New Orleans style."[4] Dodds had spoken with enthusiasm and admiration about Bechet's playing: "Bechet is really great – nobody ever played like him. Boy, he's good . . . let him hear something once – just once, and boy he'll play it like no one ever did before or since."[5] When Charles Edward Smith was preparing the notes for an album of New Orleans music for Decca in 1940 he sent a questionnaire to Johnny Dodds that included the phrase, "Who first inspired or influenced you in jazz?" Dodds wrote down his answer, "Sidney Bechet".

Johnny Dodds was not one of those who put years on Bechet's age; he thought that Sidney was younger than Louis Armstrong. Bechet saw a chance to pay homage to his friend, and collaborated (with Milton Nelson and W. C. Barnes) on a 32-bar opus entitled *Blue for you, Johnny*. Sidney was proud of the work. He gave its première on piano for writer George Hoefer, and later sent a signed song-copy to Bill Russell. Bechet decided to record the song during his forth-coming session in Chicago.

On 6 September 1940 an all-star band assembled for the date. Earl Hines was on piano, Warren 'Baby' Dodds (Johnny's brother) on drums, Johnny Lindsey on bass, and the star of Duke Ellington's band Rex Stewart on cornet. Bechet had flown to Chicago with the two RCA Victor executives, Leonard Joy and John Reid. Cornetist Rex Stewart was a highly sensitive, temperamental man. Long after the session he recalled its strained atmosphere: "I half blame myself. I found out that I was not the first choice and this made me a little jumpy. I knew Bechet in a casual way and some aspects of him disturbed me. It had been rammed down my throat by some of my Ellington band colleagues that Bechet was a genius. I knew this anyway, but their comments made me feel on edge."[6] It was no secret that Johnny Hodges (who worshipped Bechet) and Rex did not enjoy a friendly relationship, so barbed comments about the impending session might have been made in the Ellington band-room.

Earl Hines also remembered feeling apprehensive about the session. He said of Bechet: "He was a bit evil that day, and arrogant in the way New Orleans musicians often were then. He kept saying we're going to play Earl's tune and I didn't know which one he meant."[7] The tune turned out to be *Blues in Thirds*, which was superlatively recorded by a trio consisting of Hines, Bechet (on clarinet) and Baby Dodds. The composer introduces the melody during the first eight bars using richly voiced chords, then moves up the keyboard to play some inimitable octave tremolos, all the while backed by the steady pulse of Dodds's drumming. Bechet enters and plays an eloquent middle-register chorus of the melody before soaring up in gull-like flight to create a series of graceful lines; these are accompanied by some springy on-the-beat chords from Hines. The pianist takes over the melody for the final chorus and Bechet constructs an elegant counterpoint, floating down to end on a warm-sounding sixth note.

Bechet (again on clarinet) and Rex Stewart (playing tightly muted) take turns in establishing the lachrymose *Blues for you, Johnny*. Herb Jeffries sings a heartfelt vocal that is delivered in a skilful but unjazzy manner. The superior instrumental version has a purposeful piano introduction from Hines, who goes on to create a series of rhythmically daring ideas; he is seemingly unperturbed by Baby Dodds giving an uncalled-for demonstration of various percussion effects. Dodds taps out an eight-bar solo on woodblocks, then Hines ripples through the final part of his chorus. This sparks some neat counter-playing by Bechet and Stewart, who dovetail their phrases effectively.

The melody of *Ain't Misbehavin'* is established by Bechet on clarinet. Stewart, using a plunger mute, plays an acrid-sounding middle eight, then indulges in a duet with Hines, during which the musicians pitch two-bar phrases at each other – most of them cleverly curved. Bechet's solo on soprano saxophone is bold and unfaltering, and inspires Stewart to punch out a firm lead during a finale that culminates in an ingenious exchange of ideas by the two front-line musicians. A second take shows that improvisation was the key word of the session. Hines again underlines his virtuosity; the only disappointment is that the two melody instruments do not recapture their spectacular ending.

Earl Hines was in full flow by the time the group recorded *Save it pretty mama*; some of his ultra-daring phrases skip over the bar lines but miraculously resolve themselves. Stewart, giving a brief example of his celebrated half-valving technique, sounds almost tender in his recapitulation of the melody, but Bechet, with great determination, plays some powerful stop-time breaks before stepping back to work in smooth accord with Stewart. On Duke Ellington's jumpy tune *Stompy Jones*, Bechet and Stewart combine well on a descending riff (reminiscent of the *Panama* ride-out chorus) and share some fascinating two-bar exchanges. Lindsey's refined bass playing fills eight pleasant bars, then Baby Dodds is given the chance to demonstrate his ability to play melody on the drums. A rousing ensemble completes this final number.

The agitation and apprehension of the session didn't sour the music and some outstanding jazz was performed. Earl Hines probably earned top honours, both for his solos and for his zestful accompaniments, but Bechet too had great moments – his contribution to *Blues in Thirds* being the zenith of all he did that day.

Bechet had asked Mary Karoley to drive down to Chicago in the beloved Packard so that it could be used to transport him back to New York. Sidney chose not to do any of the driving on the thousand-mile run, which was shared between Mary and another passenger. Bechet soon tired of the car games the trio played and suggested that it was an opportune time to compose a song. As a result he and Mary Karoley produced *A Georgia Cabin* during the journey. Mary Karoley recalled: "He kind of looked down his nose at the finished product, and I was surprised when he recorded it."[8]

Bechet had concentrated on the clarinet during the Chicago session, but in general he devoted most of his playing time to the soprano saxophone. His publicized prowess on the instrument was mainly responsible for the dramatic come-back that it enjoyed in 1940. Jimmy Dorsey's entire saxophone section experimented with sopranos, Charlie Barnet began playing one regularly and various other players repadded instruments that they had put away ten years earlier.

Interest in the 'jazz revival' continued and many musicians listened more seriously to sounds they had previously dismissed as being old fashioned. Drummer Manzie Johnson, in a conversation with writer Johnny Simmen, shrewdly gave a reason for this rebirth of interest: "By about 1940 you could make some money playing in this style, especially when you worked for a master like Sidney Bechet. Maybe that helped to change those cats' minds."[9]

At the same time that support for the older jazz styles was growing, various young musicians were seeking ways to alter both the harmonic and the rhythmic approach to jazz improvisation. Players like Charlie Parker, Dizzy Gillespie, Benny Harris and Thelonious Monk were formulating the concepts of modern jazz, or 'bebop', as it became known. In 1940 this new method of playing jazz was only at the embryo stage. It was to be a long while before traditionalists angrily confronted modernists, but there was no lack of controversy in the jazz world, and one subject that regularly caused divisions of opinion was the playing of Sidney Bechet.

In view of the paeans of praise that had been heaped upon Bechet it was no wonder that a reaction developed, but the fierceness of the attacks on Sidney's playing took his fans by surprise. Most of the criticism was directed at the strength and insistence of Bechet's vibrato. In America this was typified by a reviewer in *Down Beat*, who likened Bechet's sound to "the whinny of a colt".[10] On the same magazine's letter page a correspondent wrote: "The last time a good note came from Bechet was when he cried 'da da' in his crib. His vibrato hasn't changed."[11]

Across the Atlantic, in war-time England, record reviewer Edgar Jackson wrote in the *Melody Maker* of 5 October 1940: "The more I hear of Bechet the more I find him, for all the ballyhoo that has been created about him in America, an over-rated pastime. What about the awful vibrato that wobbles almost as terrifyingly as an air-raid siren?" Sidney's fans rallied instantly and in the next issue, under a banner headline "In Defence of Bechet", the *Melody Maker* published various letters (amongst them one by the noted critic Charles Fox) that passionately defended Bechet's jazz talent and his individuality. These were the opening shots in a war that was to last for the rest of Bechet's life. He would have needed to have led a monk-like existence to remain unaware of the fierce attacks that were printed about his work, some of them degenerating into personal insults, usually concerning his aged appearance.

In 1940 Bechet was 43 years old, but, owing mainly to the fact that the small quantity of hair that he retained was quite grey, he was often described in print as being an old man (even when he was in his thirties he was known as 'Pops' by his colleagues in Noble Sissle's band). A misprint in the *Down Beat* issue of 15 July 1940, which gave his date of birth as 1887, helped to spread the illusion that Bechet was ancient. In an effort to correct the magazine's error as soon as possible, writer Charles Edward Smith asked Sidney's brother Leonard to provide birth and baptismal information to prove that Sidney Joseph Bechet was born on 14 May 1897. These details were duly published by *Down Beat* in its next issue, on 15 August 1940. But retractions and corrections are not always effective: some people wanted to believe that Sidney was older than he claimed, so they ignored the indisputable evidence.

During the early 1940s Bechet sometimes testily put people right on the question of his age, but it seemed to make no difference, and in the end he readily agreed with any date that was suggested. If someone told Bechet that they thought he was born in 1891, he agreed with them, and, if minutes later another person suggested 1894, Sidney nodded in affirmation. These reactions did not mean that he had said goodbye to vanity; he simply realized that he was wasting his breath in saying his real date of birth, for nobody believed him. He may also have been swayed by the fact that, in the growing swirl of romanticism that was cloaking early jazz history, several musicians whom Bechet knew well were blatantly adding years to their age in order to be considered true pioneers of jazz music.

Bechet began the year 1941 in almost exactly the same way as he had started 1940 – at the Log Cabin in Fonda, New York. Despite previous disagreements with the proprietor, Bechet agreed to play another season there, commencing in October 1940. During the ensuing three-month residency the personnel of the quartet underwent flurries of changes. Its longest-serving members were bass player Wellman Braud, pianists Cliff Jackson and Norman Lester, and drummers Eugene Moore and Joseph Smith.

Bechet and Braud journeyed in from Fonda for an RCA Victor session on 6 January 1941. The rest of the line-up on that date was Henry 'Red' Allen (trumpet), J. C. Higginbotham (trombone), J. C. Heard (drums) and James Toliver, Sidney's former colleague in Noble Sissle's saxophone section (piano). Toliver had given up playing saxophone to concentrate on piano and arranging. For Bechet's session he sketched out simple guide-sheets for the musicians, which saved a good deal of rehearsal time. Bechet was given leeway in his choice of material, and he included one standard and three numbers for which he claimed part-composer rights.

Coal Black Shine, which was attributed to Bechet and his friend John Reid, is a 'cousin' of *Polka Dot Rag*. Bechet is on clarinet throughout and plays a buoyant solo, during which he suddenly drops into a lower octave to growl out phrases that sound like musical asides; his ingenuity creates a jazz soliloquy. Allen and Higginbotham are allocated spacious solos, but, though the trombonist's early breaks are masterly, neither sounds to be in top form.

The next item, *Egyptian Fantasy*, is on a different plane, being one of Bechet's finest performances. He again remains on clarinet throughout, playing the opening minor theme accompanied only by string bass and tom-toms. Red Allen enters to take over the lead, blowing sombre, husky notes in his low register. Bechet then performs a series of startling breaks that could not be mistaken for the work of any other clarinettist. Higginbotham's role is a subdued one, his main task to supply backing notes for Bechet's clarinet solos. Sidney ends the *tour de force* with a cadenza that terminates on a spine-tingling high note.

Baby won't you please come home is taken at a fast clip. Sidney sketches out the melody, then hands over to Higginbotham who plays two brazen and ingenious choruses (he later cited this as one of his own favourite recorded solos). Red Allen lopes in and plays a series of daringly timed runs, boldly suspending notes to add flair to what is already lively improvising. Bechet returns to circle around the melody for two choruses, the second of which has some full-toned brass riffs.

Slippin' and Slidin' (by Bechet and Dave Nelson) is an undistinguished 32-bar 'swing' opus introduced by Bechet on soprano saxophone; the arrangement is highly reminiscent of Allen and Higginbotham's band style of this period. Both the brass players are featured more than is Bechet, though the last named comes to the forefront in the closing stages and blows combatitively against another burst of hefty brass riffing. A highlight of the session is the stimulating drumming of the young J. C. Heard, who is superbly inventive on the last two numbers.

The tunefulness and construction of the composition *Egyptian Fantasy* was widely praised. It was listed as being jointly composed by Bechet and John Reid but, in truth, neither man had any part in the origination of the striking melody. The tune, and all of its various strains, had been copyrighted in 1911 by Chicago publisher Will Rossiter and issued in sheet-music form as *Egyptia*. The composer was Abe Olman, an Ohioan whose other works included *Down among the sheltering palms*. Bechet had known the piece for many years: it had been a theme song for Freddie Keppard's Original Creole Orchestra.[12]

It is not unkind to conclude that Bechet deliberately chose to ignore the rules governing the use of copyright music. He had doubtless seen many instances of melodies being claimed by people who could not possibly have written them, and he may even have been the victim of these dubious practices himself. Nevertheless he was guilty on more than one occasion of registering as his own compositions themes that were indubitably the work of other people. Sometimes his efforts in this direction did not succeed: apparently he originally tried to convince people that he had written *Sweetie Dear*, but Joe Jordan was on hand to remind the record company that the song was his. Bechet and Mezz Mezzrow attempted to claim that *Ja da* (the evergreen by Bob Carleton) was a theme of theirs entitled *Jorina*, but this idea did not wash with the officials at RCA Victor.

Bechet was hard up at the time, and deprivation can easily bring temptation, but even when the going finally became smooth Bechet was not above putting his name on other people's compositions. Despite these lapses, it is abundantly true that Bechet's talents as a composer of highly original works would gain him a high place in any listing of jazz writers.

There was nothing dubious about Bechet's next session for RCA Victor; it was in fact an epoch-making display of individuality and versatility. At the recording studios on 19 April 1941 Bechet performed on six instruments – soprano saxophone, tenor saxophone, clarinet, piano, string bass, and drums, – in order to make a multi-track recording of *The Sheik of Araby*.

The idea for this had been conceived by John Reid. In Philadelphia in 1940 he had demonstrated to Sidney that it was possible to superimpose soprano saxophone and clarinet parts onto a previously recorded piano track. Bechet was intrigued, and decided to develop the plan by working out individual parts on six different instruments. The next stage took months, since Bechet had to gain some proficiency on string bass and drums; he also had to memorize the various harmony parts that he intended to play on the clarinet and saxophones. He showed immense patience and determination, but as soon as he felt confident enough to carry out the ambitious plan he told John Reid, who put the idea to Leonard Joy; Joy told them to go ahead and book the recording studio.

At 9.30 a.m. on the day of the session Bechet, John Reid, recording manager Stephen Scholes, and recording engineer Fred Maisch settled down in the RCA Victor studios to face a nerve-wracking experience. Bechet began by playing a tenor saxophone part, which became the basic track. He then added the double bass part, and one by one those of the other instruments, listening on earphones to what he had previously recorded. This was in the era before tape recording, so each effort had to be recorded on a 78 r.p.m. wax original; if a mistake occurred it meant a fresh start.

Bechet later said that he was in a "cold sweat" throughout his laborious and exacting task. There were three major hold-ups: on two occasions Bechet hit 'clinkers' whilst recording the clarinet part, and once the earphones slipped off in mid-performance, causing him to stop in confusion. But eventually, after almost two hours, Bechet had succeeded in recording all six parts of *The Sheik of Araby* (the tenor saxophone solo he played was the chorus that he had taught Johnny Hodges a decade earlier).

Bechet then began a multi-track recording of *Blues for Bechet*, but studio time ran out and he was able to complete only four of the parts (piano, tenor, saxophone, clarinet and soprano saxophone – in that order). The results were still satisfactory, and RCA Victor had a remarkable coupling to release. Margaret Hartigan, who worked in the company's press department, prepared a news release concerning the extraordinary session, and this led to dozens of news-papers throughout the USA printing long stories about Bechet's remarkable achievements.

Sidney was proud and relieved that he had managed the difficult task. Soon after it had been completed he met Fats Waller, who congratulated him on his efforts. Bechet said that it would have been better with more rehearsals –

meaning practice sessions to get used to the recording technique involved. Waller apparently exploded with laughter and said, "Man, how the hell you going to have a rehearsal with yourself?" Immediately after he left the studio Bechet said, "That ends three months of torture. Thinking about this session was giving me nightmares. I dreamt I was playing parts for the whole Duke Ellington Band." But he added, "I want to make another record like this, adding trumpet for the seventh piece."[13] This was one ambition that Bechet never got around to fulfilling.

The novelty of the enterprise, and Bechet's skills, made the project a remarkable achievement. On *The Sheik of Araby*, a series of fruity sounding tenor saxophone breaks lead into a harmonized first chorus; the tenor takes the lead and the soprano a harmony part, which allows the clarinet to create a lively, bubbling improvised line. A nimbly played riff chorus leads into an interwoven final 32 bars (containing the 'Hodges' segment). Little can be heard of the rhythm section on this piece, but Bechet's piano playing has a prominent part in *Blues for Bechet*, where his introduction and opening chorus are reminiscent of Morton. He then "plays a duet" on tenor saxophone and clarinet before creating a coalition on the soprano and tenor instruments. In the background the piano can be heard playing a series of steady chords on the beat. Even though there wasn't time to record the bass and drum parts, the track is musically more satisfying than that of *The Sheik of Araby*.

Nine days after the one-man-band session Bechet returned to more normal recording activity by leading yet another version of his New Orleans Feetwarmers; this group consisted of Gus Aiken (trumpet), Sandy Williams (trombone), Lem Johnson (tenor saxophone), Cliff Jackson (piano), Wilson Myers (string bass) and Arthur Herbert (drums).

The first tune of the date, *Swing Parade*, begins with liberal quotes by the ensemble from *Maryland, my Maryland*. Bechet then launches the highly tuneful piece on soprano saxophone (he chose not to play clarinet in this session). Gus Aiken creates an improvised second part that promises more than it achieves (though his efforts on the second take are more consistent). The overall balance is poor, particularly disappointing as most of the piece is devoted to ensemble playing. Lem Johnson on tenor saxophone only half emerges from the conglomeration of sound, but Herbert's cymbals ring out a series of stimulating patterns during the second series of quotes from *Maryland*.

Sandy Williams is virtually inaudible on the first track, but flowers in all his glory during a solo on the fast rendition of *I know that you know*. Gus Aiken's technique is strained to the limits at this tempo, but Bechet romps comfortably through two of his showpiece choruses, which highlight his technique and his remarkable breath control. Cliff Jackson's solo demonstrates that the sound of his left-hand playing was totally individual. The band made three attempts at this tune but couldn't improve on its first effort – things might have turned out differently had the tempo been reduced slightly.

Next Bechet repeated one of his long standing features, *When it's sleepytime down South*, but allows his front-line colleagues a chance to play a solo during the opening chorus. Sandy Williams's eight bars make an exquisite miniature, Lem

Johnson's eight are full of interest and Gus Aiken is close to his best in his brief outing. Bechet completes a highly skilful work-out, hands over to Jackson for eight bars, then performs an impressive climb to his final dramatic high note.

Wilson Myers's sense of musical adventure and smooth bowing technique enhance *I ain't gonna give nobody none of this jelly roll*. Bechet sets the ball rolling with a chorus of melodic variation, Myers takes a solo, and then Jackson pounds out a pugnacious 16 bars. Williams and Aiken follow with solos, but whereas Williams sounds free and easy, Aiken's pinched tone conveys anxiety. The reed players provide some effective 'jumpy' riffs behind the brass solos, but when the full ensemble regroups a near-chaotic mood develops. It seems that every man is for himself, and even Arthur Herbert, who played with restraint throughout the rest of the session, joins in the cacophonous fray.

Bechet was presented with enormous problems in assembling the musicians for his various recording sessions. He was not on the telephone at his new home (421 West 154th Street) and, as he was not given to writing letters, he usually had to trudge around seeking each and every musician he intended to use on a date. Sometimes he located them at their place of work; sometimes he had to visit them at home (as was the case with trombonist Sandy Williams). This awkward method of assembling a band was one of the reasons that the personnels change so often on Bechet's sessions of 1941. If he couldn't physically locate a musician, Bechet moved on swiftly to find someone else, and his system didn't produce the sort of continuity that reassures a record company.

Life would have been easier with a telephone, but Bechet chose not to have one. Expense was one of the reasons. In 1941 the musicians' union minimum rate for a week's work in New York City was 40 dollars. That was a fair wage, but it was not easy for any jazz musician to work for a whole week anywhere in Manhattan. In the summer of 1941 Bechet's home-town colleague Albert Nicholas temporarily gave up the struggle to earn a living playing jazz and found himself a better paid job working as a guard on the Eighth Avenue subway.

Bechet himself was short of work during several periods in 1941. Usually he kept his problems to himself when speaking to journalists, but when interviewed by Ollie Stewart for a feature that appeared in the *Baltimore Afro-American* on 7 June 1941, he said: "The trouble nowadays is that there are too many musicians. If there weren't too many there would still be good jobs left for colored boys after the white boys got through imitating them and taking away all the best jobs."

Bechet hung on and was offered the job of leading a group at the Mimo on 132nd Street in Harlem, a club part-owned by dancer Bill 'Bojangles' Robinson, which catered for black and white customers. A quartet consisting of Sidney, Wellman Braud, Cliff Jackson, and drummer Eugene Moore began the residency, but Bechet was soon invited to take over the club's main musical spot, which involved his leading a nine-piece band. The rhythm section was joined by Joe Hayman (alto saxophone), Lem Johnson (tenor saxophone), Frank Powell (alto and baritone saxophones), and Leonard Davis and Henry Goodwin (trumpets). Pianist Lloyd Phillips played within the main band, but Cliff Jackson remained on hand to accompany Bechet in the quartet's feature numbers.

Sidney's playing was done with the rhythm section; for the rest of the time he conducted the band.

Writer Leonard Feather, who had recently migrated to the USA from England, went to interview Bechet at the Mimo Club for the *Melody Maker*. He first asked Sidney if he was aware of the virulent criticisms that had appeared in print. Bechet replied, "Sure, I've read some of them and heard a lot of talk about it. The way I look at it is this: anybody is entitled to his opinion, but some of those guys need to think and listen a little more carefully before they write." Feather asked, "What about the remarks about your vibrato?", to which Sidney replied, "I play every number the way I feel it. Do you know how I get the best effect out of a piece? I look at the lyrics and try to get the same sort of effect through my instrument that the words of the song express. The vibrato is just a form of that expression and I'd do it on any instrument I might play."

Feather stayed on to hear the quartet play a set which included *Muskrat Ramble*, *Dardanella* and *Lonesome Road*, after which he wrote: "Gradually I realised that at certain tempos, in certain moods, the vibrato becomes quite secondary, and all you are aware of is that Bechet is building some fine choruses. Say what you may – and I've said plenty about that vibrato – it must be admitted that Bechet's talent is something strange and almost unique."[14]

By the time that feature was published, Sidney had left the Mimo Club to begin the first of several residencies at Camp Unity, in Allaben Acres, Wingdale, New York, some 75 miles from New York City. Camp Unity was a vacation centre with swimming and boating facilities on nearby Lake Ellis; it also offered tennis courts, horseback riding, hikes through the Berkshire countryside and camp-fire sing-songs. The only aspect of Camp Unity that irked some of the musicians who worked there was that its organizers made a point of propounding left-wing political ideas.

Sidney Bechet never refused a proffered pamphlet, but for most of his life he was totally uninterested in politics. Pianist Willie 'the Lion' Smith, who opened the 1941 season at Camp Unity with Bechet, became alarmed and angry about working in what he described as "a nest of Commies".[15] He wrote in his autobiography: "It was the most mixed-up camp I ever saw or heard about – the races, the sexes, and the religions were all mixed." Smith, bothered both by the tracts and life under canvas, made his mood known to Sidney, who apparently said, "I told them I couldn't see anything in that Communism stuff. Instead of the early bird getting the worm they wanted the early bird to cut up the worm and give away all the pieces."[16]

However, Bechet was content with several aspects of life at Camp Unity: the working schedule there only involved playing for dancing during the evenings, which left him plenty of time for other pursuits. He found some good fishing spots, enjoyed rowing on the lake and playing table tennis, and was not averse to sharing some of his time with various female holiday makers. After a week at the camp Willie 'the Lion' Smith made tracks for New York, where he hastily arranged for another pianist to take his place; the rest of Bechet's line-up was Frankie Newton on trumpet (he had worked at Camp Unity before), Everett Barksdale on guitar and Arthur Trappier on drums.

When the season ended (on 7 September 1941) Bechet returned to New York and resumed recording for RCA Victor. For the session on 13 September he was reunited with Willie 'the Lion' Smith, who, together with Wellman Braud, Everett Barksdale, Manzie Johnson and trumpeter Charlie Shavers, made four engrossing sides. At the time these recordings were issued Charlie Shavers's playing came in for a good deal of criticism, but in retrospect it is clear that his work with Bechet is full of subtleties and spontaneity. He did what Bechet asked him to do, which was to create a second voice to the soprano saxophone's melody line. His method of doing so was highly imaginative, and one that avoided fly-blown fill-in phrases.

Shavers plays one of these absorbing second parts on the medium-paced version of *I'm comin' Virginia*, after which the two front-line musicians interchange the melody. Savers's low register solo is fluent without sounding glib, and it is sympathetically backed by Bechet's adroit line. The rhythm section is sedate and restrained but Smith's piano solo is full of panache. There are no dramas in the final chorus, but there is a good deal of thoughtful and effective interplay between Bechet and Shavers.

The trumpeter provides a quasi-dramatic introduction to *Limehouse Blues*, then Bechet executes an intense version of the melody, which is interspersed by Shavers's filigree phrases. The soprano saxophone solo begins with a series of triplet variations of the kind used in his set-piece solo *China Boy*, but here they sound a little stiff. The Lion is again in good form and Shavers's solo is warm and sumptuous. Bechet re-enters with a glorious assortment of paraphrases, then he and Shavers end the final chorus with some engaging musical sparring.

Bechet sounds delightfully expressive on *Georgia Cabin* (the tune that he wrote with Mary Karoley), and there is no evaporation of intensity when Shavers takes over the theme. Bechet plays a rich-sounding second part that blends well with Shavers's fat tone, then returns to restate the tender melody. The least successful item from the session is *Texas Moaner* (which Bechet had first recorded with Louis Armstrong). Shavers plays the first chorus well enough, supported by Bechet's clarinet, but from then on fails to perform a satisfactory continuum. Bechet's clarinet chorus, couched within his full-sounding chalumeau register, is a gem. Shavers improvises a fluent, slightly whimsical solo, and then Bechet (on saxophone) modulates and piles on the drama. The last chorus liaison between Shavers and Bechet is unsatisfying because the trumpeter has abandoned all thoughts of the theme of *Texas Moaner*. Aside from this lapse, Shavers had proved to be one of Bechet's most stimulating front-line partners; it was a pity that they didn't work together regularly to build up their obvious rapport.

When the full band session ended, Bechet (on saxophone) recorded two trio sides with Smith and Barksdale. The first was a song that Billie Holiday had performed with great success, *Strange Fruit*. After some inappropriate flourishes from Smith and Barksdale, Bechet projects the tune with a superb dignity and presence, injecting an attractive nasal quality into his high notes; he never strays far from the melody, but enhances it with subtle inflections. The other item, *You're the limit*, a catchy theme by Willie 'the Lion' Smith, is played almost without embellishment by Bechet. Smith strides out with a rocking little interlude in double tempo, then Bechet returns to re-establish the primary melody. Originally neither side was considered worthy of issue, and they remained in the vaults until the arrival of the microgroove era.

Bechet's contract with RCA Victor called for 24 sides a year, so he was soon organizing yet another session. Only one player from the previous occasion, drummer Manzie Johnson, was retained. He was joined by Henry Goodwin (trumpet), Vic Dickenson (trombone), Ernest Williamson (bass), and Don Donaldson (piano). Bechet played soprano saxophone. Don Donaldson wrote the skilful arrangements used in this session, organizing each piece to move towards a logical, satisfying conclusion. There are no signs of the uneasy mêlées that mar some of the other Bechet sides from this period, but the problem remains that three of the items were manufactured from inferior material. Vic Dickenson sings two of these, *Rip up the joint* and *Suey*, and almost manages to make them sound convincing.

On the former, Dickenson shares the vocal line with some enthusiastic singing from the rest of the group. The neatly arranged passages for the front line allow Henry Goodwin to fire off some effective two-bar salvos, but Bechet takes the only solo of any duration – a neat and tidy effort in keeping with the form of the piece. On *Suey*, Donaldson's arranged voicing of a front line led by soprano saxophone is cunningly appealing – he cleverly reverts to writing for the instruments in unison at crucial points in the 32-bar sequence. Dickenson's lyrics (written by Bechet and John Reid) follow those for the genre of songs that describe new dance steps – Suey was obviously a strut that never caught on. Bechet again keeps well within his emotional limits during his 32-bar solo.

Blues in the Air, a composition by Bechet, immediately elevates the proceedings and unleashes a flowing stream of passionate phrases from the soprano saxophone. Dickenson plays some suitably atmospheric answers on muted trombone, but doesn't top Goodwin's plunger-muted tribute to the skills of Bubber Miley. Again Donaldson's scoring and his sense of form add to the overall performance. The band remains in similar mood to perform a splendid version of *The Mooche*, complete with effective tom-toms and a cutting clarinet lead from Sidney. Dickenson produces some more wry, melancholic phrases, but solo honours again go to Goodwin; his efforts apparently pleased Duke Ellington, who said that this version of *The Mooche* was his own favourite rendition. Ironically Bechet doesn't play a solo on this track.

The nadir of the session was the final song, an unfunny performance of *Laughin' in Rhythm*. Goodwin was given the job of chortling the worldless, mindless role of a man who can't stop laughing. Initially it sounds as though he is imitating a death rattle, but he warms to his task by producing some maniacal shrieks. Bechet's 32-bar solo is the only saving grace, but even he can't resist giving out some imitation chuckles.

Don Donaldson's brief solo moments occur in the introduction to *Blues in the Air* and during *The Mooche*; elsewhere he suffers from the grievously poor balance. *Laughin' in Rhythm* was howled down by the critics, and so too were *Rip up the joint* and *Suey* (though these two now seem to have quaint period charm).

Even Bechet's staunchest supporter, Paul Eduard Miller, wrote that *Rip up the joint* "was inferior musical material obviously aimed at the juke boxes".[17] But discounting the three 'failures', any session that produced music such as *Blues in the Air* and *The Mooche* can only be deemed a success.

Ten days later, on 24 October 1941, Bechet was back in the studio with another totally different personnel. With the exception of the drummer (Sid Catlett took Manzie Johnson's place), he reverted to the group used on 13th September. The two-piece front line (Bechet and Shavers) again produces some fascinating music. This team continued to be criticized by those who felt that Bechet needed an earthier partner, but after hearing test pressings of their earlier efforts together Bechet did not agree. Shavers himself was not a man to dwell on his own recordings, no matter how historic the company, but he did say that at first he felt that he was being used by Bechet simply because other trumpeters were not available. When he was rebooked for another session, things took on a different light, and he enjoyed himself immensely. He retained considerable respect for Bechet's playing, and said that he found him easy to work with – his authoritative phrasing left no room for doubt.

The old standard *Twelfth Street Rag* came first in the session, and the sextet performs it at breakneck speed. Bechet (on clarinet) takes the melody while Shavers and Barksdale (playing single notes on guitar) create the harmony parts. Shavers's increased confidence is apparent by the dare-devil way in which he articulates a complex break; his playing throughout is tackled with the similar bold approach he employed in John Kirby's band. Bechet's clarinet solo is solid and thoughtful rather than daring, and Smith's piano solo is an odd mixture of flamboyancy and delicacy. The front-line partners jam out a finale full of cleverly echoed phrases. Each of the two takes of this piece is packed with improvisation.

Those who selected a particular 78 r.p.m. issue for release were almost invariably right in their choice of take: *Mood Indigo* seems to be an exception. Both takes are outstanding, and each of them could be placed amongst Bechet's finest recordings, but the first has the edge. Shavers plays the melody open, using his broad-sounding low register; lower still, Bechet provides the perfect musical underlay on clarinet. Barksdale's plush guitar chords add another dimension to the already attractive blend of tone colours. Sidney embellishes the second theme with love and care; rarely have the marvels of his clarinet tone been so finely captured. During the final chorus Bechet, Shavers and Barksdale improvise simultaneously, creating a style of musical conversation which, in jazz terms, was years ahead of its time.

Rose Room gives the impression of being a high-class fill-in number. The group takes it at a comfortable jog, though Shavers's break leading into Bechet's restrained soprano saxophone solo is nothing less then stunning. Barksdale consolidates the existing mood with a lightweight solo, then the melody instruments regroup to share some amiable ideas. *Lady be good* threatens to be a low-energy offering; the first chorus, harmonized in thirds, is close to being dull, but once the solos begin with Bechet on saxophone, the excitement starts to mount. Smith, on piano, reconfirms his individuality but he too, like some of his predecessors, suffers from the strange balance achieved in the Victor studios in this era. All the wraps are removed by Sid Catlett's dynamic eight-bar drum break, which catapults the front line into its syncopated closing riff.

All the items in the session were famous standards, the final one being Cole Porter's *What is this thing called love*. Sidney performs a slow, romantic rendering of the tune, aided by apt fill-ins from the guitarists. Shavers's improvisations explore the bravura possibilities of the song: he moves close to a rhapsodic mood but suddenly changes course in the second eight bars to produce an amazingly intricate rhythmic pattern. Bechet picks up the melody for the final 16 bars, moving up an octave for dramatic effect. Shavers pads alongside him, offering shrewd complementary answers to the passionate outpourings of the soprano saxophone.

Unfortunately this was the last time that Bechet and Shavers worked together in tandem. The bonus in their final session together was the drumming of Sid Catlett, who was at his brilliant best throughout the date; he made use of every part of the kit to great effect and always sounded flexible and dynamic, whether playing invigorating off-beats, splashing joyful sounds out of his cymbals, or striking crisp rim-shots.

At best, Bechet's sales figures for RCA Victor during the early 1940s were little more than satisfactory. There had been disappointments, notably the one-man-band coupling, which, despite blanket-cover publicity, had sold poorly. Bechet had been given a good deal of freedom in his early sessions for the recording company, but had failed to formulate the sort of individualistic band style that would have gained automatic orders for his records. As it was, his use of a succession of arrangers and a constantly fluctuating personnel created confusion for many new jazz fans, who liked to feel familiar with both the sound and the personnels of the records they bought. Bechet's approach was not one that was likely to gain the support of the majority of America's jazz buying public.

However, Bechet's devotees bought almost everything he recorded, which meant that there was a good chance RCA Victor would renew his contract for another 24 sides. One magazine, *Music & Rhythm*, actually announced that the deal had been signed, but unfortunately the extension to the contract did not materialize. During the period that the company was mulling over Bechet's prospects, the American Federation of Musicians decided to preclude its members from making commercial recordings. When that strike officially ended, almost two years later, RCA Victor felt that the musical climate had changed so far as Bechet's sales potential was concerned and, as a result, decided not to renew his contract.

FIFTEEN

Farewell to Louisiana

During the early 1940s the record royalties from RCA Victor made Bechet's life somewhat easier, but he still could not afford to turn down gigs and, as a result, played a wide assortment of dates. The idea of public jam session featuring star jazzmen was taken up by the record producer Milt Gabler, who organized a series of lively gatherings in New York. One exciting get-together, held in February 1941, united the robust talents of Hot Lips Page on trumpet and Bechet on soprano saxophone. Gabler later said, "We paid union scale, ten dollars per man, and double for the leader. Sidney Bechet always got double, even when he was a sideman. He wouldn't work for single scale."[1]

Guitarist Eddie Condon and writer Ernie Anderson took the club jam session idea a stage further by booking the New York Town Hall to present all-star line-ups playing informal sessions on the concert platform. Bechet appeared at many of these Town Hall concerts throughout the 1940s. On 21 February 1941 he was featured in the very first of the series, which was billed in newspaper advertisements as "A Chiaroscuro Jazz Concert under the direction of Eddie Condon, with Bobby Hackett, Pee Wee Russell, George Wettling, Hot Lips Page, Max Kaminsky, John Simmons, Brad Gowans, Sidney Bechet and others". Most of these concerts took place on Saturday afternoons, commencing at 5.30 p.m.; the admission price ranged from 75 cents to $1.50. Bechet knew most of the participants from his days at Nick's Tavern. Eddie Condon always retained the highest respect for Sidney's talents and made sure that he was given prominent feature spots in the Town Hall concerts. Bechet always enjoyed working with Condon and genuinely enjoyed the guitarist's wisecracks. He later said that Condon had been one of the people principally responsible for putting him on his "come-back trail".

Bechet often organized pick-up bands for casual bookings that came his way. On one such date in 1941 he ensured that there would be no shortage of competition on the bandstand by hiring two trumpeters, Henry 'Red' Allen and Henry Goodwin, and two trombonists, J. C. Higginbotham and Sandy Williams, to work alongside him in a five-piece front line. In the rhythm section that night, Bechet used pianist James 'Buster' Toliver, who had become his permanent musical amanuensis, writing down in musical notation the various compositions that Sidney played or hummed to him.

On 19 April 1941 Bechet secured a particularly unusual booking. It was for Nesuhi Ertegun, whose father was then the Turkish Ambassador in Washington, DC; Nesuhi and his brother Ahmet were devoted jazz fans, and decided to run their own all-star sessions in the capital. Nesuhi Ertegun made the preliminary plans during a visit to the Mimo Club where Bechet was:

> . . . backing a slick show with a chorus line and singers and all that, and the band was in tuxedos. It all looked very prosperous. But the truth was that Bechet wasn't doing at all well. The next day he invited me to his apartment for a drink and something to eat. After we sat down his wife came in and said to Bechet, "Who's that? What does he want?" Bechet introduced me and said he'd brought me home for a bite. She said, "You know there's no food in this house. Now on get out and find your own food!" We went to a bar and had a drink and worked out details of the concert. Washington was still a Southern racists' town, and no concert hall would touch such an affair. Finally, the Jewish Community Center, which had a four-hundred-seat auditorium, agreed.[2]

Nesuhi Ertegun confirmed the booking to Bechet by a Western Union cable and specifically asked him to bring Sidney De Paris on trumpet, Vic Dickenson on trombone, and Wellman Braud on bass. Sidney complied, and also booked George Wettling on drums and Art Hodes on piano. This all-star line-up was booked for the sum of 136 dollars; 21 dollars each for the five sidemen and 31 dollars for Bechet as leader and contractor.[3] The date proved a memorable one for Nesuhi Ertegun:

> When the band arrived in Washington they came to the Embassy, and we had an elegant lunch. I knew Bechet loved red beans and rice, and he was astonished. He wanted to know if we had a Creole cook, and I said no, a Turkish cook, and that beans and rice was a common dish in Turkey, too. Bechet couldn't believe it and he said we must be copying the Creoles, and a very pleasant argument went on for some time about the roots of red beans and rice. The musicians were relaxed and in a good mood and the concert, which was in the afternoon, was a tremendous success musically. From then on Sidney and I were very friendly. He was deceptive. With his white hair and round face he looked much older than he was. He also had this genial, sweet Creole politeness and a beautiful, harmonious way of talking. In many ways he seemed like a typical Uncle Tom, but once you got to know him, once you had broken the mirror and got inside and found the true Bechet, you discovered he wasn't that way at all. He couldn't stand fakery or hypocrisy, and he was a tough and involved human being. He was far more intelligent than people took him for, and he knew what was going on everywhere. I never heard him play badly, even with bad groups.[4]

Although the demands of World War II recruitment had caused there to be plenty of vacancies in big-band sections, work for Bechet wasn't abundant in 1942. During the early months of that year he performed a series of solo dates in Philadelphia and also appeared as a guest with Henry 'Red' Allen's band at the Ken Club in Warrenton Street, Boston. George Frazier, one of that city's most famous columnists, wrote about Bechet's visit: "He is a courtly and gentle man who looks as if he belongs anywhere except behind a soprano saxophone. But his appearance notwithstanding, behind a soprano saxophone is just where he belongs. At his best, he seems to me a forthright and enormously gifted jazz musician. I think that I, as an outspoken needler of his in the past, should lose no time in reporting that he is at his best these nights. At the Ken, where he is featured with Red Allen's Band, he is playing better than I have ever heard him play. His work has none of the bleating quality that marred his performances on the 12-inch H.R.S. faces, which were supposed to be so utterly significant."[5]

Bechet's longest booking in 1942 was for a return season at Camp Unity. During most of the summer engagement he used Henry Goodwin on trumpet, Sandy Williams on trombone, Don Donaldson on piano, Ernest Williamson on string bass, and Gerald Hopson on drums; occasionally other players like Manzie Johnson, Wellman Braud and trumpeter Bill Coleman were booked to work as substitutes in the band.

John Reid visited Sidney at Camp Unity in June and August 1942. On his second trip there he took along his mobile recording equipment and set it up to record Bechet's band playing for a dance. He also spent a whole afternoon recording Bechet playing piano and singing excerpts from a ballet that he was composing. This project, which was an extension of his earlier work *The Negro Rhapsody*, took Sidney several years to complete, and he worked regularly on the, as yet, untitled composition during his stay at Camp Unity. John Reid was able to play for Sidney a message that had been recorded for him by trumpeter Bunk Johnson. Interest in Johnson's reputation had grown steadily since the publication of the book *Jazzmen* in 1939. Bunk's come-back moved a stage nearer when he was visited at his home in New Iberia by Mary Karoley in February 1942. Mary Karoley (who had written a long, detailed biography of Bechet for the issue of *Jazz Information* dated 6 December 1940) borrowed some portable recording equipment from John Reid and made a pilgrimage to Louisiana to record Johnson's voice and short examples of his trumpet playing.

Bunk duly sent via Mary Karoley a recorded message mentioning particularly two musicians he had known as youngsters in New Orleans. He said, "I'd be very proud to send a little message to Sidney Bechet and the whole bunch, also Louis Armstrong and group, as he promised to send me a trumpet, I haven't seen that trumpet yet. Ask Sidney would he like to work at Pitman's place with me where he first worked when we were in the Eagle Band . . . ask Sidney do he still remember our old Scott Joplin music that we used to play. Tell him that I have never forgotten any of it."[6]

Bechet was thrilled to hear Bunk Johnson's voice again, and John Reid capitalized on his delight by getting him to superimpose a recording of his playing on one of Mary Karoley's samples of Bunk performing an unaccompanied version of *Weary Blues*. It was to be three years before Bechet had another chance to record with Bunk, but when he did so the trombonist at the session was Sidney's colleague for that 1942 summer season – Sandy Williams. Williams retained vivid memories of his stay at Camp Unity: "I used to get a kick out of Bechet, but he was a moody guy. He'd be happy and jolly one minute and the next he'd be off by himself, walking through the woods. He'd tell you he was thinking. Other times he'd go out on the lake in a boat all by himself."[7]

In September 1942, when the season ended, Bechet returned to New York and had a formal meeting at the William Morris Agency at 1270 Sixth Avenue; as a result the agency took on the job of finding bookings for his group. In the past, Billy Shaw of that office had occasionally offered Bechet casual dates, but from this point onwards he could officially advertise his representation. Shaw, a former trumpet player with the California Ramblers, had good contacts within the club world and with private organizations. Sidney soon benefited financially from the connection, but musically the arrangement was less rewarding; most of the venues to which the agency introduced him were simply restaurants with a dance floor.

Late in 1942 Sidney began playing at one of these venues, Sandy's Hollywood Bar at 108 Market Street, Paterson, New Jersey. The hours were long but the pay was good. Bechet's group worked from 9 p.m. until 3 a.m. every night, and from 4 p.m. until 7 p.m. for the Sunday jam session. Sidney had never been one to tire easily, but for the first time in years he began feeling fatigued and unwell, and he didn't seek an extension of his contract at Sandy's. The ill health was stomach trouble, early warning signs of problems that were to come. He was also having problems with his teeth, and found it painful to play the clarinet, so much so that he gave the instrument he had to Mary Karoley (who later donated it to the New Orleans Jazz Museum).

Bechet had recently moved home and now lived at 455 West 141st Street, New York. He and his wife, Marilouise, were still officially together (she had spent some time at Camp Unity with him), but they were soon to separate. Bechet rested at home and soon recovered from his digestive ailment; his mouth healed temporarily and he acquired another clarinet. In March 1943 he resumed a full schedule by leading his own small group at the Colonial Restaurant in Hagerstown, Maryland, then moved on to play at the Alpine Musical Bar in Philadelphia. He was visited there by writer Bob Arthur, who was amazed to see that Sidney had dyed his sparse hair jet black. Bechet explained his action: "You can't get a job if you're old. They don't like grey-haired performers."[8]

Fortunately Bechet was soon persuaded to stop applying the odious darkener, but his action revealed just how precarious he found the work situation. His admiring fans across the Atlantic might have found Bechet's concern almost impossible to understand: in Britain Bechet's talents were constantly discussed in the jazz magazines. A new controversy erupted in 1943 after Stanley Dance, in *Jazz Record*, likened Bechet's "throaty, emotional vibrato" to the sound made by the voices of Bessie Smith and Louis Armstrong. A correspondent answered complainingly: "He uses a horrible vibrato and produces a monstrous tone." Dance stepped in with a knock-out blow: "Bechet's vibrato demonstrates his consciousness of the fact that he is playing jazz and not some posy kind of boudoir music."

In May 1943 Bechet returned to New York to play some 'guest star' bookings at various clubs, and also led a small group on relief nights at the Hurricane Club at Broadway and 51st Street. Duke Ellington's orchestra was in New York at this time, and about to begin its own residency at the Hurricane; this gave Bechet the opportunity to carry out a plan that he had been contemplating for some time. That same month he arranged to pay an afternoon call at Ellington's apartment in order to ask Duke whether he would consider performing the extended work which Bechet had so patiently composed. Duke, his mind on other things (including his own extended works), remained a model of charm and tact, but apparently never let Sidney get to the point of the visit. Every time that Bechet thought he had Ellington boxed in, the maestro deftly changed the subject. In the end Bechet gave up and took his leave. He never again raised the matter with Duke, but neither did he ever stop regarding Ellington's orchestra as his favourite big band.

During the summer of 1943 Bechet played a series of dates in Maryland, Massachusetts and Pennsylvania, and then returned to New York to work briefly at the Onyx Club, sharing the bill with Billie Holiday. When that engagement ended Bechet faced a bleak patch without much work. Accordingly he began calling at various clubs in an attempt to rustle up some bookings. He went to Nick's Tavern, carrying his soprano saxophone, and sat in with Cliff Jackson, who was working as the intermission pianist. The effect of the duo's music on the audience was little short of sensational and Nick Rongetti not only paid Sidney something for dropping in that night (a gratuity that caused some of Nick's regulars to gasp in amazement), but also invited him to work regularly with Jackson. Intermittently, for the next few weeks, Bechet shared the gig with Jackson, who never forgot the experience: "We worked at Nick's years ago, piano and soprano saxophone. He and I used to battle all night. He was a genius, millions of ideas."[9]

Jim McGraw, who was then writing for *Jazz Record* (a new magazine started by Art Hodes), got to know Bechet at Nick's:

Bechet, his hair just beginning to turn silvery, his head as round as a basketball, had a great sense of humor despite the depressing times, and kept his fellow musicians laughing. One night at Nick's, at the expense of Pee Wee Russell, whose face was as wrinkled as a prune, Bechet remarked, "Some night I'd like to see you make a face, Pee Wee". The band shook with laughter.

Bechet and I became close friends. He had an unusual intelligence for a self-taught musician. Between sets on warm nights we'd sit in the tiny park on Sheridan Square and discuss everything from Beethoven to Bobby Hackett, from politics to whorehouses, and mainly, the mistreatment of black musicians by white entrepreneurs, and the discriminations practiced by night club operators and the musicians' union. In Nick's for example, the white group would play on the stand. At intermission the black group was shunted to the dance floor, separate and unequal, they could not be allowed to dirty the white group's chairs. When our jug was empty, Bash and I would play a game with our cigarette butts, seeing which of us could flip the butts farthest and laughing heartily in the process.[10]

Bechet often spoke of his regard for Bobby Hackett's cornet playing. During an interview that Steve and Lee Smith conducted in autumn 1938, Sidney said that Hackett's approach to improvisation was similar to that of Big Eye Louis Nelson (which, he added, was very different from the usual New Orleans clarinet variation style). Three years later, in answer to a question from Leonard Feather, Bechet picked his three ideal trumpeters: Louis Armstrong, Sidney de Paris and Bobby Hackett.

Almost everyone in the pool of musicians who worked at Nick's liked Bechet as a person, and all of them revered his musical ability. Pee Wee Russell's comments were typical: "Such a great man! Nobody can take that away from him, a great jazz musician. He had his own unique way of playing and he did it well. I don't think he ever made a bad record, or if he did I haven't heard it. Power, inventiveness, and above all that great feeling that everything he played was jazz."[11]

When Bechet sat in with the house band at Nick's the atmosphere became charged with excitement. Clarinettist Johnny Mince dropped into the club late one night to play a few numbers with Bobby Hackett's band: "I was working in big bands for most of the time, so it was nice to go and jam a little in the clubs. One night at Nick's I was sitting in with Bobby's band and we had some mellow things going. Out of the corner of my eye I saw someone getting on the bandstand, but I carried on blowing. Suddenly this almighty gust of power took over and swept the whole band along with it. The place shook! I had never met Sidney Bechet before, but as soon as I heard that dramatic sound I knew it was him."[12]

In October 1943 a lack of gigs forced Sidney to work for a week in a shipyard simply to get some money together.[13] But despite this desperate step, Bechet didn't lose his optimism. Mary Karoley said, "He was very secure about his tremendous gifts and did not doubt that the time would come when he could display them."[14] A month later Bechet took his first vacation for years and went to stay at Mary Karoley's home in Mount Healthy, Ohio, a small village 12 miles from Cincinnati (just across the Ohio River from Kentucky). Mary Karoley recalled the visit:

> Racial rumblings were not uncommon. Our house was isolated on a country road, so there was no problem there. One afternoon Sidney told us he was going to take a walk (about a mile) to the village and look it over. Off he went and returned with a funny story about his adventure.
>
> I doubt in the small village there were any colored residents at all. His walk warmed him up and when he reached the village he walked into the only bar in town. The bartender stopped serving, the customers stopped drinking, and everyone seemed electrified by the appearance of Sidney, who took in the situation immediately and said, "Good Afternoon Gentlemen". To the bartender he said pleasantly, "May I have a beer please?". The silence continued for a second then the bartender spoke gruffly, "You'll have to drink it from the can". Sidney smiled and said, "Certainly it's so much more sanitary that way". You can imagine the various reactions to this remark. Another shocked silence and then one of the man with a sense of humor started to laugh at this wonderful innuendo. The bartender looked ashamed and Sidney was served his beer in a glass. By the end of the week Sidney had made friends up and down the main street.
>
> It was during the week that he electrified me by bringing home some kind of creature (in a bag). It was obviously dead. I shrieked, "What's that thing?". He said, "I'm cooking supper and this is it". I asked suspiciously, "What is it?". "I'll tell you later" he said. I knew that he was an excellent cook but I was truly uneasy as I watched him take the "thing" out to the garage. Finally I decided to leave the supper and kitchen entirely to him. In time we were called to the dinette and I must admit something smelled very good. It tasted a bit like rabbit but better, and he had made some very luscious "fixins". I remember the dessert – delicious pecan pudding. Everyone ate enthusiastically and I relaxed a bit. Over coffee I made my demand, "What was it Sidney?". Looking pleased with himself Sid replied, "Muskrat Jambalaya". I screamed, "Muskrat!", nearly passed out and was revived by some brandy and benedictine. "That's the last thing you'll cook in my house", I told him, but it wasn't.[15]

Because of the strike that affected the recording industry, Bechet made no commercial recordings during 1942 and 1943, but on 9 December 1943, with Vic Dickenson on trombone, Don Donaldson on piano, Wilson Myers on bass and Wilbert Kirk on drums, he made three titles for issue on V-discs (non-commercial recordings specially made for distribution to the US Armed Forces). On *V-disc Blues* (a thinly disguised version of *Bugle Call Rag*), Bechet launches the proceedings with the celebrated 'bugle call', then romps effortlessly through a fluent solo. The bowed bass solo is full of ideas, after which trombonist Dickenson (a notable individualist) takes four laconic choruses, leading the group into the *Ole Miss* section of the tune. Kirk's drumming locks onto a heavy off-beat, and sounds all the steadier for doing so, but the real swing comes from the two-piece front line.

Suitably warmed up, the band went on to produce a rendition of *After you've gone* that is a near masterpiece. After a bland piano introduction, Dickenson plays the familiar melody with guile and sensitivity. Bechet creates a counter-point that is nothing short of ingenious, and then steps forward to play the melody like an aria. Kirk's drum break takes the tune into double-tempo, and Donaldson strides out with a hectic piano chorus. Bechet and Dickenson re-enter and salute each other with complementary phrases, swinging effort-lessly throughout. The duration of the longer-playing V-discs allows Bechet time to establish musical peaks and then climb higher still. A smooth rallentando rounds off the exhilarating performance effectively. The group's *St Louis Blues*, with Bechet leading on both the major and minor themes, has fine solos and some powerful concluding riffs, but compared to the preceding track it is simply another excellent Bechet recording.

Bechet found one of his most effective musical partners in Vic Dickenson. He anyway enjoyed working in a front line with only a trombonist, but Dickenson's all-round musicianship and subtleties especially pleased Sidney. The difference in range between the soprano saxophone and the trombone enabled them to keep out of each other's way, and, whereas a trumpeter's top notes often threatened Bechet's sense of domination, the mellow qualities of a trombone blended effectively with all registers of his instrument.

Dickenson, as laconic a person as he was a musician, enjoyed working with Bechet. He said, "You knew nothing could go wrong when you played a number with Sidney. He always played the right harmonies behind you, and he phrased in a way that gave you a chance to slip in your own ideas, and his tempos were perfect. He had his funny ways – I don't think he ever got my name right. He'd announce me as Dick Vickerson. I never fell out with him, even when he was as mad as hell about something. I kept on the right side of him musically, and I made sure I never got too friendly with any of his girl-friends, so we had no reason to fall out."[16]

Bechet wanted everyone to be as dedicated to music as he was himself. This fervour, combined with a certain reserve, and a recurring suspiciousness, caused even established friends to approach him warily. Guitarist Everett Barksdale recalls: "We got along well together. But Sidney was a rather testy person, who was continually on a short fuse."[17] Pianist Art Hodes said: "He wasn't a man that you felt you could laugh with straight away, not that he was sour though. He was serious about his music and expected other musicians to be the same way."[18] Duke Ellington's recollections were markedly similar: "He was a serious type of man. Bechet was never a very outgoing man."[19] Writer Max Jones also spoke of Bechet's reserve: "He was always friendly to me, but he just wasn't the sort of man you greeted with a warm embrace, even if you hadn't seen him for a long time. With someone like Louis Armstrong an expansive hug seemed totally natural, but not with Sidney."[20] Bechet's sudden bursts of anger were usually reserved for anyone displaying what Sidney considered to be sloppy musicianship. Mary Karoley said, "He was unable to tolerate mediocrity, even for the sake of kindness."[21]

Early in 1944 Bechet played for a season in Springfield, Illinois. The state capital wasn't noted for a thriving jazz scene, but a local restaurant owner, Vito Impastato, decided to inject some musical excitement into the fare at his Club Rio ("Speciality Spaghetti and Fried Chicken Sandwiches"), which was situated on West Grand Avenue. The club's press advertisements read: "Just The Place To Dine And Dance. Sidney Bechet and his four piece band, with a wide variety of dance tunes".[22] In effect, the venue was like many of the club-restaurants in which Sidney had worked in the North.

At the Club Rio one of Bechet's sidemen was the New Orleans pianist Gideon Honore, who was later replaced by Cedric Haywood (soon to work with Kid Ory). Haywood said of his Springfield stay: "It was a wonderful experience for me as Sidney was such a tremendous instrumentalist and very easy to get along with. I greatly admired his playing."[23] Paul Barbarin was the group's drummer. Bechet was also reunited with a veteran New Orleans trombonist, 'Hamp' Benson (who had been an associate of Buddy Bolden). Benson had also worked briefly with Bechet in New York in 1924.

When the Springfield season ended Bechet briefly returned to the East Coast and played at another series of concerts organized by Eddie Condon and Ernie Anderson. The success of their New York Town Hall presentations had encouraged the two promoters to carry out similar ventures in other cities. Bechet was also due to play for a season in Philadelphia, but this didn't materialize. He was not worried about this cancellation because by this time he was again having considerable problems with his teeth. He finally decided that the way to remedy the situation was to pay a visit to his dentist brother, Leonard, in New Orleans. So, for the first time in more than 25 years, Bechet went home.

John Reid made the journey to New Orleans with Bechet in June 1944. Reid was permitted not only to see the return of the prodigal, he was, via his portable recording equipment, also able to capture some of the sounds of the homecoming. One of the first to greet Sidney was the ace trumpeter Manuel Perez. Some jazz history books describe Perez as being senile by this time, but this is contradicted by the recording of his effusive greeting: "Well, well, Bechet. I'm certainly glad to see you. Glad that you're here among your friends." To which Sidney replies, "Yeah Manuel, I'm pleased to be back. I'm very happy to be back. I'm very happy to meet all the old friends of mine once more, such as Louis Nelson, and Picou, and Willie Santiago. It really reminds me of the old days. You know something, Manuel, if it hadn't been for you, fixing up my passport and things, I wouldn't have had the trip all over the world as I did. And now I'm back my brother is going to fix up my mouth and I hope to get started again. I've brought a friend of mine, by the name of John Reid. He's very much interested in our race and our music."[24]

Unfortunately, John Reid's only means of recording the men's fascinating memories of New Orleans music around the turn of the century was on 78 r.p.m. discs, so the conversation went in short bursts to allow new blanks to be placed on the machine. Bechet's introduction, which specifically mentioned John Reid's interest in the music of "our race", firmed up the musicians' trust, and later in the month they recorded examples of old New Orleans favourites for the visitor. Reid also attempted to make some recordings for issue on V-discs. In a letter to Bill Russell dated 11 July 1944, Reid wrote: "I went down to New Orleans with Sidney in June and stayed ten days. I had a swell time and I stayed at Dr. Bechet's right in the heart of things. Made two V.disc sessions, one with a large Navy Band (colored), and the other with seven pieces consisting of Nelson, Picou, Bocage, Decou, George Foster, Louis Keppard and Paul Barbarin. Sidney could not play as his new teeth were not finished, but he did play piano for one side."

Both Reid and Sidney lodged at Leonard and Odette Bechet's home at 1240 St Bernard Avenue, which enabled Sidney to make the aquaintance of Leonard's children, Emelda (b1925), Leonard, Jr (b1927) and Elmo (b1932). He was also able to meet up with various old friends, many of whom had never left New Orleans. There was a reunion with bass player George 'Pops' Foster, by coincidence also visiting New Orleans. When Sidney's dental work was completed he and John Reid moved north. Their ten-day stay had been a happy one and had served to reconcile Leonard and Sidney.

Soon after this trip Sidney returned to play for another season at the Club Rio in Springfield, Illinois (commencing on 7 August 1944). Paul Barbarin began this new residency with Bechet, but was forced to leave because his wife was taken ill. On his recommendation, the New Orleans drummer Dave 'Bob' Ogden took his place within a line-up of musicians (all from New Orleans) consisting of Quentin Baptiste on piano, Erving Charles, Jr, on guitar, and Walter Spencer on bass. After Bechet's group had finished its run the New Orleans tradition continued with the arrival of trumpeter Punch Miller, who remembered the 110 dollars a week he received in Springfield as being the best pay that he ever had for a job.

One of the great champions of Bechet's talents during the late 1930s and the 1940s was the author Paul Eduard Miller, who had first come under Sidney's spell after hearing him with Noble Sissle's band in Madison, Wisconsin. In the summer of 1944 Miller, who lived in Illinois, decided to pay a visit to hear Bechet in Springfield. In order to do so he had to travel a long way across the state; his two companions on the journey were drummer Ken Smith and pianist Max Miller, stalwarts of the Chicago jazz scene. Max Miller had vivid memories of the trip:

> We had to make a round trip of about 700 miles to meet Sidney, but it was worth it. I was working in a defence plant at the time, and Paul Eduard Miller kept saying, "You must meet Sidney Bechet". So Ken Smith, who was driving a truck for a commercial

milk company, said, "Okay, let's drive to hear Bechet". So we used the milk company's truck and went down into Chicago, about a hundred miles. We picked Paul up there and then went on to Springfield, Illinois, about another 250 miles. We got there in the middle of the night, or so it seemed, but Sid was still blowing at the club, and after we were introduced we sat in and we played for the rest of the night. We hit it off straight away and later, whenever Sid came to Chicago, we usually had a session. We always got along great, he was a gentle man. He sure liked a drink in those days, but then we all did.[25]

In early October 1944, when Bechet finished his season at Springfield, he decided to call into Chicago to meet up with Max Miller and Ken Smith. This time their session, on 8th October, was privately recorded. The issue of *Down Beat* dated 15 November 1944 reported: "While in Chicago last month Sidney held forth musically in a private home. The session was organised by Paul Eduard Miller of *Esquire* magazine and featured Sidney Bechet (clarinet and soprano), Max Miller (piano) and Ken Smith (drums). Sidney went along with the advanced ideas and improvisations of Max Miller."

Bechet, accompanied by his pet Boxer dog, also met up with John Reid and Mary Karoley in Chicago. He took them with him when he visited the home of an old friend from New Orleans, Mrs Alma Molsby, who cooked the visitors a chicken gumbo. When the meal was over Sidney and Alma Molsby entertained the others by singing old Creole songs from New Orleans. Sidney revered the heritage of his home city, and rarely need much encouragement to sit down at a piano to play and sing the songs of his childhood. Amongst John Reid's private recordings is Bechet's beautifully sung version of the old Louisiana Indian theme *To-wa-bac-a-wa*.

Bechet moved back to New York and took part in several recording sessions, the most notable of which was by Sidney Bechet & his Blue Note Jazzmen on 20 December 1944. The *Jazz Record* of January 1945 noted his return: "Sidney Bechet is back in town, blowing more horn than ever", an enthusiasm that was borne out by Bechet's remarkable playing on the Blue Note recording date. He seems determined to give his new dentures a rigorous test and, unusually, plays much more on clarinet than on soprano saxophone.

The highlight of the session is *Blue Horizon*, which is totally devoted to Bechet's clarinet playing. The six engrossing choruses of the slow blues he creates constitute one of his supreme achievements, revealing, amongst other things, the vast array of tonal effects he could produce (without any hint of gimmickry) from his instrument. The performance also demonstrates how Bechet could create countless variations of the blues; each 12-bar chorus brings forth perfectly conceived ideas that are rich in melody and in feeling. His colleagues back him sympathetically, allowing him to be heard in his full glory.

Sidney also plays clarinet on the slow rendition of *St Louis Blues*, where his work has a similar timbre to that of Johnny Dodds in his playing on the New Orleans Wanderers' version of *Perdido Street Blues*. Vic Dickenson's two choruses here can be measured against his finest work, and trumpeter Sidney De Paris displays his gift of creating unexpectedly fierce phrases – his playing on the ride-out choruses is inspiringly forceful.

The relaxed ensemble playing of the front line reveals the musicians' team spirit; no amount of rehearsal could have achieved the joyful way in which they play the shared breaks on *Jazz me Blues*. De Paris is again in triumphant form, particularly during his graceful but tough solo on *Muskrat Ramble*. This is the only title of the session on which Bechet plays soprano saxophone. His solo is full of clever touches, notably the way in which he produces a discordant tension, then quickly resolves it, like an ace juggler appearing to drop the vital object. Once again Manzie Johnson's drumming is full of lift, Pops Foster on bass is his admirably robust self, and Art Hodes plays effectively without threatening anyone.

Twenty-four hours later Bechet was recording as a sideman in Cliff Jackson's Village Cats, a star-studded group that consisted of Sidney De Paris on trumpet, his brother Wilbur De Paris on trombone, Gene Sedric on tenor saxophone and clarinet, Everett Barksdale on guitar, Wellman Braud on bass, Eddie Dougherty on drums and Bechet on clarinet and soprano saxophone. The session, for the independent Black and White label, is not well recorded. Bechet is listed as the vocalist on *Walking and talking to myself* (a composition of his) but the singing sounds unfamiliar.

Cliff Jackson makes no attempt to hog the limelight, but takes effective, rumbustious piano solos on *Quite please*, *Jeepers creepers* and *Cliff's Boogie*. On this last title, which also features Sedric's placid clarinet playing and a sprightly trombone solo from Wilbur De Paris, Bechet adds some unexpected notes into a startling solo. Sidney De Paris gets the chance to demonstrate his unique, song-like, muted trumpet work.

Bechet's playing on soprano saxophone adds considerably to the merits of these recordings, but he sounds a little below his best: there are no roaring phrases or breathtaking runs. This may be connected to the fact that he had latterly been concentrating on his clarinet playing, and certainly his best moments of the session occur during his clarinet chorus on *Jeepers creepers*. The solos from everyone are satisfactory, but the principal failing of the session is the ensemble work, when it is every man for himself.

A few days later, on 26 December 1944, Wilbur De Paris acted as the promoter for a memorable session held at the Pied Piper Club in Greenwich Village. Bechet was one of the stars of the gathering. The *Record Changer* of February 1945 described it as "one of the best sessions in a long time", and it gave a young musician, Bob Wilber, an early chance to marvel at Bechet's extraordinary talents. The event was billed as a "Swing Soirée" and featured Bechet (billed as the "World's Premier Soprano Saxist"), Mary Lou Williams and her trio (Al Hall on bass and Bill Coleman on trumpet), plus various other gifted players. Bechet performed his sets with Coleman on trumpet, De Paris on trombone and a rhythm section consisting of Hank Duncan (piano), Al Hall (bass) and Eddie Dougherty (drums).

Unfortunately that event was not recorded, but many of Bechet's appearances within all-star line-ups during the mid-1940s were. These included Eddie Condon's concerts (held initially at the New York Town Hall but later in the Ritz Theatre), which were originally recorded for radio transmission, but later found their way onto various long-playing albums. During Condon's Saturday afternoon dates Bechet was able to renew his ties with ex-colleagues from Nick's. He also had the opportunity of working regularly with the superb pianist Jess Stacy. During the shows Sidney was usually featured on a jazz standard, often one of his show pieces like *China Boy*, *I know that you know* or *Dear Old Southland*, but sometimes he performed delightfully impromptu versions of tunes such as *Don't get around much anymore*. He usually opted to play soprano saxophone on these quartet numbers, retaining it for the finales, in which the entire cast of musicians blew as lustily – and as skilfully – as they could.

Bechet maintained an easy relationship with Eddie Condon and with Ernie Anderson. During this period he took the opportunity of making a strange request to Anderson:

> Sidney had been on one of his out-of-town bookings – he'd been out of New York for some months. When he returned he phoned me and told me a stranger-than-fiction story. He began by saying that he thought that all his troubles had been caused by someone putting a hex on him, a witchcraft deal. As a result he sought out a woman in Harlem who apparently had the power to make the "evil" disappear. The "cure" involved Sidney renewing his faith in the Catholic Church, but it was an unorthodox deal, and the main penance was that he had to write some music for the 23rd Psalm. He not only had to write the music, he also *had* to get it published. So Bechet was telephoning me to see what I could do for him. I contacted Johnny O'Connor, who managed Fred Waring's music companies, and he said, "Okay, bring it around". So Sidney and I went to this crummy office and talked it over with Johnny. Sidney showed the manuscript (which someone else had written out for him) to O'Connor, and stressed that he *must* have the piece published, but said that he didn't want any advance or any money for it. Johnny went along with the idea and a black-and-white song copy came out. I don't think anything happened with it as far as sales went, but Sidney was very pleased to see the music in print, and felt that his luck would start to change. And strangely enough, it did.[26]

Subsequently the work was sung by Martine Johns in a performance at the Tabernacle of the Presbyterian and United Church of Christ, in Philadelphia, Pennsylvania.

In January 1945 Bechet went back to New Orleans. He had stayed away from his home city from 1919 until 1944, but within months of that first visit of reconciliation he again returned to the Crescent City. The occasion was a concert organized in the Municipal Auditorium by the National Jazz Federation on 17 January 1945. Sidney was part of a line-up including Louis Armstrong on trumpet, J. C. Higginbotham on trombone, Paul Barbarin on drums; James P. Johnson and William Houston, Sr, shared the piano duties, and two bass players, Richard Alexis and Narvin Kimball, alternated within the group. This stellar band was augmented briefly by the legendary trumpeter Bunk Johnson. Several of the band's numbers were broadcast (and recorded off the air by enthusiasts).

Unfortunately the amalgam of Armstrong and Bechet didn't produce the expected results. It seems that both men decided simultaneously to take the initiative at the preliminary rehearsal, and clashed head-on. Other New Orleans musicians (including Alphonse Picou and Henry Allen, Sr), who were seated in the auditorium during the run-through, observed that Armstrong became very angry and showed this by yelling at Sidney, "I ain't gonna have no two leads in my band." Thereafter the trumpeter played as though he was determined not to give Bechet any room to manoeuvre. As a result the music produced has an uneven quality, although Louis's feature on *I'm confessin'* is spectacular. Higginbotham's trombone playing is disappointing, and his solo on *Dear Old Southland* has the marks of burnt-out greatness. *Basin Street Blues* offers a brief glimpse of Bunk Johnson, who plays with a rare grace and beauty, using phrasing that was quite unlike the work of any other trumpeter; he creates a golden echo of the past.

This return visit by Bechet attracted more attention than his pilgrimage in 1944. He was interviewed by E. V. Gregorie for a long article that appeared in the *Pittsburgh Courier* of 20 January 1945. Sidney made sure that he mentioned his efforts on the 23rd Psalm, saying that he was going to dedicate it to St Augustine's Church (where he had been baptised in 1897). Bechet spoke of his travels and recalled playing for "the King of England, the Maharajah of India [sic] and the King of Italy". He also reminisced with obvious affection about the old days in New Orleans. But nostalgia did not keep Sidney in his home city for long, and he left Louisiana soon after the concert, never to return.

SIXTEEN

Bunk and Boston

Bechet's association with the Blue Note company was a regular and important part of his recording activities in the 1940s. On 29 January 1945 he organized a session that featured the trumpeter Max Kaminsky, with whom he worked on various club and concert dates. Kaminsky recalled Bechet with affection: "I always got along great with him. He was kind to me, but he could be mean to people if he didn't like them – he had a New Orleans temperament. We worked all sorts of jobs together in the 1940s. He could command an audience from the moment he got on stage. He blew in a way that could break the walls down if he wanted to. He never seemed to me to drink that much, but he had lots of fire in his playing, and his time was marvellous. He was an original and in turn respected players who weren't copying other people. He said he wanted a plain lead, and that's what I gave him. He could play *High Society* like he wrote it, but when we made that record together of that number he didn't attempt to take it over. He was a master."[1]

The soulful quality of Kaminsky's middle register is one of the features of the Blue Note version of *High Society*; his lead is uncomplicated but ingenious and his final chorus is superbly assertive. Bechet is on clarinet throughout; his husky timbre and Kaminsky's mellow tone create a highly engaging blend, but his playing of the 'traditional' clarinet solo is a mixture of the slipshod and the splendid. *Salty Dog* has a perfunctory vocal performance by drummer Freddie Moore that is improved by the rich sound of Bechet's low-note clarinet backing. Hodes's piano solo seems to go off at half-cock, and Kaminsky's dark-toned plunger solo gives the impression that his lip- and hand-movements are not coordinated. Kaminsky plays a superb plunger solo on *Jackass Blues*, however, sounding fierce and imaginative. Bechet's first chorus has an uneasy aura, but his second 12 bars are a triumph. He plays soprano saxophone throughout this number, as he does for a generally undistinguished rendition of *Weary Blues*. Bechet's contribution is a bold assembly of his stock phrases, but his interplay with Kaminsky's trumpet produce some magical improvisations.

Each of the session's four tracks is flawed in some way. George Lugg was not an imaginative trombonist; he had a pleasant tone but his solos never develop, and it sounds as though he couldn't make up his mind when constructing an ensemble part. The rhythm section is solid but doesn't engender much lift. Its three members (Moore, Pops Foster and Hodes) all play energetically but not cohesively, and a good deal of Hodes's rolling piano work is haphazardly performed.

Hodes and Bechet played on many gigs together, and the pianist often booked Sidney when he was organizing jam sessions. On one particular date in Greenwich Village this led to a bitter quarrel. Hodes had booked Bechet for a club jam session, but Sidney failed to show up; fortunately, Pee Wee Russell was on hand to deputize. Bechet didn't telephone any explanation to Hodes but turned up for the following week's session ready to play. Hodes summarized the situation:

> I wasn't long on patience and tolerance. So when Bechet showed up and took out his horn and started blowing I let him. But when the evening closed and he wanted his bread I just said, "No bread", turned my back and walked away. George Brunis was in the house and when Sidney got hot and said, "I'm going to Harlem and get my knife", and some more stuff, George followed to calm him down. I guess he did 'cause Bechet didn't come back at me. But I did get a letter from our union requesting I appear before the board.
> Well I had friends up on that board and I called one of 'em. I told him the whole story and he said, "Art, don't worry 'bout a thing. We've been looking to nail the old so-and-so for a long time. This is it." That's what got me to thinking. I could see Sidney and me before a board of directors washing our dirty linen publicly, and it didn't set good. He was too big a man to have that happen. No night's pay could mean that much. So I stepped back. Oh I caught it from some of the board members for doing it. I called Sidney and told him to forget it; I was mailing him the money.[2]

Fortunately most of Bechet's freelance dates passed off without incident. In February 1945 Sidney and Pops Foster journeyed to Boston to play for the local jazz society. Whilst playing the gig (on the 26th) at the Huntington Chambers Hall, Bechet announced that he was bringing Bunk Johnson up from Lousiana, and that he intended to form a band featuring Johnson's trumpet playing. Apparently this plan had taken shape during the concert in New Orleans in January 1945.

Bechet had already lined up a recording session with Blue Note for the new group, but he had not been able to get it any bookings in New York. When Dick Schmidt, the president of the Boston Jazz Society, heard about the shortage of work, he went to Steve Connelly (who ran the Savoy Cafe at 410 Massachusetts Avenue, Boston) and suggested that he book the new band. Connelly agreed to present Bechet and Johnson at his club, and accordingly, via Bechet, booked the five-piece group. The initial agreement was for a fortnight, commencing Monday 12 March 1945; Connelly retained the right to extend the booking (an option he repeatedly implemented).

Bunk Johnson was already a legendary jazz figure. Championed originally by Bill Russell and Gene Williams (editor of the magazine *Jazz Information*), he had gained a number of passionate supporters who insisted that here, at last, was the man who could revitalize jazz by re-establishing the traditional values of the ensemble. Lovers of small-band jazz had grown disillusioned by the growing popularity of swing music, in which highly arranged big-band routines gave little scope for improvisation. Groups like Muggsy Spanier's Ragtimers and Bob Crosby's Bob Cats temporarily solved the problem for many of the small-band devotees, but a hard-core minority felt that even these units lacked the rugged sincerity that they associated with the great jazz bands of the past.

Thanks to Bechet, Armstrong and Clarence Williams, the writers of the book

Jazzmen were able to track down Johnson, who was employed as a truck driver by a rice wholesaler in New Iberia, Louisiana. He had not played regularly for several years, but through the efforts of Dr Leonard Bechet he was fitted with false teeth, which allowed him to redevelop an embouchure; well-wishers bought him a trumpet and a cornet. Bunk subsequently made his recording début in New Orleans in 1942, and during the following two years played in other sessions. All of them provoked fierce controversy.

Detractors wrote that Bunk was bunk, and criticized the veteran's technique, tone and phrasing. His followers stoutly defended all Bunk's instrumental mannerisms, protesting that he was trying to purify jazz of the tainting commercial elements that had spoilt a once beautiful music. Bunk's come-back coincided with the emergence of modern jazz, soon to be dubbed 'bebop', and for 'beboppers' Bunk Johnson became a symbol of what they despised about old time jazz or, as they called it, "moldy fig music". The resultant furore brought Bunk a good deal of publicity.

Cynics later said that Sidney Bechet had observed the interest in Bunk's come-back and decided to capitalize on it by having the trumpeter work in his band, but this allegation doesn't hold water. Sidney was not one of life's born entrepreneurs, but he was shrewd enough to know that, if there were no prospects in New York for a band featuring himself and Bunk, the chances of lucrative work elsewhere were highly unlikely.

The truth of the matter was that, having heard Johnson play at the New Orleans concert, Bechet was intrigued by the idea of working with him again. Their partnership in the old Eagle Band had been a happy one, and Bechet had, in general, enjoyed Bunk's company off the bandstand. During the late 1930s he had developed a burning ambition to form up a 'real' New Orleans band. His efforts to make this dream come true in his group with Ladnier had been thwarted, and it seemed logical to try again with Ladnier's own teacher, Bunk Johnson.

Bechet was a man of catholic musical tastes, a musician who could improvise on all sorts of themes but one who had somehow been swept into the dixieland world. During the mid-1940s he was ambitious enough to feel that there was more to life than an endless round of *Muskrat Rambles* and *Ole Miss* programme finales. Bechet revered the musical traditions of his home city, but, like some jazz devotees, he felt that vital elements of the music were likely to disappear in the superficial worship of so-called historic numbers, the mere performance of which was sometimes cited as proof that a particular group was authentic. By working with a giant of yesteryear who had not suffered years of assault by various professional recording executives and reviewers, Bechet hoped that he would be able to form the nucleus of a band that would revive the best aspects of unspoilt New Orleans music. As far as repertoire was concerned, Bunk and Bechet thought along similar lines. Johnson told Bill Russell, "Any tune can be played well, the latest pop or oldest folk song can be played just as well as the most famous 'jazz classic'."[3]

Bechet didn't ask Johnson to sign a formal contract; he simply suggested that it would be a good idea for them to work together in the North, and the trumpeter agreed. In doing so, Johnson was making a shrewd move. He had already discussed (with Gene Williams) plans to lead his own band in New York later in 1945, and his springtime visit to the North would certainly serve as useful reconnaissance.

Bunk Johnson duly arrived in New York on Thursday 8 March 1945. On the following Sunday afternoon he gained sheafs of publicity by playing in a jam session organized by Milt Gabler at Jimmy Ryan's club. A packed house saw Bunk take the stand with Bechet on soprano saxophone, Pops Foster on bass, Kaiser Marshall on drums, Hank Duncan on piano and, on trombone, Sandy Williams (whose place was soon taken by George Lugg). The tunes which the pick-up group played (*Careless Love*, *St Louis Blues*, *Weary Blues*, and *I'm confessin'*) showed no alarming diversion from the usual musical fare at Ryan's, but the manner of their performance led the experienced critic Ralph Gleason to write in *Down Beat* that Bunk's playing that day gave him "the biggest thrill I have ever gotten out of jazz". Other jazz magazines covered the event in detail. *Jazz Record* reported that Bechet was surprised that Louis Armstrong (who had closed at the Zanzibar Club on the previous night) hadn't called in to see Bunk Johnson.

On the same day as the session at Ryan's, four of the participants (Bechet, Johnson, Williams and Foster) joined drummer Manzie Johnson and pianist Cliff Jackson in a recording session for Blue Note (in which Bechet played only clarinet). The group, later billed on record labels as Bunk Johnson & Sidney Bechet and their Orchestra, produced refreshing music that was totally devoid of gimmickry. Despite the unfamiliar surroundings, Bunk remains steadfastly himself, playing relaxed legato phrases in a highly individual manner, succinctly breaking up lines by deliberately clipping his notes, and tonguing an occasional note for effective emphasis. The man was an artist, but unfortunately his technique never redeveloped sufficiently for him to implement all the impressive musical ideas at which he hints.

Bunk Johnson was undoubtedly a highly individual musician. His recordings are historical examples of the style of trumpet playing that linked ragtime phrasing with the 12/8 rhythm that became known as the jazz beat. Bunk may have blarneyed about his associations with Buddy Bolden – Bechet said of Bunk's claim, "He may have played a piece with Bolden, but not regular"[4] – but there is no doubt that Johnson was an esteemed player in New Orleans during the early years of this century. He was a jazz pioneer whose style had developed during the music's infancy, a time when an emphatic trumpet lead was not the continuous sound of a small band's ensembles. In those days it was often a violinist who played the melody; one of the two clarinettists or the trombonist also took turns in carrying the theme. During the course of one number it was not uncommon for each of the melody instruments to share the job of playing the lead. Johnson and Bechet, having listened to live music during every day of their young manhood, were more than well aware of this tradition, and they did their best to resurrect it on the recordings in March 1945.

The group's performance of *Milneberg Joys* radiates musical team spirit; no one overblows and each man listens carefully to what his colleagues are playing.

Bunk's rendition of the melody is pretty faithful to the composer's lines. His playing doesn't 'swing' in the accepted sense of the word, but his fine sense of rhythm is obvious; it is a case of someone being supremely eloquent in an archaic tongue. An energetic solo by trombonist Williams is gracefully backed by Bechet and Johnson playing in their middle registers. When the clarinettist takes over lead duties, the backing by the brass players blends handsomely. Bunk then resumes the lead, blowing an almost dainty line before a heavier last chorus, during which he plays with spirit and conviction.

On the medium-paced 'spiritual' theme *Lord let me in the lifeboat*, the band uses the 16-bar tune to convey its solid ensemble rapport. To a degree, the odd man out is Sandy Williams, who could have been a little bolder, but he shows no signs of reticence in his solo, which is rich in lively lip trills. Bechet, using his warm chalumeau register, sounds inventive and totally relaxed. The concluding ensemble, which rests on the bouncy, four-in-the-bar pulse of Pops Foster's bass playing, has an ease that suggests the band would happily have gone on playing for several more choruses. Foster is well supported by Manzie Johnson on drums, and on piano by Jackson, who concentrates on 'comping' chords rather than playing fill-in phrases.

Bunk Johnson's approach to blues playing was quite different from that of Bechet. This is abundantly apparent on *Days Beyond Recall*, on which the trumpeter takes the four opening choruses. Whereas Bechet's blues playing is intensely dramatic and passionate, Bunk's is ruminative and almost mellow. Bechet's frequent blue notes are strong and searing, but Johnson uses them sparingly – almost as an incidental ingredient. Much was made by Bunk's disciples of Johnson's "diminished fingering", a description that makes no sense in that there are no special fingerings on the trumpet for the diminished chords. What is apparent on blues such as *Days Beyond Recall* is that Johnson liked occasionally to insert phrases built on a diminished-chord arpeggio.

Porto Rico (which was not issued for 40 years) begins as a lilting rumba. Johnson leads the group firmly through the first section of pretty, chromatic motifs, then guides the musicians positively into the four-in-a-bar section. Sandy Williams plays a competent solo against firm off-beat drumming; his improvisations are backed with chirpy clarinet comments. When Bechet takes a solo, Williams returns the compliment and blows a judicious accompaniment in support. Bunk re-enters to establish the workaday melody.

Up in Sidney's Flat is virtually a feature for Sandy Williams, who performs magnificently here, his bold ideas being couched in a virile tone that creates a melancholic effect without ever sounding maudlin. His partners avoid playing riffs, but instead concentrate on blowing soft backing phrases. Bechet summed up Williams's unfettered skills when he said, "He sure could shout the blues."[5] Bechet himself creates a richly expressive chorus, then Bunk comes to the fore playing with delicacy and poise. During the last chorus there are clues that Johnson's 'chops' were starting to tire, but he retains enough control to lead his partners to a satisfying ending. Although Bunk was physically fit (having worked as a truck driver, carpenter, and handy-man in the foregoing years), this recording session was still a challenge to his lip and his lungs. However, Bechet could not have been displeased with the veteran trumpeter's efforts. Unfortunately the honeymoon didn't last long, and Sidney soon had cause to regret his invitation to Bunk Johnson.

Troubles began for Sidney when he started rounding up the musicians he had intended using for the Boston residency. Hank Duncan, his original choice as pianist, decided not to leave New York, as did drummer Freddie Moore, who couldn't get a release from his regular job at Jimmy Ryan's. As pianist, Sidney engaged Ray Parker, a widely experienced player who had recently worked with Frankie Newton; he was also the editor of the New York magazine *Music Dial*. The new drummer was George Thompson, who had just finished a long stint in Louis Metcalf's band. But having to make these late changes agitated Bechet, who was already jumpy through having to keep a close watch on Bunk Johnson; the latter was prone to disappear if joyous prospects seemed in the offing elsewhere.

It was arranged that Bunk would lodge in Bechet's apartment at 16 Hamilton Terrace, New York, prior to his departure for Boston. The arrangement soon lost Bechet some sleep. On one of his first nights in New York Bunk Johnson went missing and Bechet had to spend most of the night roaming the city before he located him. Sensing that he would have his hands full, Bechet sent to New Orleans asking his 18-year-old nephew Leonard to come to New York to "help with the band's errands". Leonard, Jr, duly arrived in time for the Sunday session at Jimmy Ryan's. He recalled the preparations for the impending trip to Boston:

> The next morning we were all to meet at 10 a.m. at Sidney's place. We couldn't find Bunk and so Sidney went looking for him with me. The rhythm section showed up on time to find no one there, so they went home. When Sidney came back at 11 a.m., there was a note saying the men had gone home. Sidney told me to find Bunk and get him to Boston while he would get the others together and meet me at the job. I finally found Bunk and got him to the station. There I was with the drums, Sidney's horn, a heavy typewriter and Bunk – who wouldn't wake up. When we got aboard the train Bunk insisted on practising his horn. We finally got to the Savoy to find that Sidney hadn't arrived, so the management got Pete Brown's group to cover for us. Sidney finally arrived at 1 a.m., and they opened on Tuesday. That was enough of the band business for me, and I told my uncle I was going back to New Orleans.[6]

The fifth member of Sidney Bechet's New Orleans Rhythm Kings (as the band was billed in Boston) was bass player George 'Pops' Foster, who had known Bechet and Johnson for 40 years; he was apparently getting a good deal of enjoyment at seeing Bunk give Sidney the sort of treatment that, decades earlier, the young Bechet had so often meted out. Bechet had toyed with the idea of adding veteran trombonist Roy Palmer to the band, but the budget didn't allow for a sixth member. The Savoy management paid Bechet 550 dollars a week to provide the band; out of this Sidney paid Bunk Johnson 100 a week, Foster a little less and the two younger men about 70 dollars each.

Owing to some extraordinarily bad weather, the group's opening nights were heard by small audiences consisting mainly of devoted local jazz fans, but attendances soon improved and the band got into its stride, playing a wide variety of material. On 8 March 1945 Bechet sent a postcard to Bill Russell from New York, saying, "Hello Bill, Bunk is here and I think I am going to have a good band." Ten days later (from 413 Columbus Avenue, Boston), Bechet sounded even more optimistic; writing to John Reid, he enthused, "We are doing very well, Bunk is knocking 'em dead."

However, grievances on and off the bandstand soon began to effect the good relationship that Bechet and Johnson had previously enjoyed. Bechet felt that Bunk was drinking too much and was in consequence unreliable; in turn, Johnson thought that Bechet should only play the clarinet (as he done on the Blue Note recordings). Johnson used a contemptuous New Orleans term – "a fish horn" – in describing the soprano saxophone, supplementing the insult by calling it a "hop pipe".[7] Johnson's friend Harold Drob wrote about problems at the Savoy: "Bunk went to Boston with the highest hopes. He even went so far as to bring some sheet music with him. When Bunk pulled out his music Sidney apparently thought he was trying to take over the band."[8]

There is no doubt that Bunk was doing a good deal of tippling during the band's stay at the Savoy Cafe. When he got drunk, he became temperamental and played only when he felt like it, sometimes abandoning his efforts mid-way through the opening chorus of a band number. Bechet found such unprofessionalism totally exasperating, and as a result played the soprano saxophone on most numbers so that he could instantly re-establish the lead in moments of crisis. The more Johnson drank, the more Bechet played the soprano saxophone; the more Bechet played the saxophone, the more Johnson drank. There were some mitigating circumstances: this was the longest booking that Bunk had played in more than a decade, and he soon developed a sore mouth. In order to speed his recuperation he wanted Bechet to play the softer-sounding clarinet. This was not only on account of the instrument's tone colour; it was also to save his having to exert painful pressure to maintain a lead against the powerful soprano saxophone.

Bechet was not a model of sympathy on this occasion and became more and more angry. Bunk told Bill Russell: "Sidney would stomp some of those numbers off so fast he couldn't even pat his foot to them."[9] Johnson went on to express his disillusionment: "I didn't come to Boston to play Dixieland, and especially racehorse Dixieland."[10] The band's penchant for ultra-fast numbers was confirmed by Chris Tyle, whose father Axel Tyle sat in with the band at the Savoy: "The regular drummer took ill so on one of the band's breaks Axel went up to Bunk and asked if they could use a drummer. Bunk said "yes" and apparently talked it over briefly with Sidney. When they came back from the break my father sat down to play and Sidney called a number at breakneck tempo. My father apparently did a good enough job to be able to play the rest of the evening. His recollections of Bunk was that he 'was a nice old fellow', and that Sidney 'didn't have much to say'."[11]

On hand at various stages of the Johnson–Bechet contretemps was an assorted bunch of eminent jazz listeners, including Bill Russell, Nat Hentoff, Wynne and Grace Paris, Ralph and Jean Gleason, Eugene Williams, Larry Hitchcock and John Reid. Each saw the situation from a slightly different point of view. Later

Bill Russell and Wynne Paris exchanged cordial letters on events at the Savoy; these were later published in an article compiled by Mike Hazeldine for the British magazine *Footnote*.

Bill Russell (on 8 June 1945) insisted that he was not going to make alibis for Johnson, but explained that what others saw as plain cussedness on Johnson's part was actually a fierce independence: "He's been in the South for 65 years, had certain things beat into him, has never gotten a 'fair' deal' by any of my standards, and yet he hasn't given up and says 'I'm a Conga Negra, you can't take my privileges away from me'." Russell also wrote of the despair that Bunk felt about the musical capabilities of the Boston band, and suggested that Johnson's behaviour in Boston was "a month-long act". He urged Wynne Paris, "Don't be fooled by the way he can act so dumb for he's one of the quickest thinkers I ever saw. As he once said, 'While the white man is talking I'm thinking and before the white man is thru talking I have the answer.'"

Gene Williams, who had edited the magazine *Jazz Information*, but who worked for Decca in 1945, visited the Savoy during the first weekend of the band's stay. He described the scene in a letter to Bill Russell: "A big dimly lit night club with no dancing and no entertainment except the two bands (the other is a local trio featuring Pete Brown). Quite large, and jammed with white and colored every night I was there . . . the bands play alternate sets between 7.30 and midnight, with a Sunday matinée, no off-nights. Bunk's lip is in very bad shape, he played wonderfully Saturday night but on Sunday he omitted to work out before the matinée and could hardly play at all. Sidney was as mad as hell . . . they're planning to rehearse some Scott Joplin numbers though Sidney has some doubt about whether the people would go for them."

According to Bechet, his and Bunk's desire to play a wide selection of tunes at the Savoy was hampered by certain aspects of that venue. In *Treat it Gentle* he wrote: "There's no dance floor. Had we been able to have taken just any number and done something to it, théy wouldn't have cared just so it had a good rhythm to dance to. But what it was at the Savoy there, it was more of an attraction like and we had to stick to the *Royal Garden Blues* kind of thing."

Gene Williams's assessment of the Boston situation seems, on the evidence of his letters, to have been fair to all parties, as does Bill Russell's, but Bechet came to suspect that both men were partly responsible for Bunk's lack of cooperation. Sidney's excessive suspiciousness had surfaced again. He later came to realize that Russell's long-term friendship and admiration remained undiminished, but he never forgave Williams. Bechet claimed that Williams was responsible for getting Johnson drunk, despite the fact that Williams was hundreds of miles away for most of the booking. He also blamed him because Bunk had made recordings before his visit to the North and criticized him for planning to bring Bunk back to New York later in 1945. In addition Sidney insisted that Williams had spoilt his friendship with a girl called Lorraine by suggesting that she go home with Bunk (instead of with Sidney). This acrimony blended in with Bechet's general annoyance about Johnson's attitude, and after one of the band's broadcasts he described the trumpeter as "a hard-headed old cocksucker".[12]

Out of desperation, and perhaps a desire that Bunk shouldn't see him drinking too much, Sidney (unusually for him) smoked marijuana during the Savoy residency. Harold Drob recalled the final stages of the Bunk–Bechet saga: "The climax came when Sidney instructed the bartender in the place not to serve Johnson. Bunk told the bartender, 'I'm not a child. I'm 65 years of age and if I want to drink some whiskey I know how to find the nearest bar."[13]

John Reid visited the Savoy during the band's fourth week there and wrote to Bill Russell: "I don't like the situation at all, and if it isn't resolved the band will never hold together." Early in April Bill Russell visited Boston, but by then his chances of mediation had disappeared; on April 8th Johnson told him that he was quitting. Bunk carried out his intention and left Boston later that week. Bechet was eventually able to take a philosophical attitude towards Bunk Johnson's conduct. He said, "I guess the *Esquire* magazine summed it up about right when they said 'This group might easily have developed into a fine unit featuring New Orleans music had it not been for the unfortunate temperamental gymnastics of the eldest member of the band'."[14]

Sidney's health suffered as a result of the Savoy traumas. He went to the doctor with eye problems and was told that he had a kidney infection. Feeling quite ill, he was faced with the problem of fixing a suitable replacement for Bunk Johnson. His thoughts immediately shifted to New Orleans, and he wired an offer to his old neighbour trumpeter Herb Morand (who was decidedly more sociable than his drummer brother Morris). Herb was forced to decline the offer because his mother was terminally ill. Bechet then made contact with another of his home-city associates, Peter Bocage. Bocage agreed to join the band temporarily, as he was planning a trip to the North to see his sister Lillian (Lorenzo Tio's widow).

In the meantime, following a series of enthusiastic recommendations from the members of the Boston Jazz Society, Bechet decided to offer the job to a young local favourite, Johnny Windhurst, then only 18 years old. Peter Bocage eventually arrived and replaced Windhurst, but returned to New Orleans three weeks later, allowing the young man to resume a place in the front line alongside Bechet.

Bass player John Field sat in with this band under curious circumstances: "Once at the Savoy in Boston, Robert Goffin was in town. Bechet had a young Johnny Windhurst on cornet with Pops Foster on bass. Bechet was trying to impress Robert Goffin. Pops Foster motioned me to join in. My ax was on the stand. So Bechet had two basses. Shook him."[15]

The full blessings of the Savoy booking only became apparent to Bechet's devotees when Johnson McRee, Jr's label, Fat Cat, released albums of broadcasts that the group made in 1945. Sometimes the changing relationships are reflected in the music but, despite the acrimony, the jazz is, at times, wonderful. The broadcasts survived through the home recording equipment of Robert and Faith Kelsey and Jim Weaver; Wynne Paris also kept acetates of his radio interviews with Bechet made at this time, and they are included on the Fat Cat releases. But perhaps the most fascinating recordings from the Savoy were made by John Reid, who captured the band (with Bunk) rehearsing during the afternoon of 3 April 1945. Even this highly productive rehearsal was loaded with ill will. John Reid recalled the scene: "Just before I left Boston Sidney called a rehearsal so I could record the band. This was set for 2 p.m. at the Savoy. On arriving with my equipment I found to my horror that the electric current at the Savoy was in the DC district of Boston. Of course, AC was required for my turntable and recording amplifier." Reid eventually managed to locate a converter, and he arrived back at the hall sometime after 4 p.m. to find that the band was packing up. Sidney persuaded the musicians to unpack and the rehearsal resumed: "No one was speaking and they barely acceded to my instructions as relayed by Bechet. Their mood was such that I didn't dare ask for repeats, so with one exception each take was the one and only take. I kept Sidney to his clarinet throughout these standards."[16] Reid was understandably delighted with the performances (which include a cardinal version of *Sister Kate*).

Bechet's broadcasts from the Savoy contained many jazz standards, but occasionally the band played pop songs like *Pistol Packin' Mama* and Edgar Sampson's swing tune *Blue Lou*. Some of the most fascinating moments come during the blues theme that serves as the signature tune of the "Jazz Nocturne" programmes. Bechet opens the treasure trove of his blues phrases during the 36 recordings of the theme taken off the air. Bunk Johnson is present on the first half dozen broadcasts, but is often badly balanced, sometimes sounding distant throughout an entire programme; the problem may have been self-induced by Bunk's deliberately turning away from Bechet on the bandstand. Happily he comes through loud and clear on a number of items, particularly *Didn't he ramble* (29 March 1945) and *I found a new baby* (5 April 1945), but if Bunk's reputation rested solely on these Savoy dates his name might never have become hallowed. It is apparent that Johnson is having recurring problems with his embouchure, but even allowing for this, the playing is full of enigmas. His feature on *I'm confessin'* utilizes quaint touches and subtle grace notes but seems practically devoid of spirit, almost as though the performer is wilfully creating an air of indifference.

On some of the broadcasts with Bunk, Bechet safeguards the opening melody by playing it himself (on soprano saxophone), often in unison with Johnson. As soon as Bechet hears that the trumpeter sounds secure he moves off to play a harmony part, but he often hovers anxiously for a bar or two. Yet when the two musicians achieve a sudden rapport, as on *I ain't got nobody* and *Sobbin' Blues*, the effect is immensely satisfying. Their contrasting tonal approach is highlighted on *Never No Lament*; Bechet alternates between cajoling entreaties and growled exclamations, but Johnson plays dignified lines that suggest a bygone world. Their differing rhythmic feel is clearly shown on *Muskrat Ramble*. Bunk, by some ingenious phrasing, gives an idea of how the tune might originally have been played. Bechet, who maintained that the theme was actually an old New Orleans favourite called *The old cow died*[17], nevertheless 'swings' his phrasing.

Johnson, in general, sounds more comfortable when Bechet plays the clarinet. On *Basin Street Blues*, Bechet begins on saxophone, but takes the unusual step of changing to clarinet (on the occasions that he changed instruments during a number he usually followed the reverse procedure). This number (like the tunes which John Reid recorded at the Savoy rehearsal) gives a glorious indication of what might have been – both front-line musicians create absorbing lines that blend perfectly. Pianist Ray Parker constructs a serene solo here, but at most times seems to be at loggerheads with an unresponsive instrument. The rhythm section suffers from variable balance, but even on a good night never seems to be inspired or particularly unified.

Bechet's own contributions to the broadcasts with Bunk are often disappointing. Even his set variations lack their usual sparkle and his performance of *When it's sleepytime down South* must rank amongst his least noteworthy. However, there are bewitching moments, particularly on the final section of *The Darktown Strutters' Ball* (on saxophone) and *Royal Garden Blues* (on clarinet). Sidney is much more authoritative and eloquent in the sessions with the talented young Johnny Windhurst, even though the two took a while to work up an effective partnership.

Windhurst, who later developed into a fine jazz trumpeter (one who never received his dues), sounds on these early dates like a technically accomplished amalgam of Bobby Hackett, Wild Bill Davison and Bunny Berigan. He had yet to find his own style, but any young trumpeter could be proud of what Windhurst plays on *Ugly Child*, *Jazz me Blues* and *Blue Skies*. Windhurst shows briefly how well he uses the cup mute; the attractive sound he produces would have blended well with Bechet's clarinet, but unfortunately the two tone colours never occur simultaneously.

Bechet plays some numbers accompanied only by the rhythm section with some formidable results. On most of these, drummer George Thompson uses brushes instead of sticks, allowing Pops Foster's powerful bass sound to cut through more easily. Sometimes Bechet plays a segue ballad medley, running through a single chorus of each piece, as in the medley by Jerome Kern which contains *Can't help lovin' that man*, *Why do I love you?* and *Make Believe*.

Johnny Windhurst handed over temporarily to the veteran Peter Bocage, who takes a sedate approach to his task, seldom sounding adventurous. This strategy sometimes achieves effective results, as on *The Sheik of Araby*, where Bechet decides not to repeat his celebrated variation and instead creates some blithe improvisation. Careful listening reveals Bocage's subtle approach, but apparently he did not enjoy working alongside Bechet on saxophone (which Sidney obstinately played through all six broadcasts with Bocage). The trumpeter shows his displeasure by sometimes dropping out of the band during the ensembles.

The Bechet–Bocage partnership is rich in confusion, which did not diminish when the two were temporarily joined by valve trombonist Brad Gowans (on 15 May 1945, when he replaced bass player Pops Foster for one broadcast). Gowans plays some elegant solos that underline his attractive use of wide intervals, but sounds bemused by the existing lack of coordination within the ensemble.

Bocage carried out his original plan and soon left for New Orleans. Later he spoke philosophically about his dates with Bechet: "He just wants you there, that's all. But he's gonna do all the playing, you understand."[18] Windhurst returned to replace Bocage and settled in quickly, obviously benefitting from things learnt during his previous stint with the band. His contributions are more consistent, both in his solos and during the ensembles. As a result Bechet allows him to develop his own lines, which he does impressively, particularly on *Marie*, *Ol' Man River* and *Dinah*.

The rhythm section benefits from the accord within the front line and, at last, settles into something like a swinging unit, albeit a heavy-handed one. But for all the increased proficiency and rapport, the band which concluded the Boston residency did not achieve the authenticity that Bechet had fervently hoped for; Sidney never again made any determined plans to form an 'authentic' New Orleans style band.

SEVENTEEN

King Jazz

Although Bechet was disappointed with the musical results of his long stay at the Savoy, socially there had been many happy times with various friends. Whilst working in Boston he met Laura, a North American Indian, who subsequently moved down to New York to live with him.

Bechet recuperated from his kidney ailment, then during early July 1945 undertook a series of dates in upstate New York. For Sidney, the big event of that month was the commencement of a series of recordings for a new company, King Jazz, the president of which was Mezz Mezzrow. Plans for this organization came into being when Mezzrow met electronics engineer John van Beuren at Jimmy Ryan's club in New York. The two men became friends, and later van Beuren and his business partner, Harry Houck, invited Mezzrow to head a recording company that they were forming. The trio settled on the name King Jazz, Inc.; Mezzrow designed the label and his partners chose the logo colours. From an office at 140 West 42nd Street, Mezzrow began planning a series of small-band dates, most of them centred around the enormous musical talents of Sidney Bechet.

Bechet's first date for King Jazz was on 30 July 1945, as part of the Mezzrow–Bechet Septet; Mezzrow was the only white musician in the group. Hot Lips Page (billed as Papa Snow White for contractual reasons) was on trumpet and vocals, and Sammy Price (as Jimmy Blythe, Jr, because of his Decca commitments) was on piano; Danny Barker was on guitar, Pops Foster on bass, and Sid Catlett on drums. King Jazz adopted a non-commercial attitude towards material, and many of the items that appeared on the label were instrumental blues. At least two takes of most of the output of the Mezzrow–Bechet group were eventually released, revealing that the performers were encouraged to improvise as much as possible on these dates.

The circumstances were almost ideal for inspired jazz performances, but there were snags – one being that Mezzrow was not adept at musical planning: often a second take was needed to sort out an aspect of a head arrangement that should have been talked over before the recording light went on. Mezzrow said, "When we were recording we never had to talk about what we were going to play"[1], but this policy caused some excellent solos to be set in muddled surroundings. There is also a distinct lack of strong themes. It is all very well to say "the blues is the blues", but most great blues performances are anchored to a strong opening melody. The same failing mars those sides where the group takes a standard chord sequence like *I found a new baby* and makes it the basis for its improvisations on *Minor Swoon*.

There is no jazz 'law' that says you must use an opening theme; in fact, there have been superb impromptu recordings (such as Lionel Hampton's *Dinah*) where the tune is played only fleetingly. But such an approach cannot be relied upon, and for all the skills on display, Bechet, Page and Mezzrow share some uneasy ensembles where no one sounds sure of his role. Bechet usually solved such dilemmas by picking up an uncertain front line by the scruff of its neck and, by the sheer power of his playing, forcing it into a cohesive unit. In deference to Mezzrow's position of command, and to his lack of musicality, Bechet decided to remain less assertive in the ensemble; he does, however, create some momentous solos.

Trumpeter Hot Lips Page is in powerful form on *House Party*, showing all his considerable skills as a blues player; when he takes over after Bechet's thrilling solo he produces no sense of anticlimax. The two versions of *Perdido Street Stomp* (a pretty 16-bar theme that had cropped up earlier that year in Boston as *Feetwarmers' Stomp*) are quite different, both in structure and in tempo. The group moves out of the opening theme by modulating from C to F, and the musicians then create their solos on a 12-bar blues sequence. The first take is marred by some wrong notes in the playing of the theme, but even so it has considerably more lift than the second attempt.

Revolutionary Blues is also taken at two different tempos, the first version slow, the second bouncy. Despite the title, it is not a blues, but a 32-bar pattern, rich in improvising prospects. Mezzrow, keen to revive the noble art of the jazz ensemble, eschewed the sort of planning that those prospects deserve. The second attempt is taken at a tempo that allows the strong rhythm section a chance to add zest to the performance, which is played by the whole ensemble from beginning to end.

The most organized number of the session, *Blood on the Moon*, produces some stirring music. According to Mezzrow, it was "composed in the studio".[2] Pianist Sammy Price creates an introduction that perfectly launches two choruses of Page's husky singing; Bechet backs him with rugged directness, and Mezzrow offers quiet support. Bechet (on saxophone) plays a passionately expansive solo, then Page sings another chorus before picking up his trumpet for an emphatic concluding chorus.

On the following tracks the septet provides instrumental backings for the New Orleans singer Pleasant Joseph, who made an impression soon after his arrival in New York by sitting in with Hot Lips Page's band at Clark Monroe's club; within weeks he was recording with Mezzrow and Co. These were early days for the singer, and his skills of vocal delivery were not fully developed. Here he tends to sound mannered and repetitive. The band gives him solid support, and on the first take of *Bad Bad Baby Blues* Bechet plays a ravishing obbligato. Mezzrow himself reaches an expressive height on *Saw Mill Blues*.

The session ended with two instrumental pieces. Of the three takes of *Minor Swoon*, take two is infinitely the best, with free-wheeling solos all round (Page sounds splendidly waspish in his tightly muted chorus), and there is some exhilarating drumming by Sid Catlett. The first of two attempts of *The Sheik of Araby* wins the prize. Here Bechet's saxophone tone is at its most opulent. Mezzrow sounds primitive but interesting, and Hot Lips Page brings back memories of the exultant playing he contributed to a V-disc recording of the same tune.

A month later Mezzrow and Bechet took part in another prolific recording session covering two days, 29 and 30 August 1945. Only bass player Pops Foster remained from the previous date. The veteran Kaiser Marshall came in on drums, and Fitz Weston played the piano. This rhythm section doesn't have the swagger of the previous unit, as is made obvious on the first recording of the date, *Baby I'm cutting out* (a vocal number by Douglas Daniels – a former member of the Spirits of Rhythm). Bechet's main role is in establishing the stereotyped melody. Mezzrow achieves a twittering effect on the two early takes, but performs with more artistry on the third. This track is one of the only blatant attempts at commercialism by the King Jazz label.

Bechet's power and conviction immediately lift *Ole Miss* into a swinging groove, and Mezzrow, who is swept along by the hurricane, plays with considerable spirit. By this time the rhythm section had achieved a sturdy union. *Bowin' the Blues* is a feature for Pops Foster's bowed bass playing; his arco work blends nicely with pianist Weston's tremolo arpeggios. Bechet and Mezzrow play a well-organized duet, in which Bechet initially leads, then creates a rich harmony part to the clarinettist's line. On the first take their blend is near elegiac, but it is less so on the second try. Mezzrow had an anecdote about this title:

> John van Buren [sic], who was in the control room at the recording, remembered that he had brought his camera to take pictures . . . he came into the studio with the camera in hand . . . Pops Foster saw it and asked to be excused from the room. This made Bechet and I furious because we were all warmed up from the last side . . . he returned with two objects in his hand . . . one was a powder puff and the other was an envelope with powder in it that he had borrowed from Mrs Van Buren, who was also in the control room. Bechet had had enough of this by this time and began to fuss with Pops, saying, "Man! You are as old as Methuselah and you want to powder your face to make a picture. I don't dig you". Pops became nervous then and grabbed his bow, which he seldom uses, and began to tune up his bass. Fitz Weston who was also nervous by that time, sounds the notes on piano for him, but ran arpeggios at the same time, leaving Pops to fish around on the bass to get his notes. This sounded very good to me and I stopped both of them and said, "That's it. We're gonna make a record of the blues now. Pops, you are gonna use your bow and the title will be *Bowin' the Blues*".[3]

I ain't gonna give no one none of my jelly roll was a cornerstone of most of Mezzrow's performances (he recorded it with Tommy Ladnier in 1938). Unfortunately, familiarity did nothing to broaden Mezz's imagination; in fact, by throwing caution to the wind (as he does here), he sounds aimless throughout most parts of the four takes. In contrast, Bechet works steadfastly to achieve a better solo at each new attempt. He sounds particularly determined on take two; Mezzrow is perhaps closest to coherence on take three, though take four has its moments.

The quintet made a new version of *Perdido Street Stomp*. It is tidier than the effort of the septet, with Bechet playing a forceful interpretation of the theme before zooming into some majestic improvisations. Bass player Pops Foster is close to his impressive best, pumping out an inspiring stream of perfectly placed, rich-toned notes. The second take is longer, and contains many differences; Mezzrow plays a more prominent role here. The group has three shies at *Old School* (again using the 32-bar *Revolutionary Blues* sequence). There are slight musical mishaps in all three versions, but each attempt is devoted entirely to ensemble playing. Alongside Mezzrow, Bechet plays his impelling improvisations with the ease that comes only with complete mastery. In the slower second take the rhythm section begins to buckle, but suddenly picks itself up and lays down a solid beat that inspires some purposeful lines from Mezzrow.

Just as inspiration was beginning to fade, Mezzrow wisely chose to record one of his own blues themes, *Gone Away Blues*, and instantly the hit-and-miss combination achieves unity and spirit. The two men in the front line re-create the mood that they had first shared on their 1938 recording of *Really the Blues*. Mezzrow plays the opening theme with Bechet blowing a soft triplet figure as accompaniment, the coalition of sounds resting on the sonorous notes of Foster's bowed bass. The harmonized second 12-bar section produces a near-tender mood, which Bechet develops with a plethora of noble sounding ideas. Mezzrow's low register gives the soprano saxophone an admirable backing, encouraging Bechet to move higher to pour out a quivering, ornate series of timeless blues stanzas. There was no need for another take – the group had achieved perfection.

The quintet cruises through *De Luxe Stomp*, which is loosely built on the final strain of *Royal Garden Blues*, and in doing so creates another fairly uneventful medium-paced ensemble work-out. Variation was at hand in the shape of another blues composition by Mezzrow, *Out of the Galleon*. Again (as in the case of *Gone Away Blues*) the group responds to the framework of a strong theme. The three takes provide a fascinating insight into how a jazz group shapes and reshapes its material, and how inspiration ebbs and flows in various attempts. A feeling of caution pervades the early part of the first take, though the final two choruses are majestic; the second take is smoother, but the tonal blend between Mezzrow and Bechet is nothing like as satisfying. On take three all the elements combine to create a masterpiece.

Perhaps weariness had generated just the right mood, for certainly Mezzrow achieves a mellowness that rarely graced his work. He and Bechet combine their ideas beautifully, and Fitz Weston's simple block-chording on piano could not have been more appropriate. Bechet, sounding very relaxed, plays with extreme sensitivity throughout his second 12 bars, then floats into a final section, establishing a mood that somehow encompasses both joy and sorrow. Again his ingenuity is enhanced by Mezzrow's hushed backing notes.

Mezzrow himself was delighted with the sessions, and said that the music he recorded with Bechet was a "welling up of our enthusiasm and our warm feeling for each other".[4] In 1945 Bechet's relationship was at the cordial stage. Suspicious though he was, Sidney sensed that Mezzrow's expansive compliments were well meant, but some of the things that Mezzrow played on his instrument bemused him.

Sammy Price, who played on some of the King Jazz dates, said: "I don't think that Bechet could ever understand why Hugues Panassié thought that Mezzrow was a great clarinettist. As I saw it, Sid and Mezzrow were never close. They might have played gigs together and made records, but they were never close friends."[5] Sidney always fidgeted when Mezzrow said that, although he had a white skin, he was really a Negro at heart. Years later Bechet told a Scandinavian friend, Dr Terkild Winding: "Mezz should know that race does not matter – it is hitting the notes right that counts."[6] It is significant that Bechet never once used Mezzrow on any recording session for which he was the leader.

The success (though deserved) of the King Jazz recordings turned Mezzrow's head in an alarming way; this is rendered obvious by the comments he made in the 1960s for the Storyville label reissues: "I'm a genius. Yes, I'm a genius and Sidney Bechet helps me to prove it on the King Jazz recordings. I'm not going to wait until I've been dead a hundred years to be acclaimed. Braggadocio, yes, but not conceit."[7] Sidney must have spun in his grave at these remarks. Mezzrow was never slow to publicize himself, but on this occasion he gives the impression that he was enough of a megalomaniac actually to believe what he said about his playing. In truth, he was a limited musician with a sour tone and a stunted rhythmic, melodic and harmonic imagination. He is at his best on the slow blues duets with Bechet because he has such a giant to cling to, rest on, and be inspired by. On the swifter pieces his ensemble playing often creates a ludicrous effect; he may well have thought he was sounding like Jimmie Noone, but his impersona-tion is as convincing as Bob Hope beating his chest and pretending to be Tarzan. But jazz listeners would have been poorer had Mezzrow never lived. His foresight, courage and enterprise enabled the world to hear many marvellous examples of Sidney Bechet performing without restraint, unhampered by drastic time curtailments on fertile, uncommercial material. Hugues Panassié was near the truth when he wrote: "Seldom, if ever, has such extraordinary music been heard on record, it is really something entirely new."[8] Bechet concurred and, on first hearing the test pressings, said: "They're different from any records I ever heard or made."[9]

The French bandleader Claude Luter, who knew Bechet and Mezzrow well, wrote of the latter: "He is a good amateur, but the sad thing is that some people wanted to consider him a genius and others as something useless. For me, the adjective amateur does not have a pejorative meaning, on the contrary, an amateur is someone who plays as he likes, if his music brings in money, good, if not, he has to find money some other way."[10] Writer Ralph Berton, who also knew Mezzrow well, said that he made up in enthusiasm what he lacked in ability, and certainly it was Mezzrow's enthusiasm that put King Jazz records into production. Mezzrow showed (probably influenced by Jimmie Noone's reed-duo recordings) that a clarinet and saxophone line-up could produce satisfying jazz, which, at the time, was a unique viewpoint amongst record producers. In proving his point, Mezzrow acted as an inspiration for many musicians (particu-larly in Europe and Australia) who did not wholeheartedly believe in the dogma that traditional jazz could only be played by a front line consisting of a trumpet, trombone and clarinet.

Throughout the mid-1940s Sidney retained his links with the William Morris booking agency. By then Billy Shaw, who had negotiated several residencies for Bechet, was running the agency's "one-night stand department", which dealt only with touring units. Bechet's small group was classified by the agency as a "cocktail unit", and all such bands were handled by the section in which Joe Marsolais, Vi Barrett and Harold Oshry worked. In the late summer of 1945 Bechet received an offer from this department which led to his taking a quartet to Washington, DC, to play a residency at the Brown Derby, 3333a Connecticut Avenue.

Bechet's bass player for this engagement was Pops Foster, whose recollections show that Sidney was still smarting over the way in which Louis Armstrong had yelled at him during their visit to New Orleans earlier that year: "Some guys wanted Sidney and I to come to New York and go on the air with Louis Armstrong. But Sidney said he was as big a name as Louis, so Louis could come to Washington. Joe Glaser (Louis's manager) wouldn't go for that, and we didn't get the job."[11]

Bechet returned to New York a few weeks later and renewed his association with the Blue Note recording company. Alfred Lion's business was flourishing. In late 1939 he had incorporated an old friend, Francis Wolff, as his partner; Wolff looked after the company's affairs during the time that Lion served in the US forces. When Lion was released from the services he implemented an ambitious series of recordings that embraced many jazz styles, old and new. His first postwar date with Bechet was on 12 October 1945. It featured Sidney with cornetist Wild Bill Davison (recently demobilized from the US Army), bass player Pops Foster, drummer and vocalist Freddie Moore, and the session's leader, pianist Art Hodes. Davison, Hodes and Moore were working as a trio at the Village Vanguard, and the session was held on their night off; it began at midnight.

Teaming Davison with Bechet seemed an inspired idea. Both men specialized in extrovert jazz, and, although Bechet was the more creative improviser, Davison was also capable of playing fiery, spirited music. Their first recorded encounter would have been more satisfying had they worked together more often as a duo. As it is, both men go in for some careful sparring, like two champion boxers in an exhibition bout: there is plenty of huffing and puffing, but too often the excitement appears contrived. Each musician possessed the ability to enflame an ensemble with a single, searing, high-register note, but, perhaps to avoid confrontation, both keep the effect under wraps for most of the session. Even so, their talent and their energies create some exciting moments on the fast tunes and a few voluptuous exchanges on the slower numbers.

Wild Bill Davison gave writer Russell Davies his views on the partnership: "I was smart enough to know when he was playing the lead to play the second part. I didn't try to step on his toes, and when I had solos he let me go – he didn't butt in on my things. We played some songs I didn't know, and he would promptly take me in a room, and he'd say, 'Here's the way it goes'. I remember one he taught me was *Save it Pretty Mama*."[12] This tune, the first of the session, is also the best. Bechet is on clarinet throughout, and during the opening chorus weaves supporting phrases around Davison's straightforward lead. Art Hodes creates a robust but lucid solo, rolling out emphatic phrases that are firmly supported by Foster's thwacking bass sound and Moore's unconstrained drumming. At this slow tempo Bechet's low-register solo needed a fuller backing sound than his three accompanists provide – Hodes's piano playing is unobtrusive to the point of inaudibility. Davison re-enters and boldly plays the recently learnt melody, inserting an occasional dirty-toned aside; Bechet provides a loose counterpoint, much as he might have done had he been playing soprano saxophone. By 1945 Bechet's ensemble work on clarinet and saxophone was almost identical; the main difference was in timbre and in volume. Davison definitely felt happier when Bechet was playing the clarinet alongside him. He said, "I can't take the sound of that horn too long."[13]

Bechet remained on clarinet for *Way down yonder in New Orleans*. Hodes's unadventurous piano solos fail to make full use of the tune's harmonic possibilities but Davison decorates the melody effectively, playing a spritely lead in the closing stages. This exuberance may have convinced Sidney that it was time to bring out the big guns; he plays soprano saxophone for the rest of the date, and acts like a typhoon against Davison's lead on *Memphis Blues*.

The quintet's version of *Shine* has been praised as jazz at its most unrestrained, but aside from an opening chorus taken hell for leather, the mood of the piece is merely frantic. The drumming is unimaginatively relentless, and Hodes on piano discovers that the pace is too fast for comfort. Davison also finds the bar-lines coming at him with disconcerting swiftness and is forced to resort to stock phrases. Only Bechet seems comfortable at the tempo (one suspects that he set it); his solo is grandiloquent, full of sweeping, rubato phrases. The best moments come in the final chorus, where the lead shuttles to and fro between Davison and Bechet.

Fred Moore's highly personal vocal style is the feature of *St James Infirmary*. Davison, unusually for him, uses a cup mute in backing one of the vocal stanzas. Bechet creates a sub-tonal effect on saxophone that can justly be called beautiful; it is regrettable that this delightful timbre wasn't captured more often on record. The group ending sounds jerky and unrehearsed, and this same lack of preparation mars *Darktown Strutters' Ball*. But, despite some uncertainty about the routines, there are some stimulating exchanges between the raucous sounding Davison and Bechet in combative mood. On a second take, Bechet plays clarinet throughout, but the gentler sound seems to induce the ensemble to move down to a lower, less suitable, gear. The rough moments of the final two numbers from the session are excusable. Only four tunes were scheduled to be recorded on the date, but things fell into place so quickly that the last two selections were hastily added to the agenda so as to make full use of the studio time. The entire session lasted only for two hours.[14]

Lorraine Gordon, who was then Alfred Lion's wife, remembers the expectancy surrounding Bechet's early sessions for Blue Note: "We made the recording sessions and then waited breathlessly for the test records to arrive. We gathered at our apartment in Greenwich Village and settled down to the real business of hearing how it all sounded. Usually there was just one take and it was always wonderful to our ears. We had a simple record player in those days, nothing like today's equipment, but Sidney filled the room with his sound and we knew it was right. Then he always cooked up a meal for us of red beans and rice, my first experience, and I've never had it better since. These sessions would last until the wee hours and then we would drive him home, somewhere in Harlem."[15]

Lorraine, Alfred Lion and Francis Wolff decided to publicize Blue Note's growing achievements by holding a celebratory concert at the New York Town Hall on 15 December 1945. Sidney Bechet on soprano saxophone and clarinet headed a star-studded assembly which included Sidney De Paris, Sandy Williams, Albert Nicholas, James P. Johnson, Sid Catlett, Wellman Braud, Danny Alvin on drums, Billy Taylor on bass and Jimmy Shirley on electric guitar. Frankie Newton made a guest appearance playing a rare instrument, the bass cornet. Pig Meat Markham and Cow Cow Davenport supplied the vocals. Bechet was apparently in an elated mood that night, happy to be a star in what was then a rare event, a New York Town Hall concert devoted almost exclusively to the work of black performers.

Bechet was not a racist and often said he was more interested in a man's musical talent than in the colour of his skin. Only days before that concert he had recorded with one of his favourite drummers, the white musician George Wettling. Both men had been part of quartet led by the white pianist Joe Sullivan; the fourth member of the group was bass player Pops Foster.

The main disappointment of this session is caused by the poor recording quality, but there are some superb moments. The opening choruses of *Sister Kate* feature Sidney sounding relaxed and inventive on saxophone, while Wettling's wristy brush work provides obvious stimulation in the background. Sullivan's solo reveals his debt to Earl Hines; nevertheless he performs brilliantly, urged on by Foster's propulsive beat. Bechet displays his remarkable rhythmic balance during his variations on *Panama*; this too has an impressive solo from Sullivan which is full of *élan*. In the July 1947 issue of *Metronome*, Leonard Feather reported on a blind-fold test he had conducted: he played this track for Count Basie, who instantly recognized Sidney's playing: "Must be that fine old man Sidney Bechet; I have an awful lot of respect for him, he always sounds interesting to me."

Got it and Gone has no theme. It is a series of improvised work-outs on the 16-bar *Saints* sequence. Bechet, on clarinet, growls out three choruses without sounding particularly inspired, but Sullivan is again in superb form. Some uneasy moments develop during the stop-time notes which back the bass and drum choruses, but impetus keeps the group going and in the finale the group achieves a joyful, spirited mood, with Foster's bass sounding at its most energetic.

Foster and Bechet worked together often during this period. They spent part of late 1945 back at the Savoy Cafe in Boston, this time appearing as guests with various local musicians and sharing the bandstand with Sabby Lewis's orchestra. The relationship between the two New Orleans giants was variable. Foster's autobiography contains some bitter comments about Bechet: "Sidney is all for himself and jealous of everyone. He and Louis Armstrong were two of a kind, you didn't make any showing when you played with them. I played with Sidney all of my life and I used to tell him 'Your name is in the lights, man, and nobody can hurt you. If you've got a good band with you, it makes you better.' But he wouldn't listen. He is the most selfish, hard to get along with guy I ever worked with." One of the problems in their latter-day collaborations concerned Bechet's use of the soprano saxophone. Pops Foster, in common with several other New Orleans veterans, didn't like the sound of the instrument, no matter who played it. He said, "Some of the notes are beautiful and some are out of tune . . . Sidney and I used to argue about that all the time."[16]

Yet there was at least one occasion on which Foster should have been grateful to Bechet. Art Hodes recalled the time when he took a seven-piece band (which included Foster and Bechet) to play a gig at Penn State University. The group went from New York in two cars driven by college students, and during the long journey Pops Foster got drunk. Hodes picks up the story: "You should have heard Sidney. He took one look at this guy and sparks flew. Sidney read him off. That was just to get his attention. Next came a cold bath, then some walking around the block. After aspirins and black coffee that musician performed the date and performed as well as any of the rest of us. Bechet didn't draw top billing this concert; it was my baby. But Sidney didn't look at the marquee. He did what he did because that was the way he operated. He gave his best no matter who was leader."[17]

Bechet's relationships with various ex-New Orleans colleagues were inclined to be unpredictable, but one of the least volatile was that with Albert Nicholas. It was not always to be so, but during the 1940s there were few problems between them. Sidney once told Mary Karoley in a jocular fashion that he was not jealous of any New Orleans clarinettists except Albert Nicholas, "because he's a heap sight better looking than me".[18]

Nicholas and Bechet shared the billing in a session held on 12 February 1946 for Blue Note which also featured Art Hodes, Pops Foster and the white Chicagoan Danny Alvin on drums. The first recording by the Bechet–Nicholas Blue Five was a superb version of *Blame it on the Blues*, an extraordinarily good tune with three strong themes. Bechet plays the melody on saxophone, cohesively aided by Nicholas's clarinet work. The rhythm section is a little too chunky; what sets out to be solid support becomes monotonous and heavy, but the flow of the front line creates an infectious swing.

Nicholas's filigree solo (on the 32-bar 'march' strain) is given some beefy support by Bechet's riffing, and when Sidney takes over, the full, contrasting piquancy of their tones becomes obvious. The two men seem perfectly matched in intent, and one of their harmonized breaks (on take two) may be compared to work in the duos by King Oliver and Louis Armstrong.

Both men play clarinets on the rapturous performance of *Old Stack o'Lee Blues*. Their linked phrasing reveals a solid mutual understanding, and their warm tones blend admirably. Nicholas's approach to the blues is more graceful than Bechet's: his blue notes never bite quite as deep, and he is content to let his tone flow from the instrument unmarked by rasps or growls. His opening solo is effectively typical. Hodes rolls out a sturdy chorus, then Bechet takes over, remaining determinedly in the low register (happily, the recording catches all the nuances of his sybaritic tone). Nicholas re-enters, his phrasing intertwining with Bechet's, then moves off to play a richly satisfying harmony part during a triumphant final chorus.

Bechet's Fantasy features Bechet on soprano saxophone throughout. This fine composition by Bechet consists of two themes: a rhapsodic 12-bar blues and a dramatically contrasting eight-bar variation. Sidney is in fine coloratura mood, but the indifferent recording quality takes the edge off the performance slightly.

The medium-paced version of *Weary Way Blues* never quite lives up to the promise of its brightly played introduction, but both reed players produce some fascinating contrasting ideas. A happy, free-for-all spirit marks the final choruses, and alternate takes show that a good deal of spontaneity blessed this fine session. Bechet knew exactly what he wanted before he ever entered the studio, but like some great generals he preferred to let adjutants work out details. In this case his subordinate was pianist Art Hodes: "I taught the *Weary Way Blues* clarinet part to Albert – not that I'm putting Albert down, it's just that Sidney knew what he wanted and I used to go over to his house and play the second parts on the piano until he got the part he wanted. Then I taught it to Albert and the record was made."[19]

Bechet's magpie approach to other people's compositions caused early issues of *Blame it on the Blues* (written by the black composer Charles L. Cooke) to be labelled as *Quincy Street Stomp*, by Sidney Bechet. 160 Quincy Street in Brooklyn was Sidney's new home address; he had moved there not long before the session for Blue Note. It was an old, solid property, and quite the most comfortable residence in which he had lived since he left the family home many years before. He shared the dwelling with his girl-friend Laura and his huge dog, Butch.

For the first time in years, Bechet had achieved a degree of financial stability. He was drawing regular recording royalties, he was getting well paid for various freelance recordings, and he was receiving top rates for his concert appearances. All this income was in addition to the money he received for playing club dates and quartet residencies. The mid-1940s saw the blossoming of the jazz concert. Such occasions were extremely rare in the 1930s, but during World War II the idea of presenting jazz on the concert platform gained strength. Eddie Condon and Ernie Anderson played a big part in the growth of the concert's popularity, and many others soon followed their example in promoting them. Hardly a week went by in 1946 when Bechet wasn't a guest at an East Coast jazz concert. The idea also spread to other parts of North America, and Sidney occasionally crossed the border to play dates in Canada.

One such concert took place at the Eaton Auditorium in Toronto on 23 March 1946. There Bechet headed an all-star unit consisting of Rex Stewart on cornet, Benny Morton on trombone, Willie 'the Lion' Smith on piano, Al Hall on bass, and Specs Powell on drums. Rex, mindful of the tensions that had surrounded his recording session with Bechet a few years earlier, decided to down a few drinks before the show. A few more followed, and the outcome led one reviewer to say bluntly that Rex was drunk on stage. Clyde H. Clark sent a report to *Australian*

Jazz Notes which read: "Rex clowned, yelled, screamed, jabbered into the mike, fluffed notes and interrupted the other soloists, while Willie 'the Lion' Smith got so far off the chords when backing Bechet that Rex, tight as he was, tried to drown out the piano with harmonic phrases, so Bechet wouldn't be completely put off. Benny Morton played well, especially on *Basin Street Blues*, but felt he wasn't in Bechet's class. When the master of ceremonies asked him to think of a closing number to play while Bechet finished 9 climactic choruses of *High Society*, he said 'What could possibly follow this?'."

The crowd gave Bechet a standing ovation and, according to Clark, left the auditorium murmuring appreciatively, "I just don't believe it". Bechet had saved the day by lifting an otherwise chaotic concert to supreme heights. It was not an experience that he wanted to repeat in a hurry and he chose not to accept a lucrative offer to return to Toronto for a concert in May 1946. But even concerts nearer home could produce drama, as was amply illustrated by events in Washington, DC, during the spring of 1946. Ernie Anderson recalled the background details:

> Sidney Bechet was due to guest with Eddie Condon at a concert we planned to hold at the Auditorium of Constitutional Hall in Washington, DC. This was a hall run by the Daughters of the American Revolution, who, a few years earlier, had barred the famous singer Marian Anderson from performing there because she was black. We felt that things might have improved, but I needed to test that out. Eddie and I went to the hall the day before the show to check ticket sales, etc, and to look things over. I said to the hall manager, "It should be a good concert, we have the great Sidney Bechet with us". The manager just looked on. Then I said, with some emphasis, "Sidney Bechet, the wonderful negro jazz musician". That did it. We were told that the concert couldn't go ahead due to previously unforeseen circumstances.
>
> I called the editor of the *Washington Star*, and we had a picture taken of Eddie Condon sitting in front of the auditorium with his guitar but holding his head in his hands; for good measure the whole background story was published. Well, Washington was also the headquarters of Associated Press. They picked up the story and it was used all over the country. We went straight ahead and booked the ballroom of a big hotel to hold our jazz concert in. The people clamoured for tickets. Sidney played as though he was on fire; he played and played, and the audience loved it.[20]

Despite his prestigious appearances on the concert platform, Bechet was still willing to play as a sideman for any recording dates that happened along. In one such session, on 7 May 1946, he was part of a sextet that backed Stella Brooks. Brooks, a singer who had worked in various clubs in Greenwich Village, was a competent vocalist; during her better moments she reveals something of the charm and style of Lee Wiley. The blues were not Stella's strong point, but nevertheless she chose to sing three on the date, a strategy that tipped the scales against the session being a triumph. Unfortunately, the instrumental interludes are tantalizingly brief.

On *As Long as I Live*, Stella Brooks sings imaginatively, applying a wry quality to her middle register and a lilting sound to her high notes. Frankie Newton contributes a relaxed 16-bar cup-muted solo, but Bechet on soprano saxophone is consigned to playing organ-likes notes in the background. None of Brooks's subsequent singing measures up to that in the opening number. Bechet plays a sparkling clarinet solo on *St Louis Blues*, unleashing a familiar burst of energy during the final vocal chorus. He has no solos on *Jazz me Blues*, *I'll never be the same* or *Little Piece of Leather*, but on this last tune plays an authoritative clarinet accompaniment to the singer's too slick blues lines. The highlight of *Little Piece of Leather* is the fiery solo from Newton, who for once excels on a blues by parading majestic ideas and exciting lip trills.

Bechet's longest contribution to the date is his 16-bar saxophone feature on *Ballin' the Jack*. The solo is, as ever, confident and ingenious, the only slight blemish occurring in the final two bars, where he fails to negotiate a chord change smoothly. The entire session, for the Disc label, is 'low-fi' (similar in sound quality to most recordings by independent labels during the 1940s). The piano, despite being expertly played by Joe Sullivan, is a poor-toned, out-of-tune instrument. As each item (except *Ballin' the Jack*) has a piano introduction, this becomes irksome, and adds to the rhythm section's unease. Bechet's solo contributions play only a small part in this date, but they dwarf the efforts of trombonist Georg Brunis, who is allotted a solitary eight-bar feature (on *I'll never be the same*).

Bechet returned to Washington, DC, in the early summer of 1946 to play another residency at the Brown Derby club. This time he used a quartet consisting of himself, Norman Lester on piano, Billy Taylor on string bass and Pleasant Joseph on guitar and vocals. When this short booking ended Sidney returned to New York and came to the decision that he had had enough of the club-restaurant circuit: his stomach problems seemed to be exacerbated when he had no chance to prepare his own food. His regular concert bookings and club dates in New York guaranteed that he would not starve, but to make up for the money that he was losing through his new routine he decided to resume teaching.

Left to Bechet's own planning, this scheme could well have been still-born – his only advertisement was a sign placed above his Quincy Street door which read: "Sidney Bechet's School of Music". However, his ally Mezz Mezzrow was a hustler, and he soon found Bechet pupils, one of whom, Bob Wilber, became an internationally famous jazz musician and Sidney's most articulate disciple:

I began studying with Sidney by visiting his home, on Quincy Street, once a week. I think the fee was five dollars a lesson. He gave me most of my early tuition from the piano. He sometimes demonstrated phrases on the soprano, but he rarely picked up the clarinet during a lesson. He was thorough, but not in a totally formal way. His method was to teach his whole approach to music; he explained how he felt about a certain piece of music, and he did so in a way that was enlightening and instructive. He didn't insist that his way of doing things was the only way – he said, "This is the way I do it".

We got along fine, in fact he was like a benevolent father to me. In a way I think he was delighted that I was interested in the older styles of jazz. At about this time many young musicians automatically 'took up' Charlie Parker when they became in-terested in jazz, but the work of Armstrong and Bechet always had more emotional appeal for me. The only problem I had was in travelling to the lessons. I had to come from my home, quite a distance, and this meant changing buses, and a lot of waiting about. After a few months Sidney suggested that I move into the house which he shared with Laura.

My parents agreed. I was around 18 at the time, so moved to Quincy Street and was able to get to know Sidney well. He was never anything but kind to me, but I knew that he could be evil and, it's not too strong a word to say, paranoic. Yet if he felt that he was with friends, and not threatened, he was jovial, courteous and good company. He liked routine. For instance, when he was playing a Town Hall concert he dressed with great care, putting on an expensive shirt, a fine tie, a gold watch and chain, gold cuff-links and a gold stick-pin, but then he'd put on white socks – totally out of key with the rest of his appearance. It was something I noticed other New Orleans musicians did. They would, almost perversely, wear one item of clothing that didn't jell with the rest.

I think bad health played some part in his irritability. He often had trouble with his digestion. When he was in pain he used to swallow huge drafts of a chalky medicine that settled his stomach for a while, but if he drank a few whiskies he'd suffer a lot the next day. He smoked a lot of cigarettes, but I don't recall him smoking 'pot'. I don't ever remember him getting really drunk. Usually after a few drinks he'd want to party. He was never an evil drunk, but he could be evil when he was cold sober. If he liked you, nothing would be too much trouble, he'd give you the shirt from his back. But if he felt that someone had slighted him, he could turn nasty in an instant. He did everything with a passionate intensity. He was a great musician and a tremendous man.

He didn't want to live in the past for the sake of reminiscing, but he got pleasure out of recalling his early days in New Orleans. The thrill that he had got from learning his instrument stayed with him, and I think that is why he was so pleased to have young pupils. He remembered how happy he had been to learn his craft; he wanted to share what had been taught to him. He never once mentioned his early experiences in France, but he did tell me that during his stay in Berlin he had lived in a brothel, and he had greatly enjoyed that experience.[21]

Bechet made many guest appearances at New York Town Hall concerts for a variety of promoters during 1946. On one of these dates he played a set with Pete Johnson on piano and Billy Taylor on bass. This was reviewed by Virgil Thompson, the distinguished critic of the *New York Herald Tribune*, who wrote that the trio had provided "the season's high in chamber music". Bechet also performed a series of Saturday concerts for the newly formed New York Jazz Club. At one of these (held at the Local Hall, 100 East 17th Street) he was reunited with an old colleague from New Orleans, Buddy Christian, who played piano and guitar on the date.

There were also regular trips to Philadelphia, where pianist Sammy Price organized his own promotions. For one of these, held at the Philadelphia Academy of Art on 15 September 1946, Sidney took along a band which included Baby Dodds on drums, George Lugg on trombone, Mezz Mezzrow on clarinet and Pops Foster on bass. Trumpeter Jack Butler was late arriving because his train had been delayed, but despite the fact that he had left New York with hours to spare he was still publicly castigated by Bechet. Sammy Price has mixed memories of those days: "When I ran concerts and various dates in Philadelphia I often booked Sidney as a guest star. It usually worked out okay, but one time I lost a lot of money by booking Art Tatum and Sidney Bechet to appear together. The music was fantastic – they sparked off of each other – but the people just didn't show up. Two great attractions like that, and I still lost money."[22]

The audiences for whom Bechet played at concerts and in clubs were racially mixed, but black people were very much in the minority. In the August 1946 issue of *Pick Up*, Bill Gottlieb remarked: "I noticed very few Negroes in the Dixieland places. This, however, is not a matter of Jim Crow. I believe the music just doesn't appeal to them."

Three of the participants in the Philadelphia concert in September 1946, Bechet, Dodds, and Mezzrow, returned to New York, and on the 18th of the month recorded a marathon session for King Jazz. On these recordings Bechet proved by the authoritative and inventive way that he tackled the blues that the inclusion of many show tunes into his repertoire had done nothing to blunt his incisive approach to the 12-bar sequence.

Breathless Blues is built on a series of busy arpeggios (phrased almost like *In the Mood*). It features Mezzrow and Bechet on clarinets, playing solo and in duet, swopping the lead to and fro; they engender a fine spirit of abandon despite the uncohesive rhythm section (Wellman Braud on bass, Baby Dodds on drums, and Wesley Wilson on piano). Wilson prefaces a new version of *Really the Blues* with an unelaborate piano introduction; the opening theme is based on the haunting duet which Mezzrow and Bechet had used as an incidental part of their 1938 recording. On this version Mezzrow creates two blues choruses that are among the best he ever played, achieving a poised solo almost worthy of Jimmie Noone. The piano solo is rather stiff-jointed, but Bechet's improvised chorus, save for a surprise squeak in the closing bars, is statuesque. Lack of recording time caused the piece to end at that point. The other side of the 78 r.p.m. disc was labelled as Part II, and featured five consecutive choruses of Bechet on soprano saxophone, during which he parades his amazing ability to create fresh phrases on a blues sequence. Sidney builds his solo to a truly dramatic conclusion, helped by the unflagging sounds of Baby Dodds's ringing cymbal.

Under normal circumstances Wesley Wilson would not have been booked to play piano throughout a prestigious instrumental date; he did so on this session for King Jazz because he was there to accompany his partner, Coot Grant, on the series of vocal pieces that form the bulk of the recordings made that day. Mezzrow and Bechet play subsidiary roles on these: there are no reed solos, only fill-ins – and those are of a mixed quality. Grant was an underrated blues singer and performs raffishly on *Fat Mama Blues* and *Hey Daddy*; her vocal duet with Wilson on *You can't do that to me* radiates the humour and charm they both shared.

Most of the vocal numbers were completed in single takes. The only repeated efforts were reserved for a slow blues, *Whoop Miss Wolf* (which has persistently been reissued as *Whoop this Wolf*), and by the third attempt Bechet and Mezzrow had organized an effective backing plan. The date ended with three instrumental attempts at *Groovin' the Minor*, a 16-bar theme similar to *My daddy rocks me*. Bechet, on soprano saxophone, again proves that he was an amalgam of artistry and stamina.

Sidney continued to appear in concerts sponsored by Eddie Condon and Ernie

Anderson. Bass player Jack Lesberg worked at many of these with Bechet, and usually shared the journeys with him when they played dates out of town: "We often went by train. Sidney and myself would sit together, mostly talking about music. He knew that I was also working with symphony orchestras, so he loved to talk about classical composers. He'd go into great detail about his own composing and asked me on several occasions if I could help him get some of his works performed."[23]

There was no doubt that Bechet loved the adulation his concert appearances brought. Both his presence and the passion of his improvisations had a dramatic effect on audiences, and dozens of reviewers called attention to this. One critic, writing about a concert promoted by Eddie Condon in October 1946, said: "Without doubt the highlight of the concert was the performance rendered by Sidney Bechet. Sidney, with Jess Stacy (piano), Jack Lesberg (bass) and George Wettling (drums), took clarinet in hand – a short cadenza warm-up – then came the Blues. He literally had the audience in his hand. It was as if he were opening and closing his fist. The audience swayed and sighed as Sidney moaned the Blues."[24]

Sidney was reliving his days on the European concert platforms. An opportunity soon arose that gave him the chance to recapture the thrills he had enjoyed as an actor in theatrical presentations of the 1920s. The issue of *Down Beat* for 15 July 1946 carried a small report: "Arthur Hopkins, who has acquired for fall production Orin Jannings' play *Hear that Trumpet*, is facing casting problems since five of the cast must be jazz musicians." The item was brought to Bechet's attention. Its effect was like the ringing of bells for an old fire horse. Sidney made it his business to be in that show. As a result he became one of a group consisting of trumpeter Bobby Sherwood, trombonist Skippy Layton, bass player Bart Edwards, pianist Ray Mayer, and Marty Marsala (who had temporarily abandoned the trumpet) on drums. Ray Mayer was an experienced actor but the rest of the group, other than Sidney, had little working knowledge of drama. The plot concerns six war veterans who return to civilian life and attempt to reorganize their jazz band.

Hear that Trumpet opened on 7 October 1946 at the Playhouse Theater on Broadway and closed after only eight performances. The critics panned the work, but praised the musicians for their dramatic abilities, particularly Bobby Sherwood (who had the leading role), Ray Mayer and Sidney Bechet. Bechet was disappointed that the show had folded so quickly; he felt that the play had failed because it had had a racially mixed cast.[25] George Simon (reporting in *Metronome*) felt that the play "was hampered by too much philosophising", and wrote that Bechet had been given an "Uncle Tom characterization, one that certainly won't do the racial situation much good".[26]

EIGHTEEN

Absent Enemy

At the end of his one and only week in the production of *Hear that Trumpet*
Bechet took a Sunday plane flight to play at a concert held at the Civic Opera
House in Chicago. His partners on the date were trumpeter Dizzy Gillespie and
reed player Eugene Sedric. The three imports from New York played on a bill
that also featured an assembly of Chicago jazzmen, including pianist Tut Soper,
cornetist Jimmy McPartland, guitarist George Barnes, drummer Ken Smith,
pianist Max Miller and tenor saxophonist Bud Freeman. In his book *You Don't
Look Like a Musician*, Freeman recalls a backstage scene: "I was raving about
Louis Armstrong's playing to Sidney Bechet. Sidney surprised me by saying,
'Well, I don't know man; I might have some things I want to play too'."

The concert gave Ken Smith and Max Miller the chance to re-establish the
warm friendship that had begun during their wartime meetings with Bechet.
Sidney was happy to see these old friends again, and during the coming years
took part in privately recorded sessions with them. Miller, who was then rated as
one of Chicago's leading modernists, loved jamming with Bechet: "We'd book
the Bachman Studio on Carmen Avenue and make recordings (78 r.p.m.), just for
fun. I was never happy with the piano there, it was an iron-foot job, but the
surroundings were great – it was a Frank Lloyd Wright house. Our sessions with
Sidney were nearly all purely improvised; we literally made the tunes up as we
went along. He played soprano mostly on the sessions we did together, and he
did so wonderfully."[1]

Sidney was much more broad-minded about music-making than any jazz
magazine ever gave him credit for. Trumpeter Max Kaminsky was often on
hand to observe this: "Bechet was more flexible than people suppose. He could
play all sorts of requests. His recordings give some indication – *Just One of those
Things* – that sort of thing, but he knew thousands of songs, ballads, etc, a lot of
interesting stuff. But some of the trumpeters he worked with knew their little set
tunes and that was all they ever did for years."[2]

Bechet always kept his ears open for interesting sounds, but in general he was
not enamoured of big-band swing. He never went out of his way to criticize it, but
Albert Nicholas recalled an occasion when he let his thoughts on the subject flood
out: "There were several guys from Jimmie Lunceford's Band at a bar in Harlem.
They were crackin' their jaws about how beautiful their arrangements were
when Sidney interrupted and said, 'Well, I'll tell you: I don't bother with reading
music – I don't bother with arrangements. As long as you've got your heads

stuck in a book reading all the time you're not doing anything. But one thing, I'm going to be playing until I die, and people are going to appreciate me.'"³

Bechet was happy to be coaching his various pupils, but the role of a stay-at-home teacher did not suit his restless personality, and he was delighted to play any gigs that were offered to him in late 1946. On Tuesday nights he was guest at Eddie Condon's recently opened club, and he regularly took part in Sunday afternoon jam sessions organized by Milt Gabler. His concert dates included some for Eddie Condon and some for Bob Maltz's New York Jazz Club. Out-of-town bookings again took him to Chicago, and the success of his October visit there prompted Paul Eduard Miller to organize a return concert booking, this time in Kimball Hall.

On Sunday afternoon, 1 December 1946, the various participating musicians assembled at the 450-seat hall. A local rhythm section consisting of Ken Smith (drums), Joe Rumoro (guitar), Mickey Simms (string bass) and Ray Dixon Oehler (piano) had the task of backing Bechet, Mezz Mezzrow and a former reed player with McKinney's Cotton Pickers, Jimmy Dudley. In order to make the programme as varied as possible, these musicians were featured in various permutations: the opening was entrusted to a duo consisting only of Ken Smith on drums and Bechet on soprano saxophone. Unperturbed, the two men played *Laura*, followed by a blues that made the crowd forget the unusual instrumentation. Gradually, more musicians were added, until the whole cast – billed as the Bechet–Mezzrow Sextet – concluded the show (which was compèred by writer Studs Terkel).

There had been no time for rehearsals, but everything went off smoothly. Pianist Ray Dixon commented: "Bechet was very easy to work with to be sure. He only needed the regular chord changes and then everything was fine."⁴ Paul Eduard Miller was delighted with the results; in *Esquire* magazine, he wrote: "To be fully appreciated Bechet must be heard in person. It is when he is able to play for a longer duration than the regulation three or four minutes of the recording studio that one comes under the complete domination of his vigor and forcefulness. His is not the cocktail lounge type of jazz, to which one can listen pleasantly for hours without being touched at the core of one's self. Bechet's music strikes boldly at the heart of the listener."

Mezz Mezzrow was involved in the concert as part of the promotion for his recently published autobiography, *Really the Blues*, in which he had expressed his unstinting admiration for Bechet's work: "How easy it was falling in with Bechet – what an instinctive mastery of harmony he has, and how marvelously delicate his ear is!" Musician and writer Richard Hadlock made a young fan's pilgrimage to hear Bechet play the date at Kimball Hall; later he wrote: "In 1946 I traveled some 900 miles to hear Sidney play a single concert in Chicago. Mezz Mezzrow, whose autobiography had just been published, was the star of the show and the lobby of the theatre was jammed with autograph-seekers, well-wishers and elbow-rubbers. Bechet remained backstage, largely unnoticed, although his music dominated the concert itself."⁵

Less than two months later Bechet was again back at Kimball Hall, this time sharing front-line duties with Woody Herman's trombonist Bill Harris and a local tenor saxophonist, Otis Finch. The musicians on bass, drums and guitar were as before but, in a sensational coup, Paul Eduard Miller persuaded the bandleader Fletcher Henderson to play piano for the concert. In his programme notes, Miller promised the audience they would hear examples of "spontaneous combustion" when Bechet and Harris played together. Apparently no one was disappointed; the two musicians gave a marvellous display of improvising as a duo, proving once again that Bechet revelled in playing with expert musical company from any 'school' of jazz.

Sometimes Bechet's out-of-town gigs led to high jinks. Writer and impresario Al Rose recalls one such occasion when he booked Bechet for "a great concert" at Princeton in 1947:

> Wild Bill Davison, Georg Brunis, Mezzrow, Pops Foster, Baby Dodds and Sammy Price were on hand. After the concert we had to wait at Princeton junction station for a railway train. Wild Bill stole a fire hose nozzle and began to play the blues on it. Sidney took out his clarinet and joined him. It was 1 a.m. and from the raised platform we could see the dormitory lights turning on, and soon, hundreds of students in bathrobes and slippers ringed the station. By the time Pops Foster had unpacked his bass Baby Dodds had his drums set up and a full session was in progress. I kept warning the musicians to pack their gear before the train came, but at 2 a.m. I had to help them drag their unpacked instrument cases into the car. Bechet wouldn't stop blowing before the end of *Shake it and break it*.[6]

Al Rose, who had first booked Bechet for concerts in the 1930s, also commented: "I always limited Sidney to one soprano solo in each half of any concert, because my sessions always emphasized ensemble playing (which Sidney resisted) and he played such fabulous clarinet." The two men did not always see eye to eye, and Rose concluded: "I found Bechet to be a very difficult person to work with, self-centered and inconsiderate of others, and never happy to share a spotlight."[7]

Bechet's New York concert schedule kept him busy throughout the early months of 1947. During this time he took part in a series of "Midnight Concerts" held at the Town Hall, which presented an amalgam of jazz and blues. These Saturday-night jamborees, sponsored by an organization called Peoples Song, Inc., featured such artists as Big Bill Broonzy, Memphis Slim and Sonny Boy Williamson. In those heady post-war days many sincere people who saw connections between racial problems and the class struggle thought concerts that outlined the history of black music might eliminate prejudice and develop political awareness. At these concerts musicians and singers were encouraged to step forward and deliver a biographical address, but Bechet chose not to do so, and let his music speak for him.

One thing that did help Bechet obtain more work was the installation of a telephone at his home. This development caused the magazine *Jazz Record* to insert a brief tongue-in-cheek news item in its issue of March 1947: "Sidney Bechet now has a phone." Sparing expense had been one reason for Bechet's not having a telephone, but he also found the sound of a phone bell irritating and distracting. His nephew Leonard, Jr, who lodged with him briefly, said: "He was always practising and would get very upset if he was called to the telephone while he was rehearsing. He wanted things to be just so."[8]

In March 1947 Bechet's own trio opened at Jimmy Ryan's club on 52nd Street, New York, a booking which marked the start of Sidney's long association with the club. The burst of publicity surrounding the opening included a double-column article in *Time* in which the reporter wrote: "Unlike his friend 'Satchelmouth' Armstrong he refuses to front for bigtime, second-rate bands." This comment didn't please Louis Armstrong, but the person who ended up most disgruntled by the feature was Bechet, who justifiably took exception to being described as looking "like a sleepy Pullman porter".

Writers for various jazz magazines were delighted to report that Sidney Bechet had a resident berth for six nights a week, and those who visited the club had enthusiastic things to say about the trio, which consisted of Bechet on soprano saxophone and clarinet, Lloyd Phillips on piano, and Fred Moore on drums and vocals. Bob Aurthur, in *Jazz Record* (May 1947), wrote: "Ryan's audience is usually an appreciative one, which gives an added lift to Sidney's playing, at worst sensational. Bob Wilber comes in almost every night and stands watching the master. When Bob plays a solo Bechet looks at him with an expression that is only seen on a mother hen watching her chick." Most nights, Wilber travelled down on the subway with Bechet and spent the whole evening listening and learning. Trombonist Georg Brunis, remarking on the inseparable nature of master and pupil, nicknamed the duo "Bash and Shay". Wilber has countless memories of his visits of Jimmy Ryan's:

> Matty Walsh did all the management at the club. Jimmy himself was something of a playboy, whose claim to fame was that he had appeared in the original production of *Roberta* (which had featured a young Bob Hope). He had many show-business friends and he loved Sidney to play the Jerome Kern melodies and the Cole Porter tunes, which Sidney didn't mind at all. Late at night, when the crowds had gone home, was just about the best time to hear Sidney. He and pianist Lloyd Phillips used to test one another's memories to see which of them could remember the most obscure tune. The results were often marvellous, and under those circumstances I first heard Sidney play his version of *Song of Songs*. When things were quiet he'd suddenly drop into a slow version of the blues and he'd play things that I'd never heard before. He didn't encourage random sitting in, but enjoyed it immensely when musicians he admired called into the club. On one occasion the front line consisted of Sidney, Hot Lips Page and Jack Teagarden on trombone. I think the version of *Struttin' with some Barbecue* they played that night still ranks amongst my most outstanding musical memories.[9]

Pianist Lloyd Phillips, who had worked and recorded with Bechet during the preceding years, came to know him better during their shared stay at Ryan's. Lloyd always felt there was something enigmatic and mysterious about Sidney's personality and never quite got used to the mixture of jocularity and fury, but he always retained the utmost respect for Sidney's musicianship:

> I always prided myself with a fair knowledge of musical form and harmony and I never remember Sidney Bechet playing any phrase that was poorly constructed, rhythmically or harmonically. Everything he blew was shaped in a way that invited listening, like a true musical story-teller. It was fascinating to accompany him,

particularly on tunes we had never tried before. He might suddenly call a song that I hadn't thought of in years; he'd blow the thing inside out and might never play it again. Other times he'd chose something he'd just heard on the juke-box and every note and every chord change would be perfect, but the most electric moments came when he played the blues. At around three o'clock in the morning I've known him put his feet up on a chair, close his eyes and play one blues solo lasting twenty minutes. The place might be empty, it didn't matter. It was ghostly because he seemed so far away. One night I think there was one customer in the place and he was so drunk he fell flat on his face, knocking a bar stool over and scattering glasses all over the floor. The noise was terrific, but Sidney remained totally oblivious and just went on playing the blues.

Nothing on record gives you this side of Sidney – even stuff like *Blue Horizon* is only the tip of the iceberg. But he could be awful mean when he felt like it. One night a customer gave him five dollars for playing *Body and Soul*. He gave me a dollar and stuffed the rest in his pocket. The drummer kept giving Sidney hard looks, but Sid said very sternly, "We played *Body and Soul*. You just went swish-swish like you would have done on any slow tune that we played, so you don't get extra."[10]

At Ryan's, Bob Wilber observed how skilfully Bechet could control an audience with his showmanship. He was also adept at getting a message across to various female listeners: "He'd point his soprano at a woman he liked and push it up slowly like a giant phallus. It was like the work of a snake charmer, and he had plenty of conquests."[11] Whilst Sidney was at Ryan's, Wilber became acquainted with one of his teacher's girl-friends, the actress Tallulah Bankhead.

Tallulah had first heard Sidney play in Paris with Noble Sissle's band and had also been a frequent visitor to Pod's and Jerry's Club during the time Bechet had worked there in the early 1930s. At some stage the two consummated their affair, creating a romance that was as durable as it was unpredictable; sometimes years elapsed between their meetings, yet each time they were reunited they picked up the excitement from where they had left off. The liaison had its bizarre features. Bob Wilber recalls answering the phone to Tallulah at Ryan's whilst Sidney was still on the bandstand: "She asked me to tell him to come over as soon as he had finished work. I told Sidney and he said, 'We'll both go and play her some duets'. So we went to the Hotel Elysée and Tallulah answered the door, stark naked. Inside the apartment was an actor who worked with Tallulah. After we'd talked for a while Sidney and I played duets to Tallulah as she lay in bed, and then we left."[12]

It was at Ryan's that Sidney introduced Bob Wilber to Shirley 'Ricky' Rickards, who was to become Bob's first wife. Ricky recalls: "A crowd of us used to go to Jimmy Ryan's to hear Sidney in 1947 and he came to know us because we were there so often. He introduced me to Bob Wilber. Later, B. W. and I frequently visited him and Laura on Quincy Street, at which house also lived his beautiful, good-natured Great Dane, Butch, who loved to try to sit on people's laps."[13]

At about this time Sidney undertook yet another of his schemes. This time it involved purchasing a motor-boat, which was moored out at Sheepshead Bay in Brooklyn. Bechet had often said that one of his ambitions was to sail around the Caribbean, calling in at New Orleans. Unfortunately the boat that he bought was not up to such a task. A mariner looked the vessel over and strongly advised

Bechet not to attempt to leave the harbour, never mind sailing across treacherous oceans. Bechet heeded the advice and never lifted the anchor. He was content to let the boat exist as a floating haven where he could entertain his friends. Ricky Wilber said: "I was delighted when he asked me to christen the boat. Something or other caused us to be late and by the time we arrived disc-jockey Fred Robbins had done the honors. We sat around on the boat drinking toasts, then had dinner in a nearby seafood restaurant and ended up seeing *Blood of a Poet* at the Fifth Avenue Cinema – Sidney being the only one of us who could understand Cocteau's dialogue."[14]

Bob Wilber recalls:

Sidney was always happy when he was on the boat, and often when we left it we'd go to an old club house near the marina. We'd drop in for a couple of beers, and Sidney invariably sat down to play the piano and entertain the people. He really enjoyed that. There was a side to him that loved to have a good time; he loved to dance.[15]

Sidney's piano playing was highly effective. He was good at keyboard voicings and at resolving harmonies – they might have sounded odd but he had a way of making progressions flow easily. He'd happily sit down at a piano for hours. With his love of such things he was one of the first to own a tape recorder; it was a big old Brush model and he must have filled countless tapes with ideas that came to him at the piano. Contrary to what most people think, he could write out his musical ideas in notation, but it was a slow and laborious process. He was impatient and much preferred to demonstrate his ideas to someone else. He could have written out various things for his recording sessions, but he didn't – he'd either walk to a piano to illustrate what he wanted or he'd play the changes, arpeggio by arpeggio, on the soprano. He played clarinet about the house, mostly for his own amusement, but I always had difficulty in getting him to take it down to Jimmy Ryan's, even though it would have been ideal in the trio. He always used to say to me, "Master the clarinet and then the saxophone will come easy". But he encouraged me to play the soprano and I began devoting most of my time to it.[16]

Bechet kept his clarinet playing in trim by practising at home. This was just as well, since he was specifically asked to play both his instruments for a "This is Jazz" radio programme on 1 March 1947. This show, which was one of a series organized by writer Rudi Blesh and broadcast on Mutual, drew on a pool of musicians which included Albert Nicholas on clarinet, Pops Foster on bass and Baby Dodds on drums. During the next eight months Bechet often performed as guest with the show's resident band, but on each of these later occasions he remained steadfastly on soprano saxophone.

Promoter Ernie Anderson decided to hold a spectacular concert at New York's Town Hall on 17 May 1947, where the two main attractions were to be Louis Armstrong and Sidney Bechet. Advance details of the show were publicized by Fred Robbins on his widely heard WOV radio show. Louis was scheduled to work within an all-star small group, which, for the entire second half, was to be joined by Sidney Bechet.

When Ernie Anderson first broached Bechet about the concert he was greeted with positive enthusiasm, but later, when Sidney was sitting in the quiet of his own home, he began to brood, slowly allowing the rancour he felt about Louis Armstrong's success to overwhelm his earlier judgment. The first hint of impending trouble came when Ernie Anderson took a telephone call at the Town

Hall from a woman who said that Sidney couldn't make the rehearsals, but he would be along in good time for the concert. As curtain-up time approached Anderson began to feel uneasy and decided to telephone Bechet's home to see what was happening. There was no reply, so Anderson assumed Sidney was on his way.[17]

Bechet maintained that he left for the concert but was taken ill on the subway. Vexation about the concert would not have helped his digestive problems, but just how ill he felt at the time of the Town Hall concert will never be known. The pressure of the impending occasion may have got to him *en route*, but somehow Peanuts Hucko, Jack Teagarden, and writers Peter Tanner and George Avakian heard that Sidney had been taken ill before they left Jimmy Ryan's to go to the concert.

Trumpeter Max Kaminsky was working close by and he feels certain that later the same night he called into Ryan's during his intermission and saw, to his surprise, that Sidney was playing there. Max wasn't that astonished because he knew that a rift had grown between Bechet and Armstrong: "He didn't get along with Louis and made up his mind that he wouldn't play the Town Hall concert."[18] Bob Wilber tends to agree with Kaminsky's analysis: "I don't know if he was taken ill on the subway. If he was, he soon recovered. I think the feeling against Louis got too strong for him to go and play at the concert."[19]

Ernie Anderson, having organized what turned out to be one of the most historic jazz concerts ever, decided to shrug his shoulders over the whole Bechet affair, but Louis Armstrong felt hurt and angry by Sidney's behaviour and never really forgave him. Louis's manager, Joe Glaser, was even more vexed. It is rumoured that, when Glaser heard about Bechet preferring to work at Ryan's rather than play in a concert with Louis Armstrong, he sent word to Sidney advising him not to spoil his health by working too often in smoky clubs. Bechet understood the message and took things easy around the New York area for some weeks afterwards.

However, Sidney did not go into hiding. On the day following his non-appearance at the concert he entertained several of his friends, including Alfred and Lorraine Lion, to a party aboard his firmly anchored boat. A week later he and Max Kaminsky went to Chicago to play in a concert at the Kimball Hall, where they were accompanied by Joe Rumoro, Ray Dixon and Ken Smith. Paul Eduard Miller's concerts were proving increasingly popular, but in New York, Eddie Condon, influenced by declining business, decided to take his summer concert recess earlier than usual. He said that during the coming winter series he intended to add acrobats and weight-lifters to his shows: "Why waste that time on music? Let's give the fans what they really want."[20]

Rudi Blesh, whose radio show "This is Jazz" was thriving, decided to revive an old form of musical promotion by chartering a boat, called the *North Haven*, to sail up and down the Hudson River with a jazz band aboard. Each weekend (on Fridays, Saturdays and Sundays), the motor vessel, bedecked with a banner announcing "Jazz on the River. Take the Cruise to Lose the Blues", left Pier 83 at West 42nd Street, loaded to the gunwales with 300 enthusiastic jazz fans.

Bechet joined the enterprise on Friday 6th June, and thereafter played for a series of these floating gigs, working at various times with Art Hodes, James P. Johnson and Ralph Sutton on piano, Danny Barker on guitar, Baby Dodds on drums, Pops Foster on bass, Albert Nicholas on clarinet and Jimmy Archey on trombone. Either Marty Marsala or Wild Bill Davison played with the band, implementing a strategy devised by Blesh: "One of my basic ideas is always to use a white trumpeter against [sic] a Negroid rhythm section."[21]

Trombonist Jimmy Archey spoke of his surprise on being asked to work for Blesh: "I've been playing first chair in big bands. I don't know whether I can play that music or even remember the tunes. I went down with Pops Foster to W.O.R. Studios. We started playing and everything worked out fine. It was a half hour show with half an hour rehearsal, and it paid 50 dollars. I thought this was lovely. Afterwards Rudi Blesh said I played fine. He then said, 'Do you think you can make the boat ride? We just run up the Hudson to Yonkers and back'. It paid 60 dollars. This was tremendous, 110 dollars a week for a half hour radio show and three nights on a pleasure boat."[22]

All went well with the cruises until the one planned for 22nd June. With a full complement of fans and musicians aboard, the boat went aground just as it was leaving the dock. No one was hurt, but Bechet derived pleasure in recounting the incident. Perhaps mindful of his own maritime frustrations, he felt glee in describing the look on the face of the "Commodore" (his pet name for Rudi Blesh) as the voyage ground to an enforced halt.

The Hudson River mishap might well have been an omen for Blesh. Soon afterwards, following months of smooth sailing, his radio show hit a hefty sandbank in the shape of a dispute with Albert Nicholas. This occurred in the middle of a rehearsal, and led to Nicholas criticizing Pops Foster, Jimmy Archey and Baby Dodds. Albert let fly in the issue of *Down Beat* dated 8 October 1947: "For my dough these men are not only being Uncle Toms of the worst sort, but are hindering the kind of jazz I have loved and played for 34 years by letting an aggressively egotistical balloon-bomb like Blesh try to run them."

The dispute rumbled on for weeks, during which time participating musicians spoke out on behalf of Blesh. Guitarist Danny Barker said: "He certainly never tried to tell me how to play my music and he's easy to get along with." Baby Dodds querulously asked why Nicholas had played the show for 30 weeks before complaining, and added: "Blesh usually paid above scale and he's always been ready to lend money to me and other musicians." Bechet averred that he had been given complete musical freedom on the show, and commented: "It's a shame that 'This is Jazz' is off the air because I know it did us all a lot of good." Wild Bill Davison summed up by saying: "Where else could a band, playing the music we do, made up of both Negro and white musicians ever get a chance to work over a network program. I like working for Rudi – period." Blesh's comments were direct and dignified: "I am, and have long been, an admirer of Albert Nicholas' clarinet playing. However he was not always co-operative on the program."[23]

One of Albert Nicholas's taunts against Blesh was that he had refused to give the band permission to record with Sidney Bechet for a record date with Columbia. Trombonist Jimmy Archey agreed that, in his case, this was true, but pointed out that Blesh was totally within his rights since he (Archey) had signed an exclusive recording contract with Blesh's own company, Circle.[24]

Bechet's contract with Columbia materialized through the auspices of George Avakian, who recalled the background: "Columbia Records couldn't care less about Sidney or jazz at the time. I was a very junior member of the staff – the youngest by far – but there were only two other producers in the pop department which of course gave me an opportunity to do a lot."[25] Avakian's help was timely. Bechet had not been in a commercial recording studio for over a year; his only recordings from this period were taken from broadcasts or concert dates. Avakian said of his dealings with Bechet: "Sidney was a serious person, warm but a bit withdrawn. I was in great awe of him at the time and we never got into anything personal. On the other hand, when we talked seriously about recording, Sidney preferred to do it at home, he lived far out in Brooklyn and I remember sitting in the kitchen chatting while he cooked up a bit of lunch – rice and vegetables 'not like we make it back home, but it's O.K.'."[26]

Bechet's first session for Columbia, on 14 July 1947, featured him with a band of young musicians led by his protégé, Bob Wilber. The date produced four sides for issue and provided the various members of Bob Wilber's Wildcats with the useful, albeit daunting, experience of working alongside a master jazz musician. Bob's band had already enjoyed a good deal of acclaim, but the prospect of recording with Bechet caused some trepidation. Even Wilber, who knew Bechet well, remembers that the impending session filled him with apprehensive excitement. Dick Wellstood, the band's pianist, who had first worked with Bechet (at the ripe old age of 19) in a jam session with Milt Gabler in 1946, said that Bechet directed the recording "like the captain of a beleaguered galley – there was no such thing as a mistake, only mutiny. The effect on me was to turn my fingers into frozen sausages."[27]

Trombonist Bob Mielke recalled his thoughts of the record date, and of meeting Bechet: "He appeared to me to be a patriarch, with all the years and dignity that word implies. That was my main impression of him, his dignified bearing. He was a man who was aware of his gifts, and his artistic stature, in short, he was a proud man. As I recall there was a rehearsal at Bechet's home. Bob Wilber conducted the rehearsals. My recollection is that Bechet didn't interact with members of the band except Wilber. If he wanted something changed, or someone to modify what he was doing, he communicated this through Bob. I stood in awe, partly because of his bearing, partly because he was a 'living legend', and partly because of the sheer power and abundance of his playing. I speak for myself, but I think the others felt the same."[28] Trumpeter Johnny Glasel expressed similar sentiments: "I don't remember a lot about the date itself, only that Sidney had a somewhat forbidding aspect, at least to my mind. I got the impression too that he was a little bit impatient with all of us."[29]

Despite their combined anxieties, the members of the band did a satisfactory job on their recordings with Bechet, and, although the sound quality is indifferent, there is plenty of spirit. Listening to them again 35 years later, Wilber said: "I hear a bunch of very enthusiastic, very nervous young players, very excited about playing with the old master. There is certainly no lack of energy there. Musically, of course, we are just not in Bechet's league."[30] However, dispassionate listening reveals that there were other occasions during Bechet's career when he received backing that was decidely more inept.

Spreading Joy (a tune loosely resembling *The Onions*) is a fast composition by Bechet which the youngsters tackle with obvious fervour. Each of them seems to be running, head down, in his own lane, but Bechet masterfully unifies the group's efforts. He takes the lead in a gutsy clarinet duet with Wilber, which gives way to a trombone solo. Bob Mielke was obviously pleased to get through this without anything going seriously wrong, but he doesn't convey any undue anxiety. Glasel, a fine, precocious trumpeter, sounds assured and Wellstood's brief piano solo is emphatic.

Wilber, sounding much like Bechet, takes the opening bars of *I had it but it's all gone now* on clarinet; Sidney then supplies his 'vocal', which consists of a ponderous enunciation of the title. The rest of the piece is a feature for his soprano saxophone. The band plays its backing precisely, but Bechet, despite a superficial flamboyance, seems to be only on half-rein, playing a theme that resembles a batch of assorted ideas.

The speedy fingering required in the opening section of *Polka Dot* (here called a stomp) gives an immediate impression of strain within the ranks, but gradually the mish-mash of parts achieves a rugged, purposive qualtiy. Wilber had certainly heeded Bechet's advice; his sound on clarinet could almost be mistaken for that of his teacher. Hugues Panassié remarked, after hearing the two play together in person: "With my eyes closed I hesitated to recognize which was which."[31] Bechet's soprano saxophone solo is full of ripe, sweeping phrases, but honours go also to the young Glasel and to Charlie Traeger for his spirited bass playing.

Bechet also chose to re-create another of his earlier triumphs by recording a new version of *Kansas City Man Blues*, on which the handsomely matched clarinet tones (and vibratos) of master and pupil are a highlight. Glasel again plays well, shaping his solo on patterns originally formulated by Louis Armstrong, but injecting his own accent. None of the young participants disgraced himself. Stomach butterflies might have carried away some of the best ideas, but the results are more than curios. Sidney was proud of the recordings, happy, according to Bob Wilber, that he was able to perpetuate a musical message amongst such young company.

Later that same month Bechet, using a quartet consisting of himself (on saxophone), Lloyd Phillips, Fred Moore and Pops Foster, recorded another session for Columbia. The main result was a strong version of Bechet's composition *Buddy Bolden Stomp*, in which the performance dwells more on the establishment of the tune's various themes than on abandoned improvisation. Some days later Bechet went back to the studio with his group, but this time used a less obtrusive drummer, Arthur Herbert.

This session, on 31 July 1947, provides an insight into Bechet's catholic tastes (which had been encouraged during his residency at Jimmy Ryan's). The first number, *My Woman Blues*, begins with a ravishing unaccompanied introduction on soprano saxophone. It is another composition by Bechet, which, despite familiar dominant seventh phrases, is an entirely new work. The next item, *Song of Songs*, takes us back to Bechet's early manhood, when he first heard Nelson Kincaid playing the satin melody. Bechet's love of grand opera is shown in a bravura performance that never strays far from the tune. His final flight into the top register is over-pitched, but this seems to underline his flow of passion. Bechet's tendency to play sharp made itself most plain when he ended a ballad with a string of high notes, but it only assumed uncomfortable proportions when he was particularly tired. A rest break taken during a recording session often alleviated the problem.

Just one of those things highlights the effective team work that had developed between Bechet and pianist Lloyd Phillips. Phillips was by nature a born accompanist – never likely to usurp a soloist, but always able to provide skilful guide-lines for both the improviser and the rhythm section. Bechet prowls around Cole Porter's ingenious melody and produces fine jazz from what purists might think unlikely material. Arthur Herbert stokes the proceedings admirably by laying down a bright-sounding 'shimmy' beat on drums. *Love for Sale*, also by Cole Porter, is a melodic performance, with Bechet singing the tune through his instrument; he deliberately trails his phrases to emphasize the composer's ingenuities, making a glissando up to a point where the unheard lyrics are at their most salient.

To while away late hours at Jimmy Ryan's, Bechet and Phillips often teased each other by inserting fleeting 'quotes' into their solos. The pianist demonstrates this 'game' by hinting at *Au clair de lune* during his piano introduction to *Laura*. Bechet picks up the melody, projecting it with obvious emotion; behind him Phillips plays a series of lush piano voicings in the manner of Eddie Duchin. The brief interlude makes a fascinating contrast, but doesn't shatter the rhapsodic mood, which is re-emphasized as the group moves smoothly back into slow tempo. The song was Sidney's tribute to the woman who was sharing his life: he slips in a fleeting reference to *Pretty Baby* during a graceful coda. The session ended with each musician being featured on Bechet's fast rendition of *Shake 'em up*, an intricate melody which contains several ideas that could have been developed further had more recording time been available.

The restricted duration of the 78 r.p.m. disc often hampered Bechet, and George Avakian remembers problems encountered on this session, especially on *Love for Sale*: "I still have the first take, which is every bit as good, but it exceeded the playing time for a 10-inch 78 r.p.m., so the ending is missing on the test pressing." Unfortunately, despite the results of this session, the recording company chose not to invite Bechet back. Avakian was disappointed: "He was at the height of his powers and I deeply regret that I didn't have the muscle to make Columbia sign him to a term contract. Even *Love for Sale* didn't sell that much, although for a jazz single it was pretty good. The thing I also regret is that the L.P. hadn't come along then."[32]

The summer of 1947 was relatively inactive for Bechet, though he made a number of guest appearances performing on various radio shows and in concerts. By then Bob Wilber had moved into an apartment on 111th Street, but Bechet continued to coach and advise him. During that summer Bechet gained another pupil, Robert Lewis, who became his life-long friend. Robert, who had been playing clarinet at school for about a year, had already developed an interest in jazz. He recalls: "I was turned upside down in amazement when one day I heard from down the hall Sidney and Muggsy Spanier on the H.R.S. label. That summer I collected Sidney's recordings in earnest. Also I went about trying to find him, just to meet him. A record dealer suggested the Brooklyn telephone directory. I called, he asked if I played Boehm or Albert. I thought he said 'band', so I said 'band'. He asked me to come down to his house on Quincy Street where I played *Steal Away Blues*, picked up from a Johnny Dodds recording. He said I had 'an idea' and suggested I come back."[33]

Thus began Lewis's regular tuition: "He was patient unless he thought (knew) I'd been goofing off instead of practicing. Once he cut through by asking me to put down my horn, staring me dead in the eye and asking 'Would you talk to me that way?' He asked me to try again. I did and he said, 'Now you sound like you're going to play something'. In many, if not all ways, it was like a father–son relationship; I think he was trying to help me grow up." Later, when Sidney moved to 155th Street, he would journey down on the subway with Lewis to visit Willoughby's camera store after a lesson was through, but the tuition would continue *en route* as Bechet urged his pupil to think of music whilst travelling: "He let me know I did not need my horn to practice all the time. He leaned toward the car floor, looked up and said I could practice there and then; I had the beat under me and all I had to do was let the music loose in my head."[34]

NINETEEN

Chicago Showdown

On Monday 22 September 1947 Bechet resumed playing at Jimmy Ryan's club, using Lloyd Phillips on piano and a succession of drummers. Bechet never learnt to tolerate any action he regarded as a sign of musical mediocrity; a player's style never bothered him, but he was always irked by a lack of prowess. He was never impressed by technique alone, but demanded that a performance should be worthy of what he sometimes called "a musicianer". He was never delighted to hear a pianist play wrong chord changes, but most of the spleen he directed at his accompanists was reserved for drummers. The world might say that so-and-so was an excellent drummer, but if Sidney thought otherwise he would have no hesitation in telling the percussionist, sometimes on the bandstand. Conversely, if Sidney thought that a drummer suited him he didn't care what anybody else, in or out of the group, thought. The problem was that so few drummers satisfied him.

Bechet usually travelled by subway to Jimmy Ryan's, but on certain nights, chosen at whim, he drove to the club in his recently purchased Cadillac. (Bechet loved good cars, and as soon as he had amassed enough money he splurged it on a new automobile.) It was, Bob Wilber remembers, "the pride and joy of his life" For a time it was garaged around the 52nd Street area, almost too precious to be used.

Guitarist Marty Grosz, then a teenager, came into contact with the illustrious vehicle when it was parked outside Jimmy Ryan's: "On a summer evening in 1947 several of us were loitering about the club in order to hear the music. Ryan's had no air-conditioning so the doors were open and Bechet's tremulous sound could be heard in the street. Off and on we would step into a bar called Reilly's for a 20 cent beer. At one point I was leaning against a large black car when a voice bellowed out, 'Get off my car. What do you think it is? A whorehouse?'"[1] The furious reprimand came from Bechet. Yet those who saw Bechet after he had finished his stint at Ryan's (at around 3.30 a.m.) recall him as a picture of jollification, wending his way around various Harlem after-hours clubs before sitting down to have his breakfast at Creole Pete's, then making his way home at the time that most New Yorkers were setting out for work.

Bechet's failure to turn up for Louis Armstrong's Town Hall concert had ceased to be a burning topic amongst New York's jazz fans. In late September 1947 their minds were on another Town Hall show, which also promised to be an historic occasion. The exciting event was to be a concert performance by Bunk Johnson. After the Boston débâcle in 1945 Bunk had played successful seasons at the

Stuyvesant Casino in New York, but had eventually moved back home to Louisiana. Bob Maltz, on behalf of the New York Jazz Club, had optimistically offered him the chance to play in a concert at the Town Hall on 4 October 1947; to his surprise, Bunk accepted.

The Town Hall line-up included Muggsy Spanier, Albert Nicholas, Georg Brunis, James P. Johnson, Fred Moore, Pops Foster, Wellman Braud, Knocky Parker, Johnny Blowers and two blues artists, Champion Jack Dupree and Brownie McGhee. Sidney Bechet was billed as the "Great New Orleans Clarinettist and Soprano Saxist", but chose to bring only his soprano saxophone. On this occasion Bunk Johnson had other things to worry about. His travel arrangements had gone awry and he had been forced, by shortage of time, to fly up for the date, and for some reason had arrived without a trumpet; one was hastily found. Almost all of the 1200 people in the audience would have loved to have heard a superb performance from Bunk, but it was not to be. Walter Schaap, reviewing the concert in *Jazz hot*, wrote: "Bunk played frightfully, disappointing all of the audience, except a handful of fanatics who consider that he is God himself."

This time Bechet wasn't the bandleader. If he was irked by Johnson's failings he didn't show it, and only stepped into the breach when he saw disaster was imminent. An unnamed correspondent provided a review for the Irish magazine *Hot Notes* (no. 12, 1947): "I am sorry to report that Bunk Johnson's career as a trumpet player must be just about over. He played, yes, but so pathetically poor that Sidney Bechet had to assume the lead himself and drown him out on soprano sax."

Later Bunk called into Jimmy Ryan's, where cornetist Jerry Blumberg and writer Harold Drob were listening to Bechet play. Blumberg recalled that Johnson was drunk and kept trying to request old tunes in the hope that Bechet wouldn't remember them, "but Bechet knew them all – many very obscure."[2] Afterwards Blumberg went to a restaurant with the two great New Orleans musicians, and over the meal Bechet agreed with Bunk that the veteran trumpeter had taught both Louis Armstrong and himself. When that subject had been covered Bunk querulously raised something that had obviously been bothering him for some time. He accused Bechet of trying to steal his girl-friend when they had worked together in New Orleans 30 years earlier. Bechet testily asked why Bunk had never mentioned this grievance before and the incident passed.

Bechet's concert successes in Chicago had been noted carefully by a young couple whose plans to open their own club in that city reached fruition in June 1947. Bill Reinhardt and his wife Ruth had tried without success to get Bechet to play for the opening season at their club. Undeterred, they made several other offers and eventually, in November 1947, Sidney relented and agreed to play a season at the new venue, Jazz Ltd (situated at 11 East Grand Avenue, on the near North Side). The booking was so successful that for the next year or so Bechet's name became synonymous with that of the club.

Manhattan-born Ruth Reinhardt (née Sato), formerly a show dancer, acknowledges her mixed parentage by quipping: "I have the pride of the Japanese and the stubbornness of the Irish." She had married clarinettist Bill Reinhardt in 1942; the two of them had shared an ambition to open a night-club that would feature jazz.

> After Bill got out of the navy we decided to carry out our plans in Chicago. We were so naive we put an ad in the paper offering a thousand-dollar bonus for information that led us to the right establishment. We didn't get a single reply. Then Bill was out strolling and found this basement, which proved ideal. Originally we thought of calling the club Jazz Inc, but a lawyer vetoed that idea, so we settled for Jazz Ltd. Paul Eduard Miller said, "You can get the news to all the jazz fans by running a concert at Kimball Hall", which we did. The one that featured Bechet and Max Kaminsky, we sponsored that with Paul. Both of us had known Bechet in New York, and Bill thought the world of his playing. Bechet wasn't known at all by the general public in Chicago, but we decided he'd be great at the club, so eventually he arrived there.
>
> It wasn't a huge place, it seated 88 people, and five of them sat at the bar. We had strict rules: men had to wear jackets, no local yokels allowed. The Mafia were big in that area, they were very tough about keeping their hands on prostitution, so we had to make it very clear to them that we were not going to cut across their path. We only had male serving staff and unaccompanied women couldn't get in the club – and no women could sit at the bar. People waited behind a velvet rope until they were seated. It all worked and we built up a tremendous atmosphere there.[3]

At that time, in common with every other night-club in the USA, Jazz Ltd would have been subject to a 20 percent tax had it allowed singing on the premises. The Reinhardts chose not to permit this, and concentrated on presenting instrumental jazz played by a five-piece group, one of whom was always a guest star. Bill Reinhardt led the band and played clarinet. When Bechet arrived the rest of the personnel was Munn Ware (trombone), Mel Grant (piano) and Danny Alvin (drums). Grant was later replaced by Floyd Bean.

Bill organized the presentation of the music and Ruth was responsible for the management and administration. She was shrewd and enterprising, and realized the value of regular publicity; soon Bechet's name was appearing in news items, gossip columns and national magazines. Ruth's dealings with Sidney were often tinged with rancour: "I was running a business and my father had always said, 'Business is business', I never looked for popularity. The only people who liked me in Chicago were newspapermen, because I gave them lots of good stories."[4]

The first collision of interests between Ruth and Sidney occurred soon after he had begun his residency at Jazz Ltd. Sales of Mezzrow's records for King Jazz were booming, so much so that Mezz was anxious to build up a stock of new titles. He sent word to Bechet in Chicago requesting that he come to New York for another studio session. Ruth Reinhardt was adamant that she would only agree to such a move if she were provided with a suitable replacement and adequate compensation. The upshot of her stand was that Mezzrow, Sammy Price, Pops Foster and Kaiser Marshall all had to drive from New York to Chicago to make the recordings with Bechet at the United Broadcasters' Studio on Erie Street.

They arrived on 16th December, rehearsed with Bechet during the following day, and then spent the next three afternoons, from 1 p.m. until 4 p.m., in the recording studio. Their first effort was an ornate 32-bar composition by Mezzrow and Bechet (which sounds more like Bechet's work than Mezzrow's) entitled *Where am I*. Three choruses of the slow, majestic tune just fitted on to a 12-inch 78 r.p.m. record. After a grotesquely inappropriate introduction by the rhythm section. Bechet (on saxophone) states the melody, slightly hampered by Mezzrow's out-of-tune support. The arrangement is a feature for Bechet but, unfortunately, at no stage does Mezzrow drop out of the proceedings. The rhythm section sounds accomplished (with Kaiser Marshall effecting a fine job on drums), its double-tempo 'feint' in the final chorus being superbly performed.

The voices of Mezzrow and Bechet announce *Tommy's Blues*, dedicated to Tommy Ladnier. It is a worthy tribute, being a subtle blues that makes telling use of a diminished chord variation. The front-line partners establish the theme, then Price takes the ensuing chorus with rolling piano figures, backed by the rock-steady efforts of Foster and Marshall. Mezzrow projects two choruses competently and sincerely before handing over to Bechet, whose solo is packed with ingenuities of timing and melody that his colleague was never able to create. A truncated, less satisfactory, version of a second take was also issued.

The 32-bar *Revolutionary Blues* sequence was one of Mezzrow's favourite musical hunting grounds; two more versions were recorded in Chicago. The first is slow, with an effectively coordinated introduction that has Mezzrow on clarinet and Bechet on saxophone (which he played throughout the date). Bechet, at his most stirring, excels himself, blowing phrases that are connective and rich in emotion. Mezzrow is more productive on the fast version that followed. Sammy Price displays some boogie-like patterns, energetically supported by Foster's springy bass playing. Bechet's tough solo completes a good all-round perform- ance. Second takes of both versions were issued, but they do not surpass the original efforts. It must be said in Mezzrow's favour that he often relinquished a take containing a better solo by himself for a performance that was of overall superiority.

Mezzrow maintained that the basic idea of *I want some* had originated in his session with Tommy Ladnier in 1938; he also suggested that Bechet took the theme away in 1946 and later used it in one of his extended compositions. Sidney plays the opening melody, supported by Mezzrow's harmony part. The two swop the lead, then Mezzrow constructs an inspired solo; it seems that the Chicago air suited him. Bechet rises to the challenge and plays with compelling assurance. Mezzrow is more subdued on *I'm speaking my mind*, an unusual 16-bar minor theme, which has an effective descending bass line. The soprano saxophone and piano solos are taken on a straightforward 12-bar blues sequence, Bechet's efforts providing another vivid example of his unfettered imagination. Each of three takes is packed with his magnificence, but the third has the edge because of the particularly expressive playing of the opening melody.

Never will I forget the blues is a pretty eight-bar theme, touchingly presented by the two reed players. They hand over to Sammy Price, whose series of 12-bar choruses make the piece into a feature for piano. The front line then repeats the opening theme, which has fleeting similarities to Bechet's later composition *Si tu vois ma mère*. Nothing epic emerged from the three days of recording, but the standard of performance and the depth and force of the improvisation rarely flagged until the last stages. After an expressive rendition of *Delta Mood* (reminiscent of *Darkness on the Delta*) the group completes its mammoth task with a loose work-out on the *Sister Kate* chord sequence, which was later entitled *Blues of the Roaring Twenties*. In all, the Mezzrow–Bechet Quintet had managed to record 30 issueable takes within the space of three afternoon sessions.

The set routine at Jazz Ltd suited Bechet's health, but, although his stomach problems eased, he was plagued with toothache during his first weeks in Chicago. There was no chance of Sidney flying down to New Orleans to be treated by his brother. Instead he sought his advice by telephone and, in doing so, discovered that Leonard was hankering for a chance to visit Chicago. So the two brothers, physically very much alike, enjoyed another reunion. Leonard had been playing trombone more regularly since their previous meeting, and had joined the Blue Eagle Melody Players, an eight-piece band that worked regularly in and around New Orleans. Sidney was delighted to hear this piece of news, but was forbidden by local union regulations from allowing his brother to sit in with the band at Jazz Ltd.

The accord that had redeveloped during their previous reunion continued to grow and, as a result, Sidney suggested that he could find work at Jazz Ltd for Leonard, Jr. Accordingly, Sidney's nephew (who decided to ignore his memories of the Boston fiasco) began working in the cloakroom at the club, a task that allowed him plenty of time to be coached on the soprano saxophone by his famous uncle.

Sidney's recent tooth extraction had eased the problem of pain, but its loss brought unfamiliar pressure on part of his dentures, making it more difficult (so he said) to play the clarinet. He specialized on soprano saxophone at Jazz Ltd, but had occasionally played clarinet duets with Bill Reinhardt. One night, as he was preparing to do this, he found that his clarinet 'bite' had become unbearable. Ruth Reinhardt observed the aftermath: "He got so mad he called his nephew Leonard over and handed him the clarinet, saying, 'Take it! I don't ever want to play that damn thing again'."[5]

Leonard recalled his uncle with affection: "He took a liking to me and showed me things on my horn. My teacher had always told me to play with no vibrato, but Sidney told me to forget all that and just play as I wanted to. Of course everything I played from then on sounded a little like him. Sidney always wanted me to be a lawyer, never a musician. He said it was too hard a life, with too little reward."[6]

The stay in Chicago during 1948 was a barren one for Sidney as far as recordings went, but there was compensation in the regular income and the growing adulation he received. Early in the year he turned down an offer to play for a week in Paris (at a fee that was equivalent to 1500 dollars). The offer came from Hugues Panassié, working in conjunction with Radio Diffusion; details of the booking were relayed to Sidney via the broadcasting company's New York office. The prospect of returning to France attracted Bechet and the 1500 dollars was inviting, but he soon found out that, under French currency restrictions, he would not be able to take the money out of the country. Negotiations ended at that point. It was also mooted that Sidney might be featured in a group with Mezz

Mezzrow at the 1948 Nice Jazz Festival. Bechet's contract with Jazz Ltd precluded that idea, but his ex-pupil Bob Wilber, now a fully fledged professional, made the trip instead, and joined Mezzrow in performing some of the Bechet–Mezzrow King Jazz duets.

Pianist Floyd Bean left the band at Jazz Ltd on 6 February 1948. His place was taken temporarily by Lionel Prouting, but his permanent replacement was a former member of Bob Wilber's Wildcats, Dick Wellstood. Wellstood recalled:

> I had not long been back from playing in Cape Cod when I got the offer from Bill Reinhardt. A few weeks later I started at Jazz Ltd. The pay was a hundred dollars a week. The hours were usually from 9 p.m. until 3.30 a.m., with Saturday from 10 p.m. until 5 a.m. – long, but nothing like as long as the hours that Lee Collins played over on Randolph Street. Although it was a night-club the atmosphere was sort of informal; the front line, who played seated, would chit-chat amongst themselves and kibbutz with the customers. Bill Reinhardt was the leader, he tapped off the tempos. Supposedly, if Bechet had any complaints he passed them on via Bill, but often he couldn't suppress his thoughts and a forceful murmur shot out. Sidney had a way of frowning disapproval that struck terror. Without doubt I was afraid of him.
>
> I never found him to be 'one of the boys'. He was the star of the proceedings and usually behaved in an imperious way. He sometimes went 'out on a bat' and got evil as a result of this over-drinking, but I never recall him using pot. His appearance was always dignified, but he could be cruel and suspicious. He epitomized the New Orleanians' sense of mistrust. Like the great old-timers, he took his music seriously. He had a fine ear, and took a pride in playing correct harmonies with a good tone, and playing good time.
>
> After I'd been at the club for about a week I learnt that Danny Alvin was leaving, so I recommended a friend of mine, Bob Saltmarsh, for the job. He'd played well during the previous summer when I worked with him on Cape Cod. So Bob joined the band at Jazz Ltd. But Bechet, for some reason, found fault with him from the off and started issueing curses to him from the side of his mouth whilst we were on the stand. You'd hear Sidney say, "Lay out, mother-fucker" . . . "Keep time, mother-fucker". I felt for Bob, but he improved greatly and stayed for the rest of the gig.[7]

Bob Saltmarsh took the criticism in good part and now says: "I am sort of proud to have been associated and worked in a band with Sidney Bechet. Relationships with all concerned seemed amicable during the time I was there in spite of the fact of an incident that happened to me. During a rare reharsal 'lull' I asked Sidney if he would autograph my original mint Okeh disc of *Wild Cat Blues* by Clarence Williams' Blue Five. He responded by saying 'Man, forget about all that nonsense and concentrate on your playing music'. He usually stayed pretty much by himself on the job, drifting away quietly into a back room cranny between sets."[8]

Dick Wellstood recalls an occasion when both he and Bob Saltmarsh were severely reprimanded by Bechet. One night, between sets at Jazz Ltd, the two young musicians decided to use the club's kitchen for some hockey practice. They found brooms and ice cubes (from the fridge) and began an energetic game, which was interrupted by Bechet in his role as headmaster. He commanded them to stop and instructed them to use their intervals more usefully by pondering on all the bad mistakes they had made during the previous set.

In the *Down Beat Year Book* for 1971, Dick Wellstood wrote about Sidney:

"Bechet was not racially prejudiced and he rather enjoyed having young musicians around. For music to him was a skill to be taught, to be learned. There was a right way to play, a right way to breathe, a right set of chords, a right tempo for each tune. The job was simply to learn the right way and then secure in one's craft one could go before the public."

Sidney revelled in the acclaim that he received from the public at Jazz Ltd. Wellstood remembers him sitting at a table during intermissions, graciously receiving the "greetings of the worshippers as they entered the temple". His manner on the bandstand was "like a Caesar . . . bowing his neck and brandishing his soprano like some enormous phallus, sending his vibrato throbbing into the far corners of the hushed club like the beating of great wings. And all the while pondering who had tried to put the poison in his Chicken-In-A-Basket, all the while thinking that they'd spoiled those publicity photos on purpose just to make him look bad, all the while thinking of the trip to Europe he was about to make, of the knife in his pocket just in case he needed it, of the money he owed, or the girl back in the hotel room. And when the tune was over someone would come up to shake his hand and say, deeply moved, 'I can tell from your music that you've had a happy life', and Sidney would smile and shake his head and answer 'oh yes . . . yes'."[9]

Bob Saltmarsh noticed one of the ploys that Bechet used to command the audience's attention: "Sidney always adjusted the bullet-shaped light above him on the low ceiling so that its rays bounced off the giant ring on his finger as he stood taking his solos."[10] This spectacular emerald ring had been given to Sidney by Tallulah Bankhead. The two old friends still enjoyed an occasional hectic get-together, and in 1948 this led one Chicago columnist to mention Tallulah's interest in "Sidney Bechet, the celebrated jazz pianist".

Bechet met up with a number of old friends during his stay at Jazz Ltd. The most illustrious of these visitors was Ernest Ansermet, the Swiss conductor and composer who had given Sidney the historic review in 1919. Both Ruth Reinhardt and Paul Eduard Miller (who had engineered Ansermet's visit to the club) managed to gain a lot of publicity over the event, but Ansermet chose not to echo the praise he had previously passed on to his readers. In 1948 he simply summarized his general view by saying: "The days of jazz are over. It has made its contribution to music. Now in itself it is merely monotonous."[11]

The distinguished conductor's latter-day view of jazz was not a direct comment on the performance he heard at Jazz Ltd; his disillusionment with jazz had grown over the years. Like others in music, he had been thrilled and inspired by the freshness and vigour that jazz had originally represented. Dismay set in when jazz practitioners began gloating over harmonic ideas that had long been regarded as commonplace in classical music.

Bechet never became deeply involved in any quest for so-called modern harmonies. He was one of the first jazz improvisers to explore the possibilities offered by 9th and 13th chords, but when he used additional notes it was to enhance the richness of the lines he was improvising; he thought of them (in musical terms) horizontally rather than vertically. When composing he constructed a melody line, and then, step-by-step, harmonized it, whereas modernists, in order to provide the basis of a new tune, often played a series of widely voiced block chords and then extracted notes. Sidney positively discouraged the use of complicated substitute chords by his accompanists, and he was never seduced by chromaticisms. But he dismissed nothing without first listening carefully. Had he found anything that he considered attractive within the new music he would have had no hesitation in using it. He was aware that he had created a unique style of improvising and saw no reason to change his methods.

Bechet's first long residency at Jazz Ltd ended on 6 June 1948. Just before the end of his stay he indulged in some end-of-term fun on the bandstand which was vividly remembered by Dick Wellstood and by Joan Hulbert (the former wife of trombonist Munn Ware). Ware, seeing Bechet sit down after playing a solo on *Tiger Rag*, came to the justifiable conclusion that Sidney had had his say; accordingly he stood up and started blowing. Bechet suddenly leapt to his feet and resumed where he had left off. Ware politely sat down and awaited the end of the soprano saxophone solo. Bechet concluded a chorus, then sat down. But again, just as Ware rose, Sidney leapt up and recommenced playing, much to the amusement of the crowd. Dick Wellstood picks up the story:

> Munn Ware sat down and fumbled under his chair for something. Once again Sidney pretended to stop, but kept going. But this time Munn didn't try to play. He took the water pistol he used to oil his slide and shot Sidney in the back of the neck with it. Right on that enormous scrotal roll of fat, the water and the oil dripping down the neck, soaking into the white collar, staining the gray pin-stripe. I was terrified. I kept playing, waiting for the sky to fall, knowing that Munn was sitting there chuckling, wondering what Sidney would do when this chorus was over. But he did nothing, just sat down and laughed. Munn laughed. Bill laughed. The people laughed. It is good to be able to join a god in laughter. I laughed too.[12]

Bechet returned to New York, confirming to himself that his long association with Laura was coming to an end. Before he left Chicago he signed a contract to return to Jazz Ltd for another season, so he was able to treat his stay in New York as something of a summer vacation. He appeared as a guest at various places, including the Stuyvesant Casino (at 140 Second Avenue and 9th Street), where a series of "Jazz Band Balls" were held, but generally he took life easy, recording his musical thoughts onto his tape recorder and poring over various camera-store catalogues. He decided to buy another clarinet, but not long after sold it to Eugene Sedric (who later gave it to Louis Metcalf's son Charlie). Bechet then began practising on a Czechoslovakian clarinet that was part Albert system, part Boehm, but soon abandoned that idea and reverted to a straightforward Albert model. Most of his clarinet playing during this period was done in the house.

By late August 1948 Bechet was back in harness at Jazz Ltd, replacing cornetist Paul 'Doc' Evans, who had been appearing as a guest with the house band. Bill Reinhardt and Munn Ware were still in the front line, but to coincide with Bechet's return Don Ewell came in on piano. Drummer Enos 'Doc' Cenardo had joined the group during Bechet's summer absence, replacing Bob Saltmarsh in late July. Bechet's return brought the crowds flocking in, and the "House Full" and "Reservations Only" signs were regularly on display. This time Bechet only

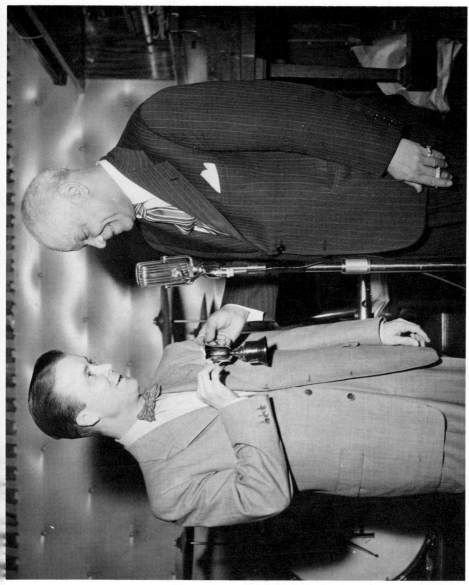

Bechet with Eddie Condon, 1949 (*courtesy Dick Hughes*)

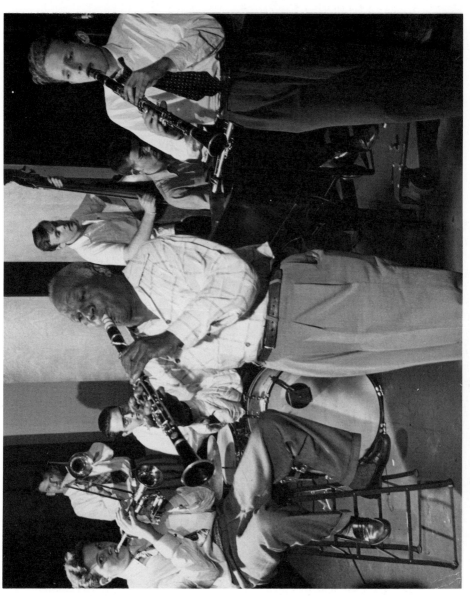

Bechet with Bob Wilber's Wildcats *(courtesy Peter Tanner)*

(left to right) Don Frye, Bob Wilber, 'Big Chief' Russell Moore, Bechet, Claude Hopkins, unknown, Lloyd Phillips (*courtesy Dick Hughes*)

Bechet in a box at the Winter Garden Theatre, London, 1949 (*courtesy Melody Maker*)

Bechet with the Swedish pianist Reinhold Svensson, November 1949 (*courtesy Dagens Nyheter*)

Sidney Bechet in his kitchen (*courtesy Dick Hughes*)

Bechet with Hot Lips Page (*photo P. Leloir*)

Hughes Panassié and Madeleine Gautier arriving in New York, February 1949, and being greeted by Happy Caldwell (tenor saxophone), Mezz Mezzrow (clarinet), Buck Clayton (trumpet), Bechet and Cliff Jackson (*photograph courtesy Buck Clayton*)

Bechet in Paris with Ray Sonin, editor of *Melody Maker*, and Charlie Parker, May 1949

Bechet with Claude Luter's orchestra (*courtesy Dick Hughes*)

Bechet with the Dutch Swing College (*photo Wouter Van Cool*)

Bechet relaxing at the home of the leader of the Dutch Swing College, Peter Schilperoort, listening to his host play the guitar (May 1951) (*fotovak engel*)

Bechet with Claude Luter, Switzerland, May 1952

Bechet enjoying late-night revels in Paris (*courtesy Dick Hughes*)

Bechet polishing his Salmson, Juan-les-Pins, 1951 (*courtesy Dick Hughes*)

Sidney Bechet, top of the bill

Bechet playing with Marty Marsala's band in San Francisco, September 1951; the pianist is Johnny Wittwer (photo John Smith)

Bechet with Marty Marsala's band, San Francisco, September 1953 (left to right): Marsala (trumpet), Bechet, Skip Morr (trombone), Billy Cronk (double bass) *(photo John Smith)*

Sidney Bechet in London (*photo Jeff Atterton*)

Bechet with his émerillon outside the
Vieux Colombier, Juan-les-Pins

Sidney Bechet: fisherman

My dear Wife
I know that this ~~broke~~ you
heart. How ~~~~ do you
like this little Fish.
I was out fishing for two
days the first day I didnot
chach nothing but, O boy the
next day I made up for
times. now Baby this is
a little Samon, 28 Ponds
so Please dort be Mad.
Good Luck to you when you go
fishing —
   your ~~great~~ fishing Husban
   Mr Sidney J. Bechet

Letter from Bechet to his wife, written on
the reverse of the photograph

An early portrait of Elisabeth Bechet

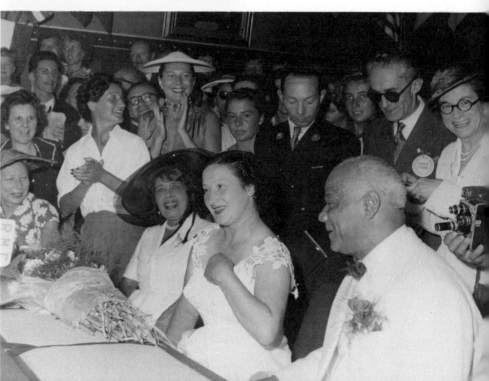

Sidney Bechet and his new bride Elisabeth, 1951 (*courtesy Dick Hughes*)

Bechet with André Réwéliotty and Humphrey Lyttelton, 1956

Bechet with Sammy Price, Paris, c1957 (*courtesy Melody Maker*)

Daniel Bechet

Sidney Bechet: a late study
(*courtesy Dick Hughes*)

signed a five-week contract, because some lucrative prospects were developing in New York.

The plum jobs consisted of a series of television dates with Eddie Condon. Condon, who was one of the first jazz bandleaders to be featured on television (in 1942), used many famous jazzmen in his 1948 "Floorshow" series. Bechet was one of them, as was bass player Jack Lesberg, who remembers the impact that Bechet made on viewers and on the production staff: "Sidney always exhibited power and presence, but on television his impact was terrific. He was so photogenic the director and the camera man loved working with him."[13]

Another small bonanza also fell Sidney's way. The details were contained in a letter that Stephen H. Scholes, of RCA Victor, wrote to John Reid on 13 October 1948: "We have released a Bechet record, *Twelfth Street Rag* coupled with *Suey*. Frankly the release was made in order to compete with the Pee Wee Hunt Capitol recording. However we have already sold over 25,000 of the record which should be some help to Sidney, no matter for what reasons the records were purchased. Any thoughts of Bechet albums have again been pushed into the future and I will let you know when things develop." Despite this brief flurry of interest, RCA Victor decided not to sign a new recording contract with Bechet.

As well as doing the television dates with Condon and some radio work, Bechet played a brief residency at Jimmy Ryan's from 18 October 1948, then after a month headed west to begin another session at Jazz Ltd on 23 November. In the period since his departure from Chicago there had been changes in the club's band: Doc Cenardo had left to join Doc Evans; his place had been taken by Johnny Vine, who was in turn replaced by Wally Gordon.

Early in 1949 the line-up of Bechet, Reinhardt, Ware, Ewell and Gordon, plus bass player, Sid Thall, recorded three titles, which were issued on the new Jazz Ltd label as part of a package set of 78 r.p.m. discs. The initial idea for making the recordings with Bechet was inspired by a local demand for Sidney's version of *Egyptian Fantasy*, which was no longer in the RCA Victor catalogue. The demand had been nurtured by a Chicago disc-jockey, Linn Burton, who had used Bechet's 1941 recording as a theme song for his programme. This exposure created a lot of interest amongst his listeners, but when they tried to buy the record at local stores they were told it had been deleted. The Jazz Ltd issue helped satisfy the demand, but musically it was considerably inferior to the earlier release.

On the new version, Bill Reinhardt takes the opening melody on clarinet, but, owing to the curious voicings adopted by Bechet (on saxophone) and Ware (on trombone), the full beauty of the tune is lost. The arrangement proceeds like a gavotte; Bechet shakes off the stiffness by projecting the melody himself during the closing stages, but the ending features a dismal series of coy, unaccompanied exchanges between Reinhardt and Bechet. The timing of this brief escapade (2 minutes 25 seconds) was designed to obtain radio plays, so too was the commercial treatment of *Maryland, my Maryland,* which is complete with a count-in in German and a military-styled drum break. *Careless Love* is the most satisfactory of the three titles. The opening chorus features Bechet playing the melody, nicely accompanied by Reinhardt's liquid-toned obbligato. After a modulation

Munn Ware blows a sparsely phrased but effective re-vamp of the tune; behind him the rhythm section sounds relaxed and swinging. Bechet soars into a final chorus that is dotted with quotes (from *Humoresque*, *The song is ended*, etc.), the inclusion of which had become part of his stock treatment of the noble old tune. The Jazz Ltd recordings are disappointing, especially as many visitors to the club invariably described the group as being capable of playing lively, interesting jazz.

Bechet returned to New York on 15 January 1949 and prepared himself for the new recording session for Blue Note that took place six days later. For this the front-line partnership of Bechet and Davison was reconstituted. Art Hodes was on piano, Fred Moore on drums, and the ex-Count Basie star Walter Page on bass. The session was under Bechet's name. He chose not to play clarinet.

Every tune on the date was familiar, but for most of them Bechet and Davison made genuine efforts to produce fresh sounding versions. *Sister Kate* moves gracefully. During a solo that contains a scintillating break, Bechet introduces some poetic descending ideas that move one step at a time. Davison takes a velvet-gloved outing, but zest surfaces in the final chorus when both musicians hit a pre-arranged series of staccato half-notes smack on the beat.

An effective loping pace enhances *Tiger Rag*; Page's bass playing provides the piece with a bouncy, flexible spine. Ensembles and solos are trim and thoughtful, and there is an inventive closing theme in which Bechet takes the lead while Davison plays a lower harmony. *Tin Roof Blues* is reflectively presented: both front-line players often make skilful use of dynamics, dropping their volume by a half, then suddenly revving up to full power.

The highlight of the session is *I've found a new baby*, in which Davison thrusts out a flamboyant lead; Bechet responds by swooping, diving and climbing all around it. Both players then link for a lively descending chromatic riff. *Nobody knows you when you're down and out* sounds makeshift. Davison creates a maudlin effect and Bechet seems unwilling to let go of the melody. Hodes has a brief moment of glory during a solo that, typically, involves tremolos. The pianist is also featured on the slow introduction to a dignified rendition of *The Saints*. This is a decidedly uncharacteristic version: vulgarity is sparse, Moore's off-beat drumming is well-behaved and Hodes's two choruses are almost prim. Bechet establishes a feeling of propulsion in his two choruses (taken in the minor key) and Davison follows on with a series of his swift octave jumps. Everything remains musicianly, epitomizing an interesting session.

Ten days later Bechet led his own group, the Circle Seven, on a recording for Rudi Blesh's label. Despite a strong line-up – Buster Bailey (clarinet), Wilbur De Paris (trombone), Albert Snaer (trumpet), James P. Johnson (piano), Walter Page (bass), and one white musician, George Wettling (drums) – the results are disappointing. The opening number, *I got rhythm*, is a prime example of the misuse of riffs; appropriate backing figures can stimulate an improviser, but here they distract and disfigure. All the soloists (including Bechet) suffer from riffs that are played too loudly. The same fault spoils *Who*. Bechet plays an ingeniously spaced opening melody (backed by scored figures), but subsequent solos by De Paris, Bailey and Snaer are all drowned out by riffs. The pity is that Bailey (flexible as ever) seems to be in an enthusiastic mood. Snaer, a veteran originally from New Orleans, performs well despite the barrage, but all merit disappears during the welter of confusion that spoils the final jammed chorus.

Bechet sounds assured and majestic when playing the opening melody of *September Song*; Bailey provides some affectionate fill-ins, then James P. Johnson composes a rippling piano solo that suddenly reveals a hard core. The black spot of the arrangement comes when the band unwisely doubles the tempo for six bars, creating cacophony; fortunately Bechet's powerful phrasing establishes the return to a slow melody, and so the earlier mood is restored.

Johnson's place at the piano was taken by James Toliver for *Casbah (The Song of the Medina)*, which Toliver had arranged. The slow, Moorish theme is replete with tom-toms and atmospheric band figures; Bechet plays it as though he were wearing a fez. There are two brief interludes in 4/4 time, but the piece is scored throughout. Critics later blamed the taste of French audiences for Bechet's use of material like *Casbah* and *September Song*, but Sidney's love of atmospheric pieces had been with him for most of his professional life. When given a free hand – or encouragement – he never shunned the chance to include such items in his programme.

TWENTY

European Acclaim

The advertisements for Bechet's appearance on 21 January at the Central Plaza, New York, included the words "soon leaving for Europe", a reference to a trip to France that was being planned by the agent Billy Shaw for the coming May. When the William Morris Agency had shut down its band departments, Shaw set up his own booking agency, which handled some of Bechet's engagements; it also dealt with work for the up-and-coming jazz saxophonist Charlie Parker. It was mooted that both Bechet and Parker would appear at the International Jazz Festival scheduled to be held in Paris from 8 to 16 May 1949.

Because of this agency tie-up, the two saxophonists played some dates on shared bills during the early months of 1949. The eminent French jazz writer and record producer Charles Delaunay, visiting New York, was present at one of these. On 21st February he presented a *Down Beat* poll-winner's plaque to Charlie Parker on a WPIX television show; Bechet was also in the programme and joined in a jammed finale. Bechet shrugged when Delaunay said that he wished he were also presenting an award to him, but the Frenchman received the clear impression that Bechet was in no way overawed by Parker's talents.

Twelve days later, at the Waldorf Astoria Hotel, Parker and Bechet were featured at a Saturday morning Youth Forum organized by the *New York Herald Tribune* as part of a presentation by Rudi Blesh entitled "A Battle of Music". Each man led his own group, which played three numbers. Parker's band, consisting of Kenny Dorham (trumpet), Al Haig (piano), Tommy Potter (bass), Max Roach (drums) and Milt Jackson (vibraphone), performed *How high the moon*, *Barbados* and *Anthropology*. In competition, Bechet's group (Buster Bailey, Wilbur De Paris, Walter Page, Ralph Sutton and George Wettling) played *I found a new baby*, *Ad Lib Blues* and *Dear Old Southland*.

No bitter animosity resulted from the encounter. Despite reports in the music magazines hinting that traditional musicians hated modernists, and vice versa, players from supposedly rival camps often socialized together. Such was the case with Parker and Bechet. They had first came to know one another during the period that Parker was working at the Three Deuces (close to Jimmy Ryan's club). Sometimes they spent their intervals together at a nearby bar. On one such occasion they were observed by writer Yannick Bruynoghe, who reported that the two men embraced warmly. He asked Bechet what he thought of Parker, and was told, "He's a great guy, a good friend."[1]

Such socializing did not mean that Bechet was planning to play be-bop. Early in 1949 he gave his views on that style of playing: "Be-bop? Why it's the best thing that ever happened to jazz! After all be-bop has caught the attention of a whole lot of people who never had any previous interest in jazz. When they get tired of be-bop they'll discover the *real* jazz for themselves."[2]

Charles Delaunay, whose visit to the USA was for business and pleasure, heard Bechet play at a jam session organized by Milt Gabler and at the Central Plaza. One of his tasks was to secure Bechet's services for the coming festival. However, there were hurdles to be overcome before the contract was signed. Arriving at a financial agreement with Sidney was one obstacle; another was the obtaining of a work permit, which, due to Bechet's previous misdemeanour, might prove difficult. Walter Schaap, who, with Delaunay, was author of the 1947 edition of *Hot Discography*, recalled the background to these complicated negotiations:

> Charles Delaunay came over here in 1949 to sign up jazz stars for the proposed festival, and wanted Bechet and 'Bird' to be what we now call the superstars. As Delaunay's American agent, I worked closely with him, and so did Billy Shaw, who represented Parker. Around the same time, Nicole Barclay, wife of Eddie Barclay of Blue Star records, came over for a rival festival, with which Panassié was associated.
>
> As you know, the problem we faced was that Bechet had once been thrown out of France, and forbidden to return. On February 26 1949, Delaunay, still in the U.S. received a cable from his associate, Souplet, saying that the ban on Bechet had been lifted by the rival group, and hoping we could take advantage of this, ("Interdiction SEJOUR BECHET LEVEE PAR DE BRY POUR PANASSIÉ POUVONS PROFITER CETTE MESURE A LEUR PLACE").
>
> Unfortunately, Bechet felt that, if he signed with us, the other group could cause troubles with French officialdom. On March 15 I wrote Delaunay, now back in France, that Bechet was about to sign with Nicole Barclay. On March 16, Delaunay cabled me that he and Barclay had now joined forces for a unified festival. I wrote Delaunay, the next day, that we can now sign Bechet for $1,600 of which he wanted $1,200 in advance. I believe that I worked things out with Sidney over the next few days, cutting the advance to 50%, when the bombshell fell: A March 26 cable from Delaunay and Franck Bauer (about to be appointed General Secretary of the festival by all the partners) broke the bad news that the French government would permit only 30% to be paid in dollars, with the balance in francs at the official rate of 325 to the dollar. This appalled Billy Shaw and myself, since our negotiations with all the musicians had been on the basis of a 50% advance in dollars and assurances that they could get the much higher free-market rate for the francs. As the contracts in my possession indicate, we got around the regulations by a necessary subterfuge.
>
> The official contract with Bechet, dated March 26, specified the permitted 30% advance and the 325 official rate. Another contract dated March 25 specified a 50% advance and the free-market exchange rate. A third document is a personal contract between Bechet and myself (undated and drawn up by Bechet's lawyer, Conrad.J. Lynn at 271 W 125 St). This would indicate incidentally, that Sidney had no intention of remaining in France at that time. Bechet's $1600 was far more than the other individual musicians received for the festival, which ranged from $200 to $350. Charlie Parker was paid $2275, but this included his band (Dorham, Haig, Potter, Roach).

Schaap added: "I adored Sidney Bechet, both as a musician and as a sweet old man who was always very nice to me. I could tell from his obstinacy during negotiations that he would be a bad man to cross, but he was certainly always kind to me."[3]

Feeling relieved that the complications surrounding his trip to France had been resolved, Bechet settled down to a new residency at Jimmy Ryan's. He led a quartet consisting of himself on soprano saxophone, Sammy Price on piano, Kansas Fields on drums and 'Big Chief' Russell Moore – so called because of his North American Indian ancestry – on trombone. At the time Moore seemed an unlikely choice for the quartet, but Bechet seemed determined to use a trombonist and not a trumpeter in the front line. Moore recalled the circumstances of his joining: "After leaving Louis Armstrong and the big band I joined Sidney Bechet. He liked my tone, that's the reason why I got in with Sidney. He taught me all about traditional jazz. I said, 'I don't know that music you play'. He told me, 'That's alright Chief, just come on with me and I'll play my notes and you play your notes'. He was so talented."[4]

Bechet continued to appear as a guest with bigger groups at various New York jazz functions. He played one session in front of the Air France reception desk at New York airport. At this unlikely spot, Sidney (on soprano saxophone), Mezz Mezzrow (clarinet), Buck Clayton (trumpet), and Happy Caldwell (tenor saxophone) assembled to greet Hugues Panassié and his friend Madeleine Gautier, who had arrived from France to visit the USA. On 27th February Bechet was part of an all-star band that played at the Village Vanguard to celebrate Panassié's 37th Birthday.

In March 1949 Wild Bill Davison was reunited with Bechet in another session for Blue Note (under Sidney's name). Art Hodes was on piano, Walter Page on bass, Wilmore 'Slick' Jones on drums and Ray Diehl on trombone. Diehl, who had not long been out of the US Navy, recalled the session: "There were no rehearsals for these recordings. The tunes were either well known to us or were quickly learned by us. A few tunes had ensemble passages written by Art Hodes, to give the band a more organized sound. The producers did a fine job of organizing, providing a relaxed mood, and a little whisky for the thirsty players. A few weeks after the album was released Bechet asked me to join his band for a tour of Europe. I declined the offer because I wanted to finish my education. Bechet was a gentleman, and an encouraging leader. He knew how to get the best out of you. Those old jazzers had an energy and vitality which made Dixieland music sound rousing and happy."[5]

Diehl acquits himself very satisfactorily throughout the session. Wild Bill Davison takes few solos on this date but flexes his ensemble muscles on *Fidgety Feet*, shouting hot, hoarse-sounding phrases on his cornet as he guides the front line through the tune's various strains. Bechet plays a glorious solo on that number, giving a new glow to ideas he had first presented on *Viper Mad*, but also adding bright-sounding new thoughts.

As the date of his flight to France drew nearer Bechet became increasingly restless, but he calmed down during the final stages of his wait and waved goodbye in a relaxed manner to Bob and Ricky Wilber, who went to the airport to see him off. Oran 'Hot Lips' Page, who was also a guest at the Paris festival, travelled with Bechet: "Flying over, Sidney Bechet and I sat together. While we were circling around, getting ready to land, Sidney turned to me and said, 'Lips, as soon as we land we'll slip over and change dollars into francs, but don't say anything to those be-bop boys. They think they know everything already, and what a surprise some of them are going to have when they run into a different kind of money.'"[6]

Bechet spent Saturday night (7th May) in a hotel, but then moved in with old friends who lived in the Latin Quarter. He did this mainly to avoid a constant stream of visits and telephone calls from well-wishers; he was also plagued by discographers eager to check on the personnels of various recordings. Representatives of many European jazz publications met Sidney at a reception held on 7th May, but even there he was bombarded with a series of "Who played what?" questions. A British contingent was overjoyed to hear Sidney say that he had recorded sides for Columbia during his stay in London in 1919.

Back home in the USA Bechet had become used to an occasional question about his old recordings, but here in Paris it seemed that some people were intent on following him night and day to ask him about long-forgotten details of his activities. He humoured most of the interrogators, but was happy to start rehearsing in the Club St Germain with a band led by an 18-year-old soprano saxophonist, Pierre Braslavsky. Denis Preston, writing in the *Melody Maker*, described this initial rehearsal; "Bechet showed himself meticulous over the smallest detail, for example, the balance of a background harmony; the type of drum-beat in a certain passage; the phrasing of introductions, bridge passages and codas; the accuracy and attack of the ensemble. When the old master swung the bell of his saxophone it was as imperious a gesture as any down beat by Toscanini. And when he said 'Doucement' in that quiet Southern voice of his, the Braslavsky boys toned down to a degree of softness which I'm sure they never before associated with jazz. On every playing Bechet's solos were identical down to the finest inflection."[7]

Finally, on the evening of Sunday 8th May, the great moment arrived for the audience at the Salle Pleyel: they were, at last, greeted with the sounds of Bechet's soprano saxophone. Writer Kurt Mohr vividly remembers the occasion: "I had been totally keyed up to the 'Old Man' through his records, and it was with somewhat mixed feelings that I went to hear him in person, accompanied by the French semi-pro band of Pierre Braslavsky. 'Bras', no mean soprano-player himself, went into a sprightly warm-up number. And then . . . there was suddenly an echo, a second soprano poking out from behind a curtain. With a devilish sense of timing the man stepped out, playing furiously and bringing the atmosphere to a climax. The rest of the concert was one big fiesta, and that's the way Bechet used to function: 'You gotta whip up a storm and keep it blowing' was one of his sayings."[8]

Bechet had certainly done a good job in rehearsing Braslavsky's band, and the musicians responded by giving a vibrant performance. Each of Bechet's solos was greeted with rapturous applause, and his deliberately spectacular phrases produced screams of ecstasy from the crowd. The same sort of intense admiration greeted every appearance he made at the theatre during that week. Most times he was accompanied by Braslavsky's band, and some of their numbers together were recorded as airshots, relayed from the hall. None is a first-class recording, but they do give an indication of the tremendous excitement that permeated the festival.

Sidney is in bold form, disregarding introspection, giving a performance that is full of swagger, growl, spirit and swing. Braslavsky's band worked without a trumpet, and this suited Bechet, even though the two soprano saxophones almost get entangled at times. Braslavsky, whose tone was much lighter than Bechet's, plays an attractive solo on *Tin Roof Blues*, and clarinettist René Franc (another disciple of Bechet, and then aged 20) sounds amazingly relaxed on *Jelly Roll*. These two titles (plus *Blues in the Air*) are the most successful of the recordings taken from the concerts at the Salle Pleyel.

During the festival Bechet also played with a band led by clarinettist Claude Luter, who had long been an admirer of Bechet. Claude wasn't overcome by nervousness, but finds hard-and-fast details of what happened on stage during that week difficult to remember. He recalls that Sidney regularly came down to the Vieux Colombier, the club where Claude and his L'Orientais band were working. Luter's trumpeter, Pierre Merlin, spoke of the excitement that surged through the band each time Bechet played with them during his visit: "The only problem was that we didn't have enough time to rehearse with him. I think we mostly played numbers from our repertoire, but Bechet made them into something quite different. He would suddenly turn round and play a backing riff for you to follow. No sooner had you got hold of that riff than he had moved on to another, more complicated one. Frankly, I found it terrifying. Also I had difficulty in understanding what he was saying. I think only one of our band spoke English fluently, so it was obvious that Sidney would speak in French, but because of his accent this made things difficult. I suppose he was out of practice, but it wasn't only accent, it was his vocabulary as well."[9]

Partisanship between fans of older-style jazz and those who exclusively supported the modern musicians marred some of the concerts, but most of the audiences settled back to hear the music. The opening concert of the festival featured Bechet in the first half and Parker in the second. Backstage, the two men's friendly accord was nearly shattered when a tense Bechet insisted on opening a window to let the fumes from Parker's marijuana escape, but for the most part all of the participating musicians were happy in each other's company. Trumpeter Miles Davis heard Bechet play live for the first time at the Salle Pleyel, and stood in the wings sampling the sound with evident pleasure. His reverie was interrupted by Maurice Cullaz, who asked Miles if he liked the music of New Orleans. Davis's reply was typically forthright: "I don't know if this is the music of New Orleans, or Texas, or wherever, but it sure is music and this old guy can really play it. He's fantastic."[10]

Hot Lips Page spoke of his trip to Paris: "Once the concerts started we got the impression that we were the ones who had been brought over to draw crowds and sell tickets."[11] Bechet usually enjoyed working with Page, but their version of *I know that you know*, recorded at a Salle Pleyel concert, is disappointing. The tempo is too fast for the rhythm section's comfort, and the atmosphere engendered by the excitable audience leads the musicians to attempt pyrotechnical solos. Bechet always got on well with Page socially, but at the festival he proved, yet again, that he could be stubborn and immovable, even when a friend was involved. The British visitor Denis Preston, knowing that an informal jam session was imminent, went looking for Bechet and found him quietly sipping a drink at a boulevard café. Preston urged him to make haste to join in the impromptu session. Bechet showed no signs of moving, whereupon Preston played what he thought was a trump card by saying, "Hot Lips Page will be there!" Sidney took this news impassively, then ended the conversation by saying, in solemn tones, "Let him be there."[12]

During a day on which Bechet wasn't engaged at the Paris festival he went to Switzerland to play a concert with Pierre Braslavsky's band at the Victoria Hall in Geneva. Recordings from this engagement (on 14th May) were issued as part of a boxed set of albums by Jazz Selection. The band performs with more relaxation (understandably) than it had displayed in the opening concerts with Bechet in Paris. The ensembles on *Sweet Georgia Brown* have a happy, lively quality, and the same track has a promising solo from the young pianist Eddie Bernard. Some of the endings sound a little ragged, but this is mainly because of the performers' enthusiasm. Bechet breezes through a set of old favourites, including *Weary Blues*, *Muskrat Ramble* and *High Society*, sounding in superb form, his fingers and embouchure working in perfect coordination. He was obviously delighted to have received a truly rapturous welcome – the opening notes of his performance of *Summertime* were greeted with gasps of pure delight.

Bechet travelled back to Paris for the grand finale of the festival, held on Sunday 15th May. A week had elapsed since the tumultuous opening and there were no signs that the excitement was abating. "The Blues Final", which featured many of the festival's leading performers (including Bechet, Lips Page, and Charlie Parker), was captured on record. It is a fine memoir of an historic jazz occasion, but despite the illustrious cast the end result is disappointing. Even Bechet and Parker, perhaps overwhelmed by the hubbub, do little more than present solos that are loaded with their stock phrases.

Next day, in the comparative peace of a studio, Bechet recorded half a dozen titles (for Eddie Barclay's Blue Star label) with a French pick-up band. The overall style is that of a jam session, which means that the ensembles do not always achieve a productive unity, but there is no lack of spirit. Unfortunately, the recording quality is poor, with the result that the rhythm section sounds muffled and ineffective. Apart from Bechet, trombonist Benny Vasseur and trumpeter Gerard Bayel are the main soloists, but sometimes, as on *High Society*, Bechet is heard throughout. Bayel plays a good, fierce plunger-muted solo on *Festival Blues*, which has some superlative improvising by Bechet. On most of the other tracks Bechet is cheerfully inventive, particularly on *Coquette* (his only recording of his tune) and *Honeysuckle Rose*, where he scatters dozens of highly melodic phrases. *On the Sunnyside of the Street* contains the blueprint of his later definitive version.

Bechet's visit had an exhilarating effect on countless listeners and musicians, particularly reed players. Music-shop owners reported a dramatic increase in the sales of soprano saxophones. Every new instrument in stock was sold within days of the end of the festival, and in meeting the continuing demand the dealers managed to find owners for their most ancient and dubious models.[13]

Sidney flew back to the USA, his ears ringing with the fervent applause of his fans and with the multitude of offers he had received from various promoters, all of whom were eager to get him back to Europe as soon as possible. Back in New York, events occurred that kept the mood of elation flowing. As if to prove (albeit temporarily) that a jazz musician could be a prophet in his own land, two honours were accorded Sidney. To coincide with his return, Jimmy Ryan arranged a special week of celebrations at his club, on each day of which a commemorative statuette was presented to Bechet. During that same week, on 20 May 1949, the Newspaper Guild of New York presented a "Page One Award" to Bechet at a vast ball held at the Commodore Hotel. This award, which had been inaugurated in 1934, was the newspaper union's way of "recognizing distinction of achievement"; other winners in 1949 were the discover of streptomycin, Dr S. A. Waksman, and the distinguished commentator Edward R. Murrow. At the ball, Bechet played a set with Brad Gowans's band, which included Bobby Hackett on cornet and Joe Marsala on clarinet. A day later, on 21st May, Bechet received the award again, this time for the benefit of those who watched Eddie Condon's weekly television show.

By this time Bob Wilber's career had moved ahead by leaps and bounds. During 1948–9 he led his own all-star band for a long residency in Boston. In June 1949 the band backed Bechet for a recording session which was full of inventive touches. None of the sounds produced has the quality of classic jazz, but if Sidney had worked regularly in this group the results could have been sensational. Here his role is that of a star soloist whose playing is well featured within arrangements that are often intricate.

The opening chorus of *I'm through, goodbye*, led by the trombonist, introduces a pleasing tone-colour. Bechet rhapsodizes masterfully throughout his solo, then trumpeter Henry Goodwin takes a chorus in his jerkily phrased muted style; unfortunately, the final ensemble is disappointingly scrappy. *Love me with a feeling* is a feature for Sidney's spoken romantic pleas; the best part of this track is Wilber's mellow clarinet accompaniment. *Waste no tears* is a deftly played clarinet duet, which highlights the wonderfully matched tones and vibratos of the two musicians (Wilber's lighter sound takes the lead).

Box Car Shorty is reminiscent of Sidney's ill-fated Haitian session, but Wilber's band gives a superior performance to that of the 1939 group. The arrangement is attractively pungent and the calypso vocal by 'the Duke of Iron' has a bright, merry lilt. The session's best item is *The Broken Windmill*, in which a strong melody line is blended with cleverly syncopated figures. The loosely played, ad-lib ensemble contrasts nicely with the previous, arranged section; Bechet's 32-bar soprano saxophone solo sounds inspired and totally appropriate. The date ended with a thoughtful mood piece, *Without a Home*; Bechet's soprano saxophone is effectively featured but the scored backing suggests a contrived production number.

The excitement over the trip to Europe gradually dispersed and Bechet settled down to his usual stints at Jimmy Ryan's. The audience there was minuscule compared with the vast numbers who had attended his European concerts, but this didn't put any sort of brake on Sidney's musical endeavours. Matt Walsh, the long-time manager of Jimmy Ryan's, never knew of an occasion when Bechet attempted to coast through a gig:

> I found Sidney easy to get along with and he made no demands to speak of. One wouldn't know that he was in the place till he got on the bandstand and started to play – then all took notice! With other musicians, at Jimmy Ryan's at least, he was the complete boss. He felt that people came to see him first, and they weren't disappointed. He did his own negotiating. He was fair and didn't 'hold me up'. He could have worked elsewhere more profitably, but he felt comfortable at Ryan's. Sidney was a gentle soul but he did carry a switch blade and wouldn't have hesitated to use it if the need arose. Perhaps he carried this knife to protect the huge ring which Tallulah Bankhead gave him, or the car he bought equipped with a burglar alarm which loudly played one of his recordings. Tallulah was a frequent visitor to Sidney at Ryan's. Same routine, quickly in the door and heading for the bandstand, dropping the mink coat in a heap, half-way down the 30 foot bar. By the time her escort retrieved the coat Tallulah was sitting on a step of the bandstand looking admiringly at her hero – Sidney.[14]

Bechet found no difficulty in coping with this sort of situation. The only occasions on which Matt Walsh sensed that Sidney was ill at east was when he was given something to read. It was rumoured that Bechet was illiterate; this was not the case, but Sidney hated to feel that his word fluency was undergoing any sort of test. Walsh noted, "He always acted very surreptitiously when he received mail in another's presence."[15] For a while Bechet received mail at Ryan's, because he had left the house on Quincy Street and was preparing to move into an apartment at 408 Edgecombe Avenue, Washington Heights. This was the fifth time during the 1940s that Bechet had moved home; the decampments were another indication of the changeable side of his nature. In a profile of Bechet, published in the September 1949 issue of *Playback*, Bob Aurthur wrote, "He is a man of shifting tastes and emotions, a confusing man whose moods and surface ideas change from moment to moment. One day he collects French perfume bottles, the next, miniature cameras. One month he will buy a Bell and Howell sound projector and will begin collecting 16 mm films with furious zeal and the next month he will sell it all."

Bechet left Ryan's early in September 1949 and went to Chicago for another residency at Jazz Ltd. There were new faces in the house band, which now consisted of Bill Reinhardt on clarinet, 'Big Chief' Russell Moore (who had also enjoyed success at the Paris Jazz Festival) on trombone, Sidney's old colleague Lloyd Phillips on piano, and Sid Catlett (who, for health reasons, had recently ceased touring with Louis Armstrong's All Stars) on drums. It was a strong line-up, but not one that Sidney worked with for long. On 20th September, with two weeks of his contract still to run, he left Chicago and made his way to New York; four days later he sailed to France aboard the liner *Ile de France*.

In some ways the move resembled the reckless, impetuous acts that had scarred Bechet's professionalism during the 1920s, but this was a more carefully planned operation; he even arranged for his beloved Cadillac to be shipped with him. The preliminary plans for the journey had been outlined during his wildly successful visit to Europe in May 1949. Charles Delaunay had assured Sidney that a tour before the end of the year would be both possible and profitable. Sidney agreed in principle and saw no objection to Delaunay's handling the enquiries that were coming in from promoters all over Europe. The outlines of a lucrative tour took shape and Bechet was advised to be ready to commence it early in October 1949. Sidney did not reveal any details of his impending trip either to journalists or to Bill and Ruth Reinhardt at Jazz Ltd. He did, however, call in at the offices of the Chicago musicians' union, where he was advised to honour the contract he had with the Reinhardts.

Sidney booked out of his hotel in Chicago on Tuesday 20th September, but, because Tuesday was the musicians' night off at Jazz Ltd, the club's owners were unaware that he had left the city until Wednesday evening, when he failed to turn up for work. The rest of the band assembled as usual and got on the bandstand, waiting for an arrival that didn't take place. Cornetist Doc Evans was located and he filled the gap; trumpeter Jack Ivett took the stand the next night, and then Muggsy Spanier came in on a regular basis. By then the picture had clarified. Sidney telephoned Ruth Reinhardt from New York and explained that he was sailing to France and had plans to live there permanently. Ruth Reinhardt had no hesitation in pointing out that she had a valid contract and that Jazz Ltd would be seeking compensation; she also brought it to Sidney's notice that Jazz Ltd had the exclusive rights to his appearances in the Chicago area. Sidney said he would be returning to the States to settle all his affairs, and there the matter rested.

Sidney disembarked at Le Havre, where he was reunited with his Cadillac. He drove to Paris, arriving there on Saturday 1st October. The young clarinettist Maxim Saury, who had been delegated to meet Sidney off the *Ile de France*, accompanied him on the road journey and showed him the small hotel in Saint-Germain into which he had been booked. An official reception was held at a club on the Champs-Elysées, and there Sidney was presented with a souvenir model of the Eiffel Tower. On 2nd October he began a series of rapturously received "Jazz Parades" at the Theatre Edouard VII. During the five-day residency there he worked in concert with bands led by Pierre Braslavsky and Claude Luter. For most of a subsequent tour of France and Switzerland he was backed by Braslavsky's group, but on 14 October 1949 Bechet made the first of his many recording sessions with Claude Luter and his orchestra.

Clarinettist Luter (who had won the *Jazz hot* poll in 1948) was then 26 years old and had a big following amongst jazz-loving students in Paris. His band had first established itself during a residency at L'Orientais, but fire regulations made it impossible for it to continue working at that club. At the time of Bechet's arrival it was firmly settled into a new residency at the Vieux Colombier. Luter said: "I had always liked Bechet, since I first began listening to jazz. People used to automatically say that our early band was styled on King Oliver's Creole Jazz Band, but there was a time before that when we had been influenced by the 1938 recordings that Sidney made with Mezzrow and Tommy Ladnier. Later, Henri Renaud played his King Oliver records to me and that marvellous music became the basis of our style. But we were very familiar with Bechet's music, so naturally we were greatly honoured to work with him."[16]

The keenness of Luter's band is apparent from the opening bars of *Ce mossieu qui parle*. The ebullient theme is presented with an infectious vitality, but this feeling rapidly diminishes with the onset of a bizarre banjo solo. Pierre Merlin and Luter play vigorous solos, then Bechet soars high to confirm his flawless superiority. A chat in French between Bechet and Luter graces the opening of *Buddy Bolden Story*. During this verbal exchange Sidney speaks briefly of his early days, then plays a theme that turns out to be *I thought I heard Buddy Bolden say*. The ensemble chorus tends to flounder but Luter shows his boldness in staying alongside Bechet. *Bechet's Creole Blues*, which begins with an attractive ostinato figure from pianist Christian Azzi, is a much more satisfying affair. Bechet takes the melody, which is not unlike that of *Summertime*, in grandiloquent style; except for a clarinet break in the style of Johnny Dodds from Luter, he is featured throughout.

Anita's Birthday, which clearly has the same opening themes as *The Hucklebuck*, has no magic moments, and the band's playing of the final, arranged riff seems lackadaisical. The jaunty mood resurfaces in the group's rendering of *Les oignons*, a tune that was to become irrevocably linked with Bechet's name, much to the chagrin of some of those who knew it as an old Creole folk song. The strong blend of Bechet's passionate soprano saxophone and Luter's forceful clarinet gives a quaint Gallic feel to the proceedings, and even the woodblocks somehow add to this attractiveness. The silent breaks and catchy main theme soon caught the public's fancy.

Bechet plays some robust blues on *Ridin' easy*, but the out-of-tune backing spoils the track. This blemish is avoided on *Blues in Paris*; Bechet is accompanied only by the rhythm section, which provides a reasonably brave support for Sidney's heartfelt five choruses. The final tune of the session is a 'composition' by Bechet entitled *Panther Dance*, which is almost a carbon copy of *Tiger Rag*. Its main blessings are a series of scorching breaks by Bechet and some fat-toned trombone calls from Mowgli Jospin. The final chorus radiates more spirit than swing, but Bechet seemed unperturbed; he was happy to be playing with young musicians who were eager to learn their craft.

In France Sidney retained his occasional habit of appropriating other people's compositions. Claude Luter caught one of his first glimpses of the fiery side of Bechet's nature when he mentioned a particular similarity: "When we first played through *Panther Dance* I said to Sidney, quite innocently, 'Oh, *Tiger Rag*'. He turned around angrily, and said, 'No! No! This is my tune! My tune!', so I didn't say anything more on the subject."[17]

On 20 October 1949 the Vogue recording company carried out the enterprising idea of gathering together a band comprised of expatriate American jazzmen who were working regularly in Europe (the one exception being the French bass player Pierre Michelot). Two members of the group, pianist Charlie Lewis and tenor saxophonist Frank 'Big Boy' Goudie, had worked with Bechet in Noble Sissle's band; drummer Kenny Clarke had been a member of Bechet's quartet in 1939 and trumpeter Bill Coleman had played various gigs with Sidney during the early 1940s. It seemed to be a homogenous mixture of musicians who were familiar with each other's styles, but familiarity bred contempt. Apparently Bechet issued orders in the manner of a sergeant-major and made it clear that he was determined to be obeyed. Bill Coleman, normally an easy-going man, could never be pushed beyond a certain point, and this stage was reached before a note had been recorded. The resultant session produced a disappointing mish-mash of jazz.

Bill Coleman sounds quite ill at ease on *Orphan Annie Blues* (which is actually a 28-bar theme: 8 + 8 + 4 + 8); Big Boy Goudie only gets a four-bar solo, and even Bechet's grandstand entry into the concluding key doesn't elevate the performance to any great heights. *Happy Go Lucky Blues* is anything but that, either in length (32 bars) or in spirit. After a couple of dull, shoddily played riff choruses Goudie steps forward to begin his solo, only to discover that Bechet has forgotten the routine; in doing so he crashes into the tenor saxophonist's lines. Sidney quickly covers his mistake by creating a backing riff, but chooses to play this fortissimo. Bill Coleman constructs another fidgety solo, then Sidney conceives two authoritative choruses that almost compensate for the previous dire happenings.

A near-chaotic ensemble tramples through a slow 12-bar blues dedicated to Kenny Clarke and entitled *Klook's Blues*, then Clarke and Bechet move into double-time to play a fascinating series of four-bar chases between drum and soprano saxophone that are full of life and ingenuity; the rest of the band re-enters for the slow ending. There is an even more spectacular drum and soprano saxophone duet on *American Rhythm*, during which Sidney builds up a kaleidoscope of phrases (most of them based on diminished chords) while Clarke produces a fine array of polyrhythmic tone-colours from his kit. Lewis and Michelot join Bechet and Clarke for a ravishing two-chorus version of *Out of nowhere*, marred slightly by the heavy off-beat keyboard rhythms. However, Lewis gives Bechet sympathetic backing on the old French favourite *Mon homme*, providing an accompaniment that slots in nicely with Bechet's out-of-tempo 'cabaret' treatment of the verse.

Besides engendering two fine tracks, *American Rhythm* and *Out of nowhere*, this session served to prove that Bechet, on European soil (even more than in America), had come to regard himself as a musical generalissimo. This strategy was to produce commendable results in many forthcoming sessions, but on dates with musicians who considered themselves Bechet's peers it invited acrimony. Yet two weeks after this session Sidney proved that he was as easy to work with as anyone.

In a fertile recording session, with a good rhythm section consisting of Kenny Clarke, Pierre Michelot, and Eddie Bernard (on piano), Bechet made quartet versions in rapid time of six evergreens and two medium-paced blues. The performance of *Wrap your troubles in dreams* may comfortably be placed in a listing of Bechet's finest recordings. Kenny Clarke felt that Bechet was happy at being able to show his versatility. At the time he said: "Bechet plays New Orleans style because he's expected to, but he prefers to play more modern stuff."[18]

Bechet always retained the utmost respect for good musicianship, but late in

1949 both he and Louis Armstrong (having been goaded by a series of derisive remarks by young 'modernists') lashed out verbally against modern jazz. Louis said: "Bebop? One long search for the right note." And Bechet, when asked about bop, replied: "That's deader than Abraham Lincoln."[19] In justification, it should be mentioned that Bechet had been deeply offended by comments made by Dizzy Gillespie after hearing a recording of *Gone Away Blues*: "I can't see how a man can spend his time learning to play a horn, maybe put in 30, 40 years at it then waste his time playing absolutely nothing."[20]

TWENTY-ONE

Beating the Ban

During his stay in Europe in late 1949, Bechet paid a brief visit to England. His trip involved only one hastily arranged guest appearance at a concert held in London's Winter Garden Theatre, but this solitary engagement created repercussions that lingered for years.

The British Musicians' Union had long been involved in a dispute with the American Federation of Musicians which concerned the banning of working visits by each other's members. The Ministry of Labour endorsed a ruling that forbade American musicians from working in Great Britain, except if they appeared on stage as variety performers or within a theatrical production.

An English promoter, Bert Wilcox, visiting Paris to hear a concert by Louis Armstrong early in November 1949, met up with Charles Delaunay and Sidney Bechet. Finding that Bechet was willing to play in Britain, Wilcox decided to try and swerve around the union and ministry restrictions by adding Bechet to the programme of an impending concert which featured a band led by trumpeter Humphrey Lyttelton. Wilcox succeeded in bringing Bechet to London for the concert on 13th November, but as a result he was charged (under Section One of the Aliens Order 1920) with breaking the law. He was found guilty at a subsequent trial and fined £100 and costs (comprehensive details of the case may be found in Jim Godbolt's *A History of Jazz in Britain, 1919–1950*).

The aftermath of this case (and a similar one involving a visit by Coleman Hawkins) affected the British jazz scene for years – until the union ban was lifted in 1956 – but memories of the music which Bechet played on that brief but sensational visit are imperishable. The austerity that affected Britain, and many other European countries, in the immediate post-war years proved, by some trick of fate, to be the perfect nurturing ground for the development of a passionate interest in early jazz. Pioneering groups in several countries had sown the seeds of this renaissance during World War II. When hostilities ended, this 'underground' musical movement made itself known via sessions in many clubs in many lands. Humphrey Lyttelton was the central figure in the British movement: he played briefly in George Webb's Dixielanders and as a result formed a productive partnership with clarinettist Wally Fawkes (an avowed disciple of Bechet), who subsequently joined the band that Lyttelton formed.

Bechet (who had just returned from playing two dates in Sweden) and his manager, Charles Delaunay, flew from France into London Airport late on the afternoon of Saturday 12th November, where they were met by a small group of well-wishers – including Max Jones from the *Melody Maker* and Bert Wilcox –

who drove the visitors to the Kingley Hotel in London. Humphrey Lyttelton and Wally Fawkes had a gig to play at the London Jazz Club, 100 Oxford Street, but before leaving they joined Bechet and a small party at Leon's, an old established Chinese restaurant in Wardour Street. Bechet chose the place himself, saying that he used to go there for meals in 1919. Remarkably, the Chinese woman who greeted the party as it entered immediately recognized Bechet and pointed to the table that he habitually used during his earlier visits.

The British musicians went off to work and Bert Wilcox took Bechet on a brief sight-seeing tour of London. Hampered by the winter darkness they nevertheless visited Trafalgar Square and other landmarks before Bechet asked to see the site of Rector's, the club in Tottenham Court Road where he had played a long residency almost 30 years earlier. Wilcox recalls: "It was arranged that Bechet would call into the London Jazz Club to hear part of the Lyttelton session. At the beginning of our drive he seemed almost reluctant to carry out that idea, but as the memories of his old days in London came flooding back he became positively enthusiastic. He kept saying how much things had changed, and was amazed by the large number of buses. We went into the club and he was almost mobbed by the excited people."[1]

Bechet sat and listened to the band play a few numbers and said complimentary things about the front line, particularly clarinettist Wally Fawkes. He had a brief conversation with Humphrey Lyttleton about a recording for Melodisc which had been planned for the following day; the two men discussed a tentative list of tunes, then Sidney made his way back to the hotel.

Next morning Lyttelton's band, feeling understandably apprehensive, turned up at the ARP studios in Denmark Street. Bechet arrived and in brisk, business-like fashion unpacked his soprano saxophone and showed Lyttelton a list of the tunes to be recorded – none of the previous night's suggestions was included. Lyttelton recalled the scene: "In the studio he never once mentioned them, but announced his intention of recording *Intermezzo* from the film *Escape to Happiness*. Having put pianist George Wcbb through the unfamiliar theme for several nerve-jangling minutes he suddenly discarded it. It had served its purpose in tying us up in knots and with a secret look which somehow combined malicious satisfaction with kindliness he got down to the business of recording."[2]

Wally Fawkes gave his memories of the occasion: "He ran through all the numbers without referring to any chords by name; he just demonstrated them by playing arpeggios. He had to teach George Webb and banjoist Buddy Vallis some of the sequences, and he got them to amend some of the chords they were intending to use. I remember him being very stern about this. But I think Sidney realized that this was not going to be one of the big days in his life, so he let things go that I'm sure he would have corrected, and worked on, if he had had more time."[3]

Lyttelton recalls a similar picture: "Nothing was written down at all, not even chord symbols. He taught us, note by note, the answer phrases he wanted on *Georgia*. He occasionally made solemn suggestions. I'll always remember him saying to our drummer, in almost biblical tones, 'Young man, you have to keep that beat going. You're pulling it back – and that's cruel to music.' He taught us a blues that he had planned to record with a French band. Its title had already been established *I told you once I told you twice*; later a critic sourly wrote that Bechet had called it that because of difficulties he encountered when rehearsing the band. That story was totally untrue."[4]

Word of the recording session had leaked out to some of the local jazz fans; as a result a number of them turned up at the studio and gained access. Their subsequent chatting created a volume of sound that did nothing to settle the British musicians' nerves. Eventually the band and its guest star recorded the first number, *Some of these days*. Lyttelton used his regular line-up, which consisted of himself on trumpet-cornet, Fawkes on clarinet, the Christie brothers (Keith on trombone and Ian on clarinet), George Webb on piano, Buddy Vallis on banjo, John Wright on string bass, and Bernard Saward on drums.

The members of the band were understandably nervous, and, to add to their problems, the placements within the studio meant that they could not all see one another; however, spirit and inspiration carried them through. Bechet allows Lyttelton to lay down a firm lead during the opening chorus of *Some of these days*. Keith Christie and Wally Fawkes take 16 bars apiece before Bechet swings into action with a powerful chorus that gathers momentum as it flows over the final, cluttered ensemble. The biggest disappointment is the poor quality of the recording.

The front line (now minus Ian Christie) plays quiet backing notes for Bechet's elegant and rhapsodic version of *Black and Blue*. Unfortunately the sound of the piano and banjo striking the same inversion, rigidly on the beat, adds nothing to the *élan* of the proceedings. The well-known but rarely recorded tune *Who's sorry now* came next. The opening ensemble is fervent rather than relaxed, but the obvious enthusiasm is infectious. Fawkes's well-constructed 16-bar solo is marred by overblown background figures but Lyttelton's solo rings out loud and clear. Bechet's chorus is full of sweeping phrases that are close to the melody; he saves his bolder ideas for the concluding chorus, commanding attention with a series of long, thrilling high notes.

At this point in the proceedings, one member of the band became perturbed by Bechet's catholic choice of numbers. Highly suspicious of anything that wasn't labelled blues, stomp, or rag, he put down his pipe and his instrument and said, "When are we going to play some jazz?" Bechet seemed to regard this as an intricate private joke and simply called up the next number, *When it's sleepytime down South*. This was the item from the session that apparently pleased Sidney most. Later that day he told Lyttelton he thought it was "a masterpiece", but, as Lyttelton has pointed out, Bechet chose not to listen to any playbacks in the studio. When offered this facility he replied brusquely, "Why should I? That don't do me no good." Lyttelton later found out that Bechet was being paid a set amount for each tune recorded, which explained his haste to move on to the next item.

The musicians find the best rapport of the date on the blues *I told you once*. Bechet states the opening theme eloquently, then Lyttelton and Fawkes share an inspired duet. Keith Christie's intonation wobbles slightly but he too plays admirably. Bechet re-enters to create some poignant and effortless blues stanzas before joining the ensemble in a recapitulation of the theme. The session ended with a medium-paced, call-and-answer version of *Georgia on my Mind*, in which Bechet grants the main solo spot to Lyttelton, who justifies the accolade by creating some highly rhythmic phrases. Bechet takes over at the final bridge and then roves over the band during the concluding bars like a parent eagle.

Before moving off to the Winter Garden Theatre to rehearse for the evening's show, Bechet again sampled some Chinese food, this time at a lunch organized by Doug Whitton of Melodisc, who wrote about the gathering in the following Friday's *New Musical Express*: "After the recording, everyone adjourned to Choy's Chinese Restaurant, where seated at the head of the long table, Sidney put to good use the experience gained when he played for a time in Kowloon, many years ago, by ordering a meal for the whole party."

Sidney was in a fairly expansive mood during his conversations with Whitton, and this induced him to mention the location in which he had gained his knowledge of Chinese food. Any cynics who doubted Sidney had ever visited Kowloon might well have been given a quick sight of the passport that Sidney had used in the 1930s. There, sure enough, on page 32 of the visa section, is a series of Chinese characters. A doubter might easily be dumbfounded, but not if he read Chinese – for the characters say simply "Pork and Chinese Cabbage". Bechet's sense of humour was bizarre and mischievous.

At the theatre a stern-faced Bechet took command of the proceedings. Humphrey Lyttelton recalls: "He directed everything with the soprano sax; it was more expressive than any baton. The jutting movements he signified as he played left no room for doubt whatsoever – the messages transmitted were unequivocal. But with us I would say he was firm, but not at all angry."[5]

Bechet's appearance at the concert had not been advertised in the press, but thousands of enthusiasts knew that he would be there and many more than the capacity crowd of 1750 applied for tickets. Because of the existing regulations, it was decided that Bechet's appearance on stage would be portrayed as a happy accident. He was seen with the Wilcox brothers, Stan and Bert, and Doug Whitton in the royal box, from where he was invited by the compère, Rex Harris, to join the band for a few numbers. Naturally Sidney obliged. He left the box and, to tumultuous applause, joined the band on stage for *Royal Garden Blues*. Sidney played four more numbers before the interval, and returned in the second half to play another seven tunes.

In its front page story the *Melody Maker* described the concert as "the most dramatic and exciting occasion in the history of British jazz"; everyone who attended the concert agreed. Something close to hysteria engulfed the audience, and those seated in the gallery stamped their feet so hard that the structure bounced, rather like a sprung dance floor. Lyttelton commented:

I've often been asked how Bechet played at that concert, and all I can say is that he played marvellously. But I just can't remember whether he improvised that night or whether he played exactly what he had played at the rehearsal. It would be like asking the rabbit about some aspect of the python. The worst moment came when he got on stage. The applause was so great we couldn't hear each other, but when Bechet began blowing it was like a sirocco. I got the impression that, despite the superb playing and authoritative showmanship, Bechet was also very nervous. At one point, when he was waiting to come on stage for the second half, I looked over and saw him pacing up and down anxiously. But when the concert was over he was relaxed and avuncular, though there was a touch of the headmaster's report in his manner. He gave a run-down on how each member of the band could improve, saying that I should take more chances and not be so nervous![6]

It was Bert Wilcox's task to get Sidney through the crowd of well-wishers at the stage-door; he eventually managed this and took Bechet to a restaurant in Newman Street for a late meal. There he was able to talk at length with Bechet about his career and his previous visit to London: "I found him absolutely charming, a man with a quiet but jolly personality – one might say the epitome of a delightful Southern gentleman. The only time I sensed a bit of animosity was when I started talking enthusiastically about Louis Armstrong, but I saw the reaction and dropped the subject. Because of the circumstances surrounding the concert I didn't pay Bechet or Delaunay direct. I gave the £200 fee to Emil Shalit, who was the Vogue recording company's representative in London, and it went via him to Paris."[7]

Early next morning Bechet and Delaunay flew back to Paris, where they formulated plans for Bechet's next trip to Europe. On the following day, just before his return to the USA, Bechet made more recordings with Claude Luter's orchestra. The series of recordings made in 1949 with Luter, Braslavsky and Lyttelton was the first example of a New Orleans jazz giant helping young European musicians to re-create a style that had come into being before they had been born. Bunk Johnson had done the same sort of thing earlier in California, with the pioneering band led by Lu Watters, but Bechet's efforts were on a much bigger scale. (Later many New Orleans veterans were to follow Johnson and Bechet's example.)

During those early years of the European jazz 'revival', Bechet could plainly see that there was a role for him as the music's patron saint. He was delighted to observe this, but the proud side of his nature also wanted to make it clear that he was not, and never had been, restricted to one particular type of musical material. He did realize, however, that many newcomers to traditional jazz preferred to hear tunes that had a romantic association with the music's so-called golden era. To meet this demand he made sure that he always included a team of old 'war-horses' in his programmes, but over the coming years in Europe his selections were often boldly experimental. By then his playing style was firmly set, but he was determined to get the young revivalists interested in ballads and standard songs.

His rendition of *Temptation Rag*, recorded with Luter's band, was almost in the style of a 1920s music-hall overture; the slow version of *Riverboat Shuffle* is also novel. These recordings show that a productive accord was developing between Luter and Bechet; their soprano and clarinet duet on *Sobbin' and Cryin'* has some excellent moments, despite the quavering nature of Luter's early style. But Bechet often assumed an autocratic role with this band, as he does on *Everybody loves my baby*, on which he allows himself space to produce some cogent and vital jazz.

Bechet left France in November 1949 laden with good wishes and gifts; his Cadillac was shipped back with him. One of his packages contained a new Selmer clarinet for Bill Reinhardt of Jazz Ltd; resolving the contractual wrangle with that club was at the top of Bechet's agenda. He arrived back in New York on 28th November, rested briefly at his home in Washington Heights, and then made his way to Chicago.

Sidney arranged to meet Bill and Ruth Reinhardt at Jazz Ltd. The reunion turned out to be amicable, with Sidney agreeing to return to play there in the spring of the coming year, 1950. Ruth Reinhardt told a *Down Beat* reporter, "All is forgiven". A group photograph was taken at one of the club's tables showing Sidney with Georg Brunis, Muggsy Spanier, Sid Catlett, Floyd Bean and Bill Reinhardt. To make the occasion complete, Sidney handed over to Bill Reinhardt the Selmer clarinet he had carried from France. Bill had asked Sidney to get one for him, whatever the cost: Sidney explained that Selmer's had given him a discount, so the price was only 250 dollars. Reinhardt's delight lasted until a representative from Henri Selmer's company, attending a trade convention in Chicago, called into Jazz Ltd and asked Bill how he liked the gift clarinet that his company had sent via Sidney Bechet.

After his one-day visit to Chicago Sidney returned to New York and fixed up a date for his return to Jimmy Ryan's. In the meantime he undertook a series of guest appearances at the Stuyvesant Casino. He also played weekly at the Central Plaza. For the first of the bookings there, in December 1949, Noble Sissle came along, doubtless to hear all about Sidney's experiences in France. Bechet's old friend Jim McGraw attended many of the sessions held at the Stuyvesant Casino:

> It was a huge ballroom, with an audience seated at large round tables. The place was smoky, the acoustics terrible and the crowd noises overwhelming, but Bash would blow his head off nevertheless, and come to sit with me and my friends and share a drink with us. When the place closed at 4 a.m., we'd walk or stagger arm-in-arm to my apartment on West 10th in the Village. He would stay over, sleeping on the rug rather than on a sofa or a comfortable chair. One morning as we headed for the subway Bechet startled me by asking if I could cash a check for him. I explained that I too was pretty broke, but asked how much was the check for? He reached in his inside coat pocket and handed me a check from ASCAP for Sidney Bechet, made out for 68 cents. It was a monthly royalty check. I cashed the check, but regretfully didn't keep it.[8]

Sidney had never been good at putting money away, but how he came to be so broke at this period of his life is nearly unfathomable. Rumour has it that he had left all of his European earnings in France to avoid any tax problems; another line of thought is that he may have been speculating in property. He was working often, regularly organizing pick-up bands for well-paid private dates. Bechet kept a hefty percentage of the fee for these gigs for himself; his talent entitled him to do this, but whenever he met Bob Wilber he always complained about the quality of the sidemen he was forced to use. Bob recalls: "When I suggested certain names Sidney pulled a face and said, 'They want too much money'. Some musicians became wary of working with Sidney, even though they admired his playing. They felt they were in a 'no-win' situation. If you played too good you were trying to steal the limelight; if you just did your job you weren't playing well enough."[9]

Writing in *Playback* magazine, Bob Aurthur dwelt on Bechet's choice of sidemen: "Sidney is a minor victim to his own feelings of insecurity, rooted deeply within himself by all those years of uncertainty. He will, for instance, surround himself with mediocre musicians if given the choice. He won't admit their mediocrity, claiming that his are the best choices, but there is that subconscious fear of too much competition. Competition is the last thing that Bechet has to fear. Actually he accepts the challenge to mix it up with anybody anytime and always his soprano sails high above the ensemble daring any player to come up and meet him on any terms."[10]

In February 1950 Bechet resumed his berth at Jimmy Ryan's, with 'Big Chief' Russell Moore, Lloyd Phillips and Art Trappier (on drums). After a few weeks these three departed and were replaced by Vic Dickenson, Kenny Kersey and Cliff Leeman; a bass player was added when the group undertook radio work.

On 19 April 1950 Bechet recorded yet another session for Blue Note with Wild Bill Davison. These two, plus Jimmy Archey (trombone), Pops Foster (bass), Slick Jones (drums) and Joe Sullivan (piano), recorded various old favourites from the 1920s, including *Copenhagen*, *China Boy*, *Jelly Roll Blues*, *Runnin' Wild*, *Mandy make up your mind* and *Shim-me-sha-wabble*. Tunes like *Copenhagen* and *Mandy* were seldom played by any bands in that era, but most of the others were old chestnuts. The arrangement and performance of *Copenhagen* is bright and breezy; Bechet's culminating solo really whips up a sense of fervour, but Foster's bass and Jones's drums never quite jell, and Sullivan's piano playing is nowhere near its best.

Both brass players perform well, and Archey creates a perfectly inflected, robust solo on *Shim-me-sha-wabble*, but, despite Bechet's sterling efforts, a feeling of *déjà vu* haunts this disappointing session. Sidney may have felt a little world-weary when playing *China Boy* for the umpteenth time, but he tried to shield his listeners from any sense of ennui. He was a devout professional who never lost his respect for tradition – and woe betide those around him who did.

Bechet encountered just such an attitude during this session, from pianist Joe Sullivan. Trouble began when Joe began making derisive noises at the titles of the tunes Bechet suggested; one in particular, *Jazz me Blues*, he greeted with a loud groan. Wild Bill Davison picks up the story: "Joe Sullivan did a lot of drinking and when he drank he became very sarcastic. Joe got very sarcastic with Bechet, and Bechet pulled a knife and went up to his throat and said, 'One more crack and I'll cut your head off'."[11] Sullivan picked up the piano stool as his weapon, and the session ended there and then.

Eight days later Bechet and Davison recorded together again, this time without Sullivan, whose place was taken by Ralph Sutton. Wilbur De Paris, who sketched out the arrangements, was on trombone, George Wettling on drums and Jack Lesberg on bass. The session was produced by Milt Gabler for the

Commodore label and featured Bechet playing clarinet (on two numbers); this was the last occasion he ever played the instrument for an American recording date. It was also one of the first sessions that Sidney recorded on tape – rather than on 78 r.p.m. masters.

Bechet plays clarinet throughout *Jelly Roll Blues*, the opening part of which closely follows Morton's arrangement (recorded by the Red Hot Peppers), though Sidney's piping, bitter-sweet tone adds an original flavour. His solo is not particularly mobile, but warmth and resilience are obvious. The final ensemble has a character all of its own, with De Paris's lines adding a distinctly individual touch.

Milt Gabler deliberately arranged the balance with Wild Bill away from the microphone. This strategy produces an attractive ensemble blend on *At a Georgia Camp Meeting*; Sutton produces sturdy, but nimble, piano phrases in a rocking solo. Davison plays a sparse, almost wary, lead, and this allows Bechet ample space in which to pour his thick soprano saxophone sounds. Bechet's clarinet adds spikes to a bustling version of *National Emblem March*, but De Paris's trombone solo has a laboured, up-hill quality. The verse of *Hindustan* provides a fascinating cameo of sounds. Davison and Bechet blow pianissimo phrases at each other, creating a near tender mood; beneath them the rich sonority of Lesberg's bass playing is faithfully captured.

George Wettling's subtle but muscular drumming was a mainstay of this session. Bechet enjoyed hearing the crisp sounds that Wettling obtained from his drum kit; he also admired Wettling's sense of light and shade. Art Hodes, for one, became well aware of Bechet's liking for Wettling's drumming: "On one of the dates we made, Bechet wanted Wettling. Now this is something you may not have known about Sidney. He was color blind when it came to music. Wettling was white; Fred Moore is black. That cut no way with Sidney Bechet. I'd done a lot of work with Moore and I wanted him on the gig and I prevailed. But it was expensive. Blue Note was doing another date with Sidney and I wasn't on it."[12] Hodes knew that Bechet could be ultra-critical of drummers: "One night when I was working with Bechet at Jimmy Ryan's, the drummer (not Fred Moore) got the crowd going with some spectacular breaks and solos. Unfortunately, in doing so he wrecked the tempo and this made Sidney bristle with anger. Sid was too much of a pro to let the audience know that anything was amiss, but as soon as we stepped out of the club for an intermission he let fly. I don't think I've ever heard a more furious verbal onslaught."

Bechet's return to the clarinet was only a temporary move, though he seems to have half toyed with the idea of resuming his regular doubling on both soprano saxophone and clarinet in preparation for his impending return to France. At the end of his visit in May 1949 Claude Luter's band had given Sidney a brand new clarinet as a going-away present. Luter persuaded the Selmer company specially to resume their production of Albert models so the presentation could be made, but even this remarkable gesture didn't rekindle Sidney's former love for the instrument; he rarely played clarinet in the 1950s.

Claude Luter had failed, just as Bob Wilber had done, in attempts to get Bechet to play clarinet regularly. Wilber himself was going through a reverse process, playing the soprano saxophone less and the clarinet more. By 1950 Wilber had established his own reputation, but some people still automatically linked his playing to that of Bechet:

At first it was wonderful when listeners came up and said, "That sounds just like Sidney", but then they wanted it to go a stage further, they wanted me to play Sidney's choruses note for note off the record. Nobody admired Bechet's playing more than I did, and still do, but we were two different people; I wanted to take what he had taught me and develop something of my own. It got to the point where it was irksome to be totally identified with Bechet. Finally I came to the decision that I had to give up playing soprano saxophone in order to lose the Bechet image, so that's what I did. For many years I played clarinet and tenor saxophone, and it wasn't until the 1960s that I returned to the soprano, this time a curved model. By then I could be myself on the instrument.[13]

Bechet never ceased to be proud about Wilber's achievements, but by 1949 he realized that the time was right for the ex-pupil to stretch his wings. He told Kay Thompson that Wilber "had not disappointed any earlier predictions". Bechet also observed: "After all, whilst most people may not know it, Wilber is not the first young person I've influenced. Years ago Jimmie Noone and others modelled their early styles on mine. The point is, once they really learned to play they asserted their individuality, developing distinctive styles of their own. I myself learned to play by patterning my work after 'Big Eye' Louis Nelson."[14]

Sidney kept in touch with a former member of Bob Wilber's Wild Cats, pianist Dick Wellstood. Wellstood worked in Bechet's quartet for a residency at the Swing Rendezvous in Philadelphia (with Fred Moore on drums and Jimmy Archey on trombone). He recalled: "The Swing Rendezvous functioned within the Hotel Senator. The sessions were organized by Lee Guber, who later became a successful show producer. By that time Bechet seemed set on the idea of only working with a trombone in the front line. Anything to keep those trumpet players away, I guess."[15]

During one of his residencies at the Swing Rendezvous Bechet gained another pupil, one who was to become an accomplished jazz player and a distinguished writer. Richard 'Dick' Hadlock had been given a soprano saxophone in 1942 by his father, who was employed by RCA in Brazil. Hadlock, Sr, had found the instrument stored above his company's recording studio in Rio de Janeiro. "It was Bechet's record of *Rose Room* on which I first heard a soprano and realized that this silly instrument given to me by my Dad was OK."[16] Years later, when Hadlock was living in Philadelphia, he met Bechet:

Sidney and I talked first. He said I sounded like someone who had played a long time when I talked but not (I presume) when I played. He charged ten dollars a lesson, not a bad fee in 1950. Mostly I learned by sitting right in front of him every night at the Rendezvous in Philadelphia. For a week he borrowed my horn while his was in the shop, and handily wiped out any mechanical excuses I might have due to playing a cranky mid-1920s soprano (I still play that old Buescher). I first found out about Hungarian taragotos from Sidney. He loved their sound. Sidney also made me more politically aware than I had been. He asked my why the US never used flame throwers (not to say A-Bombs) on Europeans.[17]

I began to understand something of what total commitment to music entailed.

Sidney would run off a complex series of phrases and leave me alone in his room for a couple of hours to wrestle with what he had played. One lesson could easily take up an entire afternoon, and Sidney favored giving a lesson every day. "Look, when you emphasize a note, you throw your whole body into it", he would say, cutting a wide arc with his horn as he slashed into a phrase. "I'm going to give you one note today", he once told me, "See how many ways you can play that note – growl it, smear it, flat it, sharp it, do anything you want to it. That's how to express your feelings in music. It's like talking. Always try to complete your phrases and your ideas. There are lots of otherwise good musicians who sound terrible because they start a new idea without finishing the last one".[18]

Even after his triumphs in Europe in 1949, back in the States he was just another jazzman scuffling. Often when we went to the automat after the job Sidney would spot other musicians he knew and it would be like a party. Bull Moose Jackson was one I remember. But outside of musicians, and 'inside' fans, Sidney was not a celebrity in his own country. Another thing I remember well is that Sidney was at his best in that little night club. He wasn't trying to smother his own players, but he was reaching out to his listeners.. His studio/radio/TV/concert performances seemed more like set pieces or musical jousts. I liked it best when he took chances.

After Sidney left Philadelphia, I would go to New York City to take my funny lessons. He stayed in a run-down hotel on the west side called The Alvin. Depressing. One time my New York room-mate (Thornton Hagert) and I had Sidney to visit our very humble loft below Greenwich Village. No hot water, no shower, soot everywhere and broken-down furniture. Bechet liked it and started making suggestions for fixing up the place. He could be a very nice man.

We showed for a concert in Philadelphia, Sidney forgot his spare reeds and simply 'ordered' me to drive back to his room and get them. Right there I decided I had had enough and could continue my studies through recordings or other teachers. But Sidney is still important to me.[19]

One of the sessions in which Bechet took part on a return trip to the Rendezvous Club in Philadelphia was privately recorded; it was later issued on Vogue's Jazz Selection label in France. Because of sound-balancing problems and unelaborate equipment there are obvious shortcomings. The work of the pianist (? Kenny Kersey) is practically inaudible, but the sound that does seep through emanates from an out-of-tune instrument. Bechet's soprano saxophone and Vic Dickenson's trombone are presented in low-fi, but Cliff Leeman's crisp drumming cuts through effectively. In spite of the sound problems, the good outweighs the bad, and Bechet and his colleagues stretch out, playing extended routines with a relaxed inventiveness.

Many old war-horses, like *High Society, Muskrat Ramble* and *China Boy*, come out of their stables, but so too do refreshing versions of *I've got a right to sing the blues* and *Stardust*. The former allows two splendid melodists, Bechet and Dickenson, to bask in their skills; there are no fireworks and no dramatic finale. A relaxed spirit marks almost everything the group did that night (24 May 1950), and Dickenson's droll quote from *Have you met Miss Jones?*, inserted in his solo on *Blue Lou*, typifies the warmth and humour of the occasion. On another issue of this same material, in an effort to enhance the poor sound quality, the recording company dubbed in the playing of Yannick Singery on piano and Georges 'Zozo' d'Halluin on bass. This move was frowned upon by some purists, but the augmentation did help to improve a grievous sound picture.

Bechet went back to New York, his mind set on the imminent trip to Europe; any thoughts about fulfilling his promise to return to Jazz Ltd in Chicago were ignored. He arrived in France on 5 June 1950 and made his way to Paris, where he soon began a residency playing with Claude Luter's band at the Vieux Colombier. In Paris the existentialist movement had exerted a strong influence on many young people; there was also an army of youngsters who simply copied that group's outward manifestations. Intermingled, these passionate adolescents became enamoured of jazz in general, and of Sidney Bechet in particular. The young fans were soon nicknamed the 'cave rats', because it seemed that most of their lives were spent underground, listening intently. These cave rats, together with a regular influx of holiday-makers (from other parts of France and from overseas), combined with local jazz followers to make up the bulk of the Vieux Colombier's audiences. Every session was hot and crowded. The owner, Annet Badel, had originally envisaged that the cellar club would be a handy meeting place for theatre-goers and actors, but jazz sessions proved to be so popular he never carried out his original plan. Claude Luter's orchestra soon established the place as its unofficial headquarters, though other bands also played there.

Several other famous American jazz musicians were working in France in 1950, including trumpeter Roy Eldridge and tenor saxophonist Don Byas. Sidney's first big concert date that summer was when he shared the billing with these two at the Clamart Music Festival. There, a critic described Sidney's playing as being "the showy old-time style", but admitted his appearance was greeted with "a roar of applause".[20] Sidney's popularity was growing rapidly in France, but he was still undecided about making his home there. When asked by a reporter whether he intended to stay, he said, "Maybe, but I guess there will be some movement back and forth between here and the States."[21] But as the summer of 1950 wore on Bechet began to make positive plans for a long stay in France; the site where he made his decision was an idyllic one, Juan-les-Pins.

Soon after his concert appearance at Clamart, Sidney moved south to play for a season with Claude Luter's orchestra at Annet Badel's seaside version of the Vieux Colombier. The enterprising club owner had built a genteel reproduction of his Parisian night-spot on a site in the Boulevard de la Pinède, close to the Juan-les-Pins Casino. The club opened at 9.30 p.m. Luter's band played for dancing, then at 11.30 p.m. Sidney (working as a cabaret attraction) came on for the first of his sessions. His next appearance was at 1.15 a.m., by which time the club was usually packed with holiday-makers.

During the day Claude Luter's band and Sidney were at liberty to do as they wished. Much of their time was spent on the nearby sands, or sitting around the Pirate's Bar which was situated on the beach. Whilst others sunbathed Sidney preferred to sit in the shade; he didn't join in the swimming, but occasionally paddled. His main maritime interests were in piloting various speed boats and fishing out in the deep. Gradually the members of the Luter band, and particularly its leader (who was also a keen fisherman), got to know Sidney well. Luter spoke of the bookings at Juan-les-Pins:

As a fisherman Sidney was the model of patience – entirely different from his musical attitude. He always seemed happy and contented when he was fishing; he was good at it. He joined in on some of the band jokes, but he had no close men friends. He loved to find the girls, but, if anyone in the band found a girl that Sidney liked the look of, he would show his displeasure by cutting out all of that musician's solos, often for nights on end, sometimes for a whole week. The band were young and carefree about girls, but for Sidney it was a very serious business. He did this to me – stopped my solos – but I made it clear to him that I wasn't going to have that sort of interference in my private life. I would take all the musical advice and instruction that he cared to give, because in comparison to his talents I was the amateur, but I would not stand for him arranging my life.

Sidney didn't sit down and listen to recordings, but he always listened out for music, wherever he was. It all went into his ears, classical, jazz, whatever. I found it difficult to get Sidney to talk about the past, in fact most of the things that I found out about his history I learned from other people. He was touchy when anyone brought up the subject of age, like certain women. He never talked about King Oliver – he'd just nod his head if the name was mentioned – and one got the definite idea that he didn't like Louis Armstrong. But Freddie Keppard meant a lot to him, and Tommy Ladnier, and he also spoke warmly about Buddy Petit; he described how Petit sometimes played a second harmony part, like a clarinettist. But if you asked specific questions you usually got nowhere. Once I asked him how he came to play the sarrusophone on the recording, and he just pulled a face.

He was not religious, and although he may have had some leanings towards communism when he was in America he certainly did not when he moved to France. He loved collecting photographic apparatus and wanted to photograph the Côte d'Azur from the air. I took him up in a plane that I piloted. It was a small aircraft and Sidney didn't take to the flight; he became frightened and angry with me, but it soon passed. He also got into a temper with me over a card game. I was winning, absolutely by luck, but Sidney took this personally. He was a bad loser, so I never played with him again. But there were no serious incidents, and I never saw him threaten anyone.

Sidney smoked quite a lot, preferring American cigarettes, but he certainly didn't use marijuana regularly. One day our bassist said to him, "I've never tried it and I want to very much", so Sidney got some for him and they both smoked it. But it didn't do anything for the bass player. Sidney said, "Me neither". Then he lectured him, saying, "It's all in the mind. You could get just as high if you did deep breathing". Sidney drank milk, Coca-Cola, beer or gin, depending on his mood. If things weren't going right with the girls he'd go on a 'bender' for two or three days, drinking gin, but he definitely wasn't an alcoholic.

He alone chose the repertoire, and sometimes he came up with a choice of tunes that surprised us; but there was no arguing, it was a case of 'march or die'. On recordings he made the decisions. If the version was alright by him, then he passed it, regardless of how anyone else played. But I must say that in all the time we worked together I never saw him in trouble with any sort of music. He was an irascible genius, marvellous![22]

The kind and gentle side of Bechet's personality was often in evidence during that summer season; he always seemed happy to talk in English with various visitors from Britain or America. One of his devoted British fans, Ken Bell, made a pilgrimage to Juan-les-Pins: "I heard from a contact that Sidney had a daily tea-time drink in a bar near the Vieux Colombier, so at 5 p.m. I ventured round. He wasn't there, but as I mooched off I bumped into him. I was too awe-struck to say much after all my preparations, but he said he'd see me in the club that evening. Entrance was free but consommation was obligatoire – and expensive. I was almost skint but by luck I came across a half-empty glass of beer on the bar, which I stood by for the rest of the evening. Bechet joined me at the interval for a short chat, then he said he'd see me in the bar outside afterwards, and sure enough he came into the bar for a night-cap."[23]

When the season of Juan-les-Pins ended Bechet and Claude Luter's band moved back to Paris, where Sidney became increasingly aware that he was gradually becoming a national celebrity. His fame had blossomed beyond the following of the *simili-existentialistes*, and several of the recordings he had made in France, in particular *Les oignons*, were being played regularly on the radio. Proof of the growing acclaim became evident when Bechet appeared at the first of a series of concerts in Paris. A 500-yard queue formed outside the theatre long before the box-office opened, and when the 'house full' notices were displayed hundreds of disappointed people rushed the doors, smashing them in order to gate-crash their way into the concert. The theatre filled to overflowing, and boxes meant to hold six people were crammed with 15 eager fans.

A similar situation occurred a few weeks later when Sidney played at Paris's first Salon du Jazz. Hundreds of fans without tickets charged the theatre's temporary box-office with such force that they carried it away – with the terrified cashier still inside. Total chaos ensued and hundreds of people who had already bought tickets were stranded outside in the rue St Dominique. Bechet worship had begun in earnest.

These huge waves of success didn't sweep Sidney off his feet, and he remained just as conscientious about his music-making. The clarinettist and bandleader Maxime Saury, who acted as an "unpaid secretary" to Sidney during the latter's visits to France in 1949 and 1950, recalled how assiduously Bechet practised, particularly if he felt he had not played at his best on the previous night:

> He was living at the Hotel Saint-Yves, rue de l'Université. I would go there every day in the late morning, Sidney was always in bed. He'd get up and order his breakfast, then, as he waited for it, and before he even got dressed he would start playing the soprano sax, which he kept on his bedside table. He never left it alone, and blew it continuously when he was home. He didn't work on the instrument in the same way as a classical musician. He'd repeat phrases that he made up, until they came out perfectly. He said, "You must have balance between technique and the ideas you are trying to express. If one has too much to say and no technique one 'stutters', but if one has lots of technique and nothing to say one will bore the listeners to death."[24]

Early in October 1950 Bechet and Luter's orchestra recorded 14 numbers for Vogue. Amongst them was *Moulin à café*, a tune that was to earn a great deal of money for Sidney (it was subsequently recorded by Humphrey Lyttelton, and others, as *The Coffee Grinder*). But long before Bechet committed this tune to record, in 1909 to be precise, exactly the same melody had been published as the work of George L. Cobb under the title of *Rubber Plant Rag*. (Cobb, who died in 1942, achieved some success as a composer; *Are you from Dixie?* is probably his best-known work.) Once again, Sidney had appropriated someone else's tune. Years later Claude Luter could not help chuckling when he learnt about this falsification: "Sidney certainly said that it was his melody. In fact he scratched his head and said, 'I don't know what to call it'. I suggested the title *Moulin à café*."[25]

In the recording session, Bechet proved that comfortable living in the South of France hadn't taken the edge off of his blues playing, and he performs formidably on *Society Blues*. Claude Luter is granted two clarinet choruses on *Ni queue, ni tête* and shows how rapidly his musical stature was growing. Cornetist Pierre Dervaux plays an admirably fierce plunger-muted solo on *Francis Blues*, but in general the members of the band are restricted to background roles.

The exception is *Moustache gauloise*, on which drummer Francois 'Moustache' Galepides is well featured. It is a curious attempt to recreate the formula of *Shag* by playing a hell-for-leather version of *I got rhythm*. Galepides and trombonist Bernard Zacharias both sing on a rumba entitled *Madame Becassine*, but this performance is eclipsed by another Latin-American number, *Lastic*, an ingenious composition by Bechet. Sidney's vocal part is not the musical highspot; that honour is achieved by the delightful blending of the soprano saxophone and clarinet.

Most of the other numbers from the session were Bechet's 'stand-bys', on which he played his own familiar phrases, but he did so in an electrifying fashion, blowing them in a way that suggested they had been conceived that very split-second. Occasionally an alternate take was recorded, more often than not it was to experiment with the tempo; mistakes were few because the band and Bechet had achieved an effective rapport. They were able to demonstrate this on the wide-ranging tour they made in the winter of 1950–51. An atmospheric concert at La Chaux-de-Fonds, Switzerland (in November 1950) was recorded, with excellent results. It includes a version of *I got rhythm* on which Bechet and Luter, on clarinets, re-create (with more success) the duet they had recorded on *Moustache gauloise*.

In March 1951 Bechet made a brief tour of Scandinavia. On Sunday 18th March he played in two concerts at the KB Hall in Copenhagen, accompanied by the band led by trombonist Peter Rasmussen. The concerts, which were underwritten by a promoter named Mr Strangeup and two Danish jazz lovers, Baron Timme Rosenkrantz and Dr Terkild Vinding, coincided with the worst snow storm of the year; in consequence the attendances were disappointing. Even so, there was some marvellous music to be heard, and one very unusual item. As Dr Vinding recalls: "I persuaded Sidney Bechet to appear on stage playing the then Danish State Radio signature tune, an old folk tune from the 13th century. He played this a cappella, saying afterwards, 'It's just like an old New Orleans dirge'."[26] Rasmussen's band was thrilled to accompany Bechet, but during the rehearsals the Danish leader kindly asked Bechet not to point the soprano saxophone at him as it made him feel nervous.

Bechet moved on to Sweden, where he played in two concerts for promoter Nils Hellström, sharing the bill with Stan Getz in Stockholm (19th March) and Gothenburg (20th March). At the Stockholm concert (held in the old National Concert Hall) Bechet was backed by a band led by pianist Charles Norman; Getz was accompanied by Arne Domnerus's orkester. Prior to the concert, the two Americans were due to share the conductor's room; the Swedish musicians were allocated a big ante-room. This arrangement was short-lived. After ten minutes Getz asked if he could also use the ante-room; from within the conductor's room Bechet's angry voice was heard to say, "I don't dig them be-bop boys."

Another solo date took Bechet into Belgium (on 1st April), where he appeared as part of an all-star line-up that included James Moody, Don Byas, Bill Coleman and Roy Eldridge. Bechet had toured Belgium with Pierre Braslavsky's band during the previous October, but for his visit to North Africa in April 1951 he was again accompanied by Claude Luter's orchestra. Soloist and band were temporarily replaced at the Vieux Colombier by Roy Eldridge and Claude Bolling's group.

Roy Eldridge's most potent memory of Bechet concerned a radio programme on which they played together in Paris. The two stars were in competition, Bechet representing the Vieux Colombier, and Eldridge the Club St Germain (run by Boris Vian). Eldridge, an inveterate musical battler, recalled: "I had heard Bechet many times over the years, and had jammed with him often, but when you had him in direct opposition, phew . . . he sure blew that day. I had to hand it to him, he sure could play."[27]

The tour of North Africa with Claude Luter proved to be a momentous one for Sidney. In Algeria he was reunited with his former fiancée, Elisabeth Ziegler. The two had not met for over 20 years, during which time Elisabeth had married and divorced. She and Sidney rapidly re-established their romance and plans were soon made for Elisabeth to leave her home on the rue Mustaphia-Ismael in Algiers and move to Paris. Sidney had recently bought his own house (8 rue Pierre-Brossolette, Grigny, near Paris). To go with the new home he had also purchased a dog called Yank, which, even by the dimensions of Sidney's previous hounds, was huge. Fishing waters were close by, and so too were friendly neighbours; all that seemed lacking was a wife. Sidney proposed to Elisabeth and she accepted, so they began to formulate plans for a truly spectacular wedding ceremony.

In France the demand for Sidney's recordings went on escalating, and in May 1951 he again undertook a long studio session with Luter's orchestra. The first number, *In the Groove*, is a disjointed composition by Bechet; even so the performance is laudable. Guy Longnon, on valve trombone, plays a prominent and skilful part on this and several other numbers from the session. Bechet sounds in a mellow mood on most of the tracks, but there are no signs of slip-shod playing; every one of his phrases is perfectly conceived. He begins a solo on *Promenade aux Champs-Elysées* (his own excellent tune) in an almost stealthy fashion, but romps into the final chorus, inspired by a relaxed two-beat backing.

On *En attendant le jour*, Bechet's saxophone sounds soft and romantic as it answers Longnon's rendering of the melody. The band moves easily through *Wolverine Blues*, playing all three strains with a non-frantic swing. Next was a re-make of *Egyptian Fantasy*, this time as a feature for soprano saxophone. Luter has two well-balanced clarinet breaks, but the piece is mainly a demonstration of how Bechet could take a new look at a familiar theme. The low spot of the session is *Blues in the Cave*, which begins with Bechet playing the piano and giving stilted verbal instructions to the band in English. For once the group seems to lack conviction. Bechet's paramount blues artistry saves the day, but the overall effect was spoilt by the stagey beginning. This was a minor blemish, however, on a productive session, one that showed that Bechet was not content simply to revel in the comforts of hackneyed crowd-pleasers; he was keen to record material that led the French band into broader, deeper waters.

A few days later, during a tour of Holland, Bechet (on soprano saxophone) recorded two numbers with the Dutch Swing College at the Hilversum studios. The first, a jaunty version of *King Porter Stomp*, has competent, but slightly marred, clarinet and trumpet solos; however, the full-sounding octet firmly supports Bechet's exciting playing. *Dutch Swing College Blues* is far superior. It is a well devised theme which opens with the trombone and trumpet playing pedal-notes into plunger mutes. This sturdy sound is piquantly answered by harmonized reeds; there are effective backing figures throughout and a subtle use of dynamics. The 12-bar solos are divided up in an unusual way: the trumpet takes eight bars, and the trombone four; then the clarinet has eight and the trumpet another four. Bechet enters to create two powerful, roving choruses before the band plays a reprise of the opening call-and-answer motif.

The Dutch Swing College, like all the other European jazz groups who worked alongside Bechet, was honoured and delighted by his musical company. Socially, things got off to a quiet start when Bechet first worked with the band (which was some while before the recording date), but soon warmed up, as the group's leader, Peter Schilperoort, explained:

We first met Sidney in Amsterdam, at a little theatre where we had been booked to accompany him for a concert. We were introduced, but Bechet seemed rather cool; he went straight off and sat down in the corner. Meanwhile a young French pianist stepped forward and told us which numbers Sidney wanted to play, the keys, tempos and routines. Nothing was written down, and there were no chords. He explained where Sidney wanted breaks and where he wanted long notes. Sidney sat there, not saying a word.

We played the concert with him, and I must say that it was a great success. Sidney, realizing that the band had good ears and were capable of doing their job, became friendlier – much friendlier in fact. Later we made the record without any problems, and in the following year he especially asked for us to accompany him in Switzerland. We became good friends, and whenever he played concerts in The Hague he stayed at my home. He loved to sit up, deep into the night, talking about old New Orleans, and discussing various old tunes. When I said that I was unfamiliar with a particular melody that he had mentioned he immediately got out his soprano and played the song for me. I got out my guitar to accompany him. This was in the early hours of the morning and neighbours soon began knocking; Sidney put a handkerchief in the bell of his saxophone to quieten it down.

During the times he played in Holland his drinking was very moderate, though he ate very well. On one trip he drank only milk. He said he loved the taste of Dutch gin, but that it upset his stomach. I think his illness was already beginning. As far as working with Sidney Bechet, well, on concerts he dominated the band. He seemed to play ten times louder than we did. I was mostly on clarinet, following his lead. He knew exactly what he wanted. He directed everyone, pointing out who was to solo, then playing the riff that backed that solo. He was playing in tune, and sounded beautiful on the ballads. His time was impeccable, and, although lots of his fast runs were worked out, he always played them with such swing, such rhythm, such spirit – his vibrato added to the excitement. When one worked with, say, Billy Butterfield or Bud Freeman, they were in with the band, but Sidney Bechet was in front of it, dominating it.[28]

TWENTY-TWO

Monsieur Bechet

Bechet resumed working at the Vieux Colombier in Paris after his cross-Continental tour, though his time-table at the club allowed him to play on radio shows and to make day-time guest appearances. On the morning of 14 June 1951, as he drove to the Clamart Music Festival, his car skidded on the Fontainbleu road, hitting a tree; as a result Bechet injured his head. Don Byas was called on to deputize at the festival, but after a few days' rest Bechet was back in action, packing his bags for another season at Juan-les-Pins. Beginning on 1st July, Bechet played a repeat season with Claude Luter's orchestra. Luter gave his reminiscences:

> Whenever we returned to Juan we soon got back into the routine, Sidney too. Although he was a restless person in many ways, the life there suited him, whereas a concert tour didn't. Before a concert all of our band would be light-hearted, fooling around, but Sidney definitely suffered from *le trac* [stage-fright]. He would be very serious and withdrawn, but he was fine the moment he got on stage.
> Annet Badel, the club owner, and Jeanine Senneville, who was the administrator at the club, both got on well with Sidney. Badel was a kind and considerate man. He needed to be, because one of Sidney's escapades at Juan would have tested anyone's patience. Sidney bought a small falcon (an *émerillon*) as a pet. He used to sit solemnly with the bird on his hand; it was on a chain which was attached to a ring on his thumb. No one was allowed to make jokes about the bird, and once Sidney reprimanded me for speaking too loudly when it was dozing. One day a girl dancer at the club, Claude Mockery, accidentally tripped over the chain and the bird got loose. It flew away and perched up in a tree. It wouldn't come down. That night Bechet refused to come to work on time, saying he had to recover what he called his "fucking oiseau". This went on for a couple of days. All his spare time was spent trying to coax the bird; he stood under the tree making clucking noises. That's all that was on his mind – no thoughts of work, music, anything else. But he wouldn't take advice and no one was to rescue the bird, only him. Then the bird simply flew off, and that was the end of that.[1]

The working routine at the Vieux Colombier in Juan-les-Pins during the summer of 1951 was as follows:

Claude Luter's orchestra	22.30–23.00
Benny Bennet's orchestra	23.00–23.30
Sidney Bechet and Luter's orchestra	23.35–24.00
Les Boulau	00.00–00.15
Benny Bennet's orchestra	00.15–00.45
Claude Luter's orchestra	00.45–01.15
Sidney Bechet and Luter's orchestra	01.15–01.45
Les Boulau	01.45–02.00
Benny Bennet's orchestra	02.00–03.20 (approx.)[2]

Benny Bennet was a black ex-GI who played drums and bongos in his own Latin-American/Cuban quintet, and Les Boulau were a boy-and-girl double act who sang, did mime, and told jokes. Usually, on the last of Bechet's numbers a couple of dancers, billed as Les Rats de Saint-Germain des Pres, came out to perform some spectacular twirls.

The growing fame of the club at Juan-les-Pins, and the presence of its celebrated guest star, attracted scores of famous visitors. Intellectuals such as Jean-Paul Sartre, Jean Genet and Simone de Beauvoir briefly sampled the atmosphere, so too did various Hollywood stars – Joseph Cotton, Alice Faye, Errol Flynn, Michele Morgan, Orson Welles and others. Even the great Maurice Chevalier paid a call. There was a procession of aristocrats, major and minor. An English jazz fan, Gerard Organ, witnessed the visit of a noted celebrity: "One night Ali Khan arrived at the Vieux Colombier with a party of friends. They occupied a favoured seat near the band and naturally spent very freely. After Bechet's set there was an interval, but the Master of Ceremonies announced that Bechet would return to play especially for dancing in honour of 'our distinguished guests'. He played right through to the small hours of the morning with Benny Bennet's orchestra. All his penchant for luxuriant tunes such as *Embraceable You, Just one of those things* and *Laura* came to the fore, and there was a marvellous stream of music from him until perhaps 3 o'clock in the morning, when the whole party folded."[3]

Bechet was usually at his happiest when playing for dancing, a fact that he readily acknowledged: "If we play for dancing then we can relax, but when it is a concert we are inclined to tense up a bit. Each concert for me is just a little like those far-off days when I first appeared in public."[4]

Sidney gradually introduced some of his favourite numbers into his performances with Luter's orchestra. Most of the members of that band were devoted jazz record collectors; they were originally taken by surprise when Bechet suggested that they play *Mon homme*, but when they heard what marvellous music he made of the song their purism evaporated. Later he performed other 'unlikely' songs with them, such as *My Yiddisher Momma* and *You are my heart's delight* (a tribute by Sidney to one of his own favourites – the tenor Richard Tauber).

The famous French stage star Mistinguett described her visit to the Vieux Colombier in her autobiography: "One evening I went with some friends to a night-club in Juan-les-Pins and watched the vivid, suntanned youth of the Riviera dance the night away. As I sat sipping my 'pastis', an old Negro with stubby jewelled fingers put his saxophone to his lips and began to play . . . I did not recognize the tune at first. It was a sad tune and everyone was looking at me. Then before I knew it my eyes filled with tears. The Negro was called Sidney Bechet. He was playing *Mon homme*. I put on my dark glasses. Others were crying too, pretty girls, who leaned their faces on their hands as they sat listening."[5]

As the summer season of 1951 passed, plans for Bechet's impending marriage became more elaborate. Annet Badel and local dignitaries joined forces with designers, float-constructors and caterers to help organize preparations for the

August wedding. On the 17th of that month, the ceremony at Cannes Town Hall went off without any alarming hitches. Sidney's witnesses were the American Vice Consul and Mrs Suzanne Blum; Mistinguett and the Mayor of Cannes acted for Elisabeth. The event was reported all over the world. Various ages for the couple were published (Elisabeth was born on 20 September 1910), and the newspapers also failed to agree on how much champagne had been drunk at the wedding luncheon (held at the Vieux Colombier). Some journals said 300 bottles, others 500; what is certain is that the 400 guests (including Princess Fawzia of Egypt) had a memorable time. The wedding procession lived up to expectations. Scores of doves were released as the couple began their slow drive through the streets in an open carriage. The thousands of well-wishers who lined the route cheered the couple, clapped the colourful floats and the parading jazz bands, and laughed approvingly at the 12-foot model of a soprano saxophone which was carried by two attendants. In all, the cortège was more than half a mile long.

The honeymoon was spent at Juan-les-Pins, where Sidney continued to play his summer season until 5th September. During the last weeks of the booking Sidney was visited by the American arranger Billy Moore, who was then the music director for the Peters Sisters. One day they were joined at a café by British writer Ronald Sweetman. Bechet began reminiscing about England, saying that he had originally been wary of going there because it was the capital of a colonial empire, but he had been agreeably surprised by the open welcome he had received. The conversation turned to world affairs, and both Bechet and Moore said that they regarded the conflicts then raging in Malaysia and Korea as racial rather than political – the white British fighting the brown Malays, and the white Americans fighting a yellow enemy. There was very little sitting in at the Vieux Colombier, but Sweetman and other listeners were treated to a bonus: Big Bill Broonzy, who had been appearing nearby at Menton, visited the club and sat in for several numbers.

Bechet returned to Paris, where he and Claude Luter were guests with André Réwéliotty's band for a recording session on 7th September. Sidney takes the opening melody on each number, and is then featured at length. Pianist Yannick Singery plays solos on most tracks and trombonist Jean-Louis Durand is granted regular space, but the two clarinettists are given only the briefest chance to shine; trumpeter Marcel Bornstein gets one brief solo (on *Darling Nelly Gray*). Bechet's simple but effective blues riff *Sidney's Wedding Day* is the only original piece on the date, which included items that Bechet hadn't recorded previously, such as the 1928 'pop' song *Together* (usually played as a waltz).

When that session ended Bechet was only able to spend a few hours at his home in Grigny; he then said goodbye to his new bride and left for a tour of the USA (which had been planned some months before). Sidney didn't take a direct flight to America; instead he spent nine days in London, holiday-making – without Elisabeth. He arrived in England on 8 September 1951 and travelled to Wimbledon (in South London) where he stayed with friends, Bobby and Bunty Blick. During his visit Sidney linked up with several people he had met previously in 1949, including Humphrey Lyttelton and writer Max Jones. He also had a reunion in London with his old friend Tallulah Bankhead, who happened to be visiting, in connection with an impending radio show. On Sunday 9th September Tallulah threw a party in her suite at the Ritz Hotel. Sidney attended the gathering, as did the Honourable Gerald Lascelles (a cousin of the Queen of England) and Randolph Churchill (the son of Sir Winston). There was no music-making at the party. When it was over Gerald Lascelles (a life-long jazz fan) took the opportunity to drive Sidney back to Wimbledon in a 1929 Speed Six Bentley. The journey took place late at night at considerable speed. The driver recalls: "Sidney reacted favourably to the trip, but seemed a little breathless as we climbed the stairs."[6]

As Sidney was in transit for the USA, he had his soprano saxophone with him, but he was careful to avoid the sort of problems that his engagement in London in 1949 had created. However, he played at a private party (held on 10th September at the Blick's home), but this was only under duress. Gerald Lascelles, who was at the party, was called on to play the piano with Sidney. He recalls the background:

> I endeavoured to accompany him that evening, due to rather odd circumstances. There was a very talented blind pianist at the party who was playing perfectly so far as I was concerned. Sidney got out his horn and started to blow but after a few moments put it down claiming that he could not blow with someone who insisted in playing such 'modern' chords. No one else played piano, and I have always made a point of never playing in front of, or with, professional musicians, but I was press-ganged that night to perform rather than let Sidney's talents go unheard. To this day I only admit to playing in the key of C, but I think Sidney persuaded me to upgrade my act to E flat, probably with disastrous results. I have no idea what tunes we played other than the blues, but I think that was the moment when I was first struck by the incredible ferocity of tone that Sidney produced when blowing freely and unhampered by studio or stage microphones.[7]

Sidney flew to the USA on 17th September and opened his tour at Frank Holzfeind's Blue Note club in Chicago. Bechet must have realized he was courting disaster in playing at a club that directly rivalled Jazz Ltd (with whom he still had an exclusive contract). Bill Reinhardt was in Bermuda, taking his first vacation in years, but as soon as his wife Ruth came to hear of Sidney's engagement in Chicago she took legal action to establish the validity of the club's agreement with him. Meanwhile Bechet began his residency, accompanied by 'Big Chief' Russell Moore on trombone, Arthur Trappier on drums, and Red Richards on piano. Richards said:

> I had never worked with Sidney Bechet before the 1951 tour. Red Allen advised Sidney to use me. It was a wonderful three months. We played at the Blue Note in Chicago, and for George Wein at the Storyville in Boston; we also did the Elks Rendezvous in Philadelphia and the Colonial Tavern in Toronto, Canada. I loved working with Bechet, he was so dynamic, and such a great musician. I learnt many tunes working with him that I had never played before. He didn't bring any written music, or chord changes – except for *Petite fleur*. I got on fine with Sidney. He always called me Buddy. But I do know that he had an awful temper. This tended to show up when he had too much to drink; he drank a lot of champagne at that time, and sometimes brandy. But no matter how much he had to drink he was always okay with me. He used to take it out a bit on drummer Art Trappier. Trappy, like Bechet, had a

short-fuse temper. Sidney liked to announce him as Art Strappier, and that really used to burn Art up.[8]

Various old friends of Sidney's visited the Blue Note club on Randolph Street, including John Reid, his wife Barbara, and Bill Russell. One evening in late September 1951 these three went with Sidney for a Chinese meal, chosen because it was the nearest thing to New Orleans rice-based food that they could find. Both Bill Russell and Barbara Reid took notes of Bechet's conversation that night. Bill Russell kept a copy of the memoir for his archive, and kindly sent me details:

Sidney's return to his native land has been anything but pleasant for him. After the calm and comparative quiet of Europe, Sidney says he finds the restaurants too brightly lit, and the streets too crowded and noisy, and although he always gets homesick, when the cards are on the table it is still France he prefers. In a rather vague way Sidney talked of going home to New Orleans for a visit, and he wants his brother Dr. Leonard Bechet to do some more work on his teeth.

Sidney mentioned one hobby that he had had for years, which he can't seem to shake, even in France, and this is the purchasing of property. Only recently he acquired a new villa outside Paris "the prettiest little house ever". His other hobby, on which he has spent thousands of dollars, is photography, and of all the equipment he has had, only 2 or 3 cameras remain. New Orleans is on Sidney's mind constantly. It is only natural then that he would prefer to play New Orleans style music. It is the style of music preferred by Paris also. Sidney was saddened by the fact that the band backing him up at the Blue Note engagement did not play New Orleans style. Almost apologetically he says, "When they drag that beat, sometimes I feel like I'm Billie Holiday". Sidney seemed to agree with Baby Dodds, and Louis Armstrong, in liking the Claude Luter Band of Paris. The Luter band can be distinguished from a New Orleans band only with some difficulty. However he did say "They ain't got that *beat*".

For sometime past Sidney has been bothered by his nerves and by stomach trouble. But by an odd chance his condition has improved in the past year. The medicine he was required to take before X-ray pictures was supposed to coat the lining of the stomach and show in the pictures. Apparently the amount to be taken was only one glass, but Sidney drank the whole pitcher and the pain immediately disappeared. Sidney refused to have the X-rays taken, and so far no further treatment has been necessary. However Sidney says that after his Chicago venture he will need treatment of some kind.

Trouble has beset him on all sides. Hardly had he set foot in Chicago before he was confronted by a law suit from Ruth Reinhardt. A few days later Sidney was called in his hotel suite and informed that the caller, a woman, was on the way up. When Sidney opened the door, the girl, a stranger whom Sidney had never laid eyes on before, placed a small child in Sidney's arms, saying "It's yours". After the shock wore off Sidney managed to straighten out the "misunderstanding". Hardly had Sidney recovered before he was informed that his ex-wife had a few unpleasant things to impart. But mention Sidney's new marriage and his face lights up. He carries a picture of Elisabeth in his watch bracelet.

Sidney noticeably relaxed when he discussed food – New Orleans food. He lectured on the various gumbos. An authority on the subject, he stated that there are three kinds of gumbo, and all variations fall into one of these groups. Zhobes Gumbo is for the spring season and contains spinach and chopped greens with ham. In the summer the dish is Okra Gumbo, and during the fall and winter the sturdier dish is the Filé Gumbo, a meat gumbo with the powdered leaves of filé.

It is a source of irritation to Sidney that when people hear him play in Paris they come up to him and say, "Sidney, you play so differently over here". And Sidney says, "I don't play no different. It's you that's listening different. I've been playing this way all my life". Sidney says it is difficult for Parisiens to adopt New Orleans style, even though it is the most popular jazz form there. This is due to the fact that their only teachers are the few jazz record imports. As a result there is a large, unsatisfied demand for jazz in Europe.

While playing in Chicago Sidney had difficulty with his horn drying out under the lights. He was presented with a new horn in Paris, but so far has not been able to use it. The horn, a Cuesnon, has had to be cut down three times already, as the pitch has not been satisfactory to Sidney. He still plays his old American Buescher.

Bechet's booking at the Blue Note was not interrupted by legal action. The group finished the run, then prepared to move off to Toronto. Bechet, Richards and Trappier went by plane, but 'Big Chief' Russell Moore refused to fly and had to make the long journey by train. After a successful booking in Canada the musicians moved down to play a residency at George Wein's Storyville club in Boston. They opened up at the club (where they remained from 15th to 28th October) playing opposite drummer Jo Jones's quartet (which featured tenor saxophonist Zoot Sims). George Wein recalls:

Sidney played for me at both Storyville clubs, at Copley Square and at Kenmore Square. But my first encounter with him took place some years earlier, I guess around 1946. I was in college but had gone to Philadelphia to see an ex-army pal. Bechet was playing at a session with Max Kaminsky. James P. Johnson had been booked to do the session, but he didn't show. Max Kaminksy spotted me in the audience. He waved, and told Bechet that I played piano. So I got up there, not feeling at all confident, because at that time I didn't know the Bechet-type repertoire. He sensed this and nursed me through the whole session. He was so sweet, he couldn't have been nicer. Later, when he came to work for me, I still found him to be a lovely man. I had heard from several people that he could be nasty, but neither me nor my wife Joyce ever saw him when he was anything else but nice. Who can blame him for settling in France? He was like a god there, bigger than he ever was in the States, yet he could have been as big as Louis Armstrong. But his suspiciousness alienated a lot of people; he had an inborn mistrust of managers and bookers.[9]

Red Richards vividly remembers a particular gig at the Storyville club: "One night in Boston the club was full of newspaper reporters and Sidney became very apprehensive. Tallulah Bankhead's maid had sold her story to a New York paper, and had described the parties that Tallulah had given and various goings-on in Connecticut. Sidney's name had been mentioned, so the reporters wanted to follow up the story. But it all passed off peacefully. I don't think Tallulah showed up during that entire tour."[10]

Dick Hadlock provided a description of one of Tallulah Bankhead's zany gatherings: "Sidney had a wacky side that surprised me. One night he went to a celebrity party thrown by Tallulah. She arranged for him to be introduced as an atomic scientist, and, of course, he couldn't discuss any of that because it was classified information. The joke was climaxed by Sidney descending the great hall while playing The Saints (on my soprano). Bankhead was a nut, but she loved jazz."[11]

The warmth of the Bechet–Bankhead friendship had begun to cool by the end of 1951. It was rumoured that they fell out over a sum of money that Tallulah had lent Sidney. For Bechet the wounding moment came in December 1952 when Tallulah made Louis Armstrong the main subject of an interview on jazz that she gave to *Ebony* magazine. She mentioned Sidney but described Louis as "the World's Greatest Musician".

Bechet's quartet was well received in Boston; various airshots taken from broadcasts that originated at the Storyville club show why. The unit had a tough, unhesitant approach. All of the tunes used were stock items in Bechet's programmes, and often they were filled with stock phrases, but here and there Sidney suddenly develops an idea that has fallen under his fingers. When he does, he shapes and delivers it with all of his old magic. Bechet himself summarized his tactics: "I play just as I feel. Sometimes I may stick to a variation for a while, and then suddenly decide to do something else. There are no rules."[12] Richards and Trappier, who were used to working together, combined well. 'Big Chief' Russell Moore hadn't the guile or the contrapuntal sense of Vic Dickenson, but he was assertive and capable of creating exciting lip trills. On harmonized passages he blended well with Bechet (particularly on *Storyville Blues*).

Sidney went out on the town after one of his nights at the Boston club and took too much champagne aboard. As a consequence his balance was affected and he fell over, injuring his mouth. The resultant swelling meant that he had to cancel a couple of dates; a quartet featuring Jimmy and Marian McPartland was hastily brought in.

Bechet's group moved on to Philadelphia, where it played from 28th October until 25th November. Bechet took brief leave from this booking to go into New York to record a session for Blue Note (preceded by a guest appearance at the Central Plaza on 3rd November). Considering the line-up – Sidney De Paris, Jimmy Archey, Manzie Johnson, Pops Foster and pianist Don Kirkpatrick – the results of this session are disappointing. A distractingly uncoordinated rhythm section seems at times to be operating on three different pulses (conceivably a time lag in the studio prevented the musicians from hearing one other properly). Pops Foster's rugged tone isn't captured by the recording; instead his efforts produce a monotonous thumping sound. The choice of tunes is unadventurous, and most of them are dixieland eternals. It is strange that when Bechet first began recording for Blue Note his selections (*Summertime*, *Blue Horizon*, etc) were much more daring.

There is a feeling that the ensembles are simply coasting along. All of the pieces are played at around medium tempo, and the solo routines unimaginatively follow the same order on several of them, but the profusion of talent ensures that some worthwhile moments occur. Sidney De Paris, who rarely played to the gallery, creates many nimble phrases without appearing to extend himself. Archey's performance, as usual, is forthright and big-toned, but he too seems to be playing with less zeal than expected. Bechet never sounds casual, but despite his efforts the band is often uninspired.

Sidney sounds ultra-determined to make something extraordinary happen on

Blues my naughty sweetie, but nothing he does proves contagious; the piano solos do not bear close scrutiny on either take. The band also made two attempts at recording *Ballin' the Jack*. The second of these achieves a degree of purposefulness and contains some bright stop-time solos from trumpet, trombone and soprano saxophone. The session ended as it should have begun with a lively version of *There'll be some changes made*, on which Bechet's efforts are positively Herculean.

Bechet returned to Boston in early December 1951 to begin another residency at Storyville, commencing on the 10th, this time backed by a trio led by George Wein on piano. Throughout his US tour Bechet had suffered more than usual with digestive problems. In Boston he decided to enter the Massachusetts General Hospital for a series of tests, which revealed that he was suffering from a stomach ulcer. Much to George Wein's astonishment, Bechet announced that he would sooner be operated on in France. Sidney contacted his wife Elisabeth, cut short his tour and flew back to France, arriving there on 22 December 1951. Sidney's plane was met by Elisabeth and the drummer Moustache Galepides, who drove the couple to their home at Grigny. The radio stations carried the news that Sidney had been forced to curtail his tour of America because of health problems. As a result of these broadcasts the telephone at Bechet's home scarcely stopped ringing, as friends and anxious fans called to ask for news of Sidney's health.

Charles Delaunay was the first visitor to arrive; his anxiety was soon diminished. Bechet was determinedly anxious to show him some new American fishing tackle that he had brought back, and he also wanted to demonstrate the new Polaroid camera that he had purchased on his travels. Next day other visitors included Léon Kaba of Vogue records, who made the 20-mile journey from Paris to see for himself that the returned traveller was feeling much better. Bechet found that the French air was so beneficial he insisted on paying a visit to the Vieux Colombier that night. News of the impending visit spread like wildfire and, despite the extremely cold weather, a crowd gathered outside the club to welcome Bechet. Waiting inside at the bar was drummer Zutty Singleton. The two men had often been at loggerheads but on this occasion they embraced warmly.

Also in the club was another musician with whom Bechet had shared an uneven relationship, Mezz Mezzrow. Bechet was slow to acknowledge Mezzrow. An onlooker said, "When Bechet saw Mezz he stiffened. It was Mezz who made the first approach, then the two sat down to a bottle of champagne."[13] The drinks with Mezzrow marked only a truce, not a cessation of hostilities. The invalid stayed in the club until three o'clock in the morning. It was a strange way to convalesce, but for Sidney it was a return to his old routine, one that he had first established as a teenager in New Orleans. He hated leaving any late-night gathering until he was sure that every drop of enjoyment had been squeezed out.

In the light of Bechet's recovery, surgery was postponed and he was able to return to work at the Vieux Colombier on 16 January 1952. For the first few nights blues singer Big Bill Broonzy and trumpeter Nelson Williams took over the opening sets to lighten Sidney's work load, but Sidney played a full second set, prefacing it by apologizing to the audience for the fact that he was still on a milk diet and not quite his old self. However, there was no lack of vigour on the recording session in which Bechet took part with Claude Luter's orchestra on 18 January 1952.

The session highlighted several fine compositions by Bechet, including his attractive tune *Ghost of the Blues* (which he had never recorded). Guy Longnon was now regularly with Luter's band on trumpet (he had formerly played valve trombone with the group). He and Luter play brief attractive solos within an ornate arrangement of *Ghost of the Blues*, but the composer chose a tempo that seems to be too fast to be effective. After some dazzling opening cadenzas from Bechet the version of *Strike up the band* sags badly, but the initial recording of Bechet's tune *Si tu vois ma mère* is absolutely entrancing. Both the melody and its rendering, first by Bechet then by Longnon, are superb. An orderly performance of *Wabash Blues* is successfully shared between Bernard Zacharias on trombone and Bechet, with the old master in full passionate flow. *Mouche à miel*, a busy tune in the mould of *Polka Dot Rag*, sounds as though it was over-exhaustively rehearsed, but *Le marchand de poissons* is full of lyricism and spirit, and demonstrates Bechet's gift for constructing ingenious musical patterns on basic arpeggios. *As-tu le cafard* is a more sophisticated affair, but it is also reminiscent of other tunes, notably *Autumn in New York*. The session ended with a stirring march, *Dans la rue d'Antibes*, which is full of panache and tunefulness; it also contains Longnon's best solo of the day. The new trumpeter's range and power had made a difference to the group, as had Claude Phillipe's banjo playing, but whereas Phillipe's work enhances some of the numbers it sounds quite out of place on others.

The recordings not only showed that Bechet had returned to comparative good health, they also provided another indication that, in presenting his compositions (with Luter's band), Sidney was creating an Afro-American-Gaulish fare that was unlike anything else being played in the jazz world. This was no accident. Not long before that particular recording session Bechet said: "I have noticed an improvement in French musicianship. It would be conceited of me to say that this is due to my playing in France, or to that of any other American musician. Nevertheless, if we examine the style closely we find this. Before the Americans became part of French music, the French played their jazz in a kind of 'straight' way. Today, the bands have much more to them. I'm not going to speak for all bands, but I can speak for the Luter combination." On that occasion Bechet added, with charm and diplomacy: "Every man has two countries, his own and France", but speaking of his audiences, he noted: "After some youngsters have heard a musician three or four times they begin to take him for granted. They listen less attentively and shout a little louder."[14]

There was certainly plenty of shouting at Bechet's first big concert of the season, held on 31st January at the Salle Pleyel in Paris, but, according to a report in *Melody Maker*, there was also some booing. This was attributed to fans who disapproved of the slow numbers in the programme and to "rival jazz organizations" – meaning the differing factions who supported either Charles Delaunay or Hugues Panassié. The post-war rift that ended the friendship and cooperation between France's two leading jazz experts, Charles Delaunay and Hugues Panassié, had, by the early 1950s, reached bitter proportions, with rival supporters eager to trade vociferous insults. The British jazz establishment was, for the most part, dismayed that two men who had done so much to enlighten the world about jazz should be in conflict, but despite the efforts of mediators the two antagonists never resumed their friendship.

Some visiting American jazzmen were able to maintain equitable social contact with both Panassié and Delaunay, but this was impossible for Bechet since Charles Delaunay was his agent. The reverse side of the coin affected Mezz Mezzrow (who had moved to France), because his association was with Panassié. But neither of the Frenchmen was responsible for the degree of rancour that existed between Bechet and Mezzrow in the early 1950s. The two musicians were never close friends, but during the mid-1930s, when Mezzrow adopted the role of a fan or even a disciple, their meetings were usually amicable. Bechet had no particular admiration for Mezzrow's musicianship but he was grateful for the opportunities that Mezzrow had presented to him, and this led him to tolerate his shortcomings. When someone remarked that Bechet's duets with Mezzrow had worked more successfully than those he recorded with Albert Nicholas, Bechet tartly replied: "I have too much respect for Albert to tell him exactly what to play."[15]

Mezzrow experienced the vicious side of Bechet quite early on. In 1938 Bechet, seeking money that was owed to him for a recording session, called on Mezzrow, who promptly chain-locked his front door to stop Sidney from entering. When Mezzrow realized that Bechet's purposeful ingenuity would soon unlock the door, he fled. Bechet assumed that Mezzrow had gone for a gun; accordingly he pulled out his knife as he entered the apartment. Mezzrow's wife, Mae, took Bechet's side in the dispute and insisted that Mezzrow pay the debt there and then. Sidney collected the cash, and the transaction allowed the relationship with Mezzrow to return, temporarily, to an even keel.

But ever after, the suspicious side of Bechet's nature worked overtime when he had any dealings with Mezzrow, a situation that did not change when Mezzrow became the principal of the King Jazz recording company. Mezzrow was never able to devise a system of royalty accounting that satisfied Bechet, who was convinced that he was not being treated fairly. Mezzrow insisted that his behaviour in the matter was exemplary, which Bechet hotly disputed; thus began their feud.

Mezzrow's quixotic way of doing business angered other musicians, but some who worked for him regularly found him to be a prompt payer and an honest man. Bechet steadfastly maintained that Mezzrow was neither, and the two men kept well out of each other's way in Paris. Claude Luter revealed: "Both Mezzrow and Bechet carried revolvers, so it was just as well they never had a fight in public, though I think it highly unlikely that they would do so. Mezzrow was always fine with me, very kind in fact."[16]

The fact that by now Bechet was a famous man in France did not stop him carrying a gun. One night in the Vieux Colombier, much to the embarrassment of his tour manager Claude Wolff, Sidney asked him to look after a revolver for the rest of the night. Bechet's public know nothing of this side of his life. He had developed an affectionate following amongst all sections of the French people, only a minority of whom would have felt at home in a Montmartre club. Most French listeners responded warmly to Bechet's unrestrained vibrato; his passion and romanticism struck a common chord within them. They were charmed by the accent in his speech, and they also liked the look of him. The fact that he had a French name wasn't a handicap either. Charles Delaunay said:

Sidney never became big-headed with the people. He liked to be recognized by them as he walked down the street, and when anyone shouted greetings to him he always shouted a friendly message back. People loved to hear him talk in French, even though it was always Creole. It never changed, or improved, it was what we would call 'petit nègre'. If he was in a bar he'd start up a conversation with anyone. Oh yes, he had great appeal for the general public.

Sidney always seemed to be happy with my work for him as an agent, but there was always a certain reserve between us. He did not want to mix business with pleasure too much. We were always friends, and I loved the man, but we never got too close on personal matters. In many respects he was like a shrewd peasant, you never knew quite what he was thinking – a little like a fox. But he was strong and positive about what he wanted to record. He could enter a studio and record ten tunes in three hours, simply because he knew exactly what he wanted before he arrived. If anyone was in any doubt, Sidney would play what he wanted on the soprano sax, or he would cross to the piano and demonstrate harmonies without any hesitation. He was a truly extraordinary musician, a proud and often serious man.[17]

Trumpeter Pierre Merlin, who had left Claude Luter's orchestra to concentrate on painting, observed Sidney's fierce pride at a club session he heard him play in 1951. Pierre commented to Sidney that he was delighted to hear him play the chorus that Johnny Hodges had recorded on Duke Ellington's *The Sheik of Araby*. Bechet bristled and said, "He stole that from me!"[18]

As if to tickle the record-buying tastes of a middle-of-the-road audience, Bechet recorded a session in January 1952 with a French all-star band, playing popular standards such as *Old Black Magic*, *I get a kick out of you* and *You're lucky to me*. He also made the original version of the hauntingly impressive *Petite fleur* and recorded two of the themes, *Blues* and *Girls' Dance*, from the musical suite that had occupied him for so long and which had recently been reshaped as the score for a ballet – *La nuit est un sorcière* (book by André Coffrant). Unlike the ballet themes, *Petite fleur* had been swiftly composed, apparently whilst Bechet was seated on the lavatory. Drummer Moustache Galepides was visiting Bechet's home when he heard Sidney's voice commanding Elisabeth to bring his soprano saxophone to the toilet. Elisabeth did what she was asked and soon the magic sounds of a new opus drifted out from the tiny, secluded room. Bechet emerged triumphant, explaining that the melody had entered his head at a most unlikely moment. Moustache suggested the work should be called *Petite fleur* and Bechet delightedly agreed.[19]

To keep record sales climbing Bechet took part in another session with Claude Luter's orchestra in January 1952. They produced a batch of 'good old good ones', including *St Louis Blues*, *Royal Garden Blues* and *Muskrat Ramble*, supplemented with re-makes of *Petite fleur* and *Les oignons*. To link in with record promotions Bechet took part in a series of publicity enterprises: he was photo-graphed with various 'pop' stars; he posed with Dizzy Gillespie on board a riverboat on the Seine; and he visited the Salon du Jazz accompanied by Elisabeth and Zutty and Marge Singleton.

The increase in Bechet's popularity meant that his concert appearances were much in demand. During the early months of 1952 he played in three concerts at the Salle Pleyel before touring Belgium and Switzerland (with Claude Luter's orchestra). He also did some concert dates with a band led by another of his devotees, clarinettist André Réwéllioty, but when summer came around he moved south as usual to play a season at Juan-les-Pins with Luter's group.

By this time Bechet was the proud owner of an emerald-green Salmson car, which had a mascot in the form of a soprano saxophone across its bonnet. Like most luxury cars it could be purchased in either left- or right-hand drive; Bechet bought a right-hand model which he could be seen polishing and repolishing in front of the Vieux Colombier.

At Juan-les-Pins fishing was still a serious business; Bechet would put on his spectacles and bait and rebait a hook several times until he was perfectly satisfied with his efforts. Despite having to give his autograph regularly (which he never refused to do) he often sat on a public bench when he felt like relaxing in the shade. Over the years many visitors to Juan-les-Pins saw him thus, contentedly smoking American cigarettes and munching French pears. Singer Herb Jeffries sat down with him one day and reminisced about the recording session they had shared in Chicago in 1940. A discussion started on how the words 'jass' and 'jazz' came into being and Sidney put forward his theory (a novel one) that the word 'jass' was inspired by an expression he had often heard used at New Orleans funerals, 'Jesus Almighty Save our Souls'.[20]

During the 1952 summer season (in July) Bechet and Luter's orchestra played an unusual date aboard the US warship *Coral Sea*. The event was a dance in aid of the French Cancer Society. When that season ended the musicians undertook a long tour of North Africa, playing in Casablanca, Fez, Meknès, Oran, Algiers and Tunisia. Sidney had mixed feelings about touring Africa. He enjoyed most of the sight-seeing, and the excellent revenue, but he was upset by the racism he observed, and sometimes encountered. In one interview he said: "The French have no call to crow over Americans . . . I've been in Dakar and I've seen what they do to Negroes there, and Frenchmen are no better than anyone else."[21]

Bechet's biggest personal upset during this period was caused by the death in New Orleans on 17 September 1952 of his brother Leonard. The two had kept in semi-regular communication since their reunion in 1944, but Leonard never got around to taking Sidney up on his offer of a free trip to Europe.

Sidney returned from Africa to Paris and began another round of club and concert dates, all the while attracting bigger, more diverse audiences. In October 1952 he undertook an unusual recording date with Zutty Singleton on drums, and former colleague Lil Hardin-Armstrong on piano. The long-playing record had come into being and the trio was able cut more than enough material for a ten-inch album. The session is full of charming moments. The trio seems to have approached the recording as though it were a friendly club date. There are some mishaps, but a happy spirit compensates. Lil Hardin-Armstrong was not the most versatile or technically agile of pianists but she plays a firm role here, and contributes a light-hearted vocal (complete with scat singing) on *Big Butter and Eggman*. The full timbre of Singleton's array of drum and cymbal sounds isn't cleanly captured, but even so a wealth of percussive tone-colours emerges, particularly on *Limehouse Blues*; this is one of the best items of the date, along with *Black Bottom*, where Sidney and Zutty share a duet. This exchange with the drummer allows Bechet to indulge in some microtonal playing, where he fiercely, and deliberately, bends his notes out of pitch.

Lil Hardin-Armstrong always had something of a sisterly feeling for Sidney and was happy to make the recordings with him. By the time of the session Sidney had taken an apartment in Paris to save himself (or so he said) from getting tired out by repeated journeys to and from Grigny. As a platonic gesture he managed to get accommodation for Lilian within the same apartment block.

Zutty Singleton, who was soon to return to the States after working in Europe for a year or more, still had an unpredictable relationship with Bechet, but most of their meetings in France were cased in cordiality. After Zutty had settled back in New York Sidney contacted him: "He wanted me to join his band. He wrote me a letter that was so full of don'ts that I got scared."[22] Humphrey Lyttelton, visiting France in 1952, saw the two men meet in the street late one night, and stood by as they shared uncomplimentary thoughts about Mezz Mezzrow: "Their putdown was animated, and they laughed wildly at each other's imitation of Mezz."[23] Lyttelton felt that Sidney respected people who stood up to him: "I really believe he found the timid adulation of the young revivalists who gathered around him in Europe irksome, and that the prodigious rages and the almost sadistic practical jokes (a favourite trick was to pretend to come in after a drum break and then to withdraw at the last minute – leaving the drummer, spent in energy and ideas, to struggle through another chorus) were designed to break it down."[24]

Bechet certainly had a mischievous streak. He delighted in throwing young musicians in at the deep end. On one occasion he commanded Maxim Saury's band to play *Petite fleur*, even though the musicians didn't know it. Years earlier, in a session that he was playing at Jimmy Ryan's with Bob Wilber, he caught trombonist Bob Mielke (who was sitting in) totally by surprise in announcing: "*Body and Soul*, featuring Bob Mielke." Mielke recalls the traumatic experience: "Only Bob Wilber understood my chagrin (actually, it was terror). But Sidney had already announced and kicked-off *Body and Soul*, so I had to make a stab at it. I groped and muttered and got a tentative impression of the melody out of my horn. They covered for me and brought it to an end without disaster."[25]

TWENTY-THREE

Stardom in France

The final months of 1952 were filled with recurrent successes for Bechet. Late in the year he made a wide-ranging tour across France with Luter's orchestra, playing at concert dates and gala balls before returning to Paris for a triumphant appearance at the Coliseum's "Nuit de Jazz" on 20th December. There was to be a few months' respite from recording following a November date with Luter's group, but Bechet was kept busy throughout the winter of 1952–3, alternating between the Vieux Colombier and touring. He also spent a lot of time checking over the music for *La nuit est une sorcière*, which was soon to be given its première.

The recording session in November 1952 produced a mixture of old favourites like *12th Street Rag*, a medley on *Showboat*, and commercially tailored versions of popular French airs. An atmosphere of haste seems to have affected the occasion, and almost everything recorded that day contains superficial mistakes, some of them committed by Bechet. But unfaltering passion triumphs in a memorable performance of *Embraceable You* – a two-chorus feature for soprano saxophone. The Luter group plays long backing notes throughout that tune but individual members frequently take solos in other numbers. Claude Luter introduces the melody of *Porter's Love Song* and plays a whole chorus solo. He does so effectively enough to prod the competitive side of Sidney's nature, with the result that Bechet roars into action. Bernard Zacharias on trombone is full of robust guile, and pianist Raymond Fol plays thoughtfully, both in his solos and in accompaniment. The missing element is the lack of recording definition.

Most of the selections from that date were aimed at the general market. Some of the tunes recorded were not in Bechet's normal repertoire, but sometimes numbers that were successfully performed in public were not considered for recording. In 1951 Dr Terkild Vinding, one of Bechet's staunchest fans, heard what he considers to be Sidney's greatest unrecorded performance. The occasion was a Catholic Convention held in Juan-les-Pins, at which Bechet and Luter played Sidney's arrangement of Schubert's *Ave Maria*. Bechet was not averse to experimenting with his repertoire, but he rarely did so on concert dates; he realized that the old traditional jazz war-horses and recorded hits received the most applause. However, the impending première of his ballet suite promised to be a departure from any of his previous presentations.

In April 1953, Bechet's long wait ended. Hundreds of his admirers trekked to the Palais de Chaillot to hear the work performed by the conservatoire's Orchestre Symphonique; the solo parts of the composition were played by

Bechet himself. Henry Kahn, reporting for the *Melody Maker*, wrote: "The music was as straight as long hair – patches of it dyed slightly blue as one recognised the Bechet New Orleans touch. And the fans just clapped, no whistling, no cries, no paper aeroplanes floating about the hall as would happen at a jazz concert. But when Sidney Bechet and Claude Luter stepped on to the stage to play for forty minutes they broke out once more into their usual frenzy of rowdiness."[1]

Backstage, Bechet was more agitated than usual and spent two hours in his dressing room nervously sifting through the same box of reeds, trying to find one he felt at ease with. James Toliver must have been almost as anxious as Bechet to get the work performed. Over a period of several years he had patiently transcribed what Bechet had played, sung or hummed to him, running through countless permutations of harmonies at the keyboard whilst Bechet deliberated on which progression suited a particular passage of melody. Toliver's orchestration received general praise. The main problems came via the classical musicians' attempts to impart jazz phrasing to the score; there was also some confusion as to whether certain passages should be played two- or four beats in a bar.

The first public performance of the ballet music left the audience "muddled and dismayed"[2]; it received the sort of polite applause that is borne of disappointment. But the initial reaction was more enthusiastic than that of record reviewers who had to listen to the music in the cold light of day. The critics, and Bechet's fans, had been intrigued by the publicity surrounding the première, but the resultant high hopes were blighted by the studio recording that Sidney made in May 1953 with the Orchestre Symphonique (conducted by Jacques Bazire).

The Coffrant–Bechet collaboration was based on the story of a young white somnambulist who kills his fiancée and his parents during their attempts to bring him out of a nocturnal trance. This carnage is observed by the killer's black valet, who leads his employer to an open window and stands by as he steps out to certain suicide. Sometimes great music can accompany an indifferent plot, but in this case the sounds were about as banal as the story. The composition is a hotch-potch of ideas, none of them monumental. The opening theme has a certain light charm, and the blues sequence provides effective contrast, but these interludes are engulfed by a surfeit of quasi-dramatic phrases, most of which would not sound out of place as the background for a low-budget film. Sidney's role as soloist is a subsidiary one, which is perhaps fortunate because he sounds ill at ease, and in these 'straight' surroundings his vibrato sticks out like a sore thumb.

After the concert Bechet put on a brave front and said how much he was looking forward to performing the work in various other cities, but he knew in his heart that the music had not achieved the impact for which he had so fervently hoped. Happily this disappointment didn't induce him to give up composing, and he soon settled down to prepare material for the recording session with André Réwéliotty's orchestra which took place on 28 May 1953. Luter's group was anxious to follow other prospects for the time being, so Réwéliotty's musicians became Bechet's semi-regular accompanists. Charles Delaunay remembers the pride and delight that Réwéliotty showed when he took over the task.

Clarinettist Réwéliotty (who died in a car crash in 1962) summarized the association with Bechet: "After listening to Bechet at the 1949 Festival I bought myself a clarinet. I always liked to listen to New Orleans music, the only music I truly love. With Sidney we whooped up a storm with tunes which probably would not have been suitable for other groups. We did a lot of travelling and played almost the same things every time. What the public wants is something it already knows."[3]

During the winter of 1952, and intermittently throughout 1953, Bechet toured in the "Jazz Varieties" show. This was organized by Charles Delauney, and at various times featured Don Byas, Big Bill Broonzy, Nelson Williams, Lil Hardin, Moustache Galepides and Claude Luter. Broadcasts from some of the shows have been issued on record and, although the results are varied, many catch the lively atmosphere. Occasionally crowd fever causes the accompanying group to get reckless, but in general Luter's band sounds spirited and inventive – the version of *As-tu le cafard* with Bechet is in some ways better than the one in the studio. Another highlight features Bechet playing *I'm confessing* in front of a big band led by Aime Barelli. Bechet sounds at his most expressive against the rich textures of a simple arrangement, and dovetails neatly with trumpeter Barelli during the closing chorus.

Bechet continued to appear at the Vieux Colombier but from the spring of 1953 his bookings there were less regular. By then he was a nationally famous star. The English singer Beryl Bryden, who was working in Paris, was delighted to observe that Sidney was famous enough to have his portrait featured on various items of merchandise, including an expensive brand of chocolates. Various instrument manufacturers were keen that Sidney should be seen playing their soprano saxophones. Bechet, eager to benefit from this, tried models made by Couesnon and Selmer but, despite having them altered to his exact specifications, he never settled on either. Selmer also made a replica of Bechet's mouthpiece, but even this didn't suit him. He had used the same mouthpiece for years (it is now in Claude Luter's possession); he continually made minor adjustments to it, but remained reluctant to change his allegiance.

During 1953 Bechet also played in a number of "Jazz Parade" concerts with André Réwéliotty's band and other guests. Like the "Jazz Varieties" shows, they finished with a vast jam session on stage, often consisting of the entire cast; but no matter how many musicians took part, Sidney could still be heard soaring above the banks of sound. In the summer of 1953 Bechet played some highly lucrative dates at Knokke in Belgium; he also appeared at several French festivals, including one (on 16 June 1953) that took place at the ancient Lutèce Arena in Paris. Open-air festivals were then an attractive novelty, and more than ten thousand people turned up. A chaotic scene developed which resulted in a thousand people getting in without paying, and the overcrowding almost caused a riot. The tumult at the arena exacerbated Bechet's habitual stage fright and some of the people in the show began to have serious doubts as to whether Sidney would will himself to go on, particularly after Don Byas's appearance was greeted with a shower of orange peel and apple cores. Sidney need not have worried: the crowd had come to see him, and when he appeared on stage he was cheered like a favourite gladiator.

A few weeks later the Lutèce Arena was again the venue for a jazz festival organized by different promoters. Bechet was featured once more, but this time only 80 people turned up. The crowds who had suffered such discomfort at the first shindig deliberately stayed away, and warned their friends to do the same. Bechet, sensing disaster, warily asked to be paid in advance. The organizers gave him half his fee, so he went ahead and played the first set, but when the balance failed to materialize he quit at the interval and went home.

Bitter experiences had led Bechet to be wary of promoters; he also tended to be guarded when anyone from the film world came to him with an offer. Over the years many people had outlined nebulous plans to feature him in movies, but few of these schemes ever advanced beyond the pipe-dream stage. However, his growing fame in France consolidated a few deals. In 1952 he appeared with Claude Luter's band in *La route du bonheur* (playing one number), and a year later he was featured briefly with André Réwéliotty's band in *Piédalu député*.

Bechet enjoyed the ambience of the film studio. He was something of a film buff and took great pleasure in going to the cinema. The only part of his filming activities that really irked him was the waiting about in the studio, which didn't suit his impatient nature. In this respect he was happier with the immediacy of television; in those days everything was transmitted live, and, although this meant many run-throughs, Bechet felt happier doing them than sitting about waiting. He was always pleased when strangers came up to say how much they had enjoyed seeing him on television. By this time he was getting regular fan mail from all over Europe. Most of it was dealt with by his secretary, Anita White (whose place was later taken by Marlene Gray).

For some while Bechet had been receiving offers to play again in the United States. He hesitated about accepting them, knowing that he might face problems caused by the injunction taken out by Jazz Ltd. But he was anxious to tidy up various aspects of his personal affairs and to sell or store those of his possessions that were still in New York City. Accordingly he decided to undertake a tour that was tentatively scheduled for five or six months.

Bechet flew into New York on 4 August 1953 and soon began a brief season leading a pick-up band at a recently opened basement club, the Bandbox, which was close to Birdland and near Broadway. Bechet was not in the happiest frame of mind during the early stages of his visit, having been made to pay US Customs' duty on the huge emerald ring that he always wore. His vehement protests that the ring had been given to him long before had no effect on the officials; later he put the matter in the hands of a Philadelphia lawyer, but to no avail. However, the New York booking allowed him to arrange the storing of various items in James and Lola Toliver's apartment at 66 St Nicholas Place.

At the Bandbox Sidney's band, consisting of Joe Thomas (trumpet), Herb Flemming (trombone), Panama Francis (drums) and Dick Wellstood (piano), played opposite groups led by Earl Hines and Muggsy Spanier. Dick Wellstood remembers the brief gig: "I was totally surprised when Sidney decided to buy band uniforms for us to wear at the Bandbox. It was a waste of money because I don't think the booking lasted for more than a week; the club folded soon afterwards. My most durable memory of the place is of seeing Sidney sitting backstage, as though he were a king on a throne. He received his loyal subjects, and there were quite a few, with imperious acknowledgments. Alfred Lion of Blue Note records came and feted Sidney with champagne, which he accepted with an egocentric but regal bow."[4]

Alfred Lion had called in to fix the details of the Blue Note session that took place on 25 August 1953. Bechet was happy to use Jonah Jones on trumpet and Jimmy Archey on trombone, but asked drummer Johnny Blowers to fix the rhythm section. Blowers recalls: "After trying many piano players and bass players I got Walter Page as he and I had worked together for Condon and others – he was great – and I got Buddy Weed from ABC Radio, and I knew Sidney would like him. The day of the date, the heads of Blue Note were very worried because they did not know Buddy, neither did Sidney, but after the first run down of the first song in which Buddy had a piano solo Sidney liked it so well he asked Buddy to play it again and the control room smiled and lit up like New Year's Eve. It was a great date."[5]

The music lives up to Blowers's assessment. It is one of the most relaxed dates of Sidney's career, with much democratic sharing of solo space. Bechet leads off *Sweet Georgia Brown* in half tempo, but for the remainder of the date makes a point of freely allocating prominence to everyone on the date, including bass player Walter Page, who takes a rare solo on *All of me*. Bechet entrusts the opening melody of that song to Harold 'Buddy' Weed, who plays delightfully. Thirty years later Weed said: "Although I had done quite a bit of recording by this time I still felt young and callow in the presence of his greatness. A bit self-conscious you might say. I do recall his kind efforts to make me feel at ease. It was a ball, although I fear the ear-marks of studio work were a bit obvious."[6]

Weed is again gracefully inventive on *Rose of the Rio Grande*, and Archey on trombone blows a typically strapping solo, full of bold, short phrases. Bechet pitches his high notes with clarity and firm control and Jonah Jones contributes an effortlessly flowing solo. The session contains some of Jonah's finest work, particularly on *All of me* and on *Ding Dong Daddy*, where he pays homage to Louis Armstrong's classic recording. Bechet never once attempts to oust Jonah, and often drops in happily with the trumpeter's phrasing, playing a productive harmony part. The front line sounds in good accord with the rhythm section and, although no one was out to make history, the session produces an abundance of swinging jazz.

Bechet's tour itinerary took in some widely differing venues. After playing a one-night stand at Child's Restaurant in New York, he topped the bill at the world-famous Harlem theatre the Apollo. He appeared there for a week (accompanied by Lucky Millinder's band) as part of a pot-pourri of variety acts which included the Congaroos ("Jitterbugs Supreme"), Tables Turner (a balancing act), the old favourites Butterbeans and Susie, Los Tropicas (a dancing troupe), and the effervescent Slim Gaillard. Slim spoke of this booking: "I never had a chance to get to know Bechet there because I drove virtually non-stop from the West

Coast to make the Friday rehearsal, and thereafter we never seemed to meet up. The Apollo crowd could be tough, particularly a team that used to be up in the second balcony, but Bechet projected straight at them, and they liked it."[7] Bechet shared the front of the stage with trumpeter Henry 'Red' Allen, who was also appearing as a guest with Lucky Millinder: "We did a duet act with Lucky Millinder. Opened with *Muskrat Ramble*, closed with *The Saints* and in between Sidney did *September Song* and I took *Ride, Red Ride*."[8] The two star soloists produced some exciting music, but business was poor throughout the week. Bechet's name meant little to the average New Yorker.

For Bechet the highspot of the tour was his first visit to California. His initial engagement there was at the Down Beat Club in San Francisco, where he opened for a three-week season on 10 September 1953 (backed by Marty Marsala's band). Marty, an old friend of Bechet, led on trumpet, Skip Morr was on trombone, Bob Bates on bass, Robert 'Cuz' Cousineau on drums and (at various times) Larry Venucci or Johnny Wittwer on piano. George Walker also played drums on some of the band's dates.

Airshots from the club show that, despite the fact that he was again suffering from the digestive problems which had plagued him during his previous visit to the USA in 1951, Sidney was in fine form. Apparently he was less than happy with the band's performance and there were several instances of his glaring at those responsible for (what he considered to be) musical misdemeanours. Sidney had no quarrel with the way that Marty Marsala played, but Marty privately expressed disappointment that Bechet no longer doubled on clarinet.

The Down Beat (situated at 90 Market Street) was basically a club that catered for modern jazz fans, and appearing opposite Bechet was a group led by Buddy DeFranco (later Miles Davis led the group that shared the sessions). Happily the audiences accepted the various performances on their merit, without consulting their jazz history books. One person who listened to Bechet as often as he could at the club was the saxophonist and clarinettist George Probert, who said: "One of the big honors of my life was that Sidney took the time, on his first night off, to come and sit and listen to me and my band over in Oakland. He was very kind and friendly and I think that he was pleased that I, in no way, was attempting to try and imitate him. I think he was getting a little tired of this by this time in his life. I had the honor and privilege of driving him around the Bay Area on both his visits. He gave me little hints about breathing and holding the horn, but we really didn't get into music that much as he wasn't feeling well and just wanted to relax and see things."[9]

Although Probert has been listed as one of Bechet's accompanists on this West Coast trip he points out: "I never once played or recorded with him." But in September 1953 Probert was delighted to join Phil Elwood, Marty Marsala and Vivian Boarman in a KRE radio interview they conducted with Sidney. Bechet, who stayed on Bush in San Francisco, enjoyed a reunion with New Orleans trumpeter Lee Collins and his wife Mary during his stay. The three went on sight-seeing trips, which allowed Bechet to test yet another new camera.

For Bechet the most prestigious date of the whole tour was his appearance at the sixth annual Dixieland Jubilee, held on 3rd October at the Shrine Auditorium in Hollywood. In preparation for this gig Bechet went with George Probert to meet the group (led by trumpeter Bob Scobey) that was to accompany him on the concert: "I took Sidney to rehearse with this band and he did not seem too happy with the situation. All he would say, in a kindly manner, was: 'At least they play together.'"[10]

The audience of 6700 that packed the Los Angeles venue gave Bechet an ecstatic welcome; the programme notes, which said that Sidney ranked "with Louis Armstrong as a titan of jazz" must have pleased Bechet almost as much as the reception. Working alongside Bob Scobey on trumpet and Jack Buck on trombone, and supported by a four-piece rhythm section, Bechet announced his own numbers (after being introduced by promoter Gene Norman). There are no other soloists; the band simply provides a musical backdrop for the visiting giant. The four tunes that Bechet played were all old faithfuls on which, for the most part, he paraded his marvellously conceived stock phrases – the notable exception being *On the Sunnyside of the Street*. After warming up on a forceful version of *St Louis Blues* Bechet launches into an unforgettable rendering of the old ballad. It was a tune he had often played before, honing and polishing his phrases over the years to shape a set solo that usually stood him in good stead. But there at the Dixieland Jubilee (despite being in poor health) he produced a version in which all the elements of his masterful projection and imagination came together. It must be considered as one of the best performances of his life, revealing a burst of supreme inspiration. His last two numbers, a buoyant rendition of *Muskrat Ramble* and a smooth version of *Summertime*, were, by comparison, ordinary performances. Fortunately all four numbers were recorded and issued.

Sidney flew to Philadelphia and began a residency there on 4th October. When that ended he moved on to play a booking at George Wein's Storyville club in Boston, working with Vic Dickenson (trombone), Jimmy Woode (bass), Buzzy Drootin (drums) and Claude Hopkins (piano). On 25 October 1953 an impressive recording was made of the group in action at the club, but with George Wein on piano instead of Hopkins. Wein recalls the circumstances: "Claude was supposed to be on that Sunday afternoon recording, but he overslept or went out and forgot all about the date, so that's how I came into it. It was a very informal affair."[11]

This informality comes through on disc. Bechet, happy to be reunited with Vic Dickenson, is relaxed and inventive, sometimes urging Dickenson, and Wein, to take another chorus. Buzzy Drootin's robust drumming kicks things along, but some of his breaks sound tense; Woode's bass playing is precise and energetic. The recording quality is generally good but balance is variable, with Wein, Dickenson and Bechet all drifting out of focus occasionally. The resultant albums are a superior memento of an impressive club date, one in which there were more evergreens than war-horses.

During this period Bechet had one of his most memorable musical encounters. Writer Dan Morgenstern was on hand to describe it: "Boston was the setting of something I'll never forget: Art Tatum was working upstairs at Storyville and Sid was downstairs at Mahogany Hall, and on Sunday afternoons George Wein would have both bands at a matinée with a concluding jam session. In this case it was Art and Sidney and a rhythm section. They did *Lady be good*, and look out! Tatum did some striding that has never been captured on record or tape, and in the outchoruses he and Sidney just blew the tune apart – you know how both of them were in terms of taking back seats, but they got together that time and it was just incredible."[12]

Meanwhile Ruth Reinhardt, holding an injunction against Bechet, watched Sidney's progress throughout his tour with interest. His next move caused Ruth to bring the forces of the law into action. Sidney was booked to appear as a guest star in a package show that featured Woody Herman's orchestra and Billy Eckstine. Most of the show's dates were in and around Chicago, and thus Bechet moved into a working area covered by his contract with Jazz Ltd.

Bechet was featured in the package playing a few numbers with a small group drawn from Woody Herman's band, which consisted of the group's rhythm section and its bass trumpeter Cy Touff. There were no problems for Sidney; the rhythm section was flexible and the bass trumpet as unobtrusive as a trombone. The pianist in the group was Nat Pierce, who recalled: "We only played standard numbers, but I seem to remember we soon achieved a good blend. The group sounded okay, but business was terrible – lots of empty seats wherever we played."[13] One of the show's dates was a Sunday concert held in a Chicago high-school auditorium. Sidney had flown into the spider's web. Ruth Reinhardt alerted a bailiff, who turned up at the hall and enjoyed a sample of Bechet's music before serving the writ. Ruth Reinhardt later commented: "I couldn't believe that the guy could be so dumb as to ignore a court ruling, but I heard later that he thought that a legal order couldn't be served on a Sunday. He found out that he was wrong, and found out the hard way. I had every right to claim the 5000 dollars that the court awarded me for breach of contract, and I did."[14]

Bechet moved off with a heavy heart to play return bookings in California, but flew east as soon as he could. His stomach problems were further exacerbated, so he decided to cancel the rest of the tour and return to France to consult his own doctor. Once again a transatlantic flight worked wonders for him. He soon felt ready to start work again, which he did at the annual "Grand Nuit de Jazz" held on 19th December. He also began playing regularly at the Metro Club with bands led by André Réwéliotty and Michel Attenoux, and for one brief period (in late 1953 and early 1954) he doubled between the Metro and his own club, Chez Sidney Bechet.

Bechet, being Bechet, had long toyed with the idea of opening his own night-club (despite his earlier unhappy experience in that field of activity). His wife Elisabeth, who had had professional experience in the catering trade and was also an expert cashier, approved of the scheme. Bechet looked around and found a site for the club at 67 rue Pierre Charron (near the Champs-Elysées). It was not quite what he wanted but there was ample space for dancing, so he commissioned various people to tidy the place up and renovate it. Finally, on 23 December 1953, he and André Réwéliotty's band played at the official opening. Unhappily the club went the way of many of Bechet's other business enterprises. Various visitors, even those who went there when the club was spick and span, were unimpressed by the decor and the clientele. Singer Beryl Bryden visited the club and later described it as "a bit of a rough house" [15] The venue never developed a conducive atmosphere, and closed after a few months.

The loss that Bechet incurred was, in terms of his earnings, negligible. By then he was commanding good fees for personal appearances and these were supplemented by his record royalties (both as a performer and as a composer). But he needed a big income to keep his two homes going – one for his wife Elisabeth in Grigny, and one for his mistress, Jacqueline Pekaldi, in Paris.

In a session with Réwéliotty's band in May 1953 Sidney took the bold step of recording a composition each for Elisabeth and Jacqueline. *Jacqueline* comes off best. It is a slow romantic ballad, full of augmented chords that spice a strong melody. Bechet and trumpeter Guy Longnon (now regularly with Réwéliotty) are poignantly featured; a tinkling celeste adds to the mood of enchantment. In contrast *Elisabeth* begins with a blues theme, reminiscent of *Blues in the Night*. After two 12-bar ensembles the pattern changes into an eight-bar sequence, which is repeated; after that things revert to an unsurprising blues.

In the same session Bechet recorded a number of popular French songs, some of them in a sing-along manner, with the melody heavily stressed by each of the soloists. Trumpeter Longnon takes a less restricted approach on *Brave Margot*, and on *Pleure pas, Nelly* Bechet shows in the obbligato he creates alongside Réwéliotty's melody that he was still capable of playing lines of delicate beauty. During the 'cod' dialogue that heralds the start of *La complainte des infidels*, Bechet commands the ensemble to take a New Orleans approach to the tune; the resultant romp is highly effective, but most of the items from this date were aimed at Sidney's 'new' fans, rather that at those who were devout jazz listeners.

In January 1954 Bechet played for a fortnight's season at the Alhambra in Paris accompanied by Réwéliotty's band (he had toured France earlier that month with Michel Attenoux's orchestra). He moved on to Geneva in mid-February and worked with a band led by another of his dedicated followers, the Swiss soprano saxophonist Claude Aubert. The hyperactive Bechet moved out of Switzerland to work in Belgium with Attenoux (a concert in which they performed together was issued on record 30 years later), then zig-zagged back to Paris for a recording with Réwéliotty's band, before returning to Geneva for a month's work at the Palladium with Claude Aubert's band.

By then Aubert's band had been augmented by the arrival of another guest, clarinet player and cartoonist Wally Fawkes, who had taken temporary leave from Humphrey Lyttelton's band (and his newspaper job in London) to play the residency with Aubert and Bechet (which lasted from 11th March to 4th April). Fawkes spoke of the visit:

> I got to know Claude Aubert when Humph's band worked in Switzerland. He also played with us when he visited London. He called me and asked me to come over to work with Sidney for a month. I was determined to go. I managed to do the cartoon strip for weeks ahead, and good friends of mine at the *Daily Mail* kept their eyes on things and did my filling out. Humph agreed that it was chance not to be missed, so I travelled over to Geneva with my first wife and two children. I deliberately arrived a few days ahead of Bechet so that I could run through the repertoire with Claude and his pianist Henri Chaix.

When we had settled into an apartment, Bechet came to visit us; he was friendly and played happily with the children. The gig at the Palladium, which was a sort of night-club, ran from about 9 p.m. until 2 a.m. Each night I'd meet up with Claude. We'd have a few drinks, then go to call for Sidney at his hotel – he was alone on this trip. One night we couldn't get an answer, and, knowing that he was quite ill, we rang and rang because the hotel had confirmed that he was in. Suddenly there was a loud explosion of laughter. Sidney had heard us coming and had run up the stairs to hide. He came down helpless with laughter.

Most days you could tell he was in pain, and you knew it was wise to leave him alone. He wasn't drinking much, just the odd brandy. Suddenly he'd feel much better and would talk away happily. He always called me 'Sport', which was what he had called me in London, simply (I think) because he couldn't remember my name. But no matter what his mood was, he always seemed to play well – powerfully, and very loudly.

Sometime during the second week of the booking I suddenly came to the conclusion that it was no use just copying Bechet as I had been doing for a long time. I could hear the difference all too clearly, so from then on I tried to develop my own way. Bechet didn't give me any technical advice, but he wasn't averse to making direct comments. One night, during an ensemble, I worked in a George Lewis run that I'd heard on record. Bechet stopped playing and said very irately, "What do you think you're doing. Playing in a fucking brass band?". On another occasion he said, "If you had Claude's beat and Claude had your feeling then you'd make players who would be formidable for me to contend with". He also said, "You're trying too hard to tell the whole story of your life every time you take a solo. Tell them a little bit at a time".

He didn't improvise very much at the Palladium. He had arrived at a solo that made a grand impact and saw no reason to change it. But one night was full of pure improvisation. That was when we played at a sanitarium quite a way out of Geneva. There were no set-pieces, no concert solos; Bechet just picked out standards and blew some marvellous stuff on them. It was like a swing-era jam session. I've always thought that Bechet was a swing player, even before the swing era was ever heard of.[16]

Bechet continued to take a different approach on non-concert dates. He said, "A concert holds a guy very tense." He was also aware of the potency of his stock phrases: "You get sort of self-conscious about a little run that you did that the public just whooped and hollered at. You don't even care about it, but you come to it just to get this boom, boom, boom of applause. Oh it's great."[17] But at heart it seems he still preferred playing for a ballroom crowd: "They like to dance, and I'm not against it. You see, when you play people are supposed to act the way they feel. That's the way we played in New Orleans. People listened and they danced. I don't see why they should get so serious about it."[18]

When the Geneva booking ended Bechet moved on to play an engagement in Lucerne. Whilst in that Swiss city he received a telegram from l'Hôpital d'Asnièrnes in France telling him that Jacqueline Pekaldi had given birth to their son, Daniel, on 3rd April. Bechet finished his contracted tour, which took him across France, then eagerly took his first look at his son, whose birth was dramatically to change his domestic arrangements.

Sidney's wife Elisabeth accepted the situation with a certain calm. She was a stoic woman and not at all vicious ("She wouldn't harm a fly", said Claude Luter). She was resigned to Sidney's way of life and saw no objection to his continuing to maintain his apartment in Paris, but Jacqueline and Sidney decided that a spacious house was needed for the new infant to grow up in. Divorce was not contemplated; Sidney continued to spend time with Elisabeth at their home in Grigny, but their marriage was never the same again.

Despite the increased severity of his stomach pains, Bechet made little attempt to curtail his working schedule during the late spring of 1954, undertaking concerts in eastern France, Switzerland and Holland. He was due to be featured at a huge Jazz Fair to be held at the Salle Pleyel in Paris throughout the first week of June 1954, but during the early hours of 1st June he was taken seriously ill and transported to the American Hospital at Neuilly. Doctors stopped the haemorrhaging and operated on the ulcer.

For the first time in years Bechet was not his own master. He was ordered to lie quietly to facilitate his recovery, but he could not resist an invitation to address the audience at the Jazz Fair via the Duplex telephone system and tape recordings. He was immensely pleased by the news that negotiations were under way to present his ballet music on British television (the plan never materialized), and sent a message from his bed: "I have written my ballet. Now I can die in peace."[19]

Fortunately Sidney made a speedy recovery. He left hospital long before the month was out and began planning a new work schedule: He had been unable to play a planned season at Knokke, but hinted that he might be ready for Juan-les-Pins in August. Sure enough he was. Trumpeter Gilbert Thibout worked alongside Bechet there, and saw him making his recovery: "He was besides himself with joy at his daily improvement. He had been advised that the best way to repair his stomach was to eat very little, very often. Every couple of hours he'd order his favourite delicacies. He worked at his recovery like he worked at his music, conscientiously and with perseverance. In the evening he'd go out for a stroll, wearing his white dinner jacket, his butterfly-bow – and felt slippers. There was a certain malice in the way he took advantage of his state of health when playing poker with fellows in the band. If he saw that the play was likely to go against him he'd leave the game saying, 'Oh-la-la my old friends, I have a bad stomach'."[20]

By September 1954 he was back into the swing of things, and proved it by making some fine recordings with trumpeter Jonah Jones, who had spent the summer in Paris after being featured at the Jazz Fair that Bechet had been forced to miss. Accompanied by a French rhythm section – André Persiany on piano, Benoit Quersin on bass, and Marcel Blanche on drums – the two Americans tally superbly in producing several exceptional duets. Their performance of *Crazy Rhythm* is a model of relaxation; the solos are highly satisfying, but it is the compatibility of the ensembles that is so outstanding. Things do not go quite as smoothly on *Lonesome Road*; nevertheless there is some neat musical side-stepping by both of the stars. Bechet proves that his illness had not diminished his skills or his power; the blue notes are delivered as forcefully as ever, and his sudden sweeps into the upper octave remain awesomely impressive.

Somebody stole my gal and *When you wore a tulip* both have exhilarating moments, but neither could be considered a show-stopper; each is a fine example of two jazz players working successfully in tandem. Jonah Jones plays boldly without sounding brash, and Bechet responds to the trumpeter's firmness and control by moving away from the centre stage at exactly the right moment. Sidney's tone had not yet regained its former fullness, but the reedy sound he produces on this session has its own astringent charm. *When you wore a tulip* and *Chinatown, my Chinatown* were issued in both long and short versions; on the briefer takes Jones and Persiany forfeit their solos. In general the extended takes are more interesting but some of the most stirring playing on the date comes from the truncated version of *Chinatown*.

Pianist André Persiany gets a chance to demonstrate his locked-hands style on *Squeeze me*, which also has a majestic solo by Bechet and an ingenious final chorus in which the two front-line partners play a delightfully understated re-vamp of the melody. Throughout the session Bechet and Jones continued to work easily together, sometimes deliberately playing call-and-answer phrases, but more often one paraphrasing an idea that the other had created a few bars earlier. The January 1955 issue of the French magazine *Jazz hot* gave the recordings a glowing review, commenting on the merits of having Jonah Jones working "with our own Sidney".

Bechet resumed his old schedules with a vengeance and returned to work at the Vieux Colombier with Claude Luter's orchestra. Just before he did so he enjoyed a reunion with Clarence Williams's daughter, Irene, who was starring in a touring version of *Porgy and Bess*. Irene said at the time: "Sidney has always known me. Even when I was a little kid. He was a friend of the family and used to rock me in his arms."[21] Irene was amongst the crowds who turned out to see and hear Sidney working again in St Germain.

Dick Hughes, the Australian pianist and writer, also visited the Vieux Colombier during the autumn of 1954. In his book *Daddy's Practising Again*, Hughes wrote of the dramatic way in which Bechet entered the club: "I've never seen such a little bloke with such a determined walk. He couldn't help knowing he was IT. Like Louis Armstrong and Duke Ellington he radiated greatness." Hughes cemented his acquaintanceship with Bechet and arranged to interview him for Australian radio. The two men shared a bottle of champagne and Bechet confided that following his operation he had been advised to wear a surgical corset in case the vigour of his blowing undid the operation scars. During the subsequent radio interview Bechet said that 'Big Eye' Louis Nelson was the best clarinettist he had ever heard, and that his favourite contemporary players were Benny Goodman and Edmond Hall. During his visits to the Vieux Colombier, Dick Hughes was fascinated by Bechet's rendering of his own composition *A moi de payer*. Eventually Hughes recorded the tune (under the title of *The Pay Off*) and gained a place in the Australian hit parade.

Bechet's stay that October at the Vieux Colombier was deliberately brief. He left the club to undertake a 40-day tour of North Africa. After his return to Paris he shared equal billing with Claude Luter's orchestra for a concert at the Olympia on 8th December. It was his first concert in Paris for two years and it proved to be a huge success. Once again Vogue took recordings of the concerts and issued the results, most of which were spirited re-creations of numbers that

Bechet and Luter had previously recorded together. They had not re-established a permanent working association, but there were plans afoot for them to act together in a movie with Viviane Romance. The film world also beckoned Sidney in another way; he was invited to write the music for a short movie, *Fantasia for a Mouse*.[22]

In a brief respite from his travels, Bechet played for another short stint at the Vieux Colombier before undertaking a wide-ranging tour of France and Switzerland, which included a musical reunion with Albert Nicholas at the Palladium, Geneva, on 19 December 1954. Nicholas had moved to France, at Bechet's suggestion, in October 1953. Sidney had warmly recommended his skills to Charles Delaunay and to various other French entrepreneurs, and these commendations made it easy for Albert to find enough work to settle in Europe. Bechet and Nicholas's initial reunions on French soil were filled with warm nostalgia, but gradually the love-hate relationship that has tattooed so many friendships between old New Orleanians began to surface. All that is needed to start such a rift is a single grudge, and Albert soon developed one concerning Bechet's highly successful recording of *Les oignons*. Albert was always quick to inform sympathetic ears that he had recorded the tune way back in June 1947, "long before Bechet ever had the idea". Sometimes envy got the better of Nicholas. On one such occasion he said to Humphrey Lyttelton: "Everybody talks about Bechet did this and Bechet did that. Listen, when we were making all that jazz history, Bechet wasn't even there."[23]

Bechet, ever watchful for a flicker of animosity, soon spotted it in Nicholas's eyes and responded with a glare. Thereafter the two men often acted as though they scarcely knew each other. Lyttelton, unaware of this shift in attitudes, met up with Bechet and asked, "And how is Albert?" Sidney's reply took a long time coming. "He didn't exactly say Albert WHO? But he came fairly close to it", admits Lyttelton, who described Bechet and Nicholas as being "separated by a chasm of animosity heavily tinged with admiration".[24]

Somewhile later another of Bechet's old friends from New Orleans, drummer Paul Barbarin, became decidedly angry over losing the credit for a tune that Bechet played. British bandleader Monty Sunshine recalled the background:

> On my first trip to New Orleans I heard Paul Barbarin's band play a marvellous tune. To smooth over any slight delay that might occur as Paul made his way to the front to make announcements the band played a brief part of this theme, then, at the end of the session, they played the whole tune. I asked Paul what it was called and he said, "That's *I keep calling your name*. I wrote that with Sidney Bechet a long while ago". I asked him to send me the music, which he kindly did. Then one day I heard Sidney's recording of *En attendant la jour*, which was the same tune. I looked into this and found there was no mention of Paul Barbarin's name. It seems that by this time Paul had made the same discovery. He went to the musicians' union and then to the publishers and eventually got his share of the royalties.[25]

Bechet seems to have been unduly worried that Albert Nicholas in residence might in some way usurp the position he held with the French public – a highly unlikely proposition. As a rule Sidney never failed to be helpful to American musicians in Paris, provided they were not stopping. In late 1954 when trumpeter Lee Collins was taken ill in France he found Bechet kind and helpful, and said in his autobiography *Oh didn't he ramble*: "I knew those Creoles would not let me down." Jonah Jones was always grateful for the friendly advice that Bechet gave him during his stay in France. But even temporary visitors sometimes had to be wary. Buck Clayton, appearing on the same bill as Sidney, innocently played *Muskrat Ramble* only to be confronted by a furious Bechet, who thought that Buck was trying to steal some of his glory.

Bill Coleman, a naturally affable man, never settled into an easy friendship with Bechet, despite both of them being expatriates. Bill was determined never to be manoeuvred into a situation where Bechet had the power to be autocratic. On one occasion, when someone was lavishly praising Bechet's work with a European band, Bill could not stop himself making a very untypical remark: "He's only happy when he can bark orders at amateurs."[26]

Benny Waters, like Albert Nicholas, settled in France in 1953. He went round the jazz clubs in Paris introducing himself, sitting in wherever he could. At the Vieux Colombier he made the mistake of playing soprano saxophone: "I had been playing soprano regularly with Bob Wilber's band in Boston, so when Claude Luter offered me his soprano to use it seemed natural to blow a few numbers on it." Bechet soon got to hear of the enthusiastic reception that had greeted Benny's guest appearance. A few days later Waters met up with Bechet in a backstage dressing room. Sidney got out his revolver and started to polish it, saying in an ominous fashion, "I never know when I might have to use this, you know." Benny concentrated on playing the tenor saxophone and clarinet for some while afterwards.[27]

In 1954, after playing engagements in Switzerland, Humphrey Lyttelton and his pianist Johnny Parker paid a visit to Sidney in Paris before they returned to London. At that time Bechet was the Honorary President of the Humphrey Lyttelton Club. The two British musicians did not have Sidney's current address, but called into Gabbi's Restaurant, where they were given his telephone number. Sidney invited the visitors round to his apartment, where they found him in company with Jacqueline and baby Daniel. Sidney asked what had brought them to Paris and was told about the gigs in Switzerland. The word 'Switzerland' caused an instant domestic explosion; Jacqueline mistakenly received the impression that the two visitors were acting as couriers, bringing a clandestine message from Bechet's Swiss girl-friend. Parker recalls: "She went bananas." Lyttelton also remembers the passionate wrath: "She really shrieked at Bechet, but he didn't look at all hangdog. In fact a gleam came into his eye at the prospect of aggro."[28] As there seemed little chance of instant calm returning to the apartment, Bechet led the visitors downstairs to meet Lil Hardin, and there Johnny Parker was prevailed upon to play Lil's piano. He was soon joined at the keyboard by Bechet, and the two played piano duets, which were captured on Lil Hardin's wire recorder.

Once again Bechet had proved that he could be charm itself when entertaining visitors to France. Big Bill Broonzy always spoke with gratitude of the way in which Sidney had helped him during his early days in Paris. Bill had apparently resigned himself to eating ham and eggs throughout his stay in France, as that was all he could manage to order in French. His luck and his diet changed thanks to the guidance of Bechet, who, according to Broonzy, taught him the French words for "food, drink and women".[29]

TWENTY-FOUR

The Birth of a Ballet

Bechet's main place of employment during the early months of 1955 was the Vieux Colombier, where he played with Claude Luter's band. But, as before, the club only served as a central base for a formidable touring schedule, which included a trip in January 1955 to Brussels to appear (with Luter's orchestra) at the Palais des Beaux-Arts. Despite their long association and the friendship they shared, Sidney could still be aggravatingly suspicious in the financial dealings he had with Luter. The latter recalls that the trip to Belgium provided a prime example of Bechet's untrusting nature:

> Sidney asked me to change some money for him from French francs into Belgian. I did exactly as he asked and kept his money entirely separate from mine, but when I handed his over, saying so many francs at such-and-such a rate, he went mad with rage and thrust a newspaper at me which gave the previous day's rate. The rate had changed overnight, which meant that the French franc was worth slightly less than the figure that the newspaper had printed. I patiently explained this to Sidney, but he wouldn't listen and insisted that I was trying to rob him. The amount involved was absolutely tiny, but he went on and on until finally I too got angry. It wasn't a happy tour, but when we got back Sidney had the nerve to go to Charles Delaunay and say that I had been unpleasant to him in Belgium. It was not the sort of row that could break up a friendship, but it did show how his mind worked on certain matters. I think that we became better friends after we had finished working together regularly – we became closer. The reason why we stopped working with him on a regular basis was money. We knew Bechet was the star, no question of that, but we wanted a better share of the fees.[1]

The trip to Belgium helped publicize a television transmission in that country of *La nuit est une sorcière*. It was one of the few notable presentations that the work achieved, but it was enough to set Bechet talking about his plans for writing another extended work. He said, with some irony: "I want to call it 'The Mississippi', but they want to link it with the River Seine, and, believe me, they are not the same thing."[2]

Most of the long tours which Bechet undertook in 1955 were with André Réwéliotty's orchestra, including a spring jaunt that took them through many hundreds of miles of France and Belgium (where they played a brief residency at Knokke). Sidney also found time to visit Switzerland to play for a broadcast with a quartet led by one of his favourite European musicians, painist Henri Chaix.

In Paris impresario Bruno Coquatrix had recently reintroduced jazz concerts at his vast hall, Olympia. Many of them featured Bechet, including one held in March 1955 to celebrate the 20th anniversary of the magazine *Jazz hot*. On the occasion of another Olympia concert Bechet took a look at the billing and saw that his name was not printed in the largest type available. He promptly said that violent stomach-ache would prevent him from going on, but after Coquatrix had filled the 'number one' dressing room with flowers Sidney made a swift recovery and went on stage to dazzle the audience.[3]

It was a period of intense activity for Sidney, but somehow he found time to act in the film *L'inspecteur connaît la musique*, in which his role demanded that he was murdered by fellow-actor Claude Luter. The murder weapon was a clarinet, and Bechet repeatedly asked Luter to make sure that he did not hit him for real when the cameras started rolling. This apprehension apart, Bechet revelled in his work on the film set, and the experience was often retold to various people he met during his subsequent season with Luter's band at the Vieux Colombier in Juan-les-Pins.

The biggest event of that year for Sidney was the first full production of *La nuit est une sorcière*. The music had been performed previously on various occasions, including one at the Salle de l'Opéra on 17 March 1955 in front of the President of France, Rene Coty (Bechet also played for the President at the Elysées Palace). But in early September 1955, at the Théâtre des Champs-Elysées, the première of the full production (with choreography by Harold Lander) took place. A cast including Claire Sombert, Pierre Lacotte, Arthur Bell, Irene Bamziger and Guy Laine had rehearsed endlessly; their efforts were rewarded by a tremendously enthusiastic reception. Bechet, who played his brief interludes within the score, was accorded nine curtain calls.

After having his photograph taken with the guest of honour, the film star Gina Lollobrigida, Sidney took the opportunity of optimistically announcing that he had decided on a title, "A Delta's Mood", for his next ballet. But despite the warmth of the first night audience, future ticket sales were extremely disappointing; the ballet soon closed and plans for a quick follow-up were shelved.

For Sidney the resultant dismay was allayed by the onset of a prestigious concert held in his honour at Olympia on 19 October 1955. This free occasion was paid for by Vogue to commemorate the fact that record sales by Bechet in France had topped 1,350,000. Thousands attempted to get into the concert to pay homage to Sidney, and the celebrations in the streets unfortunately turned into a riot; police reinforcements were called in from various other sectors of Paris.

Those lucky enough to gain admission shouted with delight when Charles Delaunay presented Sidney with a leather pouch containing a gold record achieved by the sales of *Les oignons*. In his speech, Delaunay pointed out that no foreign artist had ever sold more than a million records in France before. It was an emotional moment, but the behaviour of fans in the hall, who had already destroyed two hundred seats, got almost out of hand, and it was thought wisest to drop the fire curtain as soon as Sidney had played his final note.

Bechet was in a high state of excitement after the concert and decided to go out to celebrate. But he went alone, as he often did, even at this stage of his fame. Much as he enjoyed dining in the finest restaurants, he also liked to drop in to various less plush haunts for a drink and a gossip. Often he went out of his way to seek the company of a fellow black American. He did so after the 'gold disc' concert, calling on Bill Coleman, who was working at the Trois Mailletz club. Bechet virtually insisted that Bill accompany him on a drinking spree after that club closed. Bill pointed out that he would have to take a taxi home, but Bechet waved aside that excuse by promising to drive Coleman back. At the end of their drunken travels through the clubland of Paris Bechet had totally forgotten his promise, and Bill Coleman had to pay for his taxi journey home.

In November 1955 the need to meet up with musicians from his homeland again made itself felt within Bechet, and he decided to attend Louis Armstrong's All Stars' concert at the Olympia. Many other expatriate jazzmen, including Albert Nicholas, Peanuts Holland and Bill Coleman, went along; so too did Mezz Mezzrow. The English pianist Johnny Parker made his way backstage with Bechet, where they found Mezzrow standing guard at the door of Armstrong's dressing room. "You can go in", said Mezzrow to Parker, but turning to Bechet he hissed, "Louis doesn't want to see you." Bechet walked away fuming, and said, "Mezzrow is going to have to kiss my arse before I ask his permission to go and meet my old friend Louis Armstrong."[4]

Yet when Mezzrow's views appeared in print during this period he invariably praised Bechet: "There are plenty of people who think Bechet is simply marking time. But you know I think it is playing with the French rhythm sections who don't push him enough, also there is not enough competition here and this is why he often re-sifts the same clichés but I also think he is always great and magnificently sonorous."[5]

By the end of 1955 Bechet had completed tours of Italy and Germany accompanied by André Réwéliotty's orchestra. As the concert queues grew, Sidney's practice of playing set solos solidified. In earlier years there had always been informal occasions where he could take chances and explore new ideas, but such events were becoming increasingly rare. Yet no one hearing Bechet's solos of the mid-1950s would suspect that they were not improvised. Sidney, like Louis Armstrong, had a gift of projecting phrases with such feeling that the listener automatically assumed that they were improvised. But in the recording studio, with Réwéliotty's band, Bechet strived for freshness by tackling new material. He did so in a session on 5th December and again later that month for a date on which one of his ace pupils, clarinettist René Franc, replaced Réwéliotty.

Bechet's routine of working part of the winter at the Vieux Colombier with Luter's orchestra re-established itself. Some cynical onlookers felt that both the star soloist and his accompanying musicians appeared, and sounded, bored – fatigued by repetition. But most French musicians who worked with Bechet look back with affection, regarding the time that they spent with Sidney as an enriching experience, both musically and personally. Luter's trombonist, Bernard Zacharias, who worked regularly with Bechet during the early 1950s, is typical: "Nothing could be more satisfying for me than to recall a period of my life which left me with such joyful memories. The way that Sidney Bechet closely mixed the seriousness of his work with his good humour and love of life is almost impossible to express. Whether it be by the way he tapped Moustache [the drummer] on the head with his soprano during rehearsals ('il ne faut pas espérer pour pratiquer, mon vieux') or by the jokes he loved to make whenever he could, such as in Nancy, where, after a concert, he gave bassist Roland Bianchini a sandwich without ham in it (having eaten it himself), his cars, his women, his passion, or his parties. . . ."[6]

At the Vieux Colombier a steady trek of visiting musicians sat in with Luter's band, though they were rarely invited to do so during one of Bechet's sets. Lionel Hampton, who was visiting Paris to play for a concert at Olympia in January 1956, was a notable exception. Sidney and Luter's group spent part of January and February 1956 playing in various towns for premières of the film L'inspecteur connaît le musique (which was given mixed reviews by the popular press). As in the previous spring, Bechet undertook a two-month tour with Réwéliotty's band, sometimes playing two shows a day on a wide-ranging trip that took them all over France. Almost without taking breath the group and its star moved off to play a series of 15 galas in North Africa.

In May 1956 Bechet enjoyed a happy reunion with his old friend pianist Sammy Price, who was touring Europe with his Bluesicians: Emmett Berry (trumpet), George Stevenson (trombone), Herbert Hall (clarinet), Fred Moore (drums) and Pops Foster (bass). As ever, when meeting visitors, Sidney was at his jolliest. Price says: "I found Sidney just the same as ever, except he was rich!"[7] On the eve of its departure for home the band recorded a selection of tried-and-true numbers with Bechet; the notable exceptions were Yes we have no bananas and Back Home.

The disappointments of the session are not connected with the solos, which range from workaday efforts by Stevenson to crisply played gems by Berry, but with the ensembles, which sound messy and haphazard. Bechet adopts a vigorous approach, and performs with unmistakable panache. His intonation in the high register is persistently, but not disastrously, sharp and his tone is not as mellow as usual; however, he certainly sounds as though he is enjoying himself. The American band had just played a private engagement in Paris, at which one of Sidney's old flames passed on a message. Sidney received this with obvious pleasure, and said: "My, my, what a gal. I used to have a fine time with her when I was young – about three years ago."

At this stage of his life, Sidney was often caught in between two stools on the question of age. Because he wanted to appear as a patriarchal jazz figure he became evasive when anyone tried to ascertain his exact date of birth, but on the other hand he still loved to charm the ladies and did not want them to regard him as a grandfather figure. He could still bristle perceptively if anyone remarked that one of his accompanying musicians looked young and handsome, and, though he mistrusted doctors, it is fairly certain that during his visits to Switzerland he consulted a Dr Voronov for advice on retaining his sexual potency.

There was no question of Bechet's moving into a lower gear as he approached his sixtieth birthday. Whenever he had to attend a morning business meeting with Charles Delaunay, the latter always got the impression that Sidney hadn't been to bed, but had used the morning appointment as an excuse to stay up all night, gallivanting around Paris. Kurt Mohr (nicknamed Spo-De-Odee by Bechet) remembers Sidney's visits:

Bechet often used to drop in at the office of Vogue records, where I had a job. Charles Delaunay was there too, in a more eminent position, and we often tried to induce Bechet to reminisce about the 'way back when' days, and obscure records. Bechet willingly complied, but his souvenirs of precise personnels usually tended to be vague. Obviously his mind was more centred on girls, money, and other trivia than on such crucial topics as 'who played second trumpet . . . ?' I never assisted at a Bechet recording session, but I know it was hard work. I'm talking about the sessions with Claude Luter and André Réwéliotty's bands. The musicians came back exhausted, but always respectful of their leader. Bechet wore that wry smile: 'You gotta push 'em boy, or else you won't get nothing.'[8]

Bechet had no qualms about going along with a big publicity campaign that Vogue mounted during the summer of 1956, ostensibly to celebrate the great man's jubilee as a professional musician. But despite a half century of energetic blowing, Bechet was still eager to get back to work. Charles Delaunay observed Sidney's delight as he cast his eyes down a long list of future engagements: "He was determined to be kept busy, and this is why he accepted reasonable fees. He felt it was better to work regularly than to play occasionally for huge fees, so we played many small towns that might not have been able to afford a big price. But in those small places the people turned out in their hundreds and we were immediately offered a return booking for the following year. I think this policy played a part in making Sidney Bechet such a national figure. Usually Sidney took half of the fee; the other half was divided up amongst the band members."[9]

Most of Bechet's touring in the mid-1950s was done with André Réwéliotty's orchestra, which occasionally had to undergo changes of personnel as various of its members were conscripted for military service. Such was the case when cornetist Marcel Bornstein (who left to serve for 16 months in the forces) was replaced by trumpeter Guy Longnon. Bornstein feels that he never really got to know Bechet, but says: "I shall always retain memories of a man who was unpretentious and very sensitive, one who kept his distance from the entourage."[10] Pianist Yannick Singery's stay with Réwéliotty was also interrupted by military service (he was replaced by Eddie Bernard), but he subsequently rejoined the band. Singery (whose father was from Mauritius) spoke English fluently and came to know Bechet better than most of his colleagues. On tour he usually travelled in Bechet's huge black Lincoln (driven by tour manager Claude Wolff). Singery told Jean-Roland Hippenmeyer about those days:

To me Sidney Bechet is probably the musician who most impressed me. We were young French amateurs and to be able to play with him was so amazing and unexpected. We got on well together, though sometimes we had little arguments. I worked with Réwéliotty for almost eight years and saw Bechet almost every day. Sidney was a very possessive person, who not only took charge of the music but also of our lives. For example, Sidney used to like to walk around towns when we were on tour. He would get up early to do so, but everyone had to get up to accompany him. He'd come and knock at eight o'clock in the morning, even after a late night, and we had to walk around with him window-shopping. At first we didn't say anything, but then it became too much. So these arguments were not about music, we were his great admirers, he was so far above us.[11]

Bechet rarely drove whilst on tour, but he never lost his love of big cars. After his Cadillac, Salmson and Talbot, he finally bought a Lincoln. He enjoyed driving fast on open roads, but Claude Luter always felt that Sidney was ultra-careful when driving within a city: "He never got used to the traffic in Paris. If you travelled with him then, it felt as he was driving at four miles an hour. He bought a Talbot, which had pre-selected gears, but he never got used to it. He stayed in first gear all the time, and in a few months he'd murdered it."[12]

By 1956 Sidney's record sales in France were comparable with those of the leading pop stars. The release of his albums was accompanied by a big publicity campaign; material thought suitable for single release was extracted and then plugged heavily on the radio. Such was the case with tunes from the film *Coquin de boubou*, in which Bechet and Réwéliotty's band appeared; one of these, *Passport to Paradise*, is amongst the loveliest of all Bechet's compositions. But, despite the merits of the tune, Sidney's recording is disappointing. The tempo appears to be a trifle fast, but the main problem is caused by Bechet's intonation, which seems unduly taxed; as a result his vibrato loses its expressiveness and instead sounds distractingly wide.

Bechet and Réwéliotty had previously appeared together in *Série noire*. In that film Bechet had a brief acting role. One of its stars was another figure who had gained considerable fame in France in the late stages of his career, actor Erich von Stroheim. Unlike Stroheim, Bechet was still getting offers to work in the United States, but, as in previous years, Sidney ignored these chances, feeling certain that after a few prestigious concert dates he would be back on the arduous club circuit. But Sidney still spoke of the USA as home, and told one reporter: "I was in this place with some French movie people and a bunch of Frenchmen were drunk and raising a riot. The manager comes up and says to them, 'Behave yourself. Don't disgrace your country. You want people to think you're a bunch of Americans?' Well, I called him on that and he said, 'Oh, I don't mean you. I mean white Americans'. That's when I let him have it. He thought that was gonna go over great with me, but it made me sore. He was talking about my country and my friends. I sure gave it to that son-of-a-bitch. I live in France because that's where I can make a living. If I could make out with money back home, I'd be back in New York tomorrow."[13]

Despite these sentiments, Sidney showed no signs of returning to the USA. He did, however, agree to revisit Britain for a tour in 1956. The British Musicians' Union had finally worked out a system of exchanges with the American Federation of Musicians, which meant that Bechet, as a member of New York Local 802, could officially tour Britain. In exchange, a British group led by saxophonist Tommy Whittle went to the States. Bechet was accompanied by André Réwéliotty's orchestra throughout the hectic tour, which covered many miles and four countries – England, Wales, Scotland and Northern Ireland. He flew in on 1st September and opened the tour at London's Royal Albert Hall on the following day, playing to 7000 people. The show moved on to Norwich (3rd), Wolverhampton (4th), Cardiff (5th), Bristol (6th), Leicester (7th), Birmingham (8th), Manchester (9th), Newcastle (10th), Glasgow (11th), York

(12th), Belfast (13th), Liverpool (14th), and Sheffield (15th), ending at the Royal Festival Hall, London, on 16th September.

Humphrey Lyttelton's band (minus Wally Fawkes, who had just left the group) played the first half of the concerts for most of the tour, and also took part in a grand finale which involved a mobile version of *The Saints*, where the combined Réwéliotty–Lyttelton front lines (and Sidney) paraded crocodile-style for the audience. Lyttelton recalls:

> It was wonderful to see Bechet again, but when I looked at him I thought to myself, "I wonder if he'll be able to manage this tour". He looked so old and tired, but he saved all of his energy, or most of it, for the stage. When we travelled together he sat quietly on the band coach. He was always polite when anyone asked him questions, but he answered them very slowly. But then he'd suddenly surprise you. One day he was twisting his knuckles round to make a reflection of them in the chromium cup that was on the back of a coach seat. One felt obliged to ask what he was doing. He gave out a huge grin and said, "If the light catches your hand right, it looks just like a nude woman bending over her bath". There didn't seem to be much close camaraderie between him and Réwéliotty's band, but that's no wonder, because he seemed to treat them like a tyrant.
>
> He didn't drink much on that tour, but he pushed the boat out after we had played in Birmingham. After the concert a woman went to Bechet's hotel room and said, "Mr Bechet, I want to talk to you about your wonderful music". Sidney told us that his reply was, "That's okay with me. Take your clothes off and we'll talk". The resultant exchange put Bechet in a celebratory mood and next day we all had to drink with him.[14]

Drama occurred early in the tour. At Norwich some of the keys on Bechet's soprano saxophone stopped working and Sidney had to borrow an instrument from a local musician. The trouble recurred at Leicester. A replacement instrument was sent for, but didn't arrive in time. Undeterred, Bechet went on stage as though nothing was amiss. Lyttelton's reed player, Bruce Turner, could hardly believe his ears at the marvellous music that Bechet produced, despite being unable to use half of the instrument's keys: "It was almost like an act of Zen. Bechet willed himself to create notes that weren't really there on the instrument."[15]

For most of his life Bechet adopted a devil-may-care approach to his musical equipment. Zutty Singleton could not help but speak admiringly of the way he had seen Bechet make a reed from part of a cigar box in an early emergency. British musician Noel 'Chappie' D'Amato saw Bechet do something similar in London in 1920. Sidney, who had used up his last reed, nonchalantly razored a slice off a plywood matchbox and used that in his mouthpiece.

On the tour in 1956 Lyttelton's pianist, Johnny Parker, found Bechet affable, even jovial, during the day, but noticed that he became distinctly edgy as performance time approached:

> We played at the Rialto in York. By that time we had heard Sidney's show several times and decided to go out for a drink before we had to reassemble for the finale. Bechet spied us going out and said commandingly, "Don't be late back". We had a drink but decided to return immediately to the hall. As we crossed the car park we heard Sidney playing his final number; he'd cut his programme by 15 minutes to try and catch us out.

But when Sidney was in a relaxed mood he was wonderful company. At the Adelphi Hotel in Liverpool I sat in his room for hours as he talked of this and that. He showed me the criss-cross of abdominal scars that had resulted from his operation, all the while assuring me that he had never felt better in his life. The discussion turned to Louis Armstrong and Sidney said, "We're not on friendly terms". I asked why, and to my surprise he replied, "I'm unhappy about the way Louis treated Bunk Johnson. In the old days we used to smuggle Louis in to hear Bunk play, but now Louis says only Joe Oliver helped him. Well, Joe Oliver wasn't that sort of person. He wouldn't bother himself with helping anyone out. He was a mean type of guy, but Louis keeps saying he helped him, and not Bunk".[16]

Liverpool marked the spot where Réwéliotty's pianist, Eddie Bernard, and Bechet fell out. The show's entourage had been invited to a party organized by the local Merseysippi Jazz Band. Lyttelton's contingent accepted with alacrity, but Bechet declined the offer; this meant, *ipso facto*, that the members of Réwéliotty's band were not to attend the gathering. However, Eddie Bernard, whose association with Bechet had been long and often stormy, decided to break the 'rules' and go to the party. Bechet expected all of the French musicians to sit down with him for a late meal at the hotel and then follow his example by going off to bed. On this occasion Bernard went through the routine but then slipped away to the party, making his entrance there by announcing, "Fuck Bechet!"[17]

Next day Lyttelton shared morning coffee with Sidney. After a few sips Bechet said: "I hear Eddie enjoyed his party last night. If I had not been so tired I would have gone to that party to fetch him back myself." Bernard stood up to Bechet on various occasions. Sidney showed tolerance towards him because he liked his playing, but, according to mutual friends, Bechet always got his own back by behaving spitefully towards Bernard. Years later Eddie Bernard took a philosophical view of the contretemps by saying that he had to cease working with Bechet in order to preserve a respect for his enormous talents.

British bandleader Chris Barber heard Bechet perform in Northern Ireland:

> We had just finished a tour and went along to hear Bechet's concert at the Ulster Hall, Belfast. As we stood outside we saw Bechet's entourage arrive. A crowd of curiosity seekers had attached themselves to the jazz fans who had stood waiting for a sight of Bechet. One of these onlookers said, "Who is he?" pointing to Sidney. Another answered, "He's been brought over to wrestle Dirty Pye" [Jack Pye, 1901–85, a famous British wrestler].
>
> A local band joined in the finale, and its trumpet player obviously hadn't been told that Bechet insisted on playing the last note of *The Saints* for longer than anyone else on stage. The local musician did his manful best to carry on when everyone except Bechet had deliberately dropped out. I'll never forget the steely look, like a flashing knife-blade, with which Sidney got him to shut up.[18]

Bechet's demonic anger had shown itself on stage during a previous concert, at Manchester, also during *The Saints*. Bechet signalled local bass player Eric Batty forward to take a solo. Batty, well aware of his limitations, appeared to decline, but Bechet insisted. To show willing, Batty decided to sing a chorus, but no sooner had he warbled, "Oh, when . . .", than Bechet's soprano came down through the air like a dervish's scimitar, making Batty fully aware that his efforts were no longer required.

The tour ended at the Royal Festival Hall, where Bechet had a reunion with Maxwell Knight, the 'M' figure whom Bechet had not seen for almost 40 years. Sidney always had a poor memory for names, but his capacity for recalling sounds and faces was quite exceptional. As soon as he saw Knight in 1956 he said, "You were the fellow I sold a bass clarinet to. Do you want to sell it back to me?"[19] Bandleader Eddie Gross Bart had a similar story to tell after meeting Bechet at Juan-les-Pins. The two men had not seen each other for more than 30 years, but Bechet walked straight up and said, "Man, I played at your wedding in February 1921." In Munich during the 1950s, drummer Willi Mac Allen hesitated about contacting Bechet because the two men hadn't met since 1929, in Berlin. He telephoned Sidney and was flabbergasted when Bechet immediately recognized his voice.

Chris Barber's band took part in Bechet's Royal Festival Hall concert in September 1956, but a month later a contingent from the band played a much more important role in Sidney's life. A quartet, including clarinettist Monty Sunshine, recorded a version of Bechet's composition *Petite fleur*, which became a best-selling single throughout the world. Monty Sunshine discovered the song almost by accident: "I was on holiday in Spain, and an accordionist in a bar I went to always seemed to be playing *Petite fleur*. The melody stuck in my head as 'holiday tunes' sometimes do, but I never even asked what the piece was called. Months later I was driving home from a gig and heard on the car radio Bechet's version of *Petite fleur*. It was my 'holiday tune' so I got the record and learnt the melody."[20] Speaking of the recording, Chris Barber said: "It was done almost as an afterthought. Monty hadn't quite got the structure of the tune right, so our version had an extra bar – one more than the Bechet version. And because Monty's record player went at a fast speed he learnt it in A flat minor instead of Bechet's key of G minor. We found out later, but never bothered to change it."[21]

Bechet returned to France to find that his popularity was still in the ascendant. His record sales were booming, his concerts sold out as soon as they were announced, and it seemed as though almost every French radio station was continually playing Bechet's music. In October 1956 a Bechet Fan Club was organized in Paris. Following its inauguration a celebration was held aboard the *Coche d'eau* on the River Seine.

The general public in America was hardly aware of any of this acclaim, though any Americans who travelled to France were soon enlightened. A visitor from the USA was quoted as saying: "Sidney could have become mayor of Paris if he wanted to. Crowds of people followed him through the streets. I was never so surprised in my whole life as when I discovered that a compatriot, whom I had barely heard of, had become the darling of the French. And I was quite embarrassed when asked questions by the French about Sidney and was unable to answer. They didn't understand as an American I was so little informed about their idol."[22]

Ernie Anderson, visiting Paris, met up with Bechet: "He was a celebrity, no doubt about that, and his fame brought him even more success with women – his sexual activity was tremendous. He introduced me to five women and it was obvious that he was involved with each of them. One of them was a blonde model, aged only about 20; her mother was there to chaperone her, but from what I gathered Bechet was keeping both of them happy. He saw me look in amazement, and said, with a wink, 'I did it all with my horn'."[23]

The Bechet touring machine rolled on throughout the winter of 1956–7, visiting Germany and Italy and making massive tours of France. For a concert in March 1957 at the Salle Pleyel, Bechet and Réwéliotty's musicians dressed up as undertakers to give the première of Bechet's new composition, *New Orleans*. The fans went wild with delight.

In March and June 1957 Bechet startled his fans by recording an album with one of the leading modernists of that era, pianist Martial Solal. Algerian-born Solal, who was in his late twenties, didn't know Bechet well, but went along with recording plans devised by Charles Delaunay, who said: "I had a brainwave to pair Bechet and Solal with a good rhythm section. The contrast in styles worked marvellously, but I think the results could have been even better if Sidney had bothered to rehearse more. He liked the idea of working with Solal very much, but when it came to the sessions he was impatient to get on with things."[24]

As in most of Sidney's latter-day recordings, there are some superb moments; the pity is that such a session hadn't taken place when he was at the peak of his powers. Solal backs Bechet confidently and displays a profusion of ideas during his dextrous solos. The drummer for the March session was Al Levitt; on the June date it was Bechet's ex-sideman Kenny Clarke. The French bass player Pierre Michelot played alongside Clarke, but Levitt's partner on bass was the Canadian Lloyd Thompson. Both combinations produce what may be described as the sound of a welterweight rhythm section.

Most of Sidney's performances on the album are laced with care; on *All the things you are* he comes as close to sounding cautious as he ever did. The process of age seems to have thinned his tone, and his firm control over the vagaries of the soprano saxophone's intonation problems slackens on several tracks. By deliberately avoiding riffs, Bechet encourages a feeling of lyrical diffidence to pervade most of the final choruses. But the ingenuity of his exchanges with Solal on *The man I love* and the two-bar chases on *These foolish things* show that the veteran's musical reflexes were still in fine shape. The old panache surfaces in *All of me* and *I never knew*, and his playing on *Pennies from Heaven* is a clever mixture of flair and subtlety. Bechet carefully avoids any long, high-note finishes, and most of the numbers end with an unseemly abruptness (except for the sign-off on *Jeepers Creepers*, which sounds like a paraphrase of the tune *Slipped Disc*). Almost all of the tracks are brief and taken at medium tempo. Regretfully, no blues sequences (usually a fertile common ground for jazzmen of all schools) were included. The album is more of a memento than a masterpiece, yet most critics (impressed by the musicianship of the backings) went out of their way to lavish praise on it.

The issue of *Down Beat* for 2 May 1957 announced startling news: "Sidney Bechet definitely will return to the United States for the opening Louis Armstrong night at the American Jazz Festival to be held at Newport, Long Island." Sidney had certainly been approached about the possibility of his appearing at this festival, but the magazine's note of certainty was misplaced. History repeated itself, and Bechet again declined a chance to get on stage with

Louis. Perhaps the date of the event, 4th July (Armstrong's birthday), had something to do with Sidney's decision; he certainly must have realized that there was no chance of his getting undivided attention on such an occasion.

All of the organizers, and Louis Armstrong, knew well in advance (this time) that Bechet would not be appearing, but some of Bechet's fans took the information in *Down Beat* as gospel and trekked out to Newport to hear Sidney; the magazine later published their letters of complaint. Jack Teagarden seems to have been as keen as anyone to get Sidney there. He had remained a devout fan of Bechet's work and suggested to Louis Armstrong that it would be a fine idea for the three of them to play a set at Newport together. Apparently Louis looked decidedly unconvinced, which led Jack to say: "We may never get another chance. I hear he may be dying." Louis allegedly replied, "Well, he's not going to die on my stage."[25] As it turned out Louis's birthday evening was full of mix-ups, and few of the planned reunions, including the one with Jack Teagarden, took place.

As usual, Bechet spent part of the summer playing at Knokke. For his stint in 1957 he was accompanied by Jacqueline and their infant son Daniel. Sidney's old friend and former pupil Robert Lewis, who was on vacation in Europe, met up with the family there. He recalls that Bechet was still very interested in photographic equipment: "His deep down hobby was not just photography but the concept of optics. We'd count sun spots through his specially rigged telescope from the hall window of the Knokke hotel. Before we left Knokke he asked me to look at a new German mo-pix camera he wanted to buy. It had a built-in auto F. Stop and Meter, which was big deal in those days. He bought the camera. Certainly he admired the huge lenses of binoculars on a tripod which we saw in a second story window. He said the owner could probably see Holland if he had had a window facing Northeast."[26]

Bechet's winter schedule included, as ever, tours in France, a trip to Switzerland, and concerts at the Salle Pleyel and at the Salle Wagram. But the most publicized of his stage presentations was the production of an operetta called *New Orleans*, for which he wrote most of the music. The show opened on Christmas Eve 1957, and featured Bechet, the Peters Sisters and a cast of 72 actors and actresses. Bechet, in a white suit, played on stage with a band that included Billy Tamper on trombone, Kansas Fields on drums and Sonny Grey on trumpet. Critics complained about the lack of improvisation in the music of the show, and one wrote: "Sidney gave us plenty of Calypsos, marches and what have you. What he did not give us was the Sidney Bechet we all love."[27]

That writer's disappointment was nothing compared with Bechet's feelings about his involvement in *New Orleans*. The show was almost a complete flop at the box-office, and what money was taken was immediately swallowed up by production costs. Bechet's contract stipulated that he would be paid 50,000 francs a night, but after five weeks his total earnings from the show were only 120,000 francs. The show ended ignominiously, leaving Bechet free to play dates at the Vieux Colombier club.

Sidney, almost like a character in a Hollywood extravaganza, wanted desperately to be acknowledged as a 'serious composer', but, despite his determined and repeated efforts, all of his attempts in this direction seemed to end in failure.

Because it was so simple for him to create monumental phrases within a jazz group, he was reluctant to consider the incontravertible fact that his best solos contained more great music than any of his 'serious' composing. None of Bechet's extended works has had a belated success, but Claude Luter (in 1964) made an admirable job of recording his rhapsody-ballet *La colline du delta*.

Bechet again parried his disappointments by immersing himself in performing; in April 1958 he completed a 16-day tour of Germany with André Réwéliotty's orchestra. After this series of one-night stands Sidney rested for longer than usual and told various people, in a semi-jocular way, that he was thinking of retiring. By this time Bechet had no money worries, and was being described in the popular press as a (francs) "multi-millionaire". His life story was shown on television, and this brought forth a swarm of new female admirers. Blake Ehrlich wrote of Sidney in *Esquire* magazine: "He still continues to indulge in his simple tastes for food, drink and women. 'Women!', moaned one night club-manager, who fancies himself something of a dog with ladies, 'they just throw themselves at that old man. He does nothing. They do it all.'"[28]

Bechet soon put any thoughts of retirement out of his mind and agreed to undertake another season at Juan-les-Pins, this time accompanied by a band led by Moustache Galepides. In June 1958 he played a three-day graduation "Bal du Bac" in Paris, and again recorded with André Réwéliotty. On 4th July he took part in a recording session with visiting American trumpeter Teddy Buckner, who had flown in from the United States to appear at two big jazz festivals with Bechet. It was Buckner's first visit to Europe: "My trip had been fixed by Gene Norman and Frank Bull. I didn't know Sidney Bechet personally, but neither did I know most of the American musicians who were working at those festivals, because I had lived for so long on the West Coast and most of them were from the East Coast."[29] To help publicize their forthcoming concerts it was arranged that Bechet would meet Buckner at the airport. The two musicians cheerfully swopped good-will messages and arranged to meet again on the record date.

The recording session took place at the Salle Wagram. When the musicians assembled Bechet announced the tunes that were to be recorded. Most of them were well-known standards, but three were original pieces by Bechet (these didn't present any particular problems as they were all on familiar chord sequences). When things were under way Bechet quickly became aware that, for the first time in ages, he had come up against a trumpeter who was quite willing to contest the upper register with him. Buckner had never developed a stratospheric range, but he could punch out emphatic top Cs and Ds with the minimum of effort.

Fortunately the session didn't become a musical squabble. The music produced was satisfying and proved that Sidney was still eminently capable of playing with spirit and with finesse. His rendering of the melody of *I can't get started* shows that his tone had regained a satisfying fullness, and that his powers of expression were still highly potent. Throughout the date drummer Kansas Fields demonstrates how his superb ambidextrous skills produced driving fill-ins. The three other musicians in the band, Eddie Bernard (piano), Christian

Guerin (trombone) and Roland Bianchini (bass), were all 'on loan' from Claude Luter's orchestra.

Christian Guerin is allocated a couple of melody solos on *Sugar* and *All of me*, but makes the most of his two plunger-muted choruses on *Bravo*, a tune by Bechet, which allows the composer to demonstrate that his gift for creating blues solos full of warmth and conviction was undiminished. Buckner shows his skills with the plunger mute on *Souvenirs de la Nouvelle Orleans*, another of Bechet's compositions, this time based on the eight-bar *How Long Blues* sequence. The third piece by Bechet in the session, *Aubergines, pouvrins et sauce tomate*, is a musical recipe that had been used long before in New Orleans; here the simple ingredients never quite blend in any of the band's three attempts. Alternate takes of *Weary Blues* and *Ain't Misbehavin'* show that both Bechet and Buckner were improvising consistently. Both men must have felt reasonably satisfied with the results of the session.

Three days later Bechet was less pleased with a session that he and Buckner recorded live at the Knokke Festival. Something about Buckner's flamboyant style, full of bursts reminiscent of Louis Armstrong, really pleased the crowd. His round, happy face and projective stance made a good impression, and the audience showed their approval by clapping everything he did just as loudly as they applauded efforts by Bechet (who had been announced as the "King of New Orleans"). Bechet had become quite unused to sharing either the idolatry or the melody, and on this occasion he had to share both. Twice in the opening number, *St Louis Blues*, he and Buckner go for the same notes (the lead on the minor theme) and on each occasion it is Buckner who emerges with the melody.

Fortunately there were too many experienced musicians on the bandstand for things to get out of hand; Vic Dickenson plays cohesively, and the rhythm section of Sammy Price (piano), Arvell Shaw (bass), and J. C. Heard (drums) keeps things swinging. Buckner plays at his best on Bechet's former triumph *On the Sunnyside of the Street*, presenting a fine array of his own ideas before re-creating some of Louis Armstrong's best licks. Bechet doesn't disintegrate under this pressure, but fails to resume command during his subsequent solo. The only vintage moments on *Sister Kate* occur during Sammy Price's rocking piano solo. The treatment of *I'm comin' Virginia* verges towards brashness, but it was still cheered loudly by an enthusiastic crowd.

Bob Dawbarn, reporting for the *Melody Maker*, wrote: "The star according to audience reaction was Teddy Buckner." He then went on to describe the concert's extraordinary ending: "The climax of the entertainment came with *The Saints*, for which the group was joined by Albert Nicholas and the Claude Luter front line. In the usual arrangement Bechet holds the last note longer than the rest of the band. Buckner either didn't know or didn't care and cheated slightly by taking a second breath, outlasting Sidney. Bechet didn't take kindly to this and openly remonstrated with the trumpeter as the rest of the musicians were leaving the stage. He then went into *The Saints* all by himself until the rest of the rather puzzled group came back. Once again that last note, and once again Buckner holds out the longest. A milling bunch of arguing musicians finally left the stage."[30]

TWENTY-FIVE

The Final Bows

After the dramatic finale at Knokke the principals moved down to play at the Cannes Jazz Festival. During the ensuing three days passions had cooled and at Cannes the group performed a lively, but orderly, set, which was recorded by Vogue and filmed for television by Jean Christophe Averty. When Buckner returned to the United States he was understandably bemused by Bechet's dictatorial behaviour, but years later he saw things in a mellower light: "Bechet was a jazz giant, a marvellous player. For the most part things went smoothly, and I look back on that trip with a lot of pleasure. The only real misunderstandings occurred because no one allowed us any time to rehearse the endings."[1]

Later in that same month (July 1958) Bechet linked up with another famous jazz trumpeter, Buck Clayton, who was part of an all-American band that worked with Sidney at the World's Fair exhibition in Belgium. Sidney Bechet and his All Stars justified their billing in Brussels and produced a fine live album. The band had been assembled by George Wein, who played piano with the group during its week of concerts: "I contacted Sidney direct and read the names of the musicians I thought we'd use. He approved and this led to a happy time playing together. Buck Clayton worked superbly with Bechet. He was so sensible: when Bechet took the lead, Buck instantly moved to a harmony part. Bechet knew how to get the best out of any band. He was a true giant."[2] Buck Clayton regards those dates with Bechet as the outstanding highlight of his musical career: "I didn't have any trouble at all in working with Sidney. When he played lead, I shifted my part a third below the melody. He was real generous with the solos and didn't try to hog the show. He was serious about his music, but otherwise he was in a very good mood. He was a fine leader."[3]

Arvell Shaw echoed similar sentiments: "After I had played at the World's Fair with Benny Goodman I decided to stay to have a good look around, but George Wein heard I was there and said, 'Arvell, will you play with Sidney Bechet for a week?' I was delighted to say 'Yes'. Then he followed up by asking if I would also work with Teddy Wilson, so I had a busy time after all. Bechet was playing good and everything went smoothly, because other than the two numbers we did as a sound check we didn't do any rehearsing. Bechet talked over the routines, and individuals sorted out their own features. It all worked just fine. I don't think I ever heard Kansas Fields play better."[4] Drummer Fields, who had worked so often with Bechet in Europe, still regards the Brussels dates as something special: "Sidney looked so full of health I had no idea he was ill."[5]

Certainly the music from the Brussels Fair album offers no clues about

Sidney's impending illness. He sounds in fine, vigorous form, playing strongly on *Indiana* and leading the ensemble at the beginning and at the end of *Society Blues*. The blue notes are projected with all the old savage fervour, the fast glissandos are shaped by fingers that seemed as nimble and powerful as ever, and the tone still cannoned out of the soprano saxophone.

The climax of *St Louis Blues* is Bechet's playing of 11 consecutive choruses, boldly imitating a pearl diver in holding one of his long notes for 19 bars. He takes a richly melodramatic look at *Way down yonder in New Orleans*, playing throughout both the slow and fast choruses before stepping aside to allow Vic Dickenson to play *In a Sentimental Mood*. He also allows Buck Clayton space to create one of the best-ever versions of *All of me*. Bechet plays enthusiastic riffs in support of Clayton; on several tracks he can be heard calling out words of encouragement to his various sidemen. Sidney may not have been improvising much at this stage of his life, but he continually proves that he was still eminently capable of giving a vibrant, magnetic performance. The final number, *The Saints*, is anti-climactic. The front line reassembles uneasily after a confusing bass solo, but even so Bechet's four choruses are models of grandeur. Nobody present, least of all the performers, realized that this was to be Bechet's last album.

By 1958 Bechet's domestic arrangements had reached a state of near tranquillity. Most of his off-duty life was spent with Jacqueline and Daniel at the home they shared at Garches, north of Paris, but Sidney continued to see his wife, Elisabeth, at their home in Grigny, south of the capital. In its issue of July 1958, *Esquire* made much of the way Bechet shared his life by publishing photographs of the patron 'at home' in both of his mansions.

The arrival of Daniel had proved to be a powerful magnet for Bechet's affection: he became a doting father. His tender approach to the child was apparent in his words to Raymond Mouly: "He's always amused by the implements I keep at the back of the house. I potter about there and make furniture. I have an electrical saw and other tools that could be dangerous for a kid, but they are just the things he likes best. One time he took the clippers and dismantled all the door knobs in the house. He is fond of music. He sings the words of *Au claire de lune*, and when he hears *The Onions* he beats out the rhythm very well. He loves it when I pretend to be a horse and he rides on my back. He calls me 'Dada Papa'. He sits on my knee and I pretend to be taking a nap, then I embrace him – et voila!"[6]

In such company Bechet found contentment, and at last he began to slow down and enjoy the comforts of his earnings. He said that he planned to take Daniel to the United States to show him the school he had been to, the church he had been baptized at, and various other landmarks in his life. Sidney intended to take his camera so that he would always have a reminder of the route he had travelled as a youngster.

At this stage of his life Bechet's conversation frequently revolved around incidents that had happened to him in America. This attitude was typified by the comments he made to the *Esquire* reporter, who noted: "He is quick to say how much he loves America, because that's the place he belongs, and he is quick to defend France, because that's the place where he is, the place that loves him." Bechet had indeed learnt to adore the French way of life and never seriously contemplated making a permanent move back to the USA, even though various visiting Americans may have got that impression.

Bechet's praise of France was sincere. When, in speaking of the early days of jazz, he said: "The rhythm came from Africa, but the music, the foundation, came from right here in France"[7], he wasn't simply being diplomatic, he was echoing what he had been brought up to believe in. His elder brother, Leonard, expressed similar sentiments to Robert Goffin years earlier when he said: "Americanisation was forced upon New Orleans, and French which was spoken in most families was officially abandoned. This produced a generation of Picous and Perez. Jazz was only Creole music as it used to be played by Picou and Perez with all the changes that Perdido Street brought to it."[8]

Bechet gradually adopted a mellower approach to expatriate musicians. On at least one occasion in 1958 his nostalgic view of the past washed over the sense of rivalry and suspicion that had blighted his relationships with Albert Nicholas and Bill Coleman. One evening Bechet and Nicholas met and went to hear Bill Coleman play at the Trois Mailletz club; afterwards the three musicians sat and talked happily about the "good old days".

At about this time Bechet took part in a popular British television show, 6.5 Special. Singer Beryl Bryden helped with the organizational preliminaries for the show, which was transmitted live from the Caveau de la Huchette in Paris. Bechet, who was accompanied by Maxim Saury's band, played an energetic version of St Louis Blues, which featured his soprano saxophone throughout. Before performing the number Sidney was interviewed by compère Pete Murray, who began by asking: "Why did you settle in Paris, Mr Bechet?" Sidney replied, "Because I like it very much. I was over in Paris in 1920, and I always had a desire to come to Paris to write my book – which I did – and to compose some very serious music."

Murray then said, "I see you've got your old soprano saxophone with you. At one time you devoted your work entirely to the clarinet, didn't you. Why did you change to soprano sax?" Bechet replied, "In 1923 the clarinet began to go out of style, and I thought I'd pick a soprano because I can play the melody with a soprano saxophone and also make variations and improvise also." Murray went on, "You like the melody?" Bechet: "Very much." Murray continued, "Then may I ask you a question? As an expert on New Orleans Jazz, and very nearly a creator of it, what do you think of modern jazz?" Bechet hesitated, then said, "I can't tell you what I think, not to its favour, because I don't understand it. I like rhythm and melody. I can't follow it."

Bechet was on his best behaviour with that questioner, but an interview he gave to British journalist Steve Voce in 1956 ended abruptly when Voce brought up the subject of the clarinet: "I asked why, in the middle forties, he seemed to abandon the clarinet, because I found his sound on that instrument more appealing than the soprano. 'That's a damned good question', he said, rising to his feet, 'and I'll answer it with another one. What the hell's it got to do with you?' End of interview."[9] Sometimes Sidney parried a direct question with a humorous answer. On that same tour in 1956, writer Ernest Bornemann asked Bechet what caused his wide vibrato: Sidney replied, "Senility, old boy, senility."[10]

After his appearances in Brussels Bechet worked for ten days on the French Riviera, then moved on to play a tour of various coastal resorts, taking time out to visit a film festival in Venice. During these travels he developed bronchitis and nearly lost his voice. He saw a specialist in St Honoré les Bains, who temporarily alleviated the problem but advised Sidney to visit his own doctor for a thorough check-up. In the past Sidney might have chosen to ignore such advice, but the symptoms persisted; he went to his own doctor who sent him to see a specialist. The specialist soon diagnosed that the patient was gravely ill with lung cancer. Bechet was simply told that he must have a long supervised rest and minor surgery. All engagements were cancelled and the press informed that Bechet had a temporary indisposition. An invitation to play at the Monterey Festival in California was declined by a telegram that said Bechet felt "he was an old man, and didn't care to leave France now".[11]

A complicated course of treatments began, and by late November it seemed as if the condition was being held in check. Bechet was not yet aware how desperately ill he was and formulated plans for a project that had appealed to him for years, namely the recording of various Christmas songs. His doctors raised no objections, feeling that the psychological lift that Bechet acquired in planning (and practising for) the session would not further harm his condition.

On 12th December the invalid and his doctor made their way to the recording studio in Paris. Amazingly, Bechet set about his task with much of his former vigour. When organist Jean-Claude Pelletier inadvertently played a wrong harmony, Bechet forcefully played the right one by blowing a loud arpeggio on the soprano saxophone. Alix Bret on bass and drummer Kansas Fields were amazed to hear Bechet insist on "going back to the top" of an arrangement when a simple tape splice could have inserted a smoother beginning. That had never been Bechet's way of doing things and he made it clear that he did not intend to change his methods. Finally the wan but determined figure completed his task, having recorded (in stereo) *Silent Night*, *White Christmas* and two other seasonal themes, *Spirit Holiday* and *Blues du Papa Noel*. For good measure the old warrior cut yet another version of *Les oignons*.

The recording session was a bold gesture, but even braver was Bechet's insistence that he would play at the annual "Nuit du Jazz" (held at the Salle Wagram on 20 December 1958). Kurt Mohr witnessed Bechet's entreaties: "He persuaded Charles Delaunay to let him play a set. We were all apprehensive but once again, to the very last note, Sidney Bechet proved his uncanny sense of timing. Hardly any words were exchanged. His band was in place and Sidney stepped out, making his usual ponderous announcement, which sounded like this, 'Et maitenon je va vous jouer [sic] . . .' I don't remember what Sidney played that night but I know he managed to be his flawless, explosive self, climaxing with that old standard *Maryland my Maryland*. Everyone on stage, and a large part of the audience, knew that these were the very last notes that were winding up the career of Sidney Bechet."[12] When the concert was over

Sidney seemed determined to carry on as usual, and despite the foggy weather he spent most of the night revelling in a cabaret.

As the New Year began Bechet's condition began to deteriorate and he was forced to cancel a scheduled appearance on the first programme of Radio Cologne's jazz series. On his doctor's recommendation, Bechet entered the Clinic Hartman on the Boulevard Victor Hugo in Neuilly and began a debilitating course of radiography. The treatment brought a respite and Bechet was able to visit Paris occasionally. On one of these brief outings he was reunited with Mercer Cook (the son of his old friend Will Marion Cook), who recalled: "In 1959 I met him and his wife at a sidewalk cafe on the Champs-Elysées. I was accompanied by my younger son, aged fourteen. Bechet, obviously ill, had mellowed considerably. He spoke of Dad and added that if his throat ever healed he planned to record my father's *My Lady's Lips*. His parting words were, 'Take good care of that fine boy'."[13]

A boost for Bechet's morale came in the shape of the widespread success of *Petite fleur*. Monty Sunshine's version (on an album by Chris Barber) had been released in Germany. The German recording company issued *Petite fleur* as a single and soon had a hit on their hands. Other companies throughout the world followed suit and issued singles of the tune, which became an international success. For the first time, in the closing months of his life, Bechet's work had made an impact on the American record market. Bechet was too ill to write much to the British clarinettist, but sent a signed photograph inscribed: "To Monty who made Petite Fleur in the Sunshine."

Bechet's illness gave him time and incentive to re-examine his lapsed dedication to the Catholic Church. He again embraced the faith of his childhood and regularly spent time with his priest, Father Dupland. Sidney's physical condition worsened during the early months of 1959 and his doctors insisted that he re-enter the clinic for further treatment. Visitors found the patient cheerful, always eager to get his hands on the latest issues of *Mad* magazine. Gradually the disease re-established itself and spread. Charles Delaunay visited Bechet regularly and saw the progressive change, which was heightened by a grievous loss of weight. George Wein visited the clinic and was shocked by Bechet's appearance; so too was Albert Nicholas, who was soon to leave for a visit to the United States. Some musicians, like Kansas Fields, could not bear to go and see the former model of vigour in such a pitiable state, but Fields (like many others) sent a stream of affectionate messages.

Claude Luter kept in close touch with Bechet and clearly remembers his last visit to the clinic: "At the beginning of April 1959 I went there with Eddie Bernard and Roland Hug. We found Sidney sitting in a dressing gown watching television. He looked very ill but was determined to be cheerful with us. When he was told it was time for him to go for some X-rays, we got up to leave, but Bechet insisted on walking out with us to show that he could still manage the stairs. I said something like, "Watch out or you'll do yourself an injury', but he said, 'I just tell myself that I'm chasing Mezzrow for the money he owes me!' That was the last thing I ever heard him say."[14]

During the month of April 1959 Bechet's physical defences caved in and the malignant cells raced through his body. When his condition became hopeless, doctors agreed with his wishes and allowed him to return to his home at Garches to share his last days with Jacqueline and Daniel. His condition worsened and he lost consciousness, and, although he rallied briefly, he suffered a relapse a few days later. By 13th May he was unconscious for most of the time. A priest from the parish of Garches came to administer the last rites. By then Bechet was unable to speak, but indicated acknowledgment with his eyes. At one o'clock on the afternoon of 14 May 1959 – his 62nd birthday – Sidney Joseph Bechet died.

On 19 May 1959 more than 3000 people gathered in heavy rain outside the church of Saint Louis in Garches to pay their last respects to Sidney Bechet. In deference to Elisabeth Bechet's wishes no jazz bands performed before or after the funeral service. The organist played *Nobody knows the trouble I've seen* and *Ol' Man River* during the ceremony, which was attended by many of Bechet's old friends, including Arthur Briggs, Claude Luter and his wife, André Réwéliotty and Mercer Cook. Soon after the interment at the cemetery in Hauts-de-Seine (St Cloud) trumpeter Jack Butler stood at the graveside and played *My Buddy*.

A vast number of sympathetic messages reached Bechet's home, and jazz magazines throughout the world were filled with heartfelt tributes. All of the daily newspapers in France commented on Sidney's death. *Le Figaro* said: "His disappearance closes a capital chapter in the history of jazz." *France Soir* affirmed: "The name of Sidney Bechet will remain attached to the *belle époque* of Saint-Germain-des-Pres." Alfred Lion and Francis Wolff (of Blue Note records) took a big advertisement in *Down Beat* magazine, which simply said: "In memory of a great and good friend Sidney Bechet."

Louis Armstrong, who was touring Switzerland at the time of Bechet's death, chose not to go through the motions of deep grief, but spoke with genuine regret that Sidney hadn't guarded his health with more care: "He should have been playing for years. Sidney was no more than three years older than me."[15] He added a compliment about Bechet's tone: "It was golden . . . a jug full of golden honey."[16]

A month later on 14 June 1959, at New York's Carnegie Hall, Sidney's old friends Sammy Price and Noble Sissle organized a tribute concert to Bechet's memory, the proceeds from the event being donated to Cancer Research. The turn-out of musicians included Henry 'Red' Allen, Vic Dickenson, Omer Simeon, Eugene Sedric, Edmond Hall, Teddy Wilson, Noble Sissle, Wilbur De Paris and Sidney De Paris. The guest of honour was Coleman Hawkins, who had been a friend of Bechet's ever since their legendary battle of music had taken place in the early 1920s.

The presence of Coleman Hawkins seemed to underline the debt that so many jazz saxophonists owed to Sidney Bechet, who proved that the instrument was capable of being used for flexible improvising. Sidney also introduced a whole series of articulations and showed that it was possible to produce a robust, non-cloying tone on the saxophone. It is impossible to say which saxophonist produced the first cogent, flowing jazz solo, but Bechet must be one of the leading contenders. His legato phrasing caused countless pioneers to abandon the pervasive slap-tonguing method. Some analysts have, erroneously, restricted the sphere of his influence only to those who blatantly copied his mannerisms, but Bechet's skills were such that he has had a wide-ranging and long-lasting effect on jazz saxophonists. Musicians of the 1960s, 1970s and 1980s, intent on exploring the tonal possibilities of the soprano saxophone, acknowledge that Bechet is the father figure of their art.

Had Bechet lived for a few more years, he would have observed an enormous increase in the use of the soprano saxophone. One of the pioneers of the instrument's renaissance was Steve Lacy, who came into jazz after hearing Bechet's recording of *The Mooche*; "It was like hearing my own voice. When I heard the soprano it had an uncanny effect on me."[17]

During the 1950s musicians like James Moody and Lucky Thompson had used the instrument occasionally, as had many traditional-jazz players, but during the 1960s many began specializing on it. Steve Lacy was in that vanguard, but from 1961 John Coltrane regularly played the soprano saxophone and, in doing so, converted a whole generation of young musicians to accept it and to seek out the possibilities of the instrument. Coltrane too had a vast respect for Bechet's talents. When Richard Hadlock first played John Coltrane Bechet's 1932 recording of *Shag*, the young musician, already a virtuoso performer, was astounded and said: "Did all of those old guys swing like that?"

By the end of the 1960s dozens of superb soprano saxophonists had emerged, including Jerome Richardson, Norwood 'Pony' Poindexter, Curtis Amy and Sam Rivers. Roland Kirk spoke for all of these when he called Sidney Bechet "a black classical musician". The instrument had become so common that arrangers were not afraid to write scores that used the soprano saxophone to lead the reed section.

By the early 1970s a category for soprano saxophonists was part of all the important polls in the jazz magazines. By then Wayne Shorter was in the forefront of the instrument's exponents. Master tenor saxophonists such as Stan Getz, Zoot Sims and Budd Johnson began doubling regularly on the instrument, and many young 'free-jazz' players who were guided to Bechet's recordings were amazed to find that he had marked out paths of sound exploration and the use of microtones. Sales of the soprano saxophone continued to spiral throughout the world during the 1980s. By then skilful musicians like Grover Washington, Bill Evans, Gene Roland and Branford Marsalis had taken their places in the hierarchy of the instrument's players. Whoever emerges as a star performer on soprano saxophone always reveals direct (or indirect) links with Bechet's pioneering efforts.

While countless young modernists were adjusting and reshaping Bechet's original concepts, a whole school of players deliberately modelled their playing closely on Bechet's style, sometimes going to the point of attempting to reiterate the master's recorded work. Others like George Probert, Dick Hadlock, Wally Fawkes, Claude Luter, René Franc (and his son), Joe Muranyi and Steen Vig took their inspiration from Bechet but then developed their own individualism. At the head of this branch of the instrument's development is Bob Wilber, who made thousands of new listeners aware of a great tradition in the group Soprano

Summit (which he led with Kenny Davern) and subsequently in his own unit, The Bechet Legacy.

Bechet's influence was not restricted to the soprano saxophone. It is more than likely that Coleman Hawkins, the justly revered father of the jazz tenor saxophone, learnt more than a trick or two during his early skirmishes with Bechet. Sidney's influence on Johnny Hodges was readily acknowledged by the distinguished Ellingtonian; its effects took root during the time Hodges specialized on the soprano saxophone, but the broad outlines of Bechet's methods could still be heard in Hodges's alto saxophone solos. There is no huge gap between Hodges's playing and that of tenor saxophonist Ben Webster, particularly in tone production and construction of solos. Webster always acknowledged Hodges and Hawkins as his influences, but he also revered the parent style and automatically placed Bechet in his list of jazz immortals. Bechet's effect on the styles of Hawkins and Webster was formative; in turn these two musicians influenced almost all the big-toned jazz tenor saxophonists who came after them.

Bob Wilber has a theory that Bechet's playing had a direct influence on some of Stravinsky's compositions for clarinet. It's an idea that stands up to scrutiny. Late in his life Ernest Ansermet, the man who first championed Bechet's genius back in 1919, said: "For nearly 20 years Stravinsky and I lived like brothers. I shared his troubles, his torments and joys and I followed his work very closely."[18] In 1927 Ansermet wrote: "Stravinsky knows by heart all the good jazz dance music. Jazz, instead of harming 'classical' music, gives it new matter to develop."[19] Stravinsky himself said: "Jazz burst into my life so suddenly when the war ended."[20] It would be surprising if the subject of Bechet's playing failed to enter the Ansermet–Stravinsky conversations. Others besides Wilber feel there is a link between some of Stravinsky's compositions and Bechet's work; the idea was first mooted in the magazine *Record Changer* in July 1949.

It is conceivable that other modern composers listened with interest to Bechet in Europe during the 1920s. Maurice Ravel said in 1932: "For many hours I have sat in night clubs in London, Paris and other great cities and listened to first-class jazz bands. Some of my music owes its inspiration to jazz."[21]

A much more direct link is the acknowledged one between Bechet's playing and several of Duke Ellington's compositions. Throughout his life Ellington never ceased praising Bechet's achievements; for his *New Orleans Suite* in 1970 he wrote a section dedicated to Bechet, which was to have been played on soprano saxophone by Johnny Hodges. Hodges's unfortunate death made that part of the plan impossible, and instead the work was performed by Paul Gonsalves on tenor saxophone. In 1985 Bob Wilber gave the première of the work as a feature for soprano saxophone during a British concert.

Bechet himself was a gifted composer with a talent for creating strong, sweeping melodies. On occasions he purloined the work of other writers, but curiously, when he did so, he unashamedly lifted the piece *in toto* and made no efforts to camouflage the misappropriation. Those misdeeds should not diminish an appreciation of Bechet's own compositions, many of which are outstandingly original. Since his death a number of them have been recorded by contemporary reed players: Archie Shepp's tribute album (1981) is a fine example; so too is the late Roland Kirk's masterful version of *Petite fleur*.

The importance of Bechet's clarinet playing as a shaping force is generally overlooked. Although Bechet was always quick to cite 'Big Eye' Louis Nelson as the first of the New Orleans clarinettists to shun the legitimate approach in order to give his improvisations a 'jazzy' timbre, Sidney was the first to carry Nelson's concepts forward. With Bechet it was not only a question of tone and attack; he also played a big part in developing a linear clarinet counterpoint. Writer Martin Williams has commented on the fact that Bechet and Jimmie Noone were principally responsible for creating a clarinet line that 'moved' within a New Orleans ensemble. Considering that Noone acknowledged Bechet's influence, Sidney's role as an originator becomes even more clear-cut.

Johnny Dodds was particularly adept at creating a telling clarinet counterpoint, and he too acknowledged that his influence was Bechet. Some historians have ruled out this connection simply because Johnny Dodds was several years older than Bechet. He was, however, a late starter, and jazz history is full of examples where older players have been influenced by younger musicians; in the 1980s the work of trumpeter Wynton Marsalis has inspired performers more than twice his age.

Homages to Bechet's talents have taken many different forms. In the South of France, at Juan-les-Pins (the scene of many of his triumphs) a statue of Bechet was unveiled in 1960. Many of Sidney's disciples, including Johnny Hodges, paid pilgrimages to that site. Many of these visitors reflected that, while Bechet was much honoured in Europe, he was still virtually unknown outside jazz circles in the country of his birth. Posthumously, Bechet was further honoured when his portrait was used on postage stamps issued in the Republic of Chad and in the Republic of Gabon.

Aside from his music, one of the most lasting mementos of Bechet was the posthumous publication (in 1960) of his autobiography *Treat it Gentle*, which was hailed as the most poetic of all jazz books. Because of the poetic qualities most reviewers allowed appropriate licence for the book's various anomalies. A lack of chronology within the memoirs was generally criticized, but this was attributed to the fact that Bechet had dictated part of them directly into a tape recorder. Further reasons for the lack of continuity became obvious only after an investigation into the complex saga concerning the preparation of the autobiography.

During the 1940s Bechet began to think earnestly about passing on the detailed story of his life in book form. His good friend John Reid had acted as something of a Boswell during the late 1930s and the 1940s, keeping written and recorded examples of Bechet's reminiscences. Mary Karoley, a close friend of Reid and Bechet, assembled a long, superb biographical feature on Bechet for the issue of *Jazz Information* dated 6 December 1940 (this piece formed the basis of many later articles on Bechet, including George Hoefer's tribute in *Down Beat* in 1951). But none of the magazine articles gave more than a hint of the lyrical way in which Bechet himself described events. With the help of Joan Williams, who also did secretarial work for him, Bechet began transferring his memoirs to paper, usually from recollections he had recorded on tape.

In January 1951 Sidney announced, via the *Melody Maker*, that he had completed his autobiography. The same journal published a follow-up story in its issue of 13 October 1951, which said: "This important work is still in the hands of his American agent but may be placed with a publisher by now. Bechet told us that he hoped his book *Where did it Come from?* would appear in the New Year in America. Pops was assisted on the literary side by a young American writer, Joan Williams."

Extracts from the work, now titled as *Souvenirs de Sidney Bechet*, were published in the February 1952 issue of *Jazz hot* (translated into French by Boris Vian). These extracts were accompanied by an announcement that said they were part of a book to be published by Twayne, USA. The old established publishing house of Twayne was indeed interested in Sidney's autobiography, but pointed out to him that more details were needed and that the book should be brought up to date. Privately the company was unhappy about the style of the book, which was no longer exactly what Sidney had said; many flowery descriptions and analytical asides had found their way into the narrative.

In an attempt to restore the original qualities, Twayne commissioned the well-known poet John Ciardi to work on the manuscript with Sidney. Ciardi, who had first met Bechet at the Vieux Colombier in 1950, willingly took on the task. He later wrote that Sidney "was a magnificent man, a wise one with a metaphysic power of language exciting to listen to. I spent most of a year editing and adding material I got from later interviews with Sidney (in Boston) but when the book was ready for the press Joan claimed she was the author and threatened to sue. At that point Twayne bowed out afraid to take on litigation."[22]

One section of the book was fully shaped by the time John Ciardi began his collaboration. This concerned the long, dramatic tale of Bechet's 'grandfather' Omar; it remained at the beginning of the manuscript and gave the book its fascinating opening chapter. When *Treat it Gentle* was eventually published, the saga of Omar produced raised eyebrows amongst many of those who knew Sidney well. Some critics openly doubted the story of Omar; others felt that the language used was so evocative that truth was irrelevant. Rudi Blesh suggested that Bechet secured his inspiration from one of George Washington Cable's 19th-century tales of old Louisiana. One of Cable's stories, *Bras coupé*, has fleeting similarities to Omar's tale, but much closer in content is the factual story of *Bras coupé* (known both as Squire and Squier, who died in 1837) which was published in 1945 as part of *Gumbo Ya-ya* (a collection of Louisiana folk tales). Sidney may have read that book, or perhaps the Squier's saga had been told to him during childhood. Somehow legend triumphed over reality and became the basis of recollections about his own grandfather.

Sometimes, if he felt that an interview needed enlivening, Bechet said whatever came into his head, purely out of mischief. On other occasions, with no ill will towards the questioner, he simply invented background details. This was not a symptom of growing old; as early as 1939 he told one writer that his father was Senegalese.[23] Historian Al Rose took a blunt view of Sidney's verbal improvisations: "Much of what Bechet wrote in *Treat it Gentle* is apocryphal, to say the least. He had a way of brushing off interviewers by telling them lies so transparent as to be obvious: 'I made my first soprano sax myself in 1906, but it got stolen by Attakapas Indians when I was nine. Years later I saw it in Uncle Jake's Pawn Shop'."[24]

Sidney was not a congenital liar. If he felt that the time was right, he could be a model of truth and patience – as he was with John Reid and Mary Karoley when they asked him for biographical details. But the flair that created Sidney's music often shaped his story-telling. His friend Claude Luter said: "Sidney was positively not a born liar, but when he told a story he always wanted it to be a *good* story." John Ciardi commented eloquently on Bechet's inclusion of the Omar legend: "Sidney was a showman and much dedicated to his own image. A little ancestral re-decoration doesn't offend my sense of Sidney as a self-engrossed true genius."[25]

The book's erstwhile publishers Twayne decided to shelve the manuscript, but then had second thoughts and announced in a trade magazine that they would be interested in receiving offers for the rights. This advertisement was spotted by Dr Desmond Flower, a distinguished author, who was also a director of the British publishers Cassell & Co Ltd. Dr Flower was a passionate jazz fan, particularly devoted to the playing of Sidney Bechet, whom he had first heard in Berlin in 1931. He completed negotiations with Twayne, then settled down to edit the material that was sent to him. He knew that the book had not been kept up to date and that most of the events of the 1950s were not covered; he also realized that there were gaps in the narrative and that many details were not in chronological order. He resolved to contact Bechet in the hope that they could work together on the manuscript.

Sidney willingly agreed to meet Dr Flower, being increasingly eager to see the book in print. Accordingly, Desmond Flower visited Bechet in France and the two men sat together for hours as Sidney dictated new information for use in the memoirs. Unfortunately the tape recorder used for this purpose was in poor working order; to make matters worse the microphone picked up many extraneous noises. However, much background detail was passed on. Dr Flower returned to London where his secretary, Herda Charles, had the difficult task of transcribing tapes that contained a good deal of poorly recorded, indistinct speech. Inevitably misunderstandings occurred and names were misheard, but in general most of what Bechet had said was faithfully transcribed.

A further session with Sidney was planned in order to clear up anomalies and to bring the book up to date, but sadly by this time Bechet was already fatally ill. Dr Flower then had the onerous task of catching the mood of Sidney's verbal expressiveness in a way that presented a resumé of his latter-day activities. He did this triumphantly, and the book was, at last, finished. Unhappily Bechet didn't live to see its publication in 1960. *Treat it Gentle* was originally published in London by Cassell, and an American edition was produced by Hill and Wang. Since then the book has appeared in various editions and translations, taking its place alongside the countless albums and boxed sets of records that are testimony to the everlasting appeal of Bechet's music.

There is a growing awareness of Bechet's enormous influence on the original shaping of jazz, and the appreciation of his playing skills is more widespread than ever. Together with Louis Armstrong, he is recognized as one of the most innovative improvisers to emerge during the first decade of jazz recordings. Like Armstrong, he retained his powers as a performer almost until the end of his life, ever able to project epic phrases that were full of vitality and feeling.

In later years Bechet's amazing consistency invited blasé reactions, but the biggest obstacle to his achieving universal acclaim was unquestionably his vibrato. Detractors were well aware that Bechet was a consummate artist, whose harmonic knowledge and technique were exceptionally fine, but the fierce throbbing that marked his sound touched a nerve within them and they could not listen with pleasure to his music. Within recent years many jazz reed players have deliberately developed wildly exaggerated vibratos that make Bechet's pulsating effect seem almost smooth. These bold sounds have encouraged tolerance amongst jazz listeners and given them fresh insight into the work of an early master.

But some listeners will never fall under Bechet's spell, simply because of the intensity of his playing. The French saxophonist Alix Combelle realized this when he likened Sidney's playing to an African sun; he also compared it to "alcohol that is 30 years old, and 70 proof".[26] Nevertheless, the majority of jazz lovers appreciate Bechet's enormous gifts and realize that it was idiotic to regard him simply as a 'dixielander'. That he never was.

Bechet was a giant of traditional jazz, an originator who could be inventive within any musical line-up. His thrilling playing 'swung' before that descriptive word had ever been applied to music, and throughout a long career he remained a supremely gifted melodist. His interpretation of the blues is timeless, and all of his work contains a passion that should never be absent from jazz.

Coda

Sidney Bechet's son, Daniel, has always taken a keen interest in music. He became a drummer and was, for a time, the pupil of his father's former colleague Kenny Clarke. He was the chief beneficiary in his father's will; his mother, Jacqueline, continues to live in Garches. Sidney's widow, Elisabeth, was granted a small income by the Vogue recording company but continued to work as a cashier until her retirement.

Leonard Bechet, Jr, Sidney's nephew, carried on playing the soprano saxophone for a number of years; in February 1973 he recorded an album in California with British drummer Barry Martyn. Emelda Bechet Garrett, Sidney's niece, lived for a long time in New York, where she worked occasionally as a singer; in November 1974 (as Mel Bechet) she took part in a recording session for producer Lennie Kunstadt, but the results were not issued. Emelda subsequently moved back to New Orleans, where she brought up her family. Her brother Elmo is still a resident of New Orleans.

References

Chapter 1

1   *Down Beat* (15 Aug 1940)
2   Robert Goffin: *La Nouvelle-Orleans*, p. 151
3   Ibid., p. 151
4   *Jazz Information* (6 Dec 1940)
5   Lizzie Miles: letter to David Griffiths (18 May 1959)
6   Joe Rena: interview, Tulane Jazz Archive, New Orleans (7 April 1961)
7   Ibid.
8   F. Wynne Paris: radio interview with Sidney Bechet, Boston (April 1945)
9   Alan Lomax: *Mister Jelly Roll*, p. 96
10 *Jazz Journal* (Sept 1966)
11 Noel 'Chappie' D'Amato: conversation with author (1956)
12 Robert Goffin: *La Nouvelle-Orleans*, p. 149
13 Emile Barnes: interview, Tulane Jazz Archive (1 Oct 1959)
14 Alphonse Picou: interview, Tulane Jazz Archive (4 April 1958)
15 *Record Changer* (July 1949)
16 *Jazz Information* (6 Dec 1940)
17 John Reid: recorded interview with Sidney Bechet (June 1944)
18 Louis Tio, Jr: interview, Tulane Jazz Archive (26 Oct 1960)
19 *Jazz Journal* (Oct 1966)
20 Louis Tio, Jr: interview, Tulane Jazz Archive (26 Oct 1960)
21 Johnny St Cyr: interview, Tulane Jazz Archive (27 Aug 1958)
22 *Jazz Journal* (June 1964)
23 Alan Lomax: *Mister Jelly Roll*, p. 93

Chapter 2

1   *HRS Rag* (Sept 1940)
2   Bill Russell: letter to author (5 Feb 1985)
3   *Record Changer* (July 1949)
4   Sidney Desvigne: interview, Tulane Jazz Archive (18 Aug 1958)
5   Sidney Bechet Schedule: John D. Reid Collection of Early American Jazz, Arkansas Arts Center, Little Rock, Arkansas
6   *Storyville*, no. 57 (Feb–March 1975)
7   Emile Barnes: interview, Tulane Jazz Archive (20 Dec 1960)
8   Paul Barnes: interview, Tulane Jazz Archive (15 April 1968)
9   Emile Barnes: interview, Tulane Jazz Archive (20 Dec 1960)
10 John D. Reid Collection
11 *Down Beat* (14 Jan 1946)
12 *Second Line* (spring 1972)
13 *Dramatic Mirror* (15 Feb 1919)
14 *Dramatic Mirror* (15 March 1919)
15 Tony Sbarbaro: interview, Tulane Jazz Archive (11 Feb 1959)
16 Paul Barbarin: interview, Tulane Jazz Archive (7 Jan 1959)
17 Alan Lomax: *Mister Jelly Roll*, p. 95

18 *Melody Maker* (3 June 1939)
19 *Jazz Information* (4 Oct 1940)
20 *Jazz Information* (6 Dec 1940)
21 Peter Bocage: interview, Tulane Jazz Archive (29 Jan 1959)
22 Paul Barbarin: interview, Tulane Jazz Archive (7 Jan 1959)
23 *Jazz hot*, no.17 (1947)
24 *Storyville*, no.43 (Oct–Nov 1972)
25 Recorded interview, John D. Reid Collection
26 Lee Collins: *Oh, Didn't he Ramble*, p.63
27 Alan Lomax: *Mister Jelly Roll*, p.96
28 Louis Keppard: interview, Tulane Jazz Archive (4 Aug 1957)
29 Eddie Dawson: interview, Tulane Jazz Archive (28 June 1961)
30 *Jazz Information* (4 Oct 1940)
31 Jack V. Buerkle and Danny Barker: *Bourbon Street Black*, p.20
32 Peter Bocage: interview, Tulane Jazz Archive (29 Jan 1959)
33 Albert Glenny: interview, Tulane Jazz Archive (27 March 1957)
34 Alan Lomax: *Mister Jelly Roll*, p.98

Chapter 3

1 Henry 'Red' Allen: conversation with author (1966)
2 'Wooden' Joe Nicholas: interview, Tulane Jazz Archive (12 Nov 1956)
3 *Melody Maker* (15 July 1972)
4 *Jazz Journal* (June 1954)
5 George Foster: *The Autobiography of Pops Foster, New Orleans Jazzman*, p.88
6 Emile Barnes: interview, Tulane Jazz Archive (1 Oct 1959)
7 Ibid.
8 Samuel B. Charters: *Jazz New Orleans 1885–1963*, p.79
9 *Basin Street* (Aug 1945)
10 *Jazz Record* (March 1947)
11 *Down Beat* (15 Sept 1941)
12 *Jazz Journal* (Oct 1966)
13 *Jazz Review* (May 1960)
14 Manuel Manetta: interview, Tulane Jazz Archive (21 March 1957)
15 Donald M. Marquis: letter to author (1984)
16 Louis Keppard: interview, Tulane Jazz Archive (4 Aug 1957)
17 Bill Russell: letter to author (5 Feb 1985)
18 Sidney Bechet: *Treat it Gentle*, p.93
19 Louis Armstrong: *Swing that Music*, p.14
20 Louis Armstrong: *Satchmo, My Life in New Orleans*, p.120
21 Joe Robichaux: interview, Tulane Jazz Archive (19 March 1959)
22 Peter Bocage: interview, Tulane Jazz Archive (29 Jan 1959)
23 *Jazz Information* (20 Dec 1940)
24 Sidney Bechet schedule: John D. Reid Collection
25 *Down Beat* (20 Oct 1954)
26 John Casimir: interview, Tulane Jazz Archive (17 Jan 1959)
27 *Record Changer* (June 1949)
28 Ibid.
29 Sidney Bechet schedule: John D. Reid Collection
30 *Indianapolis Freeman* (17 Nov 1917)
31 Sidney Bechet: *Treat it Gentle*, p.114

Chapter 4

1 Paul Barbarin: interview, Tulane Jazz Archive (27 March 1957)
2 *Record Changer* (July 1949)
3 *Second Line* (spring 1985)
4 Manuel Manetta: interview, Tulane Jazz Archive (21 March 1957)

5   *Down Beat* (May 1938)
6   Tony Sbarbaro: interview, Tulane Jazz Archive (11 Feb 1959)
7   Lawrence Duhé: interview, Tulane Jazz Archive (9 June 1957)
8   Ibid.
9   Wellman Braud: interview, Tulane Jazz Archive (10 May 1957)
10 Emile Barnes: interview, Tulane Jazz Archive (1 Oct 1959)
11 *Indianapolis Freeman* (25 May 1918)
12 *Jazz hot*, no.30 (Feb–March 1939)
13 Frederic Ramsey, Jr, and Charles Edward Smith, eds.: *Jazzmen*, p.65
14 Lawrence Duhé: interview, Tulane Jazz Archive (9 June 1957)
15 Sidney Bechet: interview taped by Dr Desmond Flower (*c* summer 1957)
16 *Coda* (Sept 1959)
17 *Basin Street* (Nov 1945)
18 Richard Hadlock: letter to author (10 Oct 1984)
19 *Music & Rhythm* (Nov 1940)
20 Sidney Bechet: interview recorded by John Reid (June 1944)
21 Sidney Bechet: *Treat it Gentle*, p.118
22 *Down Beat* (15 Nov 1944)
23 *Storyville*, no.68 (Dec 1976–Jan 1977)
24 *Jazz Journal* (Oct 1966)
25 *Down Beat* (11 Dec 1958)
26 *Jazz Journal* (Sept 1966)
27 *Down Beat* (1 Jan 1941)
28 Sidney Bechet: interview recorded by John Reid (June 1944)
29 Sidney Bechet: interview on KRE radio, California (Sept 1953)
30 *The Jazz Session* (March–April 1945)
31 *Storyville*, no.74 (Dec 1977–Jan 1978)
32 *Down Beat* (1 Oct 1942)
33 Wellman Braud: interview, Tulane Jazz Archive (10 May 1957)
34 Manuel Perez: interview recorded by John Reid (June 1944)

Chapter 5

1   *Melody Maker* (19 May 1934)
2   Conversation with author (3 Jan 1985)
3   *Storyville*, no.78 (Aug–Sept 1978)
4   *Dancing Times* (Feb 1921)
5   Sidney Bechet: interview on KRE radio, California (Sept 1953)
6   *Rhythm* (July 1928)
7   Conversation with author (3 Jan 1985)
8   *Melody Maker* (9 June 1934)
9   Brian Willan: *Sol Plaatje, South African Nationalist*, p.239
10 *The Stage* (20 May 1920)
11 *Melody Maker* (21 May 1949)
12 *The Bailie* (21 Sept 1921)
13 London County Council: London Fire Brigade report (11 Aug 1920)

Chapter 6

1   Conversation with author (3 Jan 1985)
2   *Melody Maker* (12 July 1941)
3   Sidney Bechet: interview on KRE radio, California (Sept 1953)
4   *Popular Music and Dancing Weekly* (20 April 1935)
5   *West London Observer* (24 Oct 1919)
6   *Dancing World* (Oct 1920)
7   *Rhythm* (Nov 1930)
8   *West London Observer* (29 Oct 1920)
9   Conversation with author (30 Jan 1985)

10 Josephine Bradley: *Dancing through Life*, p.12
11 Conversation with author (27 Feb 1985)
12 Sidney Bechet: interview with Roy Plomley for "Desert Island Discs", BBC radio (28 June 1965)
13 *Melody Maker* (28 May 1960)
14 *Melody Maker* (16 June 1934)
15 Conversation with author (30 Jan 1985)
16 Sidney Bechet schedule: John D. Reid Collection
17 *Storyville*, no.78 (Aug–Sept 1978)
18 Clerkenwell Magistrates' Court, London: Charges 1922, Public Record Office, File 437 145 H045/24778
19 Ibid.
20 Ibid.

Chapter 7

1 Danny Barker: letter to author (Feb 1985)
2 *Record Research*, no.46 (1962)
3 *Jazz Review* (Jan 1959)
4 Chris Albertson: *Bessie*, p.39
5 Duke Ellington: *Music is my Mistress*, p.417
6 *Second Line* (fall 1972)
7 Barney Bigard: *With Louis and the Duke*, p.71
8 *Metronome* (July 1949)
9 *Down Beat Year Book* (1965)
10 Letter to author (1 Feb 1985)
11 Sidney Bechet: radio interview with F. Wynne Paris, Boston (April 1945)
12 *Down Beat* (1 Dec 1966)
13 *Jazz Journal* (Jan 1966)
14 *Second Line* (Nov–Dec 1962)

Chapter 8

1 *Record Research*, no.77 (1966)
2 *The Jazz Session* (Jan–Feb 1945)
3 Sidney Bechet: interview with Roy Plomley for "Desert Island Discs", BBC radio (28 June 1965)
4 *Jazz Journal* (Jan 1966)
5 *Variety* (22 Oct 1924)
6 *Swing Music* (May–June 1936)
7 Sidney Bechet: interview on KRE radio, California (Sept 1953)
8 Duke Ellington: *Music is my Mistress*, p.466
9 Danny Barker: letter to author (Feb 1985)
10 *Jazz Journal* (June 1961)
11 *Metronome* (Feb 1945)
12 Duke Ellington: *Music is my Mistress*, p.47
13 *Melody Maker* (17 June 1944)
14 Barney Bigard: *With Louis and the Duke*, p.72
15 *Jazz Journal* (Jan 1966)
16 Unilever Library: Soap statistics (1919)
17 *Jersey Jazz* (June 1974)
18 Josephine Baker: *Josephine*, p.46
19 Lynn Haney: *Naked at the Feast*, p.87

Chapter 9

1 Letter to author (16 March 1985)
2 Lynn Haney: *Naked at the Feast*, p.59
3 Letter to author (17 May 1985)

4   Sidney Bechet: interview recorded by John Reid (June 1944)
5   Josephine Baker: *Josephine*, p.55
6   *Jersey Jazz* (May 1974)
7   *Jazz Record* (April 1946)
8   *Jersey Jazz* (June 1974)
9   Engino Biagioni: *Herb Flemming: a Jazz Pioneer around the World*, p.29
10 *Pittsburgh Courier* (20 Jan 1945)
11 Letter to author (18 May 1985)
12 Sidney Bechet schedule: John D. Reid Collection
13 Letter to author (1 Feb 1985)
14 Ibid.
15 *Jazz Information* (6 Dec 1940)
16 *Down Beat* (26 Aug 1965)
17 *Record Research*, no.61 (1964)
18 *Jazz hot*, Special no. (1948)
19 *Jazz Information* (6 Dec 1940)
20 *Jazz hot*, Special no. (1948)
21 Ibid.
22 *Storyville*, no.57 (Feb–March 1975)
23 John Toland: *No Man's Land*, entry 88
24 Bricktop and James Haskins: *Bricktop*, p.118
25 Ibid.
26 Sidney Bechet: *Treat it Gentle*, p.150
27 John D. Reid Collection
28 *Jazz hot*, Special no. (1948)
29 Sidney Bechet: *Treat it Gentle*, p.150
30 Glover Compton: interview, Tulane Jazz Archive (30 June 1959)
31 *Jazz hot*, Special no. (1948)
32 Hugh Ford, ed.: *Nancy Cunard 1896–1965*, p.45

Chapter 10

1   *Berolina Magazine* (Sept 1930)
2   Bud Freeman: *You Don't Look Like a Musician*, p.91
3   *Jazz Journal* (Sept 1956)
4   *Storyville*, no.78 (Aug–Sept 1978)
5   *Melody Maker* (July 1929)
6   Conversation with author (30 Jan 1985)
7   Letter to author (14 Nov 1984)
8   Jean-Roland Hippenmeyer: *Sidney Bechet*, p.176
9   *Melody Maker* (29 Feb 1964)
10 *Jazz Information* (6 Dec 1940)
11 *Down Beat* (July 1939)
12 Mezz Mezzrow, Bernard Wolfe: *Really the Blues*, p.292
13 *Jazz Review* (Feb 1959)
14 *Jazz Journal* (May 1968)
15 *Mississippi Rag* (June 1978)
16 Hugues Panassié: *Quand Mezzrow enregistre*, p.72
17 *Chicago Defender* (21 Jan 1933)
18 Mezz Mezzrow and Bernard Wolfe: *Really the Blues*, p.293
19 *Jazz Information* (6 Dec 1940)
20 *Melody Maker* (2 Sept 1933)
21 *Jazz Journal* (June 1957)
22 Sidney Bechet: interview on KRE radio, California (Sept 1953)
23 *Storyville*, no.18 (Aug–Sept 1968)
24 Sidney Bechet: *Treat it Gentle*, p.159
25 Barry Martyn: interview (n.d.)
26 Sidney Bechet: interview on KRE radio, California (Sept 1953)

27 Willie 'the Lion' Smith & George Hoefer: *Music on my Mind*, p.214
28 Ibid.
29 Letter to author (14 Nov 1984)
30 *Melody Maker* (12 July 1941)
31 Sidney Bechet: interview on KRE radio, California (Sept 1953)
32 Willie 'the Lion' Smith: *Music on my Mind*, p.214
33 Sidney Bechet: interview on KRE radio, California (Sept 1953)

Chapter 11

1   Cook County, Illinois: Marriage License, 1413286
2   Letter to author (10 Sept 1984)
3   Natty Dominique: interview, Tulane Jazz Archive (31 May 1958)
4   *Tune Times* (Feb 1935)
5   *Metronome* (Sept 1936)
6   Sidney Bechet: *Treat it Gentle*, p.160
7   Letter to author (22 Sept 1984)
8   Letter to author (10 Sept 1984)
9   Lena Horne: *Lena*, p.68
10 *Record Research*, no.61 (1964)
11 *Melody Maker* (20 June 1936)
12 *Jazz Journal* (May 1964)
13 Sidney Bechet: interview with Russell Davies for "The Silver Bell", BBC radio (22 June 1984)
14 *Down Beat* (Dec 1937)
15 Sidney Bechet: interview with Russell Davies for "The Silver Bell", BBC radio (22 June 1984)
16 Letter to author (18 Oct 1984)
17 *Down Beat* (June 1938)
18 Conversation with author (6 May 1985)
19 *Melody Maker* (22 Feb 1964)

Chapter 12

1   *Down Beat Year Book* (1969)
2   *Swing* (Jan 1939)
3   *Melody Maker* (28 March 1936)
4   *Coda* (Jan 1973)
5   *Jazz hot*, no.31 (May 1939)
6   Frederic Ramsey, Jr, and Charles Edward Smith eds.: *Jazzmen*, p.283
7   Sidney Bechet: interview on KRE radio, California (Sept 1953)
8   *New Yorker* (14 Sept 1981)
9   *Jazz Journal* (June 1950)
10 Letter to author (31 Jan 1985)
11 *Jazz Journal* (June 1950)
12 Ibid.
13 *Melody Maker* (3 June 1939)
14 *Swing Music* (May 1939)
15 John D. Reid Collection
16 *Jazz Information* (6 Dec 1940)
17 *Metronome* (July 1954)
18 Letter to author (17 Oct 1984)
19 *Melody Maker* (5 Feb 1943)
20 *Down Beat* (4 Sept 1969)
21 Letter to author (5 Dec 1984)
22 Alan Lomax: *Mister Jelly Roll*, p.94
23 Ibid., p.313
24 Wellman Braud: interview, Tulane Jazz Archive (10 May 1957)

25 Letter to author (5 Dec 1984)
26 *HRS Rag* (Sept 1940)
27 Letter to author (5 Dec 1984)
28 Zutty Singleton: taped interview (n.d.)
29 *Jazz Journal* (Nov 1968)

Chapter 13

1   Willie 'the Lion' Smith: *Music on my Mind*, p.217
2   *Jazz Review* (Nov 1959)
3   Letter to author (12 Oct 1984)
4   *Jazz Information* (15 March 1940)
5   Letter to author (5 Dec 1984)
6   Wellman Braud: interview, Tulane Jazz Archive (10 May 1957)
7   Conversation with author (June 1979)
8   *HRS Rag* (Sept 1940)
9   *Melody Maker* (19 March 1960)
10 *Jazz Journal* (June 1962)
11 *Crescendo* (Aug 1968)
12 Duke Ellington: *Music is my Mistress*, p.49
13 John D. Reid Collection
14 Sidney Bechet: radio interview with F. Wynne Paris, Boston (April 1945)
15 *Jazz Information* (16 Feb 1940)
16 Letter to author (5 Sept 1985)
17 John D. Reid Collection
18 Ibid.

Chapter 14

1   Letter to author (16 Oct 1984)
2   Bill Russell: letter to Johnson McRee, Jr (18 March 1982)
3   *Footnote* (June–July 1984)
4   Sidney Bechet: radio interview with F. Wynne Paris, Boston (April 1945)
5   *Music & Rhythm* (Nov 1940)
6   Conversation with author (1966)
7   Giants of Jazz booklet: Time-Life, STL-J.11
8   Letter to author (5 Sept 1985)
9   *Coda* (Jan 1973)
10 *Down Beat* (1 April 1940)
11 *Down Beat* (1 June 1942)
12 *Jazz Information* (12 March 1941)
13 ANP Press handout: John D. Reid Collection
14 *Melody Maker* (12 July 1941)
15 Willie 'the Lion' Smith: *Music on my Mind*, p.236
16 Ibid.
17 *Music & Rhythm* (Dec 1941)

Chapter 15

1   Arnold Shaw: *The Street that Never Slept*, p.248
2   *New Yorker* (14 Sept 1981)
3   Western Union Cable: John D. Reid Collection
4   *New Yorker* (14 Sept 1981)
5   *Boston Herald* undated clipping: John D. Reid Collection
6   *Storyville*, no.43 (Oct–Nov 1972)
7   *Down Beat* (4 April 1968)

8 *Playback* (Sept 1949)
9 *Cadence* (Jan 1983)
10 Letter to author (5 April 1985)
11 *Jazz Journal* (Sept 1965)
12 Conversation with author (Oct 1985)
13 John Reid: letter to Bill Russell (2 Nov 1943)
14 Letter to author (18 May 1985)
15 Ibid.
16 Conversation with author (1966)
17 Letter to author (23 Oct 1984)
18 *Coda* (June 1959)
19 Duke Ellington: *Music is my Mistress*, p.49
20 Conversation with author (Nov 1985)
21 Letter to author (18 May 1985)
22 *Illinois State Journal* (15 Jan 1944, 12 Aug 1944)
23 *Jazz Journal* (July 1960)
24 John D. Reid Collection
25 Conversation with author (18 June 1985)
26 Conversation with author (28 Jan 1985)

Chapter 16

1 Conversation with author (13 April 1985)
2 *Jazz Report*, viii/4
3 *Melody Maker* (18 Aug 1973)
4 John D. Reid Collection
5 *Storyville*, no.116 (Dec 1984–Jan 1985)
6 *Melody Maker* (18 Aug 1973)
7 Ibid.
8 *Record Changer* (Nov 1952)
9 *Melody Maker* (18 Aug 1973)
10 Ibid.
11 Letter to author (10 Oct 1984)
12 *Footnote* (June–July 1984)
13 *Record Changer* (Nov 1952)
14 Sidney Bechet: *Treat it Gentle*, p.183
15 Letter to author (6 March 1985)
16 *Second Line* (summer 1972)
17 *Jazz Record* (July 1945)
18 Peter Bocage: interview, Tulane Jazz Archive (29 Jan 1959)

Chapter 17

1 Mezz Mezzrow and Harald Grut: King Jazz Story leaflet, Storyville Records
2 Ibid.
3 Ibid.
4 Mezz Mezzrow: *Really the Blues*, p.332
5 Conversation with author (6 May 1985)
6 Letter to author (29 Oct 1984)
7 Mezz Mezzrow and Harald Grut: King Jazz Story leaflet, Storyville Records
8 *Melody Maker* (27 March 1948)
9 Ibid.
10 *Jazz hot*, no.245 (1968)
11 George 'Pops' Foster: *The Autobiography of Pops Foster*, p.169
12 Sidney Bechet: interview with Russell Davies for "The Silver Bell", BBC Radio (22 June 1984)
13 *Down Beat* (18 Sept 1958)

14 *Jazz Notes* (Australia) no.57
15 Letter to author (1985)
16 George 'Pops' Foster: *The Autobiography of Pops Foster*, p.189
17 *Down Beat* (12 April 1962)
18 Letter to author (18 May 1985)
19 *Coda* (June 1959)
20 Conversation with author (28 Jan 1985)
21 Conversation with author (28 Sept 1984)
22 Conversation with author (6 May 1985)
23 Conversation with author (23 June 1985)
24 *American Jazz Review* (Nov 1946)
25 *Down Beat Year Book* (1962)
26 *Metronome* (Nov 1946)

Chapter 18

1   Conversation with author (18 June 1985)
2   Conversation with author (13 April 1985)
3   *Coda* (June 1959)
4   Letter to author (3 Nov 1984)
5   *Down Beat* (25 June 1959)
6   Letter to author (8 March 1985)
7   Ibid.
8   *Melody Maker* (18 Aug 1973)
9   Conversation with author (28 Sept 1984)
10 Conversation with author (1972)
11 Conversation with author (28 Sept 1984)
12 Ibid.
13 Letter to author (12 June 1985)
14 Ibid.
15 Conversation with author (28 Sept 1984)
16 Ibid.
17 Conversation with author (13 April 1985)
18 Ibid.
19 Conversation with author (28 Sept 1984)
20 *Down Beat* (18 June 1947)
21 *Melody Maker* (30 Aug 1947)
22 *Coda* (Oct 1962)
23 *Down Beat* (3 Dec 1947)
24 Ibid.
25 Letter to author (March 1985)
26 Ibid.
27 *Down Beat Year Book* (1971)
28 Letter to author (19 Oct 1984)
29 Giants of Jazz booklet: Time-Life, STL-JO.9
30 Ibid.
31 *La revue du jazz* (Jan 1949)
32 Letter to author (March 1985)
33 Letter to author (3 Dec 1984)
34 Letter to author (8 April 1985)

Chapter 19

1   Letter to author (23 Jan 1985)
2   Jerry Blumberg: interview, Tulane Jazz Archive (6 April 1961)
3   Conversation with author (23 Dec 1984)
4   Ibid.

5   Ibid.
6   *Melody Maker* (18 Aug 1973)
7   Conversation with author (25 Oct 1984)
8   Letter to author (2 Oct 1984)
9   *Down Beat Year Book* (1971)
10 Letter to author (2 Oct 1984)
11 *Jazz Notes* (Australia) (April–May 1948)
12 *Down Beat Year Book* (1971)
13 Conversation with author (23 June 1985)

Chapter 20

1   *La revue du jazz*, no.1 (Jan 1949)
2   *Record Changer* (July 1949)
3   Letter to author (12 June 1985)
4   *Mississippi Rag* (May 1983)
5   Letter to author (24 Sept 1984)
6   *Record Changer* (Dec 1949)
7   *Melody Maker* (27 Aug 1949)
8   Letter to author (July 1985)
9   Conversation with author (7 Aug 1985)
10 *Jazz hot*, no.146 (1959)
11 *Record Changer* (Dec 1949)
12 Conversation with author (Nov 1985)
13 *Melody Maker* (9 July 1949)
14 Letter to author (14 March 1985)
15 Ibid.
16 Conversation with author (20 May 1985)
17 Ibid.
18 *Melody Maker* (11 Feb 1950)
19 *Melody Maker* (19 Nov 1949)
20 *Metronome* (Jan 1947)

Chapter 21

1   Conversation with author (7 Dec 1984)
2   *Melody Maker* (23 May 1959)
3   Conversation with author (5 Feb 1985)
4   Conversation with author (4 March 1985)
5   Ibid.
6   Ibid.
7   Conversation with author (7 Dec 1984)
8   Letter to author (5 April 1985)
9   Conversation with author (28 Sept 1984)
10 *Playback* (Sept 1949)
11 Sidney Bechet: interview with Russell Davies for "The Silver Bell", BBC Radio (22 June 1984)
12 *Jazz Report*, viii/4
13 Conversation with author (28 Sept 1984)
14 *Record Changer* (July 1949)
15 Conversation with author (25 Oct 1984)
16 Letter to author (10 Oct 1984)
17 Ibid.
18 *San Francisco Examiner* (17 Jan 1965)
19 Letter to author (10 Oct 1984)
20 *Melody Maker* (5 August 1950)
21 Ibid.
22 Conversation with author (20 May 1985)

23 Letter to author (18 Oct 1984)
24 *Bulletin du Hot club de France*, no. 89 (July–Aug 1959)
25 Conversation with author (20 May 1985)
26 Letter to author (13 Dec 1984)
27 Conversation with author (30 Jan 1985)
28 Conversation with author (23 March 1985)

Chapter 22

1 Conversation with author (20 May 1985)
2 Official programme of Vieux Colombier club, Juan-les-Pins (1951)
3 Letter to author (15 Nov 1984)
4 *Melody Maker* (14 April 1951)
5 Mistinguett: *Mistinguett, Queen of the Paris Night*, p.239
6 Letter to the author (30 Nov 1985)
7 Ibid.
8 Conversation with author (28,March 1985)
9 Conversation with author (8 Jan 1985)
10 Conversation with author (28 March 1985)
11 Letter to author (10 Oct 1984)
12 *Melody Maker* (4 Aug 1956)
13 *Melody Maker* (12 Jan 1952)
14 *Melody Maker* (14 April 1951)
15 Conversation with author (1 Nov 1984)
16 Conversation with author (20 May 1985)
17 Conversation with author (24 May 1985)
18 Conversation with author (7 Aug 1985)
19 Jean-Roland Hippenmeyer: *Sidney Bechet*, p.131
20 Conversation with author (24 May 1985)
21 *Esquire* (July 1958)
22 *Melody Maker* (25 July 1964)
23 *Melody Maker* (23 May 1959)
24 Ibid.
25 Letter to author (19 Oct 1984)

Chapter 23

1 *Melody Maker* (2 May 1953)
2 *Second Line* (May 1953)
3 *Metronome* (July 1960)
4 Conversation with author (25 Oct 1984)
5 Letter to author (31 Jan 1985)
6 Letter to author (17 April 1985)
7 Conversation with author (15 Sept 1984)
8 *Record Changer* (Dec 1954)
9 Letter to author (11 Nov 1984)
10 Ibid.
11 Conversation with author (8 Jan 1985)
12 Letter to author (2 Oct 1984)
13 Conversation with author (Oct 1984)
14 Conversation with author (23 Dec 1985)
15 *Sidney Bechet Appreciation Society Bulletin*, no.5
16 Conversation with author (5 Feb 1985)
17 Sidney Bechet: interview on KRE radio, California (Sept 1953)
18 Ibid.
19 *Melody Maker* (12 June 1954)
20 Raymond Mouly: *Sidney Bechet notre ami*, p.104
21 *Melody Maker* (9 Oct 1954)

22 *Melody Maker* (6 Nov 1954)
23 Humphrey Lyttelton: *The Best of Jazz, Basin Street to Harlem*, p.52
24 *Melody Maker* (23 May 1959)
25 Conversation with author (6 May 1985)
26 Conversation with author (1966)
27 Conversation with author (23 Nov 1984)
28 Conversation with author (4 March 1985)
29 Information relayed by Johnny Parker (1 Nov 1984)

Chapter 24

1 Conversation with author (20 May 1985)
2 *Melody Maker* (26 Feb 1955)
3 *Newsweek* (undated cutting): John D. Reid Collection
4 Conversation with author (1 Nov 1984)
5 *Jazz magazine*, no.8 (July–Aug 1955)
6 Letter to author (3 July 1985)
7 Letter to author (July 1985)
8 Ibid.
9 Conversation with author (26 May 1985)
10 Letter to author (10 July 1985)
11 Jean-Roland Hippenmeyer: *Sidney Bechet*, p.190
12 Conversation with author (20 May 1985)
13 *Esquire* (July 1958)
14 Conversation with author (4 March 1985)
15 Conversation with author (1972)
16 Conversation with author (1 Nov 1984)
17 John Lawrence: letter to author (28 Oct 1984)
18 Conversation with author (5 May 1985)
19 Sidney Bechet: interview with Roy Plomley for "Desert Island Discs", BBC radio (28 June 1965)
20 Conversation with author (6 May 1985)
21 Conversation with author (5 May 1985)
22 *Metronome* (July 1960)
23 Conversation with author (28 Jan 1985)
24 Conversation with author (26 May 1985)
25 Conversation with author (Oct 1984)
26 Letter to author (8 April 1985)
27 *Melody Maker* (4 Jan 1958)
28 *Esquire* (July 1958)
29 Conversation with author (21 March 1985)
30 *Melody Maker* (12 July 1958)

Chapter 25

1 Conversation with author (21 March 1985)
2 Conversation with author (8 Jan 1985)
3 Conversation with author (April 1967)
4 Conversation with author (8 Oct 1974)
5 Conversation with author (28 March 1985)
6 Raymond Mouly: *Sidney Bechet notre ami*, p.114
7 *Esquire* (July 1958)
8 Robert Goffin: *La Nouvelle Orleans* p.149
9 Letter to author (16 Oct 1984)
10 *Melody Maker* (8 Aug 1956)
11 *Metronome* (Dec 1958)
12 Letter to author (July 1985)
13 Letter to author (16 March 1985)

14   Conversation with author (20 May 1985)
15   *Melody Maker* (6 June 1959)
16   *New Orleans Time-Picayune* (15 May 1959)
17   *Jazz Monthly* (March 1966)
18   Television programme on Ernest Ansermet, Third Eye Productions Ltd (1985)
19   Ibid.
20   Ibid.
21   *Rhythm* (Aug 1932)
22   Letter to author (28 Jan 1985)
23   *Melody Maker* (23 Dec 1939)
24   Letter to author (April 1985)
25   Letter to author (26 Feb 1985)
26   *La revue du jazz*, no.2 (Feb 1949)

Bibliography

Albertson, Chris. *Bessie: Empress of the Blues* (New York, Stein & Day, 1972)

Allen, Walter C. *Hendersonia: the Music of Fletcher Henderson and his Musicians: a Bio-discography* (Highland Park, NJ, 1973)

Allen, Walter C. and Rust, Brian. *King Joe Oliver* (London, Sidgwick & Jackson, 1955)

Armstrong, Louis. *Swing that Music* (London, Longmans Green, 1937)

——. *Satchmo: my Life in New Orleans* (London, Peter Davies, 1955)

Arstein, Helen and Moss, Carlton. *Lena Horne in Person* (New York, Greenberg, 1950)

Asbury, Herbert. The French Quarter: *an Informal History of the New Orleans Underworld* (New York, Alfred Knopf, 1936)

Baker, Josephine. *Josephine* (London, W. H. Allen, 1978)

Balliett, Whitney. *The Sound of Surprise* (New York, E. P. Dutton, 1959)

——. *Such Sweet Thunder* (London, MacDonald, 1968)

——. *Improvising: Sixteen Jazz Musicians and their Art* (New York, OUP, 1977)

——. *Jelly Roll, Jabbo and Fats* (New York, OUP, 1983)

Barker, Danny and Alyn Shipton. *A Life in Jazz* (London, Macmillan Press, 1986)

Bechet, Sidney. *Treat it Gentle: an Autobiography* (London, Cassell & Co, 1960)

Berger, Morroe, Berger, Edward and Patrick, James. *Benny Carter: a Life in American Music* (Metuchen, NJ, Scarecrow Press, 1982)

Bethell, Tom. *George Lewis: a Jazzman from New Orleans* (Berkeley, CA, University of California Press, 1977)

Biagioni, Egina. *Herb Flemming: a Jazz Pioneer around the World* (Alphen aan de Rijn, Netherlands, Micrography, 1977)

Bigard, Barney and Martyn, Barry. *With Louis and the Duke* (London, Macmillan Press, 1985)

Blassingame, John W. *Black New Orleans, 1860–1880* (Chicago, University of Chicago Press, 1973)

Blesh, Rudi. *Combo, USA: Eight Lives in Jazz* (Philadelphia, Chilton Book Company, 1971)

Bradford, Perry. *Born with the Blues: the True Story of the Pioneering Blues Singers and Musicians in the Early Days of Jazz* (New York, Oak Publications, 1963)

Bradley, Josephine. *Dancing through Life* (London, Hollis and Carter, 1947)

Bricktop [Ada Smith] and Haskins, James. *Bricktop* (New York, Atheneum, 1983)

Brunn, H. O. *The Story of the Original Dixieland Jazz Band* (Baton Rouge, LA, Louisiana State University Press, 1960)

Buerkle, Jack V. and Barker, Danny. *Bourbon Street Black: the New Orleans Black Jazzman* (New York, OUP, 1973)

Cable, George W. *The Creoles of Louisiana* (London, John C. Nimmo, 1885)

——. *The Grandissimes* (London, Hodder & Stoughton, 1898)

Carisella, P. J. and Ryan, J. W. *Black Swallow of Death* (Boston, Marlborough House, 1972)

Charters, Samuel B. *Jazz: New Orleans, 1885–1963: an Index to the Negro Musicians of New Orleans* (New York, Oak Publications, 2/1963)

Charters, Samuel B. and Kunstadt, Leonard. *Jazz: a History of the New York Scene* (Garden City, NY, Doubleday, 1962)

Clayton, Buck. *Buck Clayton's Jazz World* (London, Macmillan Press, 1986)

Coleman, Bill. *Trumpet Story* (Paris, Editions Cana, 1981)

Collier, James Lincoln. *The Making of Jazz: a Comprehensive History* (London, Granada, 1978)

——. *Louis Armstrong: an American Genius* (New York, OUP, 1983)

Condon, Eddie and O'Neal, Hank. *The Eddie Condon Scrapbook of Jazz* (New York, St Martin's Press, 1973)

Condon, Eddie and Sugrue, T. *We Called it Music: a Generation of Jazz* (London, Peter Davies, 1948)

Cripps, Thomas. *Slow Fade to Black* (New York, OUP, 1977)
Cunard, Nancy. *Negro* (London, Wishart & Co, 1934)
Dance, Stanley. *The World of Duke Ellington* (New York, Scribner's, 1970)
Dance, Stanley ed. *The World of Swing* (New York, Scribner's, 1974)
Delaunay, Charles. *Delaunay's Dilemma (De la peinture au jazz)* (Mâcon, Editions W., 1985)
Dexter, Dave, Jr. *Playback* (New York, Billboard Publications, 1976)
Driggs, Frank and Lewine, Harris. *Black Beauty, White Heat: a Pictorial History of Classic Jazz, 1920–1950* (New York, William Morrow, 1982)
Ellington, Duke. *Music is my Mistress* Garden City, NY, Doubleday & Co, 1973)
Feather, Leonard. *The Book of Jazz: a Guide to the Entire Field* (London, Arthur Barker, 1957)
Ford, Hugh ed. *Nancy Cunard: Brave Poet, Indomitable Rebel* (Philadelphia, Chilton Book Co, 1968)
Foster, George, Stoddard, Tom and Russell, R. *Pops Foster: the Autobiography of a New Orleans Jazzman* (Berkeley, CA, University of California Press, 1971)
Freeman, Bud. *You Don't Look Like a Musician* (Detroit, Balamp, 1974)
Gammond, Peter ed. *The Decca Book of Jazz* (London, Frederick Muller, 1958)
Gara, Larry. *The Baby Dodds Story* (Los Angeles, Contemporary Press, 1959)
Gillis, F. J. and Miner, J. W. eds. *Oh, Didn't he Ramble: the Life Story of Lee Collins* (Urbana, IL, University of Illinois Press, 1974)
Godbolt, Jim. *All This and 10%* (London, Robert Hale, 1976)
——. *A History of Jazz in Britain, 1919–1950* (London, Quartet, 1984)
Goddard, Chris. *Jazz away from Home* (London, Paddington Press, 1979)
Goffin, Robert. *Jazz: from the Congo to the Metropolitan* (Garden City, NY, Doubleday, Doran, 1944)
——. *La Nouvelle-Orléans, capitale du jazz* (New York, Maison Française, 1946)
Haney, Lynn. *Naked at the Feast: the Biography of Josephine Baker* (London, Robson Books, 1981)
Harrison, Max. *A Jazz Retrospect* (Newton Abbot, England, David & Charles, 1976)
Harrison, Max, Fox, Charles and Thacker, Eric. *The Essential Jazz Records*, i: *Ragtime to Swing* (London, Mansell, 1984)
Hentoff, Nat. *The Jazz Life* (New York, Dial Press, 1961)
Hippenmeyer, Jean-Roland. *Sidney Bechet* (Geneva, Tribune, 1980)
Hodeir, André. *Jazz: its Evolution and Essence* (New York, Grove Press, 1956)
Hodes, Art and Hansen, Chadwick eds. *Selections from the Gutter: Jazz Portraits from "The Jazz Record"* (Berkeley, CA, University of California Press, 1977)
Horne, Lena and Schickel, Richard. *Lena* (London, Andre Deutsch, 1966)
Hughes, Dick. *Daddy's Practising Again* (Australia, Marlin Books, 1977)
Hughes, Langston. *The Big Sea* (New York, Hilland Wang, 1963)
Johnson, James Weldon. *Black Manhattan* (New York, Alfred Knopf, 1930)
Jones, Max and Chilton, John. *Louis: the Louis Armstrong Story, 1900–1971* (London, November Books, 1971)
Kaminsky, Max and Hughes, V. E. *My Life in Jazz* (New York, Harper & How, 1963)
Kappler, Frank, Wilber, Bob and Sudhalter, Richard M. *Giants of Jazz: Sidney Bechet* (Time-Life Books, 1980)
Kimball, Robert and Bolcom, William. *Reminiscing with Sissle and Blake* (New York, Viking Press, 1973)
Larkin, Philip. *All What Jazz* (London, Faber & Faber, 1970)
Litchfield, Jack. *This is Jazz* (Montreal, Litchfield, 1985)
Lomax, Alan. *Mister Jelly Roll: the Fortunes of Jelly Roll Morton, New Orleans Creole and "Inventor of Jazz"* (New York, Duell, Sloan and Pearce, 1950)
Lord, Tom. *Clarence Williams* (England, Storyville, 1976)
Lyttelton, Humphrey. *I Play as I Please: the Memoirs of an Old Etonian Trumpeter* (London, Macgibbon and Kee, 1954)
——. *Second Chorus* (London, Macgibbon and Kee, 1958)
——. *Take it from the Top: an Autobiographical Scrapbook* (London, Robson Books, 1975)
——. *The Best of Jazz*, i: *Basin Street to Harlem: Jazz Masters and Masterpieces, 1917–1930* (London, Robson Books, 1978) ii: *Enter the Giants, 1931–1944* (London, Robson Books, 1981)
McAlmon, Robert. *Being Geniuses Together* (London, Hogarth Press, 1984)
McCarthy, Albert, Morgan, Alun, Oliver, Paul and Harrison, Max. *Jazz on Record: a Critical Guide to the First 50 Years) 1917–1967* (London, Hanover Books, 1968)

McRae, Barry. *The Jazz Cataclysm* (New York, A. S. Barnes, 1967)
Manone, Wingy and Vandervoort, Paul II. *Trumpet on the Wing* (Garden City, NY, Doubleday & Co, 1948)
Marquis, Don M. *In Search of Buddy Bolden, First Man of Jazz* (Baton Rouge, LA, Louisiana State University Press, 1978)
Mauerer, Hans J. *A Discography of Sidney Bechet* (Copenhagen, K. E. Knudsen, 1969)
Mellers, Wilfrid F. *Music in a New Found Land: Themes and Developments in the History of American Music* (London, Barrie & Rockliff, 1964)
Mezzrow, Mezz and Wolfe, Bernard. *Really the Blues* (New York, Random House, 1946)
Miller, Paul Eduard ed. *Esquire's 1946 Jazz Book* (New York, A. S. Barnes & Co, 1946)
Mistinguett. *Mistinguett, Queen of the Paris Night* (London, Elek Books, 1954)
Mouly, Raymond. *Sidney Bechet notre ami* (Paris, La Table Ronde, 1959)
Ostransky, Leroy. *Jazz City: the Impact of our Cities on the Development of Jazz* (Englewood Cliffs, NJ, Prentice-Hall, 1978)
Panassié, Hugues. *Douze années de jazz (1927–38)* (Paris, Edition Corrêa, 1946)
——. *Cinq mois à New York* (Paris, Edition Corrêa, 1947)
——. *Quand Mezzrow enregistre* (Paris, Editions Robert Laffont, 1952)
——. *Monsieur Jazz* (France, Stock, 1975)
Pleasants, Henry. *Serious Music and all that Jazz* (London, Victor Gollancz, 1969)
Ramsey, Frederic, Jr, and Smith, Charles Edward eds. *Jazzmen* (New York, Harcourt Brace, 1939)
Rose, Al. *Storyville, New Orleans: being an Authentic, Illustrated Account of the Notorious Red-light District* (University, AL, University of Alabama Press, 1974)
——. *Eubie Blake* (New York, Schirmer Books, 1979)
Rose, Al and Souchon, Edmond. *New Orleans Jazz: a Family Album* (Baton Rouge, LA, Louisiana State University Press, 1967)
Roussève, Charles Barthelemy. *The Negro in Louisiana* (New Orleans, Xavier University Press, 1937)
Saxon, Lyle, Dreyer, Edward and Tallant, Robert. *Gumbo Ya-ya: a Collection of Louisiana Folk Tales* (Boston, Houghton Mifflin, 1945)
Schiffman, Jack. *Harlem Heyday* (New York, Prometheus Books, 1984)
Schuller, Gunther. *Early Jazz: its Roots and Musical Development* (New York, OUP, 1968)
Shapiro, Nat and Hentoff, Nat eds. *Hear me Talkin' to ya: the Story of Jazz by the Men who Made it* (London, Peter Davies, 1955)
Shaw, Arnold. *The Street that Never Slept* (New York, Coward, McCann and Geoghegan, 1971)
Smith, Charles Edward, Ramsey, Frederic, Jr, Rogers, Charles Payne and Russell, William. *The Jazz Record Book* (New York, Smith & Durrell, 1942)
Smith, Willie 'the Lion' and Hoefer, George. *Music on my Mind: the Memoirs of an American Pianist* (Garden City, NY, Doubleday, 1964)
Starr, Frederick S. *Red and Hot: the Fate of Jazz in the Soviet Union, 1917–1980* (New York, OUP, 1983)
Stearns, Marshall and Stearns, Jean. *Jazz Dance: the Story of American Vernacular Dance* (New York, Macmillan, 1968)
Toland, John. *No Man's Land: the Story of 1918* (London, Eyre Methuen, 1980)
de Toledano, Ralph. *Frontiers of Jazz* (New York, Oliver Durrell, 1947)
Turner, Frederick. *Remembering Song* (Viking Press, 1982)
Walker, Edward S. *Don't Jazz it's Music* (Walsall, England, Walker, 1978)
Waters, Ethel and Samuels C. *His Eye is on the Sparrow* (New York, Doubleday, 1951)
Willan, Brian. *Sol Plaatje, South African Nationalist 1876–1932* (London, Heinemann, 1984)
Williams, Martin. *Jazz Masters of New Orleans* (New York, Macmillan, 1967)
——. *The Jazz Tradition* (New York, OUP, rev. 1983)
Winfield, George and Carr, Peter. *You Don't Know me, but . . .* (England, Storyville, 1978)
Wright, Laurie. *Mr Jelly Lord* (England, Storyville, 1980)

Selected Discography

1923	*The Sidney Bechet Story*	CBS 88084 (European)
	Contains several sides with Clarence Williams	
1923–5	*Louis Armstrong, Sidney Bechet with the Clarence Williams Blue Five*	CBS 63092 (European)
1924	*Red Onion Jazz Babies*	Fountain FJ 107 (English)
	Three tracks feature Bechet	
1923–5	*Sidney Bechet and the Blues Singers* (Volume 2)	Fat Cat's Jazz 014 (US)
	Sides with Margaret Johnson, Eva Taylor, Sippie Wallace, etc	
1931	*Noble Sissle and his Sizzling Syncopators*	Fat Cat's Jazz 199 (US)
	Featuring Sidney Bechet and Tommy Ladnier; also contains the complete sessions of 15 August 1934 and 11 March 1936	
1932	*The Complete Sidney Bechet* (Volumes 1/2)	RCA PM 42409 (French)
	Contains the six New Orleans Feetwarmers' sides	
1937	*Sidney Bechet: Unique Sidney*	CBS 63093 (European)
	Includes sides with Noble Sissle (and alternate takes) plus recordings from 1923, 1925 and 1938	
1938	*Sidney Bechet: Blackstick 1931–38*	MCA 510 100 (French)
	Includes four sides with Noble Sissle's Swingsters	
1938	*Sidney Bechet and the Blues Singers: 1938*	Fat Cat's Jazz 015 (US)
	Contains all the sides with Trixie Smith, Coot Grant'and Kid Sox Wilson	
1938	*The Sidney Bechet Story*	CBS 88084 (European)
	Includes the session with Ernie Caceres	
1938	*The Complete Sidney Bechet* (Volumes 1/2)	RCA PM 42409 (French)
	Includes the four sides with Tommy Ladnier's Orchestra	
1938	*From Spirituals to Swing*	Vogue VJD 550 (English)
	Recorded at the Carnegie Hall Concert in December 1938	
1938	*The Legendary St Regis Jam Sessions*	Alamac QSR 2445 (US)
	Includes Bechet's feature on China Boy	
1939	*The Complete Blue Note Recordings of Sidney Bechet*	Mosaic MR 6–110 (US)
	Begins with the Port of Harlem Seven titles; this six-album set covers the period 1939–53	
1939	*Jelly Roll Morton* (Volumes 7/8) (1930–1940)	RCA PM 45372 (French)
	Includes the session with Bechet of 14 September 1939	
1939	*Sidney Bechet (1939)*	Nec Plus Ultra 502001 (French)
	Contains the session recorded at Fonda, NY, in December 1939	
1939	*Sidney Bechet in Meringue Mood*	Melodisc EPM 7–79 (English)
	Contains four titles from the session in November 1939 with Willie 'the Lion' Smith (Melodisc EPM 7–114 includes a further four titles)	
1939–42	*Sidney Bechet (1939–1942) Inédits*	Nec Plus Ultra 502013 (French)
	Contains the 'proto-types' of several items subsequently recorded for RCA Victor, plus a track with Henry Levine (1941) and a session from Camp Unity (August 1942)	
1940	*The Complete Sidney Bechet* (Volumes 1/2)	RCA PM 42409 (French)
	Contains sides by Bechet's New Orleans Feetwarmers plus three titles with Henry Levine, and the entire Chicago session with Earl Hines, Rex Stewart and Baby Dodds	
1940	*Bechet–Spanier Big Four, 1940*	Swaggie S 1392 (Australian)
	Contains the entire sessions of 28 March 1940 and 6 April 1940	

1940	*Jazz Makers '38–'40* Includes the Armstrong–Bechet session of May 1940	Swaggie S 1215 (Australian)
1941	*The Complete Sidney Bechet* (Volumes 3/4) Contains Bechet's sessions in 1941 for RCA Victor, including the one-man-band date	RCA PM 43262 (French)
1941–3	*The Complete Sidney Bechet* (Volume 5) Contains Bechet's recordings for RCA Victor, and three of the titles recorded on V-discs in 1943	RCA PM 45728 (French)
1944	*Black and White Masters* Includes Bechet's session with Cliff Jackson's Village Cats	Storyville SLP 806 (Danish)
1944	*Eddie Condon All Stars, 1944* Includes Bechet's performances at Eddie Condon's concerts in the New York Town Hall	Baybridge UPS 2255–9 (Japanese)
1945	*Eddie Condon All Stars, 1945* Includes Bechet's performances at Eddie Condon's concerts in the New York Town Hall	Baybridge UPS 2260–64 (Japanese)
1945	*Bechet, Bunk and Boston, 1945* Contains a selection of titles broadcast from the Savoy, Boston, plus the rehearsal on 3 April 1945	Jazz Archives JA 48 (US)
1945	*Sidney Bechet and his New Orleans Rhythm Kings* Twelve albums featuring broadcasts and interviews from Boston: Bunk Johnson is on trumpet for the earlier dates; his place was subsequently taken by Johnny Windhurst and by Peter Bocage	Fat Cat's Jazz 001–012 (US)
1945–7	*Sidney Bechet Sessions* Contains three sides with the Joe Sullivan Quartet, concert dates from 1946, and five titles from the Bechet–Mezzrow Feetwarmers' "Wax Shop" session in 1947	Storyville SLP 4028 (Danish)
1945–7	*The King Jazz Story* Six albums and one double album containing the Mezzrow–Bechet sessions from 1945, 1946, and 1947	Storyville SLP 136, 137, 141, 142, 153, 226, 820–821 (Danish)
1946	*Songs of the 1940s* Contains Bechet's recordings with Stella Brooks	Folkways FJ 2830 (US)
1947	*Fletch, Bill and Sid, Kimball Hall* Concert recordings	Big Chief, Jerollomo SBBH 1947
1947	*The Sidney Bechet Story* Contains a session with Bob Wilber's Wildcats and sides by Bechet's quartet	CBS 88084 (European)
1947	*The This is Jazz Broadcasts* (Volume 1) Contains the complete "This is Jazz" broadcast from 1 March 1947	Rarities 33 (Danish)
1947	*The Genius of Sidney Bechet* Recordings from Bechet's "This is Jazz" broadcasts	Jazzology J-35 (US)
1947	*This is Jazz* (Volume 2) Contains complete "This is Jazz" broadcasts from 24 March and 19 April 1947	Rarities 35 (Danish)
1947–50	*Wingy Manone–Sidney Bechet Together, Town Hall, 1947* Recordings from concerts in New York and items from Philadelphia concert (February 1950)	Jazz Archives JA–29 (US)
1949	*Sidney Bechet with Eddie Condon and his All Stars* Taken from various of Eddie Condon's "Floor Show" presentations	Queen Disc 029 (Italian)
1949	*Sidney Bechet, 1949* Contains the Jazz Ltd session, titles with Bob Wilber's orchestra, and quartet sides made in Paris, 5 November 1949	Barclay 920 400 (French)
1949	*Sensation '49* Live recordings from the Paris Jazz Festival, May 1949	Phontastic NOST 7602 (Swedish)
1949	*Bob Wilber and his Famous Jazz Band Featuring Sidney Bechet, Composer and Soloist* Contains the session of 8 June 1949	Jazzology J.44 (US)
1949	*Refreshing Tracks* (Volume 2) Contains the French session in October 1949 with American expatriates	Vogue VJD 552 (English)
1949	*Giants of Traditional Jazz* Includes session with Humphrey Lyttelton's band, November 1949	Savoy SJL 2251 (US)

1950	*Bechet in Philadelphia* (Volume 2)	Jazz Archives JA–37 (US)
	Part of Philadelphia concerts (February 1950 and March 1950), plus a club date in the same city (May 1950)	
1950	*Biggest Jazz Bonanza*	Trans-Ark 1000 (US)
	American broadcasts featuring Bechet with his own group, and with Bunk Johnson (1945)	
1950	*New Orleans Style, Old & New*	Commodore XFL 15774 (US)
	Contains Bechet's session of 27 April 1950 with Wild Bill Davison	
1951	*Sidney Bechet, his Way: Boston, 1951*	Pumpkin 102 (US)
	Club recordings made during Bechet's return to the USA	
1952	*Petite fleur*	Vogue 500483 (French)
	Recordings made in France during the early 1950s with bands led by Claude Luter and André Réwéliotty	
1952	*The Best of Bechet*	Vogue 590338 (French)
	Various recordings made with Claude Luter's orchestra during the early 1950s	
1952	*Refreshing Tracks* (Volume 2)	Vogue VJD 552 (English)
	Includes the October 1952 recordings with Zutty Singleton and Lil Hardin Armstrong	
1952–3	*Sidney Bechet inédits*	Vogue 406503 (French)
	A double album featuring concert recordings made with various French bands in 1952 and 1953	
1953	*La nuit est une sorcière*	London WV 91050 (English)
	L'Orchestre Symphonique under the direction of Jacques Bazire, with Sidney Bechet as soloist: the studio recording of Bechet's ballet music, May 1953	
1953	*Jazz from California*	Jazz Archives JA 44 (US)
	Includes five titles recorded during Bechet's visit to California in 1953	
1953	*Bechet with Bob Scobey's Band*	Vogue EPV 1026 (English)
	Four titles recorded at the Californian concert, October 1953	
1953	*Jazz at Storyville Featuring Sidney Bechet*	Storyville STLP 902 (US)
	A Boston club session from late 1953	
1954	*Sidney Bechet avec Michel Attenoux et son orchestre*	Nec Plus Ultra VG 502012 (French)
	Concert recordings from Brussels, 1954	
1954	*Jonah Jones, Jonah's Wail*	Jazz Legacy JL 75 (French)
	Contains quintet sides with Bechet (including alternate takes) made in France, September 1954	
1954	*Sidney Bechet: Blues in Paris*	Vogue CLVLX 672 (French)
	A double album featuring sides made in France during the 1950s with bands led by Claude Luter and André Réwéliotty	
1954	*La grande parade de Sidney Bechet*	Vogue DP 01 (French)
	A double album featuring sides made in France during the 1950s with bands led by Claude Luter and André Réwéliotty, plus one track (*All of me*) from a session with Teddy Buckner in 1958	
1955	*Le soir ou . . . l'on cassa l'olympia*	Vogue 400316 (French)
	Live recordings made with bands led by Claude Luter and André Réwéliotty at the historic concert held in Paris, 19 October 1955	
1956	*Refreshing Tracks* (Volume 2)	Vogue VJD 552 (English)
	Includes the session of 16 May 1956 with Sammy Price's Bluesicians	
1957	*Refreshing Tracks* (Volume 1)	Vogue VJD 541 (English)
	Includes the two sessions with Martial Solal	
1958	*Sidney Bechet/Teddy Buckner: Parisian Encounter*	Vogue 500113 (French)
	A French studio recording	
1958	*Refreshing Tracks* (Volume 1)	Vogue VJD 541 (English)
	Includes the 1958 concert recordings with Teddy Buckner	
1958	*Sidney Bechet Recorded in Concert*	Vogue 500203 (French)
	Recordings from the Brussels Fair, summer 1958	
1923–54	*Giants of Jazz: Sidney Bechet*	Time Life Records TL–J09 (US)
	A three-album boxed set containing notable recordings by Bechet	

1949–59   *Sidney Bechet integrale, 1949–59*   Vogue Jazz Selection COF
           COF 21 is the first of this series of three-album boxed sets   series (French)
           covering all of the recordings that Bechet made for Vogue in
           France (including alternate takes). Recordings from Swiss
           concerts are also included in the series, which has reached the
           session of 30 May 1952 (COF 27). COF 23 and COF 24 feature
           club recordings that Bechet made in Philadelphia during May
           1950

Index

Achin' Hearted Blues, 59
Addison, Bernard, 61–2, 128–9, 132–3
Adler, Fred, 81
Ad Lib Blues, 212
After you've gone, 155
Ahaynove, Frank, 21
Aiken, Gus, 142–3
Ain't Misbehavin', 137, 281
Alderhold, Olin, 124
Alexis, Richard, 160
Algeria, 238, 252
All by Myself, 51
Allen, Henry 'Red', 18, 139–40, 149, 150, 244, 259, 287
Allen, Henry, Sr, 18, 21, 160
All of me, 258, 278, 281, 283
All the things you are, 278
Alvin, Danny, 181, 182, 203, 206
American Rhythm, 222
A moi de payer, 265
Amy, Curtis, 288
Anderson, Ernie, 118, 149, 156, 160, 183, 184, 187–8, 194–5, 277–8
Anderson, Marian, 184
Andrews Sisters, 117
Ansermet, Ernest, 39–40, 113, 207, 289
Anthropology, 212
Aquilera, Bob, 13
Aragon, Louis, 84
Archey, Jimmy, 196–7, 230, 232, 247, 258
Arley-Teets (Arley-Tiz), Correty (Coretti), 77
Armstrong, Louis, 21–2, 23, 24, 28, 30, 31, 36, 64–7, 70–71, 94, 108, 125, 128–30, 132, 136, 145, 151, 152, 153, 160–61, 163, 165, 179, 181, 182, 185, 189, 192, 194–5, 202, 223, 235, 246–7, 265, 271, 276, 278–9, 281, 287, 293
A Room with a View, 40
As Long as I Live, 184
Astoria, Long Island, 118

——, Momart Cafe, 118
As-tu le cafard, 249, 256
At a Georgia Camp Meeting, 231
Atlanta Blues, 59
Attenoux, Michel, 261, 262
Aubergines, pouvrins et sauce tomate, 281
Aubert, Claude, 262–3
Autumn in New York, 249
Avakian, George, 197, 199
Azzi, Christian, 221

Baby I'm cutting out, 176
Baby won't you please come home, 140
Back home, 272
Baquet, George, 5, 6, 7, 11, 14, 19, 23, 31, 132–3
Bad Bad Baby Blues, 175
Badel, Annet, 234, 241
Bailey, Buster, 71, 74, 125, 210–11, 212
Bailey, Mildred, 111
Baker, George, 37
Baker, Josephine, 73–7, 92
Baldwin Records, 118
Ballin' the Jack, 185, 248
Baltimore, Maryland, 71
——, Empire Theatre, 71
Bamziger, Irene, 270
Bandanna Days, 104
Bankhead, Tallulah, 193, 207, 219, 243–4, 246–7
Banks, Billy, 98–9, 102, 105
Baptiste, Quentin, 157
Barbarin, Paul, 12, 13, 14, 27, 28, 30, 156, 157, 160, 266
Barber, Chris, 277, 286
Barclay, Nicole, 213
Barelli, Aime, 256
Barker, Danny, 13, 55, 91, 174, 196
Barksdale, Everett, 144, 145, 155, 159
Barnes, Emile, 6, 11, 19
Barnes, George, 189

Barnet, Charlie, 131
Bartley, Buddy, 15, 24
Basement Blues, 88
Basie, Count, 111, 115, 181
Basin Street Blues, 161, 171, 184
Bates, Bob, 259
Bayel, Gerard, 217
Bean, Floyd, 203, 206, 229
Beatty, Josephine, *see* Hunter, Alberta
Beaumont, Texas, 23
Beautiful faces need beautiful clothes, 51
Beauvoir, Simone de, 242
Bechet, Albert Eugene (brother), 1, 3, 10
Bechet, Albertine (sister), 1
Bechet, Bertha (sister), 1
Bechet, Daniel (son), 263, 279, 283, 287
Bechet, Elisabeth (née Ziegler), *see*
  Ziegler, Elisabeth
Bechet, Elmo (nephew), 157
Bechet, Emelda (niece), 157
Bechet, Homer (brother), 1, 3, 10
Bechet, Joseph (brother), 1, 3, 7, 10, 23
Bechet, Josephine (mother), 1, 4, 5, 6, 9,
  16, 55
Bechet, Leonard Victor (brother), 1, 3, 5,
  6, 9, 10, 11, 14, 17, 55, 82–3, 136, 139,
  156–7, 163, 205, 245, 252, 284
Bechet, Leonard, Jr (nephew), 157, 167,
  191–2, 205
Bechet (née Crawford), Marilouise, 98,
  100–01, 106, 125, 152
Bechet, Omar (father), 1, 2–3, 4, 9, 13,
  16, 55
Bechet, Sidney, All Stars, 282
——, Blue Note Jazzmen, 158
——, Decca Recording Orchestra, 120
——, Feetwarmers, 120
——, New Orleans Rhythm Kings, 167
——, orchestra, 111
——, quintet, 120
——, Swingsters, 133
Bechet's Creole Blues, 221
Bechet's Fantasy, 183
Bechet's Steady Rider, 132
Belgium, 76, 238, 252, 269
Bell, Arthur, 270
Benford, Tommy, 68, 72
Bennet, Benny, 241–2
Bennett, Stanley, 71
Benson, 'Hamp', 156
Berlin, Germany, 76–7, 85–7, 89, 186
——, Haus Vaterland, 85–7, 89
Bernard, Eddie, 217, 222, 273, 276, 280

Bernhardt, Clyde, 90, 96
Bernie, Ben, 94
Berry, Emmett, 272
Beuren, John van, 174, 176
Bianchini, Roland, 272, 281
Bigard, Barney, 70, 98–9, 128
Big Butter and Eggman, 253
Birmingham, England, 51, 53
——, Palais de Dance, 51, 53
Black and Blue, 226
Black and Tan Orchestra, 24
Black and White (record label), 159
Black and White Revue, 62, 72
Black Bottom, 253
Black Flowers (show), 89
Black Revue, 73, 75–6, 77, 78–9
Blackstick, 107
Blake, Eubie, 67, 79, 104
Blame it on the Blues, 182–3
Blanche, Marcel, 264
Blesh, Rudi, 195–7, 210, 212, 291
Blind Man Blues, 59
Blood on the Moon, 175
Blount, Walter, 118
Blowers, Johnny, 116, 202, 258
Blue Eagle Melody Players, 205
Blue for you, Johnny, 136, 137
Blue Horizon, 158, 193
Blue Lou, 171, 233
Blue Note (record company), 118–20, 131,
  162–3, 165, 168, 179, 181, 183, 210,
  214, 230, 231, 247, 258, 287
Blue Skies, 172
Blue Star (record label), 217
Blue, William, 80
Blues du Papa Noel, 285
Blues for Bechet, 141, 142
Blues for Tommy, 119
Blues in Paris, 221
Blues in the Air, 146–7
Blues in the Cave, 238
Blues in Thirds, 137, 138
Blues my naughty sweetie, 248
Blues of the Roaring Twenties, 205
Bocage, Peter, 14, 17, 20, 22, 157, 170,
  172
Body and Soul, 193, 253
Bolden, Charles 'Buddy', 4, 5, 15, 17, 24,
  156, 165
Booker, Howard E., 48, 49
Boone, Harvey, 98, 100
Bornemann, Ernest, 86, 285
Bornstein, Marcel, 243, 273

Boston, Massachusetts, 71, 103, 167–71, 173, 218, 246–8, 260
——, Huntingdon Chambers Hall, 163
——, Ken Club, 150
——, Savoy Cafe, 167–71, 174, 181
——, Storyville Club, 244, 246–7, 248, 260
Boucher, James Horton, 54
Boulau, Les, 241
Bowen, Billy, 118
Bowin' the Blues, 176
Bowman, Dave, 111–12
Box Car Shorty, 218
Brandow, Jerry, 117
Braslavsky, Pierre, 215–16, 220, 228
——, band, 216–17
Brassfield, Hershel, 56
Braud, Wellman, 28, 33, 68–9, 71, 110, 122, 123, 126–8, 132–3, 134, 139, 143, 145, 150, 151, 159, 181, 187, 202
Bravo, 281
Breathless Blues, 187
Bren, Joseph, 4
Brereton, Clarence, 98–9, 101 102, 104, 107
Bret, Alix, 285
Bricktop, 82–3
Briggs, Arthur, 33, 36, 37, 40–41, 45, 46, 48, 52, 53, 72, 87, 88, 287
Bright eyes, 51
Broken Windmill, The, 218
Brooks, Henry, 98, 107
Brooks, Stella, 184–5
Broonzy, Big Bill, 243, 248, 256, 267–8
Brown, Joe, 118
Brown Pete, band, 167, 169
Brown, Tom, band, 25
Bruce and Bruce Stock Company, 25–6
Braxton, Lee, 23
Brown, Thornton, 71
Brunis, Georg, 185, 191, 192, 202, 229
Brunswick (record label), 69, 87, 108
Brussels, Belgium, 76
——, Palais des Beaux-Arts, 269
Bryden, Beryl, 256, 261–2, 284
Brymn, Tim, 34, 60
Buck, Jack, 260
Buckner, Teddy, 280–81
Buddy Bolden Stomp, 198
Buddy Bolden Story, 221
Bugle Call Rag, 155
Bullard, Eugene, 82, 84
Bull Frog Blues, 32

Bunn, Teddy, 109, 113–14, 118–20, 132
Burglar (film), 86
Burns, Wm. D., 37
Burrill, Chester, 98, 102
Burton, Linn, 209
Bushell, Garvin, 60, 77–8, 92
Bushkin, Joe, 111
Butler, Jack, 186, 287
Butterfield, Erskine, 106

Caceres, Ernie, 111–12
Caillaux, Pierre de, 36, 42, 48, 53
Cakewalkin' Babies, 67, 70
Caldwell, Albert 'Happy', 122, 214
Calloway, Cab, 94
Campbell, Arthur, 20
Cannes Jazz Festival, 282
Can't help lovin' that man, 172
Careless love, 131, 165, 209
Carey, Jack, 18–19
Carey, Mutt, 18
Carney, Harry, 58, 69, 100, 112
Carpenter, Elliott, 38
Carter, Benny, 67, 72, 90, 104
Carter, Billy, 133
Carter, Jack, 98
Carter, Lavada, 98–9, 101
Caruso, Enrico, 5, 45
Casbah (The Song of the Medina), 211
Casey, Bill, 118
Cash Away, 71
Casimir, John, 24
Catlett, Sidney, 118–20, 132, 133, 134, 147–8, 174–6, 181, 219, 229
Caulk, Joseph, 36, 37, 48, 51, 54
Ce mossieu qui parle, 221
Cenardo, Enos 'Doc', 208–9
Chaix, Henri, 269
Chaligny, Paul, 6
Characteristic Blues, 35, 37, 39, 105
Charles, Erving, Jr, 157
Chevalier, Maurice, 242
Chicago, Illinois, 25–34, 35, 87, 98–9, 195, 202–3, 205, 208, 219–20, 229, 244, 261
——, Asia Cafe, 30
——, Blue Note Club, 244–6
——, Civic Opera House, 189
——, De Luxe Cafe, 28, 32, 33, 113
——, Dreamland Cafe, 29, 31
——, French Casino, 98
——, Kimball Hall, 190, 195, 203
——, Jazz Ltd (night-club), 202–3, 205,

Chicago, Jazz Ltd (night-club) – *cont.*
219–20, 229, 234, 244, 261
——, Monogram Theatre, 25
——, Orchestra Hall, 33
——, Pekin Cafe, 31, 32, 33
——, Royal Gardens, 29, 31
China Boy, 111, 127, 128, 145, 160, 230, 233
Chinatown, my Chinatown, 265
Christian, Buddy, 20, 57, 59, 61, 65, 68, 70, 186
Christie, Ian, 226
Christie, Keith, 226
Cincinnati, Ohio, 102–3, 106
——, Moonlight Gardens Ballroom, 102–3
Circle Seven, 210
Clapham, George, 53–4
Clarke, Andy, 53
Clarke, Kenny, 125, 130, 221–2, 278
Clayton, Buck, 214, 267, 282–3
Cliff's Boogie, 159
Coal Black Shine, 140
Cole, Edward, 88, 98
Coleman, Bill, 151, 159, 221–2, 238, 267, 271, 284
Collins, Lee, 15, 16, 259
Coltrane, John, 288
Columbia (record company), 58, 196–7, 198, 215
Commodore (record company), 231
Compton, Glover, 83–4
Condon, Eddie, 110–11, 149, 156, 159–60, 183, 184, 187–8, 190, 195, 209, 218
Cook, Mercer, 75, 286
Cook, Will Marion, 33, 34, 35–6, 38, 41, 43, 57, 62, 73, 75, 286
Cooper, Jimmie, 62
Cooper, Opal, 81
Copenhagen, Denmark, 237
——, KB Hall, 237
Copenhagen, 230
Coquatrix, Bruno, 269–70
Coquette, 217
Coquin de boubou (film), 274
Cousineau, Robert 'Cuz', 259
Covington, Kentucky, 106
——, Look Out House, 106
Coxcito, Ferdinand (Manfred), 36, 41, 42, 48, 51, 54, 77
Crawford, Rosetta, 58
Crazy Blues, 58

Crazy Rhythm, 264
Creath, Charlie, 63
Creole Jazz Band, *see* Oliver, Joe 'King', Creole Jazz Band
Crosby, Bob, 163
——, Bob Cats, 163
Culley, Wendell, 98, 102
Cunard, Nancy, 84

Dabney, Ford, 56
Dance, Stanley, 152
Daniels, Douglas, 176
Dans la rue d'Antibes, 249
Dardanella, 144
Darktown Strutters Ball, 172, 180
Darling Nelly Gray, 243
Davenport, Cow Cow, 181
Davis, Leonard, 143
Davis, Miles, 216, 259
Davis, Sammy, 72
Davison, Wild Bill, 172, 179–80, 191, 196, 210, 214, 230–31
Dawson, Eddie, 16
Daybreak Express, 70
Days Beyond Recall, 166
Dean, Demas, 98, 100–01
Dear Old Southland, 72, 104, 132, 160, 161, 212
Decca (record company), 99, 102, 106–7, 117
De Courville, Albert, 42, 43
Deep River, 37
DeFranco, Buddy, 259
Delaunay, Charles, 212–13, 220, 223, 228, 248, 249–50, 251, 255–6, 269, 270, 272–3, 278, 285, 286
Delta Mood, 205
De Luxe Stomp, 177
Dennie, Frank A., 36, 37
Dent, Edward J., 39
De Paris, Sidney, 121–3, 133, 134, 135, 150, 153, 158–9, 181, 247, 287
De Paris, Wilbur, 159, 210, 212, 230–31, 287
De Pass, Arnold, 12
Dervaux, Pierre, 237
Desmond, Mope, 52
Dessieur (De Soto), Bessie, 62, 72–3
Desvigne, Sidney, 10, 11
Dickenson, Vic, 146, 150, 155, 158, 130, 233, 260, 281, 283, 287
Didn't he ramble, 171
Diehl, Ray, 214

Dinah, 173, 175
Ding Dong Daddy, 258
Disc (record label), 185
Dixon, Ray, 195
Dodds, Johnny, 19, 24, 30, 65–6, 98–9, 136, 158, 200, 290
Dodds, Warren 'Baby', 8, 18, 136–7, 186–7, 191, 194, 196
Dominique, Natty, 98–9
Donaldson, Don, 146, 151, 155
Done made a fool out of me, 70
Don't get around much anymore, 160
Dorham, Kenny, 212–3
Dorsey, Jimmy, 138
Dorsey, Tommy, 111, 131
Do that thing, 63
Dougherty, Eddie, 159
Douglas, Louis, 75–6, 78–9, 89
Doy, Daniel, 75, 77
Down in Honky Tonk Town, 129
Drootin, Buzzy, 260
Dudley, Jimmy, 190
Duhé, Lawrence, 26, 28–9, 32
——, band, 28, 30, 31
Dunbar, Rudolph, 36
Duncan, Hank, 91, 93–4, 116, 159, 165, 167
Dunfermline, Scotland, 43
Dunn, Johnny, 80
Dupree, Champion Jack, 202
Durand, Jean-Louis, 243
Dusen, Frankie, 10, 15
Dusen (Dudson), Lela, 23
Dutch Swing College, 239
Dutch Swing College Blues, 239
Dutrey, Honore, 60

Eagle Band, 15–16, 164
Early Every Mornin', 66
Early in the Morning, 65
Eckstine, Billy, 261
Edinburgh, Scotland, 43
Edwards, Bert, 188
Edwards, Sumner 'King', 91
E Flat Blues, 61
Egyptian Fantasy, 140, 209, 238
Einbrecher (film), 86
Eldridge, Roy, 234, 238
Elgar, Charles, 28
Elisabeth, 262
Elizalde, Fred, 80
Ellington, Duke, 56, 67–9, 70, 91, 94, 98, 104, 124, 131, 146, 152–3, 156, 265, 289

——, orchestra, 58, 91, 136–7, 142
——, Washingtonians, 67, 69, 70
Embraceable you, 242, 254
En attendant le jour, 238
Englin, Maureen, 62–3
Ertegun, Nesuhi, 149–50
Europe, James, Reese, 32–3
Evans, Bill, 288
Evans, Paul 'Doc', 208, 209, 220
Everybody loves my baby, 72, 229
Ewell, Don, 208–9
Exhortation, 37

Fantasia for a Mouse (film), 266
Fat Mama Blues, 187
Fawkes, Wally, 224–6, 262–3, 275, 288
Feather, Leonard, 143, 153, 181
Festival Blues, 217
Fidgety Feet, 214
Field, John, 170
Fields, Kansas, 214, 279, 280, 282, 285, 286
Filhe, George, 33
Finch, Otis, 191
Flee as a bird, 121
Flemming, Herb, 257
Flower, Desmond, 86, 87, 292
Flynn, Errol, 242
Fol, Raymond, 254
Folies Bergère, 98–9
Fonda, New York, 120–21, 124, 130, 139
——, Log Cabin Roadhouse, 120–21, 124–5, 130, 131, 132, 139
Foolin' me, 63
Forrester, John, 36–40
Foster, George 'Pops', 15, 18, 27, 132, 157, 159, 162, 163, 165–6, 167, 170, 172, 174–7, 179–80, 181–2, 186, 191, 194, 196, 198, 202, 203–4, 230, 247, 272
Four or Five Times, 126
Fox, Charles, 139
Franc, René, 216, 271, 288
Francis Blues, 237
Francis, Panama, 257
Frank, Gilbert 'Bab', 28
Frankfurt am Main, Germany, 79
——, Beethoven Hall, 79
Frasier, Smithy, 72
Freeman, Bud, 87, 111, 125, 189, 240
Frog Legs, 16
Fulbright, Richard, 109

Gabler, Milt, 149, 165, 213, 230–31

Gaines, Charlie, 30
Galepides, Francois 'Moustache', 237, 248, 251, 256, 271, 280
Galveston, Texas, 31
Garland, Ed, 15, 28
Gee, Jack, 56, 59
Gee, Lottie, 37
Genet, Jean, 242
Geneva, Switzerland, 217, 262
——, Palladium, 262–3, 266
——, Victoria Hall, 217, 262
Gennett (record label), 70
Georgia, 225
Georgia on my mind, 227
Get Happy Band, 72
Getz, Stan, 237–8, 288
Ghost of the Blues, The, 60, 62, 249
Gillespie, Dizzy, 138, 189, 223, 252
Gilmore, Buddie, 36, 37, 43
Gilmore, Mattie, 36
Glasel, Johnny, 197–8
Glaser, Joe, 195
Glasgow, Scotland, 43, 52
——, Lyric Theatre, 52
Glenny, Albert, 17
Gluskin, Lud, orchestra, 89
Goffin, Robert, 1, 70
Gone Away Blues, 177
Gonella, Nat, 112–13
Goodman, Benny, 265
Goodwin, Henry, 75, 77, 143, 146, 149, 151, 218
Gordon, Lorraine, 180–81
Gordon, Ruby, 53–4
Gordon, Wally, 209
Got it and Gone, 181
Got the bench, got the park, 88
Gothenburg, Sweden, 237
Goudie, Frank 'Big Boy', 15, 79, 221–2
Gowans, Brad, 149, 218
Grace, Toby, 132
Grant, Coot, 108, 187
Grant, Mel, 203
Gray, Marlene, 257
Grey, Sonny, 279
Groovin' the minor, 187
Grosz, Marty, 201
Guerin, Christian, 280–81

Hackett, Bobby, 110, 111, 116, 149, 153–4, 172, 218
Hadlock, Richard ('Dick'), 30, 232–3, 288
Hagerstown, Maryland, 152

——, Colonial Restaurant, 152
Haig, Al, 212–13
Haitian Orchestra, 124
Hall, Al, 159, 183
Hall, Edmond, 265, 287
Hall, Herbert, 272
Hall, Joseph, 37
Hall, Minor, 20, 28
Hall, Tubby, 15, 28
Hampton, Lionel, 58, 131, 175, 272
Happy Go Lucky Blues, 222
Hardin Armstrong, Lil, 28, 30, 66, 91, 252–3, 256, 267
Hardwicke, Otto, 80
Harris, Ben, 56, 138
Harris, Bill, 190–91
Harvey, Georgette, 56
Hawkins, Coleman, 61, 68–9, 90, 224, 287, 289
Hawkins, Erskine, 131
Hayman, Joe, 77, 143
Haywood, Cedric, 156
Hear that trumpet, 188–9
Heard, J. C., 139–40, 281
Hello Yourself (show), 80
Henderson, Fletcher, 56, 63, 191
——, orchestra, 64, 68, 91, 92
Henry, Sonny, 27
Herbert, Arthur, 142–3, 198–9
Herman, Woody, orchestra, 261
Hey Daddy, 187
Heywood, Donald, 56
Higginbotham, J. C., 118–20, 139–40, 149, 160, 161
High Society, 22, 42, 122, 162, 184, 217, 233
Hightower, Willie, 11
Hill, Ernest, 132
Hill, Howard, 98
Hindustan, 231
Hines, Earl, 98, 136–8, 257
Hippenmeyer, Jean-Roland, 273
Hodes, Art, 150, 153, 155–6, 159, 162–3, 179–80, 182–3, 196, 210, 214, 231
Hodges, Johnny, 58, 62, 67, 70, 71–2, 91, 100, 101, 104, 136, 141, 251, 289, 290
Hoff, Carl, orchestra, 98–9
Hold Tight, 116–17
Holiday, Billie, 95, 145, 152
Holland, 239, 264
Holland, Peanuts, 271
Hollywood, California, 259–60
——, Shrine Auditorium, 259–60

Holmes, Charlie, 101
Holmes, Harold, 133
Honeysuckle Rose, 217
Honore, Gideon, 156
Hopkins, Claude, 73–7, 260
Hopson, Gerald, 151
Horne, Lena (Helena), 101–3
House Party, 175
House Rent Blues, 61
Houston, William, Sr, 160
Howard, Charlie, 121, 125, 130, 132
Howard, Darnell, 32
Howell, John, 71
How Come (show), 56–7, 59
How High the Moon, 212
How Long Blues, 281
Hucko, Peanuts, 195
Hughes, Dick, 265
Humphrey, Willie, Sr, 23, 24
Hunter, Alberta, 56, 66–7
Hunter, Eddie, 56
Hurley, Sam, 50

I ain't gonna give nobody none of this jelly roll, 142, 176
I ain't got nobody, 171
I can't get started, 280
I don't know where I'm going but I'm on my way, 4
I don't love nobody, 61
If I could be with you, 127
If I let you get away with it, 61
I found a new baby, 72, 93, 171, 175, 210, 212
I get a kick out of you, 251
I got rhythm, 94, 210, 237
I had it but it's all gone now, 198
I know that you know, 142, 160, 216
I'll never be the same, 185
I'm a Little Blackbird, 66
I'm comin' Virginia, 145, 281
I'm confessin', 161, 165, 171, 256
I'm just wild about Harry, 104
Imperial Band, 3, 5, 12
I'm so glad I'm a brownskin, 66
I'm speaking my mind, 204
I'm through, goodbye, 218
In a cafe on the road to Calais, 88
In a Sentimental Mood, 283
In Bamville (show), 67
Indian Summer, 130
Indiana, 283
In Harlem's Araby, 72

In the Groove, 238
Irresistible Blues, 61
Irvis, Charlie, 65–7, 69, 70
I take to you, 102
I thought I heard Buddy Bolden say, 122, 123, 221 ,
I told you once I told you twice, 226
I've got a right to sing the blues, 233
I've got the Yes We Have No Bananas Blues, 59
I want some, 204
I want some seafood mama, 117
I want you tonight, 93
I wish I could shimmy like my sister Kate, 59
I wish I was in heaven, sitting down, 3
I wonder who made rhythm, 102

Jackass Blues, 162
Jackson, Cliff, 113–14, 133, 134, 139, 142–3, 153, 159, 165–6
——, Village Cats, 159
Jackson, Edgar, 138
Jackson, Milt, 212
Jackson, Tony, 31, 33
Jacqueline, 262
Ja da, 114, 140
James, Elmer, 113
James, Louis, 19
Jazzin' Babies Blues, 61
Jazz Kings, 42–3, 44, 48–9
Jazz Ltd (record label), 209
Jazz me Blues, 158, 172, 185, 230
Jeffries, Herb, 137
'Jazz Parade' concerts, 256
Jazz Varieties (show), 256
Jeepers Creepers, 159, 278
Jelly Roll, 216
Jelly Roll Blues, 230–31
Jersey City, New Jersey, 91
Johns, Martine, 160
Johnson, Bill, 19, 29, 30, 31
Johnson, Budd, 288
Johnson, James P., 62, 67–8, 115, 125, 160, 181, 196, 202, 210–11, 246
——, band, 67
Johnson, Jimmie, 18
Johnson, Lem, 142–3
Johnson, Manzie, 113–15, 138, 145, 146, 147, 151, 159, 165–6, 247
Johnson, Margaret, 58, 61, 70
Johnson, Pete, 186
Johnson, Willie 'Bunk', 15, 16, 17, 18, 22,

Johnson, Willie 'Bunk' – *cont.*
  24, 135–6, 151, 160–61, 163–71,
  201–2, 228, 276
Johnson, Yank, 12
Johnstown, New York, 125
Jones, Claude, 121–2, 128–9
Jones, David, 23
Jones, Isham, 94
Jones, Jimmy, 107
Jones, Jonah, 258, 264–5, 267
Jones, Max, 156, 243
Jones, Richard M., 16
Jones, Robert, 36
Jones, Wilmore 'Slick', 214, 230
Jordan, Joe, 140
Joseph, Pleasant, 175, 185
Jospin, Mowgli, 221
Joy, Leonard, 130, 136, 141
Juan-les-Pins, France, 234–6, 241–3, 252,
  254, 280, 290
——, Le Vieux Colombier, 234–5, 241–3,
  252, 270
Jungle Drums, 112
Junk Bucket Blues, 72
Just one of those things, 189, 199, 242

Kaister, Clarence, 118
Kaminsky, Max, 111, 125, 149, 162, 189,
  195, 203, 246
Kansas City, 106
Kansas City Man Blues, 57–8, 59, 198
Karoley, Mary, 133–4, 138, 145, 151, 152,
  154, 156, 158, 182, 290, 292
Kaufman, Whitey, 63
Keeling, Frank, 25
Kelly, Ernest, 12
Kent, Leonard, 117
Keppard, Freddie, 6, 7, 11, 14, 16, 19, 24,
  25, 26, 29, 30–31, 32, 92, 113, 140, 235
Keppard, Louis, 19–20, 21, 28, 157
Kersey, Kenny, 230, 233
Khan, Ali, 242
Kildare, Daniel, 46–7
Kimball, Narvin, 160
Kincaid, Nelson, 34, 46, 199
King Jazz (record company), 174, 178,
  187, 250
King Porter Stomp, 239
King Reavis, Mrs H., 37
Kirk, Roland, 288, 290
Kirk, Wilbert, 102, 104, 106, 107, 155
Kirkpatrick, Don, 247
Klook's Blues, 222

Knight, Alfred, 60
Knight, Charles Henry Maxwell, 50–51,
  277
Knokke Jazz Festival, 281–2
Krueger, Bennie, 63

Lacey, 'Little' Mack, 12, 21
La colline du delta, 280
La complainte des infidels, 262
Lacotta, Pierre, 270
Lacoume, Emile 'Stalebread', 13
Lacy, Steve, 288
Ladnier, Tommy, 29, 78, 87–9, 91–7,
  113–16, 119, 125, 164, 176, 204, 235
Lady be good, 147
Lady Luck Blues, 59
Laine, Guy, 270
Lattimore, George, 41–3, 52
Lampe, Pauline, 53–4
Lander, Harold, 270
Lange, Horst, 86
La nuit est un sorcière, 251, 254–5, 269
La Rocca, Nick, 25–6
La route du bonheur (film), 257
Lascelles, Gerald, 244
Lastic, 237
Laughin' in Rhythm, 146
Laura, 190, 242
Lawson, Yank, 111
Layton, Skippy, 188
Lay your Racket, 93
Lazy River, 127
Leeman, Cliff, 230, 233
Le marchand de poissons, 249
Lesberg, Jack, 188, 209, 230–31
Les oignons, 221, 236, 251, 266, 270, 285
Lester, Norman, 139, 185
Levine, Henry, 135
Lewis, Charles, 80, 81, 83–4, 221–2
Lewis, Dandy, 15
Lewis, Meade 'Lux', 118–20
Lewis, Robert, 200, 279
Lewis, Sabby, orchestra, 181
Lewis, Steve, 20
Lewis, Ted, 126
Lim, Harry, 125
Limehouse Blues, 130, 145, 253
Lindsay, Herbert, 20, 28
Lindsey, Johnny, 136–7
L'inspecteur connaît la musique (film),
  270, 272
Lion, Alfred, 118–20, 179–81, 195, 258,
  287

Liston, Virginia, 61, 65
Little Piece of Leather, 185
Livery Stable Blues, 25, 58
Lombardo, Guy, 94
London, England, 35–43, 45–54, 66, 87, 224–8, 243, 277
——, Breakfast Room, 53
——, Ciro's club, 87
——, Coliseum Theatre, 41
——, Embassy Club, 42–3, 44, 53
——, Hammersmith Palais, 47–8, 49, 50, 53
——, London Jazz Club (100 Oxford Street), 225
——, Kingsway Hall, 52
——, People's Palace, 39
——, Philharmonic Hall, 36, 39, 46
——, Portman Rooms, 41–2
——, Prince of Wales Theatre, 41
——, Rector's Night Club, 48, 49–50, 52, 53, 225
——, Romano's Club, 53
——, Winter Garden Theatre, 224, 227
——, Royal Albert Hall, 41, 274
——, Royal Festival Hall, 275, 277
Lonesome Blues, 132
Lonesome Road, 264
Longnon, Guy, 238, 249, 262, 273
Lopez, Vincent, 94
Lord let me in the lifeboat, 166
Los Angeles, California, 260
Louisville, Kentucky, 106
——, Chez Paree, 106
Love for Sale, 199
Loveless Love, 88, 99
Love me with a feeling, 218
Lucie, Lawrence, 122
Lugg, George, 162, 165, 186
Luter, Claude, 216, 220–21, 228, 231, 234–5, 236–7, 238, 249, 250, 254–6, 265, 267, 270, 271, 274, 280, 286, 287, 288, 292
——, orchestra, 216, 231, 234–6, 238, 241–2, 245, 249, 251–2, 254, 265, 269, 271–2, 281
Lyons, Bob, 10
Lyttelton, Humphrey, 224–8, 236, 243, 253, 262, 266, 267, 275

MacAllan, William 'Willi', 85
MacAllan Blackband, 85
McGhee, Brownie, 202
McGraw, Jim, 153

McIntosh, Arthur 'Traps', 95
McKendrick, Gilbert 'Little Mike', 83–4
McLin, Jimmy, 132
McPartland, Jimmy, 189
Madame Becassine, 237
Madera, Oscar, 98, 99, 100, 101
Magee, 'Sticks', 117
Mainz, Gerard, 54
Maisch, Fred, 141
Make believe, 172
Make me a pallet on the floor, 134
Maltz, Bob, 202
Mammy o' Mine, 37
Mandy make up your mind, 66, 79, 230
Manetta, Manuel, 20, 27
Man I love, The, 278
Manning, Edgar, 47
Manone, Wingy, 131
Maple Leaf Rag, 16, 93–4
Markham, 'Pig Meat', 181
Marrero, John, 12
Marrero, Simon, 12
Marrero, Willy, 19
Marsala, Joe, 110–11, 218
Marsala, Marty, 111, 188, 196, 259
Marsalis, Branford, 288
Marsalis, Wynton, 290
Marshall, Kaiser, 95, 165, 176, 203–4
Marshall, Saxie, 125
Martin, Sara, 58, 59
Maryland, my Maryland, 142, 209, 285
Mastren, Carmen, 111, 126–7
Matson, Charles, 60
Mathews, Emmett, 101
Mathews, George, 106
Matthews, Lewis, 20
Mayer, Ray, 188
Maysfield, John, 57
Memphis Blues, 180
Merlin, Pierre, 221
Metcalf, Louis, 68
Mezzrow, Mezz, 111, 113–15, 116, 140, 174–8, 185, 186–7, 190–91, 203–4, 205–6, 214, 248, 250, 253, 271, 286
Michelot, Pierre, 221–2, 278
Mielke, Bob, 197–8, 253
Mighty Like a Rose, 37
Miles, Lizzie, 3, 30, 55, 95
Miley, Bubber, 69, 70, 146
Milk Cow Blues, 131
Miller, Jimmy, 102, 103, 107
Miller, Max, 157–8, 189
Miller, Paul Edward, 157–8, 190–91, 195,

Miller, Paul Edward – *cont.*
  203, 207
Miller, Punch, 157
Millinder, Lucky, band, 258–9
Mills Brothers, 36
Mills, Irving, 104, 113
Milneberg Joys, 165
Milwaukee, Wisconsin, 106
Mince, Johnny, 154
Minor, Dan, 115
Minor Swoon, 175
Mistinguett, 242–3
Mitchell, Abbie, 38, 62
Mitchell, Louis A., 33, 34, 43, 47
Mitchell, William F., 48, 49, 51–2, 53, 54
Mohr, Kurt, 215, 272
Molsby, Alma, 158
Mon homme, 222, 242
Monk, Thelonious, 138
Mooche, The, 146–7, 288
Mood Indigo, 130, 147
Moody, James, 238, 288
Moon over Harlem, 117
Moore, Billy, 243
Moore, Charles, 18
Moore, Eugene, 139, 143
Moore, Fred, 162, 167, 179–80, 192, 198,
  202, 210, 231, 232, 272
Moore, 'Big Chief' Russell, 214, 219, 230,
  244, 246–7
Morand, Herb, 170
Morand, Morris, 91, 92–5, 116, 170
Morgan, Carroll, 36, 37
Morocco, 252
Morr, Skip, 259
Morris, Lawrence, 36, 37, 40
Morris, Marlowe, 132
Morris, Thomas, 57, 60, 132
Morton, Benny, 183–4
Morton, Ferdinand 'Jelly Roll', 72, 87,
  121–3, 125, 131, 135, 142, 231
Moscow, USSR, 77–8
——, Dmitrovka Cinema, 77
——, Grand Opera House, 77
Mouche à miel, 249
Moustache gauloise, 237
Mullins, Mazie, 33
Mumford, Brock, 15
Munich, Germany, 79
Muranyi, Joe, 288
Murray, Pete, 284
Muskrat Ramble, 135, 144, 159, 164, 171,
  217, 233, 251, 259, 260, 267

My Buddy, 287
Myers, Wilson Ernest 'Serious', 91, 93,
  125, 130–31, 142–3, 154
My Honey's Loving Arms, 62
My Woman Blues, 198

National Emblem March, 231
Negro Nuances, 62
Nelly, 262
Negro Rhapsody, The, 79, 81, 151
Nelson, 'Big Eye' Louis, 5, 7–8, 11, 14,
  16, 21, 23, 28, 66, 153, 156, 157, 232,
  265, 290
Never No Lament, 171
Never will I forget the blues, 204
Newark, New Jersey, 71
New Olympia Band, 19
New Orleans, Louisiana, 1–6, 8–17,
  19–29, 55, 64, 82, 96
——, Artisan Hall, 7
——, Claiborne Theatre, 24
——, George Foycault's club, 15, 16
——, Guidrey and Allen's Upstairs Club,
  20
——, 101 Ranch, 11
——, Johnny Lala's '25' Cabaret, 20, 21
——, Kinney's Hall, 15
——, Liberty Hall, 15
——, Lincoln Theatre, 23
——, Masonic Hall, 15
——, Municipal Auditorium, 160
——, Pete Lala's, 20, 24, 27
——, Poodle Dog, 24
——, Red Onion, 16
——, Rosebud Hall, 22
——, St Catherine's Hall, 11
——, Toodlum's Bar, 24
——, Villa's Cabaret, 19
New Orleans Creole Jazz Boys, 72
New Orleans Feetwarmers, 91–6, 108,
  118, 142
New Orleans Suite, 289
Newton, Frankie, 118–20, 144, 181,
  184–5
New York, 30, 33–4, 55–7, 60–64, 67–9,
  71–3, 87, 89–91, 95, 96–7, 101, 103,
  110–11, 113, 115, 118, 121, 124, 149,
  152, 159–60, 165, 167, 174–5, 179,
  185–6, 187, 191–2, 193–5, 201–2,
  208–9, 210, 212, 214, 218–19, 229,
  233–4, 247, 257, 258
——, Apollo Theatre, 56, 103, 258–9
——, Bandbox, 257–8

——, Billy Rose's French Casino, 101
——, Bob Maltz's Jazz Club, 190
——, Cafe Society, 118
——, Carnegie Hall, 115, 287
——, Casino Theatre, 99
——, Central Plaza, 212, 213, 229, 247
——, Clark Monroe's club, 175
——, Club Basha, 71–2
——, Columbia Theatre, 71
——, Connie's club, 67
——, Enduro Restaurant, 135
——, Fritz's club, 67
——, Garden of Joy, 68
——, Hickory House, 110
——, Hollywood Club, 67
——, Hurricane Club, 152
——, Jimmy Ryan's club, 165, 167, 174, 192, 194, 195, 199, 200, 202, 209, 214, 217–18, 229, 230
——, Kentucky Club, 67
——, Lafayette Theatre, 89, 97
——, Leroy's club, 67
——, Mimo Club, 143, 144, 150
——, Nest Club, 90–91
——, Nick's Tavern, 110, 113, 116, 117–18, 123, 125, 132, 149, 153–4
——, Onyx Club, 152
——, Owl Club, 67
——, Park Central Hotel, 89
——, Park Lane Hotel, 118
——, Pied Piper Club, 159
——, Pierre's Club, 87
——, Playhouse Theatre, 188
——, Pod's and Jerry's club, 90, 95, 193
——, Rhythm Club, 68, 70
——, Ritz Theatre, 159
——, Rockland Palace, 87
——, Saratoga Club, 91
——, St Regis Hotel, 111
——, Savoy Ballroom, 91–2, 95–6
——, Shelburn Hotel, 34
——, Smalls' club, 67
——, Stuyvesant Casino, 208
——, Town Hall, 149, 159, 181, 186, 191, 194–5, 201–2
——, Village Vanguard, 214
——, Waldorf Astoria Hotel, 212
——, Ziegfield Theatre, 99
New York Syncopated Orchestra, 33
Nicholas, Albert, 11, 18, 81–2, 121–2, 125, 143, 181, 182–3, 189, 194, 196, 202, 250, 266, 271, 281, 284, 286
Nicholas, 'Wooden' Joe, 18

Ni queue, ni tête, 237
Nixon, Theodore 'Teddy', 91, 93–4
Nobody knows the trouble I've seen, 287
Nobody knows you when you're down and out, 210
Nobody knows the way I feel 'dis morning, 66, 134
Noone, Jimmy, 14, 16, 29, 98–9, 178, 232, 290
Norfolk, Virginia, 56
——, Attucks Theatre, 56
Nottingham, England, 43
——, Albert Hall, 43
Nussbaum, Julius, 54

Oberstein, Eli, 94
Oehler, Ray Dixon, 190
Ogden, Dave 'Bob', 157
Oh Daddy Blues, 59
Oh didn't he ramble, 121–2
Off and on Blues, 66
Okeh (record company), 57, 58–9, 61, 62, 70
Okey Doke, 105
Old ark is moverin', The, 99
Old Black Magic, 251
Old cow died, The, 171
Old Fashioned Love, 78
Old Man Blues, 133, 134
Old School, 177
Old Stack o'Lee Blues, 182
Ole Miss, 164
Oliver, Joe 'King', 16, 18, 19–20, 21, 22, 24, 27, 29, 30, 58, 60, 64, 90, 108, 182, 235, 276
——, Creole Jazz Band, 64
Ol' Man River, 173, 287
Olympia Band, 12, 14, 19–20
One O'Clock Jump, 130
One O'Clock Stomp, 130
On the Sunnyside of the Street, 217, 260, 281
Original Creole Orchestra, 19, 23, 26, 29, 31, 140
Original Dixieland Jazz Band, 25–6, 27, 31, 35, 42, 47, 48, 51, 54
Orphan Annie Blues, 222
Ory, Kid, 24, 27, 156
——, Sunshine Orchestra, 31
Out of nowhere, 222
Out of the Galleon, 177

Page, 'Hot Lips', 111, 149, 174–5, 192, 214–15, 216–17

Page, Walter, 115, 210, 212, 214, 258
Palao, Jimmy, 28
Palmer, Roy, 28, 167
Panama, 118
Pan Americano, 37
Panassié, Hugues, 111, 113–15, 178, 198, 205, 213, 214, 249–50
Panther Dance, 221
Papa De-da-da, 71
Paris, France, 75–6, 79–85, 89, 205, 215–17, 220, 234, 248–9, 254–7, 261–4
——, Alhambra, 262
——, Ambassadeurs club, 79–80, 87, 88–9
——, Apollo, 52
——, Bricktop's club, 79
——, Casino de Paris, 33
——, Chez Sidney Bechet, 261
——, Club St Germain, 215
——, International Jazz Festival, 212–13, 215–17
——, Lutèce Arena, 256–7
——, Metro Club, 261
——, Olympia, 265, 269–70, 271, 272
——, Salon du Jazz, 236, 252
——, Salle Pleyel, 215–16, 249, 252, 264, 278
——, Théâtre des Champs-Elysées, 75, 270
——, Théâtre Edouard VII, 220
——, Théâtre l'Étoile, 76
——, Vieux Colombier (club), 216, 220, 234, 241, 248, 254, 265, 266, 269, 271–2, 279
Paris, William, 71
Paris, Wynne, 168–9, 170
Parker, Charlie, 138, 185, 212, 217
Parker, Johnny, 267, 271, 275
Parker, Knocky, 202
Parker, Ray, 167, 172
Parlophone (record company), 61
Parrish, Dan, 77
Pasquall, Jerome Don, 71
Passport to Paradise, 274
Paterson, New Jersey, 152
——, Sandy's Hollywood Bar, 152
Patrick, Edward, 36
Patrick, Jacob, 36, 53, 72
Payne, John C., 36, 37, 47
Peach Jam Making Time, 37
Pekaldi, Jacqueline, 262, 263, 279, 283, 287
Pelletier, Jean-Claude, 285

Pennies from Heaven, 278
Perdido Street Blues, 129, 158
Perdido Street Stomp, 175, 176
Perez, Manuel, 6, 7, 9, 10, 16, 17, 18, 32, 33, 156–7
Perkins, Dave, 10
Persiany, André, 264–5
Peters Sisters, 36, 279
Petit, Buddy, 11–12, 13, 14, 15, 16, 24, 29, 235
Petite fleur, 251, 253, 277, 286, 290
Peyton, Benton E. (Benny), 36, 37, 42, 48, 77, 85
——, band, 79
Philadelphia, Pennsylvania, 56, 89, 101, 118, 160, 186–7, 232–3, 247, 260
——, Academy of Art, 186
——, Alpine Musical Bar, 152
——, Dunbar Theatre, 56
——, George Wilson's Cafe, 133
——, Lincoln Theatre, 101
——, Pearl Theatre, 89
——, Swing Rendezvous, 232–3
Phillipe, Claude, 249
Phillips, Lloyd, 143, 192, 198–9, 201, 219, 230
Pickin' on your baby, 71
Picou, Alphonse, 6, 9, 11, 23, 27, 156, 157, 160
Piédalu député, 257
Pied Piper of Harlem, The, 106
Pierce, Nat, 261
Pierre, Joe, 20
Piron, Armand J., 19, 20, 22–3
Pistol Packin' Mama, 171
Pleasure Mad, 63, 107
Pleure pas, 262
Poindexter, Norwood 'Pony', 288
Poole, Alex, 71
Poet and Peasant, 33
Polka Dot, 198
Polka Dot Rag, 99, 140
Porter, Cole, 80, 148
Porter, Joseph, 36, 37
Port of Harlem Seven, 119
Porto Rico, 166
Potter, Tommy, 212–13
Pounding Heart Blues, 120
Powell, Frank, 143
Powell, Specs, 183
Preachin' the Blues, 131
Pretty Baby, 31
Prevost, Louis, 71

Price, Eddie, 120
Price, Sammy, 109, 174–5, 178, 186–7, 191, 203–4, 214, 272, 281, 287
Probert, George, 259, 288
Promenade aux Champs-Elysées, 238
Prouting, Lionel, 206
Providence, Rhode Island, 71

Quersin, Benoit, 264
Quiet Please, 159
Quincy Street Stomp, 183

Rain Song, 37
Ramsey, Frederic, Jr, 121
Ramshackle Rag, 37
Raphael, Benny, 3
Rasmussen, Peter, 237
RCA Victor (record company), 108, 121, 130–31, 133–4, 136, 139, 140–41, 145–9, 209
Really the Blues, 114, 177, 187
Reagan, Caroline Dudley, 73, 75
Redman, Don, 71, 101, 122, 125
Red Onion Jazz Babies, 66–7
Reid, John, 130, 133, 134, 136, 140–41, 146, 151, 156–7, 158, 168–71, 209, 245, 290, 292
Reinhardt, Bill, 202–3, 205, 206, 208–9, 219, 229, 244
Reinhardt, Ruth (née Sato), 202–3, 220, 229, 244, 245, 261
Rena, Henry 'Kid', 3
Rena, Joe, 3, 4
Rent Party Blues, 131
Revel, Henry, 79, 81
Revolutionary Blues, 175, 177, 204
Revue nègre, see *Black Revue*
Réwéliotty, André, 256, 261, 271, 274, 280, 287
——, orchestra, 243, 255–6, 262, 269, 271–4, 280
Rhapsodie nègre, see *Negro Rhapsody*
Rhythm of the Broadway Moon, 102
Richards, Red, 244, 246
Richards, Dave, 80
Richardson, Jerome, 288
Rickards, Shirley 'Ricky', 193–4, 214
Ricks, John, 80
Ridin' Easy, 221
Rip up the joint, 146–7
Rivera, Angelina, 36, 37
Rivera, Anthony, 36
Rivera, Santos, 36

Riverboat Shuffle, 228
Rivers, Sam, 288
Roach, Max, 212–13
Roane, Kenneth, 124
Robertson, Eddie 'Rabbit', 12
Robertson, Alvin 'Zue', 16, 19
Robeson, Paul, 53
Robichaux, Joe, 22
Robichaux, John, band, 5, 11
Robinson, Bill 'Bojangles', 143
Robinson, Eddie, 112, 117
Rochester, New York, 67
——, Lyceum Theatre, 67
Rodger, Ernest, 18
Rogers, George, 36
Roland, Gene, 288
Rollini, Adrian, 80
Roll on, Mississippi, roll on, 88
Romaine, Bert, 53
Rome, Hotel Apollo, 79
Rongetti, Nick, 110, 123, 125, 153
Rose, Al, 191, 291
Rose Leaf Rag, 16
Rosemond, E. C., 37
Rosenberg, Hermann, 110, 135
Rose of the Rio Grande, 258
Rose Room, 147
Royal Garden Blues, 169, 172, 177, 227, 251
Rumoro, Joe, 190, 195
Runnin' Wild, 230
Russell, John George, 36, 42
Russell, Luis, 128–9
——, band, 88
Russell, Pee Wee, 110, 111, 149, 153, 163
Russell, William (Bill), 131, 135, 136, 157, 163, 164, 168–70, 245
Russian Rag, 37
Ryan, Jimmy, 218

St Cyr, Johnny, 5, 7, 14, 20, 30, 31
St James Infirmary, 180
St John, Dell, 117
St Louis Blues, 56, 80, 135, 155, 158, 165, 185, 251, 260, 281, 282, 284
Saints, The, 210, 259, 275, 276, 281, 283
Sally Trombone, 37
Salnave, Bertin, 38, 53
Saltmarsh, Bob, 206–7, 208
Salty Dog, 162
San Francisco, California, 259
——, Down Beat Club, 259
Santiago, Willie, 156

Saparo, Henry, 33, 34, 36, 37, 41, 42
Sartre, Jean-Paul, 242
Saturday Night Blues, 132
Saury, Maxim, 220, 236, 284
Save it pretty mama. 137, 179
Saward, Bernard, 226
Saw Mill Blues, 175
Sawyer, Johnnie, 25
Sbarbaro, Tony, 13, 27
Schaap, Walter, 213–14
Schilperoort, Peter, 239
Scholes, Stephen, 141, 209
Scobey, Bob, 260
Sebastian, Stubby, 120
Sedric, Eugene, 159, 287
Senneville, Jeanine, 241
September Song, 211, 259
Série noire (film), 274
Seven-eleven (show), 71
Shag, 94, 237
Shake 'em up, 199
Shake it and break it, 134, 135, 191
Shapiro, Artie, 111
Sharpe, Eva, 118
Shavers, Charlie, 109, 145, 147–8
Shaw, Arvell, 281, 282
Shaw, Billy, 151–2, 179, 212, 213
Sheik of Araby, The, 91, 131, 141–2, 172, 176, 251
Shepp, Archie, 290
Sherwood, Bobby, 188
Shields, Larry, 51
Shim-me-sha-wabble, 230
Shine, 180
Shirley, Jimmy, 112
Shorter, Wayne, 288
Showboat, 254
Shreveport Blues, 61
Shuffle Along, 104
Sidney's Blues, 131
Sidney's Wedding Day, 243
Silent Night, 285
Silver Bell Band, 10, 11
Simeon, Omer, 98, 287
Simmen, Johnny, 138
Simmons, John, 149
Simmons, Rousseau, 60
Simms, Mickey, 190
Sims, Zoot, 288
Singery, Yannick, 243, 273
Singleton, Arthur 'Zutty', 110, 112, 115–16, 122, 123, 125, 128–9, 132, 248, 252–3, 275

Sissle, Noble, 32, 67, 79–81, 87–90, 97–106, 108, 109, 114, 126, 287
——, Paris Ambassadeurs Orchestra, 88–90, 101, 111, 139, 157, 221
——, Swingsters, 104–6
Sister Kate, 115, 171, 181, 205, 210, 281
Si tu vois ma mère, 204, 249
Six Brown Brothers, 31–2
6.5 Special (TV show), 284
Slippin' and Slidin', 140
Smith, Ada, see Bricktop
Smith, Ambrose, 36
Smith, Bessie, 56, 58–9, 101, 115, 152
Smith, Charles Edward, 131, 136, 139
Smith, Cricket, 77
Smith, George Mitchell, 42, 48
Smith, Harrison, 87
Smith, Jabbo, 118
Smith, Joe, 56, 67, 70
Smith, Joseph, 139
Smith, Ken, 157–8, 189, 190, 195
Smith, Mamie, 57, 58, 59
Smith, Paul, 118
Smith, Stephen W., 121, 122, 123, 126
Smith 'Sugar' Johnny, 26, 28–9, 30
Smith, Trixie, 108
Smith, Willie 'the Lion', 68, 90, 95, 118, 124, 132–3, 144, 145–6, 147, 183–4
Snaer, Albert, 210–11
Sobbin' and Cryin', 228
Sobbin' Blues, 171
Society Blues, 237, 283
Softly awakes my heart, 50
Solal, Martial, 278
Sombert, Claire, 270
Somebody stole my gal, 264
Some of these days, 226
Song of Songs, 34, 46, 192, 199
Soper, Tut, 189
Sorenson, Art, 63
Souchon, Dr Edmond, 19–20
Southern-Rag-a-Jazz Band, 51
Southern Sunset, 107
Southern Syncopated Orchestra, 34–43, 46, 52, 53, 54, 77
Souvenirs de la Nouvelle Orléans, 281
Spanier, Muggsy, 125–7, 200, 202, 220, 229, 257
——, Ragtimers, 163
Spencer, Natalie, 38
Spencer, O'Neill, 107, 109
Spencer, Walter, 157
Spirit Holiday, 285

Spirits of Rhythm, 110
Spottswood, Willie, 112, 117
Spreading Joy, 198
Spring, 37
Springfield, Illinois, 156–8
——, Club Rio, 156–8
Squeeze me, 127, 265
Stacy, Jess, 111, 160, 188
Stamford, New York, 120
——, Spruceland Inn, 120
Stardust, 233
Steal Away Blues, 200
Stevenson, George, 272
Stewart, Ollie, 143
Stewart, Rex, 136–7, 183–4
Stockholm, Sweden, 237
——, National Concert Hall, 237
Stompy Jones, 137
Stones, Cliff, 15
Strange Fruit, 145
Stravinsky, Igor, 289
Strike up the band, 249
Struttin' with some Barbecue, 192
Stuart, Dave, 135
Suey, 146, 209
Sugar, 281
Sullivan, Joe, 181, 185, 230
Summertime, 119–20, 217, 260
Sunshine, Monty, 277, 286
Superior Band, 5, 12, 16
Sutton, Ralph, 196, 212, 230
Swanee Ripples, 37
Swanee River, 37
Sweet Georgia Brown, 217, 258
Sweetie Dear, 92, 140
Sweet Lorraine, 126
Sweet Patootie, 107
Sweet Sue, 127
Swing Along, 37
Swing Parade, 142
Switzerland, 217, 252, 262, 264, 266

Tain't a doggone thing, 61
Tain't a fit night out, 102
Tamper, Billy, 279
Tatten, William T., 37
Tatum, Art, 186, 260–61
Taylor, Billy, 181, 185, 186
Taylor, Dinah, 118
Taylor, Jasper, 34
Taylor, Eva, 58, 59, 61, 66, 70–71
Taylor, Lottie, 30
Teagarden, Jack, 123, 192, 195, 279

Témptation Rag, 228
Texas Moaner Blues, 65, 145
Thall, Sid, 209
That's a plenty, 127
That's what love did to me, 102
There'll be some changes made, 248
These foolish things, 278
Thigpen, George, 132
Thomas, Joe, 257
Thompson, Egbert E., 41
Thompson, George, 167, 172
Thompson, Kay C., 116
Thompson, Lloyd, 278
Thompson, Lucky, 288
Tiger Rag, 42, 69, 86, 208, 210, 221
Tin Roof Blues, 210, 216
Tio, Lorenzo, 7
Tio, Lorenzo, Jr, 7, 11, 14, 15, 21, 91,
    95–6, 170
Tio, Luis 'Papa', 7
Tio, Luis, Jr, 7
Todd, Clarence, 11, 67
Together, 243
Toliver, James Sumner ('Buster'), 98, 99,
    100, 139, 149, 211, 255, 257
Tommy's Blues, 204
Toot it Brother Armstrong, 109
Toronto, Canada, 183–4, 246
——, Eaton Auditorium, 183
Touff, Cy, 261
Tough, Dave, 111
Traeger, Charlie, 198
Trappier, Arthur, 144, 230, 244–5, 246–7
Treat it Gentle (autobiography), 290–92
Trepagnier, Ernest 'Ninesse', 12
Trixie's Blues, 109
Turner, Henry, 110
Twelfth Street Rag, 69, 147, 209, 254
2: 19 Blues, 129

Ugly Child, 172
Under the dreamy creole moon, 99, 100
Up in Sidney's Flat, 166
Usero, Ramon, 98, 100

Vallee, Rudy, 94
Vallis, Buddy, 225–6
Valteau, Ferdinand, 20
Van Straten, Joe, 52
Van Straten, Leon, 52
Vargos, Pedro, 36
Variety (record label), 104, 106, 124

Vasseur, Benny, 217
V-disc Blues, 155
Venucci, Larry, 259
Versatile Three, 47
Vig, Steen, 288
Vigne, Jean, 16, 20
Vincent, Eddie, 19, 29
Vinding, Terkild, 237, 254
Vine, Johnny, 209
Viper Mad, 107
Vocalion (record label), 111
Vodery, Will, 56
Vogue (record company), 221, 233, 236, 270, 273

Wabash Blues, 249
Wade, Louis, 23, 25
Walker, George, 259
Walking and talking to myself, 159
Wallace, Sippie, 65
Waller, Thomas 'Fats', 57, 131, 141–2
Walsh, Matt, 219
Ware, Leonard, 111–12, 116, 117
Ware, Munn, 203, 208–10
Waring, Fred, 79, 80
——, Pennsylvanians, 79, 80
Warney, Leo, 124
Warren, Milford, 36
Washington, DC, 56, 71, 101, 179, 184–5
——, Brown Derby Club, 179, 185
——, Constitutional Hall, 184
——, Gayety Theatre, 71
——, Howard Theatre, 56, 101
Washington, Grover, 288
Washingtonians, *see* Ellington, Duke, Washingtonians
Waste no tears, 218
Waters, Benny, 267
Waters, Ethel, 63
Way down yonder in New Orleans, 180, 283
Weary Blues, 115, 151, 162, 165, 217, 281
Weary Way Blues, 183
Webb, Chick, band, 96
Webb, George, 224–6
——, Dixielanders, 224
Webster, Ben, 289
Weed, Harold 'Buddy', 258
Wein, George, 246, 248, 260, 282, 286
Welles, Orson, 242
Wells, Dickie, 111
Wellstood, Dick, 197, 206–8, 232, 257–8
Weston, Fitz, 176–7

Wettling, George, 149, 150, 181, 188, 210, 212, 230–31
What-cha-call 'em Blues, 64
What is this thing called love, 148
What ja do to me, 88
When it's sleepy time down South, 142, 172, 226
When the sun goes down, 53
When you wore a tulip, 264–5
Where am I, 204
When you and I were young Maggie, 114
Whispering, 45
White, Anita, 257
White, Ellerton 'Sonny', 125, 130
White, Gil, 107
White, Josh, 131
White Christmas, 285
White Plains, New York, 91, 95
Who, 210
Who'll chop your suey when I'm gone, 70
Whoop Miss Wolf, 187
Who's sorry now, 226
Why do I love you?, 172
Wilber, Bob, 159, 185–6, 192, 193–4, 195, 197–8, 206, 214, 218, 231–2, 253, 267, 288–9
——, Bechet Legacy, The, 289
——, Soprano Summit, 289
——, Wildcats, 197, 206, 232
Wilcox, Bert, 223, 227–8
Wild Cat Blues, 57–8, 105, 206
Wild Man Blues, 134
Williams, Clarence, 20, 22–3, 57–62, 64–6, 70–71, 74, 79, 117, 128, 163
——, Blue Five, 57, 59, 61, 70, 206
——, Creole Four Orchestra, 23
Williams, Gene, 163, 165, 169
Williams, James, 24
Williams, J. Mayo, 108
Williams, Joan, 290–91
Williams, Johnny, 118–20
Williams, Mary Lou, 159
Williams, Nelson, 248, 256
Williams, Robert, 37
Williams, Sandy, 133–4, 142–3, 149, 151, 165–6, 181
Williams, Shorty, 133
Williams, Sonny, 120
Williamson, Ernest, 146, 151
Wilson, Robert 'Juice', 32
Wilson, Teddy, 287
Wilson, Wesley, 108, 187
Windhurst, Johnny, 170, 172

Wingdale, New York, 144, 151
——, Camp Unity, 144, 151
Winin' Boy, 122–3
Withers, Frank, 77–8, 135
Without a Home, 218
Wittwer, Johnny, 259
Wolff, Francis, 179, 181, 287
Wolverine Blues, 238
Woode, Jimmy, 260
Wooding, Sam, 77–8, 90, 118
Wrap up your troubles in dreams, 222
Wyer, Paul, 36
Wynn, Albert, 91

Yes we have no bananas, 272
You can't do that to me, 187
You can't live in Harlem, 102
Young Olympians Band, 12, 13, 14
Young, Robert, 36, 37, 40
You're lucky to me, 251
You're the limit, 145
You've got the right key, 65

Zacharias, Bernard, 237, 249, 254, 271
Zeno, Henry, 15, 19, 20, 23
Ziegler, Elisabeth, 81, 85, 238, 243, 245,
    248, 252, 261, 262–3, 283

INDEX